THE RECORD INTERPRETER

THE RECORD INTERPRETER

A Collection of
Abbreviations, Latin Words and Names
Used in English Historical Manuscripts and Records

Compiled by
Charles Trice Martin, B.A., F.S.A.

With an Introduction by
David Iredale

PHILLIMORE

First published 1892
Second edition 1910

This facsimile of second edition published 1982 by
PHILLIMORE & CO. LTD
Shopwyke Hall, Chichester, Sussex

Reprinted 1994

ISBN 0 85033 465 9

Printed and bound in Great Britain by
Biddles Ltd, Guildford and King's Lynn

INTRODUCTION

By David Iredale

THE RECORD INTERPRETER was first published in 1892. Since that date 'Trice Martin' has been accepted as one of the standard local history reference sources. This compact work contains a Latin-English glossary; a key to the interpretation of abbreviations commonly found in medieval Latin or French documents; Latin forms of the names of British towns, villages, rivers and bishoprics; and Latin versions of christian names and surnames. Trice Martin is 'a must' for anyone engaged in historical or literary pursuits and the reading of old documents—teacher, research student, local historian, genealogist, heraldry enthusiast, librarian or archivist. The book occupies a prominent position on the desk in my own study; and on a shelf in the record office a copy of the 1910 edition is available for use by both searchers and staff. It is one of the tools of the archivist's trade, as indispensable to the historian as the *Handbook of dates* by C. R. Cheney, the *Handbook of British chronology* by F. M. Powicke & E. B. Fryde, R. E. Latham's *Revised medieval Latin word-list*, and A. H. Dunbar's *Scottish kings, a revised chronology of Scottish history 1005-1625*. Like these works of ready reference *The record interpreter* provides the researcher with a convenient key to the interpretation of the many and varied (often apparently incomprehensible) symbols or abbreviations which pervade the text of medieval Latin or French documents. Although common or garden Latin words and shorthand forms obviously present few problems, the more unusual ones can prove difficult, especially for the majority of present-day researchers not daily engaged and practised in the reading of medieval manuscripts. Additionally, few historians become so steeped in their period as to be able instantly to recall the correct Latin version of a British surname or place-name. Indeed if a reference work as convenient as Trice Martin lies to hand, forms like *de Vado Boum* for Oxford and *Cerda Selgouarum* for Dumfries need not be committed to memory at all by the researcher.

5

The record interpreter attempts no coverage of documentary palaeography, the reading or deciphering of handwriting. For this subject the historian must consult the standard and readily accessible textbook by L. C. Hector *The handwriting of English documents*; and, of course, the classic *English court hand A.D. 1066 to 1500* by C. H. Jenkinson & C. Johnson with Jenkinson's own *The later court hands in England*. This study may be further pursued in N. Denholm Young *Handwriting in England and Wales*, G. E. Dawson & L. Kennedy-Skipton *Elizabethan handwriting 1500-1650*, and H. E. P. Grieve *Examples of English handwriting 1150-1750*. G. G. Simpson's *Scottish handwriting 1150-1650* admirably introduces the reading of documents from north of the border.

*   *   *   *   *

Charles Trice Martin was born on 27 December 1841, at 10 Grosvenor Place, Cheltenham, the son of the Reverend Samuel Martin, 1817-1878, a Congregational minister, and Mary, daughter of John Trice of Tunbridge Wells. Samuel Martin, son of a Woolwich shipwright, had originally wanted to proselytise the natives of India, but ill-health forced him to Cheltenham instead, where at Highbury chapel he preached to an enthusiastically increasing flock of sahibs. In 1842 he heard the call to Westminster, one of the most socially unregenerate districts of the metropolis, where his 'eloquence and steady devotion to his work attracted a large congregation'. In 1862 Martin was elected chairman of the Congregational Union. His writings include essays on criminal reform and 'the useful arts', favourite preoccupations of his class and generation.

The boy Charles attended University College School, London, under its renowned headmaster Thomas Hewitt Key, 1799-1875. The boy's 'honoured schoolmaster' also officiated, unsalaried, as professor of comparative grammar in University College, compiling a *Latin grammar*, and a *Latin-English dictionary* which however remained uncompleted at his death. Key gained a reputation in educational circles for urging teachers of the classics to adopt the Sanscrit grammarians' method based on the elementary or 'crude-form' of words, omitting inflected endings. Thus Martin acquired a sound knowledge of the classical languages. He continued his studies at University College, graduating bachelor of arts during the summer of 1861. The following November he was appointed to the civil service rank of junior clerk at the Public Record

Office, Chancery Lane, in effect a trainee archivist responsible for sorting and cataloguing documentary collections. His endeavours were rewarded by promotion to senior clerk in 1873 and, 15 years later, to an assistant keepership. He served for a total of 45 years, retiring at the end of December 1906 as the most senior of the assistant keepers. The 68th annual report of the deputy keeper of the public records praised Martin's 'recognised learning and palæographical skill, and his unfailing readiness to guide and assist his colleagues', printing the brief notice of his assistant keeper's career 'in the first place', before all other items for the year 1906.

During his years as archivist he collaborated in the preparation and publication of calendars of foreign and domestic letters and papers from the reign of Henry VIII. The master of the rolls had inaugurated this project in 1856, commissioning John Sherren Brewer, professor of English and lecturer in modern history at King's College, London, to arrange and catalogue the collection. Brewer, distinguished as an editor of the works of Roger Bacon, Giraldus Cambrensis and the friars minor in England, laboured diligently in the Public Record Office, British Museum, Lambeth Palace Library and elsewhere until, it is said, the day of his death in 1879. Subsequent portions of 'the Henry VIII papers' were prepared for the press by James Gairdner, 1828-1912, historian of the reigns of Richard III and Henry VII, editor of the definitive *The Paston letters,* and, as an assistant keeper at the record office, one of Martin's colleagues. The original series extended to 21 volumes between 1862 and 1910, divided with typical Victorian thoroughness into 33 parts.

Martin also directed the printing of Latin transcripts of close rolls of Henry III's reign. These enrolled copies of documents, addressed in the king's name to royal officials and other people, and *closed* by the great seal, contain orders or information pertinent to the administration of the country. Martin's work, sorting, arranging, listing, transcribing or indexing this and other series of documents—'ancient correspondence', early chancery proceedings, patent rolls—represents a considerable, albeit anonymous, contribution to our knowledge of the nation's past and the serious study of its history through archival sources. As he himself wrote in the introduction to E. E. Thoyts's *How to decipher and study old documents,* 'all persons who interest themselves in the documents to which they may have access . . . are helping in the grand work of making clear the laws and customs and mode of living of our ancestors'.

He edited—or shared in the production of—several of the volumes in the series *Rerum britannicarum medii ævi scriptores,* chronicles and memorials of Great Britain and Ireland during the middle ages, published under the direction of the master of the rolls and commonly known as the rolls series. For this project in collaboration with J. S. Brewer he transcribed and edited the medieval Latin register of Malmesbury Abbey, preserved in the Public Record Office. His three-volume edition of the correspondence of John Peckham, a 13th-century arch-bishop of Canterbury, appeared in 1882–1885; the third volume incorporated an abstract of the entire archiepiscopal register maintained by the prelate's secretariat. His linguistic abilities included Norman-French as well as Latin. In the 1880s this skill was exhibited notably when he continued and completed Sir Thomas Duffus Hardy's project of transcribing, editing and translating into English the 12th-century *Lestorie des engles solum la translacion Maistre Geffrei Gaimar.* Gaimar's Norman-French history of the English people itself derived from the fabulous Latin chronicle, *Historia regum Britanniae,* composed by the Welshman Geoffrey of Monmouth during the early 12th century.

Martin served as secretary of the Pipe Roll Society. This learned gathering financed the publication of transcripts of the annual financial accounts rendered by sheriffs to exchequer, bulky parchment cylinders resembling pipes and so designated 'pipe rolls'. Editions of texts of ancient charters, feet of fines and exchequer records not previously printed by official bodies were also commissioned. The year 1913 witnessed the publica-tion of Martin's revised text of *Rotuli de dominabus et pueris et puellis de xii comitatibus,* an exchequer survey dated 1185 of money returnable from the widows and orphaned children of Henry II's feudal tenants in chief throughout 12 counties.

On 5 March 1874 Martin was admitted to membership of the Society of Antiquaries of London, his qualification, a 'Knowledge of English History and Antiquities'. His sponsors included Albert Woods, Garter King of Arms, Richard Holmes, librarian of Windsor Castle, and William Hardy, soon to succeed T. D. Hardy (his brother) as deputy keeper of the public records. Martin served on the society's council from

1881 and appended the letters FSA (Fellow of the Society of Antiquaries) after his name. When official duties permitted, he turned his attention to the sorting, listing, transcribing or editing of privately owned muniments such as those belonging to Oxford's All Souls College, his calendar of which was published during 1877. The next year appeared *Memorials of the Savoy, the palace; the hospital; the chapel* by William John Loftie, historian of London and assistant chaplain at the chapel royal, for which Martin undertook research among original documents and contributed some transcriptions. For the Camden Society miscellany of 1871 he edited and transcribed the journal of the Elizabethan statesman, Sir Francis Walsingham, between 1570 and 1583. And he transcribed, edited and indexed the 16th- and 17th-century 'minutes of parliament' of the Middle Temple, London, a four-volume work published in 1904–1905. These minutes of the governing assembly of that inn of court, in a mixture of Latin and English, offer apposite instances of how carefully the editor considered the appropriate and exact rendering of significant words into English. Thus because the lawyers of the temple thought of wine in hogsheads —a specific measure—rather than in casks or tuns, the Latin word *dolium,* usually 'cask' in medieval documents, appears in the translated minutes as 'hogshead'. Martin's glossary of Latin words for *The record interpreter* bears this possibility in mind:

*doleum:—*a tun *(dolium);* also used for a hogshead.

However neither glossary nor dictionary can supplant the wit and skill of a competent translator. The Latin minutes refer to men chosen *parare prandium lectoris,* literally 'to prepare the reader's meal', but the clerk himself, when employing the vernacular, simply wrote 'steward'. Martin thus follows the clerk's usage rather than the literal dictionary rendering of each of those three Latin words. His labour with these original minute books emphasises the merits of his *Record interpreter* as the product of practical—and apparently tireless—research among a wide variety of 'English historical manuscripts and records'. The translation evidences his mastery of problems associated with 'handwriting . . . very difficult to read and careless', idiosyncratic spelling, faulty Latin grammar, unfamiliar surnames, conventional phraseology or professional jargon.

Martin read and criticised the manuscript of Emma Elizabeth Thoyts's 'guide to the reading of ancient manuscripts' *How to decipher and study old documents*; and he wrote a five-page introduction for the work which was published in 1893. Because the author, a young heiress, had only recently commenced historical research among 'the various kinds of documents which are likely to be found among the title-deeds of an estate, or among the archives of a parish or a corporation', she remembered 'the difficulties and dangers of each step'. The novice accordingly described the process 'without needless technicalities, in a practical way, which will appeal to those who begin to work among such material without previous knowledge'. Her 'key to the family deed chest' did not lose its appeal, running to a second edition in 1903 and remaining in print in 1982. Emma's husband, the landed gentleman John Hautenville Cope, was also an historian, becoming fellow of the Royal Historical Society, an editor for the Oxfordshire Record Society and on the strength of the *Victoria County History*.

Martin's introduction illustrates the clarity and simplicity of his style. His message cannot be mistaken. The ability to read documents is 'the foundation of all history . . . for to attempt to get information from old writings without thoroughly knowing the forms of the letters, and the different systems of abbreviations and contractions, would be like trying to keep accounts without knowing how to add up a column of figures'. Here too his humanity shines through. Erudite and serious as becomes a professional archivist, he proves himself by no means without humour as he recounts the 'old story' of *mumpsimus,* referred to in December 1545 by Henry VIII himself during his address to parliament. The narrative concerned an old priest of those days who became accustomed to repeating *sumpsimus* 'we have received' as *mumpsimus* in the course of the canon of the mass, misreading his 13th-century manuscript missal as well as demonstrating his own ignorance. Forms of medieval *m* and *s do* have some similarities, but the priest 'made himself an everlasting name' for 'conservative stupidity' in pedantically persisting in his error even after having been corrected. As bluff king Hal averred 'Some be to styff in their old *Mumpsimus*'. Another narrative concerns the mysterious silver chest gifted to a northern abbey by its founder during the 11th century. All kinds of speculation were aroused when the abbey's modern historian first mentioned this remarkable donation. But on turning to the document itself, rather than to the printed text, the archivist can transcribe the entry as *unā marcā argenti* and extend it as *unam marcam argenti*. 'The writer of the [printed] book had not noticed the contraction over the first *a*, divided the words wrongly, and read it *unam arcam*, instead of *unam marcam*'. The donation was thus said to be 'a silver chest' instead of 'a silver mark', a coin worth 13s 4d. Martin alludes to similar howlers occasioned by the misreading of ancient scripts: a forester stealing an abbot's 'cabbages' (actually his dogs, *chens* not *chous*); farmers burning 'stones' (actually peat, *petarum* not *pet^{a}rum*).

*   *   *   *   *

In 1879 Martin prefaced the ninth edition of the lawyer Andrew Wright's standard work on the palaeography of English records. Wright's classic *Court-hand restored* first appeared in 1776 specifically to teach a generation ignorant of the 'Old Law Hands, with their Contractions and Abbreviations' how to read historical records. It was claimed by this member of London's Inner Temple that the 'Reading of the old Law-Hands is at this day very nearly (if not altogether) become obsolete', although 'Records written in those hands are daily produced in Evidence in the Courts of Law'. Clearly there was in the 1770s, and still remained for many years, a need for the lawyer to familiarise himself with court hand, the Latin language and the rules of abbreviation. Wright also hoped to educate the 'learned Historian' who, once skilled in palaeography, 'would be able . . . to examine his Copies with the *Records themselves* . . . when in search of materials to authenticate his productions'. However, 'young gentlemen of the Law' with 'large fortunes, and perhaps a natural gaiety of disposition' hardly bothered with palaeography, and the passage of time had 'gradually deprived the Law of those valuable Gentlemen', the 'Old Practitioners' capable of reading distinctive legal hands. This regrettable scarcity of competent palaeographers had resulted from the official adoption—forty years previously—of the English language and of 'a common legible Hand and Character, as the Acts of Parliament are usually ingrossed in . . . in Words at Length and not abbreviated'. Nevertheless, original records remained the best legal evidence, and 'all Gentlemen of the law should be able to read them'. And the book's subtitle underlined the author's concern: 'the student's assistant in reading old deeds, charters, records, etc.'.

Wright added 'an appendix: containing the ancient [Latin] names of places in Great-Britain and Ireland, collected from

Antoninus, Caesar's Commentaries, Matthew Paris . . . and other ancient historians. With an alphabetical table of ancient surnames. Very necessary for young Students, and others, who may have Occasion to consult Old Records . . . And a glossography of Latin words found in the works of the most eminent lawyers, and other ancient writings, but not in any modern dictionaries'. The plates of the work, engraved by John Lodge, ?-1796, illustrated 'Alphabetical Contractions of the Court Hand'; 'Words comonly contracted'; 'A Hand much used in the Reign of Ja^S 1st,'; 'the usual manner of anciently writing the names of English counties and bishoprics'; 'Court-Hand Alphabets'; and 'Christian Names Contracted'. All were copied from manuscripts in the possession of the author and 'the Contractions made as I really found them in the different originals from whence they are extracted'. Wright's book provided both the inspiration and a model for *The record interpreter*.

Court-hand restored would seem at first glance to be a rather esoteric textbook for a relatively small group of scholars, archivists, lawyers, antiquarians and students. But, taking a wider view, the publication of such a manual, embellished with reproductions of relevant documents, bears witness to the late 18th-century passion for things 'gothick', for the civilisation, traditions, architecture, literature and documentation of the middle ages. Those who turned from classicism to romanticism abandoned the equation of 'gothic' with 'barbaric'. Their enthusiastic delving into the treasury of medieval records inspired works of literature, art and history. A new generation of historians required new research aids, and among the works compiled to meet this demand were such volumes as Kelham's *A dictionary of the Norman or old French language* of 1779. A second edition of Wright appeared in 1778 followed by a third edition eight years later. Indeed Wright's *Court-hand restored* was to go through another six editions within the following hundred years before reaching a tenth edition, corrected and enlarged by Martin himself, in 1912.

Conscious of concern in academic and political circles for the better security of the nation's documentary heritage, the government eventually appointed a commission to inquire into the state of the public records. The commissioners of 1800, 'for printing the ancient Records of Domesday, and . . . other ancient and valuable Monuments of our History, Laws, and Government', commenced the publication of calendars or texts of documents considered to be 'the most important in their Nature and the most perfect of their kind'. Patriotism incited by the French war doubtless contributed to this interest in the past, and the editors made an effort to complete one or two volumes as swiftly as practicable. The earliest folios appeared in 1802: *Taxatio ecclesiastica,* the taxation imposed by pope Nicholas IV in England and Wales about 1291, and *Calendarium rotulorum patentium,* the calendar of patent rolls. All items selected for printing were for many years of medieval origin.

A new typeface was developed—known as 'record type'— because only thus (it was decided) could the peculiarities and characteristic forms of medieval manuscripts be adequately represented and the appearance of each word in a document be reproduced in type. Lithography or engraving might have been resorted to, indeed illustrations of documents *did* grace the volumes, but the record commissioners in general demanded accurate transcription, preserving capitalisation, punctuation, authentic language and special signs of abbreviation. The policy ensured that 'wherever the Manuscript is abbreviated, the Print has a Mark of Contraction, as similar to that of the Manuscript as the Types will admit'. This project relied on first-class palaeographers, expert in deciphering every letter, symbol, hairline or stroke in the manuscript, in advising on the creation and use of the distinctive typeface, and in reading the printer's proofs. Because record commission volumes *are* printed, the researcher requires, not knowledge of palaeography, but an understanding of the Latin and French languages, conversance with Latin and French forms of personal and place-names, and an awareness of the rules for extending medieval abbreviations into full words. In this sense such a researcher needs, not a *Court-hand restored,* but a 'record interpreter'.

Wright only partially satisfied this· market but, in default of some more adequate aid, was reprinted time and again. In 1846 it reached its eighth edition, corrected under the aegis of the firm started by Henry George Bohn, scholar, secondhand bookseller and originator of the cheap reprints of standard texts known as 'Bohn's classics'. Martin's enlargement of, and corrections to, Wright in 1879 met a real demand, especially as interest in the past, and gothic Britain in particular, had not waned. The Victorians' yearning for the golden age of medieval

Britain is evidenced in the gothic revival in architecture, the romantic movement in arts and letters, and the pre-Raphaelite school of painting. The 1879 edition of Wright, published by Reeves & Turner, offered seven new plates 'executed by the Photolithographic process . . . as examples of the ordinary handwritings which the Student of Records will be likely to meet with'. Martin 'throughout corrected and considerably augmented' Wright's glossary of Latin words and his topographical list. He supplied the Latin names of Scottish and Irish bishoprics (one of Wright's original plates already displayed the names of English and Welsh dioceses) and printed the Latin forms of a few christian names. He relied on the Reverend B. W. Adams, rector of Santry, near Dublin, for 'numerous corrections' of Irish place-names. It is this appendix, much amplified, that was to be issued by Martin in 1892 as *The record interpreter*. Only one further subject required investigation before 1892: abbreviations.

Contracted forms of words figured in Wright's original plates but Martin set out to develop a dictionary of abbreviations based on his own researches 'in English records and manuscripts'. He acknowledged his debt to two scholars in particular, Alphonse A. L. Chassant and Sir Thomas Duffus Hardy. The former's *Dictionnaire des abréviations latines et françaises,* published at Evreux in 1846, typifies the French interest in archives and authenticated history following their revolution of 1789 when irrecoverable losses of documentary material occurred, Chassant's countrymen guided Europe in the administration of archives: their school of archival studies was founded in 1843. The palaeographer arranged his *Dictionnaire* alphabetically according to abbreviations. These were printed from manuscript reproductions of the handwriting of medieval documents. This system permits the researcher to compare the contracted word in his manuscript with Chassant's examples, but has obviously less advantage for someone dependent on printed texts or incapable of deciphering old handwriting. However the early editions sold out rapidly, indicating 'l'utilité indispensable du Dictionnaire'.

Martin's second mentor, Thomas Duffus Hardy, was born in 1804 in Jamaica and spent his entire working life in the public records, first at the Tower of London and later at the new record office in Chancery lane, where he rose to the highest professional position, deputy keeper of the records.

He specialised in early medieval documents, collections of which were only just becoming available to scholars through the efforts of archivists like Hardy himself. For the record commissioners he edited volumes on the close, patent, Norman, liberate, fine and charter rolls. The first volume of *Rotuli litterarum clausarum,* 1833, presented the young archivist's admittedly 'imperfect' but generally useful table of abbreviations, 'supplying a requirement that was experienced by all persons desirous of reading Records'. For the rolls series he transcribed the *Registrum palatinum dunelmense,* the register of Richard of Kellawe, lord palatine and bishop of Durham between 1311 and 1316. The fourth published volume in 1878 contained an improved table of abbreviations, which influenced Martin in the compilation of *The record interpreter.* Hardy spread his abbreviations 'dictionary-wise' in double columns over one hundred and thirty pages, occasionally grouping together several ways of contracting any single word. It is not easy to compare Duffus Hardy and Trice Martin entry by entry, mainly because of their differing alphabetical order. Hardy's arrangement mixed modified and unmodified letters, and, even taking into account his double or treble entries, his list still contains only about eighty per cent of the material in Martin's glossary.

But it was accepted by both archivists that abbreviations set up in printer's type, rather than in an imitation of handwriting, facilitated research, and Martin followed Hardy rather than Chassant when he drafted his *Record interpreter* for the publisher. It should be acknowledged that both Hardy and Chassant offered extensive and useful lists, but were not in 1892 or 1910, and certainly are not today, readily available to historians on the shelves of British bookshops and libraries. Moreover, as Martin explains, Hardy's list formed merely 'a portion of the preface of a historical book', not as convenient as if combined with other information in an archival research aid separately published.

Martin persevered in his archival labours, assembling extensive indexes from the examination of thousands of printed texts and original manuscripts. Eventually in 1892 *The record interpreter* appeared, under the imprint of Reeves & Turner, the Chancery lane law publishers and booksellers. It was revised and considerably enlarged by Martin for a second edition in 1910, and was reissued in 1935, 1949 and 1976. Nor is the 1982 Phillimore edition likely to be the last printing of this most useful work.   *   *   *   *   *

Trice Martin interprets Latin into English, but not English
into Latin, and arranges all sections alphabetically only according to the Latin—and, in one part, French—forms of each word.
The glossary is no substitute for a good Latin–English, English–
Latin dictionary. The book provides no alphabetical list of
English surnames or place-names, though it is not unduly
tiresome to peruse the relevant Latin sections in order to
locate a required English word and thus its Latin translation
alongside.

The first two sections of *The record interpreter* (pages 1–176)
serve as a key to the extension of abbreviated Latin or French
words 'in English records'. The information can be used by
researchers from all over Britain because the same contractions
appear in documents from Ireland, Scotland or Wales. Medieval
scribes employed an elegant system of abbreviations for a variety
of necessary and sensible reasons: to save ink, costly parchment,
scarce paper, and the continual sharpening of quills; to avoid
the necessity of knowing the correct spelling of the extended
word and Latin ending; from habit or training; and of course
as a means of speeding the bureaucratic processes as the level
of administrative activity increased over the centuries. Although
methods of abbreviating Latin or French words changed gradually
in the course of time, the country's writing schools and scrip-
toria at any one period followed generally accepted rules. A
gothic shorthand emerged, comprehensible to the literate and
acceptable in courts of law. In a line of manuscript Latin
containing up to twenty words, ten or more marks of abbreviation may be deployed. A few practical examples will serve to
indicate the thinking behind the medieval system: memo₃ for
memorandum 'it is to be noted'; MD for *medicinae doctor*
'doctor of medicine'; AD for *anno domini* 'in the year of the
lord'; &, a sign meaning 'and'; etc̄ for *et cetera* 'and the
remainder'. Martin discusses the meaning of various 'marks of
contraction' on pages vii–ix of the preface. He explains that
his printers could not reproduce every known mark or symbol,
'which may vary with the caprice or carelessness of a scribe';
nor was it possible to represent in type abbreviations attached
to letters printed above the line.

His arrangement may be illustrated by an example of the
Latin root *secund—*, meaning 'following, second', from which
derive the adjective *secundus* 'second' and the adverb or
preposition *secundum* 'afterwards, according to'. His list notices

18 ways of abbreviating these two words, arranged *not* together but among others beginning with *s*. His method of arrangement, once grasped, truly facilitates 'finding the word wanted'.

The researcher does not need to know or guess the extended word before locating the abbreviation, but must identify correctly the individual letters and signs in the document. This presents no difficulty when the researcher studies a reliable printed text, but may prove impossible on account of illegible handwriting or scribal idiosyncrasy if an original manuscript is being perused. In general, however, the compiler's arrangement succeeds in practice.

As an alternative to Trice Martin, some historians prefer the comprehensive and scholarly dictionary of Latin and Italian abbreviations, *Dizionario di abbreviature*, by Adriano Cappelli, first published at Milan in 1899. This lexicon of over four hundred double-columned pages—longer than Trice Martin—reproduces, alphabetically, thousands of abbreviations 'quae in lapidibus, codicibus et chartis praesertim medii-aevi occurrunt'. Like Duffus Hardy, Cappelli combines into a single sequence modified and unmodified letters. Like Chassant, he prints abbreviations from manuscript reproductions of medieval handwriting, but conveniently brackets a transcript of the actual letters alongside: for example, (scd^m) secundum, (scda) *secunda,* (scdi) secundi, (scdm) secundum, (scdo) *secundo*. As archivist-palaeographer in the archives in Milan, his lengthy and erudite introduction on brachygraphy is, of course, in Italian, and his *Dizionario,* though reprinted several times, remains relatively scarce in United Kingdom libraries and bookshops.

Trice Martin confines the glossary, on pages 177–344, to medieval 'Latin words found in records and other English manuscripts, but not occurring in classical authors'. The book omits quotations from documents, passages from printed texts, dissertations on shades of meaning, variant forms of the Latin, dates of occurrence of each expression, and commonplace words such as *et, per, cum, mensa, pater,* which 'every schoolboy knows'. By these recourses, the text is held to manageable proportions, though more comprehensive than Wright's of 1776. Admittedly the information may seem to be presented 'in a rather abrupt form'. On the other hand, a functional and handy reference aid 'does not pretend . . . to take the place of a dictionary', especially the place of one executed in the grand manner like Lewis & Short's *A Latin dictionary.*

Because he chose his Latin vocabulary during half a lifetime's research into medieval and early modern records, Martin's comprehensive glossary rarely fails to come up with the required nonclassical *uncommon* word. His uncluttered layout facilitates the swift identification of relevant entries. Although he worked from sources spanning several centuries, during which meanings of words changed, the glossary cannot even indicate this development but must baldly set down only one or two most usual interpretations. Occasionally this brevity results in certain renderings which *seem,* in Martin's phrase, 'almost inconsistent', or at least unusual companions:

> *opilio*: a shepherd; a bishop
> *salsa*: a salt marsh; sauce

An instance of undoubted brevity and apparent inconsistency was presented to me only the other day when I consulted Trice Martin for a word employed by the clerk of a Scottish kirk session during the year 1671. In the minute book I read of the summoning of a woman to the next service 'to satisfie as ane adulteresse in sacco'. This appears in the glossary as:

> saccus: a sack; a cloak

A cloak is obviously very different from a sack, especially for the unfortunate woman sentenced to public humiliation on the cutty stool where she would be forced to confess her moral lapse dressed in a coarse garment in front of a congregation of her friends and neighbours. In this context a more correct translation of *in sacco*—and a reading borne out by similar Scots vernacular documents—would be 'sackcloth'. However, the rendering of all the various subtle shades of meaning is not Martin's purpose. Precise and full exposition must be sought in R. E. Latham's *Revised medieval Latin word-list* or in the bulky tomes of Charles du Fresne, sieur Du Cange, *Glossarium ad scriptores mediae et infimae latinitatis,* the encyclopaedic glossary of middle and low Latin in documents and primary sources, usually referred to as 'the Du Cange'. According to Lewis & Short, the classical *saccus* served merely as 'a sack, bag, money-bag', though by early medieval times ecclesiastical Latin permitted 'sackcloth, haircloth'.

During his long career at the Public Record Office, Martin became familiar with a large number of documents and books, and his list reflects the range of his experience: from alchemy to zoology, law and war, farming and feudalism, seamanship and science. It is no wonder that, over the years, I have located in this glossary a number of words not readily found in comparable lists, at least under the spellings in my documents, and in the course of researching this paragraph discovered *alkanea,* interpreted by Martin as 'alcanet, Spanish bugloss', *meida* 'madder' (the dye rather than a comparative lunatic), *meimmatus* 'maimed', *fala* 'siege tower', *seplassarius* 'merchant'. *Fala* actually occurs with the identical meaning in classical authors and strictly should not appear in the glossary. *Seplasiarius* is used for a 'dealer in unguents' in Roman times, and so its medieval spelling and interpretation may justifiably be included. I recently referred to the Latin word *filum* defined by Wright as 'The Middle of the Breadth of a River' and by Martin as:

> *filum*: a fillet in architecture
> *filum aquæ*: the middle of a river

The entry informs me at a glance that *filum* has two main meanings in medieval records, architectural and topographical. The latter interpretation fitted the context which was, as I recall, 'the bounds of the estate then follow the *filum* of a stream until it meets the bridge . . .'. The advantage of this definition lies in its brevity. In Latham the entry for *filum,* extending to 34 lines, begins without mentioning 'mid-stream':

> fil/um, string (of beads, *etc.*) 1387, 1388; tow
> 1295; bow-string 1279; fillet (arch.) 1253; kind
> of locust 1266; ‡ wire 1570;

Of course Latham continues with a variety of definitions, including 'mid-stream', and a number of derivative words such as *filatio* for 'file for documents'. He also dates the appearance of the word in medieval sources, as in the example just quoted. Thus Latham and Martin serve differing but related and complementary research purposes. Indeed a third source, the Lewis & Short, adds the dimension of classical Latin, excluded from the other two, to prove in the course of 62 lines that classical authors regarded *filum* originally as a common or garden 'thread or filament' and, derivatively, as 'form or texture'. The subsequent medieval development into 'mid-stream' nowhere

occurs. Finally, we must not ignore the cautionary words which
Martin includes in his introduction, that many 'words have been
found in printed editions of records and other MSS., where I
have been unable to consult the originals'. Though perforce
accepted, the spelling may not always be a correct rendering of
the manuscript. Indeed Martin appreciated this difficulty and
wrote 'in many cases I feel certain that the editor has made
a mistake in copying'.

On pages 345-422 the list of the Latin names of towns,
villages and rivers in Great Britain and Ireland comprehends
most places likely to be required by the historian, though
specifically exclusive of 'the common English names with a
Latin termination'. The local historian doubtless adds to the
list from his knowledge of documents available nowadays in
county record offices, just as Martin himself produced from
printed and manuscript sources a list that was an improved
version of Wright's glossary. The place-names of Roman Britain
exercised the minds of Victorian philologists and archaeologists,
and Martin suggests alternative localities for forts or settlements
'upon the position of which there is a difference of opinion'.
For the Cheshire *Salinæ*, 'saltpans', however, he offers only
Nantwich though some authorities prefer Middlewich. Martin
identifies the modern site of places whose names include a
common element such as *pons* 'bridge'. Some Latin toponyms
date from medieval times rather than from the era of the
Roman occupation, concocted by scribes as they compiled
charters, chartularies or chronicles. Scribes writing after 1066
commemorated the victory of king Harold over the Norsemen
at Stanfordbrycg by renaming the river crossing *Pons Belli*
'battle bridge'.

The Latin names of bishoprics in England, Ireland and
Scotland are alphabetically arranged on pages 423-428. The
list of prelacies 'in England' includes St Asaph, Bangor, Llandaff
and St Davids in Wales and Sodor & Man, *Sodorensis,* the diocese
serving the Isle of Man and the Hebrides. The latter island group
was known as *sudreyjar* or 'southern islands' in the Norse
language of the early medieval inhabitants. Four Latin forms of
Sodor & Man also appear under 'bishoprics in Scotland' (page
424). Not a few Irish dioceses, small in area and impoverished
financially, became extinct during the middle ages or were
amalgamated with neighbours, but absentee priests, ambitious
for status, revived others during times of trouble in the church.

Dromore, whose Latin name Trice Martin sets out as either *Drumorensis* or *Drunimorensis*, supported four non-resident bishops at once in the 1430s. Nowadays an Anglican prelate may sign official missives with his christian name and an abbreviated Latin form of the diocesan title. Thus the signature of the 104th bishop of Rochester, Richard David Say, reads 'David Roffen:', *Roffensis* being a Latin version of Rochester.

On pages 429–464 are tabulated alphabetically the Latin forms of English surnames and christian names, including those of Saxon or Norman immigrants into Ireland, Scotland or Wales but not native Celtic family names. The author relied mainly on documentary sources in southern England for his examples, although he records 'some Irish and Welsh [christian] names'. Proper names in documents are not always readily interpreted from the Latin, indeed English forms may be unknown, and the compiler leaves blanks against *Ibria, Orframina, Sewacus, Jerberga* and other Latin christian names not translatable. The more common Saxon or Norman names to be found in Trice Martin include *Ailwinus* for Ethelwin, *Alienora* for Eleanor, *Galterus* for Walter, *Willelmus* for William, *Galfridus* for Geoffrey. But the list really comes into its own with names that the British searcher would be unlikely to recognise and less likely to guess, such as *Caluarius* for the Irish Baldy or *Comitissa* for the Jewish Ha-Nasiah. A number of these names can appear in two or more vernacular versions. How an individual would have been addressed was known in his own village: *Radulfus* could have been Ralph or Randulph, *Randolphus* Randolf or Randal, *Johanna* Joan, Joanna, Jean or Jane, *Theobaldus* Theobald or Tybalt.

Scribes also altered surnames into Latin forms, sometimes by clumsy direct translation: giving *Pelliparius* for Skinner; *de Lato Campo* 'broad field' for Bradfield; *filius Johannis* for Johnson or, just as correctly, John's son; *de Bono Fassato* 'good faggot' for Goodrick. Some Latin names reflect the medieval writer's ignorance of etymology. In the 1770s Wright had recorded, without etymological comment, *de Umbrosa quercu* as the Latin equivalent of the English surname 'Dimoak, now Dimmock'. The Latin had been ingeniously concocted by clerks from an apparent literal meaning, 'the dim or shady oak'. In fact the surname derives not from 'dim oak' but from the village of Dymock, Gloucestershire, a place-name possibly of British (that is Celtic) origin, denoting 'pigsty'. However

Latin clerks translated 'dim oak' directly into Latin as *de umbrosa quercu.*

The retranslation into the vernacular produces the occasional headache. For instance, *rotarius* in the Latin means 'soldier or robber or wheelwright', and rarely can the researcher be certain whether such a word is being deployed as a surname, occupation or term of abuse, especially during the 14th and 15th centuries when family names were being formed. *Rotarius* offers complications, because the Latin additionally does duty for the French *le roteor*, 'a player on the rote', (a rote, the musical fiddle, rather than the routine), and hence for the English surname derived from *roteor*, namely Rutter. Rutter serves as the English version of the Latin *rotarius* or Norman French *rotier*, interpreted as 'ruffian, highwayman or soldier'. Consequently the appearance of *rotarius* in a Latin document suggests various possibilities in the vernacular: Rutter, wheelwright, Wright or wright (occupation), a soldier, ruffian, swindler, Fiddler, Vidler (a variant of Fiddler), even gallant or cavalier.

The final pages of the preface (xii–xiii) outline the interpretation of marginal dots found in financial accounts during the period when roman numerals were used. Because of the difficulty of successfully completing arithmetical calculations with the l's, x's, c's, v's, and i's of the Romans, accountants adopted various practical aids such as the abacus or the exchequer method of placing counters on a chequered cloth— and presumably the most readily available expedient of eight fingers and two thumbs. To facilitate calculation a system of lines and dots was evolved. These appear in the margins of documents, the scribe afterwards inserting the answers in roman numerals at the proper place in the text. Martin, quoting nine examples from the 1530s, does not comment on the frequency of occurrence of this 'dotting' arrangement, though N. Denholm Young in *Handwriting in England and Wales* asserts that calculation by dots 'is not common in documents at any period'.

*   *   *   *   *

Returning from *The record interpreter* to its compiler, it is pleasant to note that he did manage to drag himself away from his dusty documents to engage in more physical pursuits. Not a little of his leisure time he spent not in dim damp muniment rooms but in the countryside where his chief delight was the sport of fly fishing. And he became a familiar figure in the gymnasia of his clubs where he was a skilful exponent of the gentlemanly art of fencing. During his early career Martin resided south of the Thames, in the genteel neighbourhood, then newly developed, of Upper Tooting. His house, Number 2 The Lawn, lay in a quiet suburban street off the Balham Park Road, some seven miles from his office. Railway trains and omnibuses communicated with the city. Later, Martin moved north of the river, to Maida Vale. His house at the northern end of what was then known as Portsdown Road stood not far from Paddington recreation and cricket ground. His respectable bourgeois neighbours included Lady Hill, daughter of a chief justice of Antigua, Sir John Tenniel, the caricaturist, and a sprinkling of wealthy widows, ecclesiastics and retired military. Towards the end of his career he moved the short distance to St Johns Wood. However, he spent his retirement in the Buckinghamshire village of Wooburn Green in the Thames valley, though his villa Northcroft stood within easy reach of the London trains. His wife Catharine Heard bore his two daughters, Mary Trice and Katherine Susanna, who were eventually beneficiaries of his Royal Insurance Company life policy. But his worldly goods, albeit inconsiderable in amount, he willed to his spouse, except for three items, 'the Fern case at present in her possession' given to his sister Alice, their father's gold watch to his brother Howard, and 'my Cat's eye ring' to a Frances Henrietta Miller of Pinkneys Green, Berkshire. In 1895 Martin had expressed the wish to be buried in Abney Park cemetery, Stoke Newington, but allowed in a codicil to his will dated 1906 for cremation or burial at his wife's 'uncontrolled discretion'.

Martin died at the age of 72 on 13 May 1914. There is an 18-line obituary in *The Times,* a by no means unworthy tribute for 'a very useful officer' in the public service. And the reissuing of his renowned book in 1982 would doubtless please the compiler too. A French reviewer writing in 1862 claimed to have put Chassant's *Dictionnaire* to the surest of tests, that of practical use during several months of historical research: 'je me rencontre tous les jours en présence des difficultés dont M. Chassant s'est proposé de donner la solution, et je dois reconnaître que, sauf des exceptions assez rares, ces solutions ont été trouvées justes.' Charles Trice Martin's *The record interpreter* has, in my experience, equally well endured the test of constant reference in the archives. And is that not praise enough?

FORRES
20 FEBRUARY 1982

THE RECORD INTERPRETER.

THE
RECORD INTERPRETER:

A COLLECTION OF

ABBREVIATIONS, LATIN WORDS AND NAMES

USED IN

ENGLISH HISTORICAL MANUSCRIPTS
AND RECORDS.

COMPILED BY

CHARLES TRICE MARTIN, B.A., F.S.A.,

LATE ASSISTANT-KEEPER OF THE PUBLIC RECORDS.

SECOND EDITION.

LONDON:

STEVENS AND SONS, LIMITED,

119 & 120, CHANCERY LANE,

Law Publishers.

1910.

PREFACE.

THE present volume is really an amplification of the Appendix to the ninth edition of Wright's "Court Hand Restored," which I brought out in 1879, with the addition of a list of the abbreviated forms of Latin and French words used in English records and manuscripts.

Several such lists have been published at various times, the most used, perhaps, in England being Chassant's "Dictionnaire des Abréviations," and the list in the fourth volume of the "Registrum Palatinum Dunelmense," edited by the late Sir Thomas Duffus Hardy in the series of "Chronicles and Memorials."

This latter, however, being merely a portion of the preface of a historical book, is not so well known nor so convenient for use as if it occurred in a book devoted to information of this class.

I have endeavoured also to justify the printing of another such list by arranging the abbreviations in such a manner as to facilitate the finding the word wanted. In some lists this is not easy, unless one knows what the word is in full.

The principle acted on has been as follows:—Letters with marks of contraction attached to them, represented by a single type, are separated from the same letters printed in the ordinary way. The order thus is—the letter followed by a letter; the letter followed by a sign; the letter with a sign attached.

For instance, in the vowels the order is as follows:—

> *e.g.*, E : ea, eb, ec, to ez ;
> then—eȝ, eꞔ, e⁹, eẓ ;*
> then—ē, ẽ.

In the consonants, *e.g.*, N : na to nz ;
> then—nȝ, nꞔ, n⁹, nẓ ;
> then—ṅ, ñ, ꞟ.

In the letter C, ꞔ follows ꞓ.

In the letter P, the order of contracted forms is p⁹, ꝑ, p̃, p̉, ꝓ.

In the letter Q : q, q̃, ꝗ.

Superior letters—that is, letters printed above the line—are considered in the arrangement as if printed on the line in the ordinary way.

In manuscripts such letters often have contraction marks added to them, but it is impossible to represent these in type, and an apostrophe has had to do duty instead, as prin¹', *principalis.* In a manuscript the *l* would be struck through.

According to the correct principles of writing, the mark of contraction in a word should be placed over a letter after which letters are omitted, or over a letter before and after which letters are omitted, as p̃r, *pater ;* d̃na, *domina ;* fc̃t, *fecit ;* app̃llat,

---

* These marks of contraction, being separate types, are arranged before those which are attached to the letter, in order to keep such forms as ꞔf°ȝ, debȝ, g⁹, moẓ, pȝ, solȝ, su⁹, tȝ distinct from ꞔfõȝ, deb̃ȝ, g̃⁹, mõẓ, p̃ȝ, sot̃ȝ, sū⁹, t̃ȝ.

appellat; but such forms as pr̃, dña, fct, appttat, sometimes occur, perhaps from carelessness on the part of the scribe. Some of these false forms are inserted, but by no means all, so that if any word occurring in a manuscript is not at once found in the list, it should be looked for under some other form containing the same letters of the alphabet, but with different contractions.

The marks of contraction used in printing are intended to represent the typical forms of the contractions used in manuscripts, and necessarily appear more formal and uniform than those which may vary with the caprice or carelessness of a scribe.

Their signification is as follows :—

— means *m* or *n* following the letter thus marked ; *e.g.* ī, *in;* ōnis, *omnis;* omĩis, *omnis;* dāpna, *dampna;* dampa, *dampna.*

⁓ either over a short letter or through a long letter means the omission of some single letter not *m* or *n,* or of more than one letter either after, or before and after, the letter thus marked.

 e.g., ā, *ac, apud;* ās, *alias.*
  dñs, *dominus;* carĩa, *carmina;* fc̃is, *factis.*
  ip̃e, *ipse.*
  põita, *posita.*

⁊ means *er;* *e.g.,* inͣt, *inter;* ꝼru̅, *ferrum.*
  re; *e.g.,* p̃, *præ.*
  ir; *e.g.,* serᷓe, *servire.*

ℓ means *is* ; *e.g.*, forℓ, *foris.*

    es ; *e.g.*, om̄ℓ, *omnes* ; ꞔtℓ, *competentes.*

    Or sometimes merely the ending of a word ; *e.g.*, infℓ, *infortunium.*

ꝯ „ *us* ; *e.g.*, ipī ꝯ, *ipsius* ; ũs ꝯ, *versus.*

    os ; *e.g.*, p ꝯtea, *postea.*

    ost ; *e.g.*, p ꝯ, *post.*

ȝ „ *us* ; *e.g.*, quibȝ, *quibus.*

    et ; *e.g.*, licȝ, *licet.*

    ed ; *e.g.*, sȝ, *sed.*

    Added to q it means *quia*, and sometimes *que*, or *quæ*, though these last two words are more correctly written q̦.

    Occasionally it stands for *que*, as absȝ, *absque*, and in some MSS. for *m* or almost any final letters ; as bõȝ, *bonitatem* ; err°ȝ, *errorem.*

ᵹ „ *rum* ; *e.g.*, aïaᵹ, *animarum* ; ƀatoᵹ, *beatorum.* It is sometimes used in the middle of a word, as coᵹpere, *corrumpere.*

    ram ; *e.g.*, Alienoᵹ, *Alienoram.*

    ras ; *e.g.*, libᵹ, *libras.*

    res ; *e.g.*, Windesoᵹ, *Windesores.*

    ris ; *e.g.*, conquestoᵹ, *conquestoris* ; libᵹ, *libris.*

ꞔ „ *cum* ; *e.g.*, ꞔ, *cum.*

    com ; *e.g.*, ꞔp̃, *computus.*

    con ; *e.g.*, ꞔª, *contra.*

    cog ; *e.g.*, ꞔnouit, *cognovit.*

The marks attached to the letter P are as follows :—

p, *per, par, por; e.g.*, psōa, *persona* ; ꞔpet, *comparet* ; pta, *porta.*

ꝑ, *præ, pre ; e.g.*, ꝑsēs, *præsens* ; supꝑmus, *supremus.*

ᵽ, *pro ; e.g.*, ᵽceres, *proceres ;* ĩppⁱe, *improprie.*

p̃ indicates the omission of almost any other letters than those
mentioned above; *e.g.*, p̃ea, *postea ;* p̃a, *pœna ;* p̃cta,
puncta ; p̃pa, *papa.*

The marks attached to the letter Q are as follows :—

q, usually *quod*, but also used for *quœ, quam, que, quo,* and
followed by other letters *qui*, as qd, *quid ;* qb3, *quibus.*

q̓, *quœ, que, quem,* and as part of a word it has very various
meanings, as q̓ela, *querela ;* q̓ntum, *quantum ;* q̓one,
quœstione ; q̓ppe, *quippe.*

q̶ means *que.*

q3 „ *quia.*

A superior letter indicates the omission of two or more letters
of which this is one ; *e.q.*, qᵒs, *quos ;* cⁱlo, *circulo ;* capⁱ, *capituli.*

A point below a letter indicates that it should be deleted, and
points under or inverted commas over two words indicate that
they ought to be transposed ; *e.g.*, et " p t̃ro " it̃, *et item pro
thesauro.*

Many words will be found in this list which do not conform
to the principles here stated, but they have been found in MSS.,
and inserted accordingly.

As a rule the nominative case of nouns or adjectives is given
as the meaning, as ff, *filius ;* and sometimes the case most
frequently met with, as f̃r, *Francorum ;* but this does not exclude
other cases as well.

The glossary does not pretend, as no glossary can, to take
the place of a dictionary, where the meanings of words are
discussed, and quotations given to explain their use ; but still it

is hoped that it will be found useful, although the information contained in it is given in a rather abrupt form.

This second edition contains a number of words not included in the first, which have been noticed since that edition was printed.

Many words have been found in printed editions of records and other MSS., where I have been unable to consult the originals, and though the meaning of the word may be clear, it does not follow that the spelling is correct; in fact, in many cases I feel certain that the editor has made a mistake in copying, though I cannot suggest the right reading with any certainty.

In the case of words used in classical as well as mediæval literature, the classical meaning is not usually given, as it may be assumed that any one using this book would know it. It must not, however, be taken as excluded. For instance, *galea* is inserted as meaning " galley," but it is also used with the older meaning of " helmet." Similarly *ala* means " wing " as often as " aisle." It will be noticed that sometimes the meanings given for Latin words are almost inconsistent, but it must be remembered that the period covered by the glossary is several centuries. Words already current were used for new inventions, especially when what they once signified had become obsolete.

The list of Latin names of places in England contains most of the names which a student of history is likely to require, but of course it might be very much enlarged by adding the Latin names of a great many villages and hamlets which are merely formed from the English names.

No attempt has been made here to settle the disputed attribution of Roman stations, but rather to give the places for which their names have been used in later times.

Many of the place names and surnames have been found in classes of records which contain documents in both languages referring to the same case, like the Chancery Proceedings, in which bills and answers are in English and writs in Latin. Some of the Latin names in these are due to the ingenuity of officials or clerks, who inserted what they imagined to be a translation of an English word, of the history and meaning of which they were totally ignorant—such as *Ventus Morbidus* for Windsor, and *de Umbrosa Quercu* for Dimock. Latin inscriptions on brasses, tombstones, and other monuments, many of the sixteenth and later centuries, have afforded many very curious specimens, the English names being supplied by other sources of information.

It is worth noticing how many surnames " assimilate a vernacular origin," to use a phrase of which my honoured schoolmaster, Thomas Hewitt Key, was very fond. For instance, names ending in Latin in *villa* and in French in *ville*, are often found in later English with the termination *field* or *well*, as *de Strata villa*, Streatfield; *de Berevilla*, Berewell. Similarly, *Lotharingus, Le Loreyne*, becomes in the course of time Lorriner, or Lorimer, the English equivalent of *Lorimarius*, a harness maker. Other cases are Longfellow and Littleboy, whose ancestors were Longueville and Lillebois.

Many surnames taken from the places where their owners

lived, are not included in the list of surnames, but will be found among the list of places.

In the list of Christian names there are several blanks in the second column. These are opposite to Latin names which I inserted in my list, hoping some day to find them in English, but that day has not yet come ; so, confessing my ignorance, I leave the blanks for some more learned or more fortunate person than myself to fill up.

There is another matter of which there is no mention in the first edition, but an explanation may be of some use to those who are not already familiar with it.

In accounts of the period when Roman numerals were used, an arrangement of dots is often found in the margin, of which the following is a specimen :—

These were apparently put down while the accountant was making a calculation, and afterwards the amount which they represent, inserted in the proper place in Roman numerals. Their meaning is as follows :

The perpendicular lines mark the division into pounds, shillings and pence.

Dots on the line count as units.

Dots below the line count as units.

Dots above the line on the left hand side in the pound and shilling columns, count for 10.

Dots above the line on the right hand side in the pound and shilling columns, count for 5.

Dots above the line on the left hand side in the pence column count for 6.

A fourth column stands for farthings.

These are examples from accounts dated between 1530 and 1540 :—

$$\cdot \,|\, \cdot \ \cdot \ \overset{\cdot}{\underset{\cdot\ \cdot}{}} \qquad = \qquad 1l.\ 10s.$$

$$\overset{\cdot\ \cdot\ \cdot}{\underset{\cdot}{}} \,|\, \overset{\cdot\ \cdot\ \cdot\ \cdot}{\underset{\cdot\ \cdot}{}} \,|\, \overset{\cdot\ \cdot}{\underset{\cdot}{}} \qquad = \qquad 14l.\ 6s.\ 3d.$$

$$\cdot \ \cdot \,|\, \overset{}{\underset{\cdot}{\cdot\ \cdot\ \cdot}} \,|\, \overset{\cdot}{\underset{}{\cdot\ \cdot}} \qquad = \qquad 2l.\ 4s.\ 8d.$$

$$\cdot \,|\, \overset{\cdot}{\underset{\cdot\ \cdot\ \cdot}{\cdot\ \cdot\ \cdot}} \,|\, \overset{}{\underset{\cdot\ \cdot}{\cdot\ \cdot}} \,|\, \overset{}{\underset{\cdot}{\cdot}} \qquad = \qquad 1l.\ 16s.\ 4\tfrac{1}{2}d.$$

$$\cdot \ \cdot \,|\, \overset{\cdot}{\underset{\cdot}{\cdot\ \cdot\ \cdot}} \,|\, \cdot \ \cdot \qquad = \qquad 2l.\ 9s.\ 2d.$$

$$\cdot \ \cdot \,|\, \overset{\cdot}{\underset{\cdot}{\cdot\ \cdot\ \cdot}} \,|\, \overset{\cdot}{\underset{}{}} \qquad = \qquad 2l.\ 9s.\ 7d.$$

$$\cdot \,|\, \overset{}{\underset{\cdot\ \cdot}{\cdot\ \cdot\ \cdot}} \,|\, \overset{\cdot}{\underset{\cdot}{\cdot}} \qquad = \qquad 1l.\ 5s.\ 9d.$$

$$\cdot \,|\, \overset{\cdot}{\underset{}{\cdot\ \cdot\ \cdot}} \,|\, \overset{}{\underset{}{\cdot}} \qquad = \qquad 1l.\ 8s.\ 1d.$$

$$\cdot \,|\, \overset{}{\underset{\cdot}{\overset{\cdot\ \cdot\ \cdot}{\cdot\ \cdot\ \cdot}}} \,|\, \cdot \ \cdot \qquad = \qquad 1l.\ 7s.\ 2d.$$

C. T. M.

April, 1910.

(**xv**)

TABLE OF CONTENTS.

———

THE RECORD INTERPRETER.

———◆———

A LIST OF ABBREVIATIONS OF LATIN WORDS.

A.

A. *Alanus, Albertus, Augustinus
and other Christian names
beginning with A; quin-
genti.*

a. *ad, alta.*

aᵘ *alia, aliqua, anima, antiphona.*

aᵃm *aliam, aliquam, animam.*

aᵃndo *aliquando.*

aᵃˢ *alias, animas.*

aᵃȝ *aliam.*

aᵃẑ *aliarum, aliquarum, animarum.*

aᵃ̃ *aliam.*

abbᵃm *abbatem.*

abbᵃs *abbates, abbatis.*

abbatibȝ *abbatibus.*

abbãssa *abbatissa.*

abbⁱˢ *abbatis.*

abbĩa *abbatissa.*

abbuĩ *abbuttant, abbuttantes.*

abƀ *abbas.*

abƀa *abbatissa.*

abƀe *abbate, abbatissæ.*

abƀes *abbates.*

M.

abƀi *abbati.*

abƀia *abbatia.*

abƀiᵃ *abbatissa.*

abƀisse *abbatissæ.*

abƀs *abbas.*

abƀtē *abbatem.*

abƀtę *abbatis.*

abᶜ'ᵒ *ablatio.*

abdux̃ *abduxerunt.*

abĩ *abinvicem.*

ablaᵒ *ablatio.*

ablaĩ *ablatores.*

abła ᵒ *ablegatio.*

abło *ablatio, absolutio.*

abłõm *ablationem, absolutionem.*

abⁿᵉ *absolutione.*

abnep̃ *abnepos.*

abñ *abnepos.*

abᵒ *absolutio.*

absołȯ *absolutio.*

absqᵦ *absque.*

abstiᵃ *abstinentia.*

abstᵒ *abstractio.*

abstᵗ *abstulit.*

B

abst̃ *abstractum.*
abs₃ *absque.*
ab^{ta} *abstracta.*
ab^{te} *absolute.*
ab^{t9} *absolutus.*
ab̄b̄is *abbatis.*
ab̄lo *absolutio.*
ab̄n^{a} *absentia.*
ab̄nciū *absentium.*
ab̄ne *absolutione.*
ab̄ñia *absentia.*
ab̄tē *abbatem.*
A. C. *Anno Christi.*
a^{ca} *aliqua.*
ac^{a} *acra.*
ac^{as} *acras.*
ac^{a}ꝝ *acrarum.*
acc^{a} *accidentia.*
acc^{ales} *accidentales.*
acc^{a}l̄ *accidentalis.*
accepim^{9} *acceperimus.*
accep̃ *accepit.*
acc^{e}scit *accrescit.*
acc^{e}ūt *acceperunt.*
accēđe *accendere.*
acci^{b}₃ *accidentibus.*
accid^{do} *accidendo.*
acci^{do} *accidendo, accipiendo.*
accipe *accipere.*
accip̃ *accipere, accipit.*
acci^{r} *accidentaliter, accipitur.*
acci^{s} *accidens.*
accñ *accidentia.*
acc^{oe} *actione.*
accōmodat̃ *accommodatum.*
accōmodaū *accommodavit.*
acc^{9}are *accusare.*
acc̃ *accipe.*
acc̃a *accidentia.*
acc̃at *accusat.*
acc̃at^{r} *accusatur.*
acc̃đn^{lis} *accidentalis.*
acc̃e *accipere.*
acc̃it *accidit.*
acc̃^{m} *accensum, accusativum.*
acc̃ma *acerrima.*
acc̃n^{a} *accidentia.*
acc̃n$^{l'r}$ *accidentaliter.*
acc̃ns *accidens.*
acc̃nte *accidente.*
acc̃n^{tis} *accidentalis.*
acc̃nt^{r} *accidentaliter.*
acc̃o *accusatio, actio.*
acc̃oi^{b}₃ *accusationibus, actionibus.*
acc̃ōm *actionem.*
a^{ci} *alicui.*
ac^{is} *acris.*
ac^{m} *actum.*
a^{co} *aliquo.*
ac^{o} *actio*
acq^{i}etare *acquietare.*
acq^{i}etācia *acquietantia.*
acq^{i}r̃e *acquirere.*
acq^{itū} *acquisitum.*

acq^r *acquiretur, acquiritur.*
acr̃ *acra.*
ac^s *accidens, acras.*
acti^t' *activitatis.*
act^m *actum.*
act^r *actualiter.*
actu^r *actualiter.*
act̃ *actio, actum.*
act̃a *activa.*
act̃e *actione.*
act̃m *activum.*
act̄ōib₃ *actionibus.*
ac^ua *activa.*
ac^u⁹ *activus.*
ac̃e *accipere.*
ac̃^lis *accidentalis.*
ac̃m *acram.*
ac̃ns *accidens.*
ac̃^o *actio.*
ac̃^oē *actionem.*
ac̃s *acras.*
ac̃u *actu.*
ac̃u⁹ *acervus.*

A. D. *Anno Domini, ante diem.*
a^d *aliquid, aliquod, aliud.*
ad^at *advocat.*
ad^c *adhuc.*
ad^cat *advocat.*
addic̃o *additio.*
additam̃tū *additamentum.*
addi^tū *additamentum.*
addĩt *additionem.*

addux̃at *adduxerat.*
addux̃ūt *adduxerunt.*
add̄o *addendo, additio.*
add̄r *additur.*
add̄₃ *adderet.*
ad̃ee *adesse.*
ad̃ēē *adessem, adessent.*
adh^c *adhuc.*
adh̃ *adhuc.*
adh̃endo *adhærendo, adhibendo.*
adh̃nda *adhibenda.*
adh̃nt *adhibent.*
adh̃r *adhibetur.*
adh̃re *adhibere.*
adiac̃ *adjacens, adjacet.*
adiudic̃ *adjudicatur, adjudicatus.*
adiu^te *adjuvante.*
adīuicē *adinvicem.*
adï *adinvicem.*
a. d. k. *ante diem kalendarum.*
admīstrōm *administrationem.*
adm̃ *administrante, administratio.*
adm̃s^rat⁹ *admensuratus.*
adnep̃ *adnepos.*
adn^lat^r *adnihilatur.*
adn^l₃ *adnihilet.*
adolend̃ *adolendum.*
adop⁹ *adoptivus.*
adq^ietare *adquietare.*
adq^iet̃ *adquietatio.*
adq^ire *adquirere.*

adqⁱsic̃o *adquisitio.*

adqⁱta *adquisita.*

adq⁹ *adquisitus.*

adq̃etac̃o *adquietatio.*

adq̃siuit *adquisivit.*

A. D. R. *Anno Dominicæ Re-*
surrectionis.

ad^{ta} *administrata.*

ad^{te} *animadverte.*

ad^{t'a} *administratura.*

aduocac̃o *advocatio.*

aduocat⁹ *advocatus.*

aduocaũ *advocavit.*

aduoc̃o *advocatio.*

aduõ^{tus} *advocatus.*

adũ *adventum, advocatio.*

adũ^{d'} *advertendum.*

adũsaⁱ *adversarii.*

adũsi^{te} *adversitate.*

adũsit̃ *adversitatem.*

adũso *adverso.*

adũs⁹ *adversus.*

adũt̃e *advertere.*

ad̃lac̃o *adulatio.*

adstrand̃ *administrandum.*

ad̃t *adest, adesset.*

ad̃tor *administrator.*

a^e *aliæ.*

A. E. C. *Anno Emmanuelis*
Christi.

aecc̃ta *ecclesia.*

aecc̃tsiola *ecclesiola.*

aec̃ta *ecclesia.*

aed̃ *ædes.*

a^em *aliquem.*

aff^a *affirmativa.*

affc̃m *affectum.*

affc̃o *affectio.*

affⁱ *affidavit.*

affidaũ *affidavit.*

affid̃ *affidare, affidavit.*

affⁱmat̃ *affirmatum.*

affir^at^r *affirmatur.*

aff^{iva} *affirmativa.*

aff^o *affirmatio.*

affr̃a *affirmativa.*

aff^t *affidavit.*

aff⁹ *affirmatus.*

aff *affidavit, and other parts of*
the verb.

aff *afferatores.*

afid̃ *affidavit.*

aft̃ *affidavit.*

ag^{d'} *agendum.*

agd̃ *agendum.*

ag^eg^aa *aggregata.*

ag^em *aggregatum.*

agg^{ari} *aggravari.*

agg^at̃ę *aggravatis.*

agg^aʒ *aggravet.*

agg^edi *aggredi.*

agg̃tũ *aggregatum.*

agⁱ *agri.*

ag^m *agrum.*

agnic̃lm *agniculum.*

agñ *Agnes, agnus.*

ag° *agro.*

ag°ˢ *agros.*

ag°sc̃e *agnoscere.*

agʳ *agitur.*

ag̃ *agit, agistatos.*

ag̃đ *agendum.*

ag̃đr *aggreditur.*

ag̃m *agrum.*

ag̃nđ *agendis, agendum.*

ag̃s *agris, Augustus.*

Ag̃sti *Augusti.*

ag̃t *agunt.*

ag̃ᵗᵒˢ *aggravatos.*

ag̃đr *aggreditur.*

ag̃e *agere.*

ag̃gᵃū *aggregatum.*

aħ *archiepiscopi.*

aⁱ *alibi, alicui, aliqui.*

aⁱa *anima.*

aⁱcᵃ *aliqua.*

aⁱcⁱ *alicui.*

aⁱc⁹ *alicujus.*

aⁱd *aliquid, aliud.*

aⁱⁱ *alii.*

aⁱm *animum.*

aⁱqᵃs *aliquas.*

aⁱqᵃten⁹ *aliquatenus.*

aⁱqⁱ *aliqui.*

aⁱqⁱd *aliquid.*

aⁱqⁱs *aliquis.*

aⁱq̣ *aliquod.*

aⁱq̣ᵃ *aliquam.*

aⁱq̣ᵃr *aliqualiter.*

aⁱq̣ū *aliquam.*

aⁱq́ *aliquam.*

aⁱq́do *aliquando.*

aⁱs *aliquis, acris.*

aⁱˢ *animalis, assisis.*

aisnec̃ *aisnecca.*

aïa *anima.*

aïadũtenđ *animadvertendum.*

aïał *animal, and its cases.*

aïa₂ *animarum.*

aïe *animæ.*

aïi *animi.*

aïm *animum.*

aïo *animo.*

aïs *aliis, animis.*

aï⁹ *animus.*

a. k. *ante kalendas.*

aˡ *animal.*

Alañ *Alanus.*

Alƀ *Albertus.*

alᵈ *aliud.*

ald *aldermannus.*

aldm̃ *aldermannus.*

aldrañ *aldermannus.*

Alex̃ *Alexander.*

alⁱ *alibi.*

alicⁱ *alicui.*

alicui⁹ *alicujus.*

alic̃ *alicui.*

aliñ *aliquando.*

alioȝ *aliorum.*

aliq^a *aliqua.*

aliq^am *aliquam.*

aliq^ar *aliqualiter.*

aliq^as *aliquas.*

aliq^atlo *aliquantulo.*

aliq^id *aliquid.*

aliq^o *aliquo.*

aliq^oc̃ *aliquotiens.*

aliq^r *aliqualiter*

aliq^tr *aliqualiter.*

aliquā *aliquam.*

aliqa *aliqua.*

aliq^i *aliquid.*

aliq̇ *aliqua, aliquod.*

aliq̇d *aliquid, aliquod.*

aliq̇n *alioquin, aliquando.*

a^lis *annualis.*

alit^r *aliter.*

alit̃ *aliter.*

alïbȝ *animalibus.*

all^ao *allegatio.*

alle^at^r *allegatur.*

allec̃ *allecis.*

alle^d' *allegandum.*

allegac̃ *allegationem.*

Allex^r *Alexander.*

allocac̃o *allocatio.*

allocet^r *allocetur.*

allocuc̃o *allocutio.*

alloc̃ *allocatio, allocutio.*

alł *allegator, allegatur, allegoria.*

alłnt *allegant.*

alłta *allegata.*

alm^9 *almus.*

a^lnos *alienos.*

a^lq^o *aliquo.*

alq̃r *aliqualiter.*

alti^c *altitudine.*

alti^c̃ *altitudinem.*

alt̃a^r *alteratur.*

alt̃o *alteratio.*

alt̃ *alter.*

alt̃a *altera.*

alt̃ais *alterationis.*

alt̃i^9 *alterius.*

alt̃m *alterum.*

alt̃ȝ *alterum.*

alūis *aluminis.*

Alũed̃ *Alveredus.*

ał *alias, aliquis, alius.*

ała *alia.*

ałas *alias.*

ałd *aliud.*

ałe *animale.*

ałi *alibi.*

ałia *animalia.*

ałibȝ *animalibus.*

ałł *allegator, allegoria.*

ałła *alleluia.*

ałłauit *allegavit.*

ałło *allegatio.*

ałm *animalium.*

altnes *altitudines.*

atñ *aliquando.*

ato *alio, aliquo.*

atq⁰⁰ *aliquo modo.*

atr *aliter.*

ats *alias.*

attʳ *aliter.*

aᵐ *alium, animum, annum, argumentum.*

a.m. *anno mundi.*

am⁰ *amodo.*

amoʳ *amovetur.*

amoũ *amoverunt.*

amoᵘe *amovere.*

amoũũt *amoverunt.*

amp⁹ *amplius.*

amˢ *amictus, amicus.*

amᵗđ *amittendum.*

am̃ *amen, amicus.*

am̃al *animalia.*

am̃ciam̃ *amerciamentum.*

am̃tare *amuntare.*

am̃ciam̃ *amerciamentum.*

am̃ciāđ⁹ *amerciandus.*

an. *ante, antecessoris.*

aⁿ *ante.*

anᵃ *antea, antiphona.*

anaᵃ *anatomia.*

anatħm̃ *anathema.*

anc̃ *antecessoris.*

Anđ *Anaegaviæ, Andegavenses, Andegavorum.*

Angᶜᵉ *Anglice.*

angⁱˡˡᵃʳ' *anguillarum.*

Angloῑ *Anglorum.*

ang¹⁹ *angelus.*

Angł *Anglia.*

Angłῑ *Anglorum.*

ang̃loȝ *angelorum.*

ang̃l *angelis.*

ang̃lȝ *angelorum.*

an¹atʳ *annihilatur.*

anˡⁱˢ *annualis.*

an¹đ *angelum, angulum.*

anto *annulo.*

ann. *annos.*

ann⁰e *annonæ.*

annueῑ *annuerunt.*

anũ *annuatim, annus.*

anqᵃ *antequam.*

antᵃ *antiphona.*

antec̃ *antecedens, antecessor.*

antedc̃us *antedictus.*

anteqᵃm *antequam.*

anteqᵃ *antequam.*

anteq̃ *antequam.*

antiqⁱt⁹ *antiquitus.*

anᵗⁱ⁹ *antiquitus.*

antᵗᵉ *antecedente.*

antȩ *antecedentis.*

antῖ *ante, antecessor.*

antᵖ *antecedenter.*

anȝ *antecessorum.*

añuũ *annuum.*

añ *animalia, annus, ante, antecessor, annon.*

aña *animalia, antea.*

añcessoȝ *antecessorum.*

añcess̃ *antecessor.*

añc̃ *antecessor.*

añdc̆us *antedictus.*

añfe^r *antefertur.*

añia *animalia.*

añlo *annulo.*

añl$^{l'}$ *angelis.*

año^a *analogia.*

añpⱡta *antepenultima.*

añq^{a}m *antequam.*

añq$^{a'}$ *antequam.*

añrior *anterior.*

añs *antecedens.*

añte *antecedente.*

añt$^{l'}$ *antecedenter.*

a^o *alio, alio modo, aliquo, anno.*

a^{o}d *aliquod.*

a^{oo} *alio modo.*

a^{os} *alios.*

a^{o}t *aliquot.*

a^{o}ȝ *aliorum.*

ap^a *apta.*

ap^{ca} *apostolica.*

ap^d *apud.*

apellac̃o *appellatio.*

ap^{is} *appellationis.*

ap^{li} *apostoli.*

ap^{lus} *apostolus.*

apⱡ *aprilis.*

apⱠ *appellavit, appulit.*

apⱠac̃o *appellatio.*

apⱠat *appellat.*

apⱠat^9 *appellatus.*

apⱠi *appellari.*

apⱠm *appellum.*

apⱡȝ *apostolorum.*

ap^{num} *appellationum.*

apo^a *apostema.*

ap^{onc} *appositione, appellatione.*

apostⱡs *apostolus.*

apo^9 *apostolus.*

app^{a}t *appellat.*

app^{di} *appellandi.*

app$^{d'}$ *appellandum.*

appelⱡo *appellatio.*

appeⱡ *appellatur.*

appēdȝ *appendet.*

appēsū *appensum.*

appⱠator *appellator.*

appⱡoe *appellatione.*

app^{nc} *appellationem.*

app^{nib}ȝ *appellationibus.*

appñsū *appensum.*

app^o *appellatio.*

app^{oncm} *appellationem.*

app^{o}nes *appellationes.*

appoñe *apponere.*

appo^r *apponitur.*

apposuer̃ *apposuerunt.*

app^r *appellatur.*

app^{re} *appellare.*

app^t *appellat, apprehendit.*

app$^{t'r}$ *appellatur, apprehenditur.*

appat *appareat.*

appat^9 *apparatus.*

app$^{\bar{a}}$ *apparentiam.*

app$\bar{a}$t *appareant.*

appen^a *apparentia.*

appet *apparet.*

appicīoi *apparitioni.*

appn^a *apparentia.*

appns *apparens.*

appn̄ti *apparenti.*

apptūd *apportandum.*

app₃ *apparet, apparent.*

app̃ *appelli, appenditiis.*

app̃ciat *appreciat.*

app̃lat^r *appellatur.*

app̃llat *appellat.*

app̃llŏis *appellationis.*

app̃lłm *appellum.*

app̃lłŏis *appellationis.*

app̃m *appositionem.*

app̃ne *appellatione.*

app̃ōem *appositionem.*

app̃ui *apposui.*

app̃₃ *apparent, apparet, appendet.*

app̃ciare *appretiare.*

app̃ciaᷓ *appretiatum.*

app̃łin^{b}₃ *apprehensionibus.*

app̃is *apprehensis.*

app̃^{tr} *apprehenditur.*

appā^{ōe} *appropriatione.*

appbād *approbandum.*

appb̃tum *approbatum.*

app^{i}at *appropriat.*

app^{i}atī *appropriatim.*

appppīq^{a}t *appropinquat.*

appxi^{a}t *approximat.*

appxīat *approximat.*

Apȓ *Aprilis.*

ap^t *apud.*

ap^{tc}' *apostolicis.*

apti^c *aptitudine.*

apti$^{n\bar{c}}$ *aptitudinem.*

ap^9 *apostolus.*

ap₹ *apostolorum.*

apire *aperire.*

aptū *apertum.*

ap̃ *apud, apostolicus.*

ap̃a *apostema.*

ap̃ca *apostolica.*

ap̃d *apud.*

ap̃laũ *appellavit.*

ap̃li *apostoli, apostyli.*

ap̃lica *apostolica.*

ap̃llacõ *appellatio.*

ap̃llat^9 *appellatus.*

ap̃los *apostolos, apostylos.*

ap̃loᷓ *apostolorum.*

ap̃l^9 *apostolicus, apostolus.*

ap̃ł *apostolicum, Aprilis.*

ap̃p^9 *appensus.*

ap̃s *apostolus.*

app^i atū *appropriatum.*

aq^a *aqua.*

aq^u₃ *aquarum.*

aq^a *aquam.*

aq^e *aquæ.*

aq^i s *aquis.*

aquā *aquam.*

aq^a *aquam.*

aq̃ *aqua, aquæ.*

aq̃m *aquam.*

a^r *aliter, arguitur.*

ar^at *arguat.*

arbał *arbalistarius.*

arbo₃ *arborum.*

arƀr *arbiter.*

archid *archidiaconus.*

archidatus *archidiaconatus.*

archidis *archidiaconis.*

archiepus *archiepiscopus.*

archi^ni *archidiaconi.*

archïo *archidiacono.*

archipo *archiepiscopo.*

arcħ *archidiaconus, archiepis-*
    copus.

arcħd *archidiaconus.*

archi *archiepiscopi.*

arcħ^ni *archidiaconi.*

arcħo *archiepiscopo.*

arcħonis *archidiaconis.*

arcħpo *archiepiscopo.*

arcħs *archiepiscopus.*

arcħus *archiepiscopus.*

arcub₃ *arcubus.*

arc̃ *arcus, and its cases, archi-*
    diaconus.

arc̃eps *archiepiscopus.*

ardēd *ardendum.*

ard *archidiaconus.*

ard^n' *archidiaconum.*

arestac̃o *arestatio.*

arestaůnt *arestaverunt.*

arest̃ *arestaverunt.*

arg^i *argenti, argumenti.*

arg^m *argumentum.*

argū *argenti.*

arg^ta *argumenta.*

arg^t' *argumentum.*

argu^b₃ *argumentalibus, argu-*
    mentationibus.

argu^m *argumentum.*

arǵ *argentum, and its cases.*

arǵi *argenti.*

arǵntum *argentum.*

arǵnt̃ *argenti.*

ar^i dïi *archidiaconi.*

ar^i dn⁹ *archidiaconus.*

ar^ii *arbitrii.*

ar^io *arbitrio.*

aripū *arripuit.*

ar^lus *articulus.*

ar^m *arbitrium, argumentum.*

armatuř *armaturas.*

armig̉ *armiger.*

ar^ntum *argumentum.*

ar^{nus} *archidiaconus.*

ar$^{n'}$ *argumentum.*

ar^o *arbitrio, arguo.*

ar^{oe} *argumentatione.*

arpenđ *arpendium.*

arp̃ *arpendium.*

ar^r *argumentatur.*

arr^a *arreragia.*

arraiñ *arrainiavit.*

arrentat̆ *arrentatis.*

arrip̃ *arripuit.*

arr̃ *arrabilis, arreragia.*

ars^a *arsura.*

ar^t *arguit.*

ar^{ta} *argumenta.*

ar^{ti} *argumenti.*

arti^{b}₃ *artificialibus.*

articlo *articulo.*

arti$^{l'}$ *articulis.*

ar^{to} *argumento.*

art^x *artifex.*

ar$^{t'}$ *articulis.*

art̃^{clis} *articulis.*

ar^{um} *arbitrium.*

ar̃ *arat, arant, arantes, arabant, arabatur, aratum, aratura, arvum, articulos.*

ar̃d^{ni} *archidiaconi.*

ar̃đ *archidiaconus, and its cases.*

ar̃đ$^{n'}$ *archidiaconum.*

ar̃ep^9 *archiepiscopus.*

ar̃g̃o *armigero.*

ar̃g̃o *armigero.*

ar̃lus *articulus.*

ar̃p̃bro₂ *archipresbyterorum.*

ar̃t^{u} *argumentum.*

as. *assisa.*

a^s *alias, aliis, antecedens.*

a. s. *apostolice sedis.*

ascens̃ *ascensionis.*

asce^{on}₃ *ascensionem.*

asiñ *asinus, and its cases.*

as. mor. an. *assisa mortis antecessoris.*

as. no. dis. *assisa novæ disseisinæ.*

asp^{c}t^9 *aspectus.*

asptare *asportare.*

asptau̇nt *asportaverunt.*

asp̃cs *aspectus.*

ass^a *assisa.*

ass^{a}tus *assignatus.*

assc^{i}bi *adscribi.*

ass^c *assisæ.*

assens̃ *ascensionis.*

asses̃ *assessor.*

assēđ *assentiendum.*

assiđ *assedendum, assidendum.*

assïe *assisæ.*

assig^{a}⁹ *assignamus.*

assignãtur *assignabitur.*

assig^{n9} *assignamus.*

assigñ *assignatione.*

assitat^r *assimilatur.*

assis̃ *assisa, and its cases.*

assĩas *assisas.*

assĩaȝ *assisarum.*

ass^m *assartum.*

ass^o *assentio.*

assoc̃ *associatis.*

ass^r *assentitur.*

ass^ta *assignata.*

ass^u *assensu.*

assūpc̃oē *assumptionem.*

ass^9 *assensus.*

ass *assisa, and its cases, assessor.*

ass de m̃ anc̃ *assisa de morte antecessoris.*

ass de ñ dis̃ *assisa de nova disseisina.*

ass n. d. c. *assisa nove disseisine capienda.*

ass̃a *assisa.*

ass̃deb̃t^r *assedebatur.*

ass̃it *asserit.*

ass̃nsu *assensu.*

ass̃p^m *assumptum.*

ass̃^re *assentire.*

ass̃t *adsunt.*

ass̃u *assensu.*

ãssor *assessor.*

a^t *aut.*

a^ta *animata.*

atach̃ *attachietur, attachientur, attachiandum, attachiamentum.*

atach̃i *attachiamenti.*

athacciȇt̃ *attachientur.*

ath̃i *attachiari.*

a^tim *annuatim.*

at^n *attamen.*

atq *atque.*

att^ac̃com *attractionem.*

attach̃ *attachietur, attachientur, attachiandum, attachiamentum.*

attach̃i *attachiamenti.*

attam̃ *attamen.*

att^ib'r *attribuitur.*

att^ioe *attributione.*

attĩg̃e *attingere.*

att^m *attractum, attributionem.*

att^n *attamen.*

attorñ *attornatus, and its cases, attornavit, and other parts of the verb attornare.*

att^r *attribuitur.*

att̃ *attornatus, and its cases.*

att̃^ah̃et^r *attraheretur.*

atĩndd *attendendum.*

attĩare *atterminare.*

att̃mīat̃ *atterminata.*

a^tū *argumentum.*

atȝ *atque.*

a^t' *aliter.*

at̃ *autem.*

ãcit̃ *atrociter.*

ãts *actus.*

A.V. *annos vixit.*

aub̃gellū *aubergellum.*

auc^as *auctoritas.*

auc^re *auctore.*
auc^tc *auctoritate.*
auc^ti *auctoritati.*
aucto^ate *auctoritate.*
auc͠te *auctoritate.*
aud^do *audiendo.*
audiēđ *audiendum.*
audit^ri *audituri.*
audit^rus *auditurus.*
auditurę *audituris.*
audiũ *audivit.*
aud^r *auditur.*
auđ *audiat, audiendum, audit, audituris.*
auđia *audientia.*
a^ue *affirmative.*
auer͠ *averia.*
aufer͠ *auferre, aufert.*
Aug. *Augustus, Augustinus.*
augm^o *augmentatio.*
aug^ois *augmentationis.*
aug^t' *augmentum.*
Aug^9 *Augustus.*
Aug^9t^9 *Augustus.*
Aug͡ *Augustus, Augustinus.*
au^ifsiũ *aurifrisium.*
aum̃tū *aumentum (augmentum).*
au^or *auctor.*
aup͡ *autumpnali.*
aurif͠r *aurifrisium.*
aur͠s *aures.*
austi^tc *austeritate.*

aut^as *auctoritas.*
aut^e *auctoritate.*
aut^tc *auctoritatem.*
aut^te *auctoritate.*
autūp̃ *autumpno.*
au^t3 *auctoritatem.*
aut̃ *autem.*
aut̃n^a *autentica.*
aut̃nt^ca *autentica.*
aut̃po *autumpno.*
auunct *avunculus.*
auuncl̃^9 *avunculus.*
auunct̃s *avunculus.*
auũcts *avunculus.*
auũcls *avunculus.*
auũcl̃^9 *avunculus.*
auv^9 *avus.*
aux^m *auxilium.*
aux^o *auxilio.*
au^9 *avus, Augustinus.*
aũ *aut, autem.*
aũpo *autumpno.*
auĩa *averia.*
auioz *averiorum.*
auĩe *avertere.*
A. X. *Anno Christi.*
A. X^i. *Anno Christi.*
aysiam̃tū *aysiamentum.*
a3 *aquæ.*
a^9 *actus, albus, alius, Augustus.*
   Augustinus.
a^9us *ausus,*

aȝ *aliorum.*

Ā *5000.*

ābit *ambit.*

ābutoñ *ambulationem.*

āblare *ambulare.*

āblo *ambulatio.*

āgł *angelus, Anglus, Anglia,*
    and their cases.

āgłs *angelus, angulus.*

āgñ *Angnes (Agnes).*

āḡlus *angelus.*

āicę *amicis.*

āic⁹ *amicus.*

āiᵐ *animum.*

āiū *animum.*

āmiäˡᵉ *admirabilem.*

āmīsċo *administratio.*

āmoʳ *amovetur.*

ānoᵃ *annona.*

ānueñ *annuentes.*

ān⁹ *annus.*

āor *major.*

āorę *amoris.*

āoȝ *aliorum.*

āp⁹ *amplius.*

āp̄ *amplius.*

āqū *antequam.*

āres *majores.*

āteqᵃ *antequam.*

āteq̇ *antequam.*

ātiqⁱ *antiqui.*

āȝ *apparet, apparent.*

ā *ac, at, aut, autem, apud, ave,*
    annus, and its cases.

ãalia *animalia.*

ãaᵗⁱ *animati.*

ãatim *annuatim.*

ãaᵗˡ *annuatim.*

ãcui⁹ *alicujus.*

ãc⁹ *alicujus.*

ãd *aliquid, aliquod, aliud.*

ãdᵗᵉ *animadverte.*

ãdrd̄ *animadvertendum.*

ãe *animæ.*

ãi *animi.*

ãⁱd *aliquid.*

ãⁱⁱˢ *aliis.*

ãiᵒᵒ *aliquo modo.*

ãī *animi.*

ãle *animale.*

ãlia *animalia.*

ãlibȝ *animalibus.*

ãmal *animal.*

ãna *aliena.*

ãnga *arenga.*

ãn⁹ *annus.*

ãoᵒ *alio modo.*

ãoqⁿ *alioquin.*

ãoȝ *aliorum.*

ãqᵃ *aliqua.*

ãqᵃm *aliquam, antequam.*

ãqᵃs *aliquas.*

ãqñ *aliquando.*

ãqᵒ *aliquo.*

ãqʳ *aliqualiter.*

ãquaʳ *aliqualiter.*

ãq⁹ *aliquibus.*

ãq *aliquid, aliquod.*

ãqª *antequam.*

ãɋ *aliquem, aliquid.*

ãr *aliter.*

ãs *alias, animus.*

ãt *aut, autem.*

ãtū *argumentum.*

ãȝ *apparet.*

ãȥ *aliarum.*

B.

B. *trecenti, baptista, beatus, bere-*
wica, bordarius, bovata.

B. Ꝺ M. *berewica et manerium.*

B. Ꝺ S. *berewica et soka.*

B. A. *bixit (vixit) annos.*

babĩa *baptista.*

bᵃe *beatæ.*

balliuū *ballivum.*

balliū *ballivum, ballium.*

bal *balistariis.*

balł *ballia, balliva, ballivus.*

balłiā *ballivam.*

balłios *ballivos.*

balłis *ballivis, balliis.*

balłm *batellum.*

balłs *ballivus.*

bᵃoñ *bacones.*

bupᵃ *baptisma, baptista.*

bapᵃʳⁱ *baptizari.*

bapᵃᵗᵘˢ *baptizatus.*

bapᵗᵉ *baptistæ.*

bapĩ *baptista.*

bap̃ *baptista.*

bap̃ᵃ *baptisma, baptista.*

bap̃ᵃʳⁱ *baptizari.*

bap̃ᵃᵗᵘˢ *baptizatus.*

bap̃ta *baptista.*

barroñ *barones, baronia.*

barr̃ *barones, baronibus.*

barˢ *barones, baronibus.*

Bartħ *Bartholomæus.*

bar̃ *baro, barones, baronia.*

bᵃs *beatus.*

bastᵃd⁹ *bastardus.*

baȿ *basilica.*

bãa *beata.*

bãe *beatæ.*

bão, bã° *baro.*

bāoñ *baronem, barones.*

bā⁹ *beatus.*

beaᵐᵘˢ *beatissimus.*

beāᵃᵐ *beatissimam.*

benef *beneficiarius.*

beñ *benedictio, benedictus.*

bereū *berewica.*

beř *berewica.*

bᵉuiꝑ *breviter.*

bē m̃e *beatæ memoriæ.*

bēdᵗᵘˢ *benedictus.*

bēgnus *benignus.*

B. F. *benefactum, beneficium, bona femina, bona fide, bona filia, bona fortuna.*

bibaꞇ *bibatis (vivatis).*

B. I. C. *bibas (vivas) in Christo.*

bid *bidentes.*

bisˡⁱˢ *bissextilis.*

bix̃ *bixit (vixit).*

blad *bladum.*

blod *blodius, blodeus.*

bꝉ *blancus.*

bꞁꞁum *bellum.*

B. M. *beata Mater, beatæ memoriæ, bene merenti, bene merito.*

B. M. V. *beata Maria Virgo.*

bñ *bene, benedictionem.*

bñdc̃o *benedictio.*

bñdc̃us *benedictus.*

bñdm̃s *benedicimus.*

bñd⁹ *benedictus.*

bñd *benedicit.*

bñfïo *beneficio.*

bñfc̃oꝝ *benefactorum.*

bñio *beneficio.*

boᵃꝫ *bonam.*

boⁱᵗ’ᵉ *bonitate.*

bo. me. *bonæ memoriæ.*

boñ *bonus.*

bord *bordarii.*

boř *bordarii.*

bosc̃ *boscus.*

boᵗᵉ *bonitatem.*

bouaꞇ *bovata.*

bōa *bona.*

bõ *bona.*

bõ m̃e *bonæ memoriæ.*

bõis *bovis.*

bõm *bonam, bonum.*

bõs *beatos, bonos.*

bõꝫ *bonitatem.*

B. Q. *bene quiescas.*

BR. *bonorum, Britannia, Britones.*

braᵃli *bracali.*

bracaꝫ *bracarum.*

bʳgñ *burgensis.*

bʳǧ *burgi, burgo.*

Briǧ *Brigantiæ.*

BRT. *Britannicus.*

bř *brevis.*

břa *bracheta.*

br̃e *breve.*

br̃i *brevi.*

br̃ia *brevia.*

br̃ibȝ *brevibus.*

br̃is *brevis.*

br̃iū *brevium.*

bˢ *beatus.*

burg̃ *burgensis, burgus.*

burg̃ñ *burgenses, burgensis.*

burg̃ses *burgenses.*

bur̃ *burgus, burum.*

bus̃ *bussellus.*

buticł⁹ *buticularius.*

būe *breve.*

būis *brevis.*

BX. *bixit (vixit).*

bȝ *beatus, beatam.*

b⁹ *beatus, bos.*

B̄ *3000.*

ƀ *beatus, baptista, benedictionem, bussellus.*

ƀa *baptista, beata.*

ƀaoȝ *beatorum.*

ƀatus *beatus.*

ƀe *beatæ.*

ƀf *benefactum.*

ƀg̃ *burgum.*

ƀi *beati.*

ƀiᶜᵃ *beatifica.*

ƀido *beatitudo.*

ƀiᵈ' *beatitudinem.*

ƀiⁱˢ *beatitudinis.*

M.

ƀiⁿᵉ *beatitudine.*

ƀissimo *beatissimo.*

ƀisše *beatissime.*

ƀituⁿē *beatitudinem.*

ƀlli *belli.*

ƀltm *bellum.*

ƀm *beatum, benedictionem.*

ƀn *bene, beneficia, benedictionem.*

ƀna *bona.*

ƀnᵃ *beneficia.*

ƀndc⁹ *benedictus.*

ƀndča *benedicta.*

ƀndʳ *benedicitur.*

ƀnd *benedicit, benedictionem.*

ƀndo *benedicto, benedicendo.*

ƀndºnē *benedictionem.*

ƀndre *benedicere.*

ƀnfice *benefice.*

ƀnfiº *beneficio.*

ƀnfcoȝ *benefactorum.*

ƀnfm *beneficium.*

ƀnfo *beneficio.*

ƀnftm *benefactum.*

ƀngne *benigne.*

ƀnⁱⁱ *beneficii.*

ƀnˡⁱ *beneficiali.*

ƀnoȝ *bonorum.*

ƀñio *beneficio.*

ƀñnē *benedictionem.*

ƀo *beato.*

ƀoȝ *beatorum, bonorum.*

ƀr *brevis, and its cases; breviter.*

C

ƀruica *berewrica.*
ƀs *beatus.*
ƀta *beata.*
ƀte *beatæ.*
ƀti^me *beatissime.*
ƀti^ne *beatitudine.*
ƀtīme *beatissime.*
ƀtī^ni *beatitudini.*
ƀtoᵹ *beatorum.*

ƀts *beatus.*
ƀt⁹ *beatus.*
ƀt̆ *beatum.*
ƀue *breve.*
ƀuit^r *breviter.*
ƀuit̃ *brevitatis.*
ƀuit̄ *breviter.*
ƀui⁹ *brevius.*

C.

C. *caput, carta, carucata, centum,*
   codex, comes, conjux, cum,
   cunctis.
ca *camera.*
c^a *camera, canonica, capitula,*
   caput, carta, causa, centena,
   circa, contra.
ca^ant *capiant.*
ca^as *caritas, causas.*
c^nc *circa.*
ca^ca *canonica.*
ca^cc *canonicæ, canonice.*
ca^do *capiendo.*
ca^e *causæ, creaturæ.*
ca^i *capituli.*
cal. *calendas, calendis.*
calciam̃tū *calciamentum.*

calc̄ria *calcaria.*
ca^lo *capitulo.*
calum^ia *calumpnia.*
caluñ *calumpnia.*
ca^lñ *capitulum.*
calūnia *calumnia.*
cal̃ *calendas, calendis.*
cal̃is *calidis.*
cal̃m^ia *calumpnia.*
cal̃r *causaliter.*
cal̃us *calidus.*
ca^m *capitulum, causam.*
cam̃ *camera, camerarius.*
cam̃a *camera.*
cam̃ari⁹ *camerarius.*
cam̃ar̃ *camerarius.*
cam̃io *camerario.*

can^{ce} *canonice.*

cancellar̃ *cancellaria,cancellarius.*

cancełł *cancellaria, cancellarius.*

can^{cus} *canonicus.*

canc⁹ *cancellarius.*

canc^{c9} *canonicus.*

canc̃ *cancellarius.*

c^anispⁱuiũ *carnisprivium.*

can^{lis} *canonicalis.*

canōic̃ *canonicus.*

cañ *canonicus.*

c^{añ} *crannocum.*

cañc⁹ *canonicus.*

c^añlis *carnalis.*

cañria *cancellaria.*

cañs *canonicus.*

ca^o *capitulo.*

capc̃o *captio.*

capełł *capella, capellanus.*

capełs *capellanus.*

capⁱ *capituli.*

capiat^r *capiatur.*

capiãt^r *capiantur.*

capiend̃ *capiendum.*

capitib⁹ *capitibus.*

capiī̃ *capitulum.*

capła *capitula.*

capłł *capellanis.*

capłło *capellano.*

capłm *capitulum.*

capłni *capellani.*

capłs *capellanus.*

capł₃ *capitulum.*

cap^m *capitulum.*

cap^{nus} *capellanus.*

cappłł *capellanus.*

capt^t *captat.*

capt⁹ *captus.*

capī̃ *captus, capta, etc.*

capt̃s *captivus.*

capt̃⁹ *captivus.*

cape *capere.*

cap̃ *capellanus, capit, capitalis,*
  capitulum, caput.

cap̃d *caput.*

cap̃m *capitulum.*

cap̃t^r *capiuntur.*

cap̃tlis *capitalis.*

ca^r *capitur, causatur, causaliter.*

car^b₃ *cardinalibus.*

cardił *cardinalis.*

cardiñ *cardinalis.*

card̃ *cardinalis.*

carïa *carmina.*

c^ar^{le} *carnale.*

carł *carnalis.*

car^{mus} *carissimus.*

carⁿli *carnali.*

carña *carentia.*

carñ^{lis} *carnalis.*

carruc̃ *caruca, carucata.*

carr̃ *carucagium.*

carĩ *cartam.*

caruc̃ *caruca, carucata.*

cař *cardinalis, cariagium, carta,*
    caruca, carucata.
cařa *carucata.*
cař̃t *carucata.*
cař̃ꝯ *carnaliter.*
caˢ *causas.*
cᵃs *cras.*
cas^{lis} *casualis.*
cᵃstino *crastino.*
cᵃstiñ *crastino, crastinum.*
castᵒ *castro.*
cas̃ *castrum, castra.*
caᵗ *caput.*
catałł *catalla.*
cᵃtā *cartam.*
cath^{lis} *cathedralis.*
caĩ *catalla.*
caᵘ *casu.*
caũco *cautio.*
causał *causalis.*
cautõꝫ *cautionem.*
caūtʳ *causantur.*
caũ *casu, casum.*
caũł *causalis.*
caũłꝯ *causaliter.*
caũoē *cautionem.*
cauꝺe *cavere.*
caꝫ *causam, causas.*
caᵍ *casus.*
caꝫ *causarum.*
cābitor *cambitor.*
cābiũ *cambium.*

cācꝏo *cancellario.*
cāpio *campio.*
cā *carucata.*
cāa *camera.*
cā^{as} *causas.*
cāe *causæ.*
cāi *capituli.*
cāis *causis.*
cāitas *caritas.*
cām *causam.*
cānd *causandum.*
cānʳ *causantur.*
cāntʳ *causantur.*
cāřt *causaret.*
cās *causas.*
cāta *causata.*
cātʳ *causatur.*
cāt⁹ *causatus.*
cāu *casu.*
cāus *casus.*
cāꝫ *causarum.*
cc *circum, ducenti.*
ccᵃ *circa, contra.*
cc^{ti} *ducenti.*
ce^{b}ꝫ *celestibus.*
cᵉdidit *crediderit.*
cᵉdʳ *creditur.*
ced *cædua.*
cᵉde *cedere.*
cel. *celeres.*
cel^e *celeste.*
celebnᵒ *celebrando.*

ceł *celationes, celebravit.*

ceti *celeri.*

cetit[e] *celeritate.*

ce[m] *cœlum.*

cem̃tari[9] *cementarius.*

ceu. *centum.*

cend *cendallum.*

censr̃i *censeri.*

cer̃ *cerevisia.*

c[c]sce *crescere.*

ce[t]ę *cœlestis.*

ceĩi *cæteri.*

ceĩm *cæterum.*

ceti *cæteri.*

cetm *cæterum.*

cē[o] *centro.*

cēs[ii] *censarii.*

cēs[9] *census.*

cēt[r]io *centurio.*

Ch. *Christi.*

Chr̃o *Christo.*

churs̃ *chursetum.*

c[i] *cui.*

c[i]a *circa, citra.*

ci[b]₃ *civibus.*

c[i]ca *circa.*

c[i]cuit *circuit.*

c[i]cū[a] *circumstantia.*

c[i]cū[co] *circumspectio.*

c[i]cūsp[o] *circumspectio.*

c[i]cūsp̄c̄o *circumspectio.*

c[i]cū[to] *circumscripto.*

c[i]c̄l[9] *circulus.*

c[i]c̄tm *circulum.*

o[i]ǫ *circum.*

c[i]ǫ[cia] *circumstantia.*

c[i]ǫ[e] *circumstantiæ.*

c[i]ǫfen[a] *circumferentia.*

c[i]ǫsc[i]br *circumscribitur.*

c[i]ǫstã[a] *circumstantia.*

c[i]ǫst[is] *circumstantiis.*

c[i]ǫs̃p[i]bł *circumscriptibilis.*

c[i]ǫ[ta] *circumscripta.*

c[i]ǫ₹ *circumstantiarum.*

c[i]dū *cuidam.*

c[i]l[o] *circulo.*

c[i]l₃ *cuilibet.*

c[i]m *circum.*

c[i]mē *crimen.*

c[i]mīatr *criminaliter.*

c[i]mïb[9] *criminibus.*

c[i]m̃ *crimen.*

c[i]m̃a *crimina.*

c[i]m̃is *criminis.*

cin̂ū *cinerum.*

cir[a] *circa.*

circto *circulo.*

circts *circulus.*

circūq[a]ꝗ *circumquaque.*

circ,to *circumlocutio.*

cirog[a]pt̃ *chirographum.*

cir̃ *chirographum.*

c[i]t[te] *civitate.*

cit[ę] *citetis.*

cīt̃ᶜˢ *civitates.*

ciuťr *civiliter.*

cïũ *civitas.*

cⁱჳ *cuique.*

cïtas *civitas.*

cl. *clarissimus.*

clamanᵃ *clamantia.*

clam̃ *clamat, clamavit, clamium, clamorem.*

clᵃsʳa *clausura.*

claŝla *clausula.*

clauŝ *clausum, clausula.*

clābit *clamabit.*

clācŏe *clamatione.*

clāisᵘˢ *clarissimus.*

clām *clausulam.*

cleroŏie *cleronomiæ.*

clēᵗᶜ *clemente.*

cⁱ⁹ *circulus.*

cł *clamari, clamare, clausus, clericus.*

cła *clausula.*

cłant *clamant.*

cłcus *clericus.*

cłe *clausulæ.*

cłenᶜ *clementissime.*

cłens *clemens.*

cłi *cleri, clausi.*

cłicat⁹ *clericatus.*

cłic̆ *clericus.*

cłic̆t⁹ *clericatus.*

cłiˡⁱˢ *clericalis.*

cłis *clausulis.*

cłⁱˢ *clericis.*

cłi⁹ *clericus.*

cłm *clericum.*

cłpa *culpa.*

cłpał *culpabilis.*

cłpāˡⁱˢ *culpabilis.*

cłs⁹ *clausus.*

cłtʳa *cultura.*

cłt⁹ *cultus.*

cᵐ *capitulum, centum, cum.*

c. m. *causa mortis.*

c.mo *centesimo.*

cm̃dā *commendam.*

cm̃d̃oem *commendationem.*

cm̃s *comes.*

cⁿᵃ *centena.*

c⁰ *centesimo.*

coᵃ *contra.*

coᵃlis *corporalis.*

coᵇჳ *coloribus.*

coēm *communem.*

coēs *communes.*

cogᵃc̃o *cognatio.*

cogᵃt⁹ *cognatus.*

cogⁱⁿᵉˢ *cogitationes.*

coǵc̃o *cognitio.*

coǵnȓ *coguntur.*

coh̃cio *coercitio, coertio.*

coh̃cŏem *coertionem.*

coh̃ĩtōē *cohabitationem.*

coh̃ĩoᵐ *coertionem.*

coïā *comitissam.*

coïe *comitissæ.*

coïs *corporis.*

colĭt̄ *colitur.*

collc̆a *collecta.*

collōe *collatione.*

collōem *collationem.*

collōes *collationes.*

coll^{tur} *colligitur.*

colo^a *colonia.*

cot *color.*

cota *copula.*

cottg^{lc} *collegiale.*

cottia *collegia, colloquia.*

cotto; *collationem.*

cottr *colligitur, colloquitur.*

cotr *colitur.*

comb̄ *combustio.*

comĭt̄ *comitis, and other cases, comitissa.*

comïa *comitissa.*

comm^o *commodo.*

commō *commodum.*

com^o *commissio.*

compōi *compoti.*

compt *compareant.*

comptū *compertum.*

comp̄ *computat, computato, computum.*

com̄ *comes, comitissa, comitatus.*

com̄a *comitissa.*

com̄ūtes *commorantes.*

com̄dat̄ *commendatus, commendator, commendatio.*

com̄d *commendatus, commendatio.*

com̄e *comitissæ.*

com̄ib; *communibus.*

con^a *contra.*

con^adc̆o *contradictio.*

con^ariū *contrarium.*

con^axerūt *contraxerunt.*

concedt̄ *concederetur.*

concelam̄ *concelamentum.*

concet *concelamentum, concelatio.*

condc̆o *condicto.*

con^{dn} *concedendum.*

con^{d'} *concedendum.*

confr̄es *confratres.*

conq̄ritur *conquiritur.*

considac̄o *consideratio.*

considatū *consideratum.*

consïles *consimiles.*

conss̃^{ia} *consistentia.*

conss̃m *consensum.*

construc^o *constructio.*

const̄ *constitutis, constabularius.*

consue^{nc} *consuetudine.*

cons̃ *consanguineus, consideratio, consideratum, consilium, consuetudinem, consuetudinibus, consules.*

cons̃^{ia} *consequentia.*

conssu *consensu.*

cont^a *contra.*

contēčo *contentio.*

contēptū *contemptum.*

contīet^r *continetur.*

contïe *continue.*

contñtis *contentis.*

cont^{ui} *conventui.*

con^{tū} *conventum.*

contūa *contumacia.*

cont̃ *continens, continetur, contentum.*

coñ *contra.*

coñgeř *coningeria.*

coñ^r *communiter.*

coñsit *concessit.*

coñȝ *communem.*

coopoñ *coopertione.*

cop̄ *copia.*

co^r *commendator.*

cor^a *corpora.*

cor^aṫr *corporaliter.*

cor^ar *corporaliter.*

cor^bȝ *corporibus, corporalibus.*

corčo *correctio.*

cor^c *corpore.*

cor^cū *corporeum.*

corēte *correpte.*

corⁱbȝ *corporibus.*

corⁱs *corporis.*

cor^m *corporum, corporeum.*

corñdet *correspondet.*

cor^odit *corrodit.*

cor^onē *corruptionem.*

coroñ *corona, coronatio.*

cor^oȝ *corruptionem.*

corōačo *coronatio.*

corp⁹ *corpus.*

corpa *corpora.*

cor^r *corporaliter, corrigitur, corrumpitur.*

corrñ^r *correspondetur.*

corr^oe *corruptione.*

corrū^r *corrumpuntur.*

cor^rę *corporis.*

corř *corredium.*

corřns *correspondens.*

corřtor *corrector.*

corūte *corrupte.*

cor⁹ *corpus.*

coř *coram, coronæ, coronator.*

coř^{ct} *correspondet.*

coř^{is} *corruptionis.*

cořlē *corporalem.*

cořṫ *corporalis.*

cořndet *correspondet.*

cořn^{tes} *correspondentes.*

cořpñt *corrumpunt, corrumpent.*

cořs *corporis.*

cotař *cotarius.*

co^{tu} *comitatu.*

cot⁹ *cotarius.*

cot̃ *cotagium, cotarius.*

coūntus *conventus.*

coȝ *coronationem.*

coȝpaʳ *corrumpantur.*

coȝpᵒ *corruptio.*

coȝpᵒⁿᵉ *corruptione.*

coȝpʳ *corrumpitur.*

coȝp̄r *corrumpitur.*

coȝᵗ'ʳ *corrumpitur.*

cōburatʳ *comburatur.*

cōƀ *combustio.*

cōcelam̃ *concelamentum.*

cōcessᵗ *concessit.*

cōciliat̄ *conciliatum.*

cōcto *conclusio.*

cōcorđ *concordia.*

cōcorᵗᶜʳ *concorditer.*

cōcupᵉ *concupiscentiæ.*

cōdēpᵃtus *condemnatus.*

cōdᵒ *conditio.*

cōdⁿ̃ *concedendum.*

cōđ *commendatus.*

cōendatᵍ *commendatus.*

cōes *comes.*

cōfⁱrʳ *confirmatur.*

cōfres *confratres.*

cōfiᵍ *conferimus.*

cōfo *confessio.*

cōfōē *confessionem.*

cōfʳ *confirmatur.*

cōfres *confratres.*

cōft *confert.*

cōgnoũnt *cognoverunt.*

cōitatᵍ *comitatus.*

cōitē *comitem.*

cōito *committo.*

cōitℓ *comitis.*

cōmiss̃ *commissio, commissum.*

cōmitℓ̃e *committere.*

cōm̃dare *commendare.*

cōptio *compilatio, complexio.*

cōpō *compositio.*

cōputʳ *computatur.*

cōputᵍ *computus.*

cōp̄ *computus, compotus.*

cōpatʳ *comparatur.*

cōqⁱsiuit *conquisivit.*

cōr̃bȝ *corporibus.*

cōsecᵃc̃o *consecratio.*

cōsidat̄ *consideratum.*

cōst̄ *constabularius, constituta.*

cōsuet̄ *consuetudinibus.*

cōs̃ *consideratum, consuetudo.*

cōs̃m̃sȝ *consumpsisset.*

cōtᵃ *contra.*

cōtᵃdix̃ *contradixit.*

cōtām *contumaciam.*

cōtēᵐ *contemptim, contentum.*

cōtinȝ *continet.*

cōtʳđco *contradictio.*

cōtūaʳ *contumaciter.*

cōuᵉ *commune.*

cōuētᵍ *conventus.*

cōuictᵍ *convictus.*

cōusac̃o *conversatio.*

cō *contra.*

cõa *communa, consequentia, comitissa.*

cõam *comitissam.*

cõe *commune, consequentiæ, comitissæ.*

cões *communes.*

cõi *communi, conjugi.*

cõia *communia.*

cõib3 *communibus.*

cõicaõo *communicatio.*

cõim⁹ *committimus.*

cõione *communione.*

cõiʳ *communiter.*

cõiri *communiri.*

cõis *communis, corporis.*

cõiˢ *communis.*

cõisᵗ *commisit.*

cõitas *communitas.*

cõiter *communiter.*

cõitʳ *communiter.*

cõiẽ *communitas.*

cõiẽ *communiter.*

cõla *copula.*

cõnā *communam.*

cõnioe *communione.*

cõnis *communis.*

cõnt⁹ *conventus.*

cõnẽ *communiter.*

cõrib3 *corporibus.*

cõunis *communis.*

cõuña *communia.*

cõūe *commune.*

cp̄a *copia.*

cʳ *cur, creditur.*

crᵃ *carta.*

cʳa *cura.*

cʳabitʳ *curabitur.*

cʳant *currant, curant.*

cʳare *curare.*

cʳatᵒū *curatorum.*

cʳat⁹ *curatus.*

cʳātʳ *curantur.*

cʳca *circa.*

cʳcū *circum.*

cʳc̃m *circum.*

crᴐ *circum.*

cʳe *curæ, curiæ.*

cred *creditor, creditum.*

cʳere *currere.*

cʳia *curia.*

crïaᵵ *criminalis.*

crïaᵽ *criminaliter.*

cʳo *curo.*

cʳr⁹ *currus.*

cʳs⁹ *cursus.*

cr̃a *crimina.*

cr̃e *crimine.*

cr̃i *crimini.*

cr̃ïa *crimina.*

ctᵃ *contra.*

cᵘcc̄ *crucem.*

cᵘda *cruda.*

cuᵉ *curiæ.*

cur̃ *curia.*

cusͭ *custumarius.*

cuũ *cuva.*

cyrogᵃpħ *chirographum.*

cyr̃ *chirographum.*

c⁹ *cujus.*

c⁹ᵇ₃ *cujuslibet.*

c⁹ꝯ₃ *cujuscumque.*

c⁹di *cujusmodi.*

c⁹l₃ *cujuslibet.*

c⁹qᵃ *cujusquam.*

c⁹ꝗ *cujusque, cujuscumque.*

c⁹ꝗᵃm *cujusquam.*

c⁹₃ *cujusque.*

C̄ *centum millia.*

c̃· *cæteris, caput, capite, centum,
codex, comes, cum, cunctis.*

c̃a *causa, capitula, cetera.*

c̃ᵃ *creatura.*

c̃aᵃ *creatura.*

c̃alis *causalis.*

c̃aᵒ *creatio.*

c̃atū *causatum.*

c̃ã *creata.*

c̃ca *circa.*

c̃ditʳ *creditur.*

c̃dini *conditioni.*

c̃e *causæ.*

c̃fc̃is *confectis.*

c̃fc̃m *confectum.*

c̃g̃g̃ *congregatis.*

c̃g̃gatis *congregatis.*

c̃g̃gatę *congregatis.*

c̃iᵇ₃ *civitatibus.*

c̃is *ceteris, civis.*

c̃itas *civitas.*

c̃ius *cujus.*

c̃iux *conjux.*

c̃i⁹ *cujus.*

c̃i⁹b₃ *cujuslibet.*

c̃i⁹ꝯ₃ *cujuscunque.*

c̃ïtaˢ *civitates.*

c̃ltū *cultum.*

c̃m *cum.*

c̃ms *comes.*

c̃m̄dā *commendam.*

c̃oͭdie *quotidie.*

c̃tᵒ *centro.*

ꝯ *cerevisia.*

ꝯa *cera.*

ꝯaᵉ *creaturæ.*

ꝯari⁹ *cerarius.*

ꝯat *creat.*

ꝯatʳa *creatura.*

ꝯaũ *creavit.*

ꝯãe *creare.*

ꝯbᵒ *crebro.*

ꝯbrit⁹ *crebriter.*

ꝯbr̃ꝉ *crebriter.*

ꝯca *circa.*

ꝯci⁹ *certius.*

ꝯcū *circum.*

ꝯddᵗ *credidit.*

ꝯdibᵃ *credibilia.*

ꝯdibˡⁱᵃ *credibilia.*

čdi^bȝ *credibilibus.*

ꝰdiťe *credituræ.*

ꝰdi^a *credibilium.*

ꝰdnɗ *credendum.*

ꝰdo *credo.*

ꝰd^r *creditur.*

ꝰddi *credendi.*

ꝰddo *credendo.*

ꝰdɗ *credendum.*

ꝰde *credere.*

ꝰdem⁹ *crederemus.*

ꝰdis *credendis.*

ꝰɗndi *credendi.*

ꝰɗns *credens.*

ꝰdr *creditur.*

ꝰdt *credunt.*

ꝰd⁾e *credere.*

ꝰe *ceræ.*

ꝰea^{ia} *cerealia.*

ꝰeb^o *cerebro.*

ꝰebȝ *cerebrum.*

ꝰsc^t *crescit.*

ꝰsc̃ *crescit.*

ꝰsc̃ȝ *cresceret.*

ꝰsꝰe *crescere.*

ꝰtus *certus.*

ꝰuisia *cervisia.*

ꝰuisiores *cervisiores.*

ꝰu^sia *cervisia.*

ꝰuus *cervus.*

ꝰůnt *creverunt.*

ꝯ *con, cum. This is sometimes printed as a c reversed.*

ꝯ. *confitendis.*

ꝯ^a *contra.*

ꝯ^{aa} *contraria.*

ꝯbr̃ *contrabreve.*

ꝯ^abr̃ia *contrabrevia.*

ꝯ^actio *contractio.*

ꝯ^actū *contractum.*

ꝯ^act⁹ *contractus.*

ꝯ^ad^a *contradictoria.*

ꝯ^adc̃o^a *contradictoria.*

ꝯ^adi^oȝ *contradictionem.*

ꝯ^ad^om *contradictionem.*

ꝯ^ad^t *contradicit.*

ꝯ^adnt *contradicunt.*

ꝯ^adr *contradicitur.*

ꝯ^adre *contradicere.*

ꝯ^ah̃r *contrahitur.*

ꝯ^ai^m *contrarium.*

ꝯ^aio *contrario.*

ꝯ^aire *contraire.*

ꝯ^aiū *contrarium.*

ꝯ^{at} *concordat, considerat, conveniat.*

ꝯ^{at'} *consequatur.*

ꝯ^aȝ *consequentiam.*

ꝯ^{a'm} *contrarium.*

ꝯ^aȝ *contrariorum.*

ꝯ^a *convenientiam.*

ꝯbīatū *combinatum.*

ꝯb^rgū *comburgensis.*

ꝯbrit^r *comburitur.*
ꝯbuss^t *combussit.*
ꝯb9t9 *combustus.*
ꝯb9t̃ *combustio, combustus.*
ꝯcac̃o *communicatio.*
ꝯcat *communicat.*
ꝯce^d' *concedendum.*
ꝯce^i *concedi, concedendi.*
ꝯceł *concelamentum, concelatio.*
ꝯce^nt *concedunt.*
ꝯce^o *concedo.*
ꝯcep^ois *conceptionis.*
ꝯce^r *conceditur.*
ꝯces. *concessimus.*
ꝯcesseũt *concesserunt.*
ꝯcess̃ *concessisse.*
ꝯci^m *concilium.*
ꝯci^o *concilio.*
ꝯcipꝫ *conciperet.*
ꝯcl^oꝫ *conclusionem.*
ꝯclõe *conclusione.*
ꝯclõs *conclusionis.*
ꝯcl^r *concluditur.*
ꝯclu^r *concluditur.*
ꝯcl^ur *concluditur.*
ꝯcłd^r *concluditur.*
ꝯcłd^tr *concluditur.*
ꝯcło *conclusio, concelamento.*
ꝯcordañ *concordantia.*
ꝯcorđ *concordandi, concordantis, concordantiis, concorditer, concordia, and its cases.*

ꝯcorđi *concordandi.*
ꝯc^rnt *concurrunt.*
ꝯc^ram9 *concurramus.*
ꝯc^rẽdo *concurrendo.*
ꝯc^rẽte *concurrente.*
ꝯc^rr̃e *concurrere.*
ꝯc^rt *concurrit.*
ꝯc^rũt *concurrunt.*
ꝯcta *cuncta.*
ꝯctũ *contractum.*
ꝯcup^a *concupiscentia.*
ꝯcup^iã *concupiscentiam.*
ꝯcupi^dã *concupiscendam.*
ꝯcup^le *concupiscibile.*
ꝯcup̃ia *concupiscentia.*
ꝯc9m9 *concessimus.*
ꝯc9sio *concussio.*
ꝯc̃ *conclusio, and its cases.*
ꝯc̃^ntc *concurrente.*
ꝯc̃re *concurrere.*
ꝯc͛iue *concretive.*
ꝯc͛nit *concernit.*
ꝯdam *cujusdam, quondam.*
ꝯdẽpnꝫ *condemnet.*
ꝯdẽp^re *condemnare.*
ꝯ^di *concedi, concedendi.*
ꝯdic̃o *conditio.*
ꝯdi^o *conditio.*
ꝯdi^onꝭ *conditionis.*
ꝯdi^oꝫ *conditionem.*
ꝯdit^r *conditur.*
ꝯ^do *concedo, concedendo.*

ꝯdᵒis *conditionis.*

ꝯdōatū *condonatum.*

ꝯdʳ *contradicitur, concluditur.*

ꝯdux̃ *conduxit.*

ꝯde *condere.*

ꝯdi *concedendi.*

ꝯdo *conditio, concedendo.*

ꝯdōem *conditionem.*

ꝯdŏm *conditionem.*

ꝯdr *concluditur, contradicitur.*

ꝯᵉ *commune, consequentiæ.*

ꝯeñᵖ *convenienter.*

ꝯᵉᵗ *continet.*

ꝯeӡ *communem, conventionem, cognitionem.*

ꝯc̆m *communem.*

ꝯfessˢ *confessoris.*

ꝯfⁱmasse *confirmasse.*

ꝯfᵒ *confessio.*

ꝯfᵒӡ *confessionem.*

ꝯfōӡ *confirmationem.*

ꝯfʳ *confertur, confirmatur.*

ꝯfˢ *confessoris.*

ꝯf *confessor, confirmavit.*

ꝯfcis *confectis.*

ꝯfmac̃o *confirmatio.*

ꝯfoӡ *confessorum.*

ꝯgᶜⁱᵗ *cognoscit.*

ꝯgᵉgᵒ *congregatio, congregato.*

ꝯgⁱᵵ *cognitum.*

ꝯgnoũ *cognovit.*

ꝯgᵒ *cognitio.*

ꝯgʳ *cognoscitur.*

ꝯg̃gᵒ *congregatio, congregato.*

ꝯⁱ *communi, conveni.*

ꝯⁱa *communia.*

ꝯⁱātʳ *conveniantur.*

ꝯⁱcaᵉ *communicare.*

ꝯⁱens *conveniens.*

ꝯis *communis.*

ꝯⁱtas *communitas.*

ꝯⁱᵵ *communiter.*

ꝯˡⁱᵘᵐ *concilium.*

ꝯᵐ *communem, compotum, conceptum, concilium, convictum.*

ꝯmemᵉ *commemoratione.*

ꝯmᵒe *commotione.*

ꝯmᵗteʳ *committeretur.*

ꝯmᵗtūʳ *committuntur.*

ꝯm̃e *commune.*

ꝯm̃ndaᵒ *commendatio.*

ꝯm̃ʳⁱˢ *commentatoris.*

ꝯnoũ *cognovit.*

ꝯnouũt *cognoverunt.*

ꝯ̃s *consequens.*

ꝯᵒ *communio, communicatio, consecutio.*

ꝯᵒbr̃, ꝯᵒbr̃e, *contrabreve.*

ꝯᵒm *conclusionem.*

ꝯᵒne *conclusione, constructione.*

ꝯpar̃e *comparere.*

ꝯplectoӡ *complectorium.*

ꝯplc̄tᵗ *complementum.*

ꝯptibӡ *compluribus.*

ꝯpot⁹ *compotus.*

ꝯpʳ *computabitur.*

ꝯpʳt *comparet.*

ꝯpᵗᵃ *composita, compota.*

ꝯpᵗᵘˢ *compotus, computus.*

ꝯputator *computator.*

ꝯꝑꝫ *comparet, competit.*

ꝯpaˡᵉ *comparabile.*

ꝯpare *comparare.*

ꝯpatʳ *comparatur.*

ꝯpaͮe *comparative.*

ꝯpet *comparet.*

ꝯpit *comperit.*

ꝯpnt *comparent.*

ꝯpoꝫ *comparationem.*

ꝯp̃ *computat, computus.*

ꝯp̄latʳ *copulatur.*

ꝯp̄lᵒ *completorio, compilatio.*

ꝯp̄o *complexo, compositio.*

ꝯp̃hñˡᵉ *comprehensibile.*

ꝯqⁱsitor *conquisitor.*

ꝯꝗstu *conquestu.*

ꝯʳe *contrarie.*

ꝯʳᵉ *convenire.*

ꝯrediũ *conredium (corredium).*

ꝯʳᵉ̄ *commentatorem.*

ꝯʳę *commentatoris.*

ꝯˢ *consequens.*

ꝯsc̃ia *conscientia.*

ꝯsentᵃ *consentanea.*

ꝯsidacȯe *consideratione.*

ꝯsidati *consideratim.*

ꝯsidauūt *consideraverunt.*

ꝯsidātē *considerantem.*

ꝯsiliū *consilium.*

ꝯsiłi *consimili.*

ꝯsiᵒᶜ *consideratione.*

ꝯsñsu *consensu.*

ꝯsociū *consocium.*

ꝯsoło *consolatio.*

ꝯstiʳ *constituitur.*

ꝯstiᵗⁱ *constituti.*

ꝯstïo *constitutio.*

ꝯst̃ *constituto, constabularius.*

ꝯˢᵘ *consensu.*

ꝯsuᵈᵒ *consuetudo.*

ꝯsueⁿᵉ *consuetudine.*

ꝯsulat⁹ *consulatus.*

ꝯsułe *consulere.*

ꝯsułere *consuluere.*

ꝯs̃ *considerationem, consideratum, consilium, consuetudo.*

ꝯs̃ns⁹ *consensus.*

ꝯs̃s⁹ *consensus.*

ꝯt *comparuit, contingit, convenit.*

ꝯtᵃ *contra.*

ꝯtᵃbr̄ *contrabrevе.*

ꝯtᵃdc̃oe *contradictione.*

ꝯtᵃdiꝯe *contradicere.*

ꝯtᵃia *contraria.*

ꝯtᵃtałł *contratalliator.*

ꝯtᶜ *composite, contestatione, continuatione.*

ꝯtenc̃o *contentio.*

ꝯtentc̃o *contentatio.*

ꝯ^{ti} *compoti.*

ꝯti^bȝ *continentibus, contingentibus.*

ꝯtig̃ *contigit, contingit.*

ꝯtinet^r *continetur.*

ꝯting̃ *contingit.*

ꝯti^{te} *continente.*

ꝯt̃iuati *continuatim.*

ꝯtñtis *contentis.*

ꝯ^{tor} *commentator, conquestor.*

ꝯt^r *continetur.*

ꝯ^{tu} *conventu.*

ꝯtu^ax *contumax.*

ꝯ^{tũ} *computum, conventum.*

ꝯ^{tℓ} *competentes, compositis.*

ꝯ^{t9} *conceptus, contemptus.*

ꝯt̃ *contentum, continens, continetur.*

ꝯt̃^{ia} *continentia.*

ꝯt̃i^o *continuo.*

ꝯt̃s *contrasigillum.*

ꝯt̃ȝ *continet.*

ꝯualũ *convaluit.*

ꝯuenco̍is *conventionis.*

ꝯuēit *convenit.*

ꝯuēt⁹ *conventus.*

ꝯuiuiũ *convivium.*

ꝯuicit *convincit.*

ꝯũiā *communiam.*

ꝯũt *conveniunt.*

ꝯũnc̃one *conventione.*

ꝯũs̃ *conversis.*

ꝯ^{xũ} *complexum.*

ꝯ̃ *compotum.*

c̃a *communa.*

D.

D. *dedisse, dicens, dicit, quingenti.*

d^a *data, differentia.*

da^a *data.*

dab^r *dabitur.*

dać *dabis, dabit.*

dað̄r *dabitur.*

d^aco *draco.*

d^ac̃o *dominatio, dilatio.*

dac̃o *datio.*

dac̃oi *dationi.*

d^ac̃oi *dilationi, dominationi.*

da^m *damnum, datum.*

damp^o *dampno.*

da^o *dampno.*

dapīs *dapiferis.*

dap̃ *dapifer.*

dap̃o *dapifero.*

dᵃri *demandari, demonstrari.*

dᵃs *differentias, datas.*

dᵃˢ *differentias, datas.*

datʳus *daturus.*

dat⁹ *datus.*

dať *data, datum.*

dāpᵃreʳ *damnaretur.*

dūpᵃri *damnari.*

dāpnād⁹ *damnandus.*

dūpⁿᵉ *damnatione.*

dāpnᵘʳ *damnatur.*

dūpñ *damnum.*

dāpᵒⁱˢ *damnationis.*

dāpᵒⱬ *damnorum, damnatorum.*

dūpᵗᵘˢ *damnatus.*

dãi *dari.*

dᶜ *donec.*

dᶜᵉ *distinctione, duplice.*

dᶜᵉ̄ *distinctionem, duplicem.*

dcᵐ *dictum.*

dᶜᵒᵉⱬ *distinctionem, dictionem.*

dᶜtamē *dictamen.*

dᶜtⱬ *dictet.*

dcℓ *dictis.*

dc⁹ *dictus.*

dc̃ *ducatus.*

dc̆aīe *dictamine.*

dc̆eqₛ *dictæque.*

dc̆et *dictet.*

M.

dc̃is *dictis.*

dc̃m *dictum, ductum.*

dc̃m̃tū *decrementum, documentum.*

dc̃o *dedicatio, dictatio, dictio, dicto.*

dc̃oᵒ *dicto modo.*

dc̃oⱬ *dictationem, dictionem.*

dc̃oⱬ *dictorum.*

dc̃ur⁹ *dicturus.*

dc̃us *dictus, distinctus.*

dc̃ⱬ *dictum.*

dc̃⁹ *dictus.*

dď *David, dederunt.*

dᵉ *differentiæ, dicere, duæ.*

deᵃbʳ *demonstrabitur.*

deᵃƀlis *demonstrabilis.*

deᵃˡ' *demonstrabilis.*

deᵃʳᵉ *demonstrare, demandare.*

deᵃta *demonstrata, demandata, detracta.*

deᵃtis *demonstratis.*

deᵃtïe *demonstrative.*

deᵃt̄is *demonstrationis, detractionis.*

deaur̃ *deauratum.*

deᵃⱬ *decimam.*

debⱬ *debet.*

deƀe *debere.*

deƀ *debet, debent.*

deᵇ̊ur *demonstrabitur.*

deƀo *debito.*

D

deb; *debent, deberet.*

decenn *decennalia.*

decess *decessit.*

deceᵒo *de cætero.*

decēˡⁱˢ *decennalis.*

decid *decidendum.*

declaʳ *declaratur.*

decliᵒ *declinatio.*

decio *declaratio.*

decᵒ *de cætero.*

dec; *decet.*

decẹ *de cæteris.*

dec̃ *decanus, Decembris, decrementum, decretum.*

decãs *decimas.*

dec̃e *decimæ.*

dec̄ˡ' *decretalis.*

decĩ *decretalis.*

ded *dedit.*

dedit *dederint.*

dec̃ *deest.*

dec̃e *deesse.*

dec̃t *deessent.*

defai *defalta.*

defẽm *defectum.*

defc̃us *defectus.*

defᵈⁱ *defendendi, definiendi.*

deforc̃ *deforciatorem.*

def *defalta, defectus, defendatis,
defendens, defensionem, defenso,deforcians,deforciator,
defunctus.*

defctus *defectus, defunctus.*

defẹ *deferentis.*

deg̈tᵒ *degustatio.*

deiñ *deinde.*

deⁱta *determinata.*

deïatī *determinatim.*

deïte *determinate.*

delibⁿe *delibatione, deliberatione.*

delīq̃s *delinquens.*

deicᵐ *delectum.*

deic̃able *delectabile.*

deic̃abĩr *delectabiliter.*

deic̃aᵒ *delectatio.*

deic̃m *delectum.*

deic̃o *delectatio.*

demᵉsū *demensum.*

demᵒ *demonstratio.*

demᵒis *demonstrationis.*

demᵒstᵃc̃o *demonstratio.*

dem̃ *demum.*

dem̃dʳ *demandatur, demandetur.*

dem̃nd *demanda, demonstran-
dum.*

dem̃rans *demonstrans.*

dem̃r̃oi *demonstrationi.*

dem̃tᵃo *demonstrato.*

dem̃te *demente, demonstratæ.*

dem̃ĩ *demonstratum.*

dem̃īs *dementis, dementes, demonstrationis.*

dem̃ᵘe *demonstrative.*

denᵃ' *denarius.*

deniq̇ *denique.*

de^{nis} *denominationis.*

dentag̃ *dentagra.*

deñ *denarius, denuo.*

deñcia° *denunciatio.*

deñciãi *denunciari.*

deñci^{do} *denunciando.*

deñōi^m *denominativum.*

deñt *debent.*

deñt^r *debentur, demonstratur.*

de° *demonstratio.*

de°ne *demonstratione.*

deor^m *deorsum.*

de°ȝ *demonstrationem.*

de^{ŏc} *demonstratione.*

dep^auare *depravare.*

depo^{da} *deponenda.*

depōȝ *depositionem.*

depȝ *dependet.*

dep̄ōem *depositionem.*

derōnau^t *derationavit, deratio-cinavit.*

der̃ *Decembris.*

desc^t *descendit.*

desig^ari *designari.*

desi^m *desiderium.*

desm̃t *desumunt.*

des° *desertio.*

despa° *desperatio.*

destr^aius *destrarius (dextrarius).*

dest^uc̃o *destructio.*

des̃c^t *desicut.*

des̃r *desuper.*

des̃uiēs *deserviens.*

des̃ȿo *desertio.*

des̃uit⁹ *deservitus.*

de^t *debet, dedit.*

de^{ta} *debita, deducta, delicta.*

de^{te} *debite.*

de^{ti} *debiti, delegati.*

deⁱm̄tū *detrimentum.*

deẗis *demandatis, demonstratis.*

deȿia° *deterioratio, deteriatio.*

deȿiare *deteriorare, deteriare.*

deȿine *determinatione.*

deȿiri *determinari.*

deȿial^{is} *determinalis.*

deȿia° *determinatio.*

deȿiare *determinare.*

deȿiate *determinate.*

deuo° *devotio.*

deũ *Deum.*

deũare *devitare.*

de⁹ *Deus, debemus.*

de÷ *deest.*

dēc̃o *demonstratio.*

dĕat *debeat.*

dĕbit *debebit.*

dĕbato *deliberato.*

dĕita *debita.*

dĕliq̇ *dereliquit.*

dĕm⁹ *debemus.*

dēndi *demonstrandi.*

dēnt *debent.*

dẽrẽt *deberent.*
dẽrʒ *deberet.*
dẽt *debet, deberet.*
dẽtr· *demonstratur, determinatur.*
dẽ⁹ *debemus.*
d. g. *Dei gratia.*
di. *dilecto, distinctio.*
d^{i} *dici, diei, dirigi, dividi.*
d. i. *Dominicæ Incarnationis.*
diac̃ *diaconus.*
dic^{a} *dicra.*
dice^{m} *dicendum.*
dic̃ *dicere, dicit, dicunt.*
dic̃s *dicens.*
dic̃t *dicit, dicunt.*
dic̃us *dictus.*
diꝰent *dicerent.*
dicꝯt *dicunt.*
di$^{d'}$ *dicendum.*
diđa *dicenda, dividenda.*
diđdū *dividendum.*
diđ^{t} *dividit.*
dif^{dum} *definiendum.*
diff^{a} *diffinitiva* (*definitiva*).
diffi^{o} *definitio.*
diffīt *definit.*
diffia *differentia.*
diffo *definitio, definitivo.*
diffꝛnt *differunt.*
diffꝛñia *differentia.*
diffꝛt *differt.*
dif^{di} *definiendi.*
dig^{a}t^{r} *dignatur.*
dig^{ma} *dignissima.*
dignẽi *dignemini.*
dig^{ni} *dignemini.*
dign^{o}i *digniori.*
dig̃ *dignus.*
dig̃^{b}ʒ *dignitatibus.*
dig̃ōis *digestionis.*
dig̃tas *dignitas.*
dig̃^{t}ꝭ *dignitatis.*
dilc̃lo *diluculo.*
dilc̃m *dilectum.*
dilc̃s *dilectus.*
dilc̃us *dilectus.*
di^{le} *divisibile.*
di^{li} *divisibili.*
dili$^{d'}$ *diligendum.*
dilig̃ñr *diligenter.*
di^{lis} *divisibilis.*
dil^{o} *dilatio.*
dilōe *dilatione.*
diƚ *dilectus.*
diƚctus *dilectus.*
diƚc̃s *dilectus.*
diƚc̃us *dilectus.*
diƚim *dilatim.*
diƚns *diligens.*
diƚnꝰ *diligenter.*
di^{m} *dimidiam, dimidium, divinam, divinum.*
dimiđ *dimidium.*
dimis̃ *dimisit.*

dim° *diminutio, dimensio.*

dim°ʒ *dimensionem, diminutionem.*

dimᵗᵗe *dimittere.*

dim̃ *dimidium.*

dim̃tiū *diminutivum.*

diⁿᵉ *dilatione.*

diñ *divinum.*

di° *dimidio, divisio.*

dioc̃ *diœcesis.*

diŏe *divisione.*

diŏi *divisioni.*

diŏm *divisionem.*

diʳ *dividitur, dicitur.*

dirco͂ *directionem.*

dirᶜte *directe.*

dirᶜtiᵐ *directivum.*

dirᶜtus *directus.*

dirᶜus *directus.*

dirc̆e *directe.*

dirc̃m *directum.*

dirc̆o *directio.*

dirc̃°ʒ *directionem.*

dir̃ *dirigitur.*

dir̃c̃m *directum.*

dir̃c̃°ʒ *directionem.*

dir̃ocnauᵗ *diratiocinavit.*

dir̃onata *dirationata.*

dir̃tus *directus.*

dis. *disseisinœ, districte.*

diˢ *dicens.*

discᵈ’ *discedendum, discernendum.*

discᵉtus *discretus.*

discil’ *discipulus.*

discïdo *discindendo.*

disc̃ *discretio.*

disc̃p̃ts *discipulus.*

disc̃c̃o *discretio.*

disc̃ᵈᵘᵐ *discernendum.*

disc̃ñ *discernit.*

disⁱūt *disconveniunt.*

disˡᵘˢ *discipulus.*

displiᵃ *displicentia.*

disp° *dispositio.*

disp̃lus *discipulus.*

disp̃n° *dispensatio.*

disp̃nt *dispensant.*

disp̃° *dispositio.*

disp̃ōem *dispositionem.*

disp̃t *dispensat.*

dissᵈ’ *dissentiendum.*

dissïtᵈᵒ *dissimilitudo.*

dis̈s *disseisivit, disseisiverunt, dissensus.*

diss̈lis *dissimilis.*

dis̈s⁹ *dissensus.*

distᵃ *distincta.*

distiᵈᵘᵐ *distinguendum.*

distïtʳ *distinguitur.*

dist° *distinctio, distincto.*

distʳ *distinguitur.*

distᵘxᵗ *destruxit.*

dist̃but̃a *distributiva.*

dist̃ctu *districtu.*

dis͡to *distinctio, distincto.*

dis͡ *discretio, divisus.*

diss *divisus.*

dis͡ t̃ *discretio tua, or other cases.*

di^te *dimidietatem.*

di^tim *dimidiatim.*

dit°ʒ *ditionem.*

diu^a *diversa, divina.*

diuci⁹ *diutius.*

diu^de *diversimode.*

diu^e *diversæ, divisæ.*

diuēʒ *diversorum.*

diui^lᵖ *divisibilis.*

diui^m *divinum.*

diui^r *dividitur.*

diu^ne *diutine.*

diũdare *divadiare.*

diu̇ic̆lo *diverticulo.*

diu̇si^de *diversimode.*

diu̇^te *diversitate.*

dix^t *dixit.*

dix^ūt *dixerunt.*

dix͡ *dixit.*

dix͡nt *dixerunt.*

dix͡t *dixit.*

diissū *dimissum.*

diitte *dimittere.*

dï *Dei.*

dïa *dimidia, divina.*

dïcie *divitiæ.*

dïdat *dividat.*

dïde° *dividendo.*

dïdi *dividi.*

dïd^t *dividit.*

dï^dᵖ *dividendum.*

dïddū *dividendum, decidendum.*

dïde^r *divideretur.*

dïd̓e *dividere.*

dïe *dimidiæ.*

dï ğ *Dei gratia.*

dïğe *dirigere.*

dïnu° *diminutio.*

dïnu°ʒ *diminutionem.*

dïo *dimidio, divino.*

dïone *divisione.*

dï^r *dicitur.*

dïsil^lᵖ *divisibilis.*

dïssiōe *dimissione.*

dïssum *dimissum.*

dïsū *divisum.*

dït *dicit*

dïttere *dimittere.*

d^m *datum, dicendum, dudum.*

dm̃na *domina.*

dm̃rat *demonstrat.*

dm̃s *damus, dicimus, dominus.*

d^na *doctrina.*

d^ne *doctrinæ.*

d^ns *differentias.*

dñ *denarius.*

dña *domina.*

dñat^r *dominatur.*

dñc^a *dominica.*

dñica *dominica.*

dñs *dominus.*

dñt *dicunt, dubitant.*

dñus *dominus.*

dñū *dominum.*

dñ⁹ *dominus.*

dᵒ *Deo, dico, distinguo, domino, dubio.*

doᵃ *dominica.*

doᵃᵗ *donat.*

doᵃt *donavit.*

doᶜ *donec.*

docᵃ *dominica.*

doc̃o *documento, donatio.*

doᵉ *dominæ.*

doⁱca *dominica.*

doⁱcāus *dominicanus.*

doⁱc⁹ *dominicus.*

dᵒis *devotionis, distinctionis, dominionis.*

doⁱū *dominium.*

doᵐ *dominum, donum.*

domᵃ *dominica.*

domˡⁱũ *domicilium.*

dom̄na *domina.*

dom̄n⁹ *dominus.*

dom̃ *dominus, domus.*

donãc̃o *donatio.*

donãū *donatum.*

donᶜ *donec.*

dᵒnes *dictiones, donationes.*

doñ *donum, donatio.*

doño *donatio.*

doñū *dominium.*

doñ⁹ *dominus.*

doᵒ *dominio, domino.*

doᵒȝ *dominorum, domorum.*

dorᵗⁱ *dormienti.*

dor̄ *dormit.*

dor̄di *dormiendi.*

dor̃e *dormire.*

do⁹ *domus.*

dˢᵉ *distinctione.*

dōi *domi, domini, doni.*

dōic̃llus *domicellus.*

dōiⁱ *domini.*

dōiᵐ *dominium.*

dōiño *dominio.*

dōiãc̃o *dominatio.*

dōi *domini.*

dōii *dominii.*

dōre *dormire.*

dpo *depositio, dispositio.*

dp̄ᵒȝ *depositionem, dispositionem.*

dp̄ōes *depositiones, dispositiones.*

dʳ *dicitur, dicuntur, dirigitur, distinguitur, dupliciter.*

dʳa *dura.*

dʳatʳa *duratura.*

dʳit̃ *duriter.*

dʳ⁹ *durus.*

dĩa *differentia, dura.*

dĩe *dicere, differentiæ, docere.*

dr̃ent̃ *differenter.*

dr̆e^r *diceretur.*

dr̃ia *differentia.*

dr̃ie *differentiæ.*

dr̃iis *differentiis.*

dr̆ncia *differentia.*

dr̃ns *differens.*

ds *Deus.*

d^t *dicit, ditat, ditavit.*

d^{ta} *distincta.*

d^{te} *distincte.*

dt̆a^a *distantia.*

dt̆m *dativum.*

du^a *dubia, ducenda.*

du^at^r *dubitatur, duratur.*

dubi^{is} *dubitationis.*

dubi^o *dubitatio.*

dub^r *dubitatur.*

dub̃o *dubitatio.*

dub̃r *dubitatur.*

dub̃t^onȝ *dubitationem.*

duce^r *duceretur.*

duc^o *ducentesimo.*

duçt *ducunt.*

duⁱⁱ *dubii.*

du^m *dubium, ductum.*

du^o *dubio, dubitatio.*

du^{onis} *dubitationis.*

dupli^r *dupliciter.*

duplt̃ *dupliciter.*

dupĭr *dupliciter.*

dup^r *dupliciter.*

dup^x *duplex.*

du^r *dubitatur, duratur.*

d^{ur} *dicitur, dicuntur.*

d^ur *dicitur.*

du^{re} *dubitare.*

dur̃ *duraturam.*

dur̃o *duratio.*

du^x *duplex.*

dūmõ *dummodo.*

dū^o *dummodo.*

dūo^o *dummodo.*

dũa^t *duravit.*

dũat^ras *duraturas.*

dũāte *durante.*

dũb^r *durabitur.*

dũcet *denunciet.*

dũc^e *duplicem.*

dũ^{ci} *duplici.*

dũ^{co} *dubitatio.*

dũ^o *dummodo.*

dũre *dubitare.*

dũs *ductus, durus.*

d^x *duplex.*

dya^{ca} *dialectica.*

dya⁹ *diabolus.*

dyoc̃ *diœcesis.*

dȝ *debet.*

d⁹ *Deus, dominus, dux.*

D̄ *500000, Deus, Dominus.*

Ð *de, die, dum.*

đ *datum, de, debet, decena, dedit, deest, denarius, dicendum, dicit, dictus, die, dies, dimidium, dominicus, dominus.*

ꝺbuᵗ *debuit.*

ꝺbȝ *debet.*

ꝺca *dicta, dominica.*

ꝺcᵉ *dictæ, dominicæ.*

ꝺcᶜᵒ *discretio.*

ꝺcᵉtus *discretus.*

ꝺcᵉtū *decretum.*

ꝺciˡⁱᵃ *disciplinabilia.*

ꝺciⁿᵃ *disciplina.*

ꝺclīaͨo *declinatio.*

ꝺclat *declinat.*

ꝺcᵐ *dictum.*

ꝺcʳc̄ᵒ *discurrendo.*

ꝺcʳsū *discursum.*

ꝺcuʳo *decurio.*

ꝺcur⁹ *dicturus.*

ꝺcū *dictum, distinctum.*

ꝺcȝ *dictorum.*

ꝺc̃etū *decretum.*

ꝺc̃m̃tū *decrementum.*

ꝺc̃no *decerno, discerno.*

ꝺc̃oȝ *dictionem, dictationem.*

ꝺc̄s *dictus.*

ꝺc̃⁹ *dictus.*

ꝺc̃tū *decrementum.*

ꝺd *David.*

ꝺda *dicenda, docenda.*

ꝺdᵃ *dividenda.*

ꝺdʳ *dividitur.*

ꝺdᵗ *dedit.*

ꝺducᵒni *deductioni.*

ꝺd *dicendum, Davidem, and other cases.*

ꝺdm *dicendum.*

ꝺdr̃t *dederunt.*

ꝺelīqᵒ *derelinquo.*

ꝺeo *debeo.*

ꝺfc̃a *defecta.*

ꝺfc̃oȝ *defectionem.*

ꝺfca *defecta.*

ꝺfc̃ns *deficiens.*

ꝺ. g̃. *Dei gratia.*

ꝺi *dei.*

ꝺia *differentia, divina.*

ꝺidet *dividet.*

ꝺidᵒ *dimidio.*

ꝺidʳ *dividitur.*

ꝺidᵗ *dividit.*

ꝺie *divine, divinæ, differentiæ.*

ꝺigᵈ’ *dirigendum.*

ꝺigūtʳ *diriguntur.*

ꝺinus *divinus.*

ꝺiñ *divinum.*

ꝺio *dimidio, divino, divisio.*

ꝺiᵒᵉ *distinctione.*

ꝺisi *divisi.*

ꝺisī *divisim.*

ꝺisˢ *divisis.*

ꝺissa *dimissa.*

ꝺisȝ *divisis.*

ꝺïs̈ *divisim.*

ꝺis̈t *divisit.*

dit̜ *deitatis.*

di⁹ *dicimus.*

dīd *deinde.*

dīna *divina.*

dlcis *dulcis.*

dt *dilectus, dilectissimus, and their cases.*

dtcaⁿᵉ *delectatione.*

Dm *Deum.*

dm *differentiam.*

dᵐ *dicendum.*

dmᵈᵒ *demonstrando.*

dmᵒ *dummodo.*

dmᵒᶜ *demonstrationem.*

dmoᵗᵉ *demonstratæ.*

dmr̃at *demonstrat.*

dmr̃o *demonstratio.*

d m̃ t *de malo lecto.*

dm̃raͨo *demonstratio.*

dm̃tū *demonstratum.*

d m̃ ū *de malo veniendi.*

dna *domina.*

dnaͨo *dominatio.*

dnar̃ *denarios.*

dncᵃ *dominica.*

dnᵈᵃᵗ *defendat, descendat.*

dnd *dicendum.*

dndns *descendens, defendens.*

dne *domine, dominæ.*

dñio *dominio.*

dno *domino, dono.*

dnʳ *dicuntur.*

dnˢ *denarios, denariis.*

dnt *debent, dicunt.*

dntis *dicentis.*

dñ *denarius, dominus, and their cases.*

dñes *descendentes.*

doⁱū *dominium.*

dorᵐ *deorsum.*

dor̃ *deorum.*

dõii *dominii.*

dpēᵒʳ *dispensator.*

dpse *disperse.*

dr *dicitur, dirigitur, dividitur.*

drᵃ *differentia.*

drabile *demonstrabile.*

draz *differentiarum.*

drão *demonstratio.*

dre *dare, debere, dicere.*

drenᵗ' *differenter.*

dret *deberet, diceret.*

dria *differentia.*

drnⁱⁱˢ *differentiis.*

drnˢ *differentes.*

drnt *differunt.*

drn̯ *differenter.*

drt *differt.*

drūt *differunt.*

ds *Deus, dominus.*

dscⁱpˡˢ *discipulus.*

dscⁱpᵒ *descriptionem.*

đsiñ *desinet, desinit.*
dsīt *desinit.*
đstᵘētʳ *destrueretur.*
dᵗ *debet, dicit, distinguit.*
đta *dicta.*
đtaᵃ *distantia.*
đtᵃhēd *detrahendum.*
đtat *distat.*
dᵗᶜ *dicente, distincte.*
đtiⁱ *distingui.*
đtinᵒ *determinationem.*
đtiʳ *distinguitur.*
dᵗⁱˢ *distinguitis.*
đtiᵗ *distinguit.*

đtiᵘⁱ *distingui.*
đtorē *distributorem.*
đtᵘᵃ *distributiva.*
đtᵘᵉ *distributive.*
dᵗū *distinctum.*
dĩ *dumtaxat.*
đĩas *distantias.*
dᶛiac̃o *determinatio.*
dᶛiat *determinat.*
đueĩat *deveniat.*
đx̃t *dixit.*
dᴣ *debent.*
d)elc̃o *derelictio, derelicto.*

E.

E. *250, Edwardus, eodem.*
Eᵃ *Era.*
eappᶛ *eapropter.*
easđ *easdem.*
eū *eam, eadem.*
eūdē *eandem.*
ebdoᵃ *hebdomada.*
ebđ *hebdomada.*
ebđa *hebdomada.*
ebđe *hebdomadæ.*
ebđm̃a *hebdomada.*
ebⁱeᵗē *ebrietatem.*
ebʳat⁹ *ebriatus, eburatus.*

ecᵃ *ecclesia.*
eᶜᵃ *æquivoca.*
ecᵃᵐ *ecclesiam.*
ecᵃᴣ *ecclesiarum.*
eccᵃᴣ *ecclesiarum.*
eccᶜᵃ *ecclesiastica.*
ecclēa *ecclesia.*
eccĩia *ecclesia.*
ecc̃ *ecclesiasticus.*
ecc̃a *ecclesia.*
ecc̃ᶜᵃ *ecclesiastica.*
ecc̃i *ecclesiastici.*
ecc̃ia *ecclesia.*

ec^e *ecclesiæ.*

ecła *ecclesia.*

ec^9 *æquus, equus.*

ec̃ *etiam.*

ec̆a *ecclesia.*

ec̆^a *e contra.*

ec̃e *ecclesiæ.*

ec̨^a *e contra.*

ec̨^o *e contrario.*

ec̨r̃io *e contrario.*

edc̃m *edictum.*

edđ *edendum.*

e^di n̄e *ædificationem.*

Edw̃us *Edwardus.*

e^d' *eadem, eædem, eodem.*

eđ *edictum.*

eđc^m *edictum.*

eđc̃m *edictum.*

Edrus *Edwardus.*

Edus *Edmundus, Edwardus.*

e^e *ecclesie.*

ec̃^a *essentia.*

ec̃^alis *essentialis.*

ec̃^ałr *essentialiter.*

ec̃^am *essentiam.*

ec̃^an̄ł *essentialis.*

ec̃^e *essentiæ.*

ec̃^lis *essentialis.*

ec̃n^a *essentia.*

ec̃n^alił *essentialiter.*

ec̃n^ałr *essentialiter.*

ec̃nciałr *essentialiter.*

ec̃n^lis *essentialis.*

ec̃n^r *essentialiter.*

ec̃ña *essentia.*

effc̈iuū *effectivum.*

effic^r *efficaciter, efficitur.*

effi^n'r *efficiuntur.*

effi^r *efficaciter, efficitur.*

effi^tis *efficientis.*

eff^ue *effective.*

eff^um *effectivum.*

effu^o *effusio.*

effc̃m *effectum.*

effc̃s *effectus.*

effo *effecto.*

efftu *effectu.*

effu *effectu.*

efc̃m *effectum.*

eg^do *ægritudo.*

eg^edit^r *egreditur.*

eg^edr *egreditur.*

eg^es^9 *egressus.*

eg^inis *ægritudinis.*

eg^inū *ægritudinum.*

eg^onū *ægrotationem.*

eg^r *æger, egeritur.*

eg^rtudinę *ægritudinis.*

eğ *erga, ergo, egregius.*

eğe *egregie.*

eğo *ægro, egeo, egero.*

eğonū *egestionem.*

eğūt^r *egrediuntur.*

eğo *egero.*

e^i *enim.*

e^{ice} *æquivoce.*

$ei^{c}t^9$ *ejectus.*

$ei\hat{c}e$ *ejicere.*

e^ipołł *æquipollet.*

$e^{iu}a^a$ *æquivalentiu.*

$e^i ua^{ns}$ *æquivalens.*

$e^i ua^t$ *æquivalet.*

$e^i ua^{t'}$ *æquivalenter.*

$e^i\tilde{u}$ *æquivalet.*

ei^9 *ejus.*

$ei^9\bar{d}$ *ejusdem.*

e^{I} *enim.*

eïm̃ *ejusmodi.*

eïs *ejus.*

elem̃ *eleemosynam.*

ele^{nta} *elementa.*

e^{let} *æquivalet.*

ele^{ti} *elementi.*

ele$^{t'}$ *elementis.*

eleũ *elevato.*

elēa *eleemosyna.*

elc̃ta *elementa.*

e^{li} *æquali.*

elïa *eleemosyna.*

elo^{do} *elongando, cloquendo.*

eloq̃cia *eloquentia.*

eloq̃t^r *eloquitur.*

e^{l}ȝ *æquivalet.*

eł *æqualis, elementum, cleemosyna.*

eła *cleemosyna, elementa.*

ełaris *elementaris.*

ełari^9 *clremosynarius.*

ełco^m *electionem.*

ełconȝ *electionem.*

ełcĩo *electio.*

ełc^9 *electus.*

ełča *electa.*

ełči *electi.*

ełčio *electio.*

ełčo *electio, electo.*

ełčs *electus.*

ełčus *electus.*

ełeia *eleemosyna.*

ełi *elementi.*

ełia *eleemosyna.*

ełie *eleemosynæ.*

ełis *elementis, eleemosynis.*

ełm *cleemosynam, electuarium,
elementum.*

ełosina *cleemosyna.*

ełoȝ *elementorum.*

ełta *elementa.*

ełtoȝ *elementorum.*

ełĩm *electum.*

emđū *emendum.*

emi^{ma} *eminentissima.*

emp^{i}i *empyrei.*

empłi *emplastri.*

empłm *emplastrum.*

emp̃ *emptio.*

em^t *emanavit.*

em̃dare *emendare.*

eṁdaũ *emendavit.*

eṁd *emendam, emendet, emendum, emendationem.*

eṁdo *emendatio.*

eṁgēte *emergente.*

eṁtulatus *ementulatus.*

eṁgeñ *emergens.*

eṁg^t *emergit.*

eṁserũt *emerserunt.*

e^{nas} *eleemosynas.*

Engleš *Englesceria.*

engł *Englesceria.*

enig^{ca} *œnigmatica.*

enorł *enormiter.*

e^{nt} *erunt, exeunt.*

enūc^{le} *enuntiale.*

enū^{re} *enuntiare.*

enũare *enumerare.*

enũās *enumerans.*

eṅuat^r *enervatur.*

e^o *œquatio, e contrario, ego, eundo.*

eod *eodem.*

eodm *eodem.*

eod^o *eodem modo.*

eoʒ *eorum.*

eŏ *eodem.*

epc̃o *episcopo.*

ephifie *epiphaniœ.*

epi^{ie} *Epiphaniœ.*

epiłia *epilepsia.*

epip̃ *Epiphania.*

episc̃ *episcopus.*

eṗ *emptus, episcopus, epistola.*

eṗał *episcopalis.*

eṗatus *episcopatus.*

eṗat^9 *episcopatus.*

eṗc̃ *episcopus.*

eṗḧia *Epiphania.*

eṗḧie *Epiphaniœ.*

eṗi *episcopi.*

eṗiũ *epitaphium.*

eṗla *epistola.*

eṗlaris *epistolaris.*

eṗlas *epistolas, epulas.*

eṗle *epistolœ, epulœ.*

eṗm *episcopum.*

eṗo *episcopo.*

eṗopus *episcopus.*

eṗs *episcopus, episcopis.*

eṗsc̃o *episcopo.*

eṗtus *episcopatus.*

eṗus *episcopus.*

eq^a *œqualiter.*

eq^{a}ł *œqualis.*

eq^{a}m *œquam, equam.*

eq^{i}cũ *œquivocum.*

eq^{i}tũ *equitum.*

eq^{i}ł *equites.*

e^{q}lis *œqualis.*

eq^o *œquatio, œquo modo.*

eq^r *œquatur, œquetur.*

eq^s *œquales.*

eqʒ *œquat.*

eq̃ *œquus, eques, equus.*

eq̃lis *æqualis.*

eq̃liͭ *æqualiter.*

eq̃l̂r *æqualiter.*

eq̃° *æquatio.*

eq̃°' *æquationis.*

eq̃pat^r *æquiparatur.*

eq̃q *equites.*

eq̃^r *æqualiter.*

eq̃s *equis, equus, æquus.*

eq̃str̃ *equestris.*

eq̃ûo *æquivocatio.*

eq̶ *æque.*

e. r. *et reliqua.*

e^rat *efferat.*

er^ctā *erectam.*

ero^b' *erroribus.*

ero^u *erroneum.*

err°ȝ *errorem.*

er̃ *erat, erit, erunt.*

er̃cā *erectam.*

er̃ce *erecte, erectæ.*

er̃c⁹ *erectus.*

er̃nt *erant, erunt.*

er̃t *erant, erunt.*

esc^abiū *escambium.*

esc^agiū *escangium.*

escap̃ *escapium.*

escābiū *escambium.*

escūgiū *escangium.*

esitac̃o *hæsitatio.*

esp̃ͭ *esperdum.*

ess̃ *essoniavit, essonium, essoni-atus,*

esthr̃ *esthridinga (East Riding).*

esti^ac̃o *æstimatio.*

e^t *erat, erit, est.*

et^a *æterna.*

etc̃ *et cætera.*

et^c *æternæ.*

et^m *æternum.*

et^r *æternaliter.*

etr̃ *et reliqua.*

et̃ *esset, etiam.*

e î *eodem tempore.*

et̃^c *et sic.*

et̃m *etenim.*

et̃^m *et tamen.*

e ℓ *eodem termino.*

eℓna^r *æternaliter.*

eℓne *æterne.*

eℓni' *æternitatis.*

eℓnit̃ *æternitas.*

eℓn⁹ *æternus.*

eua^m *evangelium.*

eua^ta ȝ *evangelistarum.*

eua^te *evangelistæ.*

euāgͭ *evangelium.*

euch^a *eucharistia.*

eucha^a *eucharistia.*

eucha^c *eucharistiæ.*

euck^a *eucharistia.*

eucka^a *eucharistia.*

eucka^c *eucharistiæ.*

eue^m *eveniam, eventum.*

eue^t *evenit.*

euǧ *evangelista, evangelistæ.*

euiᵃ *evidentia.*

euiⁿˢ *evidens.*

euiꝓ *evidenter.*

eukaᵃ *eucharistia.*

eukᵉ *eucharistiæ.*

euoᵈⁱ *evocandi.*

euu. *evangelista.*

euuaᶜᵃ *evangelica.*

euuanᵉ *evangelistæ.*

euuanǧ *evangelista, evangelium.*

euuaᵒ *evangelio.*

euuaᵗᵃ *evangelista.*

euuaᵗʳ *evangelizatur.*

euuāgᶧa *evangelista.*

euuǧlia *evangelia.*

euukaᵃ *eucharistia.*

euuᶧa *evangelista.*

euuᵐ *evangelium.*

euuñᵃ *evangelista.*

euuᵒ *evangelio.*

euuˢ *evangeliis.*

euũ *evangelista.*

euũe *evangelistæ.*

euũgeᵗᵃ *evangelista.*

eũgᶧta *evangelista.*

eũo *evacuatio, evocatio.*

exᵃ *executoria, exempla, extra.*

exacc̃o *exactio.*

exadᵒ *ex adverso.*

exᵃduc̃e *extraducere.*

exᵃere *extrahere.*

exᵃhi *extrahi.*

exᵃh̃e *extrahere.*

exᵃit *extraxit.*

exᵃiuˡⁱ *extrajudiciali.*

exᵃne⁹ *extraneus.*

exᵃʳ *exemplar.*

exᵃtus *excommunicatus.*

exᵃuꝛ̃ *extrahura.*

exāiᵒ *examinatio.*

excac̃o *excommunicatio.*

excāe *excommunicare.*

exced̃ña *excedentia.*

exceᵗ *excellit.*

exciᵈⁱ *exscindendi, excipiendi.*

exᶜᵗũ *executum.*

exc̃ *excommunicat.*

exc̃aᵃ *excommunicata.*

exc̃antʳ *excusantur.*

exc̃aᵒ *excusatio.*

exc̃atus *excommunicatus.*

exc̃aui *excommunicavi.*

exc̃o *excommunicatio.*

exc̃oe *excommunicatione.*

exc̃ois *excommunicationis.*

exc̃oiᵗᵘˢ *excommunicatus.*

exc̃ʳ *excommunicatur.*

exc̃ri *excommunicari.*

excꝯⁱcare *excommunicare.*

excꝯⁱc̃o *excommunicatio.*

excꝯᵒ *excommunicatio.*

exᵉⁱ *extremi.*

exeˡᶜˢ *executoriales.*

ex^{ema} *extrema.*

exe° *executio.*

exerc⁹ *exercitus.*

exe^{re} *executore.*

exhibic̆o *exhibitio.*

exh̄ *exhibet, exhibent.*

ext̄indo *exhercendo (exercendo),*
    exhibendo.

ext̄ire *exhibere.*

ext̄iri *exhiberi.*

exⁱ *exempli.*

exibe *exhibere.*

exibi *exhiberi.*

ex^{icat} *exemplificat.*

exⁱcat *excommunicat.*

exⁱficat *exemplificat.*

exig̃e *exigere.*

exⁱn^{cū} *extrinsecum.*

exⁱns^m *extrinsecum.*

ex^{is} *exceptis, excommunicationis,*
    exemplis.

exist̃e *existente.*

exist̂e *existere.*

exit̃ *exitus, exitum, exitibus.*

ex^{la} *exempla.*

ex^{ll}ę *executoriales.*

ex^lę *exemplis.*

ex^m *exemplum.*

ex^{nis} *excommunicationis.*

ex^{ns} *existens.*

ex^{nti} *existenti.*

ex° *ex adverso, excepto, excommu-*
    nicatio, exemplo.

exopp̃o *ex opposito.*

exo^r *exoneratur.*

exo^{to} *ex opposito.*

ex°' *excommunicationem.*

ex°ʒ *extremorum.*

ex^{ōis} *excommunicationis.*

exŏria *executoria.*

exp^ctari *expectari.*

exp^ctaũ *expectavit.*

expⁱm̃e *exprimere.*

expł *explicit.*

expt̄r *expellitur.*

expñis *expensis.*

expo^bʒ *expositionibus.*

expo^{ri9} *expositorius.*

expōit^r *exponitur.*

exp^{to} *exprofecto.*

expi^a *experientia.*

expi^d' *experiendum.*

expi^e *experientiæ.*

expie^a *experientia.*

expi^{lis} *experimentalis.*

expim̃tū *experimentum.*

expi^{to} *experimento.*

expi^t' *experimentaliter, experi-*
    mentum.

expq́iaʒ *experqueriarum.*

expp̃ *expenditur, expensum.*

expło *expulsio.*

E

exp̄o *expositio.*

exp̄o' *expositionem.*

exp̄ŏm *expositionem.*

exp̄tādū *expectandum.*

exp̄ssio *expressio.*

exp̄ss̄ *expresse.*

ex^r *examinetur, excipietur.*

ex^re *excommunicare.*

exsp^ctaŭit *expectaverit.*

ext^a *excepta, extra.*

ext^actū *extractum.*

ext^aire *extraire.*

ext^aiudclr *extrajudicialiter.*

ex^te *existente.*

ext^ea *extrema.*

ext^em *extremum.*

ext^ena *externa.*

exte^r *extenditur.*

ext^etas *extremitas.*

extē^o *extensio.*

ext^ēoȝ *extremorum.*

extē̆^t *extendit.*

ex^tis *exceptis, excommunicatis.*

extīc^m *extinctum.*

extīata *exterminata.*

ex^tor *executor.*

ex^tu *exitu.*

ex^tū *exceptum, executum, exem-*
    plificatum.

exĩ *examinatis, extra.*

exĩ *excepto.*

extĩc *extunc.*

exĩn^ca *extrinseca.*

exĩn^co *extrinseco.*

exĩn^c' *extrinsecus.*

exti *exteri.*

ext^iata *exterminata.*

exupat *exsuperat.*

ex^9ne *excusatione.*

ex̃ *executio, exitus, extra.*

ex̃ci^a *exercitia.*

ex̃cis *executricis.*

ex̃i *extremi.*

ex̃ificat^r *exemplificatur.*

ex̃it *existit, extitit, extraxerit.*

ex̃iu^li *extrajudiciali.*

ex̃m *exemptum, extremum.*

ex̃me *extremæ, extreme.*

ex̃mi *extremi.*

ex̃mi^tas *extremitas.*

ex̃mi^te *extremitate.*

ex̃n^a *existentia.*

ex̃n^b' *existentibus.*

ex̃nciū *existentium.*

ex̃n^c *existentiæ, existente.*

ex̃n^m *existentiam, existentium.*

ex̃ns *existens.*

ex̃n^s *existentes.*

ex̃nt *existunt.*

ex̃nte *existente.*

ex̃ntia *existentia.*

ex̃ntę *existentis.*

ex̃ri *exemplari.*

ex̃s *exemplis.*

ex̃tat *exstat.*
ex̃ti *excommunicati.*
ex̃tis *excommunicatis, exemplatis, existentis.*
ex̃tu *exitu.*
ex̃tus *excommunicatus.*
ex̃t' *ex parte.*
ex̃tat *exstiterat.*
exci *exercitui.*
exci° *exercitatio.*
excito *exercitato.*
excitū *exercitum.*
excit9 *exercitus.*
excĩto *exercitatio.*
exce *exercere.*
e9 *ejus.*
e9đ *ejusdem.*
ē. *enim, est.*
ēd' *est dicendum.*
ēenas *essentias.*
ēī *enim.*
ēpc̄o *emptio.*
ēpł *emplastrum.*
ēpłm *emplastrum.*
ēpne *emptione.*
ēp̃ts *emptus, empturus.*
ẽ *ecclesia, enim, episcopus, erit, est.*
ẽat *erat.*
ẽea *essentia.*
ẽealis *essentialis.*
ẽeałr *essentialiter.*
ẽeam *essentiam.*
ẽeañł *essentialis.*
ẽee *essentiæ.*
ẽena *essentia.*
ẽenciałr *essentialiter.*
ẽenlis *essentialis.*
ẽenr *essentialiter.*
ẽeña *essentia.*
ẽet *esset.*
ẽẽ *esse, essent.*
ēgliū *euangelium.*
ẽiciẽr *ejicientur.*
ẽig̃er *erigetur.*
ẽī *etenim.*
ẽli *æquali.*
ẽlus *æmulus.*
ẽłr *æqualiter.*
ẽnale *essentiale.*
ẽnī *etenim.*
ẽp9 *episcopus.*
ẽto *æquato, excepto.*
ẽt̃ *essetis.*
ẽ t̃ *eosdem terminos.*
ẽualea *æquivalentia.*
ẽualet *æquivalet.*
ẽualēt *æquivalent.*
ẽualēt *æquivalenter.*
ẽuat *æquivaluit.*
ẽuata *evangelista.*
ẽuat' *æquivalenter.*
ẽuʒ *æquivalet.*

F.

F. *fabricant, faciendum, falsa,*
falsam, faustum, fecit, feli-
citas, feliciter, felix, femina,
feodum, feria, fertorem,
fertores, festum, fiat, fieri,
filia, filius, firma, fit, for-
tuna, frater, fraternitas,
frons, fundavit, fundum,
futuris, quadraginta.

fᵃ *feria, forma.*

fabᶦca *fabrica.*

faƀ *fabrica.*

faƀcᵗ *fabricat.*

faciʳ *faciliter.*

facʳ *faciliter.*

fac̃ *facias, faciendum, facit,*
factus.

fac̃ltas *facultas.*

faꞓe *facere.*

faꞓet *faceret.*

faᵈᵘᵐ *faciendum.*

faᵈ' *faciendum, facundus.*

faᵉˢ *facies.*

fᵃgilis *fragilis.*

falđ *falda.*

fallaᵃ *fallacia.*

falꞇa *fallacia.*

fam̃s *famulus.*

fanᶜᵃ *fantastica.*

fᵃncia *Francia.*

fᵃngit *frangit.*

faⁿˢ *faciens.*

faʳ *faciliter.*

farᵃ *farina.*

fariᵃ *farina.*

farīā *farinam.*

faʳ3 *faceret.*

faˢ *falsus.*

fᵃˢ *falsas.*

faᵗ *facit, faciat, faceret.*

fūilʳᵉ *familiarem.*

fät *faciant.*

fc̃a *facta.*

fc̃is *factis.*

fc̃la *fercula.*

fc̃m *factum.*

fc̃o *facto.*

fc̃s *factus.*

fc̃t *fecit.*

fc̃urᵒ *facturus.*

fc̃uᵹ *facturum.*

febᵉ *febrem.*

febⁱˢ *febris.*

Febr̃ *Februarii.*

Feƀ *Februarii.*

fec̃ *fecit.*

feċit *fecerit.*
fed *fecundus, fœdus.*
fe^{cs} *febres.*
fe^{c̃} *febrem.*
feff *feoffamentum.*
fe^{is} *febris.*
feïa *femina.*
feïe *feminæ.*
fet *felix, feliciter.*
fet rec̃ *felicis recordationis.*
femelt *femella.*
f^cmūt *fremunt, fremuerunt.*
fem̃i *feminini.*
f^eno *freno.*
f^eq̇ci⁹ *frequentius.*
f^cq̇t̃ *frequenter.*
fer^a *feria.*
fer̃ *feræ, feria, ferrum, fert.*
fer̃t *ferunt.*
fesĩ *festinando.*
fe^t *fecerunt, fecit, fecisset.*
fẽt *fecit.*
ff *fabricaverunt, fecerunt, felices, feoffamentum, filii, fratres, fundaverunt.*
ff *feoffamentum.*
fi. *fideli, fidimus.*
fi^a *figura.*
fi^abat *figurabat.*
fi^{atũ} *figuratum.*
fi^ã *figuram.*
fiãt *finalis.*

fiā^r *finaliter.*
fⁱbʒ *fratribus.*
fidei⁹oĩā *fideiussoriam.*
fide^r *fideliter.*
fide^s *fidelis.*
fi^e *figuræ, filiæ.*
fic̃t *fient.*
fic̃t *fieret, fierent.*
fie)i *fieri.*
fig^a *figura.*
fig̃a *figura.*
fig̃a^r *figuraliter.*
fig̃aĩ *figuratum.*
fig̃ū *figuram.*
fig̃c̃o *figuratio.*
fig̃e *figuræ.*
fig̃li *figuli.*
fiⁱ *fieri.*
fi^{l'} *fidelis, finalis.*
fi^m *filium.*
fi^{ma} *firma.*
fⁱma *firma.*
fⁱm^ai⁹ *firmarius.*
fⁱmatū *firmatum.*
fⁱmi^{te} *firmitate.*
fiñ *finalis, finis.*
fiñi *finiri.*
fi^o *filio.*
fir. *firmiter.*
firm̃tū *firmamentum.*
fir^{te} *firmitate.*
fir^{to} *firmamento.*

fir̃re *firmare.*

fir̃tū *firmatum, firmamentum.*

fiᵗᵃ *finita.*

fiᵗᵉ *fidelitate.*

fiᵗ' *finitum.*

fiⁿ *fidelium.*

fix̄s *fixus.*

fiʒ *finis, finem.*

fiaɫ *finalis.*

fiaʳ *finaliter.*

fie *fine.*

fiē *finem.*

fï *feria, filius.*

fïa *figura.*

fïā *figuram.*

fïbʒ *finibus.*

fïde *frigidæ.*

fïeʳ *finietur.*

filis *fidelis.*

fïos *filios.*

fïs *filius, finis.*

fïtaʒ *finitarum.*

fïus *filius.*

fi⁾et *fieret.*

fi⁾i *fieri.*

flaᵘˢ *flatus.*

flāis *flaminis.*

flē *flere.*

floɾ̃ *florenus.*

fluᵉ *flumine.*

fluē *flumen.*

fluïa *flumina.*

fluᵐ *fluminum.*

fluⁿ *flumen.*

flūē *flumen.*

flūiᵇ' *fluminibus.*

flūis *fluminis.*

flūn *flumen.*

fɫ. *falsum, filius, flumen.*

fɫa *falsa.*

fɫariū *falsarium.*

fɫas *falsas.*

fɫe *falsæ, felle.*

fɫgens *fulgens.*

fɫi *falsi.*

fɫis *falsis, fatalis.*

fɫiˢ *falsitas.*

fɫitas *falsitas, felicitas.*

fɫiᵗᵉ *falsitate, felicitate.*

fɫm *falsum.*

fɫo *falso.*

fɫoʒ *falsorum, famulorum.*

fɫs *falsas, famulus.*

fɫᵗ⁹ *falsus, famulus.*

fᵐ *falsum.*

fñ *fine.*

fᵒ *falso, folio.*

fᵒma *forma.*

fom̃t̃ *fomentum.*

fᵒntose *frontose.*

forᵃ *forma.*

forᵃlis *formalis.*

forᵃliꝉ *formaliter.*

forᵃɫm *formalem, formalium.*

for^am *formam, forestam.*
for^ar *formaliter.*
for^at *format.*
for^at̅ *formatur.*
for^{ca} *forinseca.*
for^e *forestæ.*
forⁱcādo *fornicando.*
forⁱcŏm *fornicationem.*
forⁱdīe *formidine.*
forⁱdōse *formidolose.*
for^{ine} *formidine.*
forⁱs *formis.*
for^{ius} *forestarius.*
form̃ *foramen, formam, forum.*
for^{ne} *fornicatione.*
for^o *formatio.*
for^r *formaliter.*
forr̃ *formarem.*
fort̃ *fortibus.*
forę *foris.*
foręf^ctū *forisfactum.*
foręfec̃ *forisfecit.*
foręiudicac̃o *forisjudicatio.*
forʒ *formarum.*
for̃ *foresta, forestarius, forum.*
for̃a *foresta.*
for̃cāi *fornicari.*
for̃dat *formidat.*
for̃e *formæ.*
for̃fc̃ura *forisfactura.*
for̃fec̃ *forisfecit.*
for̃i *foramini, formari.*

for̃lis *formalis.*
for̃ns⁹ *forensis, forinsecus.*
for̃sico *forensico.*
for̃t^m *formatum.*
for̃t^r *formatur.*
for̃t' *formaliter.*
for̃t̃ *fortiter.*
foʒ *forum.*
foʒ^{ca} *forinseca.*
fō *falso, festo, folio, foras, foris.*
föaⁿ *foramen.*
fr. *francorum, franci.*
fragi^{tas} *fragilitas.*
franc̃ *Francia, Francus, Francigena.*
franc̃pł *franciplegii.*
franc̃płm *franciplegium.*
fra^{tas} *fraternitas.*
frat^ueł *fratruelis.*
frat̃ *frater.*
frc̃m *fractum, fructum.*
frc̃s *fructus.*
freqñr *frequenter.*
freq̃t̃ *frequenter.*
frig̃ *frigidus.*
frig̃m *frigidum.*
fri^{tis} *frigiditatis.*
frïda *frigida.*
frïm *frigidum.*
frïssimā *frigidissimam.*
frq̃t̃ *frequenter.*
frum̃ *frumentarius, frumentum.*

fru^{nti} *frumenti.*

fr^{9}t^{a} *frustra.*

fr̃ *feria, forum, francus, frater, frequens, frumentum.*

fr̃^{as} *fraternitas.*

frc̃tā *fractam.*

frc̃t^{9} *fractus, fructus.*

frc̃tm *fractum, fructum, furcil-latum.*

fr̃es *fratres.*

fr̃ē *fratrem.*

fr̃i *fratri, freti, frumenti.*

fr̃ib^{9} *fratribus.*

fr̃ifo^{na} *ferrifodina.*

fr̃is *fratris.*

fr̃m *frigidum, frumentum.*

fr̃ni^{tas} *fraternitas.*

fr̃ni^{t}ę *fraternitatis.*

fr̃os *feriatos.*

fr̃qt̃ *frequenter.*

fr̃uet *fratruelis.*

fr̃^{us} *fructus.*

f^{t} *facit, fecit, fit, fuit.*

ft̃o *futuro.*

f^{u}ctū *fructum.*

f^{u}ct^{9} *fructus.*

fuẽrt *fuerunt.*

fugiti̇ *fugitivi.*

fug̃ *fuga, fugitivus.*

fug̃oȝ *fugitivorum.*

f^{u}i *frui.*

f^{u}ic̃o *fruitio.*

f^{u}i^{ne} *fruitione.*

fui^{t} *fuisset.*

f^{u}mēti *frumenti.*

f^{u}m̃nto *frumento.*

furat^{9} *furatus.*

f^{us}t^{a} *frustra.*

fu^{t} *fuit.*

fut^{m} *futurum.*

fut^{r}a *futura.*

fut^{r}i *futuri.*

fut^{r}is *futuris.*

fut^{r}m *futurum.*

fuîm *futurum.*

fuîs *futurus.*

fūdac̃o *fundatio.*

fūig̃o *fumigatio.*

fũ *fuit.*

fûam *fueram.*

fûat *fuerant.*

fûit *fuerit.*

fûit *fuerint.*

fûi^{9} *fuerimus.*

fûnt *fuerunt.*

fûūt *fuerunt.*

fę *festum.*

F̄. *40000.*

f *festum, foresta, fugitivus.*

fa *fallacia, festa.*

fa^{l'} *finalis.*

farius *ferrarius.*

fat^{r} *feratur.*

faĩ *furatus.*

faⱰ *frater.*

fᴄc̃o *fractio.*

fci *facti.*

fcit *facit.*

fcłm *ferculum.*

fcᵐ *factum.*

fcⁿᵉ *fractione.*

fcᵗ *fecit.*

fcta *facta.*

fcto *facto.*

fc̆ *factæ.*

fe *fere.*

fer̃ *fieri.*

ff *feoffamentum.*

fgiᵗᵉ *frigiditate.*

fi *fieri.*

fia *feria.*

fiac̃oȝ *feriationem.*

fiaʳ *feriatur.*

fiar̃ *filiarum.*

fiata *feriata.*

fiatˢ d̄ *feriatus dies.*

fiis *feriis.*

fllat *fallat.*

fllᶜ *fallaciæ.*

flłᵃ *fallacia.*

flñgeł *ferlingellus.*

flo *famulo.*

fłngi *ferlingi.*

fłs *famulus.*

fm *falsum, feodum, festum, fir-
mum.*

fma *firma.*

fmaⁿᵗᵒ *firmamento.*

fmiⱰ *firmiter.*

fmʳⁱ *fermentari.*

fmto *fermento.*

fn *forsan, forsitan.*

fnda *ferenda, fienda.*

fñg̃t *frangunt.*

fo *falso, feodo.*

fodᵃiᵒ *feodarius.*

for̃ *furoris.*

fq̈Ɒ *frequenter.*

fr *frater.*

fra *frigida.*

frᵃ *feria.*

frᵃˢ *frigiditas.*

frbᵒ *fratribus.*

frde *frigide.*

fre *facere, fratre.*

frem *fratrem.*

fres *fratres.*

frē *fratrem.*

fri *fratri, frumenti.*

fria *feria.*

fribᵒ *fratribus.*

frie *feriæ.*

frifoⁿᵉ *ferrifodinæ.*

fris *feriis.*

frī *feria.*

frm *feriam, fratrem, fratrum,
frumentum.*

frnā *fraternam.*

fro *feretro, ferro, frumento.*

fr^s *fratres.*

fruelis *fratruelis.*

frū *ferrum, fratrum, frumen-*
   tum.

fr̃a *feria.*

fs *ferens, fratres.*

f^{tas} *firmitas.*

ftⁱ *fratri.*

ftⁱb⁹ *fratribus.*

ftił *fertilis.*

ftis *futuris.*

fto *futuro.*

ft^r *fertur.*

ft^urę *futuris.*

ftȥ *fratrum.*

fℓ *frater.*

fude *fraude.*

f^uibȥ *fructibus.*

fum *fumum.*

fus *fraus.*

fũ *fervet.*

fȥ *ferrum, fratrum.*

f'rū *ferrum.*

G.

G *400.*

g^a *erga, gradus, gratia.*

gablat̃ *gablatores.*

g^abȥ *gradibus.*

gab̃ *gabulum.*

g^acā *grammaticam.*

galliñ *gallinam.*

gałł *gallo, gallum.*

gał *galo.*

g^ałr *generaliter.*

g^am *gratiam.*

g^am̃ *gramen.*

g^am̃is *graminis.*

g^am̃neũ *gramineum.*

g^anat^ai⁹ *granatarius.*

g^anđ *grandis.*

g^angia *grangia.*

g^anū *granum.*

g^añ *granum.*

garđ *gardaroba.*

g^as *gratias.*

g^aticus *grammaticus.*

g^ati^{ne} *gratitudine.*

g^aua *grava.*

g^auab̃ *gravabat, gravabit.*

g^auam̃ *gravamen.*

gᵃuare *gravare.*

gᵃuat⁹ *gravatus.*

gᵃuiʳ *graviter.*

gᵃuiℓ *graviter.*

gᵃȝ *gratiarum.*

gᵃ *gratiam.*

gᵉ *genere, gratiæ.*

geⁱᵗ *genuit.*

geīa *gemina.*

geld *geldum, geldavit.*

geldƀ *geldabat, geldabit.*

geˡᶜ *generale, gelide.*

geᵐ *gentem, gentium.*

gᶜman⁹ *germanus.*

gem̃ *geminus, gemitus.*

gem̃bȝ *gemitibus.*

geⁿᵉ *generatione.*

geⁿⁱˢ *geminis, generationis.*

geñ *generaliter, generavit, gene-rosus, genuit.*

geñalis *generalis.*

geñs *geminis,generationis,genius, gentes, gerens.*

geñꝉaᴖo *generatio.*

geñꝉm *generum.*

geoᵃ *geometria.*

gers̃ *gersuma.*

gᶜss⁹ *gressus.*

gᶜx *grex.*

ge⁹ *genus.*

geīⁱ *gemini.*

geīʳᵉˢ *genitores.*

geīt⁹ *genitus.*

geīȝ *geminorum, genitorum.*

geīa *gemina.*

gẽ *genus.*

gẽe *gente.*

gⁱ *igitur.*

giği͠t *gignitur.*

Gilℓt⁹ *Gillebertus.*

girf *girfalco.*

giřo *giratio.*

gⁱˢ *generis.*

glebaᵉ *glebale.*

gloᵐ *glossam.*

glosᵃiū *glossarium.*

glõ *glossa.*

glõᵒʳ *gloriosior.*

glõsus *gloriosus.*

gꝉa *gloria, glossa.*

gꝉatʳ *gloriatur.*

gꝉā *gloriam, glossam.*

gꝉd *geldum, gilda.*

gꝉe *gloriæ, glossæ.*

gꝉia *gloria.*

gꝉifi° *glorificatio.*

gꝉifiᵘ *glorificatum.*

gꝉifio *glorificatio.*

gꝉoᵒʳ *gloriosior.*

gꝉose *gloriosæ, gloriose.*

gꝉosiᵗᵉ *gloriositate.*

gꝉossᵐᵒ *gloriosissimo.*

gꝉosus *gloriosus.*

gꝉöiᵐᶜ *gloriosissime.*

gñ *genius, genus.*

gña *genera.*

gñalis *generalis.*

gñaℓr *generaliter.*

gñari *generari.*

gñe *genere.*

gño *generatio.*

gñs *gentes.*

g° *ergo.*

g°ᵉ *generatione.*

g°ⁱˢ *generationis.*

g°ss⁹ *grossus.*

gʳ *igitur.*

graī *grates, gratus.*

gʳbӡ *generibus, gradibus.*

gr̄ *gradus, gratia, igitur.*

gr̆a *gratia.*

gr̆as *gratias.*

gr̆u *gratiam.*

gr̄e *gratiæ.*

gr̄osus *gratiosus.*

gurǵ *gurges.*

geℓ *generis.*

g⁹ *genus, gradus.*

Ḡ *400000.*

g̈ *gaudium, geldum, genera, geni-us,genus,gilda,gratia,igitur.*

g̈bit *generabit, gravabit.*

g̈ᵇӡ *gradibus, gravaminibus.*

g̈cia *gratia.*

g̈ciℓ *gracilis.*

g̈d⁹ *gradus.*

g̈đ *gradum.*

g̈e *gratiæ.*

g̈inat *germinat.*

g̈in⁹ *geminus, genuinus.*

g̈is *generis.*

g̈iī *geritis.*

g̈le *generale.*

g̈ℓ *generalis.*

g̈ℓr *generaliter.*

g̈nabūtʳ *generabuntur.*

g̈nᵇӡ *gerentibus.*

g̈nᶜ *genere.*

g̈nᵉosus *generosus.*

g̈nᵉū *generum.*

g̈ngia *grangia.*

g̈niti *geniti.*

g̈nˡᶜ *generabile, generale.*

g̈n° *generatio.*

g̈ntibӡ *gerentibus.*

g̈nī *gentes.*

g̈nut *Cnut, Canute.*

g̈ū *generet.*

g̃ūstℓ *genistis.*

g̃ñ *gener.*

g̃ña *genera.*

g̃ñaⁱ *generari.*

g̃ñali *generali.*

g̃ñaℓr *generaliter.*

g̃ñaᵐ *generatum.*

g̃ñaᵐᵃ *generalissima.*

g̃ña° *generatio.*

g̃ñaʳ *generaliter.*

g̃ñatī *generatim.*

g̃ñbr *generabitur.*

g̃ñe *genere.*

g̃ñis *generis.*

g̃ñlis *generalis.*

g̃ño *generatio, genero.*

g̃ñōe *generatione.*

g̃oe *generatione.*

g̃rose *gloriose, gratiose.*

g̃r' *gratiarum.*

g̃s *generis, gratias.*

g̃ta *grata.*

g̃tar *gratanter.*

g̃taū *gustavit.*

g̃ti *generati.*

g̃tī *generatim, gradatim.*

g̃to *grato.*

g̃tr *generatur, igitur.*

g̃tū *gratum.*

g̃t̃ *gratum.*

g̃tm *genitivum.*

g̃ts *gentes.*

g̃uam̃ *gravamen.*

g̃uis *gravis.*

g̃ūtr *geruntur.*

g̃⁹ *gustus.*

g̃ꝫ *gratiarum.*

ꝭi *geri.*

ꝭman⁹ *germanus.*

ꝭm' *germen.*

H.

H. *ducenti, habemus, habent, habet, hac, hæc, heres, herus, hic, hoc, homo, honestus, hora, hujus, humilis, hundredum.*

H. A. *hoc anno.*

haa *haia.*

hab *habet, haberet.*

habe *habere.*

ha *hac.*

hag̃ *hagæ, hagas.*

haiū *haiam.*

hak̃ *hakeneius.*

har *habetur.*

hast̃ *hastis.*

haꝫ *harum.*

hāc *hanc.*

hāgwith *hangwitha.*

h̃et *haberet.*

hãĩts *habitationis.*

hãndn͡t *habundanter.*

hƀe *habere.*

h^c → h^c *hac, hæc, hic, hoc, huic, hunc.*

hđ *hundredum.*

hđr *hundredum.*

h. e. *hoc est.*

hereu^ađ *herewæda.*

heᷓ *heres.*

H. F. F. *hoc fieri fecit.*

hh *heredes.*

h. i. *hic invenies.*

Hierƚm *Hierusalem.*

Hierusƚ *Hierusalem.*

hinciñ *hincinde.*

Hirƚ *Hierusalem.*

Hiᷓƚm *Hierusalem.*

hi⁹ *hujusmodi.*

h. l. *hic lege, hoc loco.*

H. M: *hoc monumentum, honesta matrona, honesta mulier.*

h^o *hoc, homo, homicidio.*

ho. *homo, hora.*

ho^a *hora.*

hobedïa *obedientia.*

h^oc⁹ *hoccus.*

ho^e *hodie, homine.*

h^{oi} *hujusmodi.*

ho^{ili} *honorabili.*

hoi^m *hominum.*

ho^{is} *hominis.*

ho^{is} *hominis.*

hoi^u *homicidium.*

hoïm *hominum.*

ho^{lis} *honorabilis.*

ho^m *hominem, hominum.*

hom̃ii *homagii.*

hon^bȝ *honorabilibus.*

hon^{les} *honorabiles.*

honoᷓ *honorabilium.*

hoñ *honorabilem.*

hoñ^{b9} *honorabilibus.*

hoñ^{liu} *honorabilium.*

hoñ^lę *honorabilis.*

h^{oo} *hoc modo.*

ho^rę *honoris.*

hosp^{es} *hospites.*

hosp^{ia} *hospitia.*

hosp^{te} *hospitatæ.*

hosp̄ari *hospitari.*

hoss. *hostes.*

host^aii *hostarii.*

ho^{te} *honestate, honestæ.*

hoȝ *horum.*

h̄oestę *honestatis.*

h̄oib⁹ *hominibus.*

h̄oici^m *homicidium.*

h̄oñ *hominum.*

h̄ora^{or} *honorabilior.*

h̄ori *honori.*

h̃o *homo.*

h̃oci^m *homicidium.*

h̃oe *homine.*

hōes *homines.*

hōi *homini.*

hōim *hominum.*

hōiū *hominum.*

hōm *hominem, horam.*

hōr *honor.*

hōrē *honorem.*

hös *horas.*

hr̄des *heredes.*

huā *humanam.*

hui⁹ *hujus.*

hui⁹ceōi *hujuscemodi.*

hui⁹di *hujusmodi.*

hui⁹modi *hujusmodi.*

hui⁹m̄i *hujusmodi.*

hu¹ę *humilis.*

hum̄t *humilis.*

hum̄tr *humiliter.*

hundr̄ *hundredum.*

huōi *hujusmodi.*

hūaᵃ *humana.*

hūaᵉ *humane.*

hūaᵐ *humanum.*

hūatᶜ *humanitate.*

hūat⁹ *humatus.*

hūāi *humani.*

hūida *humida.*

hūilᵃˢ *humilitas.*

hūilis *humilis.*

hūilīa *humillima.*

hūitr *humiliter.*

hūītᵉ *humiditate.*

hūorē *humorem.*

hūa *humana.*

hūatr *habitualiter.*

hūā *humanam.*

hūe *humanæ, humane.*

hūi *humidi.*

hūior *humidior.*

hūn⁹ *humanus.*

hūōi *hujusmodi.*

hyeᵃᵇ₃ *hiemalibus.*

hyēs *hiems.*

hy⁹ *hymnus.*

h⁹ *hujus.*

h⁹cᵃles *huscarles.*

h⁹di *hujusmodi.*

h⁹i *hujusmodi.*

H̄ *200000.*

ħ *habemus, habent, habet, hac,*
    hæc, heres, herus, hic, hoc,
    homo, honestus, hora, hujus,
    humilis.

ħamⁱ⁹ *habeamus.*

ħant *habeant.*

ħat *habeat.*

ħatʳ *habeatur.*

ħāt *habeant.*

ħƀ *habet, habebat.*

ħƀe *habere.*

ħc *hac, huc, hunc.*

ħc⁹q̨ *hucusque.*

ħdib₃ *hæredibus.*

ħditat̃ *hæreditatem.*

ħdr̄ *hundredum.*
ħdū *hæredum.*
ħe *habe, habere, heredibus.*
ħeat *habeat.*
ħeāt *habeant.*
ħebat *habebat.*
ħebit *habebit.*
ħebᵗ *habebit.*
ħebūt *habebunt.*
ħebr *habebitur.*
ħebt *habebat.*
ħeᶜ' *hæreticum.*
ħeditaḡ *hereditagium.*
ħediᵗe *hereditatis.*
ħedᵗᵃˢ *hereditas.*
ħed *heredem, heredum.*
ħeds *heredes.*
ħedtᵃia *hereditaria.*
ħemiʳ' *heremitarum.*
ħemit̃ *heremitis.*
ħem⁹ *habemus.*
ħentes *habentes.*
ħeo *habeo.*
ħeʳ *habetur.*
ħere *habere.*
ħeri *haberi.*
ħerᵗ *haberet.*
ħer̄ *habere.*
ħes *habens, habes, heres.*
ħes̃ *hæresis.*
ħᶜᵗ *haberet.*
ħeticus *hæreticus.*

ħetʳ *habetur.*
ħᵉtʳ *haberetur.*
ħete *habetis.*
ħezeld⁹ *herezeldus.*
ħe⁹ *habemus.*
ħeȝ *heremitarum.*
ħēs *habemus.*
ħⁱᶜ *huic.*
ħiᵈⁱ *hujusmodi.*
ħiᵈᵒ *habitando, habitudo.*
ħieta *herieta.*
ħig̈ta *herigeta.*
ħiˡᵉ *habile.*
ħilitᵈᵒ *habilitando.*
ħil *habilis.*
ħinacõem *hominationem.*
ħiⁿᵉ *habitudinem.*
ħiᵒʳ *habilior.*
ħita *habita.*
ħitaḡ *heritagium.*
ħitᵃie *hereditarie.*
ħitaᵒ *habitatio.*
ħitare *habitare.*
ħitēt *habitent.*
ħitio *habitio.*
ħitⁱˢ *habitualis.*
ħitᵐ *habitum.*
ħitⁿᵉ *habitione, habitudine.*
ħitʳm *habiturum.*
ħitu *habitu.*
ħituᵉ *habitudine.*
ħituᵒ *habitudo.*

ħitū *habitum.*
ħitūa *habitura.*
ħitę *habitantis, habitis.*
ħiᵗę *habitationis, habitis.*
ħi⁹ *hujus, hujusmodi.*
ħi⁹i *hujusmodi.*
ħïdiaˡ' *habitudinalis.*
ħïmo' *hujusmodi.*
ħmiꞁ *humilis.*
ħmºi *hujusmodi.*
ħmō *hujusmodi.*
ħmõi *hujusmodi.*
ħm⁹ *habemus.*
ħm̃s *habemus.*
ħnª *habentia.*
ħncia *habentia.*
ħndi *habendi.*
ħndū *habendum.*
ħnđ *habendum.*
ħns *habens.*
ħnˢ *habentes.*
ħnt *habent.*
ħnti *habenti.*
ħntʳ *habentur.*
ħntę *habentis.*
ħoꞃlis *honorabilis.*
ħºˡ *hujusmodi.*
ħºi *homini, hujusmodi.*

ħoibꝫ *hominibus.*
ħois *hominis.*
ħor *honor.*
ħr *habetur, hundredum.*
ħre *habere.*
ħreⁱª *hereditaria.*
ħret *haberet.*
ħrē *haberem.*
ħri *haberi.*
ħrs *heres.*
ħrᵗ *haberet.*
ħr̃di *heredi.*
ħs *habes, heres.*
ħt *habent, habet.*
ħuäiᵗꞇ *humanitatis.*
ħueꞃt *habuerunt.*
ħui *habui.*
ħuisse *habuisse.*
ħuit *habuit.*
ħui⁹ *hujusmodi.*
ħum *humidum.*
ħunt *habuerunt.*
ħu̇at *habuerat.*
ħu̇īt *habuerint.*
ħu̇nt *habuerunt.*
ħu̇o *habuero.*
ħꝫ *habent, habet.*
ħ⁹ *hujusmodi.*

M. F

I.

I. *ibi, id est, idus, Jesus, igitur,*
in, inferi, inferis, infra,
ita, iterum, jussit.

iᵃ *illa, infra, intra, ita, prima,*
unica, una.

iactāᵃ *jactantia.*

iacȝ *jacet.*

iac̃it *jacuit.*

iac̃t *jacet.*

iamdc̃us *jamdictus.*

iañ *janua, Januarii.*

iᵃq̃ *itaque.*

iᵃȝ *primam.*

iᵃ𝔷 *illarum.*

iā *jam.*

iᵃ *primam.*

iādc̃o *jamdicto.*

iāpⁱdē *jampridem.*

ib̃m *ibidem.*

ib̃t *ibit, ibunt.*

I. C. *Jesus Christus, juriscon-*
sultus.

ic̃ *illic.*

id. *idus.*

iᵈ *illud.*

I. D. *jussu Dei.*

idcⁱco *idcirco.*

idē *idem.*

idib⁹ *idibus.*

idioᵗ⁹ *idiomatum.*

i. d. iud. *in die judicii.*

I. D. N. *in Dei nomine.*

idᵗ *id est.*

id⁹ *idus.*

id̃ *idem.*

id̃ne *indictione.*

id̃o *ideo.*

iᶜ *illæ, ille.*

iẽm *Jesum.*

ignoᵃ *ignorantia.*

ignoᵒam⁹ *ignoramus.*

ignoᵗᵉ *ignobilitate.*

igñ *ignis.*

igᵒᵃ *ignorantia.*

igᵒmïa *ignominia.*

igᵒraᵃ *ignorantia.*

igᵒrat *ignorat.*

igᵒtus *ignotus.*

igᵒt̃ *ignoranter.*

igʳ *igitur.*

ig̃ *igitur.*

ig̃s *ignis.*

i. h. *jacet hic, invenies hic.*

Ihc. *Jesus.*

Iherl̃m *Jerusalem.*

Ihl̃m *Jerusalem.*

Ihs. *Jesus.*

Ih3 *Jesum.*

Ihes *Johannes.*

Iht *Jerusalem.*

Iohes *Johannes.*

Iohi *Johanni.*

i^i *ibi.*

ij^a *secunda.*

i^{i}dc *ibidem.*

i^{i}d *ibidem.*

iij^a *tertia.*

iij^{es} *tres.*

iiij^{or} *quatuor.*

iiij^{tus} *quartus.*

iij^{us} *tertius.*

ij^o *duo.*

IIX. *octo.*

illa^o *illatio.*

illi$^{t'}$ *illicitum.*

illi^9 *illius.*

illīs *illius.*

illītā^m *illimitatum.*

ill^o *illo modo.*

illu^{es} *illuminationes.*

illuïa^o *illuminatio.*

illd *illud.*

illimus *illegitimus.*

illatus *illiteratus.*

im. *immortalis, imperator.*

i^m *illum, ipsum, irrotulatum, unum, mille.*

i. m. *in manu, in manibus.*

imīutū *imminutum.*

impl^{lis} *impossibilis.*

impp. *imperatores.*

impl^{li} *imperiali.*

imppp̃ *imperpetuum.*

impp̃ *imperator, imperant, imperante, impetrant.*

imp̃le *impossibile.*

im̃ *imperator.*

im̃do *immundo.*

in. *instantiam.*

i. n. *in nomine.*

inbri *inbreviari.*

inc^{a}ssūdū *incrassandum.*

inci^{ns} *incidens, incipiens.*

inctur̃ *inclausura.*

incor^{le} *incorporale.*

incor^{ti}e *incorruptibile.*

incp̃t *incipit.*

incr̃o *incremento.*

inc^{s}t *incurrisset.*

inc̃ *incarnationis, incipit.*

inc̃m̃to *incremento.*

inc̃p̃ *incepit, incipit.*

inc̃p̃nt *incipiunt.*

inc̃re *incurrere.*

inc̃rño *incarnatio.*

ind. *indictione.*

ind^a *indulgentia.*

indelabile *indeclinabile.*

indi^{is} *individuis.*

indi^{li} *individuali, indivisibili.*

indi° *individuo.*
i. n. D. ꝛ s. ꝛ i. T. *in nomine Dei et Sanctæ et Individuæ Trinitatis.*
inđ *inde, indebite, indictione, indus.*
inđa *indulgentia.*
inđffnꝰ *indifferenter.*
inđm *indifferentiam.*
inđra *indifferentia.*
inđrn^r *indifferenter.*
inđrns *indifferens.*
inđrnꝰ *indifferenter.*
inet *inæqualis.*
ineꝰnū *in eternum.*
inew̃ *inewardus.*
infto *inflammatio, inflato.*
infra^ta *infrascripta.*
infr̃at *infrigidat.*
inf^ta *infrascripta.*
inf *infracta.*
infꝭ *infortunium.*
infa^r *inferatur.*
infnus *infernus.*
info *infero.*
ing̃^lis *ingenerabilis.*
inhic̃o *inhibitio.*
inhic̃oȝ *inhibitionem.*
inħens *inhærens, inhibens.*
inħilis *inhabilis.*
iniun. *injungentes.*
inīū *in integrum.*
inł *inlustris (illustris).*
in ł *in libro.*
in n. *in nomine.*
inñ *innocens, innocenter.*
inobłoe *in oblatione.*
in p. *in pace.*
inp^lis *impossibilis.*
inp̃olis *impossibilis.*
inꝑ^lis *impartialis.*
inꝑpet̃ *imperpetuum.*
inp̃^lis *impossibilis.*
inp̃^l'r *impossibiliter.*
inp̃o *impositio.*
inp̃oe *impositione.*
inq^ic̃o *inquisitio.*
inq^io *inquisitio.*
inq^isic̃o *inquisitio.*
inq^isit̃ *inquisitum.*
inq̃ *inquiratur.*
ins^ciis *instanciis.*
insoł *insolidum, insolutum.*
insp^ct^ris *inspecturis.*
inspect^s *inspecturis.*
inspi^ne *inspiratione.*
insp̃cõe *inspectione.*
instãm *instantiam.*
instĩco *institutio.*
inst^li *instrumentali.*
inst^rctus *instructus.*
inst^rtle *instrumentale.*
instr̃a *instrumenta.*
instr̃is *instrumentis.*

instr̄m *instrumentum.*
instr̄o *instrumento.*
instr̄oჳ *instrumentorum.*
iusĩ *instituta, institutiones.*
iusĩn℮ *institutionis.*
insr̄ *insuper.*
insit̄ʳ *inseritur.*
instu̅ *insertum.*
intᵃ *intra.*
intᵃc̃o *intratio.*
intᵃns *intrans.*
intᵃuit *intravit.*
inteⁱᵗ *intelligit.*
inteˡᵉ *intelligibile.*
inteˡⁱᵃ *intelligibilia.*
intelʳᵉ *intelligere.*
intelᵗʳ *intelligitur.*
intelᵗuał *intellectualis.*
inteᵐ *intellectum.*
inteʳᵉ *intelligere.*
inteˢ *intellectus.*
intc̄ⁱᵗ *intendit.*
intc̄ᵒ *intentio.*
intc̃ᵍe *intelligere.*
intem̃ *intellectum.*
intᵍⁱ *intelligi.*
intⁱ *intelligi.*
intⁱᵇჳ *intrantibus.*
intⁱncʼ *intrinsecum.*
intlᶫʼ *intellectualis.*
intłłi *intelligi.*
intᵒ *intro.*

intᵒitⁱ *introitus.*
intᵒmᵗto *intromitto.*
intᵒsc̃ptū *introscriptum.*
intʳ *intratur, intelligitur.*
intropt̄a *introscripta.*
intᵘsit *intrusit.*
int̃ *inter, interest, intersit.*
intĩᵈᵒ *intelligendo.*
intĩeᵐ *intellectum.*
intĩᵍⁱ *intelligi.*
intĩligʳ *intelligitur.*
intĩllⁱᵃ *intelligentia.*
intĩlliˡᵉ *intelligibile.*
intĩlliᵒ *intelligo.*
intĩłti *intelligi.*
intĩłndū *intelligendum.*
intĩłncᵉ *intelligentiæ.*
intĩłłur *intelliguntur.*
intĩncᵃ *intrinseca.*
intĩpoło *interpolatio.*
intĩp̄ʳ *interpretatur.*
intĩtʼ *intellectus, intellectis.*
intᵱ *inter.*
intᵱcalᵃiⁱ *intercalarius.*
intᵱcalᵃo *intercalatio.*
intᵱcalar℮ *intercalaris.*
intᵱdc̃o *interdicto.*
intᵱd *interdum.*
intᵱc̃ *interest.*
intᵱc̃e *interesse.*
intᵱfc̃o *interfectio, interfecto.*
intᵱfc̃ⁱ *interfectus.*

intfice *interficere.*

inti⁹ *interius.*

intpᵐ *interpretatum.*

intpoło *interpolatio.*

intpõ *interpositio.*

intpretʳ *interpretatur.*

intp̃s *interpres.*

intp̃s *interpres.*

intp̃taᵒ *interpretatio.*

intp̃tʳⁱ *interpretaturi.*

inuenʳ *invenitur.*

inueñr *invenitur.*

inuᵐ *inventarium.*

inũcio *invencio.*

inũe *innuere.*

iñocñe *innocentiæ.*

iñõiat⁹ *innominatus.*

iñ *inde, integrum.*

iñti *incontinenti.*

iñuᵃ *insula.*

iñxe *incomplexe, innixe.*

iᵒ *ideo, illico, illo, primo.*

iᵒnᵒ *primo nocturno.*

iođ *jocundus.*

Ioħ *Johannes.*

iᵒᵒ *illo modo.*

iᵒᵹ *illorum.*

Iões *Johannes.*

Iõis *Johannis.*

i. p. *in pace.*

ipᵃ *ipsa.*

ipᵉ *ipse.*

ip̃ *ipsa, ipse.*

ip̃a *ipsa.*

ip̃aᵹ *ipsarum.*

ip̃e *ipse.*

ip̃i *ipsi.*

ip̃is *ipsis.*

ip̃i⁹ *ipsius.*

ip̃m *ipsum.*

ip̃ᵐm̃ *ipsummet.*

ip̃o *ipso.*

ip̃oᵹ *ipsorum.*

ip̃s *ipsis.*

ip̃ᵹ *ipsum.*

irraˡⁱ *irrationali.*

irrᵇ' *irregularibus.*

irreᵃritas *irregularitas.*

irretʳ *irretitur.*

irret⁹ *irretitus.*

irreᵗ' *irregularitatis.*

irreuõbiʳ *irrevocabiliter.*

irrēs *irregulares.*

irritᵃi *irritari.*

irritatʳ *irritatur.*

irriᵗᵉ *irregularitate.*

irrᵒalis *irrationalis, irrationabilis.*

irr̃is *irregularis.*

irr̃s *irregularis.*

iʳ' *illorum.*

istimᵗ *istimet.*

istimᵹ *istimet.*

ist̃ *istud.*

iᵗᵈ *istud.*

iteꝛ̄ *iterum.*

iᵗⁱ *isti.*

itiđ *itidem.*

iᵗᵘˢ *infrascriptus.*

iꞇ̄ *item.*

iꞇ̄ᵈ’ *item notandum.*

iꞇ̋aˡ’ *iterabilis.*

iꞇ̋ari *iterari.*

iꞇ̋m *iterum.*

iudicⁱᵗ *judicaverit.*

iudicit’ *judicialiter.*

iudiᵐ *judicium.*

iudiᵒ *judicio.*

iudᵐ *judicium.*

iudᵒ *judicio.*

iudʳ *judicialiter.*

iuđ *judicium.*

iuđaꞁr *judicialiter.*

iuđi *judicari.*

iuđm *judicium.*

iᵃe *jure.*

iuꞡ̄ *jugum.*

ivᵒʳ *quatuor.*

iuraᵐ *juramentum, juratam.*

iuraᵗᵒ *juramento.*

iur. cāci *juris canonici.*

iurᶜ̄ *jurisdictionem.*

iuꝛ̄dc̄o *jurisdictio.*

iuꝛ̄iuꝛ̄ *jurejurando.*

iusᵒ₃ *justitiariorum.*

iussꞌit *jusserit.*

iustᵃ *justitia.*

iustiᵒ *justificatio.*

iuuãe *juvamine.*

iuuᵉ *juvare.*

iuũ *juvat, juvabat.*

iuxᵃ *juxta.*

iũa *jura.*

iũata *jurata.*

iũatᵒes *juratores.*

iũe *jure.*

iũore *juniore.*

I. X. *Jesus Christus.*

i⁹ *Jesus, jus, illius, unius, primus.*

i⁹stiᵃ *justitia.*

i⁹tia *justitia.*

i⁹tifiᵒ *justificatio.*

i⁹t⁹ *justus.*

ī *ibi, id est, igitur, in.*

īᵃ *infra, intra.*

īᵃ *primam.*

ībꞛ̃iare *inbreviare.*

īcᵃc̄atū *incarceratum.*

īcᵃnᵒnē *incarnationem.*

īcarñ *incarnationis.*

īcarᵒ̄ *incarnationem.*

īcᵃrˢ *incarnationis.*

īcᵃꝛ̃ *incarnationis.*

īchᵒc̄o *inchoatio.*

īc̄ħac̄oñ *inchoatione.*

īclⁱaᵒ *inclinatio.*

īclˢᵒ *incluso.*

īcꞁom *inclinationem.*

īcꞇ̄sᵒ *inclusio.*

 icl^t *includit.*

īcorp^{les} *incorporales.*

īcor^{t'} *incorporatum.*

īcor̃p^{les} *incorruptibiles.*

īcōpa^{or} *incomparabilior.*

īcōti^r *incontinenter.*

ic^riā *incuriam.*

ĩcat⁹ *incusatus.*

īc,d *incommodum.*

īc,ēs *inconveniens.*

īc,i^{ta} *incognita.*

īc,o^{tē} *incommoditatem.*

īc,tīa *incontinentia.*

īd *illud.*

īdē *ibidem.*

īdēp^{te} *indempnitate.*

īdi^a *individua.*

īdid^o *individuo.*

īdign^a *indigentia.*

īdig̃n *indigentia, indignus.*

īdig̃co *indignatio.*

īdig̃n^a *indigentia.*

īdi^{is} *individuis.*

īdi^{le} *indivisibile.*

īdi^{l'} *indivisibilis.*

īdi^o *individuo.*

īdiōm *in divisionem.*

īdīdua *individua.*

ī dō *in dominio.*

īdu^t *inducit, induit.*

īdu^{tū} *indumentum.*

īd *inde.*

īdren̂⁹ *indifferenter.*

īdrnti *indifferenti.*

īe *ire, jure.*

īebⁱāt *inebriant.*

īet *inæqualis.*

īc̃ *inest.*

īc̃e *inesse.*

īc̃lia *inæqualia.*

īf^a *infra.*

īf^acta *infracta.*

īfc^m *infectum.*

īfcōm *infectionem.*

īfctū *infectum.*

īfi^{l'} *infidelis.*

īfi^m *infinitum.*

īfit['] *infinitum.*

īflu^ā *influentiam.*

īfto *inflammatio.*

īf^odac^one *infeodatione.*

īf^omac̃o *informatio.*

īfor^{iū} *infortunium.*

īfoĩt^r *informatur.*

īfra^{to} *infrascripto.*

īf̃rare *infrigidare.*

īfu^{ōe} *infusione.*

īf *infra, infracta.*

īfcōm *infectionem.*

īfc̃ *infectum.*

īfite *infinite.*

īfmis *infirmis.*

īfos *inferos.*

īfs̃tm *infrascriptum.*

īftʳ *infertur.*

igᵃrdos *inguardos.*

īǵdʳ *ingreditur.*

īǵtus *incognitus.*

īhičo *inhibitio.*

īhiᵈᵒ *inhabitando, inhibendo.*

īhitāo *inhabitatio.*

īħe *inhærere.*

īħet *inhæret.*

īħiles *inhabiles.*

īħitañ *inhabitantes.*

īⁱ *inibi.*

īⁱcaˡᵉ *incommunicabile.*

īiᶜⁱ *inimici.*

īiᶜⁱᵉ *inimicitiæ.*

īicio *initio.*

īiciū *initium.*

īⁱēs *inconveniens.*

īⁱns *inconveniens.*

īint̃ *in integrum.*

īiqᵃ *iniqua.*

īiqⁱ *iniqui.*

īiʳia *injuria.*

īitū *initum.*

īito *initio.*

īiurã *injuriam.*

īiuř *injuriis, injuriatus.*

īiᶿⁱᵃ *injustitia.*

īiᶿte *injuste.*

īī *inibi.*

īmeᵗᵉ *immediate.*

īmeᵗū *immediatum.*

īmeᵗ' *immediatim.*

īmor̃i *immemoriali.*

īmul' *immutabilis.*

īmū° *immutatio.*

īm̄le *immateriale.*

īm̄ł *immaterialis.*

īm̃siᵗᵉ *immensitate.*

īm̃sū *immensum.*

īm̃ge *immerge.*

īm̃sū *immersum.*

īnocñᵃ *innocentia.*

īⁿˢ *inconveniens.*

īnum̃is *innumeris.*

īo *ideo.*

īoq̃ *ideoque.*

īpediᵐ *impedimentum.*

īpediᵗū *impedimentum.*

īped *impedientem.*

īpedčoe *impeditione.*

īpedr *impeditur.*

īpeʳȝ *impediret.*

īpeᵗᵒ *impedimento.*

īpeᵗᵒne *impetitione.*

īpeťns *impetrans.*

īpēdᵉ *impendere.*

īpⁱmę *imprimis.*

īpłitᵃi *implacitari.*

īpłit̃ *implicita.*

īpoᵃ *impotentia.*

īpoᵉ *impossibile, impotentiæ.*

īpol' *impossibilis.*

īporᵉᵗ *importaret.*

īporī *importat.*

īpo^{tas} *impossibilitas.*

īpō *impotentia.*

īpōa *impotentia, imposita.*

īpō^r *imponitur.*

īpu^a ri *imputari.*

īpu^d' *imputandum.*

īpug̃tōs *impugnatores.*

īpu^t *imputat.*

īpf^cc̃oe *imperfectione.*

īpfc̈us *imperfectus.*

īpsoĩr *impersonaliter.*

īpt *imperat.*

īpta^m *importatum.*

īptat *importat.*

īptiri *impertiri.*

īp̃^e *impossibile.*

īp̃^le *impossibile.*

īp̃l' *impossibilis.*

īp̃me *imprime.*

īp̃o *impositio.*

īp̃s *imprimis.*

īp̃^xi *inspexi, incomplexi.*

īp̃ssiōe *impressione.*

īp̃ssōm *impressionem.*

īpp^ie *improprie.*

īp̃pare *impropriare.*

īpss̃ *improbasset.*

īq^e *itaque.*

īq^m *iniquam, inquam.*

īq̃ *inquam, inquit, itaque.*

īq̃na^r *inquinatur.*

īseq^r *insequitur.*

īsp^cto *inspecto.*

īsp̃c̃o^m *inspectionem.*

īs^t *insit.*

īst^a *instituta.*

īstāci^9 *instantius.*

īsti^ne *institutione.*

īst^ito̷ *institutorum.*

īstr^a *instrumenta.*

īstr̄is *instrumentis.*

īstr̄o *instrumento.*

īst^uet^r *instrueretur.*

īst^um *instrumentum.*

īst^umētĩr *instrumentaliter.*

īst^um ta *instrumenta.*

īst^uoc *instructionem.*

īst^u'to̷ *instrumentorum.*

īsto *institutio.*

īst̄^ti *instrumenti.*

īs̃si^le *insensibile.*

īt^a *intra.*

īte^a *intelligentia.*

īte^do *intelligendo.*

īte^e *intelligentie.*

īteg^alī *integraliter.*

īte^g' *intelligitur.*

īte^it *intelligit.*

ītel^da *intelligenda.*

īte^r *intelligitur.*

īte^s *intellectus.*

īte^t *interest.*

īte^u *intellectu.*

ītē^{bat} *intendebat.*

ītēcŏ *intentio.*

ītē^o *intensio.*

ītfc̄s *interfectus.*

ītfīc̄ *interficit.*

ītf *interfuit.*

īt^{g'e} *intelligere.*

īt^{igi} *intelligi.*

ītⁱncus *intrinsecus.*

ītlĭr *intelligitur.*

īt^{nd'} *intelligendum.*

ī^{to} *inito.*

īt^od^ctū *introductum.*

īt^odux̄ *introduxit.*

īt^oitu *introitu.*

īt^oit⁹ *introitus.*

īt^om^tat *intromittat.*

īt^om^tt^e *intromittere.*

ītōt *intonat.*

ītr^{ac̄} *intrarem.*

īt^{re} *intelligere.*

īt^{r't} *intelligeret.*

ītr̄ *intrare, intraret.*

īt^s *istis.*

īt^{t9} *intellectus.*

īt^u *intellectu.*

īt^usit *intrusit.*

īt⁹ *intus.*

īt̄ *interest.*

īt̆gle *integrale.*

ītĭllc̆m *intellectum.*

ītĭlli^e *intelligere.*

ītĭlliğe *intelligere.*

ītĭllx̄ *intellexit.*

ītĭltia *intelligentia.*

ītnd^t *intendit.*

īt̃o *initio.*

īt̃^r *intelligitur.*

ītroğo *interrogatio.*

īt̃se *intrinsece.*

īt̃^{xit} *intellexit.*

ȋt̃ *inter.*

ȋt̃dc̆a *interdicta.*

ȋt̃dⁱ *interdici.*

ȋt̃dū *interdum.*

ȋt̃d *interdum.*

ȋt̃ddo *interdicendo.*

ȋt̃ee *interesse.*

ȋt̃essen^a *interessentia.*

ȋt̃ept⁹ *interemptus.*

ȋt̃fc̄s *interfectus.*

ȋt̃fīc̄ *interficit.*

ȋt̃f *interfuit.*

ȋt̃i⁹ *interius.*

ȋt̃płł^ae *interpellare.*

ȋt̃pol^a *interpolata.*

ȋt̃poło *interpolatio.*

ȋt̃põe *interponere.*

ȋt̃põitaʒ *interpositarum.*

ȋt̃po *interpositio.*

ȋt̃pr̄ *interpretatur.*

ȋt̃ptare *interpretare.*

ȋt̃ptac̄o *interpretatio.*

ȋt̃pti *interpreti.*

ı̃ȓūp^c *interrumpere.*
ı̃ʕuei̇ete *interveniente.*
ı̃ʕuētu *interventu.*
ı̄u^as^t *invasit.*
ı̄ueı̇es *inveniens.*
ı̄ueı̇es *invenies.*
ı̄ueı̇t^r *invenitur.*
ı̄uo^e *invocationem.*
ı̄ũnt^9 *inventus.*
ı̄^xa *incomplexa.*
ı̄^9 *minus.*
ı̄ *ibi, id est, igitur.*
ı̈aȝ *illarum.*

ı̆o *illic.*
ı̆d *illud.*
ı̆dē *ibidem.*
ı̆d̃ *interdum.*
ı̈ia *injuria.*
ı̆o *ideo.*
ı̆oq̃ *ideoque.*
ı̆re *jure.*
ı̆s *idibus.*
ı̄^9 *minus.*
ı̓ʲam̃t̃ *juramentum.*
ı̓ʲāt̃ *juramentum.*

K.

K. *caput, decem, kalendarum, kalendas, kalendis.*
kalñ *kalendas, kalendis.*
kar^e *carenæ.*
karı̃la *cartula.*
karı̃lariū *cartularium.*
karˉ *carena.*
karˉm^9 *carissimus.*
kařed *cathedra.*
kāissī^9 *carissimus.*
kāi^te *caritatem.*
kāi^tis *caritatis.*
kl. *kalendas, kalendis.*
klas *kalendas.*
klaȝ *kalendarum.*

kldaȝ *kalendarum.*
kl^n *Kyrie eleison.*
klñ *kalendas, kalendis.*
klrū *kalendarum.*
kls *kalendas, kalendis.*
K̄ *10000, karta (carta).*
k̃imus *carissimus.*
k̃i^mus *carissimus.*
k̃m *carissimum.*
k̃mus *carissimus.*
k̃rmus *carissimus.*
k̃rm̃s *carissimus.*
k̃rˉ *carissimi.*
k̃rimi *carissimi.*
k̃rˉm *carissimum.*

L.

L. *lectio, libro, libris, licet, quin-*
    quaginta, vel.

lᵃ *litera, quinquaginta, quinqua-*
    gesima.

lᵃ *literam, quinquagesimam.*

lac̃ *lacu.*

lac̈ti *lacerti.*

laᵈᵒ *latitudo.*

lag. *lagemannus.*

laïa *lanina.*

laᵐ *latum.*

lap̃is *lapidis.*

latⁱa *lateralia, latria, latrina.*

latib̃m *latibulum.*

latiñ *latinarius.*

latⁱt *latitat.*

latⁿᶜ *latitudinem.*

latᵒciᵘ *latrocinium.*

latᵒi *latori.*

latᵒñ *latronum.*

latᵒus *latomus.*

lat̃ *latet, latitudo.*

lãtt *latrat.*

laud̃ *laudes, laudibus.*

laũ *laudes.*

laũb̃lis *laudabilis.*

laũlis *laudabilis.*

layc̈ *laicus.*

lãdgab̈ *landgabulum.*

lãprid̃ *lamprida.*

lb. *libra, liber.*

lc. *lucrum.*

lc̈o *lecto.*

ld̃ *laudes.*

led̃ *levandum.*

leg. *legatus, legio.*

legatar̃ *legataria, legatarius.*

legᵉ *legitime.*

legit̃ *legitime.*

legïa *legitima.*

legᵐᵘˢ *legitimus.*

legʳ *legitur.*

legᵗtio *legitimo.*

leg̃ *legalis, legem.*

leg̃uuï *legrewita.*

leᵐᵉ *legitime.*

lep̃s *leprosus.*

leʳ *legitur.*

les̃ *lesta, lestagium.*

leuiᵐᵒ *lecissimo.*

leũ *leuca.*

lg̃ *longus, longitudo.*

lⁱᵃ *linea.*

lⁱᵃ *lineam.*

libᵃs *libras.*

liber̃ *liberate, liberationis.*

libñr *libenter.*

lib̈ *liber, liberata, libra.*

lib̈a *libera.*

lib̈aᵒ *liberatio.*

liɓatʳ *liberator, liberatur.*
liɓā *liberam.*
liɓe *liberæ, libere, libræ.*
liɓllus *libellus.*
liɓtr *liberaliter.*
liɓm *liberum, librum.*
liɓns *libens.*
liɓo *libero, libro.*
liɓoȝ *liberorum, librorum.*
libs *libras, libros.*
liɓtas *libertas.*
liɓᵗᵉ *libertate.*
liɓᵗⁱˢ *libertatis.*
liceñ *licentia, licentiatus.*
liciᵐ *licitum.*
lič *licet, licitum.*
ličia *licentia.*
ličñ *licentia.*
liᵉ *libere.*
liⁱ *liberi.*
liñ *licentia.*
liᵒ *quinquagesimo primo, libro.*
liquïtia *liquiritia.*
liq̇at *liqueat.*
liᵗᵃˢ *libertas.*
liᵗᵉ̃ *libertatem.*
litt̃as *litteras.*
liᵗᵘᵐ *licitum.*
liᵗ' *licitus, licitum.*
lit̃ *litera.*
liꝑa *litera.*
līgᵃ *lingua.*

lï *liber, libra, librata, libro.*
līmačo *legitimatio.*
līmus *legitimus.*
līo *libro.*
līta *legitima, limita.*
ll. *libentissimo, liberi, liberti, libertatibus.*
lñia *licentia.*
lo. *loca, locutio, loquitur.*
lᵒ *quinquagesimo.*
loᵃꝉ *localiter.*
locᵃi *locari.*
locaʳ *localiter.*
locuʳ *loquuntur.*
locutꝰ *locutus.*
ločo *locutio.*
loᵈᵉ *longitudo, loquendo.*
loᵉ *longæ, longe.*
logᶜᵃ *logica.*
lot *localis.*
lotr *localiter.*
loᵐ *locum.*
loⁿᵉ *longitudine.*
longᵐᵉ *longissime.*
long̃a *longæva.*
loⁿū *longitudinum.*
loᵒ *loco.*
loqᵃ *loquentia.*
loqᵃr *loquar.*
loqūr *loquitur.*
loq̇la *loquela.*
loq̄r *loquar, loquor.*

loq̃t^r *loquitur.*

lo^r *localiter, loquitur.*

lorim^ai⁹ *lorimarius.*

lo^ur *loquitur.*

lōgīq^a *longinqua.*

lōg⁹ *longus.*

lōnē *locutionem.*

lõt̃ *localiter.*

lr̃ *litera, literis.*

lr̃a *litera.*

lr̃m *literam.*

lr̃s *literas.*

l^ta *quinquaginta.*

l. t. s. *liberi tenementi sui.*

lt̃me *legitime.*

lt̃m⁹ *legitimus.*

lu. *lucrandum.*

lu^a *luna.*

luc^a *lucra, lucrandum.*

luc^and̃ *lucrandum.*

luc^m *lucrum.*

luc̃a *lucentia.*

luc̃br *lucrabitur.*

luc̃tīe *lucrative.*

lud^r *luditur.*

lud̃r *luditur.*

lum̃ *lumen, luminare.*

lu^n *lumen.*

lupū *luparum.*

lup̃n^aᶜ *lupanaris.*

lux^a *luxuria.*

lux̃ *luxuria.*

lūē *lumen.*

lūīe *lumine.*

lūīm *luminum.*

lūī^si *luminosi.*

lūi *lumini.*

lūie *lumine.*

lūimag̃r *ludimagister.*

lūis *luminis.*

lȝ *licet.*

L̄ *50000.*

t *lecto, libro, libris, licet, littere,*
     lucrandum, vel.

t̃c̃ *lectio.*

t̃c̃a *lecta.*

t̃c̃is *lectis.*

t̃c̃oȥ *lectorum.*

t̃c̃s *lectus.*

t̃c̃ulo *lectulo.*

t̃c̃ura *lectura.*

t̃e^r *ligetur.*

t̃gis *legis.*

t̃g̃time *legitime.*

t̃i. *libra, librata.*

t̃ie *legitime.*

t̃ime *legitime.*

t̃is *legitimis.*

t̃tras *literas.*

t̃m *litigationem.*

t̃mus *legitimus.*

t̃m̃ *lumen.*

t̃r *legitur.*

t̃ra *litera.*

ł̄ra^r *literaliter.*
ł̄re *licere, literæ.*
ł̄ribus *latoribus.*
ł̄ris *literis.*
ł̄rs *literas.*
ł̄r^ti *literati.*
ł̄r̄ *litera, literis.*

ł̄ł̄at^9 *literatus.*
ł̄t *libet, vult.*
ł̄timus *legitimus.*
ł̄tie *legitime.*
ł̄ïis *legitimis.*
ł̄x *lux.*

M.

M. *magister, magistratus, manerium, manibus, marcas, maritus, marmor, martyris, mater, materia, matrimonium, matutinum, maximus, mea, mei, memor, memoria, menses, mensis, meritus, mihi, milia, miliaria, mille, millesimo, minus, minuta, missus, mœrens, mœrenti, moneta, monumentum, mors, mortuus, mulier, municipium.*

ma. *manet, Maria, materiam.*

m^a *marca, Maria, materia, mea, milia, mina, minuta.*

ma^a *mara.*

mac̄la *macula.*

ma^e *materiæ, Mariæ.*

mag^do *magnitudo.*

mag^ie *magnificentiæ, magnitudine.*

mag^ies *magnitudines.*

mag^iē *magnitudinem.*

mag^ificñ *magnificentia.*

mag^ificn^a *magnificentia.*

mag^iis *magnitudinis.*

mag^ne *magnitudine.*

mag̃ *magis, magnus, and its cases.*

mag̃f^ia *magnificentia.*

mag̃r *magister.*

mag̃ro *magistro.*

mai^oe *majore.*

mai^9 *majus.*

ma^let'r *maculetur.*

m^ali *manuali, materiali.*

m^atr *materialiter.*

ma^m *manifestum.*

man. *mandamus.*

man^m9 *mandamus.*

manuc̃ *manucaptor.*

man^9 *manus.*

mañ *mandamus, manum.*

mañtɇ *mandatis.*

ma^r *materialiter.*

marcħ *marchio.*

marc̃ *marca, marcata.*

ma^{ret} *maneret.*

ma^{ri} *magistri, manifestari.*

ma^{ro}rū *magistrorum.*

mᵃroȝ *magistrorum.*

Marĩ *Martini, Martis, Martyris.*

marƚis *Martyris.*

marῖ *mara, mare, mariscus, maritus, martyr.*

mascƚs *masculus.*

ma^{te} *manente.*

mat^{io} *matrimonio.*

matⁱs *matris.*

ma^{tis} *mandatis.*

mᵃtis *martis.*

mat^m *matrem, matrimonium.*

ma^{tū} *mandatum.*

maῖ *mater, matris.*

matƭa *matertera.*

ma^u *manu.*

max^a *maxima.*

max^e *maxime.*

maxx. *maximi.*

max̃ *maximus, maxime.*

mᵃ *minam.*

mādañ *mandantes.*

mūd^cđ *manducandum.*

māi^{do} *manifestando.*

māi^m *manifestum.*

māip̃l *manipulus.*

māi^{re} *manifestare.*

M.

māi^{ta} *manifesta.*

māi^{ta'i} *manifestari.*

mū^{tum} *mandatum.*

māuc̃ *manucaptor.*

māum̃tēs *manumittens.*

māutc̃atis *manuteneatis.*

mā. *mandantes.*

māie *Mariæ.*

mā^{lā} *maculam.*

māli *materiali.*

mālę *materialis.*

mām *materiam.*

mās *materias.*

M. B. *memoriæ bonæ.*

Mcc. *mille ducenti, millesimo ducentesimo.*

M.D. *medicinæ doctor.*

m^e *Mariæ, materiæ, memoriæ, mille.*

me^a *medicina, memoria.*

me^{um} *memoriam.*

me^bȝ *mediantibus.*

me^{da} *memoranda.*

medie^s *medietas.*

med^{na} *medicina.*

med^{re} *mediatore.*

med^{te} *mediante.*

medῖ *medicamentum.*

me^e *mere.*

me^{is} *mereberis.*

melā^{ci} *melancholici.*

melācoƚ *melancholia.*

G

melt *mellis.*

me^m *medium.*

memoȝ *memorandum.*

mem^r *memor, meremur.*

mem̃ *memoriam.*

me^{na} *medicina.*

menbȝ *membris, membrum.*

me^{ne} *medicinæ.*

mens̃ *mensem, mensuram.*

me^{nte} *mediante.*

me^o *medio.*

me^oria *memoria.*

meoȝ *meorum.*

me^oȝ *meliorem, meliorum.*

me^r *meretur.*

meridioñ *meridionali.*

mes. *mensibus.*

me^{te} *mediate, mediante, medietate.*

met^opoⁿ *metropolitanum.*

me^tꝑ *medietatis.*

mēc̃õ *mencio.*

mēo^a *memoria.*

mēo^{dum} *memorandum.*

mēora^a *memoranda, memorata.*

mēor^{le} *memoriale.*

mēor̃a *memorata.*

mēs̃ *mensis.*

mẽa^r *mereatur.*

mẽis *melius.*

mẽi⁹ *melius.*

mētⁱx *meretrix.*

mēt^r *meretur.*

mēt̃ci *meretrici.*

mg̃ *magis.*

mg̃ro *magistro.*

mⁱ *mei, mihi.*

mi^a *minima.*

miã^{lo} *miraculo.*

miãl' *mirabilis.*

mião *miraculo.*

Micħem *Michaelem.*

Micħis *Michaelis.*

mi^{di} *minuendi.*

mi^{le} *meridionale.*

millēio *millesimo.*

millⁱ *millesimi.*

mill^o *millesimo.*

miltimo *millesimo.*

milto *millesimo.*

mil^o *millesimo.*

milt *miles, miliario.*

mi^m *minimum.*

min⁹ *minus.*

mⁱꝗ *mihique.*

mir̃ *mirabiliter, mirifice, mirum, misericorditer.*

m^{is} *magis, marcis, meis, modis.*

mis̃dia *misericordia.*

mis^{dn} *ministrandum.*

mise^r *miseretur.*

mis^{iã} *misericordiam.*

mis̃s *missa, missis, missum.*

mⁱst^ant *ministrant.*

mⁱstio *ministerio.*

mĩš *misit.*

mĩšā *miseram, miseriam.*

mĩšcđa *misericordia.*

mĩšc°s *misericors.*

mĩšc̃di *misericordi.*

mĩš h. ex. f. *misit hæc extra fir-mam.*

mĩšⁱᵃ *miseria.*

mĩš ī m. *misit in manerium.*

mⁱus *minus.*

mⁱuĩ *minuta.*

mīoӡ *minorum.*

mĩut⁹ *minutus.*

mĩ⁹ *minus.*

mĩ *minimus, minus, minuta, miseri.*

mĩa *misericordia.*

mĩabiliĩ *miserabiliter.*

mĩam *misericordiam.*

mĩas *misericordias.*

mĩdi *misericordi.*

mĩdiᵽ *misericorditer.*

mĩe *minimæ, misericordiæ.*

mĩenta *munimenta.*

mĩm⁹ *minimus.*

mĩors *misericors.*

mĩstᵃndo *ministrando.*

mĩstᵃnt *ministrant.*

mĩstⁱ *ministri.*

mĩstrare *ministrare.*

mĩstr̃ *ministris.*

mĩstt̃o *ministratio.*

mĩsᵽ *minister.*

mĩsᵽio *ministerio.*

ML. *malum.*

mˡᵉ *materialem.*

M.M. *martyres, memento mori, memoria, meritissimus, mœst-issimus, monumentum.*

mᵐ *manifestum, materiam, meum.*

mᵐᵒ *millesimo.*

mñsʳa *mensura.*

mo. *modus, mota, motus, movet, movetur.*

m° *meo, modo, millesimo, matri-monio.*

moᵃ *monasteria.*

moᵃc⁹ *monachus.*

moᵇӡ *moralibus, morbus, motibus.*

mođ *modis.*

m° e. *modo episcopi.*

m°i *modi.*

moic̃oe *monitione.*

moĩalis *monialis.*

moĩtoñ *monitione.*

molđ *moldra, moldera.*

molᵛ *mobilis.*

moł *molestia.*

mołioӡ *molendinorum.*

moᵐ *modum, morem, moverem, monitum.*

moneĩ *monetarius.*

monⁱⁱˢ *monasteriis.*

monuᵗᵘ *monumentum.*

moñ *monasterium, moneta, monachi, moniales.*

moñdi *monendi.*

moñsȼ *monasteriis.*

mor. *mortis.*

mor* *morina.*

mora^{te} *moralitate.*

mora^{ter} *moraliter.*

mo^{re} *monstrare.*

mo^{rii} *monasterii.*

mo^{rio} *monasterio.*

mor^{l'r} *mortaliter.*

mor^{os} *mortuos.*

mor̃ *mora, more, morina, mortem, mortis.*

mor̃lis *mortalis.*

mor̃līs *mortalitas.*

mo^s *modius.*

m^{os} *modos.*

m^{o}taɫ *mortalis.*

mou^r *moventur.*

mo^{u} *motum.*

mōialis *monialis.*

mōitōio *monitorio.*

mōsȼ *monstra.*

mōdū *movendum.*

mōe *more.*

mōi *modi.*

mōia *monasteria.*

mōio *monasterio.*

mōis *modis.*

mōm *monasterium.*

mōrii *monasterii.*

mōrio *monasterio.*

mōrū *modorum.*

mōsȶiū *monasterium.*

mōsȶm *monasterium.*

mōȥ *modorum, majorum.*

m^r *magister, mater, materialiter, multipliciter.*

m^ra *mara.*

m^{re} *matre.*

m^{ris} *matris, majoris, martyris.*

mr̃ *martii, martyr.*

m^s *marcas.*

MT. *mater.*

m^{ta} *multa.*

m^tti *mitti.*

m^tȶe *mittere.*

muïe *munimine.*

multipɫr *multipliciter.*

multi^{ri} *multiplicari.*

multi^{t'} *multipliciter.*

mu^{l'} *mutabilis.*

muñe *munere.*

mu^o *mutatio.*

mu^{oe} *mutatione.*

mur̃ *mutaret.*

mu^{t'} *mutatus.*

mut̃ *mutatus.*

mūicipɫi *municipali.*

mūicōm *munitionem.*

mū^r *mutatur.*

mūri *mutari.*

m˟ *multiplex.*

m⁹ *mandamus, manus, mos.*

M̄ *manerium, mille, milia.*

m̄dax *mendax.*

m̄dic⁹ *medicus.*

m̄diū *medium.*

m̄. f. *manerium francum.*

m̄. h. *manerium hoc.*

m̄. ꝉ b. *manerium et berewica.*

m̃ *malo, manerium, manus, misericordia, morte, multones.*

m̃ᵃˡⁱ *manuali.*

m̃bᵃ *membra.*

m̃bⁱˢ *membris.*

m̃bᵒ *membro.*

m̃bra *membra.*

m̃bro *membro.*

m̃br̃ *membro.*

m̃bʒ *membrum.*

m̃ces *merces.*

m̃cii *Marcii.*

m̃cis *marcis.*

m̃curii *Mercurii.*

m̃dax *mendax.*

m̃di *mundi.*

m̃dⁿᵒ *mundano.*

m̃do *mundo.*

m̃đ *mundum.*

m̃e *medietate, mille.*

m̃gāitis *margaritis.*

m̃gⁱˢ *magnitudinis.*

m̃gⁱtuᵉ *magnitudine.*

m̃gnis *magnis.*

m̃ğ *magister.*

m̃ğʳ *magister.*

m̃ğraᵗ *magistratum.*

m̃ğt *magnificat.*

m̃iali *matrimoniali.*

m̃iis *matrimoniis.*

m̃io *matrimonio.*

m̃is *meis, muris.*

m̃ïa *misericordia.*

m̃lc̆ *mulcet.*

m̃le *male.*

m̃lē *materialem.*

m̃leʒ *mulierum.*

m̃li *materiali.*

m̃libʒ *materialibus.*

m̃lier *mulier.*

m̃lis *materialis.*

m̃liʒ *militem.*

m̃liʒ *mulierum.*

m̃lïes *mulieres.*

m̃lⁿˢ *multotiens.*

m̃lta *multa.*

m̃lticᵃ *multiplica.*

m̃lticᵃ’ʳ *multiplicantur.*

m̃lticᵉ’ⁱ *multiplicemini.*

m̃ltiē *multitudinem.*

m̃ltiloᵒ *multiloquio.*

m̃ltiᵒ *multitudo.*

m̃ltiᵒᵉ *multimode, multiplicatione.*

m̃ltiᵒm *multiplicationem.*

m̃ltip^do *multiplicando.*
m̃ltip̃tr *multipliciter.*
m̃lti^r *multipliciter.*
m̃ltis *multis.*
m̃lti^ti *multiplicati.*
m̃ltĩd^m *multitudinem.*
m̃lti^x *multiplex.*
m̃ltoc̃ *multoties.*
m̃ltoñ *multones.*
m̃ltope *multopere.*
m̃ltũ *multum.*
m̃lĩ *multum, multis.*
m̃^l' *materialis, mentalis.*
m̃l *milliaria.*
m̃la *multa.*
m̃leȝ *mulierum.*
m̃lm *multum.*
m̃lo *multo.*
m̃lr *materialiter, mulier.*
m̃lri *mulieri.*
m̃m *matrimonium.*
m̃^mo *millesimo.*
m̃m̃a *murmura.*
m̃m̃ialr *matrimonialiter.*
m̃m̃u^er *murmuretur.*
m̃ndi *mundi.*
m̃nr̃ *manerium.*
m̃ns^ra *mensura.*
m̃o *meo, monasterio.*
m̃os *meos, modos.*
m̃r *magister, mater.*
m̃ra *monstra.*

m̃rare *monstrare.*
m̃rari *monstrari.*
m̃raũ *monstravit.*
m̃rcet *marcet.*
m̃rch *marchio.*
m̃rc̃ *marca.*
m̃rc̃it *marcescit.*
m̃re *matre.*
m̃rē *matrem.*
m̃res *martyres, matres.*
m̃ri *magistri, martyri, matri,*
        monstrari.
m̃ri^bȝ *matrimonialibus.*
m̃rices *matrices.*
m̃ricē *matricem.*
m̃rii *martyrii.*
m̃ri^le *matrimoniale.*
m̃ri^o *matrimonio.*
m̃ris *magistris, martyris, matris.*
m̃^ris *majoris.*
m̃riũ *martyrium.*
m̃rīo^m *matrimonium.*
m̃rīo^o *matrimonio.*
m̃rīo^t' *matrimonialiter.*
m̃rīoi^li *matrimoniali.*
m̃rīoio *matrimonio.*
m̃rm *martyrium, martyrum,*
        matrem, matrimonium.
m̃rna *materna.*
m̃ro *magistro.*
m̃rona *matrona.*
m̃rt̃ *martyris.*

m̃rū *martyrum.*

m̃rȝ *marcarum.*

m̃r̃ *martyr.*

m̃r̃s *marcas, martyris, mors.*

m̃s *majestas, materias, mens, mensis, meus.*

m̃strat *monstrat.*

m̃str̃a *menstrua.*

m̃sur̃ *mensura.*

m̃s̃a *mensura.*

m̃s̃ā *mensuram.*

m̃tacõ *mutatio.*

m̃tat^r *mutatur.*

m̃ta^t' *mentaliter.*

m̃tē *mentem.*

m̃tēđ *mittendus.*

m̃tiri *mentiri.*

m̃tit⁹ *mentitus.*

m̃tit̃ *mentitum.*

m̃tõm *mentionem.*

m̃t^t *mittit.*

m̃t̃o *mentio.*

m̃x^a *mixta, maxima.*

m̃x^e *maxime.*

m̃xi^s *maximis.*

m̃chetę *merchetis.*

m̃cu^ii *Mercurii.*

m̃c̃ *marca, marcata.*

m̃c̃ii *Mercurii.*

m̃idioñ *meridionalis.*

m̃ito *merito.*

m̃ito^a *meritoriam.*

m̃ito^e *meritoriœ, meritorie.*

m̃itor^a *meritoria.*

m̃ir̃ *meritis.*

m̃lēḡ *merlengis.*

m̃u^t *meruit.*

N.

N. *enim, natus, nec, nepos, neptis, nimis, nisi, nobilis, nobis, nomen, nomine, non, nonaginta, nonas, noster, nota, notum, Novembris, nullus, numini.*

n^a *natura, nostra, nota, nulla.*

n^aalis *naturalis.*

n^am *naturam.*

nar̃ *narratur.*

narr̃o *narratio.*

nasĉet^r *nasceretur.*

na^{te} *nativitate.*

n^atē⁹ *nullatenus.*

na^{tis} *nativitatis.*

natiu^{t's} *nativitatis.*

natĭat^s *nativitatis.*

natĭo *nativo.*

nat^rā *naturam.*

naĩ *natalis, nativitas.*

naĩe *naturæ.*

naĩs *nativus.*

naĩt^{te} *nativitate.*

nauib₃ *navibus.*

nau^{ile} *navigabile.*

nauiū *navium.*

naũ *navis.*

nāura *natura.*

nãa *nata.*

nãt *naturalis.*

nãm *naturam.*

nb̃ *nobis.*

n^c *nec, nunc.*

n^cne *necne.*

n^cnō *necnon.*

nc̃ca *necessaria.*

n. e. *non est.*

n^e *naturæ, necesse, neque.*

nec^{ate} *necessitate.*

necc^a *necessaria.*

nec^{ib}₃ *necessitatibus.*

nec^{ie} *necessariæ, necessarie.*

nec^{ite} *necessitate.*

nec^m *necessarium.*

necñ *necnon.*

nec̃as *necessitas.*

nec̃e *necesse.*

necc̃e *necesse.*

nec̃ie *necessariæ, necessarie.*

nec̃iis *necessariis.*

nec̃^{ite} *necessitate.*

nec̃^{it'} *necessitatis.*

nec̃^m *necessarium.*

nec̃o *necessario.*

nec̃s *necessarius, necessitas.*

nec̃t^ę *necessitatis.*

ne^{d'} *negandum.*

neđ *nedum.*

negłia *negligentia.*

negłnt *negligunt.*

neḡ *negotiis, negotium.*

neḡa *negotia.*

neḡat *negotiat.*

neḡ^{do} *negando, negotiando.*

neḡm *negotium.*

neḡo *negotio.*

neⁱⁿⁱ *nemini.*

nem̃ *nemus.*

ne^o *negatio, negotio.*

ne^{oib}₃ *negationibus, nemoribus.*

neq^aq^ā *nequaquam.*

neq̃ *neque.*

neq̃o *nequeo.*

neq_b *neque.*

ne^r *negatur.*

nesci^a *nescientia.*

nesc̃ *nesciunt.*

ne^te *necessitate.*

ne^ua *negativa.*

ne^ue *negative.*

ne^u' *negativum.*

neũ *neuter.*

nẽinꝑ *neminis.*

nẽīē *neminem.*

nẽo *nemo.*

nc̃ *neque.*

nẽandū *negandum.*

nẽi *nemini.*

nẽnt *negant.*

nẽri *negari.*

nẽti^m *negativum.*

nẽti^u *negativum.*

nẽt^r *negatur.*

n^i *nihil, nisi.*

nichilo⁹ *nichilominus.*

nichilōi⁹ *nichilominus.*

nich^oi⁹ *nichilominus.*

nicħ *nichil.*

nicħlō⁹ *nichilominus.*

nicħōi⁹ *nichilominus.*

nig^edo *nigredo.*

nig^eđis *nigredinis.*

nig^enē *nigredinem.*

nig^esc̃ *nigrescit.*

nig^ido *nigritudo.*

nig^iđis *nigritudinis.*

nig̃đ *nigredinem.*

niħ *nihil.*

n^io⁹ *nihilominus.*

n^l *nihil.*

n^lo *nihilo.*

n^lomī⁹ *nihilominus.*

n^lo⁹ *nihilominus.*

n^lōi⁹ *nihilominus.*

nłłs *nullus.*

n^m *nullum.*

nn. *nostri, nostrorum, numeri.*

n^n *nomen.*

no. *nobis, nomen, nostro, novæ.*

n^o *nocturno, nullo, numero.*

no^a *nomina.*

no^andū *notandum.*

nobił *nobilis.*

nobī^m *nobilissimum.*

nob *nobis.*

nobc̃ *nobiscum.*

nob^ra *nobiliora.*

noc̃ *nocumentum.*

noc̃o^le *notionale.*

no^do *nolendo.*

no^d' *notandum.*

no^e *nomine.*

no^is *nominis.*

noïa *nomina.*

noïa^o *nominatio.*

noïat^r *nominatur.*

noïe *nomine.*

no^le *nobile.*

nole^m *nolentem, nolentium.*

no^lis *nobilis, notabilis.*

no$^{l'}$ *nobilis.*

no$^{l'r}$ *notabiliter.*

nolt *nolunt.*

nomīe *nomine.*

no^{mus} *nobilissimus.*

nom̃ *nomen.*

nom̃ibȝ *nominibus.*

non. *nonas, nonis.*

no^{n} *nomen.*

nonag^{o} *nonagesimo.*

n^{oo} *nullo modo.*

n^{o}o *nullo modo.*

no^{or} *nobilior.*

no^{r} *notatur.*

no^{ra} *nobiliora.*

Norhī̃ *Norhampton.*

no^{rius} *notarius.*

noī̃ *notarius.*

nos̃ *noster.*

not^{a}i^{9} *notarius.*

notat^{r} *notatur.*

notãa *notata.*

noth^{9} *nothus.*

noti^{a} *notitia.*

notic^{s} *notities.*

notĩ *notat, notatis.*

notõ^{le} *notionale.*

noũ *Novembris.*

noủitę *noveritis.*

noủiĩ *noveritis.*

nō *non.*

nõale *novale.*

nõalia *novalia.*

nōdū *nondum.*

nōïti *nominati.*

nōïti^{m} *nominativum.*

nõa *nomina.*

nõale *nominale, novale.*

nõbil *notabilis.*

nõbi^{r} *notabiliter.*

nõbr̃ *Novembris.*

nõbĩr *notabiliter.*

nõi *nomini.*

nõibȝ *nominibus.*

nõie *nomine.*

nõis *nominis.*

nõïo *nominatio, nominativo.*

nõn^{m} *notandum.*

nõnt *notant.*

nõnℓ *noctanter.*

nõri *nostri.*

nõrie *notorie.*

nõroȝ *nostrorum.*

nõr̃ *notariis, notario.*

nõs *nonas.*

nõtr̃ *nostris.*

nõℓ *noviter.*

nõȝ *nonarum.*

nq. *namque, nunquam, nusquam.*

nr. *noster.*

n^{r} *naturaliter, noscitur, noster.*

n^{r}a *natura.*

nr̃a *nostra.*

nr̃ā *nostram.*

nr̃e *nostræ.*

nr̃i *nostri.*

nr̃m *nostrum.*

nr̃o *nostro.*

nr̃oᵐ *nostrorum.*

nr̃oꝛ *nostrorum.*

nr̃oȝ *nostrorum.*

nr̃s *nostris.*

nˢ *nullus.*

nᵗ’ *naturaliter.*

nullaĩs *nullatenus.*

nullⁱ *nullibi.*

nulťr *nulliter.*

numᵐ *numerum, nummum.*

numᵒ *numero.*

numꝰus *numerus.*

nunc̃ *nunciante, nuncius.*

nuᵒ *numero.*

nup̃s *nuptias.*

nup̃ȝ *nuptiarum.*

nusq́ *nusquam.*

nutⁱm̃tū *nutrimentum.*

nutⁱt *nutrit.*

nutⁱᵗe *nutritive.*

nutⁱtʳa *nutritura.*

nutⁱꝛ *nutrimentum.*

nutⁿᵗᵒ *nutrimento.*

nutĩia *nutritiva.*

nutᵘʳ *nutriuntur.*

nuᵗę *nuncietis.*

nuꝰ *numerus.*

nūa *numina, nuncia.*

nūciꝰ *nuncius.*

nūcq́ *nunquam.*

nūctiꝰ *nuncius.*

nūẽñ *numerentur.*

nūmū *nummum.*

nūmoȝ *nummorum.*

nūq́ *numquid, nunquam.*

nūaᵇȝ *numerabilibus.*

nūaᵒ *numeratio.*

nūaʳ *numeraliter, numeratur.*

nūat *numerat.*

nūatʳ *numeratur.*

nūã *numerare.*

nūi *numeri, nummi.*

nūm *numerum.*

nūo *numero.*

nūs *numerus.*

nꝰuator *numerator.*

nūo *numero.*

nȝ *neget, neque.*

nꝰ *nullus.*

nꝰqᵃ *nusquam.*

nꝰq́ *nusquam.*

N̄. *nonaginta milia, 90000.*

n̄ *non.*

ñe *naturæ.*

n̄m. *numerum.*

n̄n *nomen.*

n̄n̄ *necnon.*

ñ *enim, natus, nec, nepos, neptis,
nisi, nobilis, nobis, nomen,
non, nonas, noster, nota,
notum, Novembris, nuper.*

ña *natura.*

ñalē *naturalem.*

ñaĩr *naturaliter.*

ña° *narratio.*

ña^oem *narrationem.*

ña^r *naturaliter.*

ñaᵗ' *naturaliter.*

ñ̄ᵃ *naturam.*

ñā *naturam.*

ñbĩ *nobilis.*

ñᵇȝ *naturalibus.*

ñb̃ *nobis.*

ñc *nunc.*

ñc^a *necessaria.*

ñcc̃ai⁹ *necessarius.*

ñceē *necessitatem.*

ñcēe *necesse, necessitate.*

ñcēia *necessaria.*

ñciās *nuncians.*

ñc^s *necessariis.*

ñdū *nedum, nondum.*

ñd⁹ *nodus.*

ñđ *nedum, nondum.*

ñe *naturæ.*

ñi *nemini, nostri.*

ñis *nimis, notionis.*

ñiū *nimium.*

ñli *naturali.*

ñlla *nulla.*

ñllate⁹ *nullatenus.*

ñlli *nulli.*

ñlli⁹ *nullius.*

ñllo° *nullo modo.*

ñll⁹ *nullus.*

ñlĩm *nullum.*

ñlĩs *nullus.*

ñ¹ū *nihilum.*

ñĩ *naturalis.*

ũĩr *naturaliter.*

ñm *naturam, nostrum.*

ñm̃ne *nomine.*

ñnas *nonas, nonnas.*

ñnaȝ *nonarum, nonnarum.*

ñne *nonæ, nonnæ.*

ño *nihilo.*

ñ° *notio.*

ñquā *nunquam.*

ñq̃ *numquid, nunquam, nusquam.*

ñr *noscitur, noster.*

ñra *natura, nostra.*

ñs *naturas, nos, numerus.*

ñsra *nostra.*

ñstrū *nostrum.*

ñst̃s *nostris.*

ñtia *nuncia.*

ñtiᵗ' *nititur.*

ñtĭtas *nativitas.*

ñtm *nominativum.*

ñtra *nostra.*

ñtr̃s *nostris.*

ñui *nervi.*

ñus *numerus.*

ñū *numerum.*

ñ⁹ *numerus.*

ñȝ *naturarum, nostrum, nostro-*
      rum.

n̂u⁹ *nervus.*

O.

O. *obiit, obitus, obolus, officium,*
    olla, omega, omnibus, omnis,
    oportet, optimo, oratio, ordi-
    nis, oriens, ossa, ossuarium,
    ostenditur, otio, undecim.

oᵃ *omnia.*

obᶜo *objecto.*

obᶜoȝ *objectorum.*

obeđ *obedientia.*

obeđie *obedientiæ.*

obeⁿˢ *obediens.*

obẽ *obest.*

obẽe *obesse.*

obẽie *obedientiæ.*

obiᶜ' *objectum.*

obiĉ *objicit.*

obiẽs *obientis.*

obⁱg̃o *obligatio.*

obisŝt *obisset.*

oblc̃am̃t̃ *oblectamentum.*

obliḡᶜo *obligatio.*

obliḡe *obligatione.*

obłm *oblatum, obolum.*

obło *oblatio, obolo.*

obłoe *oblatione.*

obłoᵐ *oblationem.*

obłone *oblatione.*

obłonibȝ *oblationibus.*

obstñ *obstantibus.*

obs̃ *obstat.*

obᵗ *obiit.*

obᵗ⁹ *obligatus.*

oƀ *objicitur, obitus, oblatio, obo-*
    lus.

oƀa *objecta.*

oƀas *obliquas.*

oƀene *obedientiæ.*

oƀi *objecti.*

oƀia *obedientia.*

oƀiarius *obedientiarius.*

oƀie *obedientiæ.*

oƀm *objectum.*

oƀo *objecto, objicio.*

oƀr *objicitur.*

oƀt *objicit, obtinuit.*

oƀm̃ *objectum.*

occãñ *occasione.*

occili *occidentali.*

occoñ *occasione.*

occoȝ *occasionem.*

occĭo *occasio.*

occĕltū *occultum.*

occĕnli *occidentali.*

occĕns *occidens.*

occññlis *occidentalis.*

occ̆o *occasio.*

occ̆oatr *occasionaliter.*

occ̆oe *occasione.*

occ̆one *occasione.*

occ̄paut *occupavit.*

oct̄ *octabas, octabis, Octobris.*

octĭa *octava.*

octĭas *octavas.*

oc̄lo *oculo.*

oc̄tm *oculum.*

odil' *odibilis.*

odõ *odorem.*

ođ *odium, odoris.*

ođo *odio.*

oe *omne.*

offet *offert.*

offlis *officialis.*

offa *officia, officina.*

offim *officium.*

offm *officium.*

offo *officio.*

oi *olei, omni.*

oiƀ *omnibus.*

oim *omnium.*

oipoa *omnipotentia.*

oipons *omnipotens.*

oiū *omnium.*

oïa *omnia.*

oïbȝ *omnibus.*

oïm *omnium.*

oïo *omnino.*

oïoda *omnimoda.*

oïode *omnimode.*

olī *olim.*

oł *oleum, olim.*

om *objectum, oleum, omnium, oppositum.*

om. *omnem.*

oma *omnia.*

omisnis *omissionis.*

omna *omnia.*

om̃ *omelia (homilia), omnis.*

om̃a *omnia.*

om̃aꝗ *omniaque.*

om̃bȝ *omnibus.*

om̃i *omni.*

om̃ip̃i *omnipotenti.*

om̃ip̃s *omnipotens.*

om̃is *hominis, omnis.*

om̃p̃ *omnipotens.*

om̃p̃is *omnipotentis.*

om̃p̃s *omnipotens.*

om̃s *omnes, omnis.*

on⁹ *onus.*

oñs *omnes, onus.*

oñ︢a *onera.*

oñ︢ibȝ *oneribus.*

oñ︢ū *onerum.*

o⁰ *omnino, opinio, oppositio, ora-*
   tio.

o⁰nē *orationem.*

o⁰nis *orationis.*

op. *opinio, oportet, oppositio,*
   opus.

opc̃o *optio.*

opᵉ *optime.*

opi. *opiniones.*

opiᵈ' *opinandum.*

opilac̃o *oppilatio.*

opit̃o *oppilatio.*

opĭo *opinio.*

opᵐ *oppositum.*

opᵒ *opinio, oppositio.*

opᵒ͒ⁱˢ *opinionis, oppositionis.*

oppⁱm̃ti *opprimenti.*

oppᵐ *oppositum.*

oppᵒ *oppositio, opposito.*

oppoᵃ *opposita.*

oppoⁿⁱˢ *oppositionis.*

oppoʳ *opponitur.*

oppoȝ *oppositorum.*

oppŏito *opposito.*

oppõs *oppositos.*

opptᵘ *oppositum.*

opptᵗ' *oppositum.*

opp̃o *oppositio.*

oppⁱo *opprobrio.*

opᵗ *oportet.*

optimᵉˢ *optimates.*

optᵒᵒ *opposito modo.*

opt̃ *optio, optulit (obtulit).*

opt̃ⁿᵉ *optione.*

op⁹ *opus.*

opa *opera.*

opaᵇȝ *operationibus.*

opac̃o *operatio.*

opaᵒ *operatio.*

opaᵒᵉ *operatione.*

opatʳ *operatur.*

opᵈ' *operandum.*

opibȝ *operibus.*

opm *operum.*

opⁿᵗ *operant.*

opo *operatio.*

opoᵐ *operationem.*

opões *operationes.*

opŏm *operationem.*

opr̃i *operari.*

opt *oportet.*

opte *operte.*

optet *oportet.*

optun⁹ *opportunus.*

optuᵗ *oportuit.*

optūa *opportuna.*

optũe *opportune.*

optūitas *opportunitas.*

opõo *opinio.*

opõm *opinionem.*

opˉs *omnipotens.*

opˉt *obtinet.*

opˉta *opposita.*

opˉto *opposito.*

opˉt *omnipotens, oportet.*

opˆtͻe *oportere.*

oʳ *oneratur.*

ordic̆o *ordinatio.*

ordiᵒ *ordinatio.*

ordiᵗ' *ordinatum.*

ordᵒ *ordinatio.*

ordʳ *ordinatur.*

ordđ *ordinis.*

orđi *hordei.*

orđo *ordinatio.*

origᵗ' *originaliter.*

origͤ *originis.*

oriˡ' *originalis.*

oritʳ *oritur.*

orˡe *originale.*

orⁿᵉ *ordinem.*

orões *orationes.*

orõm *orationem.*

orʳe *ordinare.*

orˉatᵉ⁹ *ornatus.*

oͬ *oras, oratio, orator.*

oͬes *oratores.*

oͬibȝ *oratoribus.*

oͬno *organo.*

oͬo *oratio.*

oͬoᵐ *orationem.*

oͬri *oriri, ornari.*

oͬt *ornat.*

oͬtᵃ *ordinata.*

oͬt⁹ *ornatus.*

oͬum *oratorum.*

oˢ *omnes.*

osc̃la *oscula.*

osĩndᵗ *ostendit.*

osĩnđ *ostendit.*

osĩnˢ *ostensum.*

osĩnᵗ *ostendit.*

oᵗ *occurrit, oportet, ostendit.*

oᵗᵃˢ *oppositas.*

oᵗū *objectum, oppositum.*

oᵗͻ *oppositis.*

oȝ *oportet.*

ōiʳ *oritur.*

ōnis *omnis.*

ōnĩo *omnino.*

õ *obolus.*

õa *omnia, ora.*

õbȝ *omnibus.*

õe *omne, ore.*

õem *omnem.*

ões *omnes.*

õē *omnem.*

õi *omni.*
õia *omnia.*
õibȝ *omnibus.*
õida *omnimoda.*
õie^li *orientali.*
õig̃ *origo.*
õi^li *originali.*
õi^m *omnium.*
õim° *omnimodo.*
õines *origines.*
õino *omnino.*
õipo^a *omnipotentia.*
õip^s *omnipotens.*
õip̃ *omnipotens.*
õip̃ti *omnipotenti.*
õi^r *oritur.*
õis *omnis.*
õi^s *omnibus.*
õium *omnium.*
õiu^r *oriuntur.*
õiū *omnium.*
õiũt^r *oriuntur.*
õĩo *omnino.*
õndāt *ostendant.*
õnde^9 *ostendemus.*
õndit *ostendit.*
õndo *ostendo.*
õnd^t *ostendit.*
õn^d' *ostendendum.*
õnđ *ostendere, ostendit.*

õndđd^m *ostendendum.*
õnđe *ostendere.*
õnđet *ostenderet.*
õnđ^r *ostenditur.*
õn^r *ostenditur.*
õns *ostendens.*
õnsi^m *ostensivum.*
õnsū *ostensum.*
õnš *ostensus.*
õn^t *ostendit.*
õntat *ostentat.*
õntℓ *ostendentis.*
õñs *ostendens.*
õñt^r *ostenditur.*
õo *omnino.*
õpo^tℯ *omnipotentem.*
õpotētis *omnipotentis.*
õp̃ *omnipotens.*
õp̃s *omnipotens.*
õp̃ns *omnipotens.*
õs *omnes, omnis.*
õt *occurrit, oportet, ostendit.*
õtas *oppositas.*
õti *oppositi.*
õto *horto, opposito.*
õto° *opposito modo.*
õtoȝ *oppositorum.*
õtuit *oportuit.*
õtū *oppositum.*
õtℓ *oppositis.*

M.

H

P.

P. *pateat, patent, pater, pater-*
nitas, patet, per, pius, post-
modum, postquam, præmissa,
præpositus, præsens, prin-
ceps, publicus, quadringenti.

pa. *passio, pater.*

p^a *parochia, persona, prima.*

pacē *pacem.*

paci^{te} *patiente.*

paci^{tia} *patientia.*

pac^{te} *patiente.*

pac^{tia} *patientia.*

p^actica *practica.*

pac̃ia *patientia.*

pac̄orē *patientiorem.*

palfr̃ *palfridus.*

pa^{l'} *passibilis.*

pałium *palatium.*

p^am *primam.*

pa^{nes} *passiones.*

pa^{ns} *patiens.*

pa^o *passio.*

pa^{õe} *passione.*

pa^{õis} *passionis.*

papaũe *papavere.*

pap^m *papam.*

pap̃ *papa.*

par^a *parochia.*

parch⁹ *parcus.*

parc̃ *parcus.*

par^c *parochiæ.*

parlam̃tũ *parlamentum.*

paro^{lis} *parochialis.*

parõ *parochia.*

partibȝ *partibus.*

par̃ *parochia.*

par̃a *parochia.*

par̃e *parochiæ.*

pas^l *passim.*

pas^{l'} *passibilis.*

pas^o *passio.*

pas^s *passus.*

pass^bȝ *passibus.*

passī *passim.*

past^bȝ *pastoralibus.*

past^ra *pastura.*

past^ragiũ *pasturagium.*

pas̃ *passus.*

p^ata *prata.*

patⁱa *patria.*

pati^{d'} *patiendum.*

patⁱe *patriæ.*

patⁱs *patris.*

p^atis *pratis.*

patiũt^r *patiuntur.*

patñ *patentes.*

pat°niū *patrocinium.*

paĩ *pateat, pater.*

paĩia *patientia.*

paĩtus *patratus.*

paℓ *pater.*

paℓfaℓ *paterfamilias.*

paℓnaℓr *paternaliter.*

pa^ue *passive.*

pa^uo *passivo.*

paup *pauper.*

p^auū *pravum.*

p^au^℩ *pravus.*

p^axis *praxis.*

p^ā *primam.*

pãper *pauper.*

pƀr *presbyter.*

p^ccatū *peccatum.*

p^cca^℩ *peccamus.*

p^ctore *pectore.*

p^ctū *peccatum.*

p^ct^℩ *pectus.*

p̃ci *peccati.*

p̃co *pactio.*

p̃cor *peccator.*

p̃coȝ *peccatorum.*

p̃cȝ *peccatum.*

p̃ce *parochiæ.*

p̃cto *pacto.*

p^e *primæ.*

pe. *peccatis.*

pe^a *pœna.*

pe^alis *pœnalis.*

pe^aℓr *pœnaliter.*

pe^as *pœnas.*

pe. ca. *pœna canonica.*

pecc̃m *peccatum.*

pecc̃or *peccator.*

pecūia *pecunia.*

pecĩa *pecunia.*

peđ *pedites.*

pellefr̃ *pellefridus.*

pelℓ *pellit, pelleret.*

pelū *pelvium.*

p^emiū *præmium.*

penℓ *penicillum.*

pen^s *penes.*

pensaĩ *pensatas.*

peñ *penes.*

peñlĩo *penultimo.*

p^epõit^℩ *præpositus.*

pet^aia *petraria.*

petič̃o *petitio.*

pet°ni *petitioni.*

petõem *petitionem.*

peĩo *petitio.*

peĩonē *petitionem.*

peĩrās *penetrans.*

peĩt *petunt.*

pēitēs *pœnitens.*

pēit^℩ *penitus.*

pēiĩ *pœnitet.*

pēs̃ *pensionem.*

pēteč̃ *Pentecostes.*

pẽ *pœnæ.*

pē̆s *penes, pœnas.*

pē̆to *peccato.*

pē̆n̄t *penetrant.*

phiᵃ *philosophia.*

phiᶜᵘˢ *physicus.*

phī̆ *Philippus.*

phꞇus *Philippus.*

ph⁹ *philosophus.*

pħ *Philippus.*

pħa *philosophia.*

pħos. *philosophus.*

pħs. *philosophus.*

pⁱ *pii, primi, pridem, principatus.*

pⁱdie *pridie.*

pieᵗę *pietatis.*

p. i. f. *pedes in fronte.*

pigᵐ *pigrum.*

pig⁹ *pignus.*

pⁱmeuo *primævo.*

pⁱmi *primi.*

pⁱmĩto *primitivo.*

pⁱmo *primo.*

pⁱm⁹ *primus.*

pⁱm̃ *primum.*

pⁱnciꞇr *principaliter.*

pinc̃ *pincerna.*

pⁱnc̃ *principalis, principaliter.*

pⁱnⁱ *principii.*

pⁱnᵐ *principem, principium.*

pⁱn° *principio.*

pⁱnʳ *principaliter.*

pⁱnᵗr *principaliter.*

pⁱñ *principia.*

pⁱñli *principali.*

p^{io} *primo, primario.*

pⁱoꝫ *priorum.*

pⁱõa *priora.*

pⁱõē *priorem.*

pⁱs *primas, primis.*

pⁱsa *prisa.*

piscᵃia *piscaria.*

piscãbꝫ *piscationibus.*

piscãia *piscaria.*

pⁱso *priso.*

pistⁱnū *pistrinum.*

pⁱstinū *pristinum.*

pĩsiū *piscium.*

pitāciar̃ *pitanciarius.*

pⁱuᵃ *privata.*

pⁱua° *privatio.*

pⁱuaʳ *privaretur.*

pⁱuaᵗ *privavit.*

pⁱuat⁹ *privatus.*

pⁱuiᵃ *privilegia.*

pⁱuileᵃ *privilegia.*

pⁱuiꞇ *privilegium.*

pⁱuiꞇioꝫ *privilegiorum.*

pⁱuiꞇiū *privilegium.*

pⁱui° *privilegio.*

pⁱu° *privatio.*

pⁱuõm *privationem.*

pⁱus *prius.*

pi⁹ *pius.*

p^{i⁹} *prius.*

pᶦᵃ *prima.*

pl. *placitum, plegii.*

plaᵃ *planeta.*

plac̃ *placitum, placita.*

plac̃ foresĩ, when extended, in
the Pipe Rolls, is usually
Placita Forestariorum, not
Foreste.

plac̃m *placeam, placitum.*

pl̃ae *planetæ.*

ple. *plene.*

plebᶦⁿ *plebem.*

pleƀs *plebanus.*

pleᵈᵒ *plenitudo.*

ple. fi. *plene fidimus.*

plenar̃ *plenarie.*

pleⁿᶜ *plenitudinem.*

pler̃q̃ *plerumque.*

pleuᵃm *plevinam.*

plēitⁿᵉ *plenitudine.*

plēituᵉ *plenitudine.*

plēū *plenum.*

pˡⁱ *possibili.*

plʳa *plura.*

plʳes *plures.*

pluũ *plurinam.*

plūat̸r *pluraliter.*

plᵉ *plus.*

pt *placet, placuerit, placitum,
plegiavit, plegius, plenam,
pleno.*

pƚa *plura.*

pƚaliṕ *pluraliter.*

pƚaʳ *pluraliter.*

pƚbanᵉ *plebanus.*

pƚƀm *plebanum.*

pƚƀno *plebano.*

pƚƀs *plebanus.*

pƚƀᵉ *plebanus.*

pƚ com̃ *pleno comitatu.*

pƚe *planete.*

pƚes *plures.*

pƚeta *planeta.*

pƚibȝ *pluribus.*

pƚies *pluries.*

pƚiᵐ *plurium.*

pƚima *plurima.*

pƚimi *plurimi.*

pƚim̃ *plurimum.*

pƚiq̃ *plerique.*

pƚita *placita.*

pƚitas *pluralitas.*

pƚitis *placitis.*

pƚitℓ *placitis.*

pƚiᵗℓ *pluralitatis.*

pƚiū *plurium.*

pƚie *plurimæ, plurime.*

pƚm *placitum, plaustrum, plegium, populum.*

pƚmo *plumeo, plurimo.*

pƚmq̃ *plerumque.*

pƚr *pluraliter.*

pƚra *plura.*

pƚres *plures.*

pƚrᵐ *plurimum.*

pĭs *pulsus.*

pĭta *planeta.*

pĭtim⁹ *penultimus.*

p. m. *passus mille, piæ memoriæ, plus minus.*

pᵐ *populum, primum.*

pñia *pœnitentia.*

pñiari⁹ *pœnitentiarius.*

pñlĭ *penultima.*

pñs *penes.*

pñt *possunt.*

p° *porro, primo.*

poᵃ *potentia.*

poᵇȝ *possibilibus.*

počĭm *poculum.*

poᵈ' *ponendum.*

poᵉ *potentiæ.*

p°ea *postea.*

poᵉᵐ *possessionem.*

poïa *posita.*

poˡᵉ *possibile, potentiale.*

poˡⁱˢ *possibilis, potentialis.*

poᵐ *positionem.*

ponᵇȝ *pontificalibus.*

pond *ponderis.*

poⁿᵉᵐ *positionem.*

pontiᵗᵘ *pontificatu.*

ponᵗᵘ *pontificatu.*

pont⁹ *pontificatus.*

ponĭ *pontifex, pontificatus.*

poñr *ponuntur.*

poñs *ponentes.*

poñt *possunt.*

poñȝ *ponderat, ponderis.*

po° *positio, possessio.*

p°° *primo modo.*

popⁱ *populi.*

popˢ *populus.*

pop̃laris *popularis.*

pop̃l⁹ *populus.*

poʳ *ponatur, ponitur.*

porc̃o *portio.*

por° *portio.*

pořetʳ *portaretur.*

poˢ *potius.*

posˡᵉ *pòssibile.*

posˡ' *possibilis.*

poso' *possessionem.*

possiᵃ *possibilia.*

possiᵈ' *possidendum.*

possid *possidendum.*

poss° *possessio.*

possõis *possessionis.*

poss̃ *possessiones, possunt.*

poss̃a *possessa.*

poss̃o *possessio.*

poss̃t *possunt.*

posᵗ *posuit.*

post̃um *posterum.*

posŭit *posuerit.*

poss̃o *possessio.*

poss̃° *possessorio.*

poss̃õm *possessionem.*

pos̃t *possunt.*

pote^a *potentia.*

poten^a *potentia.*

pote^s *potens, potentes.*

pote^t *potest.*

pot^ra *potura.*

po^t℮ *positis, potentis.*

poĩ *potestas.*

poᷱit *poterit.*

po^ui *positivi.*

po^uɑ̃ *positivum.*

p°ᴣ *posteriorum, primorum.*

pōere *ponere.*

pōi^r *ponitur.*

pōt^s *pontificatus.*

pŏdū *postmodum.*

pŏe *ponere, positione.*

pŏi *positioni, posteriori, priori.*

pŏibᴣ *positionibus.*

pŏi° *positio, posito.*

pŏit *posuit.*

pŏitīe *positive.*

pŏit⁹ *positus.*

pŏm *potentiam.*

pŏn^a *potentia.*

pŏnē *possessionem, positionem.*

pŏnis *possessionis, positionis.*

pŏnł *potentialis.*

pŏn^m *possessionum.*

pŏnū *possessionum.*

pŏñiis *potentiis.*

pŏr *possessor.*

pŏrio *possessorio.*

pōs *potentias.*

pŏt *potest, potuit.*

pŏ^t *ponit.*

pŏtatē *potestatem.*

pŏt^r *ponitur.*

põ^uɑ̃ *positivum.*

põᴣ *potentiarum.*

pp. *patres, pedes, perpetuum, piissimus, populus, præpositus, principes, provinciæ.*

p. p. *professor publicus.*

pp̃ *præpositus.*

pp̃tus *prepositus.*

pq *postquam.*

p^ra *parochia, pura.*

pr̃br *presbyter.*

p^re *pure.*

pres̃ *presentatio.*

pretᷱ *præter.*

prẽb. *presbyter.*

p^rgac̃o *purgatio.*

p^rga^r *purgatur.*

p^rgādū *purgandum.*

p^rg°'^m *purgationem.*

p^r̃gōm *purgationem.*

prid *pridie.*

p^rif^s *purificationis.*

prin^l' *principalis.*

p^rissim⁹ *purissimus.*

p^ritas *puritas.*

p^rit℮ *puritatis.*

priuiłiū *privilegium.*

p^ro *puro.*

proħns *prohibens.*

proℓ *propter.*

p^rp^est^ra *purprestura.*

p^rpⁱse *purprisæ.*

p^rp^ra *purpura.*

p^rp^rat⁹ *purpuratus.*

p^rp^re⁹ *purpureus.*

p^rp̃sĩa *purprestura.*

p^r' *priorissa.*

p̃r *præmissa, præsentatum, presbyter, prior, proviso.*

p̃rare *patrare, præstare.*

p̃ri *presbyteri.*

p̃ro *presbytero.*

ps. *postscriptum.*

psalℓiū *psalterium.*

pss. *postscriptis.*

p^t *post, potest.*

p^tate *potestate.*

p^{to} *precepto.*

p^tq̃ *postquam.*

p^ttas *potestas.*

pu^a *pura, puta.*

pub^{co} *publico.*

pub^c' *publicum.*

puƀ *publicus.*

pu^{ca} *publica.*

pu^{ce} *publice.*

pu^{co} *publico.*

pu^c' *publicum.*

p^ude^a *prudentia.*

p^ude^e *prudentiæ.*

p^udeñ *prudens, prudentia.*

puđ *pudica.*

p^uđr *prudenter.*

puelℓ *puella.*

pucĩ^a *pueritia.*

pugni^o *punitio.*

pug̃^a *pugnantia.*

purp^est^ra *purprestura.*

puȓ *purificationis.*

put^edīe *putredine.*

pūire *punire.*

pūit^{us} *punitivus.*

pūiss^{us} *purissimus.*

pūitas *puritas.*

pǔ *puer.*

pǔū *puerum.*

px̃a *proxima.*

pℨ *patet.*

p⁹ *post, primus.*

p⁹ea *postea.*

p⁹q̃ *postquam.*

p⁹siđ *possidet.*

p⁹sim⁹ *possimus.*

p⁹sit *possit.*

p⁹si^t' *possibiliter.*

p⁹sīt *possint.*

p⁹s^t *possit.*

p⁹s̃ *posset, possunt.*

p⁹s̃t *possunt.*

p⁹t^em̃ *postremum.*

p⁹tmođ *postmodum.*

p⁹tmõ *postmodum.*

p⁹tr̃ *posteris.*

p⁹tulauᵗ *postulavit.*

p⁹tuło *postulatio.*

p⁹ℓgat⁹ *postergatus.*

p⁹ti *posteri.*

p⁹ti⁹ *posterius.*

p⁹uit *posuit.*

p⁹ũũt *posuerunt.*

p⁹ᷠ *posterorum.*

p *par, per, por, perdendum, per-venerint.*

pᵃ *persona.*

pabᵗ *parabit.*

pabũt *parabunt.*

padisũ *paradisum.*

pafna *parapherna.*

pagiũ *paragium.*

pagʳ *peragitur.*

palipom̃ *Paralipomena.*

pᵃlis *personalis.*

pᵃliẽ *personaliter.*

pᵃlʳ *personaliter.*

pambło *perambulatio.*

paʳ *paratur.*

pᵃˢ *personas.*

patũ *paratum.*

pˢtũ *personatum.*

pᵃᷠ *personarum.*

pā *personam.*

pᵇᴣ *partibus.*

pcepl' *perceptibilis.*

pcepᵒ *perceptio.*

pcẽdo *parcendo.*

pcẽs *parcens.*

pciᵈᵒ *percipiendo.*

pciũ *partium.*

pcoᷠ *parcorum, porcorum.*

pcus *parcus, porcus.*

pcũctᵃi *percunctari.*

pc⁹ *parcus, porcus.*

pc̃ *percipiendo, percipiente.*

pc̃sa *percussa.*

pc̃sio *percussio.*

pc̃sor *percussor.*

pc̃tari *percunctari.*

pc̃e *parcere.*

pdc̃o *perditio.*

pdic̃o *perditio.*

pdiʳ *perditur.*

pdᵒ *perditio.*

pdoñ *perdona, perdonatus.*

pdᵗ *perdit.*

pd̃ *perdet.*

pđ *perdendum.*

pđr *perditur.*

pᵒ *personæ.*

pegⁱn⁹ *peregrinus.*

pempt̃ *peremptorie.*

penĩ *parentum.*

pc̃ptoᵐ *peremptorium.*

pēs *parens.*

pc̄te *parente.*

pc̄tˢ *parentis.*

pf̃ca *perfecta.*

pf̃ce *perfecte.*

pf̃cis^e *perfectissime.*

pf̃cm *perfectum.*

pf̃cor *perfectior.*

pf̃c⁹ *perfectus.*

pficiēd *perficiendum.*

pfice *perficere.*

pfc^m *perfectum.*

pfc^ma *perfectissima.*

pgit^r *pergitur.*

pg^t *perget, pergit.*

pgūt *pergunt.*

pg̃nt *pergunt.*

phendī^ae *perendinare.*

phend *perendinantium, perendinavit.*

phenis *perennis.*

phib *perhibet.*

ph̃ *perhibet.*

p̃indīa^do *perendinando.*

p̃indat^r *perendinatur.*

pi *pari.*

pibe *perhibere.*

picl *periculis.*

piclm *periculum.*

piclos⁹ *periculosus.*

piclo *periculo.*

pimi^r *perimitur.*

piñ *perinde.*

p^is *personis.*

pit *parit, perit.*

pitia *peritia.*

pit^r *pariter, paritur.*

pīta *paritura, peritura.*

pit̃ *pariter.*

pīcps *particeps.*

pīpes *participes.*

plam̃tū *parliamentum.*

ple *personale.*

plis *personalis.*

pl *personalis.*

pm *parum.*

pmp *parumper.*

pm^tte *permitte.*

pmu^l' *permutabilis.*

pmu^r *permutatur.*

pm̃p̃ *peremptorie.*

p^na *persona.*

p^ns *parens.*

pñt *parentes, parentum.*

po^lis *parochialis.*

pol *parochialis.*

p°nis *personis.*

p̃oa *persona.*

p̃om *personam.*

ppe^a *perpetua.*

ppe^c *perpetuæ, perpetue.*

ppe^m *perpetuum.*

ppe^o *perpetuo.*

ppe^ris *perpendicularis.*

ppet^at *perpetrat.*

ppetta *perpetrata.*

pplm *per plegium.*

ppā *perperam.*

pp̃ *perpetuum.*

pp̃i^m *participium.*

pp̃t^ato *perpetrato.*

pp̃uo *perpetuo.*

pp̃uū *perpetuum.*

pq^r *perquiratur.*

pq̃rēs *perquirens.*

p^r *pariter, paritur.*

p^ris *particularis.*

proł *parochialis.*

pr̃ *personarum.*

pr̃a *parochia.*

ps *pars, personas, personis.*

p̃^s *partes.*

pseq^o *persecutio, persequendo.*

pseq̃o *persecutio.*

pso^a *persona.*

psołr *personaliter.*

psona^r *personaliter.*

psonł *personaliter.*

psōa *persona.*

psōr *personaliter.*

psōʒ *personarum.*

psti^se *perstitisse.*

psuał *persuasibilis.*

p̃s *persolutio.*

pta *porta.*

pt^actare *pertractare.*

ptare *portare.*

pt^bʒ *partibus.*

pti *parti.*

ptibʒ *partibus.*

pticip^o *participatio.*

ptic^m *participium, particulatim.*

ptic̃la *particula.*

ptic̃łr *particulariter.*

pti^la *particula.*

pti^l⁹ *partialis.*

pti^ne *participatione.*

ptinē^a *pertinentia.*

ptinētibʒ *pertinentibus.*

ptiñ *pertinenciis, pertinet.*

ptiñbʒ *pertinentibus.*

ptiñciis *pertinenciis.*

ptio'^m *participationem.*

pti^r *particulariter, partitur.*

ptire *partire.*

pti^re *participare.*

pti^r⁹ *particularis.*

pti^t⁹ *partialiter.*

ptit⁹ *partitus.*

ptī *partim.*

ptĭciis *pertinenciis.*

pt^m *partem, partium, partum, portum.*

pt^rba^or *perturbator.*

ptr̃tare *pertractare.*

pt^s *partis.*

pt⁹ *portus.*

pt̃ *pertinet, pertinentiis.*

pt̃bat^r *perturbatur.*

pt̃ *personaliter.*

pue. *pervenerit.*

puehlit *pervenerit.*

pum *parum.*

puuł *parvulis.*

puū *parvum.*

pu⁹ *parvus.*

pū *parum.*

pūp *parumper.*

pūs⁹ *perversus.*

p₃ *paret, patet per.*

P̂ *quadringenta milia.*

p̃ *plegiavit, post, potest.*

p̃ᵃ *pœna, postea.*

p̃alis *pœnalis.*

p̃bᶜᵉ *publicæ, publice.*

p̃blic⁹ *publicus.*

p̃blic̆o *publicatio.*

p̃b̄r *presbyter.*

p̃ᶜᵃ *publica.*

p̃ᶜcaⁿ *peccamen.*

p̃ccᵐ *peccatum.*

p̃cc⁰ *peccato.*

p̃cc̃ *peccato.*

p̃c̃a *peccata.*

p̃c̃m *peccatum.*

p̃c̃o₃ *peccatorum.*

p̃cta *puncta.*

p̃cto *peccato, puncto.*

p̃ᶜᵘˢ *publicus.*

p̃c̆ *puncta.*

p̃c̈ca *practica.*

p̃c̃oᵐ *peccatum.*

p̃c̃o₃ *peccatum.*

p̃c̄tū *peccatum.*

p̃c̄tę *peccatis.*

p̃e *pœnæ.*

p̃ea *postea.*

p̃eᵃ *pœna.*

p̃ebᵗ *patebit.*

p̃ens *pœnitens.*

p̃ẽia *pœnitentia.*

p̃iđdū *possidendum.*

p̃iđᶫe *possidere.*

p̃lcᵉ *pulchre.*

p̃lcer *pulcher.*

p̃lchᵐ *pulchrum.*

p̃lcriⁿᶜ *pulchritudine.*

p̃ˡᵉ *possibile, prædicabile, principale.*

p̃ˡⁱˢ *possibilis, prædicabilis, principalis.*

p̃llic̈las *pelliculas.*

p̃ˡ' *possibilis, prædicabilis, principalis.*

p̃ĭtᵃ *penultima.*

p̃m *primam.*

p̃m⁹ *possumus.*

p̃na *pœna.*

p̃nᵃ *pœnitentia, præsentia, principia.*

p̃nᵃˡ' *pœnitentialis, principalis.*

p̃nał *pœnalis.*

p̃nᵇ₃ *principibus.*

p̃nciᵃ *principia.*

p̃nciaʳ *præsentialiter.*

p̃nciˡ' *principalis.*
p̃nciᵐ *principium.*
p̃nciᵘ *principum.*
p̃ndiū *prandium.*
p̃nđt *pendunt.*
p̃nd⁾e *pendere.*
p̃nⁱᵒ *principio.*
p̃nⁱᵒʳ *principalior.*
p̃niter̃ *pœniteret.*
p̃nitēs *pœnitens.*
p̃nĩlis *pœnitentialis, principalis.*
p̃nĩliῢ *pœnitentialiter.*
p̃nˡᵉ *principale.*
p̃nˡⁱˢ *principalis.*
p̃nˡ'ʳ *principaliter.*
p̃nᵒ *principio.*
p̃ns *prœsens.*
p̃nsatˢ *pensatas.*
p̃nsū *pensum.*
p̃ña *pœnitentia, prœsentia.*
p̃ñia *pœnitentia.*
p̃ñiariⁱ⁹ *pœnitentiarius.*
p̃ñie *pœnitentiœ.*
p̃ñt̃nt *penetrant.*
p̃o *positio.*
p̃one *positione.*
p̃ᵒʳ *possessor, posterior.*
p̃or̃ *prioribus.*
p̃ᵒ'ᵃ *posteriora.*
p̃pa *papa.*
p̃pe *papœ.*
p̃plice *publice.*

p̃plic⁹ *publicus.*
p̃płm *populum.*
p̃pᵐ *papam, populum.*
p̃pᵒ *populo.*
p̃p⁹ *populus.*
p̃pū *pauperum.*
p̃p̃lis *papalis, populis.*
p̃p̃lᵐ *papalem, populum.*
p̃p̃lo *populo.*
p̃p̃łris *popularis.*
p̃p̃łs *populus.*
p̃r *pater, presbyter.*
p̃rᵃ *prœterea.*
p̃ʳᵃ *plura.*
p̃ranđ *patrandum.*
p̃raʳ *patratur.*
p̃rari *patrari.*
p̃re *patre.*
p̃ʳᵉ *posteriore.*
p̃res *patres.*
p̃rē *patrem.*
p̃ri *patri, presbyteri.*
p̃ʳⁱ *posteriori.*
p̃ria *patria.*
p̃rib₃ *patribus.*
p̃rie *patriœ.*
p̃ʳⁱᵉˢ *pluries.*
p̃riñiū *patrimonium.*
p̃riᵒniū *patrimonium.*
p̃riȭle *patrimoniale.*
p̃rno *paterno.*
p̃rn⁹ *paternus.*

p̃rn̄ *paternum.*

p̃rochia *parochia.*

p̃rociniū *patrocinium.*

p̃ron⁹ *patronus.*

p̃rōa *patrona.*

p̃rˢ *paternitas, patris.*

p̃ruelis *patruelis.*

p̃ru⁹ *patruus.*

p̃ʳ'ˢ *plures.*

p̃so *possessio.*

p̃sōe *possessione.*

p̃t *patet, post, potest.*

p̃taᵉ *potestate.*

p̃tas *potestas.*

p̃taᵗ *portavit, præsentavit.*

p̃tatᵃ *potestativa.*

p̃tatē *potestatem.*

p̃tatę *potestatis.*

p̃te *potestate.*

p̃tebᵗ *patebit.*

p̃tet *patet.*

p̃teᵗ *patebit.*

p̃ᵗtis *potestatis.*

p̃tuit *patuit.*

p̃ĩis *potestatis.*

p̃ĩtas *potestas.*

p̃ẽn⁹ *paternus.*

p̃ue *parvæ, parve, pravæ, prave.*

p̃uileᵃ *privilegia.*

p̃uił *privilegium.*

p̃uitioᶻ *privilegiorum.*

p̃uiłiū *privilegium.*

p̃uiᵐ *privilegium.*

p̃uoᶻ *parvorum, pravorum.*

p̃u⁹ *parvus, pravus.*

p̃ *præ, pretium, præscriptum, præsentes, præsentatum, præcipimus.*

p̃abetʳ *præhabetur.*

p̃abit⁹ *præhabitus.*

p̃allᵗᵃ *præallegata.*

p̃bēda *præbenda.*

p̃bēdari⁹ *præbendarius.*

p̃bēd *præbendam, præbendum.*

p̃ᵇⁱˡⁱˢ *prædicabilis.*

p̃bȝ *præbet.*

p̃ƀ *præbet, presbyter.*

p̃ƀe *præbere.*

p̃biᵇȝ *prædicabilibus.*

p̃ƀnda *præbenda.*

p̃ƀnⁱˢ *præbendis.*

p̃ƀns *præbens.*

p̃ƀntis *præbentis.*

p̃ƀr *presbyter.*

p̃ƀrū *presbyterum.*

p̃ƀȝ *præbent.*

p̃ƀ'e *præbere.*

p̃caͦ *prædicatio.*

p̃aui *præcaveri.*

p̃ceᵇȝ *præcedentibus.*

p̃ceⁿˢ *præcedens.*

p̃cepᵃ *præcepta.*

p̃cepᵐ *præceptum.*

p̃cep̃m *præceptum.*

p̄ce^re *præcedere.*

p̄ce^t *præcedit.*

p̄ce^ti *præcedenti.*

p̄ci^e *præcipue, præcise.*

p̄cios^9 *pretiosus.*

p̄cip^e *præcipue.*

p̄cipi^do *præcipiendo.*

p̄cip^9 *precipimus.*

p̄cip̄r *præcipitur.*

p̄ci^r *præcipitur.*

p̄ciū *pretium.*

p̄cog^o *præcognitio.*

p̄c^ta *prædicamenta.*

p̄cū *precum.*

p̄c̃ *præceptum, prece.*

p̄c̃io *prædicatio.*

p̄c̃o *prædicatio.*

p̄c̃öm *prædicationem.*

p̄c̃ti *prædicati.*

p̄da *præda.*

p̄dat^9 *prædatus.*

p̄dc̃a *prædicta.*

p̄dc̃m *prædictum.*

p̄dc̃us *prædictus.*

p̄desti^ois *prædestinationis.*

p̄des̃ *prædestinatus.*

p̄det̃iare *prædeterminare.*

p̄det̃mīare *prædeterminare.*

p̄di^b3 *prædicabilibus.*

p̄dica^ntę *prædicamentis.*

p̄dicão *prædicatio.*

p̄dict^9 *prædictus.*

p̄dic̃s *prædictus.*

p̄dit̃cis *prædilectis.*

p̄dit̃cū *prædilectum.*

p̄di^o *prædictio.*

p̄di^re *prædicare.*

p̄di^tę *prædicamentis.*

p̄di3 *prædicatorum.*

p̄dōīari *prædominari.*

p̄^d' *prænotandum.*

p̄d *præda, prædicatur, Prædica-
tores.*

p̄dm *prædium.*

p̄dnañ *prædominantia.*

p̄dos *prædictos.*

p̄do3 *prædictorum.*

p̄dr *prædicitur.*

p̄emi^a *præeminentia.*

p̄est *præest.*

p̄expta *præexperta.*

p̄ex̃ns *præexistens.*

p̄ē *præest.*

p̄c̃ *præest.*

p̄ee *præesse.*

p̄c̃et *præesset.*

p̄faĩ *præfatus.*

p̄ft^r *præfertur.*

p̄gna^m *prægnantium.*

p̄gnās *prægnans.*

p̄g̃nicio *præcognitio.*

p̄g̃ni^o *præcognitio.*

p̄g̃n^o *præcognitio.*

p̄hita *præhabita.*

p̄h̄it⁹ *præhabitus.*

p̄issa *præmissa.*

p̄issis *præmissis.*

p̄iss̃ *præmissa, præmissis.*

p̄ittiʳ *præmittitur.*

p̄lib̄t⁹ *prælibatus.*

p̄ᶫⁱˢ *prædicabilis.*

p̄liū *prælium.*

p̄mᵒ ı̆c̄o *præmonitio.*

p̄mōst̃r *Præmonstratensis.*

p̄m̄ta *prædicamenta.*

p̄nᵃ *præsentia.*

p̄noia *præsentia.*

p̄nciaʳ *præsentialiter.*

p̄ncie *præsentiæ.*

p̄ndi *prædicandi.*

p̄nditʳ *prætenditur.*

p̄ndūt *prætendunt.*

p̄nia *præsentia.*

p̄nᵐ *præsentium.*

p̄nⁿ *prænomen.*

p̄noᵈ' *prænotandum.*

p̄noᵉ *prænomine.*

p̄noⁿ *prænomen.*

p̄noı̆o *prænotato.*

p̄nōē *prænomen.*

p̄nõiaˢ *prænominatis.*

p̄ns *præsens.*

p̄nse *prætense.*

p̄ntaʳ *præsentatur, præsentia-*
    liter.

p̄ntatȩ *præsentatis.*

p̄ntat⁹ *præsentatus.*

p̄ntᵇჳ *præsentibus.*

p̄nte *præsente.*

p̄ntᶜ *præsentiæ.*

p̄nteʳ *præsentetur.*

p̄ntē *præsentem.*

p̄nti *præsenti, prædicamenti.*

p̄ntia *præsentia.*

p̄ntibჳ *præsentibus.*

p̄ntie *præsentiæ.*

p̄ntis *præsentis, prædicamentis.*

p̄nto *prædicamento.*

p̄ntˢ *præsentibus.*

p̄ntȩ *præsentis.*

p̄nı̃o *præsentato.*

p̄nūatȩ *prænumeratis.*

p̄ñ *præsentia, præsentibus.*

p̄ñcᵃe *prænuntiare.*

p̄ñc̆at *prænuntiat.*

p̄ñia *præsentia.*

p̄ño *principio.*

p̄oñsʳi *præostensuri.*

p̄oñsū *præostensum.*

p̄pⁱ *præpositi.*

p̄pⁱᵗ' *præpositus.*

p̄poᵈᵒ *præponendo.*

p̄poˢ *præpositis.*

p̄põs *præpositus.*

p̄põtʳ *præponatur.*

p̄põi *præpositi.*

p̄põus *præpositus.*

p̄pı̃ *præpositi.*

ꝓptm *præpositum.*

ꝓpts *præpositus.*

ꝓp⁹ *præpositus.*

ꝓpabᵗ *præparabit.*

ꝓpaco *præparatio.*

ꝓpamta *præparamenta.*

ꝓpare *præparare.*

ꝓpatū *præparatum.*

ꝓpaui *præparavi.*

ꝓpād *præparandum.*

ꝓp̃i *præpositi.*

ꝓp̃it⁹ *præpositus.*

ꝓp̃m *præpositum.*

ꝓp̃o *præpositio, præposito.*

ꝓp̃s *præpositus.*

ꝓp̃te *præpositæ.*

ꝓp̃ti *præpositi.*

ꝓp̃tis *præpositis.*

ꝓp̃to *præposito.*

ꝓp̃tū *præpositum.*

ꝓp̃t̃ *præpositi, præposterus.*

ꝓppo *præpropero.*

ꝓr *prædicatur.*

ꝓrᵃ *præterea.*

ꝓre *prædicare.*

ꝓreʳ *prædicaretur.*

ꝓri *prædicari.*

ꝓrito *præterito.*

ꝓrogaᵃ *prærogativa.*

ꝓsᵇ₃ *præsentibus.*

ꝓsꝑ *presbyter.*

ꝓsꝑi *presbyteri.*

M.

ꝓsꝯr *presbyter.*

ꝓsciᵖ⁰ *prescriptio.*

ꝓscripᵇ₃ *præscriptionibus.*

ꝓsc̃bitʳ *præscribitur.*

ꝓscia *præscientia.*

ꝓsc̃pco *præscriptio.*

ꝓsᵈᵒ *præservando.*

ꝓsᵉ *præcise.*

ꝓsenᵃ *præsentia.*

ꝓsenca *præsentia.*

ꝓsenᵐ *præsentium.*

ꝓsenta *præsentia.*

ꝓsento *præsentatio.*

ꝓsēᵃ *præsentia.*

ꝓsēm *præsentem, præsentiam.*

ꝓsctiaꝉr *præsentialiter.*

ꝓsē *præsepe.*

ꝓˢⁱˢ *præmissis.*

ꝓsñia *præsentia.*

ꝓsñta *præsentata.*

ꝓsñti *præsenti.*

ꝓsso₃ *præmissorum.*

ꝓssoe *pressione.*

ꝓstaco *præstatio.*

ꝓstās *præstans.*

ꝓstātē *præstantem.*

ꝓstiᵗ *præstitit.*

ꝓstitᵐ *præstitum.*

ꝓsūitʳ *præsumitur.*

ꝓsūp⁰ *præsumptio.*

ꝓs̃ *præsentat, præsentant, præ-*
  sentibus.

p̃sns *præsens.*

p̃snte *præsente.*

p̃spp̄it *præsupponit.*

p̃spp̄to *præsupposito.*

p̃st *præstet, præsunt.*

p̃stī *præsertim.*

p̃sua^e *præservare.*

p̃ꝰstī *præsertim.*

p̃sua^e *præservare.*

p̃t *prædicat.*

p̃ta *prædicata.*

p̃^ta *prædicamenta.*

p̃tĕa *præterea.*

p̃tēt *præteritum.*

p̃t^m *prædicatum, præteritum.*

p̃t° *prædicato, præterito.*

p̃t°io *prætorio.*

p̃to^m *prætorem.*

p̃tor *prætor.*

p̃^tor *prædicator.*

p̃t^r *prædicatur.*

p̃tū *prædicatum.*

p̃t̃ *præteriti.*

p̃ta *præterea.*

p̃tea *præterea.*

p̃ti^m *præteritum.*

p̃ti° *præterito.*

p̃titū *præteritum.*

p̃tꝗ *præterquam.*

p̃t̃ *præter.*

p̃ea *præterea.*

p̃tib^t *præteribit.*

p̃ti^m *præteritum.*

p̃ti° *præterito.*

p̃tit *præteriit, præterit.*

p̃titū *præteritum.*

p̃tit̨e *præteritis.*

p̃tm̃t^e *prætermittere.*

p̃tꝗ *præterquam.*

p̃uēi^e *prævenire.*

p̃uēiēt *præveniente.*

p̃ᵹ *prædicatorum.*

p *pro.*

p^a *propterea, proxima.*

pbac̃o *probatio.*

pba^le *probabile.*

pba° *probatio.*

pba^r *probabiliter, probatur.*

pbat *probat.*

pbāĩ *probatum.*

pbā^r *probantur.*

pbe^r *probetur.*

pbē *probem.*

pbi *probi.*

pb° *probatio.*

pboñ *probationum.*

pbos *probos.*

pbõe *probatione.*

pbõm *probationum.*

pbū *probum.*

pb⁹ *probus.*

pbᵹ *probrum.*

pb̃ *probat, probavit, probi, probos.*

pb̃ores *probatores.*

ꝓbr *probabiliter.*

ꝓceanꝺ *procreandis.*

ꝓceat *procreat.*

ꝓceaȶ *procreato.*

ꝓcedo *procedendo.*

ꝓceꝺꝺ *procedendum.*

ꝓcem *processum.*

ꝓcent *procedunt.*

ꝓcentę *procedentis.*

ꝓcer *proceditur.*

ꝓceres *proceres.*

ꝓceribȝ *proceribus.*

ꝓcet *procedit.*

ꝓceȝ *procerum.*

ꝓcȶare *proclamare.*

ꝓcȶo *proclamatio.*

ꝓcoȝ *procorum.*

ꝓcrabo *procurabo.*

ꝓcratoiū *procuratorium.*

ꝓcrio *procuratorio.*

ꝓcrium *procuratorium.*

ꝓcoĩ *procreati.*

ꝓcurañ *procurationis.*

ꝓcuroriū *procuratorium.*

ꝓcuĩ *procurator.*

ꝓcuꝛē *procuratorem.*

ꝓcuꝛïo *procuratorio.*

ꝓcuꝛtes *procuratores.*

ꝓcuꝛū *procuratorium.*

ꝓc̃ *procurator.*

ꝓc̃ac̃o *procuratio.*

ꝓc̃are *procurare.*

ꝓc̃at *procurat.*

ꝓc̃ator *procurator.*

ꝓc̃etr *procuretur.*

ꝓc̃l *procul.*

ꝓc̃o *probatio.*

ꝓc̃re *procurare.*

ꝓc̃es *proceres.*

ꝓc̃ibȝ *proceribus.*

ꝓc̃ū *procerum.*

ꝓꝯsul *proconsul.*

ꝓdctū *productum.*

ꝓdet *prodest.*

ꝓdẽe *prodesse.*

ꝓdio *proditio.*

ꝓdo *probando.*

ꝓdt *produxit.*

ꝓdud' *producendum.*

ꝓdur *producuntur.*

ꝓꝺ *probandum, prodest.*

ꝓꝺc̃m *productum.*

ꝓꝺc̃ꝰ *productus.*

ꝓꝺt *produnt.*

ꝓe *prope.*

ꝓea *propterea.*

ꝓfc *profecturus.*

ꝓfc̃o *profecto.*

ꝓfc̃om *profectionem.*

ꝓfeo *professio.*

ꝓfꝰ *profectus.*

ꝓfar *proferatur.*

ꝓfom *professionem.*

ꝓfoȝ *professorum.*

i 2

ꝓfri *proferri.*
ꝓft^{r} *profertur.*
ꝓg^{e}ssū *progressum.*
ꝓg̃đ^{r} *progreditur.*
ꝓg̃ss̃o *progressio.*
ꝓhe^{o} *proœmio.*
ꝓhēiū *proœmium.*
ꝓhēs *prohiberes.*
ꝓhic̃o *prohibitio.*
ꝓhic̃om *prohibitionem.*
ꝓhi^{re} *prohibere.*
ꝓh^{r} *prohibetur.*
ꝓħ *prohibet.*
ꝓħa *propheta.*
ꝓħet *prohibet.*
ꝓħitū *prohibitum.*
ꝓħndo *prohibendo.*
ꝓħn^{r} *prohibentur.*
ꝓħ^{t} *prohibet.*
ꝓħuit *prohibuit.*
ꝓ^{i} *probi.*
ꝓ^{i}o *proprio.*
ꝓ^{io} *proprio.*
ꝓ^{i}us *proprius.*
ꝓ^{i}ū *proprium.*
ꝓīa *proxima.*
ꝓĩa *proxima.*
ꝓł *prolis.*
ꝓłr *probabiliter.*
ꝓmptꝰ *promptus.*
ꝓm^{t}t̾e *promittere.*
ꝓ m̃ *pro manerio.*
ꝓm̃tēs *promittens.*
ꝓndū *probandum.*
ꝓn^{n} *pronomen.*
ꝓno^{e} *pronomine.*
ꝓ^{nt} *probant.*
ꝓnūciac̃o *pronunciatio.*
ꝓnūc^{o} *pronunciatio.*
ꝓñc *pronunc.*
ꝓñt *probant.*
ꝓñtiare *pronuntiare.*
ꝓ^{o} *probatio, probo, propositio.*
ꝓ$^{o'm}$ *probationem.*
ꝓ$^{\tilde{o}e}$ *probatione.*
ꝓp^{a} *propria, propterea.*
ꝓpe *prope.*
ꝓp^{ea} *propterea.*
ꝓpħa *propheta.*
ꝓp^{i} *proprii.*
ꝓp^{i}a *propria.*
ꝓp^{i}e *propriæ, proprie.*
ꝓp^{i}et^{m} *proprietatum.*
ꝓp^{i}i *proprii.*
ꝓp^{ime} *proprissime.*
ꝓpin^{r} *propinquior.*
ꝓp^{i}o *proprio.*
ꝓp^{i}tas *propietas.*
ꝓp$^{it'e}$ *proprietate.*
ꝓp^{i}ū *proprium.*
ꝓp^{m} *proprium.*
ꝓp^{o} *propositio, proposito.*
ꝓp^{oc} *propter hoc.*
ꝓpo^{em} *propositionem.*

ppo^{ib}ȝ *propositionibus.*

ppo^m *propositionum, propositum.*

ppoñr *proponuntur.*

pporciōƚ *proportionabiliter.*

ppor^{oƚ} *proportionaliter.*

ppor^{o'lis} *proportionalis.*

ppor^{o'm} *proportionem.*

ppor^{ta} *proportionata.*

pposse *proposse.*

ppo^{ur} *proponuntur.*

ppõ *propositionem.*

ppõi^m *propositum.*

ppõis *propositionis.*

ppõitū *propositum.*

ppõ^r *proponitur.*

ppōt *proponat, proponit.*

ppria *propria.*

pprie *propriæ, proprie.*

ppr^one *proportione.*

pptū *promptum.*

ppt⁹ *promptus.*

ppt̃or *promptior.*

ppƚ *propter.*

ppƚea *propterea.*

pp⁹ *proprius.*

pp *prope, propter.*

ppare *properare.*

ppāt *properant.*

pp̃ *propter.*

pp̃e^bȝ *proprietatibus.*

pp̃e^s *proprietas.*

pp̃e^{te} *proprietate.*

pp̃iis *propriis.*

pp̃is *propriis.*

pp̃nq^o *propinquo.*

pp̃o *propositio, proprio.*

pp̃r *propter.*

pp̃s *proprius.*

pp̃^{te} *proprietate.*

pp̃to *prompto.*

pp̃^{to} *proposito.*

p^r *probabiliter, probatur, prorogatur.*

pre *probare, procurare.*

pri *probari, procurari.*

prs⁹ *prorsus.*

pr⁹ *prorsus.*

ps *probus.*

pse^r *prosequitur.*

psⁱ *prosequi.*

psp *prosper.*

pspa *prospera.*

pspi⁹ *prosperius.*

psĩt⁹ *prostratus.*

pstñet^r *prosterneretur.*

ps̃ *prosecutor, prosequendo.*

pt *probat.*

p^t *prout.*

pt^a *protestata.*

pt^ah⟩e *protrahere.*

pte. *protegatis.*

ptecõ *protectio.*

ptest^bȝ *protestationibus.*

ptē⁹ *vrotenus.*

ꝑthoɱ̃ *protomartyr.*
ꝑthoñ *protonotarius.*
ꝑ^{tor} *protestator, protestor.*
ꝑt^r *probatur, prorogatur, pro-testatur, protestor, protur-batur.*
ꝑtū *probatum.*
ꝑ^tȝ *prout patet.*
ꝑ͠t *protectio, protegatis.*
ꝑ͠thi *protrahi.*
ꝑ͠to *probatio.*
ꝑ͠t^{tur} *protestatur, proturbatur.*
ꝑ͠tuia *protervia.*
ꝑᵭ *propter.*
ꝑᵭuia *protervia.*
ꝑᵭuiᵭ *proterviter.*
ꝑᵭuïas *protervitas.*
ꝑueñ *proventus.*
ꝑue^t *provenit.*
ꝑuēt^ra *proventura.*

ꝑui *probavi, protervi.*
ꝑuiden^a *providentia.*
ꝑuid^ꝯe *providere.*
ꝑuīcia *provincia.*
ꝑuõnē *proventionem, provoca-tionem.*
ꝑut *prout.*
ꝑuũȝ *prout patet.*
ꝑũ *prout.*
ꝑx^a *proxima.*
ꝑxi^a *proxima.*
ꝑxi^c *proxime.*
ꝑxi^m *proximum.*
ꝑxīa *proxima.*
ꝑx^m *proximum.*
ꝑx^o *proximo.*
ꝑx̃ *proximus.*
ꝑx̃a *proxima.*
ꝑx̃i *proximi.*
ꝑx̃m *proximum.*

Q.

Q. *cur, qua, quacunque, quæ, quæcunque, quædam, quæri-tur, quam, quantum, qua-que, quasi, quatenus, que, quem, quemcunque, qui, quia, quibus, quid, quingenti, quintum, quod, quodcunque.*

q^a *qua, quacunque, qualibet.*
q^ad^aǧ *quadragesimam.*
q^adrages^a *quadragesima.*
q^ai *quasi.*
q^ainta *quadraginta.*
q^alē *qualem.*

qᵃlis *qualis.*

qᵃlitʳ *qualiter.*

qᵃ+ *qualis.*

qᵃmp+m *quamplurimum.*

qᵃntūcūꝗ *quantumcunque.*

qᵃnt⁹ *quantus.*

qᵃñcūꝗ *quandocunque.*

qᵃor *quatuor.*

qᵃꝑpꝓ *quapropter.*

qᵃr *qualiter.*

qᵃrñtⁿᵃ *quarentena.*

qᵃrt⁹ *quartus.*

qᵃῖ *quare.*

qᵃten⁹ *quatenus.*

qᵃti⁹ *quatinus.*

qᵃꝓ *quater.*

qᵃӡ *quarum.*

qā *quam.*

qb; *quibus.*

qꝺs *quibus.*

qꝺ; *quibus.*

qᵈā *quidam.*

qᵈ' *quidem.*

qꝺ *quadrans, quidem, quod.*

qᵉ *quæ, quare.*

qᵉdā *quædam.*

qᵉ̃ *quem.*

qⁱ *qui.*

qⁱa *quia.*

qⁱb; *quibus.*

qⁱꝺliꝺ *quibuslibet.*

qⁱcqⁱd *quicquid.*

qⁱcꝗ̃ *quicquam, quicquid, quicunque.*

qⁱcūꝗ *quicunque.*

qⁱc̃ *quicunque.*

qⁱd *quid.*

qⁱdā *quidam.*

qⁱꝺ *quidem.*

qⁱescᵗ *quiescit.*

qⁱesꞔe *quiescere.*

qⁱetaũ *quietavit.*

qⁱīo *quinimmo.*

qⁱn *quin.*

qⁱnꝗ *quinque.*

qⁱntā ꝺ *quintam decimam.*

qⁱnto *quinto.*

qⁱnӡ *quinque.*

qⁱqꞔñiū *quinquennium.*

qⁱꝗ̃ *quinque.*

qⁱˢ *quamvis, quis.*

qⁱsqⁱs *quisquis.*

qⁱˢꝗ *quisque.*

qⁱ' *quibus, quicunque.*

qᵐ *quem, quidem.*

qⁿ *quando, quin.*

qñ *quando, quoniam.*

qñᵃᵗᵉ *quantitate.*

qñcūꝗ *qnandocumque.*

qñm *quoniam.*

qñꝗ *quandoque.*

qñӡ *quandoque.*

q⁰ *quæstio, quo, quoque.*

q⁰c̃ꝗ̃ *quocunque.*

q°d *quod.*
q°dam° *quodammodo.*
q°dā *quodam.*
q°dāo° *quodammodo.*
q°d°° *quodammodo.*
q°ŧib *quolibet.*
q°liȝ *quolibet.*
q°ŧ *quolibet.*
q°m° *quomodo.*
q°m°cūq, *quomodocunque.*
q°m°libȝ *quomodolibet.*
q°m°ŧ *quomodolibet.*
q°nā *quonam.*
q°ne *quæstione.*
q°niā *quoniam.*
q°ns *quotiens.*
q°ñm *quonam, quoniam.*
q°qᵉ *quoque.*
q°q° *quoquo.*
q°q°m° *quoquomodo.*
q°q̃° *quoquo.*
q°q, *quoque.*
qᵒʳ' *quorum.*
q°s *quos.*
qᵒᵗ *quot.*
q°tŧib *quotlibet.*
q°ȝ *quorum.*
qõe *quæstione.*
qõm *quæstionem.*
qᑫ' *quinque.*
qʳ *quæritur, qualiter, queritur.*
qᵗᵃˢ *qualitas.*

qᵗ' *qualiter.*
qᵗℂ *qualitatis.*
q. v. *qui vixit, quod vide.*
quadsīo *quadragesimo.*
quaŧ *qualibet.*
quaŧr *qualiter.*
quaᵐ *quamquam.*
quanŧ *quantitatem.*
quaʳ *qualiter.*
quaᵗℂ *qualitatem.*
ᵴuat⁹ *quatenus.*
quaĩ *quatenus.*
quaĩus *quatenus.*
quaȝ *quarum.*
quā *quam.*
quãi *quasi.*
queĩ *querentem.*
quesĩ *questum.*
quē *quem.*
quĕla *querela.*
quĕones *quæstiones.*
quĕᵗ *quæreret.*
quĕᵗʳ *quæreretur.*
quisᵴ́ *quisquam.*
quisq, *quisque.*
quoᵇᵉᵗ *quomodolibet.*
quoᵇȝ *quomodolibet.*
quoc̃ *quotiens.*
quodāᵒᵒ *quodammodo.*
quoᵐ *quoniam.*
quom° *quomodo.*
quoñm *quoniam.*

quoᵒ *quomodo.*

quoᵒꝗ *quomodocunque.*

quō *quomodo.*

quŏdolibȝ *quomodolibet.*

quŏm *quoniam.*

quŏqᵘᵉ *quomodocunque.*

quŏꝗ *quomodocunque.*

qūo *quomodo.*

qȝ *quia.*

q⁹ *quatenus, quibus, quietus.*

qȝ *quorum.*

qȝꞓꝗ *quorumcunque.*

qȝdā *quorundam.*

ꝗ *quæ, quam, que, quod (mostly).*

ꝗa *quia.*

qᵃ *quam.*

qᵃas *quantitas.*

qᵃ𝑔̃ *quarteragium.*

qᵃpłm *quamplurimum.*

qᵃqᵃ *quamquam.*

qᵃꝗ *quamque.*

qᵃtū *quantum.*

qᵃtꝑ *quantitatis.*

qᵃт̃ *quantum.*

ꝗãoᵒ *quodammodo.*

ꝗbȝ *quibus.*

ꝗƀ *quibus.*

ꝗᶜ *quod sic.*

ꝗd *quid, quod.*

ꝗdāmõ *quodammodo.*

ꝗdãᵒ *quodammodo.*

ꝗdãoᵒ *quodammodo.*

ꝗdđ *quoddam.*

ꝗđ *quidem, quoddam.*

q̊ᵉ *quem.*

qⁱ *quid, quidem.*

qⁱqⁱ *quidquid.*

qᵐ *quantum.*

qᵐꞓȝ *quantumcunque.*

ꝗꝗ *quodquod, quoque, quoquo.*

ꝗꝗ *quoque.*

q̃ *500000, quæ, que, quem.*

q̃a *quia.*

q̃adᵈ̅ *quemadmodum.*

q̃admoᵐ *quemadmodum.*

q̃ađ *quemadmodum.*

q̃ađm *quemadmodum.*

q̃ae *quæ.*

q̃a𝑔̈ *quarteragium.*

q̃am *quam.*

q̃ᵃˢ *quantitas.*

q̃ā *quam.*

q̃āꞓꝗ *quamcunque.*

q̃āꝗ *quamque.*

q̃ā *queat.*

q̃ãmoᵐ *quemadmodum.*

q̃ãoᵒ *quodammodo.*

q̃ᵇ' *quælibet, quodlibet.*

q̃bȝ *quælibet, quodlibet.*

q̃b⁹ *quibus.*

q̃ƀs *quibus.*

q̃cꝗ *quæcunque, quamcunque, quicquid.*

q̃cūᵉ *quæcunque, quantumcunque.*

ꝗc̈o *quæsitio.*

ꝗc̈uᵉ *quibuscunque.*

ꝗᵭ *quid, quod.*

ꝗdam *quadam, quædam, quen-dam, quidam, quodam.*

ꝗdamō *quodammodo.*

ꝗdā *quadam, quædam, quendam, quidam.*

ꝗdāo *quodammodo.*

ꝗdᵭ *quoddam.*

ꝗdē *quidem.*

ꝗdⁱc̈ii *quadriennii.*

ꝗdⁱga *quadriga.*

ꝗdⁱgentꝑ *quadringentis.*

ꝗdo *quando.*

ꝗdꝗ *quidquid, quodque.*

ꝗdʳ *quadrupliciter.*

ꝗdragesᵃ *quadragesima.*

ꝗdᵘpeᵃ *quadrupedia.*

ꝗdᵘpᵗ *quadruplex.*

ꝗdᵘpʳ *quadrupliciter.*

ꝗdˣ *quadruplex.*

ꝗᵭ *quædam, quibusdam, quidem, quoddam.*

ꝗᵭnˡⁱ *quadranguli.*

ꝗᵭns *quadrans.*

ꝗᶜ *quoque.*

ꝗela *querela.*

ꝗet⁹ *quietus.*

ꝗi *quasi, qui.*

ꝗid *quid.*

ꝗiᵐ *quæsitum.*

ꝗiti *quæsiti.*

ꝗlec̈ *qualecunque.*

ꝗlibeᵐ *quotlibetum.*

ꝗlibᵘˢ *qualitatibus.*

ꝗlibꝫ *quælibet, qualibet, qualibus.*

ꝗlibꝫ *qualitatibus.*

ꝗlitas *qualitas.*

ꝗlitⁱ *quotlibeti.*

ꝗlitⁿ *qualitatum.*

ꝗlitᵛ *qualitatem.*

ꝗliᵗ *qualiter.*

ꝗlīs *qualitas.*

ꝗlʳc̈ *qualitercunque.*

ꝗˡᵛ *qualibet, qualis.*

ꝗlꝫ *quælibet, quilibet, quemlibet, quodlibet.*

ꝗᵗ *quælibet, &c., as above.*

ꝗᵗt *quælibet, &c., as above.*

ꝗm *quam, quem, quoniam.*

ꝗᵐ *quantum, quidem.*

ꝗmadm̃ *quemadmodum.*

ꝗmaᵭ *quemadmodum.*

ꝗmoᵗt *quomodolibet.*

ꝗᵐ' *quantumcunque.*

ꝗm̃s *quæsumus.*

ꝗn *quando, quin.*

ꝗnc̈ꝗ *quandocunque.*

ꝗndo *quando.*

ꝗngēti *quingenti.*

ꝗnio *quinimmo.*

ꝗnꝗ *quandoque, quinque.*

ꝗnta *quanta.*

q̃ntaᵉ *quantacunque.*

q̃ntᵃˢ *quantitas.*

q̃ntc̃ *quantumcunque.*

q̃nᵗᵉ *quantitate.*

q̃ntᵐ *quantum.*

q̃nto *quanto.*

q̃ntū *quantum.*

q̃nᵗę *quantitatis.*

q̃nĩ *quantum.*

q̃nꝫ *quandoque.*

q̃ⁿ' *quando.*

q̃ũ *quando, quandoque, quando-cunque, quoniam.*

q̃ũm *quoniam.*

q̃o *quæstio, queo, quo.*

q̃º *quomodo.*

q̃od *quod.*

q̃odā *quodam.*

q̃ođ *quodam.*

q̃one *quæstione.*

q̃ºº *quomodo.*

q̃oꝗ *quoque.*

q̃ᵒʳ *quatuor.*

q̃ᵒʳ t̃ *quatuor temporum.*

q̃os *quos.*

q̃oꝫ *quorum.*

q̃ōe *quæstione.*

q̃ōc̄ *quæstionem.*

q̃ōis *quæstionis.*

q̃õm *quæstionem.*

q̃ppe *quippe.*

q̃ppꝉ *quapropter.*

q̃p̢p̃ *quapropter.*

q̃qᵈ *quicquid.*

q̃qᵐ *quemquam, quicquam, quis-quam.*

q̃q̃ *quamquam.*

q̃q̃ā *quamquam.*

q̃q̃d *quicquid.*

q̃qꝗ *quæque, quique, quamque, quoque.*

q̃ʳ *quæritur.*

q̃raʳ *quæratur.*

q̃rat *quærat.*

q̃re *quare, quærere.*

q̃rela *querela.*

q̃reˢ *quærens.*

q̃rimoᵃ *querimonia.*

q̃rīōa *querimonia.*

q̃ro *quæro.*

q̃rº *quarto.*

q̃ror *queror.*

q̃rʳ *quæritur.*

q̃rto *quarto.*

q̃rtū *quartum.*

q̃rt⁹ *quartus.*

q̃r̃ *quare, quæret, quæris, quæ-ritur.*

q̃s *quas, quamcitius.*

q̃ˢ *qualitas.*

q̃si *quasi.*

q̃siᵗⁱ *Quasimodo geniti.*

q̃so *quæso.*

q̃sqᵐ *quisquam.*

q̃sq̃ *quisquam.*

q̃sq̃s *quisquis.*

q̃sꝗ *quisque.*

q̃st⁹ *quæsitus, quæstus.*

q̃s̃ *quæsumus.*

q̃t *quærit, quæsivit.*

q̃ᵗᵃ *quanta.*

q̃ᵗᵃˢ *qualitas, quantitas.*

q̃ᵗᵉ *quantæ.*

q̃ᵗⁱ *quæsiti, quanti.*

q̃ᵗⁱᵒ *quæstio.*

q̃tis *quæsitis.*

q̃ᵗⁱˢ *quantitatis.*

q̃tiᵗℭ *quantitatis.*

q̃tiᵘᵉ *quantitative.*

q̃t̃s *quantitas.*

q̃tᵐ *quantum.*

q̃to *quæsito.*

q̃tõ *quantocunque.*

q̃tuor *quatuor.*

q̃tus *quartus.*

q̃tū *quantum, quartum.*

q̃ᵗℭ *quantitatis.*

q̃t⁹ *quartus, quatenus.*

q̃t̃ *quatenus.*

q̃t̃o *quæstio.*

q̃t̃s *quatenus.*

q̃t̃us *quatenus.*

q̃t̃ *quater.*

q̃t̃n⁹ *quaternus.*

q̃ᵹ *quarum.*

ą *quam, quem.*

ąadᵈᵘ *quemadmodum.*

ąadmõ *quemadmodum.*

ąađ *quemadmodum.*

ąq̃ *quamquam, quemquam.*

ąsi *quasi.*

ꝗ *que, quia.*

ꝗᵃ *quaque.*

ꝗᵒ *quoque.*

R.

R. *octoginta, Radulfus, regni, rex, requiescat, Ricardus, requiratur, reverendus, runcini.*

rᵃ *regula.*

racħ *rachetum.*

racõe *ratione.*

racõ *ratio.*

Radto *Radulfo.*

Rađ *Radulfus.*

rᵃᵗ *rationalis.*

rᵃᵐ *regulam.*

ra^{me} *rarissime.*

rariĩs *ramulus.*

ra^o *ratio.*

ra^one *ratione.*

r^aris *regularis.*

r^ariũ *regularium.*

r^atiua *regulativa.*

rat^oci^ai *ratiocinari.*

r^at^r *regulatur.*

ratñōe *ratiocinatione.*

ratoni *rationi.*

r^a *regulam.*

rãa *rata.*

rã^{lis} *rationabilis.*

rão *ratio, rato.*

r^cti^{nc} *rectitudine.*

rc̃a *recta.*

rc̃e *recte.*

rc̃m *rectum.*

rc̃or *rector.*

rc̃s *rectus.*

rc̃⁹ *rectus.*

r^d *respondendum.*

r^{da} *reverenda.*

r^{dus} *reverendus.*

re. *recognitura.*

r^e *recipe, regulæ, require.*

reã^{tc} *remanente.*

reã^r *realiter.*

reãris *regularis.*

reb၁ *rebus.*

recc̃n^{ne} *recognitione.*

recep^o၁ *receptionem.*

recep^{tor} *receptator.*

recogñe *recognitione.*

recog̃ *recognitura.*

recōño *recognitio.*

rec̃ *recens, receptum, recessit, recognitio, recognitionibus, recognitores, recognitura, recognovit, rectatus.*

rec̃asti *recusasti.*

rec̃at *recusat.*

rec̃^b၁ *recognitionibus.*

rec̃^{ea}o *recreatio.*

rec̃o *recognitio.*

recၠēdare *recommendare.*

recၠmēdare *recommendare.*

recၠmēdão *recommendatio.*

recၠñ *recognitione, recognoscit.*

redd^{da} *reddenda.*

red^{d'} *reddendum.*

redđ *reddit, reddunt, redditionem, redditum.*

redđe *reddere.*

reddr *redditur.*

redđt *reddunt.*

redd)e *reddere.*

redēp^{ois} *redemptionis.*

redc̃es *redeuntes.*

redūdñ *redundantia.*

red *reditum.*

re^e *regulæ, require.*

reedif *reedificare.*

refēt *refecit.*

refīgat^{r} *refrigeratur.*

refor^{a}ta *reformata.*

ref *reficiendum.*

refg^{a}t^{r} *refrigeratur.*

refg̊at^{r} *refrigeratur.*

reg^{a}re *regnare.*

reg^{i}cola *regnicola.*

regīē *regimen.*

regïe *regimine.*

regła *regula.*

reg^{m} *regnum.*

regn^{te} *regnante.*

regñ *regnante, regni.*

reḡ *regem, regis, regni, regnum.*

reḡbr *regenerabitur.*

reḡis *regiminis.*

reḡra *registra.*

reḡra^{io} *registratio.*

reḡrio *registrario.*

reḡris *registris.*

reḡro *registro.*

rehire *rehabere.*

rehit *rehabet.*

reīgr̄o *redintegratio.*

rel^{a} *reliqua.*

relačo *relatio.*

relaȓs *relativus.*

rela^{us} *relativus.*

relča *relicta.*

relče *relictæ.*

releū *relevium.*

relig^{o} *religio.*

reliḡ *religiosus.*

reliōē *religionem.*

relïo *religio.*

rełii *relevii.*

re^{m} *redditum.*

reme^{m} *remedium.*

remō^{t} *removet.*

rem^{t}tim^{9} *remittimus.*

rem̃ *remanens, remanet.*

rem̃ntia *remanentia.*

re^{ne} *reginæ.*

re^{o} *recordatio, restitutio.*

repli^{dum} *replicandum.*

repl^{o} *repletio, replicatio.*

repł *replegiamentum.*

reppim^{9} *repperimus.*

repug^{es} *repugnantes.*

rep^{io} *repertorio.*

reptare *reportare.*

rept^{9} *repertus.*

rep̄riare *repatriare.*

rep̄hin^{le} *reprehensibile.*

repb^{o} *reprobatio.*

req^{a} *requisitam.*

req^{i}siȶ *requisitum.*

requiš *requisitus.*

req *requirendus.*

req̄re *require, requirere.*

req̄t *requirit.*

re^{r} *realiter, requiritur, responde-*
tur.

resčm *respectum.*

res^d *respondendum.*

residen^a *residentia.*

resiđ *residentiarius.*

resig^are *resignare.*

resig^auit *resignavit.*

resigčo *resignatio.*

resign° *resignatio.*

resi^re *resaisire, resistere.*

reso^lis *resolvibilis.*

resp^ive *respective.*

respond *respondendum.*

resp^t *respondet, respondit.*

resp̄ *respectu.*

res^rccio *resurrectio.*

resti° *restitutio.*

resti^r *restituitur.*

resõ *restitutio.*

res̃ *residuum, respectum, resump-
    tionem.*

rescm *respectum.*

res̃gna^t *resignavit.*

ret^a hit *retrahit.*

retem̃to *retencmento.*

reti^nt *retinent.*

retño *retentio.*

re^t' *realiter, receptæ.*

ret̃ *retinet.*

ret̃ct^9 *retractus.*

re^u *respectu.*

re^ua *regulativa.*

reuel *revelatio.*

re^u *respectivum.*

reũncia *reverencia.*

reũnd^9 *reverendus.*

reũsio *reversio.*

reũti^r *revertitur.*

re^xive *respective.*

re^9 *reus, respectus.*

re₹ *rerum.*

rēā₹ *remanet.*

rēīo *remissio.*

rēīse *remisse.*

rēo^do *removendo.*

rcõue *removere.*

rẽ *regit, rex.*

rẽa *regula.*

rẽaris *regularis.*

rẽmēdāe *recommendare.*

rcñd^)e *respondere.*

rc̃ns *recens.*

rc̃nsal *responsalis.*

rc̃ñ^t *remanet.*

rc̃r^cio *resurrectio.*

rc̃r^s *resurrectis.*

rc̃ti *recenti.*

rc̃us *reversus.*

rfcčo *refectio, refractio.*

rfgañ *refragari.*

r^i *rei.*

ri^l' *risibilis.*

r^io *repertorio, responsio.*

riũ̃s *rivulus.*

rĩulũ *rivulum.*

r^m *respectum, responsorium, reverendum.*

r^{ma} *reverendissima.*

r^{me} *reverendissimæ, reverendissime.*

r^{m9} *reverendissimus.*

r^{nda} *reverenda.*

r^{nd9} *reverendus.*

Ro. *Roma, Romanus.*

r^o *ratio, regio, responsio.*

r^oalis *rationalis*

rob^oata *roborata.*

r^{ol}' *rationalis.*

ro^m *rationem.*

rom^a *Romana.*

rom̄na *Romana.*

rom̃ *Romanorum.*

rond^t *respondent.*

roñ *Romanæ.*

ro^s *Romanos.*

ro^{tes} *rogantes.*

r^o' *resurrectionem.*

rōa *Roma, Romana.*

rōā *Romam.*

rōāā *Romanam.*

rō *rotulo.*

rōab^{ter} *rationabiliter.*

rŏbi^b' *rationabilibus.*

rōbilis *rationabilis.*

rōbir *rationabiliter.*

rōbi^t' *rationabiliter.*

rōb̄r *rationabiliter.*

rōci^m *ratiocinium.*

rōcina^s *ratiocinatis.*

rōcināi *ratiocinari.*

rōci^o' *ratiocinationem.*

rōciac̄o *ratiocinatio.*

rōe *ratione, Romanæ.*

rō^{lis} *rationalis, rationabilis.*

rōm *rationem.*

rōnos *Romanos.*

rōnoȝ *Romanorum.*

rōn^s *Romanos, Romanus.*

rō^r *rationaliter, rationabiliter.*

rōs *Romanos.*

r. p. *reverendus pater.*

rq^r *requiratur.*

rqt^r *requiritur.*

rq̃ *requiritur.*

r^r *redditur, rependitur, requiratur, respondetur.*

rr. *requiratur, reverendissimi.*

r^s *regulativus, requisitus.*

r^{sū} *responsum.*

r̃s *respondit.*

r^t *reddit, respondet, restituit.*

r^{ta} *registrata, rescripta.*

rt^onat⁹ *retornatus.*

r^u *redditu, respectu.*

rubⁱca *rubrica.*

rub̄ *ruber, rubeus.*

rubica *rubrica.*

ru^o *rubeo, rubro.*

r^ur̃ *resurrectis.*

r̄ᵘ *redditum, respectum, respon-*
  sum.

℞ *recipe, Regis, Regum (Book*
  of Kings in the Bible), re-
  quisitus, Rex.

℞bit *respondebit.*

r̄ *receptor, reddit, rei, relevio,*
  respondendum, responsum,
  80000.

r̄alę *realis.*

r̄at *realis.*

r̄atr *realiter.*

r̄aᵐᵃ *realissima.*

r̄aʳ *realiter.*

r̄at, r̄ᵃᵗ *registrat, regulat.*

r̄atoȝ *registratorum.*

r̄aⱡ *realiter.*

r̄bᵗ *reddebat, respondebat, respon-*
  debit.

r̄oc̃o *resurrectio.*

r̄ce *recte.*

r̄cepᵒ *receptio.*

r̄ciᵈᵒ *recipiendo.*

r̄ciᵈⁿ *recipiendum.*

r̄ciⁿᵉ *rectitudine.*

r̄ciⁿˢ *recipiens.*

r̄cipᵗ *recipit.*

r̄cipc̄ātʳ *reciprocantur.*

r̄ciᵗ *recipit.*

r̄ciᵗᵃ *recitata.*

r̄cit̃ *recitat.*

r̄coor *rector.*

r̄cores *rectores.*

r̄corę *rectoris.*

r̄coȝ *rectorum.*

r̄cte *recte.*

r̄ctiⁿᶜ *rectitudine.*

r̄ctos *rectos.*

r̄ctös *rectores.*

r̄c̃ata *recitata.*

r̄c̃or *rector.*

r̄c̃re *recurrere.*

r̄c̃us *rectus.*

r̄ꞇgᵒ *recognitio.*

r̄ꞇnosꞔe *recognoscere.*

r̄da *reverenda.*

r̄daʳ *recordatur.*

r̄daȝ *reverendarum.*

r̄dā *reverendam.*

r̄ddeᵒ *reddendo.*

r̄ddᵐ *reddendum.*

r̄ddʳ *redditur.*

r̄det *respondet.*

r̄dēpc̃o *redemptio.*

r̄duᵃ *redundantia.*

r̄ducⱼʳ *reducuntur.*

r̄duᵈ' *reducendum.*

r̄duʳ *reducitur.*

r̄dūʳ *reducuntur.*

r̄de *respondere.*

r̄dnᵈ' *respondendum.*

r̄e *respondere.*

r̄fiꞔe *reficere.*

r̄fiᵈⁿ *reficiendum.*

r̄fořta *reformata.*
r̄fctºiū *refectorium.*
r̄fnᵗ *refrenet.*
r̄ft *refert.*
r̄gał *regalis.*
r̄gᵃta *registrata.*
r̄gē *regem.*
r̄gǵti *reaggravati.*
r̄gim̃ *regimen.*
r̄gīa *regina.*
r̄gīe *reginæ.*
r̄gīe *regimine.*
r̄gīn *regimen.*
r̄gᵐ *regem, regum.*
r̄gn̂atᵍ *regeneratus.*
r̄gº *regno, regulo.*
r̄gʳ *regitur.*
r̄gˢ *regis, regulis.*
r̄gᵗ *regnavit.*
r̄gułtᵗ *regulariter.*
r̄guʳ *regulariter.*
r̄gla *regula.*
r̄glaʳ *regulatur.*
r̄gm *regulam, regulum, regnum.*
r̄gº *recognitio.*
r̄hre *rehabere.*
r̄ipuᶜᵉ *reipublicæ.*
r̄iss̃ *remissis.*
r̄la, r̄ˡᵃ *regula.*
r̄laᵃ *regulata.*
r̄labr *relabitur.*
r̄ˡᵃ'ᵉ *regulare.*

r̄le *regale, regulæ.*
r̄libȝ *realibus.*
r̄ˡibȝ *regularibus.*
r̄lineᵉ *religione.*
r̄liñʳ *relinquitur.*
r̄liº *religio.*
r̄liqʳ *relinquitur.*
r̄lᵐ *relativum.*
r̄lōis *relationis.*
r̄lteᵉ *relative.*
r̄ł *regulis.*
r̄ło *relatio.*
r̄lteᵉ *relative.*
r̄łtïa *relativa.*
r̄łtoȝ *relatorum.*
r̄łuaʳ *relevatur.*
r̄m *regulam, rem, respectum, reum.*
r̄memᵐ *remedium.*
r̄mēoʳ *rememoratur.*
r̄mïsceᵃ *reminiscentia.*
r̄moᵃ *remota.*
r̄moºᵗ *remotionem.*
r̄mʳ *regulamur.*
r̄mˢ *remittimus.*
r̄mᵗ *remanet, remansit, remittit.*
r̄m̃tēˢ *remittemus.*
r̄ⁿ *regimen.*
r̄ndemᵍ *respondemus.*
r̄ndet *respondet.*
r̄ndetʳ *respondetur.*
r̄ndit *respondit.*

r̃nd^t *respondet.*
r̃n^d' *respondendum.*
r̃nđ *respondet.*
r̃nđdo *respondendo.*
r̃nđe *respondere.*
r̃nđi *responderi.*
r̃n^e *respondere.*
r̃n^o *respondeo, responsio, responso.*
r̃ns *respondens.*
r̃nsał *responsalis.*
r̃nsio *responsio.*
r̃ns^m *responsum.*
r̃nso *responso.*
r̃ns^t *responsit.*
r̃nt *respondent.*
r̃n^t *respondet, respondit.*
r̃ntans *repræsentans.*
r̃ntē *referentem, respondentem.*
r̃nt^r *regulantur.*
r̃ñb^t *respondebit.*
r̃ñr *respondetur.*
r̃ñt *respondet.*
r̃o *ratio, recepto, rotulo.*
r̃oał *rationalis.*
r̃o^do *ratiocinando.*
r̃oe *ratione.*
r̃oē *rationem.*
r̃om *rationem.*
r̃one *ratione.*
r̃oni *rationi.*
r̃on^les *rationabiles.*
r̃o^s *rationis.*

r̃o^t' *rationabiliter.*
r̃oe *ratione.*
r̃^oe *responsione.*
r̃oē *rationem.*
r̃oi *rationi.*
r̃ois *rationis.*
r̃om *rationem.*
r̃pet^ur *repetuntur.*
r̃per̃^r *repetatur.*
r̃pti *rescripti.*
r̃pt^m *rescriptum.*
r̃ptū *rescriptum.*
r̃ptę *rescriptis.*
r̃pĭ *rescriptum.*
r̃pugn^a *repugnantia.*
r̃pûbāt *reputabant.*
r̃pačo *reparatio.*
r̃patū *reparatum.*
r̃pit *reperit.*
r̃pit^r *reperitur.*
r̃piût^r *reperiuntur.*
r̃pt *reparat.*
r̃ptare *reportare.*
r̃ptū *repertum.*
r̃pll^ͻe *repellere.*
r̃plsā *repulsam.*
r̃pls^ͻ *repulsus.*
r̃png^a *repugnantia.*
r̃phe^t *repræhendit.*
r̃pn^t *repræsentat.*
r̃pntañ *repræsentantes.*
r̃psn^di *representandi.*

r̄p̃ᵗ *repræsentat, repræsentet.*

r̄p̃ᵗᵃᵗ *repræsentat.*

r̄pmissiᵒē *repromissionem.*

r̄qⁱʳ' *requireret.*

r̄qᵗ *requirit.*

r̄q̇ʳ *requiritur.*

r̄q̇rit *requirit.*

r̄q̇ritʳ *requiritur.*

r̄rē *regularem.*

r̄ribȝ *regularibus.*

r̄ris *regularis.*

r̄rit̃ *regulariter.*

r̄rᵐ *rerum.*

r̄rᵒm *resurrectionem.*

r̄rᵒ' *resurrectionem.*

r̄rȝ *rerum.*

r̄r̄ *rerum.*

r̄s *regulas, res, respondet.*

r̄sᶜⁱᵒ *resurrectio.*

r̄sᵒ'ᵐ *resurrectionem.*

r̄spᵗᵘ *respectu.*

r̄stiᵒ *restitutio.*

r̄s⁹ *rursus.*

r̄s̃ *residuo.*

r̄s̃uare *reservare.*

r̄s̃uaĩ *reservatum.*

r̄s̃uātʳ *reservantur.*

r̄ᵗ *regulat.*

r̄ᵗᵃ *registrata.*

r̄tᵃc̃s *retractis.*

r̄tᵃhᵗ *retrahit.*

r̄tᵃnsiēs *retransiens.*

r̄th̃t *retrahit.*

r̄ti *recti.*

r̄tīeʳ *retinetur.*

r̄tīere *retinere.*

r̄tīēcia *retinentia.*

r̄tïa *regulativa.*

r̄to *recto.*

r̄tᵒ *retro.*

r̄tᵒgᵉ *retrograde.*

r̄tᵒg̃de *retrograde.*

r̄tᵒnare *retornare.*

r̄tᵒnatū *retornatum.*

r̄tʳ *regulatur.*

r̄troᵗę *retroscriptis.*

r̄ᵗᵘ *redditu, respectu.*

r̄ᵗ⁹ *respectus.*

r̄ctū *retractum.*

r̄th̃ʲe *retrahere.*

r̄r̄nsiuit *retransivit.*

r̄ᵘᵃ *relativa.*

r̄uereᵃ *reverentia.*

r̄uocare *revocare.*

r̄uocatū *revocatum.*

r̄uõre *revocare.*

r̄uõt *revocat.*

r̄ᵘˢ *respectus.*

r̄ūᵃ *revera.*

r̄ūb̄ātʳ *reverberantur.*

r̄ūentia *reverentia.*

r̄ūlsis *revulsis.*

r̄ūb̃'ātʳ *reverberantur.*

r̄ũenᵃ *reverentia.*

r̃uencia *reverentia.*

r̃ūēd⁹ *reverendus.*

r̃uet̃ *reverenter.*

r̃usio *reversio.*

r̃utaʳ *revertatur.*

r̃uti *reverti.*

r̃utiʳ *revertitur.*

r̃x *rex.*

r̃xiue *respective.*

r̃xᵗ *rexit.*

r̃⁹ *redditus, requisitus.*

r̃ʒ *rerum.*

S.

S. *sanctitas, sanctus, scilicet, scriptum, secundus, sed, seisina, septuaginta, sepultus, sequitur, serenissimus, servi, sibi, sigillum, signum, siliginis, sine, sit, sive, socmanni, soka, solidi, subscripsi, subscripsit, sunt, supra.*

s. ꝉ. b. *soka et berewica.*

s. ꝉ. so. *saca et soca.*

sᵃ *secunda, substantia, supra.*

sabb̃i *sabbati.*

sacᵃ *sacramentum.*

sacᵃˡ' *sacramentalis.*

sacᵃm̃tū *sacramentum.*

sacⁱfⁱᵃ *sacrificia.*

sac°rū *sacrorum.*

sac°sc̃e *sacrosanctæ.*

sacrᵃ *sacramenta.*

sac̃ris *sacramenʤis.*

sac̃ʳᵐ *sacramentum.*

sac̃ro *sacramento.*

sac̃ *saca, sacerdos, sacramentum, sacrificium.*

sac̃ᵇʒ *sacerdotibus.*

sac̃ˡⁱˢ *sacerdotalis, sacramentalis.*

sac̃ꝉii *sacrilegii.*

sac̃m̃tū *sacramentum.*

sac̃m̃t̃ *sacramenʤum.*

sac̃ᵗᵃ *sacramenta.*

sac̃ᵗᵉ *sacerdote.*

sac̃ᵗⁱ *sacramenti.*

sac̃ᵗᵘᵐ *sacerdotum, sacramentum.*

sac̃tę *sacramentis.*

sᵃdc̃s *supradictus.*

saec̃ *sæculum.*

sᵃempt̃ *supraemptus.*

saēna *saenna.*

sagēa *sagena.*

saisiēđ *saisiendum.*

saisit°e *saisitore.*

saisīa *saisina.*

sal°tū *salictum.*

salinař *salinarum.*

salīⁱⁱ *salinarii.*

salu° *salutatio.*

salūᵐ *salvagurdiam.*

sal̵ *salina, salis, salutem.*

sal̵m *salutem.*

sal̵ⁿᵉ *salvatione.*

sal̵ᵒʳ *salvator.*

sal̵ĩ *salutem.*

sancx̃ *sanxit.*

sanᵉ *sanguine.*

sanⁱˢ *sanguinis.*

san⁹ *sanus.*

sapᵃ *sapientia.*

sapᵉ *sapiente, sapientiæ.*

sapᵉʳ *sapienter.*

sapiᵃ *sapientia.*

sapiᵗᵘ *sapientum.*

sap̃ia *sapientia.*

sᵃsᵃ *suprascripta.*

sasīa *sasina.*

sasīe *sasinæ.*

saᵗᵘ *sacramentum.*

satȩ *satis.*

satȩfaĉe *satisfacere.*

sat̃fc̃m *satisfactum.*

sat̃ⁿᵉ *satisfactione.*

sᵃuenđ *supravenditus.*

sᵃ *secundam.*

sāgᵉ *sanguine.*

sāgⁱnȩ *sanguinis.*

sāgⁿᵉ *sanguine.*

sāgˢ *sanguis.*

sāg̃ĩē *sanguinem.*

sāg̃is *sanguinis.*

sāg̃s *sanguis, sanguinis.*

sāine *saisinæ.*

sāitas *sanitas.*

sāiᵗᵉ *sanitate.*

sāiᵗȩ *sanitatis.*

sāū *sanum.*

sā⁹ *sanus.*

sāina *saisina.*

sāia *saisina.*

sb̃ *sub.*

sb̃a *substantia.*

sb̃t⁹ *subtus.*

sc. *sciant.*

sᶜ *sic.*

sᶜᵃ *sancta.*

scacc° *scaccario.*

scacc̃ *scaccarium.*

scaĉi *scacci.*

scᵃc̃m *scaccarium.*

scābiū *scambium.*

scāgiū *scangium.*

scđ *secundum.*

scⁱ *scripsi, scriptum.*

sci^a *scientia.*

sciat℮ *sciatis.*

scⁱbi *scribi.*

scⁱb͛e *scribere.*

sci^{d'} *sciendum.*

sci^e *scientiæ, scire.*

sciĕꝶ *scienter.*

scit *scilicet.*

scⁱpt^ra *scriptura.*

scⁱptū *scriptum.*

scⁱpt̃ *scriptum.*

scⁱpt̃e *scripturæ.*

sci^{ter} *scienter.*

sci^t℮ *scientis.*

scīm *sciendum.*

scł *scilicet.*

scłaris *secularis.*

scło *sæculo.*

sco. *scola.*

sco^{rium} *scolarium.*

sc^rbtur *scribitur.*

scrib̄r *scribitur.*

s^ct℮ *sectis.*

scuⁱ *scutiferi.*

sc^upul⁹ *scrupulus.*

scutełł *scutellarius.*

scutuł *scutularius.*

scuῦ *scutifer.*

scũ *scutiferi.*

s^{c'}o *significatio.*

sc̃ *sanctus, sciant.*

sc̃a *sancta.*

sc̃ā *sanctam.*

sc̃bi^r *scribitur.*

sc̃b^t *scribit.*

sc̃b̄e *scribere.*

sc̃bet^r *scriberetur.*

sc̃b̄r *scribitur.*

sc̃b͛e *scribere.*

sc̃b͛ ēt *scriberent.*

sc̃da *secunda.*

sc̃do *secundo.*

sc̃d⁹ *secundus.*

sc̃ꝺm *secundum.*

sc̃ꝺs *secundus.*

sc̃e *sanctæ, sancte.*

sc̃i *sancti.*

sc̃ia *scientia.*

sc̃iā *scientiam.*

sc̃ie *scientiæ.*

sc̃ific^o *sanctificatio.*

sc̃iis *scientiis.*

sc̃imōiał *sanctimonialis.*

sc̃io *sanctio.*

sc̃is *sanctis.*

sc̃iss̃⁹ *sanctissimus.*

sc̃iśm⁹ *sanctissimus.*

sc̃i⁹ *sanctius.*

sc̃lare *sæculare.*

sc̃lū *sæculum.*

sc̃ł *scilicet.*

sc̃m *sanctum.*

sc̃mbiū *scambium.*

sc̃o *sancto.*

sc̃°em *sanctionem.*

sc̃oʒ *sanctorum.*

sc̃pt^r a *scriptura.*

sc̃pt^r e *scripturæ.*

sc̃ptū *scriptum.*

sc̃ptҫ *scriptis.*

sc̃p̃a *scriptura.*

sc̃p̅^m *scriptum.*

sc̃s *sanctus.*

sc̃uariū *sanctuarium.*

sc̃us *sanctus, secundus.*

sc̃ũio *sanctuario.*

sc̃⁹ *sanctus.*

s^d *sed, sicut.*

s. d. *salutem dat, sine die, sub die.*

se. *sede.*

sec^e ta^i⁹ *secretarius.*

sec^e tҫ *secretis.*

sec^r i *securi.*

seculʒ *sæculorum.*

secūt^r *sequuntur.*

sec̃ *secum, secus.*

sec̃la *sæcula.*

sec̃lū *sæculum.*

sec̃m *securum.*

sec╻ *secum.*

sed^s *sedis.*

sed^t *sedit.*

sed̃ *sedem, sedes, sedis.*

se^e *sæpe.*

se^e dc̃s *sæpedictus.*

seĩs *seisina.*

seïa *semina.*

seïaɫ *seminalis.*

seïant^r *seminantur.*

se^lo *senescallo.*

semp *semper.*

sem̃ *semen.*

sem̃l *semel.*

sen^a *sententia.*

sen^a o *senescallo.*

sen^b ʒ *sensibilibus.*

sen^c tute *senectute.*

senes. *senescallus.*

sen^le *senile, sensibile, sensuale.*

sen^ua *sensitiva.*

sep^a *septima.*

sept^a m *septimanam.*

septēt^i o *septentrio.*

septi^a *septimana.*

septim̃ *septimana.*

septĩa *septimana.*

septuãsīa *septuagesima.*

sep̃t *septimana.*

sepuɫ̃t *sepultura, sepultus.*

sep^a *separata.*

sepab^r *separabitur.*

sepac̃o *separatio.*

sepalҫ *separalis.*

sepaɫ^ℓ *separaliter.*

sepatī *separatim.*

sepc̃o *separatio.*

sep^dū *separandum.*

sep^lis *separabilis.*

sepnt^r *separantur.*
sepŏ *separatio.*
sep̃ *separate, sepes.*
sep̃^a *septima.*
sep̃^e *septimæ.*
sep̃lc̆m *sepulcrum.*
sep̃lis *separabilis, separalis.*
sep̃^lis *septentrionalis.*
sep̃na *septimana.*
seq^ela *sequela.*
seq^encia *sequentia.*
seq^estrū *sequestrum.*
seq^i *sequenti, sequi.*
seq^it^r *sequitur.*
seq^r *sequitur.*
seq^tę *sequentis.*
sequeñ *sequentium.*
seq̃oē *sequacem.*
seq̃ł *secularibus, sequela.*
seq̃r *sequitur.*
seq̃s *sequens.*
seq̃^s *sequentes.*
seq̃st^ari *sequestrari.*
seq̃t^r *sequuntur.*
se^r *sequeretur, sequitur.*
seruic̆ *servicium.*
seru^iiū *servitium.*
seru^t *servit.*
serū *serviens, servitium, servus.*
serū^tes *servientes.*
se^ta *separata.*
se. ua. *sede vacante.*

se^ue *sensitive.*
sex^a *sexagena, sexaginta.*
sext^aiū *sextarium.*
se^9 *secus.*
sēē *semen.*
sēis *seminis.*
sēp^m *sempiternum.*
sēp *semper.*
sēp̃rnū *sempiternum.*
sēsiēciū *sentientium.*
sēis *seminis.*
sēl *semel.*
sēre^r *sequeretur.*
s^i *sibi.*
sicci^te *siccitate.*
sic^t *sicut.*
sic^tas *siccitas.*
sic̃ *sicut.*
si^d *sicut.*
sig^am^9 *significamus.*
sig^auit *significavit.*
sig^cre *significare.*
sig^m *sigillum, signum.*
sig^o *sigillo, signo.*
sig̃care *significare.*
sig̃^cat *significat.*
sig̃cās *significans.*
sig̃ołm *signaculum.*
sig̃co *significatio.*
sig̃c̃t *significat.*
sig̃fi^re *significare.*
sig̃icare *significare.*

sig̃lli *sigilli.*

sig̃ltm *sigillum.*

sig̃lū *sigillum.*

sig̃t *sigillum.*

sig̃o *sigillo, significatio.*

sig̃ºm *significationem.*

sig̃ones *significationes.*

sig̃r *significatur.*

sig̃tū *signatum.*

silig̃ *siligo, siliginis.*

siliqȝ *siliquarum.*

silū *silva.*

silūre *silvestre.*

silȝ *scilicet.*

silę *siliginis.*

silt *siligo.*

sila *similia.*

silc *scilicet.*

silit *similiter.*

silr *similiter.*

sitt *scilicet.*

simª *similia.*

simtr *similiter.*

simpⁱ *simplici.*

simptr *simpliciter.*

simpr *simpliciter.*

simr *simpliciter.*

simˣ *simplex.*

sim̃l *simul.*

sim̃t *simpliciter.*

sinᵇȝ *singularibus.*

sing̃ *singulos.*

sing̃la *singula.*

sint *singulis.*

siñla *singula.*

siñˡᵒˢ *singulos.*

siñʳⁱˢ *singularis.*

sine *sinere.*

sⁱpta *scripta.*

sⁱptʳa *scriptura.*

siqª *siqua.*

siqᵉ *siquem.*

siq̇ *siquis.*

siq̇s *siquis.*

siʳ *similiter.*

sirothecaȝ *chirothecarum.*

sⁱˢ *suis.*

sⁱt *sicut.*

siū *sive.*

sībolū *symbolum.*

sīᶜᵉ *simplicem.*

sīᶜⁱᵇȝ *simplicibus.*

sicm *sincerum.*

sīgˡ' *singulis.*

sīgʳ *singulariter.*

sīgᵗ' *singulariter.*

sig̃bȝ *singularibus.*

sīistm *sinistram.*

sīᵒʳ *simplicior.*

sīptr *simpliciter.*

sīpt *simpliciter.*

sīpʳ *simpliciter.*

sīpˣ *simplex.*

sīpᶜⁱ *simplici.*

sīr̃ᵉ *singularem.*

sīrib₃ *singularibus.*

sīx *simplex.*

sīcit̃ᵖ *simpliciter.*

sīe *sive.*

sīia *simonia.*

sīl *simul.*

sīlac̃o *simulatio.*

sīlat *simulat.*

sīle *simile.*

sīlet *simulet.*

sīlē *similem.*

sīli *simili.*

sīlib₃ *similibus.*

sīliᵈᵒ *similitudo.*

sīliᵉ *similitudine.*

sīliᵒ *simili modo.*

sīlis *similis, singulis.*

sīlituᵉˢ *similitudines.*

sīlit̃ᵖ *similiter.*

sīlīdᵐ *similitudinem.*

sīlīr *similiter.*

sīlla *sigilla.*

sīllᵇ₃ *syllabarum.*

sīllᵉ *syllabæ.*

sīˡᵒ *singulo, symbolo.*

sīˡᵒˢ *singulos.*

sīła *similia.*

sīłr *similiter.*

sīstᵃm *sinistram.*

słm *salutem.*

sło *solutio.*

sĩt̃ *salutem.*

sł̃t *scilicet.*

smᵃ *summa.*

sᵐᵃ *sanctissima.*

sᵐᵘˢ *sanctissimus.*

sm̃ū *summum.*

sⁿ *sed tamen.*

sñ *sine.*

sñia *sententia.*

sñiałr *sententialiter.*

sñia₃ *sententiarum.*

soᵃ *sola.*

socɧ̃ *soca, socemannus.*

sock̃₃ *socarum.*

soc̃ *socæ.*

soldᵃii *soldarii.*

solidatᵽ *solidatis.*

solid̃ *solidus.*

solliⁿᵉ *solicitudine.*

solʳ *solvitur.*

soluᵒᵒ *solummodo.*

solūᵒ *solummodo.*

sol₃ *solet.*

soł *solent, solidata, solidus, solum.*

soło *solummodo, solutio.*

sołor *solicitor.*

sołõm *solutionem.*

sołr *solvitur.*

soł₃ *solent.*

soᵐ *solum.*

soᵒ *solo, solutio.*

sō *solet, solum, solus, solutio.*

spa^a *spatia.*

spa^m *spatium.*

spa^o *spatio.*

spāo *spatio.*

sp^c *spectantem.*

sp^cta^s *spectamus.*

sp^ctat *spectat.*

sp^ctās *spectans.*

spe^{ce} *specifice.*

speci^{ti} *specificati.*

spečo *speculo.*

spečl^{uo} *speculativo.*

spec^ū *speculativum.*

sp^eta *spreta.*

sp^eu^ai⁹ *spervarius.*

spĕalis *specialis.*

spĕa^{mc} *specialissimæ.*

spĕer *specialiter.*

spēi *speciei.*

spēliꝑ *specialiter.*

spēs *species.*

spē^{ua} *speculativa.*

spⁱalis *spiritualis.*

sp^{ib}ȝ *spiritibus.*

spiīū *spirituum.*

sp^{itu} *spiritu.*

spĩtalis *spiritualis.*

spīetū *spinetum.*

spī^{is} *spirationis.*

spĩalis *spiritualis.*

spīaria *spiciaria.*

spībȝ *spiritibus.*

spī^{lis} *spiritualis.*

spō^{lia} *sponsalia.*

spōsa *sponsa.*

spōsa *speciosa.*

sp *semper.*

sp^a *sperma.*

ꝰpare *sperare.*

spāt^r *sperantur.*

spꝑgit^r *spargitur.*

spnend *spernendum.*

spn̂e *spernere.*

spu^ai⁹ *spervarius.*

sp̃ *speciem.*

sp̃a^bȝ *specialibus.*

sp̃alis *specialis, spiritualis.*

sp̃aliꝑ *specialiter, spiritualiter.*

sp̃aliū *spiritualium.*

sp̃ałbȝ *specialibus, spiritualibus.*

sp̃ałr *specialiter, spiritualiter.*

sp̃a^m *specialem.*

sp̃a^{mc} *specialissime.*

sp̃a^r *specialiter, spiritualiter.*

sp̃a^{te} *specialitate.*

sp̃e *specie.*

sp̃ea^{mc} *specialissime.*

sp̃eā^r *specialiter.*

sp̃ē *speciem.*

sp̃ialis *specialis.*

sp̃it⁹ *spiritus.*

sp̃lis *specialis.*

sp̃liꝑ *specialiter.*

sp̄m *spatium, spiritum.*

sp̄o *spatio.*

sp̄ralis *spiritualis.*

sp̄ralit̃ *spiritualiter.*

sp̄rli *spirituali.*

sp̄s *species, spiritus, suspensus.*

sp̄tactm *spectaculum.*

sp̄u *spiritu.*

sp̄ualis *spiritualis.*

sp̄ulē *spiritualem.*

sp̄ut *spiritualis.*

sp̄utr *spiritualiter.*

sp̄us *spiritus.*

sp̄uᵗ' *spiritualiter.*

sp̄ūr *spiritualiter.*

sp̄⁹ *spiritus.*

sp̄tis *spretis.*

sqⁱllᵃia *squillaria.*

sqⁱllari⁹ *squillarius.*

sʳ *super.*

sʳgūt *surgunt.*

sʳg̃ *surgent, surgit, surgunt.*

s. r. i. *sacrum Romanum impe-*
rium.

ss. *sacerdotes, sancti, sanctissi-*
mus, scilicet, secundus, sen-
sus, sestertii, Spiritus Sanc-
tus, suis, sunt.

stᵃ *strata.*

stabilic̄o *stabilitio.*

stabᵗᵃˢ *stabilitas.*

stᵃciatū *straciatum.*

stᵃg̃tur *strangulatur.*

stᵃīe *stramine.*

stᵃmē *stramen.*

stᵃta *strata.*

stᵃtag̃a *stratagema.*

statᵐ *statutum.*

statuᵐ *statutum.*

stᵃtum *stratum.*

staî̃ᵐ *statutum.*

stāgnū *stangnum (stagnum).*

sᵗᵉᵐ *sanctitatem.*

stⁱct⁹ *strictus.*

stⁱg̃e *stringere.*

stⁱmān⁹ *stiremannus.*

stip̄to *stipulatio.*

strāē *stramen.*

strīg̃e *stringere.*

sĩcte *stricte.*

sĕct⁹ *strictus.*

sĩlla *stella.*

sĩmē *stramen.*

sĭmīa *stramina.*

sĭngᵗ *stringit.*

sĩng̃tur *strangulatur, stringitur.*

sĩo *statuto.*

st̃ *stermannus.*

sl̃ilᵗᵃˢ *sterilitas.*

sl̃it *sterilis.*

sl̃man⁹ *stermannus.*

sᵗ *sed.*

suᵃ *summa.*

subalt̃ñ *subalternative.*

subpōnes *suppositiones.*
subs⁰ *sub sigillo.*
suƀa *substantia.*
suƀaᵃ *substantia.*
suƀalis *substantialis.*
suƀā *substantiam.*
suƀe *substantiæ, substantive.*
suƀis *substantiis.*
succᵘᵉ *successive.*
succõ *successio.*
succõom *successionem.*
succ͂ᵗ *succedit, succidit.*
sudõe *sudore.*
suᵉ *summæ.*
suffiᵃ *sufficientia.*
suffic͂a *sufficientia.*
suffiⁿˢ *sufficiens.*
suffiⁿᵗ’ *sufficienter.*
sufᵗ *sufficit.*
sum⁹ *sumus.*
sum̄a *summa.*
sum̄⁹ *summus.*
sum̃ *summonitio, summonitor,*
    summonitum.
sum̃a *summa.*
sum̃ᵃi⁹ *summarius.*
sum̃s *sumens, sumptus.*
suõre *summonere.*
supᵃ *supra.*
sup⁰ *supplicatio.*
suppᶜᵃᵒ *supplicatio.*
suppᶜᵃᵗ *supplicat.*

suppeᵃ *sub pœna.*
suppʳ *supplicatur, supponitur.*
suppp̃ᵈⁱ *supplicandi.*
suppp̃ᵉ *suppone, suppositæ.*
suppp̃ᵐ *suppositum.*
suppp̃o *suppositio, supposito.*
suppp̃ᵗᵃ *supposita.*
suppp̃ᵗᵘ *suppositum.*
sup *super.*
supb⁹ *superbus.*
supciliū *supercilium.*
suphiɗ *superhidagium.*
supiᵇℨ *superioribus.*
supiᵒitas *superioritas.*
supiᵒitᵗᵉ *superioritate.*
supioᵐ *superiorem.*
supi⁹ *superius.*
supnū *supernum.*
supᵒtas *superioritas.*
suppl⁹ *superplusagium.*
supsƀalis *supersubstantialis.*
supus̃ *supervisor.*
sup̃ᵗᵘ *suppositum.*
sup̃m̃ *suppositum.*
sup̃mū *supremum.*
sup̃m⁹ *supremus.*
surcɩs *surculus.*
suᵃ *suis, superius.*
susp̃cm *suspectum.*
susp̃ns⁹ *suspensus.*
sustenɩ͂ *sustentandum.*
sustẽɗ *sustinendum.*

sustñ *sustentationem.*

su^t *sunt.*

suū *suum.*

sū^a *summa.*

sūend *sumendum.*

sūi *summi.*

sūi^r *sumitur.*

sūit *sumit.*

sūma *summa.*

sūmagiū *summagium.*

sūm^a i^9 *summarius.*

sūmāie *summariæ.*

sūme *summæ.*

sūmoïa *summonita.*

sūm^9 *summus.*

sūm̃ *summonita.*

sū° *summo.*

sūope *summopere.*

sūpc̃o *sumptio.*

sūp̃^ne *sumptione.*

sūū *summum.*

sū^9 *sumus.*

sū *sive.*

sy^a *symonia.*

sȳo^a *symonia.*

sȳo^a ̈ *symoniacis.*

s3 *sed.*

s3o *secundo.*

s; *sed.*

s^9 *suspendatur, suspensus.*

s^9 cipied *suscipiendum.*

s^9 cipe *suscipere.*

s^9 pect^9 *suspectus.*

s^9 pēd^j e *suspendere.*

s^9 pēsū *suspensum.*

s^9 pic̈e *suspicere.*

s^9 p̃cm *suspectum.*

s^9 p̃i^r *suspenditur.*

s^9 p̃ns^9 *suspensus.*

s^9 tent̃ *sustentaculum, sustentatio, sustentum.*

s^9 tiñe *sustinere.*

s^9 tiēd *sustinendum.*

S̄ *70000.*

s̃ *scilicet, semper, septimana.*

s̃a *secunda, sua.*

s̃arie *secundariæ.*

s̃ario *secundario.*

s̃ā *secundam, suam.*

s̃b *sub.*

s̃bbo *sabbato.*

s̃b^c e *subjectæ.*

s̃b^c o *subjecto.*

s̃bdel *subdelegatus.*

s̃b^c *subjectæ, substantiæ.*

s̃bē *subest.*

s̃b^ia *substantia.*

s̃bic̃tū *subjectum.*

s̃bic̃o *subjectio.*

s̃bic̃s *subjectus.*

s̃biūg^t *subjungit.*

s̃bītltndo *subintelligendo.*

s̃bli^tas *sublimitas.*

s̃b^m *subjectum.*

s̄bp̄o *supposito.*

s̄bsc̄b^m *subscribendum.*

s̄bstā^cio *substantiatio.*

s̄bsĩco *substractio.*

s̄bsĩ^tis *substitutis.*

s̄bsĩ^to *substituto, substrato.*

s̄bs̃t *subsunt.*

s̄bs̃tn^ia *subsistentia.*

s̄bs̃ťe *subsistere.*

s̄bt^accio *subtractio.*

s̄bt^ah)e *subtrahere.*

s̄btiť *subtilis.*

s̄bti^tas *subtilitas.*

s̄bt⁹ *subtus.*

s̄bĩco *subtractio.*

s̄bĩh)e *subtrahere.*

s̄bĩxīt *subtraxerint.*

s̄bũsōm *subversionem.*

s̄b̄a *substantia.*

s̄b̄aliť *substantialiter.*

s̄b̄aɫ *substantialis.*

s̄b̄a^r *substantialiter.*

s̄b̄ū *substantiam.*

s̄b̄ā^m *substantivum.*

s̄b̄e *substantiæ.*

s̄b̄i *subjecti.*

s̄b̄ia *substantia.*

s̄b̄iis *substantiis.*

s̄b̄iua *substantiva.*

s̄b̄m *subjectum, substantiam.*

s̄b̄t *subest.*

s̄b̄t⁹ *subitus.*

s̄ca *sancta.*

s̄cac̄o *significatio.*

s̄ca^r *significatur.*

s̄cas *sanctas.*

s̄cat *significat.*

s̄caȝ *sanctarum.*

s̄cci^tē *siccitatem.*

s̄cep^o *susceptio.*

s̄cia *scientia.*

s̄cie *scientiæ.*

s̄c^ifi^o *sacrificio.*

s̄ciis *scientiis.*

s̄cio *sanctio.*

s̄ciōū *sanctionum.*

s̄cip̄dū *suscipiendum.*

s̄cip̄e *suscipere.*

s̄cir^t *sanciret.*

s̄ci⁹ *sanctius.*

s̄cla *sæcula.*

s̄clare *sæculare.*

s̄cli *sæculi.*

s̄clo *sæculo.*

s̄cloȝ *sæculorum.*

s̄cɫm *sæculum.*

s̄cɫris *sæcularis.*

s̄c^oem *sanctionem,significationem.*

s̄co^m *significationem.*

s̄c^r *significatur.*

s̄cs *sanctus.*

s̄c^t *significat.*

s̄cus *sanctus.*

s̄c⁹ *sanctus.*

s̄c̄ *sacer, sanctus.*

s̄c̄a *sacra, sancta.*

s̄c̄e *sacræ, sanctæ.*

s̄c̄la *sæcula.*

s̄c̄lare *sæculare.*

s̄c̄li *sæculi.*

s̄c̄lo *sæculo.*

s̄c̄loꝛ *sæculorum.*

s̄c̄s *sanctus.*

s̄dc̄us *supradictus.*

s̄dᵒ *surdus.*

s̄đus *supradictus.*

s̄ᵉ *substantiæ.*

s̄ffⁱᵉⁿˢ *sufficiens.*

s̄ffⁱᵗ *sufficit.*

s̄ffᵗ *sufficit.*

s̄fᵗ *sufficit.*

s̄gⁱ *signi.*

s̄gᵒ *significatio.*

s̄g̃abit *significabit.*

s̄g̃at *significat.*

s̄g̃ūs *significans.*

s̄g̃āt *significant.*

s̄g̃bit *significabit.*

s̄g̃nt *significant.*

s̄g̃t *significat.*

s̄g̃tᵉ *significative.*

s̄g̃tʳ *significatur.*

s̄i *sciri, secundi.*

s̄ies *series.*

s̄ⁱˢ *secundis.*

s̄l *simul.*

s̄la *singula.*

s̄lē *substantialem.*

s̄lis *similis, singulis, substantialis.*

s̄lt̄m *salutem.*

s̄lͤ *similis, singulis.*

s̄tm *similem.*

s̄to *solutio.*

s̄te *salute.*

s̄m *secundum, summum.*

s̄ᵐ *subjectum.*

s̄mᵗ *sibimet, submittet.*

s̄m̃gᵗʳ *submergitur.*

s̄nᵃ *sententia.*

s̄nᵃᵐ *sententiam.*

s̄ndū *significandum.*

s̄nia *sententia.*

s̄niaᵗr *sententialiter.*

s̄nias *sententias.*

s̄niaꝛ *sententiarum.*

s̄niā *sententiam.*

s̄niādo *sententiando.*

s̄nie *sententiæ.*

s̄niis *sententiis.*

s̄ⁿˢ *significans.*

s̄ⁿᵗ *significant.*

s̄ñ *sine.*

s̄ᵒ *secundo, sermo.*

s̄ᵒ'm *sermonem.*

s̄ᵟᵉ *sermone.*

s̄pᶜᵗᵒ *suspectus.*

s̄pēđr *suspenditur.*

M.

L

s̅p̄ed)e *suspendere.*

s̅pēs *serpens.*

s̅pēˢ *suspendens.*

s̅pēs⁹ *suspensus.*

s̅pēt⁹ *suspectus.*

s̅pⁱᵗ' *simpliciter.*

s̅ppoꝫe *supponere.*

s̅p̄pto *supposito.*

s̅pʳ *simpliciter, super.*

s̅pˣ *simplex.*

s̅p *semper, super.*

s̅p̄c̄s *suspectus.*

s̅p̄iʳ *suspenditur.*

s̅p̄iꝉ *simpliciter.*

s̅p̄t⁹ *suspectus.*

s̅qᵉla *sequela.*

s̅r *super, superior.*

s̅ʳ *similiter, substantialiter, super.*

s̅rare *superare.*

s̅rāte *superante.*

s̅rbia *superbia.*

s̅rb⁹ *superbus.*

s̅rc̄lū *surculum.*

s̅rᵉˢ *superficies.*

s̅rexᵗ *surrexit.*

s̅rē *superficiem.*

s̅rēiᵗ *supereminet.*

s̅rfiᵇꝫ *superficiebus.*

s̅rfiᵉ *superficie.*

s̅rfiˡⁱˢ *superficialis.*

s̅rn̄nᵃ *superabundantia.*

s̅rior *superior.*

s̅riŏⁱ *superiori.*

s̅riʳᵉᵐ *superiorem.*

s̅ri⁹ *superius.*

s̅rna *superna.*

s̅rnaʳ *supernaturaliter.*

s̅rnꞁ *supernaturalis.*

s̅rnoꝫ *supernorum.*

s̅rnʳ *spernitur.*

s̅rn̄ʳ *supernaturaliter.*

s̅rn̄ *supernaturaliter.*

s̅rogat⁹ *surrogatus.*

s̅roḡe *surrogare.*

s̅rpl⁹ *superplus.*

s̅rpōdatʳ *superponderatur.*

s̅rpōt'ʳ *superponitur.*

s̅rᵗ *superest, supersit.*

s̅s *suis.*

s̅sᵃ *substantia.*

s̅scⁱbʳ *subscribitur.*

s̅sⁱ *subscripsi.*

s̅sⁱᵇlis *sensibilis.*

s̅siˡᵉ *sensibile.*

s̅siˡⁱᵃ *sensibilia.*

s̅sit *sensit.*

s̅siᵗᵃˢ *sensibilitas.*

s̅sitⁱᵘˢ *sensitivus.*

s̅siꞁ *sensibiliter.*

s̅su *sensu.*

s̅sᵘᵃ *sensitiva.*

s̅sualiꞁ *sensualiter.*

s̅suaꝉ *sensualis.*

s̅sū *sensum.*

ſsᵌ *sensus.*

ſſ *seisinam.*

ſſaᵒ *sensatio.*

ſſaʳ *sensualiter.*

ſſm *sensum.*

ſſsi *subscripsi.*

ſſᵗ *subscripsit.*

ſt *sit, sunt.*

ſᵗ *significat.*

ſᵗᵉ *significatæ.*

ſtenⁱ̃ *sustentaculum, sustentum.*

ſᵗⁱ *subjecti.*

ſtinēᵃ *sustinentia.*

ſtinᵗ *sustinet, sustinuit.*

ſtiɳe *sustinere.*

ſᵗᵒ *scripto, significato, subjecto.*

ſtʳ *significatur.*

ſᵗᵘ *scriptum, significatum, subjectum.*

ſũ *sive.*

ſx *simplex.*

ꝗico *serico.*

ꝗies *series.*

ꝗiē *seriem.*

ꝗpēs *serpens.*

ꝗpētē *serpentem.*

ꝗta *serta.*

ꝗuare *servare.*

ꝗuād *servandum.*

ꝗuiciū *servitium.*

ꝗuiēs *serviens.*

ꝗuił *servilis.*

ꝗuitᵇᣫ *servitutibus.*

ꝗuitʳa *servitura.*

ꝗuᵗ *servet.*

ꝗuū *servum.*

ꝗuᵌ *sercus.*

ꝗũs *servus.*

T.

T. *centum sexaginta, talis, taliter, tempus, tenent, tenet, tenetur, ter, terra, tertius, testamentum, testata, teste, testibus, theologiæ, tibi, titulum, tunc.*

tᵃ *talia, tertia.*

taᵃ *tabula.*

tabaɍ *tabardum.*

tᵃbs *trabs.*

tᵃctare *tractare.*

tᵃctaᵘ *tractatu.*

tᵃctᵌ *tractus.*

tᵃctᵗᵌ *tractatus.*

tᵃdc̄co *traductio.*

t^{a}dc̄o *traditio.*

t^{a}de^{r} *tradetur.*

t^{a}di *tradi.*

t^{a}dic̄o *traditio.*

t^{a}d^{o} *traditio.*

t^{a}đdo *tradendo, traducendo.*

t^{a}đr *traditur.*

t^{a}đt *traderet, tradit.*

t^{a}d⁾e *tradere.*

t^{a}hūt^{r} *trahuntur.*

t^{a}h⁾e *trahere.*

taiñ *tainus.*

ta^{la} *tabula.*

talēt̃ *talentum.*

tal^{s} *talis.*

tała *talenta.*

tałnt^{m} *talentum.*

tałr *taliter.*

tałs *talis.*

ta^{m} *tantum.*

tam̃ *tamen, tantum.*

t^{a}n$^{\bar{o}e}$ *transmutatione.*

t^{a}nq^{l}litas *tranquillitas.*

t^{a}nquillis *tranquillis.*

t^{a}ns *trans.*

t^{a}nsacc̄o *transactio.*

t^{a}nscē^{r} *transcenditur.*

t^{a}nsc^{i}b^{ur} *transcribitur.*

t^{a}nsc̄bi *transcribi.*

t^{a}nsgrōm *transgressionem.*

t^{a}nsgr̃one *transgressione.*

t^{a}nsi^{o} *transitio.*

t^{a}nsire *transire.*

t^{a}nsit^{9} *transitus.*

t^{a}nsi^{ue} *transitive.*

t^{a}nsla^{a} *translata.*

t^{a}nsło *translatio.*

t^{a}nsm^{o} *transmutatio.*

t^{a}nsm^{r} *transmutatur.*

t^{a}ns^{o} *transmutatio.*

t^{a}nsp̱ens *transparens.*

t^{a}ns^{te} *transeunte.*

t^{a}ns$^{t'}$ *transmutatum.*

t^{a}nsūpt^{9} *transumptus.*

t^{a}ns̃ *transgressio.*

t^{a}ns̃ƀa^{o} *transsubstantiatio.*

t^{a}ns̃^{lia} *transmutabilia.*

t^{a}n^{t9} *transitus.*

tant̃đ *tantundem.*

tant̃m^{o} *tantummodo.*

ta^{r} *taliter, tangitur, tardatur.*

t^{a}sło *translatio.*

tā *tam.*

tāq̃ *tanquam.*

tā^{t} *tangit.*

tātū *tantum.*

tã^{t} *tardescit.*

t^{ci} *triplici.*

tc̄ *tunc.*

te. *tenet.*

t^{e} *tempore.*

te^{a} *tenura.*

te^{do} *tenendo.*

te^{e} *tempore.*

teïoalis *testimonialis.*

temp⁹ *tempus.*

tempe *tempore.*

tᵉm̃di *tremendi.*

tem̃e *temere.*

tem̃itas *temeritas.*

tenᵃ *tenura.*

tenᵃmē *tentamen.*

tenñ *tennus (tainus).*

tenᵒē *tenorem.*

tenʳ *tenentur, tenetur.*

teñ *tenens, tenuit.*

teñs *tenens.*

teñt *tenent.*

teñtʳ *tenentur.*

teoĺn *teoloneo.*

teʳ *tenentur, tenetur.*

tᵉs *tres.*

tesm̃to *testamento.*

testamētū *testamentum.*

testāte *testante.*

testātʳ *testantur.*

testārius *testamentarius.*

testibӡ *testibus.*

testiᵐ *testimonium.*

testiō *testimonio.*

testiū *testium.*

testīoïm *testimonium.*

testīoᵐ *testimonium.*

testĩi *testamenti.*

testĩii *testimonii.*

testĩm *testamentum, testimonium.*

tesĩo *testamento, testimonio.*

tes̃ti *testamenti.*

tetrᵐ *tetricum.*

tᵉuga *treuga.*

tᵉ⁹ *tempus.*

tēᵃdʳis *tenandriis.*

tēens *tenens.*

tēet *tenet.*

tēpm *templum.*

tēpᵒ *temptatio.*

tēptaᵒ *temptatio.*

tēptio *temptatio.*

tēp⁹ *tempus.*

tēpanᵃ *temperantia.*

tēpe *tempore.*

tēp̃ *tempore.*

tētʳ *tenetur.*

tēaʳ *teneatur.*

tēbātʳ *tenebantur.*

tēbᵒsit *tenebrositatem.*

tēbᵒs⁹ *tenebrosus.*

tēbs *tenebras.*

tēmʳ *tenemur.*

tēor *teneor.*

tēre *tenere.*

thᵃm *thaxam (taxam).*

theoᵉ *theologiæ.*

theoĺ *theologiæ.*

thom̃s *Thomas, tomus.*

thōᵉ *theologiæ.*

thōs *Thomas.*

th̃ *thesauro.*

tĥa *tethinga, thaxa, thema.*

tĥata *themata.*

tĥau*ri⁹ *thesaurarius.*

tĥaurari⁹ *thesaurarius.*

tĥauȓ *thesaurum.*

tĥaũi *thesauri.*

tĥo*ȝ *theologicarum.*

tĥoł *theologicum.*

tĥri *thesauri.*

tĥrio *thesaurario.*

tĥrm *thesaurum.*

tĥro *thesauro.*

tⁱ *tibi.*

tⁱa *tria.*

tⁱas *trinitas.*

tⁱbunᵉ *tribunale.*

tⁱbȝ *tribus.*

tⁱb⁹ *tribus.*

tⁱƀło *tribulatio.*

tⁱᶜᵃ *triplica.*

tⁱᶜᵉ̄ *triplicem.*

tⁱᶜⁱ *triplici.*

tⁱe *trinitate.*

tⁱē *trinitatem.*

tⁱis *trinitatis.*

tiˡᵒ *titulo.*

ti¹⁹ *titulus.*

tim̃tes *timentes.*

tⁱni *trini.*

tⁱniᵗᵉ *trinitate.*

tⁱniᵗę *trinitatis.*

tⁱnođ *trinoda.*

tⁱnᵒtiū *trinoctium.*

tⁱn⁹ *trinus.*

tiᵒ *titulo.*

tⁱpᶜⁱ *triplici.*

tⁱpȓ *tripliciter.*

tⁱpˣ *triplex.*

tⁱp̄ʳ *triplicatur.*

tⁱp̄ł *tripliciter.*

tⁱs *trinitas.*

tⁱstiᵃ *tristitia.*

tⁱstisᵃ *tristissima.*

tⁱstis̃i *tristissimi.*

tⁱstˢ *tristis.*

tⁱte *trinitate.*

titło *titulo.*

tⁱtę *trinitatis.*

titłᵃi *titulari.*

titłatū *titulatum.*

titło *titulo.*

titĩm *titulum.*

titĩs *titulus.*

tⁱū *trium.*

tⁱūphātę *triumphantis.*

tⁱūphū *triumphum.*

tiˣ *triplex.*

tⁱ'ʳ *tripliciter.*

tñ *tamen, tenementa, tenentium.*

toᵃ *tota.*

to^alit̃ *totaliter.*
tociēs *totiens.*
toci⁹ *totiens, totius.*
toⁱ⁹ *totius.*
tolit^r *tollitur.*
tolła^{le} *tolerabile.*
tolłan^a *tolerantia.*
tolłr *tollitur.*
tołam⁹ *toleramus.*
toła^s *toleramus.*
tołr *totaliter.*
t^o *tertio.*
to^m *tomum, totam, totum.*
t^om^o *tertio modo.*
to^{ns} *totiens.*
tonŝ *tonsionem, tonsionis.*
to^o *toto.*
to^r *totaliter.*
torū^{tū} *torneamentum.*
toī̃^{tū} *torneamentum.*
totałr *totaliter.*
tot^r *totaliter.*
tōm̃tę *tormentis.*
tp̃e *tempore.*
tp̃r *tempore.*
tr^a *transgressione.*
trað *trabes.*
tranq̃lł *tranquillus.*
transit⁹ *transitus.*
transiu^t *transivit.*
trā *tractum.*
t^rba^r *turbatur.*

t^rbau^t *turbavit.*
t^rbū *turbam.*
t^rbē *trabem.*
t^rbȝ *tribus.*
t. r. e. *tempore regis Edwardi.*
tremēdū *tremendum.*
trēēdū *tremendum.*
tripł *tripliciter, triplum.*
triptita *tripartita.*
trip̃ *tripliciter.*
tri^r *triplicatur, tripliciter.*
tristi^a *tristitia.*
tri^{tum} *triplicatum.*
t^rñ *turnum.*
t^rpē *turpem.*
t^rpi^{do} *turpitudo.*
t^rpis *turpis.*
t^rpissīa *turpissima.*
t^rpit̃ *turpiter.*
t^rrē *turrem.*
t^rribȝ *turribus.*
t^rris *turris.*
tučo *tuitio.*
turoñ *Turonensium.*
turī̃b̃ìm *thuribulum.*
tuř *Turonensium.*
tut^oū *tutorum.*
tutoȝ *tutorum.*
tutę *tutis.*
tuĩla *tutela.*
tȝ *tenet.*

t̄ *160000, etiam, tallia, tam, tamen, tempore, tenementum, tenet, terræ, titulum, totum.*

t̃a *tria.*

t̃bla *tabula.*

t̃c *tunc.*

t̃cq, *tuncque.*

t̃ctare *tractare.*

t̃ctaᵘ *tractatu.*

t̃ct⁹ *tactus, tractus.*

t̃cᵗ⁹ *tractatus.*

t̃c' *triplicis.*

t̃de *tarde.*

t̃e *tempore, tertiæ.*

t̃hᵉ *trahere.*

t̃hr *trahitur.*

t̃h⁾e *trahere.*

t̃id⁹ *timidus.*

t̃is *terminis.*

t̃ⁱˢ *temporis.*

t̃le *tale.*

t̃les *tales.*

t̃lē *talem.*

t̃lia *talia.*

t̃liᵗ *taliter.*

t̃liū *talium.*

t̃lo *triplo.*

t̃t *talis.*

t̃m *talem.*

t̃r *taliter.*

t̄m *tamen, tantam, tantum.*

ĭmđ *tantundem.*

ĭmm° *tantummodo.*

ĭmm̃o *tantummodo.*

ĭm° *tantummodo.*

ĭm°o *tantummodo.*

ĭmp⁹ *tempus.*

ĭmpe *tempore.*

ĭn *tamen.*

ĭndū *tenendum.*

ĭnᵐ *tantum.*

ĭnta *tanta.*

ĭnto *tanto.*

ĭñbⁱs *tenebris.*

ĭñb°sa *tenebrosa.*

ĭñr *tenentur.*

ĭpla *templa.*

ĭplāii *templarii.*

ĭplū *templum.*

ĭptᵃi *temptari.*

ĭptⁱ° *temptatio.*

ĭpus *tempus.*

ĭp⁹ *tempus.*

ĭpa *tempora.*

ĭpᵃ *temperata.*

ĭpaᵇ₃ *temporalibus.*

ĭpam̃tū *temperamentum.*

ĭpam̃t̃ *temperamentum.*

ĭpanᵃ *temperantia.*

ĭpanᵉ *temperantiæ.*

ĭpaʳ *temporaliter.*

ĭpare *temperare.*

ĭpatū *temperatum.*

t̃paũite *temperaveritis.*	t̃ebntīa *terebinthina.*
t̃pāt *temperant.*	t̃go *tergo.*
t̃pe *tempore.*	t̃ia *tertia.*
t̃pi *tempori.*	t̃im *tertium.*
t̃pibʒ *temporibus.*	t̃ini *termini.*
t̃pies *temperies.*	t̃inm *terminum.*
t̃pis *temporis.*	t̃ino *termino.*
t̃ple *temporale.*	t̃inos *terminos.*
t̃pm *temporum.*	t̃inū *terminum.*
t̃pū *temporum.*	t̃in⁹ *terminus.*
t̃p̃mr *temptamur.*	t̃iñ *terminum.*
t̃p̃ra *tempora.*	t̃ial' *terminabilis.*
t̃p̃re *tempore.*	t̃ia⁰ *terminatio.*
t̃p̃ri *tempori.*	t̃iar *terminatur.*
t̃p̃ribʒ *temporibus.*	t̃iari *terminari.*
t̃p̃rlis *temporalis.*	t̃iato *terminato.*
t̃p̃s *tempus.*	t̃iatū *terminatum.*
t̃qa *tanquam.*	t̃ier *terminetur.*
t̃s *tempus.*	t̃ii *termini.*
t̃tam⁰ *testamento.*	t̃io *termino.*
t̃tm⁰ *tantummodo.*	t̃iom *terminationem.*
t̃t *tituli.*	t̃ios *terminos.*
t̃ti *tituli.*	t̃is *terminis.*
t̃tm *testamentum, titulum.*	t̃ius *terminus.*
t̃x *triplex.*	t̃m *tertium.*
t̃ʒ *tenent.*	t̃m *terminum.*
t̃ *ter, termino, terra, tertiam.*	t̃mis *terminus.*
t̃cete *trecentis.*	t̃mīo *termino.*
t̃cia *tertia.*	t̃m̃ *terminum.*
t̃ciā *tertiam.*	t̃m̃i *termini.*
t̃ciū *tertium.*	t̃na *terrena.*
t̃ci⁹ *tertius.*	t̃nū *terrenum.*

ꝑo *tertio.*
ꝑōꝝ *terminorum.*
ꝑra *terra.*
ꝑraꝝ *terrarum.*
ꝑrā *terram.*
ꝑre *terræ.*
ꝑreꝰ *terrenus.*
ꝑribl̄r *terribiliter.*
ꝑrili *terribili.*
ꝑris *terris.*
ꝑror *terror.*
ꝑrōe *terrore.*
ꝑr̃ *terræ, terris.*
ꝑs *terminus.*
ꝑsi *tersi.*
ꝑtia *tertia.*
ꝑtio *tertio.*
ꝑtiū *tertium.*
ꝑtiꝰ *tertius.*
⁊ *et.*

U.*

V. *quinque, quintus.*
u. *vale, valent, valet, ubi, ubicunque, vera, verbum, versus, verum, vestra, victus, videlicet, videtur, vidua, vir, virgo, vivas, vivens, vixit, una, unum, vobis, voluit, votum, vovit, ut, uti, utrique, utrum.*
ua. *vacante.*
uª *una.*
uªiatī *variatim.*
uaĭt *variat.*
uald̄ *valde.*
ualt *valebat, valet.*
ualȝ *valet.*
uariāt *variant.*
uarit' *variatum.*
uarĭne *variatione.*
uarōm *variationem.*
uat *valet.*
uāiat *variat.*

* In this list *u* is printed throughout for *u* and *v*, except for the numeral, as most early MSS. use only the one letter. In some MSS., however, the letter *v* is always used for an initial, even when it is a vowel; as ***vnus*** for ***unus***, ***vmbra*** for ***umbra***, ***vua*** for ***uva***.

ubiꝗ, *ubicunque.*

ubił *ubilibet.*

ubiꝗ *ubique.*

ub. *vobis.*

ubiorē *uberiorem.*

ue. *venit.*

ue^as *resperas.*

ue^d *velut.*

uegc̄le *vegetabile.*

uehūt^r *vehuntur.*

uehn̄r *vehementer.*

uel *velis.*

ueld *velut.*

uena^bȝ *venationibus.*

uen^abȝ *venerabilibus.*

uend *venditum.*

uen^{lis} *venerabilis.*

ueñ *venalis, venerabilis, veneris,*
   venerunt, venit.

ueñis *veneris.*

ueñl' *venerabilis.*

ueñnt *venerunt.*

uertn *verumtamen.*

uesc̄et^r *vesceretur.*

uesp *vesper.*

uesptū *vespertinum.*

uesti^m *vestimentum.*

uet^ꝰ *vetus.*

ueťa *vetera.*

ueťibȝ *veteribus.*

uēd^t *vendidit, vendit.*

uēdit *vendidit.*

uēd⁾e *vendere.*

uēiebt *veniebat.*

uēi^{le} *veniale.*

uēit *venit.*

uēit' *venialiter.*

ue^{li} *veniali.*

uē^t *venit.*

uētⁱs *ventris.*

uēt^rm *venturum.*

uētū *ventum.*

uēt^ꝰ *ventus.*

uc̄ti *ventri.*

ueť *venter.*

uēisīle *verisimile.*

uēitū *vetitum.*

uēit̨ *veritatis.*

uc̄o *veneno, vero.*

ug̃ *virgo.*

ug̃e *virgine.*

ug̃i *virgini.*

uⁱ *ubi.*

ui^a *vigilia.*

vj^a *sexta.*

uicar̃ *vicaria, vicarius.*

uice^bȝ *vicecomitibus.*

uicecom̃ *vicecomes.*

uicecōitat̃ *vicecomitatus.*

uici^m *vicinum.*

uicīs *vicinis.*

uⁱcꝗ *ubicunque.*

uic^{rie} *vicariæ.*

uic^{riꝰ} *vicarius.*

uic̃ *vicecomitatum.*

uᶦcūq̵ *ubicunque.*

uic̃ *vicarius, vicecomes, vicesima,*
          vicinarum.

uᶦc̃ *ubicunque.*

uic̃is *vicinis.*

uic̃la *vincula.*

uᶦc̃q̵ *ubicunque.*

uic̃ᵗ *videlicet.*

vic̃ᵗⁱ *vicecomiti.*

uic̃ĩ *vicecomitatum.*

uᶦç̃q̵ *ubicunque.*

uideʳ *videtur.*

uidჳ *videlicet.*

uid *videndum, vidua.*

uiddi *videndi.*

uiddᵐ *ridendum.*

uidemʳ *videremur.*

uidite̦ *videritis.*

uidr *rideatur, videtur, videntur.*

uidჳ *videndum.*

uigᵃ *vigilia.*

uᶦginē *virginem.*

uigiᵗⁱ *viginti.*

uᶦgīs *virginis.*

uigīti *viginti.*

uigł *vigilia.*

uᶦgo *virgo.*

uᶦgˢ *virginis.*

uig̃ *vigent, viginti.*

uᶦg̃ *virgata, virgo.*

uig̃i *viginti.*

vijᵃ *septima.*

vijᵉᵐ *septem.*

vij° *septimo.*

uill. *villa, villanus.*

uillañ *villanus.*

uillā *villam.*

uilł *villa, villani, villis.*

uilti *villani.*

uiltus *villanus.*

uilł⁹ *villanus.*

uiᵐ *vinum.*

uincła *vincula.*

uinc̃la *vincula.*

uiñ *vineæ.*

vj° *sexto.*

ui°ne *visione.*

ui°'ᵐ *visionem.*

uiʳ *videtur.*

uirgᵃ *virgata.*

uirgaĩ *virgata.*

uirg̃ *virgata, virginis, virgo.*

uisc̃a *viscera.*

uisʳe̦ *visuris.*

uis⁹ *visus.*

uisˢ° *visio.*

uiᵗ *videlicet.*

uiᵗᵉ *virtute.*

uitᵉe *vitreæ.*

uitᶦc̃ *vitricus.*

uᶦtt' *virtutem.*

uᶦtuᵒʳ *virtuosior.*

uᶦtuˢᵃ *virtuosa.*

uᵗute *virtute.*

uⁱt⁹ *virtus.*

uiᵗ⁹ *virtus.*

uiĩ *vitalis, vitulum.*

uiĩloȝ *vitulorum.*

niĩoȝ *vitiorum.*

uiuᵃiū *vivarium.*

uiũnt *vivunt.*

uiůe *vivere.*

uⁱ' *ubicunque.*

uiȝ *videlicet.*

uīa *vina.*

uībȝ *viribus.*

uiĉla *vincula.*

uiđce *vindictæ.*

uīoȝ *vinorum.*

uīū *vinum.*

uī *viri.*

uīƀ *viribus.*

uïde *viride.*

uiĩr *viriliter.*

uīo *viro.*

uīoȝ *virorum.*

uīre *vitare.*

uīs *verbis.*

uĩᵗ *vivit.*

ulᵃ *ultima.*

uˡᵉ *universale.*

uˡⁱˢ *universalis.*

ullo° *ullomodo.*

ul° *ultimo.*

ulʳᵉᵐ *ulteriorem.*

ultᵃ *ultra.*

ultiᵐ *ultimum.*

ultīo *ultimo.*

ult° *ultimo, ultro.*

ulĩ *ultima.*

ulĩi *ultimi.*

ulĩo *ultimo, ultio.*

ulĩoᵐ *ultionem.*

ulĩ p̃ *ultima presentatio.*

ulĩi⁹ *ulterius.*

uᵗt *valete.*

uᵐĩn *verumtamen.*

unañi *unanimi.*

unaꝗᵃ *unaquaque.*

unãiĩ *unanimiter.*

unĉ *uncia.*

undiꝗ *undique.*

unđ *unde.*

unđꝗꝗ *undequaque.*

unǧm *unguentum.*

uni°e *unione.*

uⁿⁱˢ *virginis.*

uniuᵗꝑ *universitatis.*

uniũsis *universis.*

uniũsis *universis.*

unīōe *unitione.*

uno° *uno modo.*

uñ *unde, unum.*

uñis *universis.*

uñusꝑ *universis.*

uñũ̃ *universis.*

uo. *vobis.*

u° *vero.*

u°ant^r *vocantur.*

uo^ant^r *vocantur.*

uo^as *voluntas.*

uoca^e *vocatæ.*

uoc̃^ter *vocaliter.*

uoc̃tꝑ *vocatis.*

uola^bȝ *volatilibus.*

uoleñ *volentes.*

uolc̄^s *volentes.*

uoli^ne *volitione.*

uo^lis *vocalis.*

uol⁹ *volumus.*

uoł *voluntatem.*

uołis *voluntatis.*

uołt *volunt.*

uołtē *voluntatem.*

uo^ns *volens.*

uoñr *vocantur.*

u°° *uno modo.*

u°q°ꝗ *unoquoque.*

uo^r *vocatur.*

uo^rie *voluntarie.*

uo^s *vocamus.*

uo^tas *voluntas.*

uo^tus *vocatus.*

uo^t' *voluntatum.*

uotꝑ *votis.*

u°t̃m *vocativum.*

uõ^do *volendo.*

uõlē *vocalem.*

uõm⁹ *vocamus.*

uõnt^r *vocantur.*

uõ *vocatur.*

uõs *voluntas.*

uõt *vocat.*

uõ^te *voluntate.*

uótoȥ *vocatorum.*

uõt^r *vocatur.*

uõt^s *vocatus.*

uõtꝑ *vocatis.*

uõ^tꝑ *voluntatis.*

v^que *quinque.*

uȓm *vestrum.*

usꝗ° *usquequo.*

usꝗq^aȝ *usquequaque.*

us^rā *usuram.*

usȝ *usque.*

us̈ *usque, usum.*

ut^aꝙ *utraque.*

utē° *utendo.*

ut^i *utri.*

v^ti *quinti.*

utiłr *utiliter.*

ut^iꝗ *utrique.*

ut^i⁹ꝗ *utriusque.*

utlagaũ *utlagavit.*

utł *utlagatus.*

ut^m *utrum.*

ut^mꝗ *utrumque.*

ut° *utro.*

v^to *quinto.*

ut°biꝗ *utrobique.*

ut°bȝ *utrobique.*

ut^r *utlagetur, ut probatur.*

uts. *ut supra.*

ut^t *ut dicit.*

v^{tus} *quintus.*

uĩ *ut patet.*

uĩ⁹q̇ *utriusque.*

ut̃ *uter.*

ut̃q̇ *uterque.*

uũt *vult.*

ux̃ *uxor.*

ux̃c̃ *uxorem.*

ux̃ę *uxoris.*

u3, v3 *verch (Welsh for daughter).*

u⁹ *versus.*

v̄ *quinque milia.*

ūaq^aq̇ *unaquaque.*

ūā *unam.*

ūb^e *umbræ.*

ūbra *umbra.*

ūc̃o *unctio.*

ūi^{as} *unitas.*

ūi^{ter} *universaliter.*

ūi^{te} *unitatem.*

ūiusat̃ *universalis.*

ūiusat̃r *universaliter.*

ūiusis *universis.*

ūi⁹ *unius.*

ūi⁹c̃q̇ *uniuscujuscunque.*

ūĩc̃q̃ *uniuscujuscunque.*

ūl 'vel.

ūllo^o *nullo modo.*

ūo^o *uno modo.*

ūoq^oq̇ *unoquoque.*

ūoquoq̇ *unoquoque.*

ūq̃ *unquam.*

ūũ *unum.*

ū⁹ *unus.*

ũ *ubi, ut, verbi.*

ũ^a *vera.*

ũɓ *vobis.*

ũc̃q̇ *ubicunque.*

ũgi^e *virgine.*

ũgi^{is} *virginis.*

ũgi^{tas} *virginitas.*

ũgĩm *virginum.*

ũgñs *virginis.*

ũgo *virgo.*

ũg̃ *virginis.*

ũg̃i *virgini.*

ũg̃l' *virginalis.*

ũg̃e *vergere.*

ũi *viri.*

ũis *visis.*

ũl *vel.*

ũl^c *vel sic.*

ũle *universale.*

ũl^e *valete.*

ũles *universales.*

ũlia *universalia.*

ũlib^t *ubilibet.*

ũli^m *universalium.*

ũlio͂rs *universaliores.*

ũli^r *universaliter.*

ũlis *universalis.*

ũlŧ *vellet.*

ũlt *vult.*

ũŧ *valet.*

ũŧe *valete.*

ũŧi *reluti.*

ũm *verum.*

ũm⁹ *videmus.*

ũnᵇჳ *venerabilibus.*

ũnᶜ̃ *virginem.*

ũntʳ *videntur.*

ũntū *ventum.*

ũñr *videntur.*

ũo *verbo.*

ũº *virgo.*

ũq̃ᵉ *unaquaque.*

ũq̃q, *unaquaque.*

ũr *vester, vestitur, videtur, vir, vomer.*

ũra *vestra.*

ũre *vestræ, videre.*

ũris *vestris.*

ũrm *vestrum.*

ũroჳ *vestrorum.*

ũˢ *virtuosus.*

ũs⁹ *versus.*

ũꝫ *versiones, vesperas.*

ñ̃ᵗ *videlicet.*

ũᵗᵉ *virtute.*

ũᵗᵉˢ *virtutes.*

ũtuˢ *virtutes.*

ũtutᵐ *virtutum.*

ũtuᵗ' *virtualiter.*

ũtū *ventum.*

ũᵗℓ *virtutis.*

ũt⁹ *virtus.*

ꞅu *ver, versus.*

ꞅua *vera.*

ꞅuᵃ *verba.*

ꞅuacē *veracem.*

ꞅuaciꝭ *veraciter.*

ꞅuã *veram.*

ꞅuba *verba.*

ꞅubiᵃ *verbi gratia.*

ꞅubo *verbo.*

ꞅubū *verbum.*

ꞅuᵇჳ *versibus.*

ꞅuƀ *verbis, verbum.*

ꞅuƀa *verbera.*

ꞅuƀaʳ *verberatur.*

ꞅuƀat *verberat.*

ꞅuƀeʳ *verberetur.*

ꞅuƀibჳ *verberibus.*

ꞅue *vere.*

ꞅuecūđ *verecundus.*

ꞅuget *verget.*

ꞅugēs *vergens.*

ꞅuᵷe *vergere.*

ꞅui *veri.*

ꞅuⁱ *verbi.*

ꞅuiᵃˢ *veritas.*

ꞅuⁱᵇჳ *verberibus, veritatibus.*

ꞅuiᶜᵃ'ʳ *verificatur.*

ꞅuifiʳ *verificatur.*

ꞅuis *veris.*

ꝰⁱˢ *verbis.*

ꝰⁱˢ *veritas.*

ꝰisite *verisimile.*

ꝰisīlit *verisimiliter.*

ꝰitas *veritas.*

ꝰⁱᵗᵉ *veritate.*

ꝰⁱᵗⁱ *veritati.*

ꝰⁱᵗₑ *veritatis.*

ꝰⁱ⁹ *verius.*

ꝰm *verum.*

ꝰᵐ *verbum.*

ꝰmec̃ *verumetiam.*

ꝰmē *vermem.*

ꝰmₑ *vermis.*

ꝰo *vero.*

ꝰᵒ *verbo.*

ꝰoᷓ *verorum.*

ꝰᵒᷓ *verborum.*

ꝰs *rerus.*

ꝰsi *versi.*

ꝰsū *versum.*

ꝰs̃ *versus.*

ꝰsₑ *rersus.*

ꝰtātʳ *vertantur.*

ꝰtor *vertor.*

ꝰte *vertere.*

ꝰuex *vervex.*

ꝰū *rerum.*

ꝰūptn *verumptamen (verum-tamen).*

ꝰūtⁿ *verumtamen.*

ꝰ ꝰ *veredictum versus.*

W.

wᵃātizaꝫm⁹ *warantizabimus.*

wᵃāto *waranto.*

wᵃde *wardæ.*

waīagiū *wainagium.*

wapentac̃ *wapentacium.*

wapentag̃ *wapentagium.*

wapentak̃ *wapentakium.*

wap̃ *wapentagium.*

warant̃ *warantum.*

warꝰ *warantia, warantizabunt, warantum.*

warᵒ *waranto.*

withꝉnam̃ *withernamium.*

wlgarit *vulgariter.*

wlg⁹ *vulgus.*

wln⁹ *vulnus.*

wln̄a *vulnera.*

wlpes *vulpes.*

M.

M

wlt *vult.*

wlt^r *vultur.*

w^{r}ccū *wreccum.*

wrecō *wrecco.*

wthnam̃ *withernamium.*

X.

X. *Christus, decem, denarii.*

x^a *decima.*

xannalib̃ *decennalibus.*

xc *Christus.*

x^{cē} *decem.*

x^i *Christi.*

xi^a *undecima.*

x^{i}an^9 *Christianus.*

x^{i}i *Christi.*

xii^a *duodecima.*

xii^{cī} *duodecim.*

xii^9 *duodecimus.*

x^{i}n^9 *Christianus.*

xi^9 *undecimus.*

xl^a *quadragesima, quadraginta.*

xl^e *quadragesimæ.*

x^{lis} *decimalis.*

xl^{lis} *quadragesimalis.*

xl^{ma} *quadragesima.*

xlmal̃ *quadragesimalis.*

xlme *quadragesimæ.*

xlsima *quadragesima.*

x^m *decem.*

x^{ma} *decima.*

x^o *Christo.*

xp̃c *Christus.*

xp̃e *Christe.*

xp̃i *Christi.*

xp̃ianoȝ *Christianorum.*

xp̃ian^9 *Christianus.*

xp̃m *Christum.*

xp̃o *Christo.*

xp̃ofor^9 *Christoforus.*

xp̃s *Christus.*

xr̃i *Christi.*

x^{ti} *Christi.*

xv^{mo} *quindecimo.*

x^9 *decimus.*

x̄ *decem milia.*

x̆ *decem, decimus.*

x̆ana *Christiana.*

x̆an^9 *Christianus.*

x̆aȝ *decimarum.*

x̆^{e} *decimæ.*

x̆i *Christi.*

x̆m *Christum.*

Y.

Y *150*.

ydoᵃ *ydonea.*

ydᵗᵃˢ *ydentitas.*

yeᵃle *yemale* (*hiemale*).

yēał *yemalis* (*hiemalis*).

yēe *yeme* (*hieme*).

yēs *yems* (*hiems*).

ymaḡ *ymaginibus.*

ymⁿᵉ *ymagine.*

ymᵒ *ymago.*

yᵒ *ymago, ymmo* (*immo*).

ypᶜᵃ *ypotheca.*

ypoᶜᵉ *ypothetice.*

yủnaḡ *yvernagium* (*hiberna-gium*).

y⁹ *ymnus.*

ȳ *150000*.

ȳaḡ *ymaginibus.*

ȳno *ymno* (*hymno*).

ȳnū *ymnum* (*hymnum*).

ȳn⁹ *ymnus* (*hymnus*).

ỹizare *ymnizare.*

ỹizāt *ymnizant.*

Z.

Z *2000*.

zoᶜⁱ *zodiaci.*

zōa *zona.*

Z̄ *200000*.

ꝛ *et.*

ȝ *et, que, us.*

÷ *est.*

FRENCH ABBREVIATIONS.*

A.

about *aboutant.*
acāe *à cause.*
aeq^r *acquéreur.*
aĉs *acres.*
ad^{at} *advocat.*
ad^{cat} *advocat.*
adio^{ner} *adjourner.*
affes *affaires.*
aǧable *agréable.*
aiañ *à jamais.*
am̃de *amende.*
angł *Angleterre.*
aŏn *action.*
ape^{ans} *appellans.*
app^{on} *appellation.*
appꝑa *appartiendra.*
appꝑe *apparoistre.*

app^s *appartenans.*
appt *appert.*
appteñ *appartenant.*
appu *approuver.*
apteñ *appartenant.*
aꝑs *après.*
arꝑ *arpent, arpens.*
arrest *arrester.*
arr^s *arrérages.*
asceñ *ascension.*
assig^{on} *assignation.*
assi^r *assigner.*
ass^r *assavoir.*
asse *assise.*
assõn *assignation.*
assr *assavoir, assigner.*
attempm̃t *attemprement.*
aud *audit.*
auecꝗs *avecques.*

---

* In French writing of the 15th and 16th centuries, in a cursive hand, the abbreviations are often very carelessly made—as ă for ā, p̃ for ꝑ, so that type does not exactly represent the forms used. If a word is not found in this list with the exact abbreviation occurring in a MS., it may be found with some similar form.

aueñe *aventure.*

aulˢ *aultres.*

aur̃ *auroit.*

aut̃ *autre.*

aut̃m̃t *autrement.*

aut̃pt *autrepart.*

aut̃s *autres.*

aũ *avoit.*

aũe *autre.*

aũes *autres.*

aũr *avoir.*

aũt *avoit.*

aṽ *avoit.*

aṽr *avoir.*

aṽᵗ *avoit.*

ãon *action.*

B.

baill̃ *bailli, bailliage.*

bal̃ *bailli, bailliage.*

bapt̃ *baptiste.*

bñ *bien.*

bñs *biens.*

boiss̃ *boisseau.*

bourɗ *Bourdeaux.*

bourg̃ *bourgeois.*

bout̃ *boutant.*

bō *bon.*

bōe *bonne.*

bõiois *bourjois.*

bĩ *bout.*

ƀ *bien, boisseaux.*

ƀn *bien.*

ƀnfice *bénéfice.*

ƀns *biens.*

ƀt *bout.*

C.

caũe *cause.*

caũon *caution.*

caũt *causant.*

cãe *cause.*

ceɗ *cedit.*

celᵉ *céleste.*

cestass̃ *cest assavoir.*

ce⁹ *ceus (ceux).*

chandel̃ *chandeleur.*

chapʳᵉ *chapitre.*

chap̃e *chapitre.*

chap̃re *chapitre.*

chãl *cheval.*

chãu *château.*

chãux *châteaux, chevaux.*

cheũ *chevalier.*

chl̃r *chevalier.*

chs̃ *choses.*

cñ *cher, chevalier.*

cñal *cheval.*

cñaux *châteaux, chevaux.*

cñcñ *chercher.*

cñl *cheval.*

chler *chevalier.*

chĩr *chevalier.*

chn *chacun.*

chr *chevalier.*

chre *chartre.*

chĩrs *chevaliers.*

chs *choses.*

chun *chacun.*

chū *chacun.*

ciçuencõn *circonvention.*

ciee *criée.*

cinq^e *cinquante.*

cinq^{te} *cinquante.*

clc *clerc.*

cog^{re} *cognoistre.*

colãon *collation.*

colt *collation.*

coltg^{le} *collégiale.*

compoir *comparoir.*

cond *condamné.*

con^{er} *conseiller.*

con^{ers} *conseillers.*

con^{eur} *controlleur.*

cont̃ *contre.*

conueñ *convenance.*

cop̃ *copie.*

corpelm̃t *corporelment.*

co^{rt} *court.*

coũ *court.*

cõe *comme.*

cõfess *confesser, confesseur.*

cõf^{i}mer *confirmer.*

cõis *commis.*

cõmãdʒ *commandements.*

cõme *comme.*

cõmtt̃ *commettons.*

cõpte *compte.*

cõpoir *comparoir.*

cõpte *comporte.*

cõt^e *contre.*

cõteñ *contenant.*

c^r *cœur.*

c̃tain *certain.*

c̃a^e *créature.*

c̃ace *créance.*

c̃tain *certain.*

cʒbn *combien.*

cʒd *condamnons.*

cʒdon *condamnation.*

cʒe *comme.*

cʒ^e *contre.*

cʒmand *commandons.*

cʒme *comme.*

cʒmẽdt *commendement.*

cʒmiss̃es *commissaires.*

cʒm̃dem̃t *commandement.*

cʒm̃e *comme.*

cʒm̃t *comment.*

cʒpetẽt *compétent.*

cʒpte *compte.*

cʒpoir *comparoir.*

cʒpuz *comparuz.*

cʒseil *conseil.*

cʒseñ *consentement.*

ꝯ^{te} *communauté.*
ꝯteñ *contenant.*
ꝯtēs *contens.*
ꝯt̃ *contre.*

D.

dar̃ *d'arrérages.*
dauĩ *d'autre.*
dauĩpt *d'autre part.*
db. *d'un bout.*
dc̃ *a'un costé.*
dc̃e *dicte (dite).*
decton *déclaration.*
dec̃nons *décernons.*
deff^r *deffendeur.*
deff^t *deffaut, deffunct.*
deff *deffaut, deffunct.*
dem̃ *demourant.*
dem̃d^r *demandeur.*
deñ *deniers.*
deũs *deniers.*
depp̃on *depposition.*
dep̃s *depens.*
derech̃ *derechef.*
der̃ *derrain.*
desm̃t *desmaintenant.*
dess⁹ *dessus.*
dess̃ *dessus.*
dess̃d *dessusdit.*
des̃d *dessusdit.*
deuem̃ *deuement.*

deũ *devant.*
deũs *devers.*
deũs *devers.*
dẽes̃ *demanderesse.*
dh̃iãon *d'habitation.*
dignor̃ *d'ignorance.*
dilig̃ *diligemment, diligence.*
dillig̃ *diligemment, diligence.*
distr̃ *distrent (dirent).*
dom̃^{le} *domicile.*
donñ *donner.*
d^t *devant.*
dud *dudit.*
dunept *d'une part.*
dũb *d'un bout.*
dũant *durant.*
dyoc̃ *dyocèse.*
đ *dans, de, denier, dit.*
đb *d'un bout*
đc̃ *d'un costé.*
đees̃ *demanderesse.*
đpt *d'une part.*
đquel *duquel.*
đt *devant, dit.*
đte *dite.*

E.

egte *église.*
ench̃em̃t *enchérement.*
ench̃i *enchéri.*

enꝤ *ensuit, ensuivant.*
entꝰier *entériner.*
enū *envers.*
enùs *envers.*
ep̄al *episcopal.*
escħer *eschiquier.*
escꝛ̃ *escrit.*
escꝛ̃r *escuier.*
esđ *esdit, esdites.*
espāl *espécial.*
esp̄al *espécial.*
esp̄aulx *espéciaulx.*
estīe *Estienne.*
esꞇ̃ *establi, estoit.*
euāgł *évangile.*
exᵃorđ *extraordinaire.*
execūon *exécution.*
exepꞇ̃ *excepter.*
exẽ *exécution.*
exẽon *exécution.*
expł *exploit.*
expoꝫ̃ *exposant.*
expꝰssem̃ *expressement.*
exʳᵉ *exécutoire, extraordinaire.*
exᵗꞌᵉ *exécutoire.*
ex̃on *exécution.*
ēꞇbres *encombres.*
eꝰꞇigner *entérigner.*
ẽ *est.*

F.

faiꝫꞩ *faissons.*
fc̃e *faicte.*
febʳ *Febvrier.*
feʳ *faire.*
fēme *femme.*
fẽ *femme.*
foiꝫ̃ *foison.*
forᵃt *format.*
forꝰece *forterece (forteresse).*
fourfaitʳe *forfaiture.*
from̃ *froment.*
fꝛe *frère.*
fuꝛ̃ *furent.*
fᵐᵉ *femme.*
fre *faire.*
ft *fait.*
fᵗe *faite.*
fꝰme *ferme.*
fꝰmier *fermier.*

G.

gᵃce *grâce.*
gᵃnd *grand.*
gᵃns *grans (grands).*
gᵃnt *grant.*
gᵃraūt *guaraunt.*
garꝛ̃ *garrant.*
geñal *général.*

gñalite *généralité.*
gñal *généralement.*
gñaulx *généraulx.*
goꝛ *gorce.*
gouûmt *gouvernement.*
gr̃e *grâce.*
guᵃant *guarant.*
guilꝉe *Guillaume.*
guoꝛ *gorce.*
g̃ñal *général.*
g̃e *guerre.*

H.

hebgem̃t *hébergement.*
hebg̃ *héberger.*
herit̃ *héritage, héritier.*
herit̃ *héritier.*
hᵉʳˢ *héritiers.*
honᵇˡᵉ *honorable.*
hoñ *honneste.*
hō *hon (homme).*
hōe *homme.*
hōme *homme.*
hōs *hons (hommes).*
huictᵉ *huictiesme.*
h̃bgem̃t *herbergement.*
h̃bg̃ *herberger.*
h̃biage *herberiage.*
h̃ile *habile.*
h̃irs *hoirs.*
h̃itage *héritage.*

h̃itans *habitans.*
h̃itãon *habitation.*
h̃itˢ *habitans.*
h̃rs *hers, hoirs.*
h̃s *hers, hoirs.*
h̃ˢ *héritiers.*

I.

iad̃ *jadis.*
ieh̃ *Jehan.*
imp̃ *impetrant.*
inpõle *impossible.*
inp̃ˡᵉ *impossible.*
intᵉes *interes (intérêt).*
intest *interest (intérêt).*
ioʳ *jour.*
ioux̃ *jouxte.*
iõ *jour.*
iʳ *jour.*
iug̃ *jugement.*
iurᵗ *jurèrent.*
iur̃ *jurèrent.*
iur̃dc̃on *jurisdiction.*
iusq̃s *jusques.*
iũg *Juing.*
īpe *impossible.*
ĩʳ *jour.*

K.

katine *Katerine.*
kꝉ *kalendes.*

L.

laq̃le *laquelle.*
lasˢ̃ *l'assise.*
lᵬ *libvres.*
lᵬz *libvres.*
led *ledict.*
legᵗe *l'église.*
leʳ *leur.*
leʳs *leurs.*
leuʳ *lever.*
leù *lever.*
lexc̃on *l'exécution.*
leᵌs *leurs.*
liceñ *licencié.*
lic̃ *licencié.*
lieuteñ *lieutenant.*
lordoñ *l'ordonnance.*
lq̃l *lequel.*
lr̃e *lettre.*
lr̃es *lettres.*
lᵨd *lesditz.*
ł *livres.*
łitage *l'héritage.*
łre *lettre.*
łres *lettres.*

M.

M. *Monsieur.*
Magd *Magdeleine.*

mandem̃ *mandement.*
mand *mandons.*
maniᵈ.e *manière.*
maꞑe *manere, manière.*
marᵃˡ *mareschal.*
Marğ *Marguerite.*
maᵗe *majesté.*
mᵉ *maistre.*
meᵉ *mère.*
mesm̃ *mesmement.*
messʳ *messeigneur.*
messˢ̃ *messeigneur, messire.*
mestʳ *mestier.*
mest̃ *mestier.*
meˢ̃ *messire.*
meuᵬ *meuble.*
Micħ *Michel.*
misˢ̃icors *misericors.*
mĩt *moult.*
moĩt *moitié.*
mond *mondit.*
monsʳ *monsieur.*
monst̃ *monstrer.*
monˢ̃ *monsieur.*
moñ *monnoie.*
moust̃ *moustier (monastère).*
mōstᵈ *monstier (monastère).*
mōˢ̃ *monsieur.*
mʳ *maistre.*
m̃e *mère.*
m̃s *moins.*
m̃ci *merci.*

m̃credi *mercredi.*

m̃cy *merci.*

m̃e *mère.*

N.

nᵇʳᵉ *nombre, Novembre.*

neantm̃ *néantmoins.*

noᵇʳᵉ *nombre, Novembre.*

noƀ *noble.*

noƀre *Novembre.*

nor̃ *notre.*

nos̄ *Notre Seigneur.*

not̃ *notaire.*

not̃d *notre dict.*

no⁹ *nous.*

nōe *nommé.*

nōer *nommer.*

nōes *nommés.*

nōobst̃ *nonobstant.*

nōe *notre.*

nr̃e *notre.*

nr̃edāe *Notre Dame*

nr̃edt *notre dit.*

nr̃esʳ *Notre Seigneur.*

nr̃es̃ *Notre Sire.*

ñ *ne.*

ñl *nul.*

O.

oct̃ *octave.*

opᵒⁿ *opposition.*

oppõᵒⁿ *opposition.*

ordᶜᵉ *ordonnance.*

ordⁿᵉ *ordonné.*

ordʳᵉ *ordinaire.*

orr̃ *orront.*

ostʳ *oster (ôter).*

ottⁱer *ottrier.*

oulᵉ *oultre.*

oũtem̃t *overtement.*

P.

paier̃t *paieront.*

parcȟn *par chacun.*

parlem̃t *parlement.*

parrᵉ *parroisse.*

par̃ *Paris, Parisis.*

patᵒnaige *patronaige.*

pƀre *presbtre (prêtre).*

pescȟie *pescherie.*

pȟe *Philippe.*

pⁱere *prière.*

pⁱnce *prince.*

pⁱncipale *principale.*

pⁱns *prins.*

pⁱons *prions.*

pⁱōs *prions.*

pⁱs *pris.*

pⁱse *prise.*

pⁱsiee *prisiee (prisée).*

pⁱue *privé.*

pⁱuileg̃ *priviléges.*

plēte *plenté.*

pluš *plusieurs.*

plušrs *plusieurs.*

pñce *présence.*

pñs *présens.*

pñt *présent.*

pñtãon *présentation.*

pñtem̃t *présentement.*

po^r *pour.*

po^rforcem̃t *pourforcement.*

portℯ *porteur.*

poss̃ *possession.*

poss̃on *possession.*

pourpⁱs *pourpris.*

põon *possession.*

pò⟩ *pour.*

pò⟩forcem̃t *pourforcement.*

p^r *pour.*

preseñ *présentement.*

prom̃aon *proclamation.*

proucheñ *prouchenement.*

p^rpris *pourpris.*

p^rueu *pourveu.*

p̃real *présidial.*

p̃ronaige *patronaige.*

puiss̃ *puissant.*

p *par.*

pcȟ *perches.*

pcȟun *par chacun.*

pcyd^t *parcydevant.*

pdeůs *pardevers.*

---

pdonñ *pardonnent.*

pd^t *pardevant.*

pđ *pardevant.*

pe *père.*

plem̃t *parlement.*

pł *parlement.*

pmiss̃ *permission.*

pm̃pt^{re} *péremptoire.*

poisse *paroisse.*

pp̃tuelm̃t *perpétuellement.*

pq̃s *perques.*

pre *pierre.*

proiss̃ *parroisses.*

prℏ̃ *parroisse.*

pℏ̃ *parroisse.*

ps *pars (parts).*

psōe *personne.*

pt *part.*

ptℯ *parties.*

p̃mieℏ̃ *premièrement.*

p̃nce *présence.*

p̃ns *présens.*

p̃nt *présent.*

p̃ntãon *présentation.*

p̃ntem̃t *présentement.*

p̃pal *principal.*

p̃sent̃ *présentes.*

p̃st̃ *prestre.*

p̃decess̃ *prédécesseurs.*

p̃lat *prélat.*

p̃mier *premier.*

p̃mieℏ̃ *premièrement.*

p̃nce *présence.*
p̃ndre *prendre.*
p̃neur *preneur.*
p̃ns *présens.*
p̃sent̃ *présentation.*
p̃st̃ *prestre.*
p̃udes *preudes.*
p̃uost *prevost.*
p̃uot *prevót.*
pced *procéder.*
pces *procès.*
pchaiñ *prochainement.*
pcħi *prochain.*
pcurãou *procuration.*
pcur̃ *procureur.*
pcur̃s *procureurs.*
pdes *prodes.*
peue *proeve (preuve).*
pfit *profit.*
pmetōs *prometons.*
pm̃ttōs *promettons.*
pp^{i}ete *propriété.*
pposee *proposée.*
ppos̃ *proposer.*
ppre *propre.*
ppe *propre.*
pp̃s *propres.*
p^r *procureur.*
pucħi *prouchain.*
pue *prouvé.*
puis^n *provision.*

Q.

q^{a}nq̨ *quanque.*
q^{a}nt *quant.*
q^{a}resme *quaresme.*
q^{a}rt *quart.*
q^{a}rtier *quartier.*
q^{a}rĩ *quartier.*
q^{a}tre *quatre.*
q^{i}cte *quicte.*
q^{i}elx *quielx (quels).*
q^{i}ex *quiex (quels).*
q^{i}l *qu'il.*
q^{i}tie *quitie.*
q^{i}tt ℓ *quittes.*
quelcōq̨ *quelconque.*
q^{a}t *quant.*
q̃ *que.*
q̃elle *qu'elle.*
q̃l *quel.*
q̃lcōq̨ *quelconque.*
q̃lles *quelles.*
q̃lq̨ *quelque.*
q̃lx *quelx.*
q̃lz *qu'ils.*

R.

racħi *rachat.*
ranĩ *rantiers.*
recħon *reclamation.*
reg̃re *registre.*

relĭḡ *religieuse, religieux, religion.*

relt *relation.*

relton *relation.*

renōc̃ *renonçant.*

rep̃nter *représenter.*

req^te *requeste.*

req̃rōs *requerons.*

res̃ue *réserve, réservé.*

retorn̂oit *retorneroit.*

reũent *révérent.*

reũeñ *révérence.*

rẽgnut *recognut.*

robt *Robert.*

r̃yal *royal.*

S.

S. *Saint, solz.*

sach^e' *sachent.*

sacrm̃t *sacrement.*

sac̃m̃t *sacrement.*

salt *salut.*

scaũ *sçavoir.*

sc̃t *sainct.*

sc̃te *saincte.*

seḡd *segond (second).*

seign^r *seigneur.*

semb^l *semblable.*

semest̃ *semestre.*

sen^al *seneschal.*

sens̃ *s'ensuit.*

sent̃ *sentence.*

sent̃e *sentence.*

sept̃ *Septembre.*

septs̃ *septiers.*

sets̃ *setiers.*

se^)mēt *serment.*

sf *sa femme.*

slt *salut.*

soffis̃s̃ *soffissament.*

soub^e *soubsigné.*

soubz̃ *soubzagé.*

souff℮ *souffisant.*

sōe *somme.*

sp̃al *spécial.*

sp̃aulx *spéciaulx.*

s^r *seigneur, sire.*

s^t *saint.*

st̃ *sont.*

subg℮ *subgiet (sujet).*

subtilm̃t *subtilement.*

success̃ *successeur.*

succ℮ *successeurs.*

suffis̃ *suffisant.*

supp^ant *suppliant.*

suppt *suppliant.*

s3 *sans.*

s°dc̃e *susdicte.*

s°sistāt *sussistant.*

s̃ *seigneur, sieur, sire, solz.*

s̃^a *servira.*

s̃^ct *sainct.*

s̃dit *susdit.*

s̃ᵉ *sire.*

s̃emēt *surement.*

s̃ianℓie *serjanterie.*

s̃iāz *serjanz (sergents).*

s̃m̃t *serment.*

s̃oient *seroient.*

s̃ont *seront.*

s̃ʳ *seigneur, sieur.*

s̃rem̃t *serrement.*

s̃rial *seigneurial.*

s̃ʳⁱᵉ *seigneurie, sieurie.*

s̃t *saint, sont.*

s̃te *sainte.*

s̃tȝ *solz Tournois.*

ꝫa *sera.*

ꝫᵃ *servira.*

ꝫe *sire.*

ꝫgℓ *sergent.*

ꝫiās *serjans.*

ꝫiaℓie *serjanterie.*

ꝫm̃t *serment.*

ꝫoiēt *seroient.*

ꝫōt *seront.*

ꝫuir *servir.*

T.

tabelℓ *tabellion.*

tab̃ *tabellion.*

tᵃnscript *transcript.*

tᵃũs *travers.*

tã *tabellion.*

tem̃ *témoins.*

tend̃ *tendant.*

tenem̃t *tenement.*

ten⁹ *tenus.*

teñȝ *tenements.*

tesm̃ *tesmoing.*

testam̃t *testament.*

tes̃ȝ *tesmoins.*

tⁱnite *trinité.*

toᵃˡ *total.*

toʳnois *Tournois.*

toʳñ *Tournois.*

toucȟ *touchant.*

tourñ *Tournois.*

tous̃ *Toussaints.*

tʳ *Tournois.*

traũs *travers.*

tʳnois *Tournois.*

tȝ *Tournois.*

tℓ *Tournois.*

t̃ *Tournois.*

t̆me *terme.*

t̆re *terre.*

ℓē *terme.*

ℓme *terme.*

ℓre *terre.*

ꝫrouer *terrouer (terroir).*

ꝫsor *trésor.*

ꝫsoῖ *trésorier.*

U. V.

valencĥ *Valenchiennes.*

vall^r *valloir.*

vaɫ *vallant.*

v^e *veuve.*

vend *vendeurs.*

veñ *venant.*

vergę *vergées.*

vesp̄s *vespres.*

vēde^rs *vendeurs.*

viĉ *viconte.*

vigę *vignes.*

vo⁹ *vous.*

v^rʒ *verront.*

vr̃e *vostre.*

ūs *uns.*

ṽgę *vergées.*

ṽite *vérité.*

ṽront *verront.*

ṽue *veuve.*

ṽʒ *verront.*

ꝉite *vérité.*

v̅ōt *verront.*

ꝉtu *vertu.*

X.

xp̄he *Christophe.*

xp̄ien *Chrétien.*

xp̄ofle *Christofle.*

GLOSSARY OF LATIN WORDS

FOUND IN RECORDS AND OTHER ENGLISH MANUSCRIPTS, BUT
NOT OCCURRING IN CLASSICAL AUTHORS.

A.

abaciscus :—a small square tablet.

abactor :—a cattle lifter, who steals sheep or cattle in herds, not singly.

abacus :—a calculating board; and hence, arithmetic; a sideboard; a cupboard.

abandonnare :—to permit or forbid by proclamation.

abandonum, abandum :—anything sequestered, proscribed, pledged, or abandoned.

abarnare :—to prove, legally, a secret crime.

abastardare :—to bastardize.

abaso :—an infirmary.

abatamentum :—an entry by interposition.

abatare :—to beat down; to defeat a writ or appeal; to enter into property void by death of the possessor before the heir takes possession.

abatis :—an officer who distributes corn, an avener or hostler; a ration of corn.

abator :—a person who by interposition enters into property.

abatudus :—diminished, esp. clipped, as money.

abbas :—an abbot.

abbatatus :—the office of abbot.

abbatia, abbathia :—an abbey; the office of abbot.

abbatis. See *abatis.*

abbatissa :—an abbess.

abbatizare :—to be abbot.

abbayum :—a milldam.

abbettamentum :—abetment.

abbettare, abettare :—to abet; to instigate.

abbettator :—an abettor.

abbettum :—abetment.

abbottare :—to abut, or bound.

abbreviamentum :—an abridgement.

abbreviare :—to abridge.

abbrocamentum :—abbrochment, or forestalling a market or fair.

abbrocator :—a forestaller; a broker.

abbuttare :—to abut.

abcariare :—to carry away.

abdicare :—to renounce an office before the term of service is expired.

abditorium :—a chest for keeping plate or relics.

abecedarium :—an alphabet.

abecedarius :—a scholar learning to read.

abecula : —the back of a sword or knife.

aberemurdrum :—manifest murder.

abettare, &c. See *abbettare, &c.*

abeyantia :—abeyance. Property is in abeyance when it is in expectation, in the intendment of the law, not in actual possession.

abgatoria, abgetorium :—the alphabet ; rudiments of a science.

abhæres :—a future holder of property, not the next heir.

abiaticus :—a nephew (*aviaticus*).

abigevus :—a cattle stealer. See *abactor*.

abjectire : — to be non-suited ; to make default.

abjudicare :—to take away by judicial sentence.

abjurare :— to renounce the realm for ever.

ablactatus :—weaned.

ablatum :—a wafer. O. E. obley (*oblata*).

abra :—a maidservant.

abrenunciatio :—renunciation.

abrocagium : —brokerage.

abrocarius :— a broker.

abrogabilis :—fit to be repealed.

absconcius :—a casket.

absconsa :—a dark lantern ; a sconce.

absis :—an apse ; a church porch.

absolutionis dies :—M a u n d y Thursday.

absoniare :—to shun, or avoid.

abutare. See *abbuttare.*

acatum. See *accatum.*

accalvaster :—bald in front.

accannellare :—to chamfer.

accapitare, accaptare :—to pay a relief.

accapitis, accapitum, accaptamentum :—a relief.

accatum :—an acquisition.

accearium :—steel.

accendile :—a lamp or candle wick.

acceptilatio :—discharge, acquittance.

acceptor :—a hawk.

acceptor de arbore :—a brancher.

acceptor de pertica :—a hawk off the perch.

acceptor domitus :—a reclaimed hawk.

acceptor intra clavem repositus :— a hawk in the mew.

acceptor mutatus :—a mewed hawk.

acceptoricius canis :—a spaniel used for falconry.

accessorius :— guilty of a felonious offence, not principally, but by participation.

accidia :—sloth.

accidinetum :—gorse.

acciptrarius :—a falconer.

accitulium :—cuckoo sorrel.

acclaudicare :—to lame, esp. a horse, with bad shoeing.

accola :—a colonist ; a cultivator of land where he was not born.

accompliamentum : — accomplishment.

accrescendi jus :—right of increase.

acedia :—melancholy.

acega :—a woodcock (*scolopax rusticola*).

acellarius :—" a spenser," cellarer.

acentus :—increase.

acerrum, acerum :—steel.

aceta :—a snipe, or woodcock.

achaptare. See *accapitare.*

achatum :—purchase, bargain.

achersetus :—a measure of corn, conjectured to be a quarter.

achevare :—to finish.

acitula :—henbane.

acolabium :—a farm, a tenement.

acoluthus :—an acolyte. O. E. a colet.

acopatus. See *acupatus.*

acordum :—accord ; assent.

acquestra : —acquisition.

acquietantia :—a discharge in writing, of money paid or debt due ; quittance.

acquietare :—to pay ; to free or discharge.

acquirere, adquirere :—to purchase ; to acquit.

acra :—an acre of land ; a judicial combat, holm gang.

acra anglicana :—20 English acres in the reign of Richard I. are said to be equal to 22 acres.

acroisia :—blindness. For *aorisia.*

actachiare. See *attachiare.*

actilia :—armour and weapons ; gear. See *atilium.*

actio :—a legal demand of a right.

actionare :—to prosecute.

acto : —a haqueton, a padded or quilted tunic worn under the mail.

actor :—a proctor or advocate in civil courts.

actor dominicus :—the bailiff or attorney of a lord.

actor ecclesiæ :—the advocate or pleading patron of a church.

actor villæ :—the steward or head bailiff of a town or village.

actornatus. See *attornatus.*

actuarius :—the clerk who registers the acts of convocation.

acuarium :—a needle case.

acucio :—sharpening.

aculus, acula :—an aglet, a metal tag.

acupatus :—charged with (*adculpatus*).

acuperium :—a whetstone.

acupictor :—an embroiderer.

acusile .—a trinket.

acustumabilis, acustumatus :— liable to custom.

acustumare :—to exact custom ; to exempt from custom.

acuta :—ague.

acutecula :—a steel ; a hone.

ad. Sometimes used for " at " not " to " a place.

adalingus :—an etheling.

adaquare :—to water (cattle); to drown.

adaquarium :—a watering place.

adasia :—a ewe.

adbreviare :—to abridge.

adcredulitare :—to purge oneself of an accusation by oath.

addictio :—used for *additio.*

additio :—a title setting forth a person's estate, degree, trade, &c.

addresciare, addressare :—to redress; to restore; to make amends for; to render account of.

adirare :—to lose.

adiratus :—a compensation for goods lost or stolen.

adjacentia :—neighbourhood; a thing near other.

adjectire :—to cite.

adjornamentum, adjurnamentum : —adjournment, putting off to another day or place.

adjornare :—to adjourn.

adjudicatio :— pronouncing a judgment or decree.

adjurnare :—to adjourn.

adlegiare :—to purge oneself of a crime by oath. (Fr. *aleier.*)

admensuratio :—admeasurement, a writ for remedy against persons who usurp more than their share.

adminiculum, adminiculatio :— aid, support.

admiraldus :—an admiral.

admiraldus :—sometimes used for *emeraldus.*

admiralis :—an admiral.

admiralitas :—admiralty.

admiralius, admirallus :—an admiral.

admiravisus :—an emir vizier.

admissionalis :—an usher.

admissivus :—an usher.

admonitor :—a watch dog, "a wappe."

adnichilare, adnullare :—to annul.

adquietare. See *acquietare.*

adramire. See *arramire.*

adrectare :—to do right; to make amends.

adresciare. See *addresciare.*

adsecurare. See *assecurare.*

adulterinus :—unlawful, esp. of castles and guilds.

adunare :—to collect.

aduncare :—to draw with a hook.

advallacio anguillarum :—eelbucks.

advanciamentum :—advancement.

advantagium :—advantage; the right of the lord to redeem a fief removed by the vassal from his lordship.

adventale :—a ventail or visor.

adventare :—to arrive.

adventura :—an adventure, or venture.

adventurare :—to adventure, or venture.

adventurarius :—an adventurer.

adventus :—casual profit.

adversaria :—memoranda.

advisamentum :—advice; consideration.

advisare :—to advise.

advocare :—to advow ; to vouch ; to justify an act done ; to avow, *i.e.* in boroughs, to falsely allege that goods belong to a freeman so as to evade duty.

advocaria :—avowry ; the justification of having taken a distress, when the party sues forth a replevin.

advocatia :—an advowson.

advocatio :—advowson, the right of presentation to an ecclesiastical benefice; allegation of protection or authority.

advocator:—a voucher; a pleader.

advocatus :—a counsellor or pleader ; patron of a church, avowee, advowee, vouchee ; protector of a community.

ædituus :—a verger, a keeper of relics.

Ægyptiacus, Ægyptius :— a gypsy.

aeraria, aeria :—an eyry, a nest, usually of hawks.

aerarius :—nesting.

aereus, aerius :—sky blue.

aericius canis. See *herecius.*

aerrarius. See *aerarius.*

aesnescia. See *esnecia.*

affadilla :—a daffodil.

affeagium. See *affidagium.*

afferamentum :—affeerment, assessment.

afferare :—to assess a fine.

afferator :—an affeerer, a person who assesses fines in courts leet and courts baron.

affeteiare :—to break or train hounds or hawks.

affeyteiare. See *affeteiare.*

affidagium :—assurance ; safety.

affidare :—to certify ; to swear fealty ; to affiance ; a term used at the game of tables.

affidatio :—an oath.

affidatus, affidus :—one who has pledged his faith to another.

affilare : —to put on a file with.

affilatorium :—a steel, a hone.

affina :—a workshop.

affinare :—to fine (gold) ; to finish.

affirmare :—to let to farm.

affodillus :—a daffodil.

afforare :—to appraise.

afforciamentum :— a fortress ; compulsion ; the coercive power of a Court.

afforciare :—to increase, or make stronger ; to compel.

afforciatus :—pure, unadulterated. Applied to cloth and other goods.

afforestare :—to turn land into forest.

affra. See *affrus.*

affraia :—an affray.

affraiare :—to frighten.

affrectamentum, affretamentum :— freight.

affrectare, affretare :—to freight.

affriare :—to frighten.

affrus :— an ox or horse for farm work, usually a horse.

affuramentum. See *afferamentum.*

agalauda :—a plover, probably a pewit.

agalma :—an image on a seal.

agaseus :— a gazehound.

agellarius :—a hayward ; a herd-ward.

agellus :—a hamlet.

agenda :—business ; the office of the Mass or other service ; a priest's daily office.

agenfrida :—a lord or owner.

agerarius :—a farmer's dog.

aggreare se :—to agree.

agillarius :— a hayward or herd-ward ; a keeper of cattle on a common.

agisámentum :—a masquerade.

agistamentum :—right of pastur-age ; the sum paid for this right ; assignment of it.

agistare :—to assign pasturage for cattle, esp. in a forest.

agistatæ terræ : — lands whose owners are bound to keep up sea walls.

agistator :—an agister or gyst taker, an officer who assigns the pasturage in a forest.

agistiamentum. See *agistamen-tum.*

agitatio animalium in foresta :— the drift or view of beasts in the forest.

agna :—a gold coin, 14th cent.

agnatio :—lambing.

agnellatio, agnilatio :—lambing.

Agnus Dei :—an oval piece of white wax, stamped with the figure of a lamb, and consecrated.

agontea :—a champion (*agonista*).

agreamentum :—agreement.

agreare se :—to agree.

agredula :—a titmouse.

ayri :—arable land in the com-mon fields.

aimellatus :—enamelled.

ainescia :—the right of the eldest. See *esnecia.*

aira :—an eyrie, the nest of an eagle, a falcon, or a swan.

aisiamentum, aisimentum :—li-berty of passage ; easement.

aisnecca :—a ship. (A.-S. *snacc.*)

aisya :—convenience.

akermannus :—a small farmer. (A.-S. *æcer mon.*) Their holding was less than that of the *virgatarii*, but from comparison of rent must have been more than an acre.

aketonum :—a haqueton, a gam-beson, a padded or quilted tunic.

ala :—the aisle of a church.

alabastarius :— a crossbowman (*arcubalistarius*).

alabrum :—a reel.

alamandina :—a stone coloured like a garnet.

alanerarius :— a keeper of dogs (alans) or hawks (lanners).

alanus :—a large hound.

alatera, alatoria, alatorium, ala-tura :—a covered way or walk ; a piazza.

alaudarius : — a hobby hawk (*falco subbuteo*).

alba :—an alb, a long white tight - sleeved vestment ; dawn.

alba firma :—a yearly rent payable to the chief lord of the hundred in white money, *i.e.* silver; white rent, blanch farm.

Albæ :—the weeks after Easter and Whitsunday.

albatorium :—southernwood.

albergata :—the right of lodging in a vassal's house; money paid in lieu thereof.

albergellum, albergio :—a habergeon, a tunic of mail shorter than a hauberk.

albesteria :—a loophole for shooting through.

albesterius :—a crossbowman.

albinus :—a foreigner. (O. E. a comeling.)

alblasta :—a crossbow (*arcubalista*).

alblastarius :—a crossbowman. See *arcubalistarius.*

aldermannus :—an alderman.

aldermanria :—a district under the jurisdiction of an alderman.

alea :—a passage, an alley.

alebrodium :—a warm drink ; broth ; caudle.

alecenarium :—a lanner (*falco lanarius*).

alecia (sing.) :—herrings (*clupea harengus*).

alecium, alectum :—a herring, herrings. On the Continent the word included sardines and anchovies, but probably not in England.

aleium :—alloy.

aleptes :—a chamberlain.

alficus :—a leper.

alfinus :—a bishop, at chess.

alfita :—flour. *Alfita Herbarum* is the title of a book.

algorismus :—arithmetic.

aliblasterius :—a worker in alabaster.

alices :—contortions.

alietus :—a hobby (*falco subbuteo*).

aliquilitas :—essence.

aliteum :—a crime.

alkamia :—alcamyne, a mixed metal.

alkanea :— alcanet, Spanish bugloss.

alkemonia :—alchemy.

allativus :—bringing.

allaya, allaia :—alloy.

allecia. See *alecia.*

allectium, allectum. See *alecium.*

allegiantia :—allegiance.

allegiare :—to defend or justify by course of law.

alleviare :—to levy or pay a fine.

allocabilis :—allowable.

allocare :—to allow.

allocatio :—allowance ; award.

allocatus :—a proctor.

allodium. See *alodium.*

allorium. See *alura.*

allosa :—a shad. See *alosa.*

allota, alluta :—cork ; cordwain leather.

allottare :—to allot.

allox :—a toe.

allucium. See *allota.*

alluminare :—to illuminate, to decorate books with colour.

alluminator :—a limner, an illuminator.

allutarius. See *alutarius.*

almaria, almerium :—a cupboard; an aumbry. See *armaria.*

almariolum :—a little cupboard.

almicia, almicium. See *almucia, amictus.*

almonaria :—an almonry.

almonarium :—a cupboard; an ambrey.

almonarius :—an almoner.

almonera, almoneria : — an almonry; a pouch or purse from which alms were given.

almucia, almucium :—an amess or amuse, a cloth or fur hood worn by canons and monks.

alna :—an ell. See *ulna.*

alnagium :—measurement by the ell; duty paid by the ell.

alnetum :—a place where alders grow, an alder grove.

aloarius, alodarius :—the lord of a free manor.

alodium :—a free manor.

alorium. See *alura.*

alosa :—a shad, probably used for both the twaite shad and the allice shad. (Cuvier's *alosa finta* and *alosa communis.*)

aloverium :—a purse.

alphita. See *alfita.*

altaragium :—altarage; offerings made upon the altar; small tithes.

altarigium. See *altaragium.*

altarista : — a priest assigned to one altar in a church.

altellus :—an alien.

altera pars :—half.

alterare :—to change, to alter.

alteratio :—alteration.

altile :—a fatted beast or fowl; a capon.

altiragium. See *altaragium.*

alura (Fr. *aleur*) :—an alure, a passage, alley; a parapet; a walk behind a parapet; a gutter.

alutarius :—a cordwainer; a tanner; a tawyer; dressed leather.

alver :—the same as *aloverium* (?).

alveus :—a barge.

alviolum :—a maund, a basket.

amalare :—to enamel.

amanda :—an almond.

amatista :—an amethyst.

ambactus :—a servant; a client.

ambana :—an enclosure round a house; an outbuilding.

ambassiata :— an embassy.

ambassiator :—an ambassador.

ambidexter :—a juror who takes money from both sides; a swindler.

ambis :—a vase.

ambisiata. See *ambassiata.*

ambo :—a pulpit, or reading desk.

ambra :—a measure of wheat or salt, four bushels ; a wine jar ; amber.

ambro :—bold, greedy ; a prodigal.

ambrum :—amber.

ambularius :—an ambling horse.

ambulatorium :—a passage, a gallery.

amelare :—to enamel.

amensuramentum : —m e a s u r e- ment ; assessment ; estimate.

amensurare :—to measure ; to assess.

amera :—willow.

amerciamentum :—a pecuniary punishment.

amerciare :—to amerce, to fine.

amesuramentum. See *amensuramentum.*

amicia. See *almucia.*

amictus :—an amice, a linen sacerdotal vestment forming a hood or collar.

amirellus :—an admiral.

amittena :—a sheeptick.

ammaylare :—to enamel.

amminiculum. See *adminiculum.*

ammobragium, amobragium, a kind of service ; a fine ; the Welsh form of *Mercheta.*

amodo :—then, afterwards.

amortizamentum : —amortization.

amortizare :—to alien lands in mortmain, to amortize.

amortizatio :—amortization.

amotibilis, amovibilis : —removeable.

amphibologia :—ambiguity.

amphibolus :—a cloak, an overall.

amphistrum :—the helm of a ship.

ampliatio :—deferring judgment till a cause is further examined.

amplicare :—to enlarge.

ampulla :—a vessel for holding holy oil ; a reliquary.

amullus :—some farm animal, a ram (?).

amuntare :—to amount.

amuntia :—amount.

anabatrum :—a curtain.

anachoreta :—a hermit ; an anchorite.

analogium :—a reading desk.

anamelatus :—enamelled.

anata :—a duck.

anatus :—a drake.

anca :—a haunch ; an ancle.

ancareus :—with a handle.

ancoragium :—duty paid by ships when they anchor in a haven.

ancus :—long (of gloves).

andena : — a swath ; as much ground as a man can stride over ; an andiron.

andreseya :—a dairy.

androchia, androgia :—a dairymaid.

androchiarium :—a dairy.

anelacium :—a knife ; a dagger.

anella :—a manacle, a handcuff.

angaria :—a vexatious personal service ; distress ; the Ember weeks.

angarialis :—grievous.

angariare :—to compel.

angarius :—a catchpole, an officer who arrests.

angeldum, angildum :—the single valuation or fine imposed on a criminal.

Angleria :—Englishry.

Angliceria :—Englishry.

Anglici, probatio :—proof of Englishry.

animalia :—oxen.

animequus :—contented.

anitergium :—a wisp of grass.

ankerissa ;—an ancress, a female hermit.

annales :—yearling cattle.

annatæ :—first fruits ; annates.

annatus :—first-born ; one year old.

annuale :— yearly income of a prebendary ; or of a priest for celebrating an anniversary.

annuarium :—an anniversary ; a calendar of anniversaries.

annuatim :—yearly.

annulatus :—ringed (of a pig).

anquiromagus :—a ship's stern.

ansea :—a truss.

ansorium :—a shoemaker's knife; a razor.

antecessor :—an ancestor ; a predecessor in office ; also the name of a servant attending on a dean and chapter.

antecinerales feriæ :—days before Ash Wednesday.

antegarda :—vanguard.

antela :—a poitrel.

antemurale :—a barbican.

antenatio :—the right of an elder child.

antependium :—hangings in front of an altar.

antephalarica :—a portcullis.

antesellum : —a package carried in front of the saddle.

antesignatus (antesignanus) :—a soldier posted in front of the standard.

antianitas :—antiquity, *i.e.* seniority ; ancienty.

antianus :—old, ancient.

antibata :—an opponent.

antica :—a hatch.

anticopa :—a countertally.

antidoron :—a gift given in exchange.

antigraphus :—a scribe, a copyist.

antilopia :—an antelope (heraldic).

antipera :—a screen.

antiphona :— alternate verses sung by the halves of the choir.

antiphonarium :—a book containing anthems or antiphons.

antiphonista :—an antiphoner, a leader in singing antiphons.

antiquitas :—seniority; ancienty.

antistes :—a bishop ; an abbot.

antistita :—an abbess.

antistitium : —a monastery.

antithetarius :— an accused person who charges his accuser with the same crime.

apanagium :—the portion of a younger child.

apatisare :—to agree ; to ransom.

apechiamentum :—impeachment.

aporia :—poverty ; trouble.

aporiare :—to impoverish.

apostare :—to transgress.

apostolos petere :—to appeal to Rome.

apothecarius :—a shopkeeper ; a keeper of a granary or store ; a druggist.

apparator :— a messenger who serves the process of a spiritual court, an apparitor.

apparella : —items of miscellaneous excess beyond current regulated expenditure. (Middle Temple.)

apparens lex :—ordeal.

apparentia :—appearance.

appares : —equals.

apparura : — furniture ; equipment.

appatizare. See *apatisare.*

appellare :—to appeal.

appellum : —an appeal.

appendens :—a thing of inheritance, belonging to a greater inheritance.

appenditia : — appendages ; appurtenances.

appendium : —a reel.

appendix, appendicium :—a pentice, a penthouse.

appennagium. See *apanagium.*

appensamentum :—delay ; postponement.

appensura :—payment of money by weight.

appenticium :—a pentice, a penthouse.

applauda :—sauce.

applicium :—an inn ; lodging.

applita :- harness ; fittings.

appodiare :— to prop up ; to sustain.

appoisonare :—to poison.

apponere :—to pledge ; to pawn.

apporia, apporria. See *aporia.*

apportionamentum : — apportionment.

apportionare :—to divide proportionally.

apportum :—revenue or profit ; corrody or pension ; rent or tribute.

appreciare :—to appraise.

apprenticius :—an apprentice.

apprentisagium, apprenticiamentum :—apprenticeship.

approbare :—to augment the value of, as to increase the rent of land.

approbator :—a person who confesses felony and accuses others, an approver.

appropriare :—to annex a benefice to the use of a spiritual corporation or person ; to appropriate.

appropriatio, appropriamentum : —appropriation.

approvamentum :—profits : crop.

approviare, approware, appruare se :—to use for one's own profit, as to enclose waste land.

appruator :—an officer in some towns (*e.g.* Wakefield) appointed to look after the interests of the lord of the manor.

appruntare :— to borrow.

appunctuare :—to appoint.

aprisa, aprisia :—an inquisition, information.

aquagium :—a watercourse ; a holy water stoup.

aqualitium :—a gutter.

aqualium :—the top of the head.

aquare :—to water.

aquarium :—a ewer.

aquebachelus :—a holy water clerk.

aquestus :—acquisition.

arabilis :—a maple tree.

aracium :—a stud of horses. See *haratium*.

aralis :—arable.

arallus :—a ploughfoot.

aralus :—a maple tree.

aratrum terræ :—as much land as can be tilled with one plough.

aratum :—a charter.

aratus :—a day's ploughing.

arbalista, arbalistarius. See *arcubalista*.

arbalisteria :—loopholes.

arcare :—to be charged with ; to build an arch ; to vault.

arcarius :—an archer ; a keeper of an *arca*, a chest for the deposit of treasure or deeds.

arcenarius. See *arconarius*.

archearius :—a bow bearer. See *arcarius*.

archemecherus :—some officer in the household of Henry VI., perhaps chief cook.

archenius :—a rick of corn.

archeria :—archery.

archerius :—a bow bearer.

archidiaconus :—an archdeacon.

archiepiscopus :—an archbishop.

archifenium :—a croft of land.

archionium :—a stack.

archipresbyter :—chief priest in a collegiate church.

archisigillarius :—chief keeper of a seal, a chancellor.

architector :—a thatcher.

architenens :—an archer.

archivum :—a place where records are kept.

archivus :—a keeper of records ; a secretary.

archonista :—a bowyer.

archus :—a bow.

arcista. See *artista*.

arcisterium :—a monastery (*asceterium*).

arconarius :—a man engaged in some trade connected with wool.

arconium :—a rick, a stack.

arconizare :—to stack.

arcuare :—to play a musical instrument which requires the use of a bow.

arcubalista :—a crossbow, an arblast.

arcubalistarius :—a crossbow-man, an arblaster.

arcubius :—a watchman.

arcubus, curia de :—the Court of Arches, so called from the church of St. Mary de Arcubus (le Bow), where it was formerly held.

arcuere :—to shoot with a bow.

arculius :—a watchman.

arculus :—a saddle bow.

arcussit :—shot.

ardeda :—a firegrate.

area :—an open space ; a cemetery.

arenga : – a preamble; harangue.

areniare :—to rein.

arentare :—to let for a rent; to arrent; to rate.

arentatio : — rental ; assessment of rent.

aresta, pannus de :—arras.

arestare :—to arrest.

arestum :—arrest.

a retro : —in arrear.

argumentosus :—ingenious.

argutarius canis :—a greyhound.

arista, pannus de :—arras.

arivagium :—toll paid by ships on mooring at a wharf or port.

arivare :—to approach the shore ; to arrive.

arlechatus :—equipped.

arma dare :—to make a knight.

armaria :—a cupboard ; an aumbry ; a study.

armariolum :—a little cupboard.

armarium. See *armaria*.

armarius : — a librarian in a monastery.

armatura : — armour ; military exercise.

armelausa :—a cloak.

armicudium : —a dagger.

armiger : —an esquire.

armilausa :—a cloak.

armilustrium :—a tournament.

armiturium :—a dagger.

armurarius :—an armourer.

arnaglosa :—plantain.

arnaldia :—a disease, perhaps baldness.

aromatarius :—a grocer; a spicer.

arpa :—a young eagle.

arpendum, arpennum, arpentum : —a small plot of land ; an acre.

arquilla :—a linchpin.

arquillus :—a saddle bow (?) ; an ox yoke.

arquinecca :—some drug or spice.

arrabilis :—a maple tree.

arraiamentum :—array, in reference either to a jury, or to soldiers.

arraiare :—to array.

arraiatio. See *arraiamentum*.

arraiatores : —arrayers, officers whose duty it was to see that soldiers were properly accoutred.

arrainamentum :—arraignment.

arrainare, arrainiare :—to claim; to arraign, to accuse.

arramiare. See *arrainare*.

arramire, adramire :—to promise, esp. in a court of law.

arraria :—arrears.

arratum :—a charter.

arraya. See *arraiamentum*.

arrectatus :—suspected ; accused.

arrenamentum :—arraignment.

arrenare. See *arrainare*.

arrenda :—rent.

arrentare. See *arentare.*

arrepticius :— possessed by an evil spirit.

arreragium :—arrearage ; respite of payment.

arrestare :— to arrest.

arrestum :—arrest.

arriolari :—to foretell (*hariolari*).

arrivagium. See *arivagium.*

arrivare. See *arivare.*

arrura. See *arura.*

arsina :—arson ; house-burning.

arsinale :—an arsenal.

arsura :— trial of money by fire.

artavum :—a small knife.

articulare :—to draw up in articles ; to article.

articulus :— an article ; esp. a complaint exhibited in a Court Christian.

artificium :—handicraft.

artillator :—a maker of artillery.

artilleria :—artillery.

artista : —one who has taken a degree in arts.

artitus :—skilfully made or arranged.

arura : —ploughing ; a day's work with a plough ; a ploughland ; a tilled field ; crops.

arvambulus :—a tramp.

ascella :—the part where the arm joins the shoulder; the armpit (*axilla*).

ascerra :—a ship for incense.

asceterium :—a monastery.

asiamentum. See *aisiamentum.*

asinare :—to ride on an ass.

aspersorium :—a sprinkler ; a vase for holy water.

aspiculna :—a ladle or fork used in frying.

assacella :—a stove.

assaia, assaium :—assay ; examination of weights and measures, bread, beer, &c.

assaiare :—to assay, to examine.

assaiator :—an assayer.

assallire :—to assault.

assaltus :—an assault.

assartare :—to bring forest land into cultivation by grubbing up the roots, &c.

assartum :—assart, land brought into cultivation.

assaturis :—a gridiron.

assaysiare (of judges):—to call others to assist them.

assecurare :—to make secure by pledge or oath ; to assure.

assedare. See *assidare.*

assemblare :—to assemble.

assemblata, assemblatio :—an assembly.

asseratus :—wainscotted.

asserrum :—steel.

assessare :—to assess ; to fine.

assessio :—assessment.

assessor :—an assessor.

asseurare. See *assecurare.*

asseware, assewiare :—to drain marsh ground.

assidare, assidere :—to tax equally ; to assess.

assidella :—a table dormant.

assidiare :—to besiege ; to attack.

assignare :—to transfer a right ; to appoint a deputy ; to declare ; to pledge.

assignare se ad :—to attack ; to lay hands on.

assignatio :—assignment ; transference of interest.

assignatus :—an assignee ; a deputy.

assimulare :—to put together ; to collect.

assisa :—a fixed measure ; a tax or fine ; a sitting of justices to hear causes ; a jury ; certain statutes and writs are also called *assisæ*.

assisa panis et cerevisiæ :—the power of examining the weight and measure of bread and beer.

assisores :—assessors.

assisus :—rented or farmed out.

assisus redditus, redditus assisæ :—rent of assize ; fixed rent.

assoniare :—to essoin.

assueare :—to drain.

assuera :—a drain.

assultus :—an assault.

assumare :—to kill.

assumptio :—the anniversary of the death of a saint.

assurantia :—assurance.

assurare :—to assure.

astela :—a staff.

astrarius hæres :—an heir who occupies his inheritance during his ancestor's life.

astrium :—a hearth ; a house.

astructus :—instructed.

astrum. See *astrium*.

astula :—a piece of firewood.

astur. See *austur*.

asura :—azure.

aszeisia. See *azesia*.

atachiare, &c. See *attachiare*.

athia, atia :—hatred, malice.

atilium, atillium :—an utensil ; an implement ; gear ; the rigging of a ship.

atinctus. See *attinctus*.

atirare :—to equip.

atratus :—a mourner.

atriamentum :—a courtyard.

attachare :—to affix.

attachiamentum : — attachment ; apprehension of a person or seizing goods ; articles seized with a criminal, showing his guilt ; right of using (underwood, water, &c.).

attachiamentum forestæ : — the lower court of a forest.

attachiare :—to take in pursuance of a writ ; to attach.

attachiator :—an officer who makes attachment ; a bailiff.

attagiare :—to attach.

attaincta, attincta : — attaint, a writ against a jury for giving a false verdict.

attamiare, attaminare :—to broach.

attaxare :—to assess.

attegia :—a little house.

atterminare :—to put within certain boundaries ; to postpone to a certain day ; to atterm.

atthagiare. See *attachiare.*

attilamentum. See *atilium.*

attiliaria : — military engines ; artillery.

attilliamentum. See *atilium.*

attilliator :—a maker of artillery or military engines.

attilium. See *atilium.*

attincta :—attaint.

attinctare :—to attaint.

attinctus :—attainted.

attirare :—to equip.

attornamentum :—an acknowledgment by a tenant of a new lord, attornment.

attornare : — to assign goods to some special use ; to appoint an attorney ; to pack (?).

attornata :—a commission.

attornatus : — an attorney.

attractorium :—a train ; a trace.

attractus :—carriage by dragging, draught ; store.

atturnare, &c. See *attornare,* &c.

aubergellum :—a habergeon, a tunic of mail.

aubobulcus : — an oxherd.

auca :—a goose ; some article of plate, perhaps an ewer ; an enclosed piece of land.

aucipiter :—a falcon.

auctenticare :—to declare authentic.

auctionarius, auctionator :—a retailer ; a broker.

aucubaculare :—to catch birds after dark, to batfowl.

aucula :—a gosling.

aucuntacio :—used for *augmentatio.*

aucupia :—game.

auditor : — a catechumen ; an examiner of accounts.

augea :—a cistern.

aula :—a court baron ; the nave of a church.

auleum :—a hanging, tapestry.

aunciatus :—antiquated.

auncinium : — an afternoon meal.

auracio :—gilding.

aurare :—to gild.

aureolus :—a golden oriole (*oriolus galbula*), or goldfinch (*fringilla carduelis*).

auricalcum :—latten.

auriculare :—a cushion ; a defence for the ears of a horse.

auricularis digitus : —the little finger.

auricularius :—a secretary.

aurifex :—a goldsmith.

aurificium : —goldsmith's work.

aurifilum :—gold thread.

aurifragium. See *aurifrigium.*

aurifraser, aurifresarius : — an embroiderer.

aurifriatus, aurifrigiatus : —having an orphrey.

aurifrigium, aurifresium, aurifrisium, aurifrixium :—an orphrey, golden embroidery on clerical vestments.

aurisia :—blindness (ἀορασία).

auroca, aurocus :—a haycock, a hayrick; the quantity of hay which can be lifted on the handle of a scythe.

aurus. See *averus.*

austur, austurcus :—a goshawk (*astur palumbarius.* Fr. *autour*).

austurcharius :—a falconer.

ausungius :—fat.

autela :—a horse's breastplate or poitrel, probably an error for *antela.*

autumnus : — translated " summer " in the books of the Middle Temple.

autumpnare :—to bring the harvest home.

auxilium :—an aid.

auxionarius. See *auctionarius.*

avagium :—payment for right of pannage in the lord's wood.

avalagium :—a fixed engine to take fish; eelbucks; the descent of a river; toll paid therefor.

avalare :—to descend a river.

avantagium. See *advantagium.*

avaragius :—one who looks after draught cattle.

avellana nux :—a hazel nut.

avenagium :—avenage, rent paid in oats.

avenarius :—an avener, purveyor of oats.

avencia :—advance.

aventallum :—a ventaile, or visor.

aventura. See *adventura.*

avera :—a day's work of a ploughman.

averagium :—service with horse and carriage due by the tenant to his lord; contribution by merchants towards losses of cargo by tempest.

averarius :—a man who looks after farm cattle.

averia :—horses or oxen for the plough; cattle generally.

averia de pondere, or *ponderis* :— avoirs du poys, *i.e.* fine goods, such as spices, weighed by the pound at the king's small balance when the duty was charged.

averium :—goods, merchandise.

averrare :—to carry goods in a wagon, or on horseback.

averus :—a farm horse, or draught ox.

aviaticus :—a nephew.

avironatus :—rowing.

avironus :—an oar.

avis :—used like the Fr. *oiseau,* for a hawk or falcon.

avisagium. See *avagium.*

avisamentum :—advice.

avisare :—to advise.

avoare. See *avocare.*

avoaria :—avowry.

avocare :—to avow, confess; to justify.

avragium. See *averagium.*

avrus. See *averus.*

awardium :—an award.

axare :—to make or fit an axle-tree.

axiliare :—to help.

M.

O

aymellatus :—enamelled.

ayziamentum. See *aisiamentum.*

azaldus :—an inferior horse.

azarum :—steel.

azesiæ :—tiles (?), shingles (?).

B.

babatum :—a horseshoe.

baca :—an iron hook or staple.

bacar :—a turnip.

baccalarius, baccalaureus :—a bachelor.

baccile, baccinium :—a bason.

bachelarius :—a young knight; a knight disqualified from youth or poverty from carrying a banner in war. See *baccalarius.*

bacheleria :—the commonalty, as distinguished from the baronage.

bacho. See *baco.*

bacile, bacina, bacinus :—a bason.

bacinettum :—a basinet, a helmet smaller than a helm and usually pointed at the top.

bacium :—a horsecloth. O. E. base. See *bassum.*

baco :—a hog; a salted pig's carcase; a flitch of bacon; a ham.

bactile :—a candlestick, esp. of wood.

bacularius :—a bachelor.

baculus :—a crozier.

badius :—bay (horse).

baffa :—a flitch of bacon.

baga :—a bag or purse.

bagatinus :—a small brass Venetian coin, worth in the 17th century about $\frac{1}{16}$ of a penny.

bagea :—a badge.

bagus :—bay (horse).

bahuda, bahudum :—a chest; a trunk, called a barehide in English.

baia :—rumour; a bay.

baiardus :—a bay horse.

baila, bailium :—bail.

bailius, baillivus :—a bailiff.

baillia :—bailiwick.

baillium :—a grant in trust; the " bailey " of a castle.

baius :—bay (of a horse).

bajula :—a pitcher; the office of *bajulus;* a nurse.

bajulator :—a bearer; a guardian.

bajulus :—a bearer; a bailiff.

bajulus aquilæ :—an officer in the military order of St. John of Jerusalem, the Bailly of the Eagle.

bakeria :—a bakehouse.

bala :—a bale.

balancea, balancia :—a pair of scales.

balasius :—a balasse ruby, of a pale colour.

balca :—a balk (of land).

balcanifer :—the standard-bearer of the Knights Templars.

balcanum :—the Templars' standard.

baldacinifer. See *balcanifer.*

baldekinum, baldicum :—baudekin, a kind of brocade of silk and gold, originally brought from Bagdad; a canopy.

baldrea :—a baldric.

balducta :—a posset.

balengaria, balingarium :—a balinger; a barge.

balesius. See *balasius.*

baleuga. See *banleuga.*

balidinus :—bay (of a horse).

balista :—used for a cross-bow, which is properly *arcubalista.*

balistarius :—an arblaster, a cross-bowman.

balla. See *ballia, balliva.*

ballare :—to sweep; to dance.

ballatio :—a ballad.

balleuca. See *banleuga.*

ballia :—the "bailey" of a castle. See *balliva.*

ballium :—bail; the "bailey" of a castle; wardship; a grant in trust.

ballius :—a bailiff.

balliva, ballivatus : — bailiwick ; office.

ballivus :—a bailiff.

balneare :—to bathe.

balneo, miles de :—a knight of the Bath.

balneta :—some sort of whale.

balus :—a bale.

balustraria :—loopholes.

bamba :—a bed.

bancale, bancarium :—a banker, a covering for a bench.

bancum, bancus :—a bench.

banda :—a band (of soldiers).

bandum :—a pennon.

baneale :—error for *bancale* (?), *q.v.*

banera, baneria :—a banner.

banerettus :—a knight made in the field, by cutting off the point of his pennon and making it a banner.

banidium :—a badge.

banleuga, bannaleuca : — the bounds of a manor or town ; the circuit of a monastery over which it has jurisdiction. (Fr. *banlieue.*)

bannezare :—to banish.

banniare, bannire :—to proclaim ; to summon by proclamation ; to banish.

bannum, banum :—a proclamation; a boundary; (pl.) bans of matrimony.

banum :—a bane.

baractator, barator :—a barretor, a common mover of suits and quarrels.

barbacana, barbakena. See *barbicana.*

barbator :—a barber.

barbatus :—barbed, of an arrow.

barbecana. See *barbicana.*

barbelatus :—barbed.

barbicana : — an outwork of a fortress.

barbicanagium :—contribution for the maintenance of a barbican.

barbillus :—a barbel (*barbus vulgaris*) or mullet (*mullus barbatus*).

barbitonsor :—a barber.

barbitura :—shaving.

barbota :—a barge ; an armed vessel.

barbulus :—a barbel (*barbus vulgaris*).

barca :—a barque.

barcaria. See *bercaria* and *barkaria.*

barcarius. See *bercarius.*

barcius :—a fish, probably perch (*perca fluviatilis*), perhaps also bass (*labrax lupus*).

bardatus :—barded, armed with a bard (of a horse).

barellus :—a barrel.

baresta :—a barrister.

barettus :—probably the same as *warectus.*

barga. See *barca* and *bargea.*

bargania :—an agreement; a bargain.

barganizare :—to bargain.

bargea, bargia :—a barge ; part of a horse's trappings.

barhuda, barhuta, barhuzia :—a chest ; a trunk, a barehide.

barillum, barrillus :—a barrel.

barka :—a barge ; a barque.

barkaria :—a tan-house.

barmbraccus :—a lap-dog.

barnagium :—baronage.

baro :—a baron.

baronagium :—baronage.

baronatus :—barony ; baronage.

baronettus :—a baronet.

baronia :—a barony.

baronissa :—a baroness.

barra, barrha :—a bar, a barrier ; a bar to an action.

barractator :—a barretor, an instigator of suits and quarrels.

barragium :—toll for crossing a bridge.

barrare :—to put bars to.

barrasterius :—a barrister.

barratria :—dissension ; barratry.

barrista :—a barrister.

barruzia. See *barhuda.*

bartona :—demesne lands ; a manor house.

barutellum :—a cask.

bascinus :—a bason.

basculus :—a basket.

basena. See *bazeyna.*

basilardum :—a long poniard ; a falchion ; a cutlass. (Early Chanc. Proc. 47, 256.)

basnetum :—a basinet. See *bacinettum.*

bassare :—to lower.

bassaria camera :—a base chamber.

basselardus. See *basilardum.*

bassellus :—a coin abolished by king Henry II.

bassum :—a pack saddle.

bassus :—low.

bastardia :—bastardy.

bastardus :—one born out of wedlock.

bastida, bastita :—a castle, a word used especially in Southern France.

basto :—a staff.

bastonicum :—close custody.

basum. Per basum tolnetum capere, to take toll by strike.

batalia :—battle.

batella, batellus :—a small boat.

batellagium :—boat-hire.

batellarius :—a boatman ; a bateller, the lowest order in Oriel College.

batellatus :—embattled.

batellus :—a boat. See *batillus.*

bateria :—battery, beating.

batilda :—toll for boats (?).

batillagium :—carriage by boat; boat-hire.

batillare :—to send by boat.

batillus :—a bat ; a beetle ; a clapper ; a boat.

batitoria :—a fulling mill.

batium. See *bacium.*

bativa, batura :—battery.

batleuga. See *banleuga.*

batus :—a boat ; a measure, 12½ gallons ; a peck ; a vessel used in feeding horses ; a bat.

baubare :—to bark ; to bay.

baubella :—jewels.

bauca :—a bason.

baucaria :—a tapster.

baudekinum. See *baldekinum.*

bausanus :— a badger, a bawson.

bausia, bosia :—treason, felony.

bausiare, bosiare :—to rebel.

bauzanus :—piebald. (Fr. *bauçant, bauzant.*)

baya. See *baia.*

bazantius. See *bisantius.*

bazeyna : — basil, prepared leather.

bechare :—to dig ; to use a pick-axe.

becnus :—some sort of fish.

beconagium :—contribution for the maintenance of beacons.

bedelaria :—the office of beadle, or district to which his office extends ; bedellary.

bedellus :—a beadle, or bedell.

bederipa. See *bedrepium.*

bedrepium :—bedripe, harvest work done by tenants as a customary service ; it sometimes means a definite amount, perhaps a day's work.

bedripus. See *bedrepium.*

bedum :—the portion of a mill-stream which turns the wheel and is boarded up to increase the force of water.

belfredus :—a belfry.

belgiga :—a car, a chariot.

bellicrepa :—a muster.

belligerare :—to make war.

bellum :—a battle ; used, as the English word is, to denote a portion of an army ; a judicial combat, duel.

benda :—a band, either metal or stuff ; a bar ; a bend (heraldic).

beneficiare :—to confer a benefice on ; to enfeoff.

beneficium :—a benefice, an ecclesiastical living or promotion.

benevolentia :—a voluntary gratuity given by subjects to the king.

benwrda :—benerthe, service with plough and cart.

beodum :—a table.

bera :—a bier. See *beria, bersa.*

berbiagium :—a rent paid in sheep, or tax paid on sheep.

berbicaria :—pasture for sheep.

berbix :—a sheep.

bercaria :—a sheepfold, sheepcote ; a sheepwalk.

bercarius :—a shepherd.

bercelettus. See *bracelettus.*

berdare :—to beard or bard wool, *i.e.*, to cut the head and neck off the fleece.

berebrutus :—a man who takes charge of and distributes beer (?).

berefredus, berefridus :—a belfry.

berewicha :—a village or hamlet.

berfrarium :—a military engine.

beria :—an open plain.

berkeria. See *bercaria.*

bernaca :—a bernicle goose (*anser bernicla*).

bernarius :—a forest officer ; a bearward ; a beardog.

bernix :—varnish.

berra :—a heath, or moor.

bersa :—the fence inclosing a park ; an inclosure.

bersare :—to hunt ; to shoot.

bersarius :—a hunter ; a forester or park-keeper.

berseletta, berseretta :—a small hound, used for fallow deer.

berthona, bertona. See *bartona.*

berwica :—a village or hamlet.

berziza :—beer, or perhaps wort.

besacutum. See *bisacuta.*

besantus. See *bisantius.*

besca, bescha :—a spade ; a shovel.

bescare :—to dig.

bescarium :—a spade.

bescata :—as much land as a man can dig in a day.

beschillum :—a spade.

bestiæ :—beasts (deer or cattle, usually the former).

betagius :—a serf whose lord is a church or convent.

beudum :—a table.

bever :—a beaver (*castor fiber*).

beverinus, beverius :—of beaver.

bibatio :—drinking.

biberagium :—beverage.

biberia, biberrium :—an afternoon lunch, bever.

bibina. See *biberia.*

bibis, cum suis :—error for *vivis* (?), livestock.

bibletum :—a place where rushes grow.

bibona :—a spout.

bica :—a bees' nest ; a beehive.

bicarius :—a bee-keeper.

bicoca :—a turret.

bidellus :—a bedell ; a beadle.

bidens :—a pitchfork.

bidripa. See *bedrepium.*

bidua :—a female sheep from 1 to 2 years old, a gimmer.

biduana :—a fast of two days.

biforalis :—with two doors or shutters.

biga :—a two-wheeled cart; its load. *"Anglice,* a wagon," in a deed *temp.* Jac. I.

bigarius :—a carter.

bigata :—a cart load.

bigera :—a doublet.

bigustrum :—a primrose.

bilagines :—bye-laws.

bilheta :—a bill; a billet.

bilettum :—a billet.

bilinguis :—(of a jury) part English and part foreign.

billa :—a bill.

billetum :—a billet; a stake.

billia :—a branch; a post.

billio :—money of copper, or copper and silver; bullion.

billus :—a staff or stick.

bilneta :—a passport.

bina :—a pair-horse cart.

bindum :—a bundle; a bind of eels is 250 ; a stalk of hops ; used also for skins.

binnarium :—a fishpond, an error for *vivarium* (?).

bino :—a ploughtail ; a cart pole.

bipalium :—a spade.

birrettum :—a thin close-fitting cap ; a coif.

bisacuta :—a two-headed axe ; a black bill, a twybill.

bisantius :—a besant, a gold coin, first issued by the emperors of Byzantium, worth about a ducat ; a bezant in heraldry.

bisantius albus :—a silver besant, worth about 2*s.*

bisantius de plata :—The same.

biscoctus, biscotus :—biscuit.

bisius. See *bisus.*

bisquetta :—part of a castle.

bissa :—a hind.

bisus :—lawn ; cambric.

bisus panis :—brown bread.

bivernagium :—second crop.

bizachius :—a baselard, a cutlass.

bizantium. See *bisantius.*

bladarius :—a cornchandler.

bladum :—corn.

blanchetta, blanchetum :—a woollen garment worn under armour.

blanchetus :—a blanket.

blanchiatura :—reduction of base money to its true value.

blanci :—white money, sterling.

blancum :—a silver coin, worth 8*d.,* coined by Henry V. in France.

blancum argentum : — money tested at the Exchequer as to its fineness.

blancum firme :—blanch farm.

blandella :—a cloak ; a blanket.

blanhornum :—a horn. (A.-S. *blauhorn.*)

blaserius :—an incendiary.

blaudius. See *blodeus.*

blaunchetta. See *blanchetta.*

blaundella. See *blandella.*

blendus. See *bluedius.*

blestia :—turf.

blestro :—a branch.

blestura :—branches.

bleta :—peat.

blettro :—a branch.

bleuius :—blue.

blida, blidus :—a catapult.

blodeus, blodius:—deep red; blue.

blondus :—yellow; fair-haired.

bluedius, bluetus :—blue.

blundus. See *blondus.*

blurus :—bald.

bocardo :—a prison.

bocca :—a boss.

bocellus. See *botellus.*

boculus :—a bullock.

boga :—budge, lamb fur.

bogetta :—a budget.

boia. See *buia.*

boisiare :—to rebel.

boissellus :—a bushel.

bokorammus :—buckram.

bolare :—to play at bowls.

boldagium, bolhagium :—a cottage.

bolengarius :—a baker.

bolla :—a bowl; three-quarters of a pint; a boll, 6 bushels.

boloninus :—a boloner, an Italian gold coin of two kinds, old boloners and Papal boloners, bearing on one side the Resurrection, on the other S. Thomas the Apostle of India or Mary Magdalene, the former being slightly more valuable.

bombarda, bombardus:—a cannon.

bombicina :—a hacqueton, a jack, a quilted tunic.

bombosus :—noisy.

bombycinium :—padding.

boncha :—a bunch; a bank.

bondagium :—villenage; slavery; a tenement held by a villein.

bondemannus :—a bondman.

bondus :—a serf; a slave.

borachia :—an erection for fishing. See *burochium.*

borda :—a plank; a hut; a small farm.

bordagium :—tenure by which *bordarii* hold.

bordaria :—a cottage.

bordarius :—a cottier; also probably a farm-labourer living at the farm-house; a table servant; an inferior domestic servant.

bordellus :—a small house.

bordus, bordum :—a board.

boriens, borientalis :—north.

boscagium :—food which trees yield to cattle, as mast and acorns.

boscar. See *bostar.*

boscarium :—a wooden house; a cowhouse.

boscarius :—a woodman.

boscus :—a wood.

bosia, bausia :—treason, felony.

bosiare, bausiare :—to rebel.

bosonus :—a weapon, perhaps an arrow. See *buzo.*

bostar, bostarium :—a stable for oxen.

bostarius :—a gravedigger.

bostio :—a cattle driver.

bota, botta :—a boot; a bunch; a bundle; a bottle (of hay).

botellarius :—a butler; a bottle maker.

botelleria :—a buttery, or butlery.

botellus :—a bottle; the stomach.

botescarlus :—a boatman.

botha :—a booth.

bothagium :—payment for permission to erect booths at fairs and markets.

bothena :—a barony, lordship.

bothna, buthna :—a park for cattle.

botillum :—a boltell, *i.e.* a round moulding or bead; a small shaft in a clustered column.

boto :—a button.

botonare :—to button.

botracium :—a buttress.

botrus :—a cluster.

botta. See *bota.*

bottellaria. See *botelleria.*

bounda :—a boundary.

bovaria :—a cattle-shed.

bovarius :—an ox-herd.

bovata terræ :—an ox-gang.

boveria, boverium : —a cattle-shed.

bovetta :—a heifer.

bovettus :—a steer, a young ox.

boviculus :—a young ox, but not the same as *bovettus.*

bovina :—a stable for oxen; a cow-house.

bozetum :—cowdung.

braca terræ :—a ridge of earth, a balk. (**Fr.** *braye.*)

bracalia :—breeches.

bracco :—a brache, a small hound; often means a bitch.

bracelettus :—diminutive of *bracetus.*

bracenarius :—a huntsman.

bracetus, bracheta : —a brachet, a hound for hare and fox, a beagle (?).

bracha :—a cloak. See *bracco.*

brachanum :—a carpet (?).

brachia :—some fixed fishing engine.

brachiare :—to brew.

brachiata :—an armful; a fathom.

brachinum :—a kneading trough.

braciare :—to brew.

braciatorium :—a brewhouse.

bracinum :—a brewhouse; a brew.

braconarius. See *bracenarius.*

braelli :—breeches.

braesium :—malt.

bragetum :—bragwort, or bracket, a drink flavoured with honey and spice.

bragmannus :—a robber, marauder.

brandium :—buckram.

branda, brando :—a torch.

brandones :—the first week in Lent.

brandonis vel brandonum dies :— the first Sunday in Lent.

branis :—brawn, muscle.

brannus :—a fish, probably a bream (*abramis brama*).

brao :—a ham; a gammon, possibly a misreading of *baco*.

braseum :—malt.

brasiare :—to brew.

brasiaria :—a malthouse; a brewery.

brasiator :—a maltster; a brewer.

brasina :—a brewhouse.

brasinagium :—brewing.

brasinum :—the quantity of beer brewed at one time.

brasium :—malt.

brasorium :—a brewhouse.

brassata :—a measure of 6 feet.

brattea :—a leaf of metal, foil.

bravium :—a prize.

breca :—half a virgate (Worcester Priory Reg.).

brecca, brecka :—a breach. See also *braca*.

brechia. See *braca, brecca.*

bredna :—a bream.

breidura :—embroidery.

breisna :—wethers.

brella :—starch.

bremia :—a bream.

bremium :—bran.

bremulus :—a bream.

brenagium :—a rent paid in bran, for the feed of the lord's hounds.

brenna, brennia :—a bream (*abramis brama*).

brennium, breno :—bran.

bresmia, bresna, bresnia :— a bream.

bretaschia :—a stockade.

bretechia, bretesca :—a stockade.

brethachia :—a stockade.

brethachiare :—to fortify with stockades.

bretnia :—a bream.

breve :—a writ.

breviarium :—a breviary.

brevigerulus :—one who carries and serves writs.

brevis :—a brief.

brevitor :—a writer of writs.

bria :—a liquid measure.

brianneum seruitium :—same as *brenagium* (?). (Selby Coucher, f. 122*b*.)

briga :—contention; tumult.

brigandinarius : — an officer in command of a brigade.

brigata :—a brigade.

Brigittensis :—a nun of the order of St. Bridget.

broca :—a tap. See *brocha*.

brocagium, broccagium :—a broker's hire; brokerage.

brocatus :—stitched. See *brocha*.

broccarius, broccator :—a broker.

brocella :—a wood.

brocellum :—brushwood.

brocha, broccus : — an awl; a packing needle; a spit.

brochia :—a pitcher.

brochus :—a stick of eels, *i.e.* 25.

broculator :—a brewer.

brodiellum :—brewet, pottage.

brodium :—broth.

broidare, broiderare : — to embroider.

brokettus :—a brocket, a stag in its second or third year; but in Cl. R. 21 Hen. III. m. 12, the word is applied to *damos*, *i.e.* fallow deer.

brollium :—wood, esp. for game.

broncheria :—Palm Sunday.

brossus :—bruised.

bruarium : — heather ; heath ground.

brudatus :—embroidered.

bruera :—heath.

bruilletus :—a small coppice.

bruillium. See *brollium.*

bruisdatus, brusdatus :—embroidered.

brullium. See *brollium.*

brumillus :—a bream (*abramis brama*).

brunda :—a stag's horn.

bruneta. See *burneta.*

brunus : — brown.

bruscare :—to browse.

bruscia :—a wood.

bruscus :—brush; broom plant; a beehive.

brussura, brusura :—a bruise.

brusua, brusula :—browse; brushwood.

bucca, bucia. See *bussa.*

buccare :—to puff.

buccula. See *bucla.*

bucecarlus :—a boatman.

bucellum :—a leather bottle.

bucetum :—a cattle stall.

bucla :—a boss; a buckle.

buclarium :—a buckler.

bucula :—a buckle.

buculus :—the rim of a shield.

buda :—a mat.

budellus. See *bedellus.*

bufetum :—a board, a cupboard.

buffa :—a large ship (error for *bussa ?*).

bugerannum :—buckram.

bugo :—a stump, a log. (Fr. *buche.*)

bugula :—a buckle.

buhurdicium :—a tournament.

buia, buio :—the two parts of a fetter.

buillo. See *bullio.*

bujectum :—budge, lamb fur.

bukelarius :—a buckler.

bulengerius :—a baker.

buletellum :—a sieve. See *bultellum.*

bulettare :—to boult.

bulga, bulgium :—a budget; a portmanteau; a bale.

bulla :—a seal; a papal bull, sealed with lead or gold.

bullare :—to append a *bulla* or seal.

bullaria :—the office where the *bulla* was appended.

bullatus :—sealed.

bulleria :—a salt house (?).

bullio :—a measure of salt, 12 gallons; a measure of almonds; bullion.

bullire :—to boil.

bultellum, bultellus :—a sieve ; bran ; the refuse of meal after it is dressed by the baker.

bunda :—a boundary.

bundare :—to bound.

bundellus :—a bundle.

bura :—a lock of hair or wool.

burbalia, burbilia :—the numbles of a deer.

burbulium :—a bubble.

burburium. See *burbalia.*

burcerius :—the captain of a ship.

burcida :—a thief, a cutpurse.

burdare, burdeare :—to jest ; to joust.

burdeicia, burdicium : —a tournament.

burdo :—a staff. (Fr. *bourdon.*)

burdus :—a board.

burellarius :—a bureller, maker of borel, or maker of yarn.

burellator : — a bureller. See *burellarius.*

burellatus : —barred.

burellus : —borel or burrel, a coarse brown or grey woollen cloth made in Normandy as well as in England (Fr. *bureau*) ; a cupboard ; a borrell, a boring tool.

burgagium :—the service whereby a borough is held ; a dwelling-house in a borough ; burgage.

burgare : — to break into a house, to commit burglary.

burgaria :—burglary.

burgarius : —a burgess.

burgator :—a burglar.

burgemotus :—an assembly of burgesses.

burgensis : —a burgess ; a townsman.

burgeria :—burglary.

burgesaticum :—land held by burgage tenure.

burghgeritha :—a fine for breach of the peace in a town.

burglaria :—burglary.

burgulariter :—burglariously.

burgus :—a borough.

burlemannus :—the constable's assistant at a Court leet.

burneta, burnetum :—cloth made of dyed wool ; a kind of bird.

burniciator :—a burnisher.

burochium :—a small weel for taking fish, a burrock.

burrellus. See *burellus.*

bursa :—an exchange, a meeting place of merchants.

bursaria :—a bursary.

bursarius :—a bursar ; a purse maker.

burscida :—a cutpurse.

bursesaticum. See *burgesaticum.*

burum :—a room.

burus :—a husbandman.

busca :—underwood ; firewood.

buscardus : —a transport ship.

buscare :—to cut underwood.

buscarlus :—a seaman.

buscellum. See *bucellum.*

buscha, buscia :—underwood. See *bussa.*

busellus :—a bushel.

busones :—chief persons (*barones ?*).

bussa :—a great ship. The English buss is a fishing boat.

bussellus :—a bushel.

bussio :—a bush.

busta :—a box.

butarius :—a butler ; a bootmaker (?).

buteleria, butellarium :—a buttery.

butellus. See *botellus.*

buteus :—a boat.

buthsecarlus. See *buscarlus.*

buthum. See *buttum.*

buticularia :—a buttery.

buticularius :—a butler.

butirum :—butter.

butisellus :—a small bottle.

butta, butticum :—a butt of wine.

butticella :—a buttery.

buttileria :—a buttery, or butlery.

buttum terræ :—a butt of land, the end of a ploughed field.

buturum :—butter.

buxeria :—a plantation of box trees.

buya. See *buia.*

buzardum :—a transport ship.

buzo :—the shaft of an arrow.

bycus :—boxwood.

byzantius. See *bisantius.*

C.

caabla :—a cable.

caabulus :—a machine for throwing stones, a perriere. (Fr. *chaable.*)

caballus :—a horse.

cabana :—a cabin.

cabdellus :—a chief judge at Dax. (Fr. *chadelerre.*)

cabdolium :—a castle or chief building in a town.

cabla :—a cable.

cableicium, cablicia, cablicium :— windfall wood; brouse wood, cablish.

cabo :—a stallion.

cacepollus :—a catchpole, or inferior bailiff.

cacherellus :—a catchpole.

cachiagium :—packing, or payment therefor.

cacor. See *chasor.*

cada :—a cade of herrings, 600 of 6 score to the 100.

cadaverator morine :—a man who removes the carcases of sheep dead of murrain.

cadia :—a piece of firewood.

cadicla :—a weaver's shuttle ; the woof.

cadium :—a quay.

Cæsar :—the emperor.

cæsareus :—imperial.

cafagium :—a stall ; a cage ; a pen.

caffa :—some silk stuff.

cagia :—a net for hunting ; a coop ; a cage.

cairellus :—a quarel, a crossbow bolt.

calacha :—a shoe. (Fr. *galoche*.)

calafurcium :—gallows.

calamandrum :—a kerchief.

calamar :—a penner.

calamistratus:—lazy; effeminate.

calangia, calangium : — a challenge ; a claim.

calbla :—a cable.

calcari :—to be assessed for.

calcaria, una :—a pair of spurs.

calcarius :—a spurrier.

calcea, calceia: —chalk; a causey, or causeway; a street; pavement.

calceatura :—livery.

calcesta :—white clover.

calceta, calcetum : — lime ; a causey, or causeway ; a street ; pavement.

calcifurnium :—a limekiln.

calcitura :—shoeing horses.

caldaria :—a caldron.

caldearium, caldellum :—caudle.

calderium :—a caldron.

caldo :—entrails.

caledeus :—a Culdee.

calefactor ceræ :—a chafewax, an officer in the Court of Chancery.

calefagium :—the right of taking fuel.

calefurcium :—gallows.

calendæ :—rural chapters held on the first of the month.

calendare :—to make a list; to calendar.

calendarium:—a list; a calendar; a table of contents.

calengiare :—to challenge.

caleptra :—a cap.

calfagium :—fuel.

calificare. See *qualificare*.

caligarum, unum par de :—" one pair of woollen cloth Venetians " (1601).

calix :—a chalice.

calixtorium :—a limekiln.

calmacia :—calm weather.

calmetum :—marsh.

calopodium:—a shoemaker's last.

calumnia:—a challenge ; a claim.

calumniare :—to challenge ; to accuse ; to claim.

calumniatio:—right of challenge.

calumniator :—a claimant; an accuser.

calyx :—a chalice.

camacatus :—made of camaca.

camahutum :—a cameo.

camaka :—camaca, a material of which ecclesiastical garments were made, perhaps silk, camlet (?).

cambellanus :—a chamberlain.

cambiare, cambire:—to exchange; to trade; to keep a bank.

cambiator. See *cambitor*.

cambipartia. See *campipartitio*.

cambire. See *cambiare*.

cambitio :—exchange.

cambitor:—an exchanger, a moneyer.

cambium:—an exchange; a mint.

cambra. See *camera.*

cambuca, cambuta :—a pastoral staff, a crosier.

cambucarius :—one who bears a crosier.

cambutio :—exchange.

cambuttæ :—stilts; crutches.

camelotum :—camel's hair cloth.

camera :—a crooked plot of ground; a chamber.

camera stellata : — the Star Chamber.

cameralis :—chamber (adj.).

cameraria :—the office of chamberlain.

camerarius :—a chamberlain.

cameria :—the office of chamberlain.

camerlengus :—a chamberlain.

camicia :—a shirt.

caminus, caminum :—a road; a chamber; a chimney; a stove.

camisia :—a shirt; an alb.

camoca :—a silken garment.

campana :—a bell.

campanarium :—a belfry.

campanarius :—a bell founder.

campanella :—a little bell.

campania :—open country.

campanile :—a belfry.

campanus :—country (adj.).

campartum :—part of a larger field, which would otherwise be in common; or the right of the lord to take a certain share of the crop.

campedulum : —a cope.

campertum. See *campartum.*

campestralis :—open country.

campestratus : — wearing short drawers.

campio :—a champion.

campipars. See *campartum.*

campiparticeps :—a champertor.

campipartitio :—champerty, a bargain with the plaintiff or defendant in a suit to have part of the thing sued for.

campsare :—to exchange, to traffic.

campsor :—a banker; an exchanger; an exchequer officer.

campus :—field (heraldic).

canabasium, canabus :—canvas.

canapeum :—a canopy.

canardus :—a great ship.

cancella :—the chancel of a church.

cancellare :—to delete writing by drawing lines across it; to cancel.

cancellaria :—chancery.

cancellarius :—a chancellor.

cancellatura :—cancelling.

cancellum :—the chancel of a church.

cancera : —a crab, a sort of capstan for moving heavy weights.

candelaria :—Candlemas.

candelarius :—a chandler.

candelatio :—Candlemas.

candelossa :—Candlemas.

candidare :—to wash clothes.

candidarius :—a launder, a whitster.

candredum. See *cantreda*.

canella :—cinnamon.

canellus :—a gutter, a kennel; a tube or tap for drawing wine.

canestellus :—a basket.

caneva :—a buttery; a cellar.

canevacium :—canvas.

canfara :—ordeal by hot iron.

canipulus :—a short sword; a knife.

canna :—a rod used for measuring land; a can.

canniare :—to heap up straw or reeds.

canonia, canonicatus :—a canonry.

canonicus :—a canon, a prebendary.

cantaredus. See *cantreda*.

cantaria :—a chantry.

cantarista :—a chantry priest.

cantellum :—a lump; that which is added above measure.

cantera :—a gantry, or gantril, a four-footed stand for barrels, or for a travelling crane. Perhaps the same as *cancera*.

canto :—a canton (heraldic).

cantor :—a chanter; a precentor.

cantreda, cantredus :—a cantref, a Welsh division of a county, a hundred villages.

cantus :—a corner; an angle; some part of a wheel.

capa :—a mantle; a cope; a cap.

capana :—a pot-hook.

caparo :—a hood.

capella :—a cap; a chaplet; a short mantle; a reliquary; a chapel; the furniture of a chapel.

capellania :—a collegiate church; a chaplaincy; a chapelry; a vicarage.

capellanus :—a chaplain.

capellaria :—a chapelry.

capellarius :—a capper.

capelletum :—a headpiece.

capellula :—a small chapel.

capellum, capellus :—a cap; a helmet.

capicerius :—a vestry keeper.

capicium. See *capitium*.

capillare :—a coif.

capisterium :—a sieve; a barn, a granary; a bed-curtain.

capistrius :—a maker of halters.

capitagium :—chevage, poll-money; a bolster.

capitale :—a chattell; a thing which is stolen, or the value of it; a hood; a pillow.

capitale vivens :— live cattle.

capitalis :—chief.

capitales acræ :—headlands, the parcels of a common field at right angles to the long strips.

capitalitium :—poll money.

capitaneus :—a captain.

capitare :—to abut.

capite, tenere in :—to hold in chief.

capitegium :—a hood, a cap.

capitellum :—the capital of a pillar.

capitiarius. See *capicerius.*

capitilavium :—Palm Sunday.

capitium :—a hood ; a cap ; the head of a bed ; a headland ; the east end of a church.

capitula. See *capitulum.*

capitulare :—to divide into chapters ; to make articles of agreement ; to meet in chapter.

capitulariter :—in chapter.

capitulum :—a chapter ; a chapter-house.

cappa :—a mantle ; a cope ; a cap ; the top part of a flail.

cappilegium :—the strap whereby the two parts of a flail are united.

caprarius :—a goatherd.

capsella :—a chest.

captennium :—protection ; tax or homage as an acknowledgment thereof, esp. in Guienne.

captio :—capture ; custody ; a prison ; ransom.

captivus :—a caitiff ; a wretch ; unfortunate.

captura :—a weir.

caput :—the first day of a month.

caputagium. See *chevagium.*

caputium. See *capitium.*

carabus :—a lighter ; a coracle.

caracalla :—a cloak ; a hood.

caracca, caracta :—a carrack.

caragius :—a sorcerer.

caraxare :—to write.

carbonare :—to make charcoal.

M.

carbonarius :—a collier.

carbonator :—a charcoal burner.

carbonella :—a steak.

carcannum :—pillory ; prison.

carcare :—to load ; to charge.

carcasium, carcoisium :—a carcase.

cardetum :—a carr, a low marshy place where alders grow.

cardinalis :—a cardinal.

cardiolus :—a snipe.

cardus :—a card, for carding wool ; a playing card.

carea :—a cart.

careata :—a cartload.

carecta :—a cart.

carectarius :—a carter.

carectata :—a cartload.

careia :—a cart ; a load.

careium, careyum : —service of carriage.

carellus :—a quarel, a crossbow bolt.

carelta :—a cassock.

carentinilla, carentivillus :—canvas.

careta, caretta :—a cart.

caretarius :—a carter.

cargare :—to load.

cariagium : —service performed with a cart ; a baggage train.

cariare :—to carry.

cariatio :—carriage.

carica :—a fig.

carinutus :—a cockney.

cariscus :—an evergreen tree.

P

caristare :—to make dear.

caristia :—dearth.

caritativus :—charitable.

carix :—sedge.

carnarium :—a charnel-house.

carnator morine :—a man who slaughters sheep affected with murrain.

carnebrevium. See *carniprivium.*

carnellare :—to crenellate; to embattle.

carnes ferinæ :—venison.

carnicapium :—Shrove Tuesday; carnival.

carnifex :—a butcher.

carnificium :—a meat market.

carniprivium (carnis privium) :— fasting; Lent; Shrovetide.

carogium :—a car which bears a standard.

carolare :—to sing.

caronator, caroynator. See *carnator.*

carpatinæ :—thick boots. (O. E. okers.)

carpentagium :—payment for wood-work.

carpentarium :—wood-work.

carpentarius :—a carpenter; a cartwright.

carpetor, carpetrix :—a carder of wool.

carptare :—to card.

carra :—a car.

carracutium :—a chariot.

carrata :—a cartload; a carat.

carrea, carreia :—a cartload; a cart; the right of carriage through a place.

carreta :—a cartload; a carat.

carrica, carrucha :—a ship of burden; a large Portuguese ship.

carrietare :—to carry.

carrochium :—a standard on a cart.

carruca, &c. See *caruca, &c.*

carta, &c. See *charta.*

cartallus :—a creel; a hamper.

cartare :—to convey by charter or by cart.

caruagium. See *carucagium.*

caruca :—a plough; a plough team; a plough land.

carucagium :—a tribute imposed on ploughs or plough-lands; liability to plough service.

carucarius :—a ploughman.

carucata :—a plough-land, the size of which varied. It is mentioned as containing " *centum acras ad perticam nostram* " (Cl. Roll. 19 H. iij. m. 8); and in the 15th cent. we find "ij. carewes and a half of lond conteynyng lxxx. acres." (E. C. P. 51, 314.) In some places it was 240 acres, or 8 oxgangs; a team of oxen sufficient to work a carucate, *i.e.,* eight.

carucatarius :—one who holds land by plough tenure.

carucator :—a carter; a ploughman.

carula :—a box. See *karula.*

carvana :—a caravan.

carvela :—a caravel, a sailing ship with a square poop, about 120 tons.

casale :—a village.

casamentum. See *casata.*

casata, casatum, casatura :—a house with land sufficient to maintain a family; a hide of land.

casatus :—a tenant.

caseatrix :—a maker of cheese.

cassare :—to quash, to annul.

cassatio :—nullification.

cassatus :—a tenant.

cassea :—a box.

cassidile :—a purse, pocket, or small coffer; a gamebag, a pouch.

cassus :—a case, a box.

castellania :—the office of keeping a castle.

castellanus :—the owner or captain of a castle.

castellaria, castellarium :—the precinct or jurisdiction of a castle.

castenaria :– a chestnut tree.

casto :—the bezil of a ring.

castrimergus :—a woodcock (*scolopax rusticola*).

castro :—a wether.

casula :—a small house or church; a chasuble; a casket (?).

casuma :—cinders.

catabulum :—a shed.

catacrina :—the hip.

catallum :—cattle; chattels; capital; principal.

catantrum :—a trendle.

catapulta :—a broad arrow.

catascopus :—an archdeacon; a bishop.

catatista :—a scolding cart.

catator :—a cathunter.

catellare :—to tickle.

catellarius :—a pedlar.

catenare :— to chain.

cathedraticum :—See due, a pension paid by parochial ministers to the bishop as composition for his interest in first fruits and offerings.

cathedratus :—consecrated (of a bishop).

cathenare :—to chain.

cathenarius :—a watchdog, a bandog.

catillare :—to mew, as a cat.

cattinus :—of catskin.

cattus, catus :—a cat; a military engine to protect from missiles soldiers attacking the wall of a town, called in classical Latin *vinea.*

catzurus. See *chacurus.*

caucettum :—a causey.

caula :—a sheepfold.

caulamaula :—a flute.

caulare :—to fold sheep.

cauma :—thatch.

cauniare. See *canniare.*

cautelis :—careful, cautious.

cautio :—a bond.

cauzea :—rubble.

cavalgata :—a cavalry expedition.

cavanna :—an owl.

cavaria :—a coin; a narrow path.

cavilla :—the ancle ; a peg.

cawagium :—a stall, cage, pen.

caya :—a quay.

caymiticus :—fratricidal, murderous (from Caym, a medieval form of Cain).

cayrellus :—a quarel, a crossbow bolt.

cayum :—a quay.

cebum :—tallow.

ceculicula :—a spark.

cedula. See *schedula.*

celarium :—a spence, a buttery, a cupboard.

celatorium :—a coverlet.

celda :—a chaldron, 36 bushels ; the same as *selda*, a stall.

celdra :—a chaldron.

celena ferrea :—a scythe (?).

celer : — the ceiler or canopy of a bed.

celeragium : — cellarage, payment for storing goods in a cellar.

celia :—ale made from wheat ; wort.

cella :—a cell ; a small monastery depending on a superior house ; a close stool ; a saddle (*sella*).

cellarium :—a cellar.

cellarius, cellerarius :—a cellarer.

celura :—a ceiler.

cementarius :—a mason.

cenaculum :—breakfast or luncheon ; a parlour.

cenapium :—mustard.

cendalum :—cendal, thin silken cloth.

cendula :—wood for roofing a house.

cenella :—an acorn.

cenivectare :—to carry in a barrow.

cenivectorium : — a mudcart, a wheel-barrow.

censa :—rent ; farm ; tax.

censaria, censeria :—a rent ; a farm let at a standing rent.

censarius :—a farmer.

censualis :—a person bound to pay a rent to a monastery or church, in return for protection.

censuarius :—a farmer.

census :—tax, tribute.

centena :—a hundredweight ; a hundred.

centenarius :—a petty judge under the sheriff ; a hundredor ; a centener, an officer commanding 100 soldiers.

centenus, centuria :—the division of a county called a hundred.

centonizare :—to arrange for singing.

centuclum :—cloth.

centum : — sometimes used declinable in the plural.

ceola :—a long boat or ship ; a keel.

ceorlus :—a churl.

cepa :—a sand eel (?).

cepes :—a hedge (*sepes*).

cephalia :—headache.

cephalus :—a blockhead.

ceppa :—stocks.

ceppagium :—the stump of a tree.

ceppus :—a stump.

cepum :—tallow (*cebum*).

ceragium : — waxscot, payment for the supply of candles in a church.

cercella :—a teal (*anas crecca.* Fr. *sarcelle*).

cerchia :—a search.

ceresum :—a cherry.

cerevisia, cervisia :—beer.

cerisum :—a cherry.

cerna :—choice; sort.

ceroferarius :—a candle bearer, an acolyte.

ceroteca :—a glove (*chiroteca*).

certificare, certiorare, certorare:— to certify, to inform.

certitudinaliter :—certainly.

certum letæ :—cert money, paid yearly by the tenants of some manors to the lord.

cerura :—a mound or fence; a lock.

cerussa :—white lead.

cerverettus, cervericeus, cerreritius, canis :—a staghound.

cervicale :—a bolster.

cervisiarius, cervisior:—a brewer; a tenant who pays rent in beer.

cespitare :—to stumble.

chacea :—a chace; the right of hunting; a right of way for cattle, droveway.

chaceare : —to hunt.

chaceatus :—chased (of plate).

chacepollus. See *cacepollus.*

chacia :—a countertally.

chacurus :—a horse or hound for hunting.

chalendra. See *chelindra.*

chalo :—a scapulary; a counterpane, a chalon.

chamberlaria : — the office of chamberlain.

champertor. See *campiparticeps.*

chamus :—a horse's bit; a headstall.

charactare, charaxare :—to write.

charnarium :—a charnel-house; a cemetery.

charreya :—a cartload.

charta :—paper; a charter.

charta partita :—a charter-party.

chartare :—to convey by charter.

chartula :—a small charter.

chartulare :—a cartulary, a register of charters.

chasor :—a horse for hunting.

chatia zabuli :—silting up with sand.

chaudmella : — chaudmedley, much the same as chance medley.

chauma :—reeds or sedge.

cheldrum :—a chaldron or chaldern, 36 bushels.

chelindra :—a flat boat.

cheminagium :—cheminage, chiminage; a toll paid for a road through a forest.

cheminata :—a chimney.

cheminus :— a road ; the right of carting crops through another's land.

chepingabulum : — tax paid at market.

cherechsectum :—church scot.

cheresettum :—church scot.

cherigmannus:—one whose duty it was to inspect and fix the boundaries of a manor.

cherisetum, chersettum : — church scot.

cheruca :—a vane, a weathercock.

cheva :—a shive, the bung in which the vent peg is inserted.

chevacia selionum :—the heads of the furrows.

chevagium:—poll money paid by villeins to their lord, "*ne vocentur per capita*," or on their marriage or for licence to leave his land ; or to a man of power for his protection ; also used for payment by the king at shrines.

chevalchia :—cavalry ; a cavalry expedition ; military service as cavalry.

chevantia :—a loan of money.

cheverillus :—a cockerel ; a roebuck.

cheveringus, chevero :—a rafter ; a joist ; a chevron.

chevicia :—a loan.

cherescia, cheriscæ, chevitiæ :— heads of ploughed land, headrigs.

chevisare:—to obtain by agreement.

cheviserum :—a headstall.

chimenea :—a chimney ; a fireplace.

chimera :—a riding cloak; a cope.

chiminachium, chiminagium. See *cheminagium.*

chiminus. See *cheminus.*

chintura :—a strip of land.

chirographare :—to grant by indenture.

chirographarius : — a chirographer, writer of chirographs.

chirographum :—a chirograph, a public instrument of conveyance, attested by witnesses ; an indenture.

chirographus :—an officer of the Common Pleas who engrosses fines.

chirotheca :—a glove, a gauntlet.

chivagium :—payment by *nativi* to their lord for liberty to leave his lordship. See *chevagium.*

choercere:—for *coercere.*

chorepiscopus : — a suffragan bishop.

chorista :—a chorister.

chorus : —the choir of a church ; a crowth or crowd, a musical instrument of Wales and Scotland, played with a bow.

chrisma : —consecrated oil ; any ceremony at which it is used, as extreme unction.

chrismale :—the cloth laid over a child's head at baptism.

chrismatorium :—a chrismatory, a vessel to contain consecrated oil.

Christicola, Christianicola :—a Christian.

chrotta :—a crowd, a fiddle.

chursetum :—church scot.

chymera :—for *camera.*

ciborium :—a canopy or ceiler over the altar ; a metal vessel to contain the sacramental bread.

cibutum :—a meat safe.

ciccus :—for *siccus.*

cicer :—cider.

ciffus, cifus :—a cup (*scyphus*).

cilicium :—a hair shirt.

cillaba :—a table dormant.

cimbia :—a churn ; a fillet.

cimeria :—the crest on a helmet.

cimiflo :—a stoker.

ciminum :—cummin.

cindalum :—cendale.

cindula, scindula : — shingles, lath for roofing.

cingnottus, cingnotus :—a cygnet.

cingula. See *cindula.*

cipha :—a sieve, a measure of about 5 qrs.

cipharius :—a cup maker.

ciphra :—a cipher.

cippus :—the stocks.

circa :—a watchman.

circada, circata :—a fee paid to the bishop or archdeacon at his visitation ; church shot, a measure of corn or other produce paid by each householder to the bishop.

circator :—a person whose duty it was to go the rounds, esp. in a cathedral or monastery.

circinatorium :—a covering for the altar.

circinnare :—to arrange in a circle.

circulare :—to put hoops to ; to turn.

circulator :—a cooper ; a turner.

ciricsetum :—church scot.

cirografum. See *chirographum.*

cirotheca. See *chirotheca.*

cirpi :—rushes.

cisara, cisera :—cider.

cisimus :—ermine.

cissor (*scissor*):—a tailor ; a shearman.

citherator, cithero :—a harper.

citolla :—a cittern.

citula :—a jug.

civera, civeria :—a wheelbarrow.

cives :—in some cases an elected body of citizens who afterwards became aldermen.

civilista :—a civil lawyer.

claccare :—to clack wool, *i.e.*, to cut off the sheep's mark, whereby it weighs less and yields less custom.

clada, clades :—a hurdle or wattle.

claia :—a hurdle or wattle.

clamancia :—a claim.

clamare :—to claim.

clamatio :—a claim.

clamator :—a crier ; a claimant.

clameum, clamium :—a claim.

clamivus :—an accuser.

clamor :—complaint ; demand.

clamor popularis :—hue and cry.

clamum :—a claim.

claretum :—a liquor made of wine, honey, and spices ; red wine.

clarificatio :—anniversary of a saint's death.

clarigarius armorum :—a herald.

clario :—a trumpet.

classatorium :—a clapper.

classicum :—a peal of bells.

clates :—a hurdle or wattle.

clatravus :—a latch.

clatrum :—an enclosure.

clausa :—a clause.

clausella :—a closet.

clausicula :—a closet.

clausio :—fortification.

claustralis :—living in a cloister.

claustraliter :—in convent manner.

claustrum :—the precinct of a monastery; the cloister.

claustura :—brushwood used for fencing, &c.

clausum :—a close.

clausum Pasca or *Paschæ* :—the Close of Easter, the Sunday after Easter, Low Sunday.

clausum Pentecostes :—Trinity Sunday.

clausura :—an enclosure.

clavia, clava :—a club or mace.

clavica :—a privy (*cloaca*).

clavicula :—a notch, a nock.

clavigarius :—a lorriner, a bit maker.

clavinarius :—a keeper of keys (?).

clavis. See *clavium, clavus.*

clavium :—a clove.

clavus :—a clove, a weight used for wool and other goods, 7 lbs. or 8 lbs.

clawa :—a close of land.

claya :—a hurdle or wattle.

clea, cleda, cleia :—a hurdle or wattle.

clenodium :—a jewel, a present.

clericatura :—the status of clergyman; clergy.

clericus :—a clerk, a clergyman.

clerimonia :—an assembly of the canons of a cathedral or of the members of a convent; religion; sobriety.

cleronomus :—an heir.

clerus :—the clergy; a clerk.

cleya, clida :—a hurdle or wattle.

clipsadra :—a waterclock (*clepsydra*).

clito :—a prince; an ætheling.

clitorium :—a clicket; a latch.

clitunculus. See *clito.*

clittum :—a tire for a wheel. See *clutium.*

cloca, clocha :—a bell; a cloak.

clocarium :—a belfry.

clocherium :—a belfry.

clostura. See *claustura.*

cluarium :—a forge.

clucetta :—a clicket.

clunabulum :—a dagger, worn at the side.

clusa :—a sluice; a fish stew; a monastery; a pass between mountains.

clustella :—a lock of hair.

clutarium :—a forge.

clutium, clutum :—a shoe; a horse-shoe; the tire for a wheel, or perhaps knobs to serve the same purpose.

clutus :—a cloth; a clout.

cnipulus :—a knife, a short sword.

cnolla :—a knoll, the top of a hill.

cnusticium :—a rivet.

coadunare :—to collect.

coagulatorium :—a churn.

cobba : —a cobloaf ; a bun.

cocarius :—a cook.

coccula :—a coarse woollen blanket or mantle.

coconellus :—a cockney.

cocula :—a cogue, a drinking-cup in form of a boat.

codificatio :—repairs.

codrinus :—poor.

cœnobium :—a convent.

cofa :—a cup.

cofata :—a cupful.

cofeoffatus :—a joint feoffee.

coffera :—a coffer.

cofferarius :—a cofferer.

coffinum, coffinus :—a coffer ; a coffin.

coffra, cofrum :—a coffer.

coga, cogga : — a cock-boat or coggle, a small sailing-boat.

cogniare :—to coin.

cognitio :—homage ; cognisance ; armorial bearings.

cognitor :—a judge; an informer.

cogo. See *coga.*

cohuagium :—a toll paid at a market or fair.

coifa :—a coif, the head-dress worn by serjeants-at-law.

coigniare : —to coin ; to stamp.

coinagium. See *cunagium.*

cokettum :—a custom-house seal ; a receipt for the payment of custom.

cokettus :—cocket bread, a superior, but not the finest sort.

cokilla :—a shell.

cokinus :—an inferior servant.

coksetus : — a coxswain.

colarium :—a collar.

colatorium : — a sieve; a colander.

colera :—a collar.

colerettus :—a necklace.

colerium : —a collar.

colibertus :—a tenant in socage.

colideus : —a Culdee.

colingaria. See *coningeria.*

collactanea :—a fostermother.

collardum. See *cuillardum, cullardus.*

collare :—a ruff.

collarius : —carrying a load on the neck.

collationare : —to collate.

collecta :—a collection.

collectaneus :—a companion.

collectare, collectarium :—a book containing collects.

collistrigium : —a pillory.

colobium :—a tunic without, or with short, sleeves ; a tabard.

colonellus :—a colonel.

color : —rhyme.

colorare :—to rhyme.

colpicium :—a pole.

colpo :—a fragment ; a small wax candle.

columbare :— a dovecote.

columbaria :—putlog holes.

columbarius : — a keeper of pigeons.

columbella :—a pigeon.

colustrum :—new milk.

comba : — a combe, valley.

combustio :—trial of money at the Exchequer.

comes :—an ealdorman ; a count; an earl.

comestio :—dinner.

comitatio, comitatus : — a county ; a county court.

comitiva :—a company.

commandare. See *commendare.*

commarchia :—a frontier.

commater, commatrix :—used for the relationship between one who has held a child at baptism and the mother, O. E. gomm ; a godmother.

commenda : — a deposit ; when a benefice is given to a layman, or to a clerk for a time, it is said to be given *in commendam ;* a commandry, a benefice in the order of the knights of St. John.

commendare :—to lend, to deposit ; to order ; to put oneself under the protection of another.

commendatarius :—one who holds a living *in commendam.*

commendatitius :—of commendation, esp. *literæ.*

commendatus :—a person who puts himself under the protection of his superior by doing voluntary homage.

commensale :—board ; diet ; commons.

commensalis :—a fellow-boarder, fellow-commoner.

commensare :—to begin.

commissarius :—a commissary, one who exercises spiritual jurisdiction by commission of a bishop.

commissio :—a commission.

commissionarius :—one who acts by commission ; a commissioner.

commonitio :— summons.

commorancia :—dwelling, residence.

commothum : — a commote, a quarter, or some say a half of a cantred.

communa :—common land or property ; right of common ; commons ; a community ; a fiscal regulation.

communantia :—the communance, the folk having the right of common.

communare : — to enjoy the right of common.

communaris :—a fellow-citizen.

communarius, communiarius :—a commoner.

communes :—commons at a college or Inn of Court.

communia : — a corporation or community.

communia (pl.) : — commonalty ; commons ; ordinary business of a court.

communiæ :—commons.

communiare :—to have right of common.

communicare :—to have right of common.

communis clericus : — common clerk, or clerk of the commons, now called town clerk.

communis pasture :—common of pasture.

communitas : — commonalty ; sometimes all the citizens, but in this case usually *communitas civium*.

communitas civitatis :— the commonalty of the city, the court or council.

comortha : — a collection, especially that made at marriages, and when a priest said his first mass.

comothus. See *commothum*.

compagator :—a suffragan bishop.

companagium :—anything eaten with bread ; the right of having meals together.

comparticeps, compartionarius :— a copartner.

compassare :—to compass.

compater :—a godfather.

compausare :—to cease, to rest.

compellare :— to cite ; to accuse ; to compel.

compellativus :—an accuser.

compertorium : — a judicial inquest in the civil law made by delegates.

compestralis. See *campestralis*.

compestratus. See *campestratus*.

complectorium, completorium :— compline, about 7 p.m. ; supper.

complicatorium : — a counting board, a counter.

compostiare :—to manure.

compostum :—manure.

compotus :—an account.

comptista :—an accountant.

compurgator :—one who swears to another's innocence.

computatorium :—a counter, a reckoning board ; the Counter, the name of two prisons in the Poultry and Wood Street.

computoria :—a counting-house.

computorium. See *computatorium*.

computorum rotulator :—a comptroller.

computus :—an account.

conalis murus :—a gable wall.

concelamentum :—concealment.

concelare :—to conceal.

concelatio :—concealment.

concelator :—a concealer, a man who finds out concealed lands.

concernere :—to belong ; to concern.

concides :—felled trees.

conclave :—a parlour.

concubiculum, concubile :—a bed for two.

condare :—to give at the same time.

condictum :—a mandate, an edict ; a tribunal, a court.

condigena :—a fellow-countryman.

condorsum :—a ridge or low hill (?).

conductarius :—a man employed on water works.

conductus :—a conduit.

conductus, salvus :—a safe-conduct.

condulus :—a buzzard (*buteo vulgaris*).

conduus :—a pear tree, esp. Quarendon.

conestabulus, conestabilis :—a constable.

confinium :—a boundary.

confiscare :—to confiscate.

confortamen :—comfort.

confraga :—breaking down trees.

confratria :—brotherhood ; conspiracy.

confrustare, confrustrare :—to break in pieces.

congius :—a measure containing about a gallon and a pint.

congrua, congrus :—a conger (*conger vulgaris*).

coninga :—a rabbit ; a rabbit skin.

coningeria :—a rabbit warren.

conjecturare :—to guess.

conjunctorius :—a joiner.

conquestare :—to acquire, to conquer.

conquestus :—property acquired (by inheritance or conquest or otherwise).

conquinare :—to defile.

conredium. See *corredium.*

conscisorium : — a guidon, a small standard.

consequentia :—a precedent.

considerare :—to decree ; to award.

consistorium :—a council or assembly of ecclesiastical persons, or place of justice in a spiritual court ; a seat at table ; a meal.

conspicatio :—cleaning.

constabilia :—ward.

constabilis :—a constable.

constabularia :—the office of constable.

constabularius :—a constable.

constuma :—custom.

consuetudinarius :—customary ; a custumal, a book containing the rites of divine offices, or the customs of a monastery ; a man subject to feudal services.

consuetudo :—custom, used, as the English word, for a payment imposed on merchandise.

consuetura :—use.

consulator :—a counsel, a councillor, used especially in Guienne.

consultarius :—a councillor.

contenementum :—freehold land attached to a man's dwelling-house ; what is necessary for a man's maintenance.

contentare :—to pay ; to denote.

conthoralis :—husband or wife.

contiguari :—to be near.

contra :—against, *i.e.* in time for.

contrabreve :—a counter writ.

contrada :—a country.

contrafacere :—to imitate, to counterfeit.

contrafactor : — an imitator, a forger.

contrafactura : — a counterfeit.

contraiare : — to oppose.

contramandatum : — a lawful excuse which a defendant alleges by attorney, to show that the plaintiff has no cause of complaint.

contramurale : — an outwork.

contraplacitum : — a counter-plea.

contrapositio : — a plea or answer.

contrariare : — to oppose.

contrariparius : — a corrival, a dweller on the opposite bank ; a beater on the opposite side of a river when hawking.

contrarotulatio : — comptrolment.

contrarotulator : — a comptroller.

contrarotulum : — a counter-roll.

contrata : — a country.

contratallia : — a counter-tally.

contratalliator : — a counter-talleyer.

contrivare : — to contrive.

controfacere : — to counterfeit.

contus : — a pestle.

conus : — a corner.

conveancia : — conveyance.

conveare : — to convey.

conveiancia : — a conveyance.

convenire : — to summon, to convene.

conventinare : — to covenant.

conventio : — a covenant.

conventionare : — to covenant.

conversus : — a lay monk, lay brother ; a converted Jew or Mahommedan.

conviator : — a fellow traveller.

convitiare : — to rail at.

cooperlectorium : — a coverlet.

coopero. See *coprones.*

coopertia, coopertio : — bark and broken wood of felled trees.

coopertor : — a tiler ; a thatcher.

coopertorium : — a coverlet ; a roof ; a cuirass.

coopertum : — covert.

coopertura : — a covert ; a cuirass ; coverture, the condition of a married woman ; thatch.

coopertus equus : — a barded horse.

coopicium : — coppice.

copa : — a cop of corn, " sc. xx. garbæ " (Sussex) ; of peas, 15 or 16 sheaves.

coparcenaria : — coparcenary.

coparticeps : — a coparcener.

copecia : — coppice.

copero. See *coprones.*

coperosa : — copperas.

copertorium. See *coopertorium.*

copertum : — cover for game.

cophinus : — a coffer ; a coffin.

copia : — a copy.

copiare : — to copy.

copicia : — a coppice.

copla : — a couple.

copo : — twigs.

coppa. See *copa.*

coppatus : — coppice.

coprones :—twigs.

copucium :—a coppice.

copula :—a couple for hounds ; a joist ; a tiebeam.

coqua. See *coga.*

coquarius :—a cook.

coquinarius : —t h e kitchen steward in a monastery.

coraagium :—a tribute of certain measures (*corus*) of corn ; or perhaps the same as *cornagium.*

coralius :—a currier.

corarius :—a currier.

corballum, corbella :—a basket.

corbanus :—a rural dean (*plebanus*) in Ireland.

corbellus :—a corbel, a projecting piece of timber to support a weight.

corbio :—a basket maker.

corbis :—a hive.

corbona :—a priest's treasury or strong box.

corda :—a cord ; a measure of land, 22 feet ; a cord of wood, 8 or 10 feet by 4 feet by 4 feet.

cordarius :—a rope maker.

cordebanarius, corduanerius :—a cordwainer.

cordelatus :—corded.

corderius :—a rope maker.

cordewana, corduana :—cordwain, Cordovan leather.

corduanarius :—a cordwainer.

cordula :—a string.

corerius :—a courier.

coretes :—weirs. (Welsh, *cored.*)

corgigatorium :—a churn.

corigia, corigium. See *corrigia.*

coriletum :—a hazel copse.

corluvus :—a curlew (*numenius arquata*).

cormusa. See *cornamusa.*

cornagium :—cornage, horngeld, payment for right to graze cattle ·on moor or common ; a rent or tax paid on oxen.

cornamusa : — a cornemuse, a Cornish bagpipe.

cornare :—to blow a horn.

cornarius :—a horner ; a horn blower.

cornellatus. See *carnellare.*

cornera, corneria, cornerium :—a corner.

cornicallus :—a corn on the foot.

corniculare :—to blow a horn.

cornisare, cornuare :—to blow a horn.

corodium, &c. See *corredium.*

coronale :—a wreath, a crown.

coronamentum :—coronation.

coronare :—to crown ; to make a person a priest ; to perform the tonsure.

coronarius :—a coroner.

coronatio :— coronation.

coronator :—a coroner.

coronellus :—a colonel.

coronix :—a cornice.

corositas :—rottenness.

corporale, corporarium :—a corporas.

corpus castri :—the castle without the surrounding town, &c.

corralius :—a currier.

correctarius :—a licensed broker.

corre harius :—the holder of a cerrody. See *corredium.*

corredium, corridium : — a corrody, money or allowance due by a monastery to the founder for the maintenance of one of his servants; an allowance of any kind; a livery.

corrigia :—a strip of land, leather, &c.; a girdle; a shoe latchet.

corrigiarius :—a girdler.

corrodium. See *corredium.*

cortina :—a curtain.

cortinarius :—a curtain maker. See *cortinetus.*

cortinatus :—curtained.

cortinetus :—a man in charge of the king's tents.

cortis :—a courtyard.

cortularium :—a farmyard.

corulus :—hazel.

corus :—a corn measure, perhaps 8 bushels,

corusta :—used for *chorista.*

corvata, corveia :—compulsory work done by tenant for lord.

corversarius, corvisarius : — a cordwainer; a cobbler.

cosduma :—custom.

costa :—a rib, a side; a basket; cost.

costamentum :—cost.

costera :—coast.

costerillum :—a flagon.

costillagium :—a rent in the Channel Islands.

costiterunt :—they cost.

costrellus :—a drinking cup, often of wood.

costula :—clove (of garlic, &c.).

costuma :—custom.

cota :—a cot; a tunic; a hat; a sheepcote.

cotagium :—a cottage, originally meant the land attached to a cot.

cotarius :—a cotter.

cotellus :—a cottage.

coterellus :—a servile tenant; a bandit.

coteria, coterium :—a cottage.

cotmannus : —a cottager.

cotsethla :— a cottage, a small farmhouse.

cotsethus, cotsetlus, cotsetellus :— a cottager.

cotuca :—a cloak; coat armour.

couperagium :—cooper's work.

coupiator :—a woodman.

courba. See *corvata.*

courearius :—a currier.

courtepia :—a courtepye, a short cloak.

covina, covinia :—covin, a compact for purposes of fraud.

covinosus :—fraudulently.

craantare. See *creantare.*

craiera :—a crayer, or smack.

crampo :—a crampon, a grappling iron, or metal fastening in jewellery.

cranagium :—liberty to use a crane; profit made by a crane.

cranare :—to lift goods with a crane.

crannocum :—a crannock, a measure of corn ; a basket.

crariolus :—a rake.

craspiscis :—a whale.

crassipulum :—a cresset.

cratera :—a chest or coffin.

craticula :—a gridiron ; a lattice.

cratis :—a wattle ; a crate.

cravare :—to impeach.

creancia :—credit.

creantare :—to give security for.

creantum :—security.

creca, crecca :—a creek.

credentia :—faith, belief ; a small table to hold the vessels of the altar.

crementum :—increase.

cremium :—refuse tallow.

crenellare. See *carnellare.*

creputellus :—a cracknel.

crescens :—a crescent.

cressans :—a crescent.

cresta :—the crest of a bank.

crestare murum :—to complete the top of a wall with coping stones.

crestura :—coping ; the ridge of a roof.

cretena, cretinus :—a torrent.

crevacia :—a crevice, a crack.

crevina :—increase (?).

crimisinum :—crimson.

crinium :—the skull.

cristianare :—to convert to Christianity.

crocardus :—a crocard, bad money, prohibited by statute 27 Edw. I.

croccus :—a crowbar.

crocea, crocia :—a crook ; a crosier ; investiture of episcopal sees ; dress worn by regular canons.

crociarius :—a cross-bearer.

crocus :—a crook.

croeria :—a shrike (*lanius excubitor*).

croffeta, crofta, croftum : — a croft ; a close.

cromio :—a strap. (Fr. *creim.*)

cronarius :—a man in charge of farm stock.

cronnus :—a measure of four bushels.

cropa, croppa, croppus :—a crop ; twigs.

crotia. See *crocea.*

crotta :—a crowd, a fiddle.

crucesignatus :—a crusader ; one who has taken the cross.

crucibulum :—a cresset.

crucifer :—a Crossed or Crutched Friar.

crufta :—a croft.

cruppa :—a horse's croup.

crupparium :—a crupper.

crusiatus : — having taken the cross.

crustare :—to daub ; to plaster.

crustum :—embossed plate.

crux :—sometimes used for *crus*.

crypta :—a chapel or oratory under ground.

cubare :—to lie down.

cubicare :—to go to bed.

cucneus. See *cuneus.*

cuculla, cucullus :—a long, full garment without sleeves ; a cape ; a cowl.

cucullatus : —wearing a cowl ; a monk.

cufa :—a cup.

cufata :—a cupful.

cuillarda : — a chilver, a ewe lamb.

cuillardum :—a spoonful, ladleful.

culagium :—placing a ship in dock ; keelage.

culcitra :—a cushion, a bed.

Culdeus :—a Culdee, clergy in Scotland and Ireland from the 6th to 11th centuries whose chief place was Iona.

culigna : —bellows.

cullardus :—a wether (?).

culmus : —sometimes used for *culmen.*

cultellarius :—a cutler.

culvertagium : —confiscation; servitude.

cumba :—a coomb, a measure of corn, 4 bushels.

cumbla :—a roof ; a ridge.

cumgruus :—a conger.

cumelingus :—comeling, *i.e.* newly arrived, used of cattle.

cumillia :—equality (?).

cuminum :—cummin.

cumulus :—the chancel of a church ; vaulting ; a straw-rick or pook of corn.

cuna :—coin.

cunagium :—coinage ; stamp.

M.

cunare, cuneare :—to coin.

cuneragium :—some toll.

cunere :—to coin.

cuneus : — a stamp ; a coinage ; a mint.

cunicularium :—a rabbit warren.

cuniculus :—a coney, a rabbit.

cuningeria :—a rabbit warren.

cuninus :—a rabbit.

cupa :—a cup.

cuparius :—a cooper.

cupatorium : —a vat.

cuperagium :— cooperage.

cuperius :—a cooper.

cuppa :—a ship of burden ; a lighter ; a cup.

cupperius :—a cooper.

curagulus :—a caretaker.

curallum : —coral ; some kind of corn or meal.

curator :—an attorney in ecclesiastical cases.

curatus :—careful ; a clergyman in charge ; with cure of souls (of a benefice).

curba :—some piece of timber.

curcula :—a cable.

curda : — a measure used for spices.

curetarius :—a curator ; an examiner.

curia :—a court ; frequently used for *curia Romana,* meaning simply Rome.

curialis, littera :—court hand.

curialitas :—courtesy.

currifrugium : —a riddle, a sieve.

Q

cursalis :—current.

cursaria. See *cursoria.*

curserius :—a courser (horse).

curso :—a ridge of land.

cursor :—a courier ; a crier.

cursoria :—a swift ship.

curta. See *curtis.*

Curtana :—Curteyn, the name of the sword of Edward the Confessor.

curtena :—a curtain.

curtilagium : — a curtilage, a courtyard or piece of land near a house.

curtiles terræ :—court lands ; demesne lands.

curtillum. See *curtilagium.*

curtina :—a curtain.

curtinatus :—curtained.

curtis, curtus :—a court ; a courtyard ; a house and farm ; a pound, a pinfold.

curtisanus :—a courtier.

curuca :—a carrack, a large Portuguese ship.

cussina :—a cushion.

custa, custagium, custamentum, custantia :—cost.

custamentum :—sometimes used for *custodia.*

custare :—to cost.

custodes bonorum ecclesiæ : — churchwardens.

custodia :—wardship ; a ward of a town.

custuma :—custom.

custumannus : — a customary tenant.

custumare :—to assess for payment of custom ; to pay custom.

custumarius :—customary ; subject to payment of custom ; a collector of customs.

custus :—cost.

cutellarius :—a cutler.

cutellus :—a knife.

cuteus :—of skin.

cuva : — a vat.

cuvarius :—a cooper.

cyclas : — a long garment, close at the top and wide below.

cylicium :—a hair shirt.

cyrenarumpilus :—sealskin.

cyrographum, &c. See *chirographum.*

cyula :—a ship.

D.

dacra, daker. See *dicra.*

dadus :—a die.

daeria :—a dairy.

dagus :—a dais.

daia : — a dairymaid, or man.

daiera :—a dairy.

daila, dailus :—a ditch ; a certain measure of land.

daimeretta. See *damerettus.*

daina :—a bushel ; a day's work.

dalmatica :—a dalmatic, a deacon's vestment ; a tunicle.

dalus. See *daila.*

dama :—a buck or doe.

damerettus, damericius: —a hound used for fallow deer.

aamisella. See *domicella.*

damma :—a dam.

dammus :—a buck.

damnum :—damage.

damus :—a buck.

danegildum :—danegeld.

dangeria :—a payment made by forest tenants for liberty to plough and sow during pannage time, lessilver, or lefsilver.

dangerium :—liability to confiscation.

dapifer :—a sewer ; a steward of the household ; a cellarer ; a bailiff of a manor.

dapiferatus :—stewardship.

dapiscida :—a carver.

dapsiferus :—festal.

dapsilitas :—an act of liberality.

dardus :—a dart.

darsis :—some kind of fish.

data :—the date of a document.

datarius :—a datary, an officer of the Roman chancery.

datilis, dattilus :—a date (fruit).

datium :—tribute ; tax.

dauberium :—plaster work, dab.

davata :—a "daywercke," or four perches.

daya :—a dairyman, or maid.

dayaria, dayeria :—a dairy.

dayla. See *daila.*

deadvocare :—to disavow ; to refuse ; to give up a suit.

deafforestare :—to disafforest, to bring forest land into cultivation.

dealbare :—to whiten.

dealbatio :—a white dress worn by a candidate or novice.

dealbator :—a whitewasher, dauber.

deambulatorium : — an ambulatory.

dearestare :—to free from arrest.

deawarennare :—to dis-warren.

debata, debatum :—a debate, a dispute.

debatabilis :—debateable.

debere :—sometimes means "is supposed to."

debilis :—worn.

debitatus :—indebted.

debriare :—to intoxicate ; to inundate.

debriatus :—drunk.

decaisatus :—decayed.

decalcare :—to whiten.

decanatus :— a deanery.

decania, decenna :—a deanery ; a tithing ; a friburgh.

decanica :—an ecclesiastical prison.

decanus :— a dean ; a borsholder, chief of the friburgh ; a dozenner, a tithing man.

decarnellatus :—having the crenellation destroyed.

decasus :—decay.

decaudare :—to dock the tail.

decena. See *decania.*

decendium :—a period of ten days.

decenna :—a tithing.

decennaria :—the jurisdiction . of a tithing-man.

decennarius : — a tithing-man, a dozenner.

decimabilis :—titheable.

decimæ :—tithes.

decimare :—to tithe.

decimatio : — tithes ; paying a tenth part.

decimus primus :—eleventh.

decipula :—a trap, a snare.

decius :—a die.

decolpare :—to cut down.

decostare, decosticere :—to cost.

decretales : — decretals, papal letters containing decrees, or on matters in which the popes were consulted.

decretista :—a person learned in the Decretals.

decretum :— a decree, especially of the Pope.

decrustare :—to strip off.

decuria :—a tithing.

decuriare :—to bring into order; to try (?).

decurio :—a rural dean ; a tithing-man.

dedilectio :—loss of affection.

deductus :—game ; hunt.

defalcare :—to weaken ; to deduct.

defalta :—default ; negligence.

defeasancia :—defeasance, a condition relating to a deed on the performance of which the deed is void.

defendere :—to prohibit; to refuse.

defensa :—a fenced park, an enclosure.

defensabilis :— easily defended.

defensare :—to defend.

defensio :—a prohibition.

defensiva :—fortification.

defenso, in : — in defence; of ground, enclosed for a time.

defensum :—an enclosure ; a prohibition.

defensus :—custody.

deferrare :—to unshoe a horse.

defesancia. See *defeasancia.*

defetus :—exhausted (*effetus*).

defigurare :—to disguise.

deflorare :—to pick flowers.

deforciamentum : — deforcement, illegal occupation of property.

deforciare :—to deforce.

deforciatio :—holding goods in satisfaction for debt.

deforciator :—a deforcer.

deforestare. See *deafforestare.*

deforis :—outside.

defustare :—to beat, to cudgel.

degelare :— to thaw.

degistatus :—without joists.

degradus :—stairs.

deguttare :—to drop on ; to pour over.

deia :—a dairyman, or maid.

deimericius. See *damerettus.*

deis, deisium : — a dais. See *dagus.*

deiwerca :—a day-work, or four perches.

dekernellatus :—having the crenellation destroyed.

delatura :—an accusation.

delia : — some metal found in Derbyshire.

delicius :—" a cokeney."

demanda :—a demand.

demandare :—to demand; to cite.

demanium, demenium. See *dominium.*

demembrare :—to dismember.

demorare :—to govern.

demorari : —to demur.

demullare :—to dread.

dena :—a glen ; a coppice.

denariata, denariatus :— a pennyworth.

denariata terræ :—land worth a penny per annum, varying from one perch to one acre.

denariis, in :—in coin.

denarius :—a penny ; a pennyweight, *i.e.*, 32 grains of wheat from the middle of the ear.

denbera: —a pasture for pigs (swinecombe).

denerata : —a pennyworth.

denizatus : —a denizen.

denna. See *dena.*

densescere : —to grow thick.

dentes :—gratings.

dentrix :—a pike (*esox lucius*).

deobligatio :—a release.

deodanda, deodandum :—an animal or thing forfeited for having caused a person's death.

deosculatorium :—a tablet handed round to be kissed at mass, a pax.

departura : —a departure.

depersonare :—to insult; to degrade.

depictare :—to paint an image of.

depositio :—the death of a saint, not a martyr.

depreculæ :—beads.

derationare. See *disrationare.*

derobare :—to rob, to plunder.

desamparare :—to yield, to release.

descus :—a dais.

desicut :—as.

despitus :—a contemptible person.

desponsalia :—a betrothal.

destitutio :—deprival (of an office).

destrarius. See *dextrarius.*

desubitare :—to attack suddenly.

detachiare :—to seize goods by attachment.

de tallia :—retail.

deteriare :—for *deteriorare.*

detesticulare :—to castrate.

detius :—a die.

detractari :—to be torn in pieces by horses.

detunicare :—to discover.

devadiatus :—without sureties.

devadimonizare:—to redeem from pledge.

deverium :—duty.

devestire :—to give up possession.

devillare :—to leave town.

devisamentum :—a devise ; a device.

devisare :—to devise ; to bequeath.

devisatio, devisum :—a devise.

dextrale :—a bracer, a vambrace or wardbrace. (Fr. *gardebras.*)

dextrare :—to turn to the right ; to walk on the right of.

dextrarius :—a war horse, a charger.

deya. See *daia.*

deyla. See *daila.*

diaconatus :—the office of deacon.

diaconus :—a deacon.

diapretus. See *diasperatus.*

diarium :—daily food.

diasperatus :—of various colours ; diapered.

diatim :—daily.

dica :—a tally ; a deed ; foolish talking.

diccus :—a dike.

dicenarius. See *decennarius.*

dicra :—a dicker, ten skins or pairs of gloves, ten bars of iron.

dictator :—a person charged with the duty of considering and redressing infractions of a peace or truce ; an umpire.

dictor :—an umpire. See *dictator.*

dieta :—a day's journey ; an assembly ; regimen ; diet, *i.e.*, the daily scrapings of metal in taking assays at Goldsmiths' Hall, which were periodically melted up ; a daywork of land.

diffacere :—to maim, to destroy.

diffagium :—neglect.

difficultas :—a tax.

diffidare :—to defy ; to renounce allegiance to ; to warn off.

diffodere :—to dig up.

difforciare :—to deforce.

difusculus :—diffuse.

digitale :—a thimble.

digitare :—to point at.

dignarium :—a dinner.

dilatura :—an accusation (*delatura*).

diligiatus :—outlawed.

dimidicare :—to halve.

dimidietas :—a half, a moiety.

dimissio :—demise, making over properties by lease or will.

dimissoriæ literæ :—letters from a bishop for the ordination of a person in another diocese.

diœcesis :—a diocese.

dirationare. See *disrationare.*

diribare :—to take away.

dirmutia :—for A. S. *deornett,* a hunting net (?).

disadvocare :—to deny, to disavow.

disboscatio :—bringing woods into cultivation.

discantus :—a chant.

discare :—to make dishes.

discarcare, discargare, discariare, discaricare, discarkare :—to unlade, to discharge.

discifer :—a sewer ; a steward.

disclamare :—to renounce a claim.

disclausus :—open.

disconfortare :—to cause uneasiness to.

discontinuare : —to cease attendance.

discopulare :—to uncouple ; to let loose.

discrasia :—a disease.

discredencia : — unbelief, misbelief.

discrimen :—the parting of the hair.

discus :—a dish ; a desk.

disfacere : — to dismember, to mutilate.

disforceare. See *deforciare.*

disgerbigator :—a haymaker.

disgradare :—to take away a man's rank.

dishabilitare :—to disable.

disheritor :—one who deprives another of his inheritance.

diskippagium :—unshipping.

disonerare :—to discharge.

disparagare :—to disparage ; to marry to an inferior.

disparagatio : — disparagement, marrying an heir or heiress below their degree.

dispensa :—a warehouse.

dispensarius, dispensator : — a steward.

dispensatorium :—a steward's room.

dispersonare :—to insult ; to degrade.

displicare :—to display.

disportum :—amusement, sport.

disratiocinare. See *disrationare.*

disrationamentum : — deraignment ; proof.

disrationare :—to prove ; to deraign.

disrobare, disrobbare :—to plunder.

dissaisina, disseisina :—an unlawful dispossessing a man of his land ; disseisin.

dissaisire, disseisire : — to dispossess ; to disseise.

dissaisitor, disseisitor : — a disseisor.

dissignare : — to break open a seal.

dissimulare :—to refuse ; to delay.

dissipare : — to disappear, to scatter themselves.

distemperantia :—disease.

distigius :—a distych.

distillare :—to drop ; to distil.

distonatio :—discord.

distreniatus :—rigorous.

districtæ :—a strait ; a defile.

districtio :—distress.

districtus :—tax ; fine ; territory.

distrigiare :—to stride.

distringere :—to distrain.

distringibilis :—liable to distress.

disturbancia, disturbatio : — disturbance.

disturbare :—to send away ; to disturb.

disvadiare :—to receive or to redeem a pledge.

diurnalis :—as much land as can be ploughed in one day with one ox.

diurnare :—to pass the time ; to remain ; to journey.

divadiare. See *disvadiare.*

dividenda :—a dividend.

divisa :—a device ; a devise ; a boundary ; a dole.

divisibilis murus :—a party wall.

doageria :—a dowager.

doarium. See *dotarium.*

dobelettum :—a doublet.

docillus :—a faucet.

docinna, documa : — a tithing, error for *decenna.*

dodarium. See *dotarium.*

dola :—a portion, a dole ; a faucet.

dolare :—to distribute.

dolea. See *dola.*

doleum :—a tun (*dolium*) ; also used for a hogshead.

dolfinus :—the Dauphin.

domanium. See *dominicum.*

domesticus :—of the same house (monastery).

domicella, domicilla :—a young lady ; a servant ; a nun.

domicellus :—the young son of a nobleman ; in the Roman Court, the same as *camerarius ;* a servant in a monastery.

domifex :—a carpenter.

domigerium :—danger ; power.

domina :—a lady ; a dame.

dominatio :—a demesne.

dominatus :—lordship.

dominica :—Sunday.

dominici panni :—Sunday clothes.

dominicum :—a demesne.

dominicus :—of a lord ; used on Sunday.

dominicus panis :—bread used at the Mass.

dominigerium. See *domigerium.*

dominium :—lordship.

dominus :—a title applied to a peer, to a lord of a manor, to a clergyman, and to a bachelor of arts.

domnus, dompnus : — a contraction of *dominus,* used especially for clergymen.

donatissia :—as a gift.

donativum :—a benefice given by the patron without presentation or institution.

donator, donatorius :—a donor.

donatus :—a donee.

doracus :—a john-dory (*zeus faber*).

dormiens mensa :—a table dormant, a fixed table.

dorrea :—a john-dory.

dorsale, dossale :—a dorser, dorsal, dossal, tapestry hung against a wall, especially a cloth hung above an altar ; a packsaddle.

dorsamentum :—used for *endorsamentum.*

dorsorium :—a dosser, a basket to carry on the back. See *dorsale.*

dortorium :—a dormitory, dortour.

dos :—a dowry, sometimes dower.

dosserium. See *dorsorium.*

dotalicium :—dower.

dotarium :—a dower, the portion of a widow or wife.

dotata, dotissa :—a dowager.

dracena :—a tiller.

dragetum, dragium : — drage, a coarse kind of corn.

dragma :—an ornament; a gem.

drana :—a drain, a watercourse.

draparius :—a draper; a standard bearer.

drappus :—cloth.

draschium, drascium : — draff; malt; grains.

drathium : —draff.

drava :—a drove.

draya :—a dray.

drecca. See *drana.*

drengagium : — the tenure by which *drengi* held.

drengus :—a drench, the name given to certain military tenants who were put out of their lands at the Conquest and afterwards restored.

dressorium :—a dresser; a cupboard.

dreva :—a thrave of corn, 12 or 24 sheaves.

dreya :—a dray.

droitura :—right.

dromo, dromunda :—a dromound, a long, swift ship for passengers; a warship, larger than a galley.

drovia :—a drove.

droviare :—to drive cattle.

drowa :—a drove.

druggeria :—a druggist's shop.

duaria :—jointure; dowry.

dubbare :—to dub, *i.e.*, to beat cloth with teazles to raise the nap.

dubbator :—a dubber.

duca :—a mould ; a last.

ducatus :—a dukedom; a ducat, first coined in the duchy of Apulia ; a safe-conduct.

ducillarius, ductillarius :—a tapster.

ducillus :—a stopple.

ducissa :—a duchess.

ductillus :—a tap.

ductor canis :—a lymehound.

duellio : —a champion ; a duel.

duellium, duellum :—trial by battle.

dukketta :—a ducat.

dumbula maris :—seaweed (?).

duna :—a down, or hill.

dunio :—a dungeon.

dunnarium, dunum :—a down.

duodena :—a dozen ; a jury of twelve men.

duplachium : —error for *duploytum*, a cloak (?).

duplicatus :—lined.

duploma :— a document with a counterpart; a hasty journey, two days' stages in one day (*diploma*).

duribuccus :—a slow speaker.

duritia :—duress.

dux :—a duke.

dygnarium, dygnerium :—dinner.

dytenum :—a ditty, or song.

E.

eabalus :—an alehouse (A. S. *ealahus*).

ealhorda :—the right of assising and selling ale and beer.

eastintus :—the east coast, or the eastern side of a place.

ebba :—ebb.

ebdomada :—a week.

ebdomadarius :—a canon of a cathedral church, appointed weekly to take charge of the choir ; a priest appointed for weekly duty in a monastery.

ebiculum :—the back of an edged tool.

ebrietor :—a drunkard.

ecclesia :—a church.

edestium :—a building.

edia :—help ; ease ; food.

educamen :—a brood of chickens.

efforcialiter :—by force of arms ; forcibly ; in force.

efforciamentum :—distraint ; inquisition.

efforciare :—to fine ; to distrain ; to compel ; to fortify ; to defend.

effugare :—to drive or hunt out.

egeator :—the skipper of a ship.

eia :—an island, an eyot.

einescia, eilnecia. See *esnecia.*

eisiamentum. See *aisiamentum.*

ejectum :—jetsom, wreck.

ela :—an aisle.

elargamentum :—liberation ; increase.

elargare :—to set free ; to put off ; to increase.

elargatio :—liberation.

elbidus, elbus :—russet.

eleemosyna :—alms.

eleemosynaria :—an act of donation ; a place where alms are distributed ; the office of almoner.

eleemosynarius :—an almoner.

elemosina libera, pura, et perpetua :—frankalmoign.

elemosinare :—to grant in alms, or in frankalmoign.

elemosinarium :—an almonry ; an almery, an aumbrey.

elephantia :—leprosy.

elongare :—to remove to a distance ; to eloign.

eluvio :—a sewer.

emarcidus :—withered.

embassaria, embaxaria :—an embassy.

embaxator :—an ambassador.

embaxatura :—an embassy.

emenda :—amends ; a fine.

emendare :—to make amends ; to correct ; to restore.

emendatio :—the power of correction ; the right of assize ; a fine ; repair.

emigranea :—megrim, migraine.

emissarium :—a sluice.

emissarius :—a stallion.

emolare :—to grind tools.

emologare :—to confirm.

emphyteusis :—a lease in perpetuity or for a long term.

emphyteuta, emphyteota : — the holder of such a lease.

emprisa :—an enterprise.

emprumptum :—a loan.

emunitas :—for *immunitas*.

enamelare :—to enamel.

enarnatio :—flogging.

encaustum :—ink.

encrochiare :—to encroach.

endorsamentum : — an endorsement.

endorsare : —to endorse.

endroma :—rough cloth, falding.

endurare :—to endure.

energumenus :—possessed by an evil spirit.

enfranchiatus :—enfranchised.

engleceria : — Englishry ; being an Englishman.

engleria. See *engleceria.*

engrallatus : — ingrailed, with curved indentations (heraldic).

engrossare. See *ingrossare.*

enitia. See *esnecia.*

enquesta :—an inquisition.

ensaisinare :—to put in possession ; to give seisin.

enterclausum :—a screen (?).

entrare :—to enter ; to enter in a book.

epicaligæ :—overshoes or boots.

epimenium :—a monthly present, or expense.

episcopalia :—synodals or other payments by the clergy to the bishop.

episcopare :—to make a bishop ; to act as a bishop.

episcopatus :—a bishopric.

episcopium : —a bishopric ; a bishop's palace.

episcopus :—a bishop.

epistolare :—a service-book containing the epistles.

epitilium : —a birdbolt.

epitogium :—a gown.

equalens : —a corrupted form of *equivalens.*

eques :—a knight.

equicium :—a ruler.

equillus :—a hackney.

equitarius :—on horseback ; horse, as applied to a carriage or plough, &c.

equitator :—a rider, a forest officer.

equitatura :—a riding or baggage horse ; cavalry ; knighthood.

equitibia :—the hock of a horse.

equitium :—a stud of horses.

equivalentia :—equality.

eramentarium :—a saltpan.

eremita : —a hermit.

eremitorium :—a hermitage.

eremodicium :—a non-suit.

erifilum :—brass wire.

eriquia. See *hericius.*

ermina : —ermine.

ernasium. See *harnesium.*

erodius :—a gerfalcon (*falco islandicus*).

erpica :—a harrow.

erra:—a pledge (*arrha*).

errarius cygnus : — a nesting swan (?).

erraticum : — a waif or stray.

erthmiotum :— a court held on the boundary of two lands

erubiginator :— a writer of rubrics ; a painter in red.

eruginator :—a furbisher.

esbrancatura : — c u t t i n g o ff branches ; lopping.

escaere :—to escheat ; to claim as escheated.

escaeta :—an escheat ; a fallen branch ; entrails.

escaetatio :—escheat.

escaetator, escaetor :—an escheator.

escaetria :—escheatorship.

escaetus :—escheated.

escaldare :—to scald.

escambiare : —to exchange.

escambiator : — an exchanger, money changer.

e s c a m b i a, e s c a m b i u m :—exchange ; a place for changing money.

escangia, escangium :—exchange.

escantio :—a butler, a cup bearer.

escapiare :—to escape from arrest.

escapium : — escape ; a thing that comes by chance.

escaptura : —escape.

escarius :—a carver.

escarleta, escarletum :—scarlet.

escarta. See *scarta.*

escaudare :—to scald.

escawardus : — applied to fish, "calvered" or "scarved" (?)

esceppa :—a skep, a measure of corn, salt, fruit, &c. ; a straw or rush basket.

eschaeta. See *escaeta.*

eschaetor. See *escaetator.*

eschambia, eschambium : — exchange.

escheccum :—a jury, or inquisition ; a check.

escheppa. See *esceppa.*

escheweita : — sentinel service done by folk of Bordeaux. (Fr. *eschauguette.*)

eschina :—a chine.

eschippare:—to equip; to embark.

esclavus :—a slave.

esclenka :—a leg of mutton or beef. (Fr. *esclanche.*)

esclusa :—a dam or sluice.

esclusagium :—payment for permission to make a sluice.

escomarius :—a boatman ; a pirate.

escruatio :—cleaning (ditches).

escuagium. See *scutagium.*

escuilliare :—to castrate.

escurare:—to scour ; to cleanse.

esgardia, esgardum :—a reward ; an award.

esgardiator :—an arbiter.

esgardium :—an award.

esiamentum :—easement.

eskaere, &c. See *escaere.*

esketor :—a robber.

eskiper, gen. *eskipri* :—the skipper of a ship.

eskippa. See *esceppa.*

eskippare :—to equip.

eskirmire :—to fence.

esmaelitus :—enamelled.

esnamiare :—to distrain.

esnecca :—a ship.

esnecia, esnaccha, esnechia :— primogeniture ; the limited right of primogeniture of the eldest coparcener.

espaltare, espeltare. See *expeditare.*

esperdum :—an axe (O. E. sparthe).

esperiolus :—a squirrel.

esperkeria :—a duty on dried fish in the Channel Islands, consisting of a right of preemption of congers ; 2*d.* Tournois on every 100 mackerel ; 2 sols Tournois on every bushel of fish ; and 2*d.* on every salt conger exported to Normandy or elsewhere, not in the kingdom of England.

espervarius, esperverius :—a sparrow-hawk (*accipiter fringillarius*).

espicurnantia : — the office of spigurnel.

espleta. See *expletiæ.*

espletiamenta. See *expletiæ.*

essaetor :—an assayer.

essaia :—say, sometimes means fine woollen cloth (serge), sometimes silk. (Fr. *soie*.)

essarta, essartum. See *assartum.*

essonia :—essoin, excuse for nonappearance at a court baron, &c.

essoniare :—to give an excuse ; to essoin.

essoniator :—an essoiner.

essonium. See *essonia.*

establiamentum :—a settlement.

estallagium. See *stallagium.*

estallamentum : — a mortgage ; pawning ; au instalment.

estallare :—to mortgage ; to pawn.

estangnum :—a pond (*stagnum*) ; a bank or stank ; a measure of land less than an acre.

esterlingus :—an Easterling ; sterling.

estermannus :—a pilot.

estintus. See *eastintus.*

estoverium :—estovers, allowance of wood for repairs, or of necessary food and clothes ; stover, provender.

estreciare :—to make narrow ; to straiten.

estrepamentum, estrepinamentum :—estrepement, injury done to lands by a tenant for life.

estresius :—an Easterling.

estuffamentum :—stuff ; material.

esturare. See *escurare.*

esturus. See *austur.*

esuniare :—to essoin.

esuniator :—an essoiner.

eucharistia :—the sacrament ; the consecrated bread ; a *ciborium.*

evaginare :—to unsheath.

evangelare : —a servic -book containing the gospels.

evangelizare : — to preach ' the gospel.

eventio : —profits (of a church).

evitaneus :—eternal.

ewagium : —toll paid for water passage.

ewanglia :—the gospels.

exactor :—a collector ; a sheriff; a beadle.

exallar :—an axletree (?).

examitum :—samite, a silk stuff, sometimes interwoven with silver or gold ; also used for an amice.

exartum. See *assartum*.

exbannire :—to banish.

exbrancatura :—outer branches.

excacta, excaeta :—an escheat.

excaldare :—to scald.

excambia :—exchange.

excambiare :—to exchange.

excambiator :—an exchanger ; a broker.

excambium :—an exchange.

excarletum :—scarlet.

excaturizare : —to scald.

excaudare : —to scald.

excayare :—to escheat.

exclusa. See *esclusa*.

exclusagium. See *esclusagium*.

excrustare : —to remove the crust of ; to spoil.

excudia : — a swinglestock, a wooden instrument used in beating flax.

excurtare, excurtiare :—to dock the tail of a horse or dog.

excusatorius : — containing or giving an excuse.

excussio :—driving out ; sometimes used for rescue ; thrashing corn.

excussorium. See *excudia*.

exelerarius :—a cup bearer.

exemplificare :—to copy.

exempnium, exennium :—a present ; a new year's gift.

exercituale :—a heriot.

exfrediare :—to break the peace.

exhibere :—to provide food and lodging for, to entertain.

exhibitio :—entertainment ; provision.

exigenda :—a writ of exigent.

exigendarius :—an exigenter, an officer of the Court of Common Pleas.

exigendis, in :—in exigent.

exilium : —waste, ruin.

eximperatrix :—late empress.

exire :—to issue.

exitus :—issue, in all senses, family, result, expenditure ; entrails.

exkippare, exkiupare :—to equip ; to embark.

exlegalitus :—outlawed.

exleyare :—to outlaw.

exonium. See *essonia*.

exorcista :—an exorcist, a benett, one of the lesser orders of the church.

exordinare :—to degrade.

expedatus, expedicatus :—having the feet cut off ; hambled, lawed.

expediencia : —management.

expeditamentum : —hambling.

expeditare :—to hamble, hamel or law a dog, *i.e.*, to cut out the ball of the foot or three claws ; to root up trees.

expeditio :—the obligation of accompanying the lord to war.

expedores :—outriders.

expeltare. See *expeditare.*

expenditus :—spent.

expensabile vinum :—wine usually served.

experquaria. See *esperkeria.*

explacitare :—to plead successfully.

expletiæ :—esplees ; rents ; profits.

explicit :—it is finished or ended.

expressatum :—expressed.

exprexum :—for *expressum.*

expulsare :—to expel.

expulsatio :—expulsion.

exsartum. See *assartum.*

exscahetor :—an escheator.

extendere :—to value lands.

extensor :—a valuer.

extenta :—extent ; valuation.

extermino :—to bring without the boundaries.

extimare :—for *æstimare.*

extocare :—to grub up.

extolneare :—to free from toll.

extrabarrista :—an utterbarrister.

extracta, extractum : —an estreat, a true extract or copy.

extrahura :—a stray.

extraneus :—a foreigner, *i.e.*, not a citizen.

extravagantes : —certain papal constitutions, not included in Gratian or the Decretals.

extumæ : —relics.

exulatus :—an exile.

exuperare :—for *exsuperare.*

eysiamentum. See *aisiamentum.*

F.

faber :—a smith.

fabrica :—a smithy.

facescia :—used for *facetia.*

facitergium :—a facewipe, a towel.

factum :—a deed, a document.

fagatum :—a faggot.

faginum :—beech mast.

fagottum :—a faggot.

faida :—feud, enmity.

faidinus, faiditus : —an enemy, an exile, a banished man.

fala : — "a somer castel," a wooden tower used at sieges and on board ships ; a scaffold.

falanga. See *falinga.*

falcabilis :—fit to mow.

falcare :—to mow.

falcatura : — a day's work at mowing.

falcidium :—a swathe.

falco :—a falcon.

falcona :—a falcon ; a small cannon, 2½ inch bore.

falconaria :—the service of supplying falcons.

falda :—a fold.

faldæ cursus :—a sheepwalk.

faldagium :—faldage, the right to set up folds.

faldicium :—a fold ; foldage, fold-penny ; payment for folding sheep, or for leave to set up a fold.

faldistorium : — an arm-chair ; esp. a bishop's throne.

faldum :—a fold.

falera :—trappings (*phalera*).

falerarius :—a sumpter horse.

falerator : — a sumpter man.

falescere :—to cease ; to fail.

falesia :—a rock, a cliff.

falinga :—a cloak or jacket, used in Ireland (falding ?).

falla, fallum :—a measure of land ; tin ; a fault.

fallire :—to fail.

falmotum :—a folkmote.

falsare :—to deceive ; to falsify ; to forge.

falsarius, falsonarius :—a forger.

falsator :—a forger.

falsitas :—forgery.

falsitia :—treachery.

falsonaria, falsoneria :—forgery ; making false coin.

falsonarius :—a maker of false coin.

famen :—a speech.

familia : — a set of chess or draughts men.

fanatio : —the fawning season in forests.

fancielus :—some kind of tenant.

fanula :—a fanon, a maniple.

farcinula :—a package, a parcel.

fardella, fardellum :—a fardel, the quarter, or eighth of a yard land.

fardellarius :—the holder of a fardel.

fardellus : — a bundle ; a fardel ; the holder of a fardel.

farinagium :—toll of meal or flour.

farricapsium :—the hopper of a mill ; a bin.

farsatura :—stuffing.

farundella :—a quarter of an acre.

fascennia, fascina :—a bastile, a wooden fort used in besieging a town.

fasianus :—a pheasant.

fassus :—a faggot.

fausetum : —treble ; a faucet.

faverca : —a forge.

febrimatio :—ploughing or digging up land.

feida : — a feud.

feira :—a fair.

feissa :—a strip or stripe (?).

felagus : —faithful ; a companion.

felo :—a felon.

felonia :—felony.

felonice :—feloniously.

felparia, feltrum :—felt.

femoralia :—drawers, breeches ; cuisses.

fenestra :—a window.

fenestreola :—a small window.

fengera :—fern.

fennatio. See *feonatio.*

fenissa :—a haymaker.

fensura :—a fence.

fenticius. See *finticius.*

feodalis, feudalis :—feudal ; a vassal.

feodalitas, feoditas :—fealty.

feodamentum :—feoffment.

feodare :—to enfeoff.

feodarius, feodatarius :—a feodary, an officer of the court of wards ; a feudal tenant by service.

feodelitas :—fealty, which is correctly *fidelitas.*

feodi firma :—fee farm.

feoditas :—fealty.

feodum :—a fee ; a fief.

feodum talliatum :—fee tail.

feoffamentum : — a feoffment, grant of tenements, &c. in fee.

feoffare :—to enfeoff, to grant in fee.

feoffator :—a feoffor.

feoffatus :—a feoffee.

feonatio :—the fawning season, fence month, a fortnight before and a fortnight after Midsummer.

feoragium :—straw.

fera :—a wild beast, used especially for deer.

feragium :—forage.

ferandus. See *ferrandus.*

M.

ferculum :—a dish ; a mess ; a litter.

ferdella, ferdellum. See *fardella.*

ferecia :—a quilt.

feretriarius :—a man in charge of a bier or shrine.

feria :—a fair ; a day of the week ; a ferry.

Feria prima :—Sunday.

Feria secunda :—Monday, and so on.

feriagium :—payment for ferrying.

ferialis. See *feriatus.*

feriatio :—a holiday.

feriatus dies :—a feast day, saint's day, holiday.

ferinæ carnes :—venison.

feritorium :—a swingle ; a beetle.

ferlingata, ferlingus :—four acres ; a quarter of a yard land.

ferlingellus :—a measure of corn.

ferlingus :—a farthing.

fermina :—custody.

fermisona :—the winter season for killing does.

fernere :—to empty.

fernigo :—waste land, covered with fern.

ferragia :—pasture, land where forage is grown.

ferramentum :—an iron tool or instrument ; a horseshoe ; a ploughshare ; a tire ; irons for a prisoner.

ferrandus, ferrantus :—iron grey.

ferrare :—to shoe a horse ; to put an iron tire on a wheel.

ferrarius, ferrator :—a smith.

R

ferratura : — ironwork ; esp. horseshoeing.

ferrifodina :—an iron mine.

ferrifilum :—iron wire.

ferripodium :—a patten.

ferro, ferronarius : — an ironmonger or ironworker.

ferrura :—a blacksmith's trade ; a wheel tire.

ferthendellum :—a quarter of an acre.

fesana, fesans, fesantis, fesantus :—a pheasant.

fessum, fessus :—a truss.

festinancia :—haste.

festrum :—a roof-tree.

feto cervi :—a fawn.

feudalis. See *feodalis.*

feudum, &c. See *feodum,* &c.

feugera :—fern.

feutrum :—felt.

fico :—a boat.

fidelitas :—fealty.

filacia lana :—woollen yarn.

filacium :—a file, for documents.

filare :—to file.

filarium :—a steel, a hone.

filatrix :—a spinster.

filatum :—a net ; thread.

filazarius :—a filacer, an officer of the Common Pleas who files writs.

filetum. See *filatum.*

filiaster :—a son-in-law, stepson, nephew, sister's son.

filiastra :—similar feminine relatives.

filiatio : — sonship, subjection, obedience ; used chiefly of monastic houses.

filicetum :—ferny ground.

filiolus :—godson.

filtrum :—felt ; a mattrass.

filtum : —error for *filtrum* (?).

filum : —a fillet in architecture.

filum aquæ :—the middle of a river.

fima :—dung, manure.

fimare, fimere :—to manure.

fimarium : —a manure heap.

fimarius :—a scavenger.

financia :—ransom ; fine.

finare :—to pay ; to exact ; to refine.

finire :—to pay a fine ; to exact a fine.

finis : —a fine ; a final concord.

finticius :—of trees, split or fit for splitting.

fiola, fiolum : —a beaker ; a phial (*phiala*) ; a cruet.

firgia :—a fetter.

firma : —a farm ; rent.

firmaculum :—a buckle. O. E. fermayle.

firmare :—to fortify ; to seal or sign ; to give security ; to grant a farm ; to rent a farm.

firmarium : — a corruption of *infirmarium,* an infirmary. O. E. " a fermarie."

firmarius :—a farmer.

firmatio :—doe season ; provisions.

firmitas :—fortification.

firmura :—a lock ; the right of closing.

fisantum :—a pheasant.

fistuca :—a fishing-rod.

fistulator :—a piper.

fixula :—a buckle ; a button.

flabellum :—a vane.

flaccum :—an arrow.

flaco :—a marsh ; a flagon ; a cake. See *flato.*

flagellum :—a flail ; a door-bar.

flaketta :—a flask.

flameola :—a garment, usually of silk.

flameum :—a kerchief.

flamicia : —flawn, custard.

flao. See *flato.*

flare dolia :—to hoop (?) casks.

flasca :—a flask.

flato, flauto :—a cake, a custard.

flecharia :-- service of supplying arrows.

flecharius, flecherius :—a fletcher.

flechia :—an arrow.

flechiare :—to make arrows.

flecta :—an arrow ; a hurdle.

fleebotimacio :—bleeding.

fleta : —an arm of the sea.

flexarius :—a fletcher.

flocci : — flock, refuse wool.

floccus. See *frocca.*

floratus : — embroidered with flowers ; scented.

florenus :—a florin, a gold coin, first coined at Florence, 1252.

flota, flotta :—a fleet ; a raft.

foagium :—a rent paid in the Channel Islands. See *focagium.*

focagium :—focage or housebote ; hearth-tax.

focale, focalia :—fuel ; the right of taking fuel.

focaria :—a housekeeper.

focarius :—a fireman ; a stoker.

fodera :—a fother (of lead), 1,950 lbs. or 2,000 lbs. ; 20 cwt. (E. C. P. 59 ; 215).

foderaticum :—fodder.

fodertorium, foderum, fodrum :— fodder.

foenatio. See *feonatio.*

foesa :—grass.

fogagium :—fog, rank grass.

folgare :—to follow ; to enter into service ; to serve.

folgarius :—a follower ; a servant.

follus : -- a fool.

fongia :—stockfish.

foo :—a fawn.

foracra :—a foracre, the headland of an arable field.

foragium :—straw ; forage ; the right of exacting it or obligation to provide it.

foraneus :—foreign.

forarium :—the office of harbinger.

foratus :—of fur.

forbannitus :—a banished man.

forbare :—to clean, to furbish.

forbarrare :—to bar or deprive.

forbator :—a furbisher.

forbatudus :—a person killed in self-defence.

forbire. See *forbare.*

forcelectum :—a fortress.

forceria, forcerium : —a casket; a strongbox, often of leather.

forcescettum :—a fortress.

forcia :—power, force, usually unjust; forcible exaction.

forciare :—to fortify.

fordellus : – a measure of land larger than *fardella.*

forefacere. See *forisfacere.*

forejudicatio :—a forejudger.

forellus :—a sheath; a corporas case.

forenna :—the outskirts or suburbs of a town.

forensis :—foreign.

forera, foreria :—a headland; a furrow (?)

foresta :—a forest.

forestagium :—a duty paid to the king's foresters.

forestallagium, forestallamentum : —obstructing the highway; forestalling.

forestallare :—to forestall; to waylay.

forestallator : —a forestaller.

forestallum :—a crime committed on the highway.

forestare :—to afforest.

forestaria :—the office of forester; forestership; forestry.

forestarius :—a forester.

foreta :—a headland.

forgia :—a forge; forage.

forhelna :—concealment.

forhurtha. See *foruhtha.*

foriare :—to forage.

foricus :—furred.

forigo :—list.

forinsecus :—outside; foreign.

forisbannire :—to outlaw.

forisburgum :—suburbs.

forisfacere :—to do amiss; to forfeit; also used actively, to exact a forfeit from.

forisfactum : — transgression; forfeiture.

forisfactura :—forfeiture.

forisfamiliare :—to remove from the family; to give a son his portion on his leaving home; to emancipate.

forisjudicare :—to pronounce forfeited; to outlaw.

forisjurare :—to abjure.

foristallarium, foristeallum, foristalria :—forestalment.

forjudicare. See *forisjudicare.*

forlandum : — land at the extremity of an estate; a promontory.

forlangum. See *furlangus.*

forma :—a form, a bench; a copy; a drain.

formannus :—a foreman; a headman.

formaticum :—cheese.

formela :—a formaylle, a female hawk.

formella :—a shoemaker's last; a weight of about 70 lbs.

formelus :—trained, of a hawk.

formipedia :—a shoemaker's last.

formula :—a little bench.

fornagium :—payment by tenants bound to bake in the lord's oven, or for the right to use their own ; a baker's profit ; hearth-money ; fuel.

fornire :—to heat.

forpices :—shears.

forprisum :—an exception.

forrare, forrari :—to forage.

forrerius :—a harbinger.

forsefacere :—to forfeit.

forstallare, &c. See *forestallare, &c.*

forsula :—a fortress.

fortalicium, fortallissium : — a fortress, a castle.

fortelecium, fortellescum. See *fortalicium.*

fortericia :—a fortress.

fortia :—power. See *forcia.*

fortiare :—to force ; to fortify.

fortificare :—to fortify.

fortilagium :—a fortress.

fortitudo :—force ; an army.

fortuna :—treasure trove.

fortunare :—to happen.

fortunium :—a tournament.

foruhtha :—a measure of land.

forulus :—a bin ; a sheath.

forum :—often means " price."

forura :—fur.

forurda :—a measure of land.

forus : – right or custom.

fossa : – a mound, a dike, as well as a ditch.

fossagium :—contribution for making ditches.

fossare :—to ditch.

fossatum :—a place surrounded by a ditch ; a ditch ; a dike ; a mound.

fossatura : — fortification by ditches.

fossiculus : — a basket (?) ; a fostle, *i.e.* a stake used in making a fold.

fossorium :—a mould.

fossus :—a ditch.

fotmellum :—a measure of lead ; a fother (?).

fotor :—a lapdog, "a comforter."

founinare :—to bring forth young (of deer).

founinus : —of a fawn.

founum :—a fawn.

fousura :—work done by a mason ; digging foundations (?).

fovea : – a burial-place.

foveator :—a gravedigger.

fractillosus :—dagged, jagged (of clothes).

fractillum :—a pepper mill.

fractillus :—a dag, jag.

fractitium :—arable land.

fraellum, frahellum :—a frail ; a basket ; a weight of raisins, 70 lbs.

fraeria :— a fraternity ; a brotherhood.

fraginellus :—a cracknel.

fragus :—the wrist or other joint.

fraillum. See *fraellum.*

framatura :—making a frame ; framework.

franca petra :—freestone.

francbordus : — freebord, land claimed outside a fence.

franchesia : — freedom ; franchise.

franchilanus :—a freeman.

franchire, franchisare :—to enfranchise.

franchisa :—a franchise.

francigena :—a foreigner.

franciplegium :—frankpledge.

francolanus, francolensis : — a franklin.

francus :—free.

frangibulum : — a kneading trough.

fraria :—a fraternity ; a brotherhood.

frassetum :—an ashwood (*fraxinetum*).

frater :—a friar.

fratriagium :—a younger brother's inheritance.

frecta, frectum :—coarse cloth, as used for horse cloths, frieze (?) ; embroidery, usu. with metal ; a fret ; fretwork.

frectagium :—freight.

frectatus :—frettee (heraldic).

frectum :—freight. See *frecta*.

fredum :—a composition paid by a criminal.

frescus :—fresh.

fressencia porci :—a flitch (?).

fretare, frettare :—to load ; to freight ; to ornament with fretwork.

fretinum :—a silver coin (Fr. *fretin, freton*).

fretta. See *frecta*.

frettum :—freight. See *frecta*.

fretum :—freight.

frideburgum : — frithburgh, the same as frankpledge.

frisca forcia :—fresh force, *i.e.*, newly done.

friscus : — fresh ; also uncultivated ground.

frisium :—frieze.

frithbregium :—breach of the peace.

fritum :—fry of fish.

frixura :—a fried dish ; a pancake.

frocca, froccus, froggus : — a frock ; that worn by monks was a long garment with long, wide sleeves.

fronciatus :—wrinkled.

frontale:—a frontal, a cloth hung above an altar.

frontellum :—a frontal.

frontinella :—moulding, in goldsmith's work ; the ball of the throat.

frontispicium :—a gable end.

frontuosus (*frontosus*) :—shameless.

fructuarius :—a fruiterer ; a receiver of rent.

fruissire. See *frussare*.

frunes, frunio :—a tanner.

frunire :—to tan.

frusca :—waste lands.

frussare :—to break up land.

frussatum :—land newly broken up.

frusshiare. See *frussare*.

frussire. See *frussare.*

frussura : — breaking into a house ; ploughing.

frustrum, frustum :—a piece ; a small plot of land.

frutectum :—a shrubbery; a herb garden.

fuagium :—hearth-tax.

fuallia :—fuel.

fuga :—a drove ; a chase ; hunting ; the right to drive cattle on to a place.

fugacia :—a chase ; right of hunting.

fugare :—to hunt ; to drive.

fugarius :—a hunter (horse) ; a drover.

fugatio :—a chase.

fugator :—a hunter (horse) ; a driver ; a drover.

fugatorius :—a hunter (horse).

fugera :—fern.

fugillus :—a poker.

fulcrari :—to make a bed on a bedstead.

fulcrum :—a leg of a bedstead ; a bedstead.

fuleratium, molendinum : — a fulling mill.

fullare, fullire, fullonare :—to full cloth.

fullaticum. See *fuleratium.*

fullum aquæ :—a stream of water.

fulreticum :—a fulling mill.

fultra :—a cushion.

fultrum. See *fulcrum.*

fumagium :—manure ; chimney-money.

fumarium :—a chimney.

functorium :—a foundry.

funditor :—a founder ; a pioneer.

fundum :—ground.

funerius : — a ropemaker.

fungia :—stockfish.

funifex :—a roper.

funtura : — founding, casting (metal).

furare :—to steal.

furatio :—theft.

furbire :—to furbish.

furcare :—to pitch corn or hay with a fork ; to fourch, to delay a suit brought against two persons jointly, by alternate appearance or essoin.

furectare :—to ferret.

furfuraculum :– a sieve.

furigeldum :—a fine for theft.

furlangus, furlongus :—the eighth of a mile ; the eighth of an acre.

furmelum. See *formella.*

furnagium. See *fornagium.*

furnarius :—a baker.

furnesium :—a furnace.

furniare :—to bake.

furnire :—to heat up an oven or furnace.

furnus :—a bakehouse.

furra :—fur.

furragium. See *foragium.*

furrare :—to line with fur.

furratio :—furring.

furratura :—furring, work done in fur.

furratus :—furred.

furrellus :—a sword sheath ; a bow case.

furrura, fururia :—fur.

furulus. See *furrellus.*

fuscamen :—fustian.

fusillatim :—fusilly.

fusillus :—a fusil (heraldic).

fusor :—a founder, a caster, a melter ;. a fusour, an officer in the Exchequer.

fusoria :—the office of fusour.

fustarius :—a joiner.

fustianum :—fustian.

fustum :—a beam, a log, a stump.

fusus : — a spindle ; a fusil (heraldic).

G.

gabella :—rent ; service.

gabellus :—a gable.

gablagium :—the same as *gabella.*

gablare :—to pay rent.

gablator :—a rent payer ; a farmer.

gablum :—a cross. See also *gabella.*

gabulagium. See *gabella.*

gabulum :—a gable ; rent ; interest. See *gabella.*

gabulus. See *gabella.*

gachum :—an oar or scull ; a staple ; a cake.

gafra :—a wafer.

gafrarius :—a waferer.

gayeria :—a promise, an engagement, a pledge.

gagnagium, gaignagium, gainagium :—gain, profit.

gaila :—a gaol, a prison.

gaineria :—a tilled field ; a crop.

gaiola. See *gaila.*

gaivelettum. See *gaveletum.*

galathia :—pickle for preserving fish.

galea, galia :—a galley.

galearia :—a gallery.

galeasia :—a galliasse, a large galley.

galeo :—a galleon.

galeta, galetum :—a gallon ; shingle.

galida :—a galley, a low flat-built ship with both sails and oars.

galio : — a galleon, a large Spanish sailing ship, with three or four decks.

galiota, galiotus :—a galliot, a small galley ; a master of, or man serving on a galley.

galirum :—something used by a silk weaver.

galla :—a shoemaker's last.

gallecta :—collection of dues.

galliare :—a mitre.

gallicantus :—cockcrow.

gallicidium :—Shrovetide.

gallinaceus :—a capon.

galliottus. See *galiota.*

gallivolatium :—a cock-glade, a glade along which woodcocks fly in the morning and evening ; a cockshoot, a net set for them in such places.

gallo, gallona, galo, galona, galum :—a gallon.

galya :—a galley.

gamarus : — a stickleback (*gasterosteus trachurus*).

gamberia :—armour for the legs. Fr. *grevières*.

gambeso, gambesum :—a gambeson or haqueton, a quilted jacket worn under the armour.

gambria. See *gamberia*.

ganagium. See *gagnagium*.

ganea :—a dart or arrow.

ganerium :—gainery, profit arising from tillage.

gannatura :—yelping, derision.

gannocare cerevisiam :—to jockey beer.

gansellium :—a gosling.

ganta, ganteletus :—a gauntlet.

gaola :—a prison, a gaol.

gaolagium :—prison dues.

gaolarius :—a gaoler.

gara terræ :—a gare or gore, a wedge-shaped corner of a field left after ploughing a number of strips.

garancia :—madder.

garandisare :—to warrant.

garantum :—warrant.

garba : — a sheaf ; a sheaf of arrows was 24.

garbana :—a granary.

garbelagium : — garbelage, the office of garbler ; the refuse removed by garbling.

garbellare :—to garble, to pick out the refuse.

garbellator : — a garbler, who visited shops, &c. to examine the purity of spices sold.

garcifer. See *garcio*.

garcio :—a boy ; a groom.

garciolus : — a diminutive of *garcio*.

garda : — a ward of a town ; wardship. See *warda*.

gardaroba, garderoba :—a wardrobe.

garderobarius : — a wardrobe-keeper.

gardia :—ward.

gardiana :—the office of warden.

gardianus : — a guardian ; a warden.

gardiare :—to guard, to protect.

gardiator : — a guardian, a warden.

gardinarius :—a gardener.

gardinum :—a garden.

gardropia :—a wardrobe.

gardum :—a garth.

garenna : — a warren. See *warenna*.

gargarare :—to brag.

gargata :—the throat.

garilatrix :—a scold.

gariso :—protection ; provision, living ; healing.

garita :—a watch tower.

garlanda :—a chaplet ; a garland, sometimes of gold or silver.

garnamentum :—a garment.

garnestura :—victuals, arms, &c., necessary for a garrison ; a garrison.

garniso:—protection ; a garrison.

garnizare:—to adorn ; to garnish.

garra. See *yara.*

garrettum:—a garret.

garrita:—a watch tower.

garrolum, garrulium:—a barrier.

garterium: —a garter.

gastaldus:—a governor of a town or province.

gastella:—wastel bread, fine white bread.

gastum:—waste.

gata:—a bowl.

gatgeria:—a parcel.

gauda, gaudo:—woad.

gaugeare:—to gauge.

gaugetum:—gauging, a gauge.

gaugiator:—a gauger.

gaveletum:—gavelet, a writ of *cessavit*, used where gavelkind obtains.

gavelmannus:—a tenant liable to tribute.

gavelocus:—a javelin

gayra. See *gara.*

geburus:—a villager, a peasant.

geldabilis:—liable to pay tax.

geldabulum:—land liable to payment of *geldum.*

geldare:—to enforce or to pay a *geldum.*

geldatio:—payment of a *geldum.*

geldum, geldus:—tax ; compensation ; fine.

gelima: —a sheaf.

geloffium:—a gillyflower.

geltum. See *geldum.*

gemala:—a hinge.

gemellus:—a clasp with similar ends, or double brooch. O. E. gemewe.

gemotum:—an assembly.

genealis:—native.

generale:—the commons of a monk.

generosa:—a gentlewoman.

generosus:—a gentleman.

geneta:—a genet, a beast of the weasel tribe, used for fur (*genetta vulgaris*).

genimen:—an offshoot.

genoboda:—a moustache.

gens:—often used for an army.

genuscissio:—hocking or hambling dogs by cutting the sinew of the hind leg.

geola, &c. See *gaola, &c.*

gerarchia:—used for *hierarchia.*

gerca, gercia, gercis:—a ewe lamb.

gerentarius:—an officer in a convent, probably a friary, who was not compelled to reside therein (*granatarius ?*).

gerlanda:—a garland.

gernarium:—a granary.

gersa:—starch.

gersuma:—a fine ; a reward ; an earnest. O. E. "gryssume."

gerulus:—a packhorse.

gerusa:—a goad.

gesa:—a gisarme. See *gisarma.*

gesta:—(pl.) deeds; a history.

gesta, gestum:—yeast; food.

gestrum:—a jesterne or jestorne, a sleeveless jacket of scale armour.

getti :—a hawk's jesses.

getticium :—a jetty.

gewineda :—an assembly.

ghestum :—food ; a meal given to a guest. See *gistum.*

gialda, gyalda :—a guildhall.

gifra :—cypher.

gifta :—a stream ; sometimes used for *gista.*

giga :—a cittern.

gignasium, i.e., gymnasium.

gihalda :—a guildhall.

gilda :—a fraternity, a guild.

gilda aula :—a guildhall.

gildare. See *geldire.*

gildatio. See *geldatio.*

gildaula, gildeaula, gildhalla :— a guildhall.

gildhalla Teutonicorum : — the Steelyard, or company of Easterling merchants.

gilfalco : — a gerfalcon (*falco Islandicus*).

gilla, gillus :—a mug.

gillagium :—tax paid on wine sold by retail.

gilofera :—clove or gillyflower.

gimphus. See *gumfus.*

gingibrattum :—ginger.

gipo :—a doublet (*pourpoint*).

gipsura :—pargeting.

girgillare :—to wind up.

girgillus :—a reel with a handle for winding thread.

girivagus :—wandering.

giro :—an apron, a skirt.

gisarma :—a gisarme, a weapon resembling a halberd, having a spear point, with a small axe at the foot of the point, and sometimes a spike on the opposite side : but in Matthew Paris (Rolls Ed. I. 470) the phrase occurs, " *sica, id est, gisarme.*"

gista :—a joist. See also *gistum.*

gistare :—to furnish with joists ; to recline on a litter.

gistarius :—borne on a litter.

gistum :—the duty of entertaining the lord when on a journey ; yeast.

glandines plumbei :—" *Anglice* hail-hot."

glaneare :—to glean.

glasia :—ice.

glavea, glavia :—a glaive.

gleba :—land belonging to a parish church, glebe ; a corpse.

glebalis terra :—glebe land.

glebaria :—turf.

gleniagium :—gleaning.

gleniare :—to glean.

glis :—mud.

gliseria :—clayland.

glomellus : — a clew.

glomerarius, glomerellus :—a commissioner appointed to settle disputes between the scholars of a university and their servants (?).

glorietta :—a gloriet, an upper room in a tower.

glossum :—a shrine.

glutum :—glue.

gobonatus :—embossed.

godetus :—a mug.

golda :—a drain ; a mine (?).

goliarda :—buffoonery ; a juggler's art.

goliardisare :—to act as a *goliardus*.

goliardus :—a buffoon; a juggler.

gonella, gonellus :—a gown.

gora. See *gara*.

gordus :—a weir, a weirpool; a gorce.

gorgeria :—a gorget.

gorgona :—a gargoyle.

gota :—a gut, a drain.

gouna :—a gown.

grabatum :—a couch.

gracemannus :—the head of a guild at Lincoln.

gracia :—an indulgence.

gradale, graduale :—a gradual, or grail, a book containing the musical portion of the mass.

gradiens :—passant (heraldic).

graduatus :—a graduate, one who has taken a degree in a university.

grafia, graffia :—the dignity or territory of a *graffio*.

graffio :—a count, an earl ; a reeve.

graffium, grafium :— a register, or cartulary ; a pen.

grana :—scarlet. See *granum*.

granata :—a garnet.

granatarius : — a keeper or steward of a granary.

grancia :—a grange, esp. a farmhouse belonging to a monastery.

graneta :—a garnet.

granetarius. See *granatarius*.

grangia. See *grancia*.

grangiarius :—the keeper of a grange.

grantum :—security. See *creantum*.

granum :—grain ; the *coccus ilicis* and *coccus arborum*, used in dyeing red.

grapa :—a putlog hole.

graphium. See *graffium*.

gratare :—to scratch.

gratarium :—a grate.

gratia :—an indulgence.

gratiare :—to thank.

grava :—a grove.

gravetum :—a grove.

gravia :—a grove. See also *grafia*.

gremium :—the nave of a church.

grenetarius : — a keeper of a granary.

greseus, gresius :—grey.

gresmannus :—a tenant of some sort.

gressia :—grease time, the season for killing harts and bucks.

gressibilis :—able to walk.

grisengus, grisetus, griseus :— grey.

griseum opus :—greywork, gris, fur of badger skin, or more likely the " *mus Ponticus*."

grisillones :—handcuffs, manacles.

grisium. See *griseum.*

grissus :—grey ; gris.

gristarius :—an official of a convent, probably in charge of the mills.

grisus :—grey ; gris.

groceria :—grocery.

grocerius :—a grocer.

gromes, grometus, gromus :—a groom.

gronna :—a place whence peat is dug.

gropus :—a hook, perhaps a skid.

grossa :—a groat.

grossare :—to engross, to make a fair copy, or to buy up.

grossarius :—an engrosser, a grocer.

grossum :—the revenue of a benefice ; gross.

grossus :—(adj.) large, gross.

grossus (subst.) a groat. (Fr. *Gros.*)

groundagium :—payment for permission to anchor in a harbour.

grova :—a grove.

grovetta :—a little grove.

grovum :—a grove.

gruarius :—a chief forester ; a falcon used for cranes.

gruellum :—gruel.

grumus :—gruel ; a mound ; a balk of land.

grunda :—a gutter. See *alura.*

gruta :—grouse.

grutum :—grout.

guadagium. See *guidagium.*

guadium, guagium. See *vadium.*

gualda :—woad.

guannagium. See *wainagium.*

guarda :—ward.

guardaroba :—a wardrobe.

guardia :—wardship.

guardiania :—the office of warden or guardian.

guardianus : — a warden ; a guardian.

guardiare :—to guard, to protect.

guarectare. See *warectare.*

guarenna :—a warren.

guarennarius, guarnerius : — a warrenner.

guaretare. See *warectare.*

guarniso :—provision.

guastum :—waste.

guerra :—war.

guerrare :—to make war.

guerrator :—a warrior.

guerreare :—to make war.

guerria :—war.

guerrificare :—to make war.

guerrinus :—at war ; warlike.

guiare :—to lead.

guidagium : — safe-conduct ; a payment for safe-conduct.

guidare :—to lead ; to take toll for leading.

guido :—a guidon.

guihalla :—a guildhall.

guilda :—a guild.

guildhalda :—a guildhall.

gula :—a tippet.

gula Augusti : — the first of August, Gulaust, Lammas Day.*

Gulaustum. See *gula Augusti.*

gulfus :—a whirlpool ; a gulf.

gulla :—a gully, a watercourse.

gumfus, gumpha :—a hinge, a joint; glue.

guna :—a cupping glass (*guva*); a gown.

gunca :—reeds.

gunellus :—a short gown.

gunna :—some part of the machinery of a mill ; a cannon, a gun ; a gown.

gunnarius :—a gunner.

gunnum :—a cannon, a gun.

gupilierettus :—a foxhound.

gupillius :—a fox.

gurda :—a handmill (?).

gurgeria :—a gorget.

gurges, gurgitum :—a weir.

gurgulio :—a gargoyle.

gurtus :—a weir.

guttatorium, guttorium : — a gutter.

guttera, gutteria, guttura : — a gutter.

gutturna :—quinsy.

gutturus :—a gutter.

guuarda :—ward (*guarda*).

guyalda :—a guildhall.

guysa :—manner, form.

gwafra :—a wafer.

gwalstowum :—a place of execution.

gwastum :—waste.

gyalda :—a guildhall.

gydagium :—payment to a guide.

gylda :—a guild.

gysa :—manner, form.

gysarma :—a gisarme. See *gisarma.*

H.

habentia :—riches.

habilis :—fit; capable.

habilitatio :—qualification.

habitualiter : — by estimation ; figuratively.

habitudinalis :—figurative.

habundancia. For *abundancia.*

haccus :—a hake (*merlucius vulgaris*).

hachia :—a pickaxe ; a hatchet.

hada :—a small piece of land.

haderunga :—hatred.

hadocus :—a haddock (*morrhua æglefinus*).

haerarius :—nesting.

hæreditas, &c. See *hereditas, &c.*

hærela. See *harela.*

haeria :—an aery, a nest.

---

* This name is said to have originated from the cure by Pope Alexander I. of a wen in the throat (*gula*) of Balbina by the application of St. Peter's chains on that day.

haga :—a hedge ; a house in a city or borough.

hagabulum :—a rate or tax paid at Cambridge.

hagardum :—a rickyard.

hagia, haia, haicia :—a hedge.

hainescia. See *esnecia.*

hairus :—a heron ; haircloth.

haka :—a hake (*merlucius vulgaris*).

hakedus :—a hake.

hakeneius, hakenettus :—a hackney, a nag.

hala :—a hall.

halberga :—a hauberk, a coat of mail.

halbergettum :—a coarse cloth.

halberiolum :—a haubergeon, a tunic of mail.

halda :—a hall.

halgardum :—a shed.

halimotum : — hallmote ; court baron.

halla :—a hall.

halsfagium :—pillory ; a fine.

hamella, hamelettum :—a hamlet.

hamleta, hamlettus :—a hamlet.

hamma :—a home-close ; a little meadow ; an edge or hem in the common field.

hamsoca :—the privilege of a person's house ; a fine for forcible entry.

hanaperium, hanepurium : — a hamper. The Hanaper is an office in the Court of Chancery.

hanchia, hancia :—a haunch. See also *hansa.*

handana, handayna, handena :—a day's work.

hangardum :—a shed.

hangwitha :—a fine for wrongfully hanging a robber or letting him escape.

hansa :—a house, or company of merchants ; a city with reference to its foreign mercantile dealings.

hara :—a stye.

haracium :—a stud of horses.

harare :—to plough.

haratium :—a stud of horses.

harciare :—to harrow.

harela :—a conspiracy ; a society ; a riot.

harenga :—a harangue ; a herring.

harengaria :—the herring fishery, or season.

harengus : — a herring (*clupea harengus*).

harepipa :—a snare for hares, called a harepipe.

harnesiare :—to put on armour ; to harness ; to decorate.

harnesium, harnisium :—armour ; harness ; rigging.

harpare :—to play on the harp.

harpica :—a harrow.

harpicator :—a harrower.

harrectus :—a harrier.

harreum :—a herd, troop, esp. of horses.

haspa :—a hasp, a door-fastening.

hasta :—a spit.

hastalaria, hastellaria :—a spittery, a place where spits are kept.

hastellarius :—a turnspit.

hastiludium :—a tournament.

hatchettus :—a hatchet.

haubercum :—a hauberk, a long coat of mail with sleeves.

haubergellum, haubergeo :—a habergeon, a short sleeveless coat of mail; sometimes used for hauberk.

haubergettum :—a habergeon, not necessarily of metal; a sort of parti-coloured cloth. O.E. haberject.

hauberionus, hauberiunus : — a habergeon.

hauborio :—a habergeon.

hauritorium :—a ladle; a pump.

haustrum :—a bucket; a pump.

havenator :—a harbour master.

haverocum :—a haycock, a hayrick; the quantity of hay which can be lifted on the handle of a scythe, or bound with one cord.

haya, haycia :—a hedge; a net; an enclosure.

haydagium. Same as *hedagium* (?). (Selby Cartulary, f. 126.)

hayea :—a hedge.

hayum :—a meadow.

hebdomada :—a week.

hebdomadarius :—a canon of a cathedral church, appointed weekly to take charge of the choir; a priest appointed for weekly duty in a monastery.

heccagium :—rent for heckles, fishing engines used in the Ouse, and at Pevensey.

hechium :—a hatch; a hedge.

heccagium. See *heccagium.*

heda :—a wharf; a hithe.

hedagium :—toll paid at a wharf.

heiria :—an eyry, a nest.

heiro :—a heron.

heiwardus :—a hayward.

heltum :—a hilt.

heraldus :—a herald.

herbagium :—herbage; right of pasturing cattle; payment therefor.

herbarius :—a haymaker.

herbergagium :—lodgings.

herbergare, herbigare :—to lodge; to entertain. See also *herbergiare.*

herbergeria : — a harbour; a halting place; a lodging.

herbergiare :—to build; to furnish. See also *herbergare.*

herbergiator :—a harbinger: an innkeeper.

herbiseca :—a mower.

hercarius :—a harrower.

hercea :—a hearse.

hercia :—a harrow; a frame to hold candles.

herciare :—to harrow.

herciatura :—harrowing; service by harrowing.

herebannum :—a fine for refusing to perform military service.

herecius : — a hound used for stag hunting.

heredipeta :—the next heir.

hereditamentum :—hereditament, all property that may be inherited.

hereditare :—to cause to inherit.

hereditas :—an inheritance.

herellus :—a kind of small fish.

heremina :—ermine.

heremita :—a hermit.

heremitorium :—a hermitage.

herenesium :—harness.

heresista :—a heretic.

heretagium : — hereditament ; heritage.

heretochius :—a commander of soldiers.

heretrix :—an heiress.

herettius canis :—the same as *harrectus* (?) or *herecius*.

heretum :—a courtyard for the use of soldiers.

herezeldus : — military service, scutage.

herga :—a harrow.

hericius :—a hedgehog ; a revolving bar with spikes used in fortresses.

herietum :—a heriot.

herigaldum : — a surcoat.

herigeta : —a heriot.

herilis :—there are two adjectives spelt thus, one derived from *hæres*, the other from *herus*.

heriotum :—a heriot.

heriscindium :—division of household goods.

herminus :—ermine.

hermitagium, *hermitorium* : — a hermitage.

hernasii :—irregular soldiers.

hernasium, *hernesium*. See *harnesium*.

herodius :—a gerfalcon (*falco Islandicus*).

heroudes :—a herald.

herpex :—a harrow.

herpicatio :—a day's harrowing.

hersia :—a hearse.

hersium :—a metal frame to hold candles.

hesia :—an easement.

hesta, *hestha* :—a small loaf ; a fowl.

heuedrata : — a headland (?) ; perhaps the right to store manure on headlands.

heura :—a hure. See *hura*.

heymectus :—a rabbit-net.

heyretheca :—a heriot.

heyronagium :—a heronry.

heyronus :—a heron.

hibernagium :—the winter season for sowing corn, Michaelmas to Christmas ; corn sown in winter ; winter services ; the court at which they were assigned ; rye.

hida :—a hide of land, sufficient land to maintain a family or to work with one plough team, reckoned about 120 acres. 4 hides=1 knight's fee.

hidagium :—a tax levied on every hide of land ; a fine paid by persons of servile condition instead of receiving corporal punishment for offences (*hydgild*).

hidare :—to divide into hides.

higra :—the bore or eager of a river.

hilla :—a sausage.

hiltra :—an engine for catching salmon.

M.

S

hiltum :—a hilt.

hindagium :—loading.

hippocomus :—a master of the horse.

hiremannus :—a servant.

hiritinum :—a harrow (?).

hirna :—a sausage.

hirquicallus :—squinting.

hirsepa :—a torch.

hiruco. See *hericius.*

hispaniolus :—a spaniel.

historia :—a story, in a building.

hitha :—a wharf; a hithe.

hivernagium. See *hibernagium.*

hlammator :—a fisherman of some kind.

hobellarius : —a hobbler, a light horse soldier who rode a hobby.

hobelus :—a hobby (*falco subbuteo*).

hoberarius. See *hobellarius.*

hoccus salis :—a salt pit.

hocium :—the housing of a horse.

hoga :—a mound; a pit caused by making a mound.

hogacius :—a hogget.

hogaster : —a pig; a sheep in its second year, a hogget.

hogettus, hogietus :—a hogget.

hoggus :—a hog.

hogrus :—a sheep.

homagium :—homage.

hominatio :—muster; homage.

hominium :—homage.

homiplagium :—maiming.

hopa :—a hopper, a basket.

hora :—ore (*ora*).

horarius, horarium :—a breviary; a book of Hours.

hordarius :—the keeper of a granary.

hordera :—a treasurer.

horderium :—a granary; a treasury.

hordicium :—a hurdle.

horisonium :—a clock.

hornagium, hornegeldum :—a tax on cattle.

horologiarius :—a clock maker.

horologium :—a clock ; a watch.

horoscopus :—a dial.

horripilatio :—shuddering.

hortarius :—a gardener.

horula :—a short time (dim. of *hora*).

hosa :—a small wooden cask.

hosæ :—hose.

hosarius :—a hosier.

hospitalaria : — the hostry or guest-house of a monastery.

hospitalarius :—a knight of the Order of St. John of Jerusalem ; a hospitaller or hostillar, a monk whose duty is to attend to guests, the steward of the guest-house ; a guest-master.

hospitale, hospitalitas :—an inn ; a guest house ; a hospital.

hospitare terram :—to enclose (?); to build a house on.

hospitarius. See *hospitalarius.*

hospitator :—an innkeeper.

hospitium :—a house for receiving guests ; an inn, a hostel; an Inn of Court or Chancery ; procuration or visitation money.

hostagium :—hostage. See also *hospitium* and *hostelagium.*

hostelagium :—a lord's right of being lodged by his tenants.

hostelarium. See *hospitalaria.*

hostellarius :—an innkeeper. See also *hospitalarius.*

hosteria :—a *ciborium,* q.v.

hosterium :—a hoe.

hostia :—the consecrated wafer.

hostiagius :—a hostage.

hostiaratus, hostiaria :—the office of usher or doorkeeper, one of the minor orders.

hostiarius :—an usher.

hosticius :—a porch.

hostilagium. See *hostelagium.*

hostillaria. See *hospitalaria.*

hostillarius : — an ostler. See *hospitalarius.*

hostium. For *ostium.*

hostorcus : — a goshawk (*astur palumbarius*).

hostorium :—a strickle for measuring corn.

hostorius :—a goshawk.

hostria. See *hospitalaria.*

hostricus :—a goshawk.

huca : — a hewke, a frock or mantle.

hucea : —housing of a horse; a gown.

huchea :—a hutch.

hudagium. See *hidagium.*

hugia :—a hoy ; a hutch.

huisserium :—a ship for conveying horses.

huisserius :—an usher.

hulcus. See *hulka.*

huldare : — to plank, to put campsheathing on a bank.

hulka :—a large ship, a transport ship.

hullus :—a hill.

hulmus :—a holm, a meadow on a river bank, or an island.

humagium :—a marshy place ; homage.

hummulina :—beer.

hundreda. See *hundredum.*

hundredarius :—a hundredor, a juror in a case concerning land who lives in the hundred in which the land is ; a bailiff of a hundred.

hundredum :—a hundred, a division of a shire ; a hundred court; payment due from a hundred; fine from the hundredors for non-appearance at the court.

hura :—a hure, a coarse cap.

hurarius :—a hurrer, a maker of hures.

hurdicius :—a hurdle; a military engine to protect the assailants of a fortress; a hoarding.

hurtardus, hurtus :—a ram.

husa :—a horsecloth ; housing.

husbandrea :—a farmhouse ; a farm.

husbandus :—a farmer; a peasant.

huscarla, huscarlius :—a household servant ; a military retainer attached to the lord's household.

huscus :—a holm.

husebondus :—a husband, in the sense of economy.

s 2

husgablum, husgabulum :—house-
tax, or rent, husgable.

hussus :—holly.

*hustengium, hustengum, hustin-
gum* :—hustings ; the Su-
preme Court of the City of
London.

*hutagium, hutasium, hutellum,
hutesium* :—hue [and cry].

huterellum :—drift wood (?).

hyda. See *hida.*

hydromellum :—mead.

I.

ibanum :—ebony.

ibernagium. See *hibernagium.*

icona, iconia :—an image, a figure.

iconomia :—housekeeping.

idago. See *indago.*

idoneare :—to prove innocence,
to purge.

idriola :—a holy water stoup.

ifungia :—cocket bread, the
second best white bread.

ignitegium :—curfew.

illegitimitas :—bastardy.

illicite :—translated in a document of 1385, "aukewardly."

illimitatus :—unlimited.

illuminare :—to paint. (O. E.
limne.)

imaginarius :—an image maker.

imbassiator :—an ambassador.

imbesilare :—to embezzle.

imbreviare :—to abridge ; to put
in writing.

imbricatus :—engrailed. See *engrallatus.*

imbrocus :—a brook.

imbulus :—a pentice, a penthouse.

imbursare :—to put in one's own
purse.

immeabilis :—immoveable.

immeliorare :—to improve.

immerciatus :—fined, amerced.

imminorare :—to diminish.

impalare :—to impound.

impanellare :—to enter the names
of a jury ; to empanel.

imparcamentum :—the right of
impounding cattle.

imparcare :—to impark ; to impound.

imparcatio. See *imparcamentum.*

impechiamentum : — hindrance ;
impeachment.

impechiare :—to accuse, to impeach.

impedia :—the upper leather of a
shoe.

impediare :—to mutilate a dog's
feet, to law. See *expeditare.*

impedientes :—defendants.

impennare :—to feather arrows.

imperator :—the emperor.

imperpetuum :—for ever.

impersonare :—to institute a
rector.

impersonata, persona :—parson
imparsonee, a lawful incumbent in actual possession.

impescatus :—impeached.

impetere : — to accuse, to impeach.

impetitio :—an impeachment; a claim.

impignoratissia : —adj. as a pledge.

impinguare :—to fatten.

implacitare :—to implead, to sue.

implementum :—complement ; an utensil.

implicatio :—a landing-stage, a mooring-place.

impoisonare :—to poison.

impomentum :—a dessert of fruit.

importancia :—importance.

imposterum : —hereafter.

impotionare : —to poison.

impressor :—a printer.

impressus :—an adherent, a partisan.

impretiabilis :—invaluable.

imprimere :—to print.

imprisa, imprisia :—enterprise.

imprisius :—an adherent.

imprisonamentare :—to imprison.

imprisonamentum : —imprisonment.

imprisonare :—to imprison.

imprisus :—an adherent.

improbatio : — disapproval ; disproof.

improperare :—to blame ; to impute.

improperatio :—disgrace ; insult.

impropriatio : — an ecclesiastical benefice in the hands of a layman.

impruiamentum :—the improvement of land, sometimes written *appruiamentum*.

impruiare :—to improve land.

inabilitas. See *inhabilitas*.

inactitare :—to register.

inamelatus :—enamelled.

inancia :—advantage, advance.

inannulatus :—not ringed (of a pig).

inantea :—henceforth.

inbasciator :—an ambassador.

inbladare :—to sow with corn.

inbladatio :—growing crops.

inblaura :—the product of land (*imbladatura*).

inbreviare. See *imbreviare*.

inbrochiare : —to broach.

inbullare :—to insert in a bull.

incarcare :—to imprison.

incartare :—to grant by a written deed.

incastellare :— to fortify.

incausare :—to implead.

incaustorium :—an inkhorn.

incaustum : —ink.

incensare :—to use incense ; to confer an office.

incerchare :—to seek.

incertum opus :—rubble work.

incharaxare :—to put in writing.

inchartare. See *incartare*.

inclaudare :—to fetter.

inclausa. See *inclausura*.

inclaustrum :—a cloister.

inclausura : — an enclosure, a home close.

inclavare :—to prick with a nail.

includere : —to enclose.

inclusa :—a nun ; an anchoress.

inclusarius, inclusorius :—a pinder.

inclusorium :—a pound.

inclusus:—a monk; an anchorite.

incluvium :—some instrument of torture.

incombrancia :—encumbrance.

incombrare:—to hinder ; to stop up a road ; to pawn.

incompatibilitas : — incompatibility, of benefices which cannot be held together.

incopare :—to accuse.

incopolitus :—a proctor ; a vicar.

incordare :—to string a bow or crossbow.

incortinare : —to adorn with hangings.

incrastinum :--the morrow.

incredens :—infidel.

incrocamentum :—incroachment.

incrocare, incrochiare :—to encroach.

incrustator :—a tinker.

inculpare :—to blame ; to accuse.

inculpatio :—blame ; accusation.

incumbrare. See *incombrare.*

incurramentum :—liability to a penalty.

incurrimentum :—a fine.

incussa. For *inconcussa.*

incussorium :—a hammer.

incustodia :—carelessness.

indago :—a park.

indebitatus :—indebted.

indecimabilis : —not liable to tithes.

indefensus :—one who refuses to answer to an accusation.

indefesibilis :—indefeasible, that cannot be made void.

indempnis. For *indemnis.*

indentare :—to indent.

indentura :—an indenture.

index : —a pointer or setter dog.

indicibilis :—unspeakable.

indictamentum :—an indictment.

indictare :—to indict.

indictio : —indictment ; indiction, a cycle of fifteen years by which writings were dated at Rome.

indictor :—an accuser.

indistanter :—immediately.

indistringibilis :—not distrainable.

indivisibilis murus:—a main wall, not a party wall.

indivisum :—held in common.

indorsamentum : —endorsement.

indorsare :—to endorse.

indorsatio :—endorsement.

indossare. See *indorsare.*

inductio :—induction, putting a clergyman into possession of his church.

indula :—strong thread.

indus :—indigo.

inedicibilis :—unspeakable.

inewardus :—a watchman.

infaidare : — to be at enmity with.

infalistatio :—a capital punishment inflicted at Dover, drowning (?).

infeodare :—to enfeoff.

infeodatio decimarum :—granting tithes to laymen.

infeofare :—to enfeoff.

inferius :—lower down, in a roll; further on, in a book.

infirmaria :—the infirmary of a monastery. O. E. fermory, farmery.

infirmarius :—the guardian of the sick in a monastery.

infirmatorium :—an infirmary.

infiscare :—to confiscate.

inflechiare :—to make shafts for arrows or bolts.

inforciare :—to fortify.

informator :—a tutor.

infortiare :—to fortify.

infossare :—to surround with a ditch.

infra :—further on, in a reference to a book or roll.

infraclusus. For *inclusus*.

infractura :—breach; violation.

infraudulentus :—without fraud.

infrontare :—to stop.

infrontare sese :—to resist.

infrunitas :—madness.

infugare :—to put to flight.

infula :—a cassock; a coif.

infunditur :—is flooded.

ingaignia :—an engine; a machine; a trap.

ingenerabilis :—without the power of procreation.

ingeniator :—an engineer.

ingenium :—a machine; an engine; a gin.

ingenuitas :—freedom; nobility.

inglisheria :—Englishry.

ingradatus : — engrailed. See *engrallatus*.

ingrangiare :—to deposit in a granary.

ingravare :—to engrave; to demand.

ingrediatus : — engrailed. See *engrallatus*.

ingressus :—the relief paid by an heir on entering upon his lands.

ingrossare :—to engross, to copy out fairly, or to buy up.

ingrossator :—a copier; a wholesale dealer.

inguardus :—a guard; a watchman.

inhabilitas :—unwieldiness; unfitness; want of power.

inhokare, inhoc facere :—to enclose.

inhokum :—" any corner or part of a common field, ploughed up and sowed with oats, &c., and sometimes fenced in with a dry hedge, in that year wherein the rest of the same field lies fallow and common " (Jacob).

inhospitatio :—lodging.

inhundredum :—the central portion of a hundred (?).

inimicare :—to be at enmity with.

injuriatio : — wrongdoing; injury.

inlagare : — to restore to the benefit of the law.

inlagatio :—the restitution of an outlaw.

inlagatus :—one who is not an outlaw.

inlantale :—demesne land.

inlegiare :—to satisfy the law; to restore to the benefit of the law.

innamiare :—to distrain.

innamium, innamum :—a pledge. See *namium.*

innire :—to inn, to carry corn or hay.

innocare :—to enclose.

innocum. See *inhokum.*

innodare :—to knot; to bind.

innodius :—the nave of a wheel.

innonia :—an enclosure.

innoxiare :—to purge; to absolve.

inofficiare :—to provide with the services of the church.

inordinatus : —intestate.

inpennatus :—feathered.

inprisius, inprisus :—an adherent.

inquesta, inquestum, inquisitio :— an inquest; an inquisition.

inquisitor :—a sheriff, coroner, &c., who has power to hold inquests; a retriever.

inrotulare, inrollare :—to enrol.

inscalare :—to climb by ladder, to scale.

insectator :—a prosecutor.

insellatus : —unsaddled.

insertum opus : — bonded masonry.

inservire :—to bring into slavery.

insigillare :—to seal.

insigne :—a coat of arms.

insilium :—bad advice.

insolercia :—unskilfulness.

insolutus :—unpaid.

installare :—to instal; to quit-claim, to compound.

installatio :—a composition.

instauramentum. See *instauratio.*

instaurare :—to stock (a farm).

instaurarius :—a stockkeeper.

instauratio, instaurum :—store; stock of a farm; furniture of a church, books, vestments, &c.

instirpare :—to plant, to establish.

instita :—a rochet.

institutio :—institution, the granting by a bishop to a clerk of the cure of souls in his benefice.

instuffare :—to stuff.

instructus :—furniture; tools.

insubulus :—a trendle.

insuetus :—accustomed. For *assuetus.*

insula :—a detached house or block of buildings; an aisle.

insularius :—a keeper or porter of a detached house (*insula*).

intabulare :—to write on tables; to register.

intachgara :—a gore of land newly enclosed.

intassare :—to heap up hay in cocks.

intendentia :—submission.

interceptio :—enterprise, aggression.

intercipere :—to attack; to seize wrongfully.

interclaustrum :—a walk or passage between cloisters (?).

interclausum :—an enclosure.

interclausura :—the setting of precious stones ; chasing of metal.

interclusorius :—enclosing.

interclusum. See *interclausum.*

intercommunicare :—to intercommon, where the tenants of two manors use the commons of both.

interesse :—interest.

interessens :—being present at.

interessentia :—interest ; fee to those performing divine service.

interfinium :—a space ; the bridge of the nose.

interlinearis :—between the lines.

interlocutorius :—conversational.

interloingnium. See *loingium.*

interludium :—play, mumming, as at Christmas.

intermedium :—intercession.

internamentum :—burial.

interpeditatus :—not completely hambled. See *expeditare.*

interplacitare :—to interplead.

interprisa :—an attack.

interpugnare :—to fight together.

interranea :—the bowels.

intersignum :—a token ; a countersign.

intertenere :—to entertain.

intertiare :—to sequester.

intestinum opus :—wainscot.

inthronizare :—to enthrone.

intitulare :—to enter in a book or list ; to write titles on books ; to entitle.

intorcinium :—a torch.

intrare :—to enter, or inn, *i.e.* drain and cultivate, marshes, which are then called *innings.*

intrastagnum :—a seat in a row, a stall (?).

intrinsecus :—a dweller within, a citizen, opp. to *forinsecus.*

introducere :—to marry.

introitus :—an introit, an antiphone sung while the priest is going to the altar.

intronizare :—to enthrone.

intrussare :—to pack up.

inumbliare :—to trim the branches of trees.

invadiare :—to mortgage ; to pawn.

invadiatio :—a mortgage.

invadimoniare :—to pledge, to put in pawn.

inventarium :—an inventory.

inventio :—treasure trove.

inventorium :—an inventory.

inveritare :—to prove.

investio, investimentum :—investiture.

investire :—to invest, to give possession.

investitura :—investiture.

involutorium :—a kerchief.

inwardus :—a watchman.

ipoporgium :—an andiron.

irrectus :—unjust.

irremiscibilis :—unpardonable.

irreplegiabilis, irrepleviabilis :—irreplevisable, that which ought not to be replevied or delivered on sureties.

irrotulamentum :—an enrolment.

irrotulare :—to enrol.

irrotulatio :—enrolling.

irrugire :—to roar.

iter :—the circuit, or eyre, of a judge.

iterans justiciarius :—a justice in eyre.

iterare :—to make a journey; to hold an eyre; to rejudge; to repeat.

iterato :—again, repeatedly.

iteratus :—repeated.

itineratio :—a circuit or eyre.

itura :—an alure. See *alura.*

ivernagium. See *hibernagium.*

J.

jacens :—in abeyance.

jactacula :—a hawk's jesses.

jacti :—jesses.

jactivus :—one who loses by default.

jahones :—furze, gorse.

jampnum, jannum :—furze, gorse.

jantare :—to breakfast.

jardinus :—a garden.

jarellum :—a barrier.

jarrum :—a jar.

jarruyllium :—a gutter.

jaula, &c. See *gaola, &c.*

jauones :—furze (?).

jercia :—a lamb.

jesa :—a gisarme.

jetti :—jesses.

jocale :—a jewel.

jocarius :—a jester.

jocillator :—a juggler.

joellum :—a jewel.

joppus :—a fool.

jornale. See *jornata.*

jornancia :—a day's work.

jornata :—a day's work or journey; an acre of land. (Fr. *journau.*)

Jovis dies :—Thursday.

judaismus :—Jewry.

judicator :—a doomsman, a man called in to assist a Court in difficult cases, esp. in Cheshire.

jugulare :—to yoke.

juguliettum :—the neck.

jugum :—a yoke of land, half a plough-land.

juisa, juisium :—judgment; trial by ordeal or battle; execution; pillory.

jumentarius :—a man in charge of mares.

jumentum :—a mare.

juncare :—to strew rushes.

juncata :—cream cheese.

juncta :— a joint.

junctum :—a measure of salt.

junctura :—jointure.

jupa :—a petticoat; a gown open in front. O.E., a chymmer.

jupellum :—a coat, a frock; a kind of banner.

jurata, juratio :—a jury; a body of jurates.

jurator :—a juror.

juratus :—a jurate ; a person in Bordeaux, Bayonne, and other French towns, equivalent to an alderman in England ; also in Maidstone for a time in the 17th century aldermen were called jurates.

jurista :—a lawyer.

jurnale :—a diary. See *jornata.*

jurnedum :—a day's journey.

justa, justea :—a joust, a tournament ; a flagon.

justicia :—jurisdiction ; a fine ; right, due ; a justiciary or justice ; a joust.

justiciabilis : — under jurisdiction.

justiciare :—to bring to trial ; to exercise or administer justice ; to compel, to punish.

justiciare se :—to appear or plead before a justice.

justiciaria :—the office of justice or justiciary ; a writ to justices ; the day when they sit.

justiciarius :—a justice.

justificare :—to bring to trial.

justificator :—a compurgator.

justitiaria. See *justiciaria.*

justitium : —cessation from the exercise of justice.

justorium :—a mill clapper.

juttare :—to jut out.

K.

kaia, kaium :—a quay ; a wharf.

kaiagium :—toll paid for unloading goods at a wharf ; quayage.

kalendæ, &c. See *calendæ.*

kaneva :—canvas.

kanevacius :—with canvas mail. "Mail" is the word used for the plumage of a hawk over a year old.*

karetta :—a cart.

karisma : —grace.

karistia :—dearth.

karrata :—a cartload.

karula : —a carrel, a small square chamber or cell, sometimes found in cloisters.

karvana :—a caravan.

karvannum :—a baggage train.

katallum. See *catallum.*

kauma :—thatch.

kayus, kaya :—a quay ; a wharf.

kebbatus multo : — a worthless sheep, a kebber.

kembelina : — a kemeling, or keeler, a tub.

kemmotus :—a cymwd or comot, the quarter of a cantref. See *cantreda.*

kernellare :—to embattle, to crenellate.

kernellum :—a battlement ; a pinnacle.

---

* "Hawkes have white maill, canvas maill or rede maill, and some call rede maill, iren mayll. White maill is soone knawe. Canvas maill is betwene white maill and iren maill. And iron maill is varri rede." Boke of St. Albans, 1486, f. 7, b.

keveronus. See *cheveringus.*

kidellus :—a kiddle or kettle, a contrivance for catching fish set in a weir.

killagium :—keelage, the right of demanding money for ships lying in a harbour.

kintale:—a weight, about 100 lbs. See *quintale.*

kiprus :—kipper, of fish.

kivil'a :—a pin.

klammator. See *hlammator.*

knipulus :—a knife.

knopa :—a knob; a knop.

kokettus. See *cokettus.*

kranagium. See *cranagium.*

kunupulus :—the clapper of a bell.

kydellus. See *kidellus.*

L.

labilitas :—liability to slip.

labina :—a marsh; a fen.

laborarius :—a labourer.

laccus :—a lock (of hair or wool).

laceatus :—fringed; laced.

lacescibilis :—weary.

lacerta :—a fathom.

lacinia :—a lappet.

lacista :—a cade of herring.

lacta :—defect in weight; lack.

lactagium :—rent for milch cows.

lactare :—to lack.

lacticinium : —milky food.

lactum :—alloy.

lacum :—lack.

lacunar :— a candle beam.

lada :—purgation; a watercourse, lode; a load; a lathe, a division of a county.

ladiare :—to purge oneself of a crime.

lædorium :—reproach.

læstum :—a lathe. See *leda.*

laga :—a lane; law.

lagemannus: — a lawman, a judge.

lagena :—a gallon, an eighth of a bushel.

laghdagha :—a law-day.

layhelmotus :— a law hallmote.

laia :—a broad way in a wood; a wild sow.

laicus :—a layman.

laidare. See *ladiare.*

lairvita :—punishment for incontinence.

lambella :—a label (heraldic).

lambriscare, lambrissare, lambruscare, lamburchare :—to wainscot; to ceil; to ornament with fretwork.

lamen :—a plate, a blade. (For *lamina.*)

lampreda :—a lamprey (*petromyzon marinus*), sometimes a lampern (*petromyzon fluviatilis*).

lampro :—a lampern.

lanarius :—a woollen draper.

lanceare :—to extend, to abut (of land).

lancearia :— a loophole for thrusting lances through; a long narrow ship.

lanceicia :—an adjective applied to hides. (Pat. 14 H. iij., p. 2, m. 6).

lancentagium, lancettagium : — a base or servile tenure.

lancetus,lancetta :—a tenant holding by such a tenure. (A. S. *landsæta* or *landsittend.*) At Bury St. Edmunds the *lancetti* had to clean out certain chambers in the abbey.

lanciator :—keeper of lances in the Tower.

landa :—a lawn ; land.

landea :—a ditch for draining a marsh.

lanerius, lanerus : — a lanner (*falco lanarius* or *feldeggi*). In the Middle Ages used for the female.

langabulum :—tax or rent from land.

langellum :—swaddling clothes.

langemannus :—the lord of a manor.

langeolum, langeolus :—a woollen shirt, reaching to the knees, worn by monks.

laniarius. See *lanerius.*

lanlordus :—a landlord.

lano niger :—a kind of base coin.

lanterium :—the top of a steeple.

lanterna :—a lantern.

lapicidium :—a stone quarry.

lappatus :—shaggy.

lappiare :—to lop.

lardanarium, lardarium : — a larder ; a salting house.

lardanarius, lardarius :—a larderer, or clerk of the kitchen.

lardearium :—a larder.

lardenarius. See *lardanarius.*

larderarius. See *lardanarius.*

larduarium :—a larder.

lardum :—bacon.

largitio :—largesse.

larricinium :—robbery, larceny (*latrocinium*).

lasirium :—azure.

lassatinus :—an assassin.

lasta, lastum :—a last, a measure used for fish, hides, corn, wool, &c.

lastagium :—custom paid for wares sold by the last ; ballast. See *lestagium.*

lastum :—a lathe, a division of a county.

lata :—a lath ; a latch.

lateranea :—a bedfellow ; a wife.

laterna (*lanterna*) :—a prison in a convent.

laterare :—to lie sideways (of land).

latha :—a lath.

lathamus. See *latomus.*

latia :—framework.

laticium :—lattice.

latinarius :—an interpreter, a latimer or latiner.

latius :—a lath.

latomia :—masonry.

latomus :—a stonecutter.

latro :—the right of punishing thieves.

latronissa :—a feminine robber.

latta :—a lath.

latthacio :—lathing work.

lattrinum, lattunum :—latten.

latunatus :—made of latten.

latunum :—latten.

laturia :—a book containing the Litany.

latus :—a sidesman.

laubia :—a porch, a gallery.

laudare :—to arbitrate.

laudator :—an umpire.

laudes :—Psalms 148, 149, 150.

laudum :—an award.

lavandaria :—a laundry; a lavatory.

lavatorium :—a lavatory; a laundry; sometimes used for *piscina*.

laxa :—a leash.

laxis :—an implement used in cookery.

laya :—a wild sow.

lecator :—a person of bad character, a lecher.

leccacitas :—lechery.

leccator :—a lecher.

lechia :—rushes or sedge.

lecia :—a leash.

lecteria. See *litera.*

lectica :—litter for cattle.

lectio :—a lesson.

lectionarium :—a book containing lessons, composed by St. Jerome; or the epistles read at mass.

lectis :—a brother's daughter.

lectisternium :—bedding; a mattrass.

lectoratus :—the office of reader, one of the minor orders.

lectorium :—a reading-desk; a lectern.

lectrinum. See *lectorium.*

lecturire :—to lecture.

lecturium. See *lectorium.*

leda :—a lathe, a division of a county.

ledo, ledona :—tide.

lega :—alloy. See also *leuca.*

legalitas :—status as a lawful man; jurisdiction.

legamannus :—a lawful man, or man of law.

legancia. See *ligancia.*

legatarius :—legatary; a legatee; a legate.

legatia :—legation; the district over which a legate has jurisdiction.

legatus a latere :—a legate sent by the Pope with the amplest authority.

legatus natus :—a legate in ordinary, an archbishop or bishop possessing legatine authority in his diocese.

legenda :—a book containing the lessons for church service, or the lives of saints.

legia :—the hanging part of the ear.

legiosus :—litigious.

legius. See *ligeus.*

legrewita :—a fine for adultery.

lemniscus :—a label (heraldic).

lenga :—a ling (*asellus longus*).

leones :—false coin prohibited by Edw. I.

lepa :—a lip, or lepe, a basket holding about two-thirds of a bushel.

lepidare :—to speak fair.

leporarius :—a greyhound.

leporium :—a hare-warren.

leprosaria :—a lazarhouse.

lesca :—a slice.

lescare :—to slice.

lesia :—a leash.

lessa :—a legacy ; a lease.

lessia :—a leash.

lesta, lestum :—a last ; a lathe. See *lasta.*

lestagium :—toll paid at a port on landing goods ; or at a market or fair for licence to remove goods.

lestum :—a lathe, a division of a county.

lesura :—a leasowe, a pasture.

leta :—a court-leet.

letania :—a litany.

leuca :—a league, 1,500 paces, or 480 perches ; sometimes used for a mile, and other distances ; a covenant.

leucata :—a league ; banlieue.

leuga. See *leuca.*

leugata. See *leucata.*

leugator :—a scout or forager (?).

levabilis :—leviable.

levanum :—leavened bread.

levare :—to collect, to levy ; to remove ; to carry hay ; to make hay.

levare mercatum : — to hold a market.

levator :—a lever.

levellus :—level.

leverarius :—a harrier.

leverio, breve de :—writ of relief.

levescere :—to become light.

levia :—a span.

levinarius :—a lymehound, " a leviner."

levita :—a deacon.

lex :—sometimes used for ordeal.

lezura :—a leasowe, a pasture.

liardus :—dapple grey.

libellare :—to put in writing ; to convey by charter.

libelli supplicum, magister :— Master of Requests.

libellus :—a declaration ; a libel ; a charter.

liber lapis :—freestone.

libera :—delivery of a portion of grass or corn to a tenant who has been engaged in cutting it.

liberare :—to deliver.

liberata : — a gift ; livery. The word " clothing " was used for the liverymen of a City Company as late as the Stuart period.

liberate :—a writ ordering a payment to be made, commencing with this word.

liberatio. See *liberata.*

liberatura. See *liberata.*

libertare :—to set free.

libertatio :—freedom.

libitina :—a bier, a hearse.

libra :—a pound, in weight or money.

librarium :—a library.

librarius :—a scribe ; a librarian.

librata terræ :—land worth 20*s.* yearly ; 4 oxgangs, or 52 acres.

librillare:—to chatter; to babble.

liceæ :—lists ; barriers.

licentiare : — to give leave ; to take leave of.

licentiatio :—leave.

licere :—to license.

lichinius :—the wick of a candle.

lichinus : —a candlestick.

lichitus :—an oil flask.

liciæ :—lists ; barriers.

liciarium :—a bid, in dealing.

liciatorium :—a loom.

licitamentum :—a bid.

liemarius :—a lymehound.

liga :—a league, a confederation.

ligamen :—a bond ; an oath.

ligancia :—allegiance, homage.

ligatus :—a liegeman.

ligeancia : — allegiance ; breach of allegiance.

ligeus, ligius : — liege ; lawful ; simple, unconditioned.

lignagium :—the right of cutting fuel in woods.

lignamen : —timber.

lignarius : —a wharfinger.

ligniculum :—a small image of wood.

lignile :—a wooden cupboard.

lignipodium :—a wooden leg ; a stilt.

ligula :—a fillet, a file.

limas :—an apron.

limbus :—a shallow boat ; a punt.

liminiscus :—a point or stop in a MS.

limo :—a cartshaft.

limus :— an apron.

lina lintea : —" Anglice lynnen yarne." (Pat. 8 Jac. I., pt. 5, No. 3.)

linare :—to line.

linarium :—a place where flax is grown.

linealiter :—in a straight line.

lineare : —to line.

lingius :—of linen.

lingua :—loin.

linguaris miles :—a pursuivant ; a knight of the tongue, *i.e.* a lawyer, &c., as opposed to a knight of the sword, a soldier.

liniare:—to line.

linteamen, linthiamen : —linen stuff ; a sheet ; an apron ; a neckerchief ; a ruffband.

linura :—lining.

linus :—clay.

lipsana :—relics.

liquiritia : —liquorice.

lira :—a measure of land (York-shire).

liripipium :—the tail of a hood, or the peak of a shoe.

lista :—an edge ; a strip ; a catalogue ; lists for a tournament.

lisura :—list (of cloth).

litera, literia :—litter, straw ; a litter ; bedclothes.

litiæ. See *liceæ.*

litor :—a dauber.

litteria, litura. See *litera.*

lixus :—boiled.

lobbum :—a large fish in the North Sea, of the cod species.

lobia :—a porch ; a gallery.

lobium :—a portico ; a lobby.

locagium :—a lease ; rent.

locare :—to let ; to hire.

loccum :—a lock on a river.

lochia :—a stone-loach (*cobitis barbatula*).

locutorium :—a parlour.

loda :—a load.

lodium :—a louvre.

loerenium :—a rein.

loga :—a truss (?) of hay.

loggiare :—to cut wood into logs (?).

logia :—a lodge ; an outhouse.

logiare :— to lodge, to dwell.

logium. See *logia.*

loingium, loingnium :—a lewne, or lune, a strap attached to a hawk's jesses.

lokettum :—a locket ; a flock of wool.

lolidodium :—a cart saddle.

longellus :— a coverlet ; a long cloak.

lonnia :— a loin.

lopare :— to lop.

loquela :—imparlance ; a plea ; a suit.

loquenda :—a point reserved by a court for consideration.

M.

lorarius :—a lymehound.

lorema :—a bridle bit.

loreinum :—a bridle rein.

lorengum, lorenna, lorenum. See *loreinum.*

lorica :—a hauberk.

loridium :—a belt.

lorimaria : — lorimery, bits, buckles, and other metal work for harness.

lorimarius :—a lorimer or loriner; a spurrier ; a girdler.

lotorium :—a wash-hand basin.

lottum et scottum :—lot and scot.

lovera, loverium :—a louvre.

lucarius :—a woodward; a parker.

lucea :—a taper.

lucellus :—a bier, a hearse.

lucernarius :—a watch dog.

luces :—pike (*esox lucius*) (pl.).

lucina :—a gore in a dress.

lucubrum :—a lantern.

lucupletare :—to enrich.

ludator :—a player.

ludricus :—a beast of burden.

ludum :—a device ; a motto.

luigna :—a loin.

lumbale, lumbare :—a belt, a girdle.

luminarius :—a dealer in lights ; a chandler.

luminio :—lighting.

lunæ, dies :—Monday. *Lunæ* is also used for Monday by itself, not declined, as—*infra Lunæ*, before Monday ; and the same is true of the names for the other days of the week.

T

lunarius :— a watch dog.

lunda :—a bind of eels, *i.e.* 250 ; two timbers of skins, *i.e.* 80.

lundeni :—men whose service was on Monday.

lundinarium :—a quarter of a virgate.

lunivagus girus :—the moon's orbit.

luparius :—a wolfhunter.

luplicetum :—a hop garden.

lupulatus :—made of hops.

lupus :—a cutaneous eruption.

lura :—a bung.

lurale :—a lure.

lusceus :—a pike (*esox lucius*).

lussus, lusus :—a brother-in-law.

luta :—a lute.

luter :—a basin, a laver, a font.

lutrarius :—an otter hound.

lutrea :—an otter.

lutricius :—an otter hound.

luuebona :—work done gratuitously.

luvare :—a louvre.

luvereticus canis :—a wolfhound.

luverus :—a louvre.

lymputta :—a lime pit.

M.

macarius. See *macellarius.*

macea ⸱—a mace.

macellarius, macerarius :—a victualler ; a fleshmonger.

maceria :—the outer wall of a convent.

machecaria :—a meat market.

machecarius. See *macellarius.*

machecollare :—to add *machecoulis* to a castle.

macia :—a mace.

macuellus :—a small mace.

macula :—mail ; silver halfpence.

madera :—madder.

madialis :—adj. of May.

madius :—the month of May.

maeremium, maerennium :—timber.

magnagium :—a house.

magnalis :—great.

magthura :—same as *mangura* (?).

mahemiare :—to maim.

mahemium :—mayhem, maim.

mahumeria :—a mosque.

maialis :—adj. of May.

maignagium :—a brazier's shop.

maior :—a mayor.

maiorare :—to increase, to improve.

maioria, mairia :—mayoralty.

maisneda :—a household.

maisremum, maisremium :—timber.

makerellus :—a mackerel (*scomber scombrus*).

mala :—a budget for carrying letters ; a mail ; beech mast (?).

malandrinus :—a pirate.

malecredere :—to suspect.

maleficare :—to bewitch.

maleficium :—witchcraft.

maleficus :—a wizard.

maletta :—a small mail or trunk.

malignare :—to maim.

malina :—spring tide.

mallardus :—a mallard, the male of *anas boschas.*

mallia :—mail.

mallium :—a mesh.

malmaria :—a mosque.

maltra :—a combe, 4 pecks.

malveisina :—an engine to cast stones.

mana :—an old woman.

managium :—a house.

manbota :—compensation paid for murder to the victim's master.

manca :—a square gold Saxon coin, value thirty pence, in the 12th century, from 6*s.* to 7*s.* 6*d.* ; a silver coin, ⅕ oz. ; a mark ; a fishing boat ; a defect.

manceps :—a manciple, clerk of the kitchen.

mancipulus :—a panier man (Middle Temple).

mancinus :—lefthanded.

mancus :—the curve of a sickle or scythe.

mancusa. See *manca.*

mandatarius :—a mandatory, a commissioner.

mandatum :—maundy ; an extra allowance of food in a convent ; footwashing in a monastery on Saturday.

mandibile festum :—a feast.

mandra :—a shed, a hovel.

maneleta :—tares, weeds.

manens :—a tenant who was confined to the land.

manensis :—a house, a farm.

manerium :—a manor.

manga, manganum :—a mangonel, for casting stones.

mangerium :—the right of receiving food, &c., at the house of a tenant.

mangiatorium :—a manger.

mangonale, mangonelus : — a mangonel, for casting stones.

mangonare :—to traffic at a market.

mangonelus, mangonellus. See *mangonale.*

mangura :—food.

maniamentum : — administration of justice ; possession.

maniculare :—to handcuff.

maninga :—jurisdiction ; a court of law. (A. S. *manung.*)

manipularis :—a corporal, in the time of James I.

manipulum :—a maniple, worn by a priest on the left arm.

mannagium :—a house.

mannire :—to cite.

mannus :—a horse.

manopera :— a day's work.

mansa :—a farm ; a dwelling-house ; sometimes a hide of land.

manser :—a bastard.

mansia, mansio. See *mansa.*

mansionarius :—a harbinger ; a sexton.

mansum, mansura, mansus. See *mansa.*

mantea :—a mantle.

mantellum :—a cloak ; a mantlet.

mantiare :—to fit a handle to.

mantica :—a wallet.

mantile :—a long robe.

mantum :—a cloak, a mantle.

manuale :—a manual, a book containing what is necessary for the administration of sacraments and sacramentals.

manualis obedientia :—sworn obedience.

manubriator :—a maker of hilts or handles, a hafter, a helver.

manucapere :—to mainprise, to become mainpernor for.

manucaptio :—mainprise, surety.

manucaptor : — a mainpernor, bail.

manulevare :—to raise (money).

manumola, manumula :—a handmill.

manuopera :—stolen goods taken on a thief ; cattle and farm implements ; handwork.

manuoperarius :—a handicraftsman.

manupastus :—a domestic servant ; domestic service.

manupes :—a foot in length.

manupositum :—a deposit ; an earnest.

manurare :— to manure.

manus :—used for an oath.

manusmola :—a handmill.

manus mortua :—mortmain.

manutenentia : — maintenance ; the unlawful upholding of a person or cause.

manutenere :—to maintain.

manutensionis pileum :—a cap of maintenance.

manutentor :—a maintainor. See *manutenentia.*

manutentum :—a handle.

manutergium :—a handwipe a towel.

manzer :—a bastard.

mapparius :—a keeper of linen.

mara :—a lake, a mere ; a moor.

marabotinus :—a gold coin used by the Arabs in Spain ; an account temp. Hen. III. states " *marabotinus seu talentum.*" In later times it appears to mean a maravedi.

marca :—a mark, a silver coin, 8 oz. troy weight, in money 13*s.* 4*d.*

marca auri :—in 1130 was worth 6*l.* ; in Stephen's reign, 9 silver marks ; in the reign of Henry II., 12*l.* ; in John's reign, 10 silver marks.

marcanda villa :—a market town.

marcapetum :—a footstool.

marcarda villa :—a market town.

marcare :—to mark ; to take by right of letters of marque.

marcata :—a rent of a mark.

marcator : —a merchant.

marcatum :—a market. See *mercatum.*

marcatus :—a rent of a mark.

marcha. See *marca.*

marchalsia :—the Marshalsea, a prison in London.

marchantesia :—merchandise.

marcheium :—a market.

marchesia :—the March ; the Court of the March.

marcheta. See *merchetum.*

marchetum :—a market.

marchia :—the March or border land between two countries.

marchiare :—to adjoin, to border on.

marchiatus :—a marquis.

marchio :—a marcher ; a marquis.

marchionatus :—a marquisate.

marchionissa :—a marchioness.

marchisus, marchisius :—a marcher, a dweller on a March.

Marcialis :—in the month of March.

marcula :—diminutive of *marca.*

marearchus :—an admiral.

maremium :—timber.

marescalcia, marescallia, marescaltia :—the right of taking fodder for horses ; the office of marshal ; the Marshalsea, London ; a stable.

marescalcus, marescaldus, marescallus :—a farrier ; a marshal ; a harbinger.

mareschum :—a marsh.

maretum :—a marsh.

margia :—a border, a margin.

Mariale :—a book containing the Hours of the B. V. M.

marietare :—to marry.

marina :—the seashore.

marinarius :—a seaman, a mariner.

marinellus :—a mariner.

mariola :—a small image of the Virgin Mary.

marisarchus. See *marearchus.*

mariscalcia. See *marescalcia.*

mariscus :—a marsh.

maritagium :—marriage ; a marriage portion ; the right of giving in marriage.

maritatio :—a gift by the husband to the wife on marriage.

marla :—marl.

marlare, marliare :—to spread marl over land ; to dig marl.

marleputtum :—a marlpit.

marlera, marlerium, marletum :—a marlpit.

marlia :—marl.

marlura :—marling.

marna :—some clay used in pottery ; marl.

marneria :—a marlpit ; a moat.

marqua :—the right of reprisals, marque.

marquezius :—a marquis.

marquisia :—a marchioness.

marquisius :—a marquis.

marra :—a moor ; an iron tool like a pickaxe.

marscallare :—to do a farrier's work.

martellus :—a hammer.

marterina pellis :—marten fur.

martilogare :—to insert in a register of martyrs.

martilogium :—a register of martyrs (*martyrologium*).

martina : — a marten (*martes foina*).

martineta :—a kingfisher (*alcedo ispida*).

Martis dies :—Tuesday.

martologium. See *martilogium.*

martrina, martrix, martro :—a marten.

marutia :—some additional outwork to a castle.

masagium :—a messuage.

masca :—a masque.

mascea :—a mace.

maserus :—a maser, a bowl, often of wood, especially maple.

masnagium :—a dwelling-place.

massa :—a club ; a mass.

massare :—to chew ; to hammer.

mastinus, mastivus :—a mastiff.

mastruca :—a cloak of skin, fur inside.

mastrum :—a kneading trough.

mastus :—a mast.

masuagium. See *messuagium.*

masuella :—a small club.

masura. See *mansa.*

matare :—to mate at chess.

matinellum :—breakfast.

matracia, matracium :—a mattress ; quiet.

matria :—a pantry.

matricula :—a list ; a register.

matrimonium : — marriage ; inheritance descending by marriage.

matrina :—a godmother.

matutini :—lauds, in the Rule of St. Benedict.

matutinale :—a book of lauds.

matutinellum :—breakfast.

maupigyrnum :—a sort of pottage.

maviscus : — a thrush (*Turdus musicus*).

maxima :—an axiom ; a maxim.

maximus senex :—oldest.

mazenarius :—a keeper of mazers.

mazonarius :—a mason.

meandrum :—a rubbish hole.

meanialis. See *menialis.*

meatim :—in my own way.

medaria :—a place for making or stowing mead.

medarius :—a mead maker, or seller ; an official in charge of the medary in a convent.

mederia :—a house where mead is sold.

mediamnis :—a dyke ; a canal.

medianetum :—arbitration.

meda :—mead.

medicus digitus :—the third finger.

medie manus, homo :—a man of low rank.

medietas :—mesnalty, the right of the mesne lord.

meditentum :—the cap of a flail.

meditullium :—middle.

medius :—mean ; mesne.

medlea, medleta, medletum :—a fray ; a medley.

medo :—mead.

megadomesticus :—a chief officer of the household, a major domo.

megarus : — mackerel (*scomber scombrus*).

megucarius :—a white tawyer, a leather dresser.

meida :—madder.

meimmatus :—maimed.

mela :—a measure of corn and cheese (Scotch).

melleta. See *medlea.*

mellibrodium :—bracket or bragwort, a drink flavoured with honey and spice.

mellitarius :—a beekeeper.

melotus : — a badger (*meles taxus*).

memorandorium :—a catalogue.

memorator :—a remembrancer.

memprisa. See *manucaptio.*

menagium :—a family.

mencia. Perhaps an error for *meneia.*

meneia : — appearance ; obeisance (?).

menestrallus : — an artisan ; a minstrel.

menetum :—a wooden horn.

menialis : — m e n i a l. F r o m *mœnia.*

meniare :—to wall.

mensacula :—a carving knife.

mensura :—a bushel; standard measure ; a candle of the length of or perhaps image in wax of a sick person or limb sent to a shrine.

mensurare :—to measure for the purpose mentioned above.

menusa :—reeds, rushes (?).

mera :—a marsh ; a mere ; unpressed wine. (Fr. *mère goutte.*)

merarius :—a midday meal.

merca. See *marca.*

mercancia, mercandisia :—merchandise.

mercandizare :—to trade.

mercantia :—merchandise.

mercatoria villa :—a market town.

mercatum, mercatorium : — a market.

mercearius :—a mercer.

mercenarius :—a hireling.

merceria :—mercery.

mercerius, mercerus :—a mercer.

merchandizare :—to trade.

mercheta, merchetum :—a fine payable by a villein for licence to give his daughter in marriage, and in Scotland at his own marriage.

mercia :—traffic; a fine.

merciamentum :—a fine.

merciarius :—a mercer.

mercimoniatus :—impost on merchandise ; custom.

mercinarius :—a mercer.

mercum :—a mark, a sign.

Mercurii dies :—Wednesday.

meremium :—timber.

merendula :—an afternoon refreshment, a bever.

mergulus :—a sink, of a lamp or a lavatory.

mergus :—a bucket ; a water dog.

merketum :—a market.

merlare. See *marlare.*

merlengus, merlingus :—a ling (*asellus longus*).

merscum :—a marsh.

meruca :—a cod (*morrhua vulgaris*).

merulus : — a merlin (*falco æsalon*).

mesagium. See *messuagium.*

mescheninga :—wrongful prosecution (*miskenning*).

mesfacere :—to do wrong.

meslea, mesleia, mesleta :—a fray, a melée.

mesprisio. See *misprisio.*

messaria :—the office and profits of a farm bailiff.

messarius :—a mower or reaper ; a farm bailiff.

messina :—harvest time.

messuagium :—a messuage ; a dwelling-house.

mestaria, mestera, mesterum :— art ; trade ; mistery.

mestelenium :—the remains of a meal given as alms.

mesticare, mestificare :—to make sad.

mestilo :—mesline, wheat and rye mixed.

meta :—a mete, a boundary.

metallifodina :—a mine.

metebona :—work done for food.

meya :—a stack or heap of hay or corn, a mow.

micatorium :—a grater.

michia :—a loaf.

miles :—a knight.

miliare :—a thousand ; a mile ; a milestone.

miliatium :—millet.

milicentum :—a millstream.

militare :—to be knighted.

militia :—knighthood ; a knight's fee ; a body of knights or soldiers ; tenure by knight service.

milium :—millet.

millenarium :—a thousand.

milliare :—a thousand ; a mile ; a milestone.

millo :—a hayrick.

millum :—a hound's collar.

milwellus. See *mulvellus.*

mimilogium :—minstrelsy.

mina :—a measure of corn, &c., 3 to 7 skeps ; a measure of land, 120 ft. square ; a measure of wine ; a mine.

minagium :—toll paid on corn sold by the *mina.*

minare :—to drive ; to guide.

minaria :—a mine.

minator :—a miner.

minera :—a mine, ore.

minerarius :—a miner.

mineria :—a mine ; a quarry.

minetarius :—a miner.

miniator :—an illuminator.

minietum verrum :—miniver.

minigunga :—warning. (A. S. *mynegung.*)

minister :—a thane ; a bailiff.

ministeriales :—traders.

ministerium :—a trade ; a credence, among Carthusians, Cistercians and Premonstratensian canons.

ministralcia :—minstrelsy.

ministrallus, ministraulus :—a minstrel.

minorissa :—a Minoress, a nun of S. Clare.

minstrellus :—a minstrel. See *menestrallus.*

minitor :—a miner.

minorare :—to lessen.

minta :—mint.

minuare :—to damage.

minuere :—to let blood.

minuta :—a draft, a minute.

minutio :—bleeding.

misa :—agreement ; arbitration ; cost, expense.

miscuare :—to mix.

misdocere :—to misinform ; to misadvise.

misellus :—a leper.

misericordia :—an arbitrary fine ; a gratuitous portion of food given in addition to commons ; a hall in a monastery where additional commons were given ; a dagger ; a wooden turn up seat in the choir of a church.

misevenire :—to fail.

misprisio :—misprision, culpable concealment of crime.

missa :—mass. See also *misa.*

missale :—a massbook, a missal.

missaticum :—a message.

missaticus :—a messenger.

missum :—a gift given to the King or Prince of Wales on entering Wales.

missura :—religious ceremonies at death.

missurium :—a dish, or mess.

mistera, misterium :—trade ; mistery (*ministerium*).

mitra :—a kerchief.

mitta :—a measure of corn, &c.

mixtilio. See *mestilo.*

mixtorium :—a rudder, an implement used in mixing malt.

mixtum :—breakfast of bread and wine in a monastery ; translated "pottage" in the Rule of St. Benedict, cap. xxxviij. (1875).

modiatio :—duty paid on wine or corn, measured by the *muid.*

moeta :—a half.

mola :—a millstone.

molatio :—multure.

molda :—a mould.

moldera, moldra :—multure.

molendinarius :—a miller.

molendinator :—a miller.

molendinum :—a mill.

molestra :—a sheepskin.

molinum :—a mill.

molitura, moltura :—grinding ; corn taken to a mill to be ground ; grist ; payment for grinding, multure ; a lord's right to make tenants grind at his mill.

molliare :—to knead.

mollicio :—grinding.

molneda :—a millpool.

molta :—toll paid by vassals for grinding corn at the lord's mill.

molumentum :—toll for grinding.

molutus (*molitus*) :—ground.

monaca, monacha :—a nun.

monachaliter : — in monkish fashion.

monacare, monachare :—to make a man a monk ; to receive him into a convent.

monacus, monachus :—a monk.

monagium :—error for *menagium*.

monasterialis :—monastic.

monasterium : — a monastery, a minster.

moneta : — money ; a mint.

monetacio :—coining, minting.

monetagium :—mintage, right of coining ; tribute paid by tenants to the lord that he should not change the money he had coined.

monetare :—to coin ; to mint.

monetarius : — a moneyer ; a coiner ; a banker.

monetatio :—coining.

monetum :—a mint.

moniale :—a nunnery ; a mullion.

monialis :—a nun.

monstra :—a muster.

monstrantia : — a reliquary, a monstrance, or ooster.

monstrare :—to muster.

monstratio :—a muster.

monstrum :—a muster ; a reliquary.

moota :—a seamew or seagull. (Fr. *mouette*.) See also *mota, muta.*

mora :—a moor ; a mere.

moracum :—pure wine (*merum*). See *moratum.*

morayium :—rent or service for tenure of moorland.

moratum :—a drink, supposed to be wine flavoured with mulberries.

mordaculum :—the tongue of a buckle.

moretum : — brown cloth. See also *moratum.*

morgabulum :—rent of moorland.

morgagium :—mortgage.

morgagifa. See *morganegiba.*

morganegiba : — the husband's gift to the wife on the wedding-day, or the day after.

moriatio :—residence.

morina :—murrain.

morosus :—boggy, delaying.

morsella : — a small piece [of land].

morsellatim :—piecemeal.

morsellus. See *morsella.*

morsus :—a morse ; a clasp.

mortarium :—mortar ; a mortar ; a stone or metal cup to hold a night light ; a lamp over a grave or shrine. See also *mortuarium.*

mortellum. See *mortarium.*

mortgagium :—a mortgage.

morticinium :—murrain.

mortificare :—to alienate in mortmain.

mortitivus :—dead of murrain.

mortizare. See *amortizare.*

mortua sesona :—close time for foxes, in the forests, 1 May to 1 Sept.

mortuarium :—a bequest to the testator's parish church in recompense for tithes not duly paid ; a duty payable to the lord on the death of a tenant.

mortuum vadium :—a mortgage.

morua, moruca : — a codfish (*morrhua vulgaris*).

mos :—custom, in the sense of tax on goods entering the kingdom.

mossa :—a moss or bog.

mota :—a mote ; a moot ; a pack of hounds ; a moat ; a castle mound.

motaculum :—a rudder, an implement used in mixing malt.

motibilis :—moveable; a vagrant.

motivum :—a motive.

motor :—a mootman.

motulinus :—mutton.

motum :— a moat.

motura. See *molitura.*

mua :—mews.

mucetta :—a hole.

mueta :—a watchtower ; mews a pack of hounds

muffulæ :—fur gloves ; muffs

mugettum :—musk.

muia :—mews.

muillo :—a haycock or hayrick.

muiolus (Fr *muid*) :—a measure of corn, salt, &c., about 5½ qrs.

mulcto. See *multo.*

mulecius :—a mullet (*mullus barbatus* or *mugil capito*).

mulier :—lawful issue.

mulio, mullo :—a hayrick.

mulneda :—a mill pool.

multa :— a fine.

multiplicium :—a cloak.

multo :—a sheep, a wether ; a French gold coin bearing the *Agnus Dei*, worth 12*s.* 6*d.* Tournois ; an engine of war.

multoties :—many times.

multra, multrum :—a pail.

multura. See *molitura.*

mulvellus :—melwell, milwin, greenfish, perhaps coalfish (*merlangus carbonarius*) or pollock (*merlangius pollachius*). It cannot be the green streaked wrasse(*labrus lineatus*), which is in some parts called greenfish, as suggested in Wright's Dialect Dictionary, on account of its rarity.

muncellus :—a mound, a heap of corn, sometimes 10 sheaves.

mandare :—to purge by ordeal.

mundifractura : —mundbrech, breach of enclosures, privileges, or the king's peace.

municeps :—a magistrate of a town.

manimen :—a grant, a charter.

munimenta : —records.

muntator :—a soldier serving with a knight, on the Welsh March.

muragium :—toll exacted in a town for repairing the walls.

murale :—a wall.

muratio :—a walled town.

murdra :—murder.

murdrare :—to murder.

murdrator :—a murderer.

murdredum :—murder ; tax imposed for the escape of a murderer.

murdrire :—to murder.

murdritor :—a murderer

murdrum :—murder.

murena :—a lamprey (*petromyzon marinus*).

murilegus :—a cat.

muripellus, muripula :—a buttress.

murra :—a maser.

murrena :—murrain.

murrus :—a maser.

murtrarius :—a murderer.

murtrum :—murder.

musardus :—lazy, stupid.

musca :—musk.

muscata nux :—nutmeg.

muschettus :—the male sparrow hawk (*accipiter fringillarius* ; also called *fragellus*).

muscidus :—mossy ; mouldy.

muscula :—a mussel.

museum, museolum :—a study (room).

mussa :—a moss or bog.

mussetum :—a mossy place.

musta : — must, unfermented wine.

mustrum :—muster. See *monstrum*.

muta :—a pack of hounds ; a mew of hawks ; moulting.

mutare :—to mew hawks.

mutarius :—mewed.

mutilamen : — a mutilation, a maim.

muto. See *multo.*

mutalare (*mutilare*):—to hamble. See *expeditare.*

mutulinus :—mutton.

mutulus :—a bracket ; a corbell.

mutus, mutatus :—mewed.

mystax :—a moustache.

mysterium : — mystery ; sometimes used for mistery. See *mistera.*

N.

nabulum :—freight.

naca :—a small ship ; a smack.

nacella, navicella :—a skiff ; a boat.

naivietas :—naifty, bondage.

naivus. See *nativus.*

namare :—to distrain ; to take into custody.

namatio : — distraining ; impounding.

namiare. See *namare.*

namium, namma : — distress ; pledge.

nammiare, namtire :—to distrain; to take into custody.

namum. See *namium.*

napa :—a cloth ; a napkin.

naparia :—napery.

nappa :—a rib.

napparius :—a keeper of napery.

napta :—tow.

narrator :—an advocate.

nascella :—a small ship.

nascula :—a button.

nasellus :—a small ship.

nassa :—a kiddle or fishweel.

nata :—a mat.

natale :—the condition of a man.

Natalicium :—the day of martyrdom of a Saint.

natalis dies :—Christmas day.

Natalis Domini, tempus:—Christmastide (temp. Car. II.).

nativa :—a born bondwoman; a nief.

native:—by the tenure of a bondman.

nativus :—a born serf, or bondman.

natta :—a reed mat.

naulum :—passage money by ship.

nauta :—a sailor, a bargee.

navagium :—the duty of carrying the lord's goods by ship.

narata :—a ship load.

naviagium :—navigation, sailing.

navicella, navicula :—an incense cup in the shape of a boat.

navicularius :—a shipowner; a shipwright.

navigalis :—seafaring.

navigium :— a fleet. See also *navagium.*

navis :—the nave of a church; the same as *navicella;* an ounce.

navithalamus :—a state barge.

nayvus. See *nativus.*

nebula :—a wafer (bread).

nebularius :—a baker of wafers.

nefrendus :—a boar.

neotegeldum. See *notegeldum.*

nepos :—a nephew.

nepta, neptis :—a niece.

nequare. For *necare,* to kill.

nervicia :—strength.

netus :—a bondman (*nativus*).

nigellare :—to ornament with black enamel.

nigra moneta :—copper money.

nigromanticus :—a necromancer.

nisus :—a fish-hawk (*falco haliaetus*).

noa :— a marshy pasture.

nobile :—a noble, a gold coin value 6*s.* 8*d.*

noca, nocata :—a nook of land, the quantity uncertain, in some places 12½ acres.

noctanter :—by night.

noctare:—to be dark; to spend the night.

noctuatim :—nightly.

nocturnum :—religious service performed at night.

nocumentum :—nuisance; damage.

nodare:—to decree.

nodulus :—a button.

noka. See *noca.*

nola :—a small bell.

nona :—none, from about 2 p.m. to vesper.

nonæ :—ninth part, paid to the church by church tenants.

nonagium :—ninth part of moveable goods paid at death to the clergy.

nonna :—a nun.

nonneria :—a nunnery.

nonnus :—word used by young monks when addressing elders.

nonsecta :—a non-suit.

nontenura :—nontenure.

Noragenus :—Norwegian.

Northintus :—Northern region.

nota :—a note ; a memorandum.

notarius :—a notary ; a scrivener

notegeldum, noutegildum :—payment for beasts on common pasture. The same as *cornagium*.

novale :—newly tilled land.

novercare :—to behave like a stepmother.

novitius :—a novice.

numacius :—a tollman.

numeralia :—beads.

numerator :—a teller.

nummata : — a pennyweight ; *nummata terræ* is the same as *denariata;* price.

nummosus :—rich.

nummus :—a penny.

nuncius :—an apparitor ; a sergeant ; a beadle.

nundinæ :—a fair, or tournament.

nunna :—a nun.

nutriciaria :—a nursery.

nutrius :—a foster child.

O.

obaudire :—to disregard ; also to obey.

obbatus :—a jugful.

obediencia: —any office in a monastery ; a rent.

obedientialis, obedientiarius :—an inferior officer in a convent ; an advocate of a convent.

obgrunnire :—to murmur at.

obiculum :—a chace at tennis.

obitus : —funeral service, or anniversary of death ; obit.

oblata :— an offering ; a gift ; a wafer ; the Eucharistic bread. See *obolata.*

obligar :—a garter.

obligatorium : — obligation ; a bond.

obnoxius :—sometimes used for *obnixus.*

obolata :—a halfpenny worth ; a measure of land varying from half an acre to half a perch.

obolus :—a halfpenny.

obrizus :—pure, of metals.

obsella :—a coffer (?).

obstaculum :—a tribute.

obstinatus :—deaf.

obstupare :— to stop up.

obstupatio :—stopping up.

obturacio :— filling up ; stopping up.

obulata. See *obolata.*

obventio :— an offering ; tithe ; profit.

occasio :—a tribute on a special occasion ; a hindrance ; a complaint.

occasionamentum : —molestation.

occasionare :—to molest.

occasionari :—to be liable to some special tribute ; to be hindered, vexed.

occatio :—assart. See *assartum.*

octaba, octava :—the eighth day after a feast, utas.

ocularium :—the visor of a helmet.

oculus :—a circular window.

odditorium : — a miscellaneous collection , a lumber room.

odorisequus :—hunting by scent.

œconomicus : — an administrator of property ; an executor.

œconomus :—a treasurer.

ofasium :—caudle.

offerenda : — an offering ; the sacrament of the Eucharist ; an antiphone sung at that time.

offertorium :—offerings ; an offertory ; a piece of cloth in which the offerings or the chalice is wrapped. See also *offerenda.*

officialis :—one who exercises the jurisdiction of a bishop or archdeacon.

officiare :—to serve.

officiarius. See *officialis.*

officiator :— an officer.

officium : trade ; an office, a room where a man works.

offrum : —an offer.

ofnama :—an enclosure.

olosa :—a shad. See *alosa.*

olosericum : — entirely of silk ; bawdekyn.

olyverum ferri :—a foundry (?) ; a heavy hammer worked by a treadle.

omelia :—a homily.

omnimodus :—of all sorts.

onophorium :—a costrel, a wooden bottle.

opella :—a shop.

operabile :—a handicraft.

operabilis dies :—a working-day.

operaria :—the office of works.

operarius :—a tenant who did bodily work for his lord ; a clerk of the works.

operatio :—a day's work.

operatus :—chased.

opertius :—not lawed (of a dog).

opertura :—lining.

opilare :—to hinder.

opilio :—a shepherd ; a bishop.

opirus :—sour ; mouldy (of bread).

opisie :—harness.

oplondina :—uplands.

oppidanus :—the keeper of a town.

oppilio. See *opilio.*

opprimentum :—oppression ; also used for *operimentum.*

ora :—ore ; a Saxon coin worth 16*d.* to 20*d.* ; an ounce.

orarium :—a hem ; a border ; a kerchief ; a stole. See *horarius.*

orator :—an ambassador.

oratoriolum :—an oriel or oriole.

orbi ictus :—dry blows.

ordalium :—ordeal.

ordeum :—used for *hordeum.*

ordinale :— an ordinal.

ordinarius :—an ordinary, "he who hath the proper and regular jurisdiction, as of course and of common right."

ordinator testamenti :—the administrator of a will.

ordinatus :—in holy orders.

ordinium :—posterity.

orditura :—the warp in weaving.

ordolaium :—ordeal.

oretenus :—vocally, by word of mouth.

organa :—a pair of organs.

oriolum :—a portico; a gallery; an oriel.

oritimum :—a clock.

ortellus, ortillus :—a claw.

ortolagium :—a garden plot.

ortus :—used for *hortus.*

orynale :—used for *urinale.*

osceptrus :—a hawk.

osculatorium :—a paxbrede, a small tablet to be kissed.

oseria :—osiers.

osorium :—a strickle.

ostagiamentum :—security.

ostagiare :—to give security or a hostage.

ostagius :—a hostage.

ostensio :—toll paid by tradesmen for leave to expose their goods for sale; a muster.

ostentatus :—a muster.

ostiarius :—an usher. See *hostiarius.*

ostigare :—to release on security.

ostilium :—a gate; an entrance.

ostria. See *hospitalaria.*

osturcus, osturus. See *austur.*

otriare :—to grant.

oustitrix :—a midwife.

outorius. See *austur.*

ovare :—to lay eggs; to rejoice.

ovenana. See *ofnama.*

overhernissa :—contumacy.

oversamessa :—fine for neglecting to pursue malefactors.

oviale :—a sheepfold; a sheepwalk.

oviare :—used for *obviare.*

oxillare :—to turn sour.

P.

paagator :—a collector of *paagium.*

paagium. See *passagium, pavagium.*

pacabilis :—payable, passable.

pacagium : — payment ; pasture (?).

pacare :—to pay.

pacatio :—payment.

paccus :—a pack, a bale.

paceri :—to be at peace, be discharged.

pacificarius : — an official at Benauge, in the 13th century.

padnagium. See *pannagium.*

paduencia : — a paddock.

paga : — payment.

paya : — a country ; a district ; a county.

pagania : — heathendom.

paganus : — a heathen.

pagare : — to pay.

pagella : — a panel.

pageta, pagettus : — a page (servant).

pagus. See *paga.*

paiare : — to pay.

paisa : — a wey. See *waga.*

paisso : — pannage.

pakellum : — a pack.

pala : — a pale of wood ; a pale (heraldic) ; a baker's peel.

palaciatum : — the office of *palator.*

palacium : — a palace ; a palisade.

palafredus : — a palfrey.

palatinus : — a courtier.

palator : — a paler, a forest officer.

palchum : — a stage ; a floor, a story. (Ital. *palco.*)

palefridus : — a palfrey.

palestarius : — a paler.

palettus : — a palet, a headpiece of *cuir bouilli.*

palicium : — a paling.

palistrum, palizium : — a paling.

palla : — a canopy ; a funeral pall ; an altar cloth.

pallagium : — a duty paid to lords for loading or unloading ships at their ports.

pallamentum : — used for *parlamentum.*

palliare : — to cover.

pallium : -- a pall, a pontifical or archiepiscopal vesture ; an altar cloth.

palma : — tennis.

palmarius : — a pilgrim, a palmer.

palmata : — a bargain ; a handful or handbreadth ; a stroke on the hand.

palmatia : — a palm grove.

palmiferus : — a palmer or pilgrim.

palmitare : — to bargain.

palmula : — a rudder, an implement used in mixing malt.

paltenerium : — a pautener, a purse.

paltenerius, paltonarius : — proud, savage.

palum : — a pale, paling.

pana : — a counterpane.

panagia : — holy bread.

panarius : — a place in a church where bread was distributed to the poor.

panatus : — fortified with piles (?).

Pandicularis dies : — All Saints day.

pandoxare : — to brew, or sell beer.

pandoxator : — a brewer.

pandoxatorium : — a brewhouse.

panduca : — a bagpipe.

panella, panellum :—a panel ; a list of jurors' names.

panellare :—to empanel.

panellus :—a panel ; a cushion ; a net ; a small loaf.

panerius :—a panier, a bread-basket.

panesculus :—a small loaf.

panetaria : —a pantry.

panetarius, panetrarius : — a pantler, or panter.

panetria :—a pantry. In some cases this word is used as if it were derived from *pannus*, not *panis*.

panicius :—a baker.

panigeria :—a fair or market.

panna :—squared timber supporting the rafters, or a gutter between the roofs of two houses ; a cross beam. (Fr. *panne*).

pannagiare :—to pasture pigs ; to pay pannage.

pannagium :—pannage ; mast ; payment or licence for feeding swine in a forest.

pannarius :—a clothier.

pannicipium :—a closet, a press.

panniculus :—a napkin.

pannideusium :—a button.

pannucia :—party-cloth, cloth of divers colours.

pannus :—cloth ; a weaver's spittle or spool.

pantaria, pantria :— a pantry.

paonacius :—purple.

papa :—a pope.

papatum :—pap, child's food.

papatus :—popedom ; papacy.

papilio :—a tent, a pavilion.

papilonarius :—a tentmaker.

papirium :—a record room ; a register.

par :—a pair ; a peer.

par civitatis :—a citizen ; a freeman.

parachinus, parachina : — a parishioner.

parafredus :—a palfrey.

paragium :—equality of condition or property ; a tenure between parceners.

paramentum :—equipment ; ornament.

paraphernalia : — f u r n i t u r e, clothes, &c., which a widow may claim in addition to her dower or jointure.

paraphonista :—a chorister.

paraphus :—a paragraph.

pararia. See *petraria*.

pararius :—a cloth dresser.

parasceue :—Good Friday ; any Friday.

parastica :—the step of a mast.

paraticum. See *paragium*.

parcaminarius : — a seller of parchment.

parcare :—to enclose.

parcarius :—a parker , a pinder ; a foldkeeper.

parcella :—a parcel (of land).

parcella terræ : — " Anglice vocata : A Noke Land." (Valor Eccl. iij 35.)

parcellare :—to parcel out.

parcenarius :—a joint holder of land, a coparcener ; parcenary.

parcopollex :—a shoe-horn.

parcus :—a park ; a pound, a pinfold.

pardona :—pardon.

pardonare :—to pardon.

pardonatio :—pardon.

pargulum :—a parclose.

paria :—a pair.

pariagium, pariatio :—grant of portion of lands to lord or king in return for protection.

pariettare :—to parget or plaister.

purificare :—to equalise.

purius lapis :—freestone.

parlamentalis :—of parliament.

parlamentare : — to confer together.

parlamentum :—parliament.

parlatorium : — a parlour; an audience chamber.

parliamentum, &c. See *parlamentum,* &c.

parlora :—a parlour.

parmentarius :—a tailor ; a fripperer.

paro :—a small ship.

parochia :—a diocese ; a parish.

parochianus :— a parishioner; a parish priest.

parrio :—a small ship.

parterra :—a plot of ground.

partibilis :—divisible.

partica :—a perch.

particula :—a parcel.

particulariter :—by retail.

particus. See *parcus.*

partionarius :—a partner.

parura :— apparel ; embroidery on an alb, amice, or altar frontal, &c.

parvisa :—the cloisters or circuit of a convent; the cemetery ; a church porch; a chamber over it. Perhaps a corruption of *Paradisus.*

parvisiæ :—an exercise for law students ; a moot.

parvisium, parvisus. See *parvisa.*

pasaiarius :—a ferryman.

Pasca. See *Pascha.*

pascarium :—dues or tithes paid for pasture.

pascere :—to feed, is used of men as well as beasts.

Pascha :—Easter. In the 13th cent. acc. *Pascha,* gen. *Paschatis* or *Pasche,* abl. *Pascha.*

Pascha Floridum :—Palm Sunday.

pascua :—a meadow ; pasture.

pascuagium :—pasturage.

pascuarium :—pasture ; payment for pasture.

pasnagium :—pannage.

passagiarius :—a person crossing a ferry ; a traveller.

passagium :—passage over water, ferry ; payment for passage; payment by military tenants in lieu of serving abroad.

passare :—to pass ; to cause to pass.

passarius :—a ferryman.

passator :—the owner of a ferry ; a ferryman.

passiagiarius :—a ferryman.

passiator. See *passator.*

passionerius :—a passioner, *i.e.,* book containing Saints' lives.

passus :—a portion of a book or poem, "fytte" ; a mountain pass.

pasta :—dough ; pastry.

pastea :—pastry.

pastellarius :—a pieman.

pastellum :—woad.

pasteria :—pastry.

pasticium :—a field for pasture.

pastillus :—a pie.

pastum :—paste ; dough.

pastura :—pasture.

pasturare :—to depasture.

pastus :— provisions which a tenant is bound to supply to his lord.

patella :—a pan ; a tool used in building.

patena :—a metal plate ; a paten.

patenarius :—an acolyte.

patens, patenta :—letters patent.

pathnagium :—pannage.

paticium :—an allowance.

patriaster :—a stepfather.

patricinium :—used for *patrocinium.*

patrina :—a godmother.

patrinus :—a godfather.

patronicatus :—commanded (of a ship).

patronizare :—to defend.

paunagium :—pannage.

pausa :—a barrel.

pausatio :—repose.

pavagium :—pavage ; payment for paving the roads.

pavare :—to pave.

paveillo :—a tent.

pavesium :—a pavice, a large shield.

paviare :—to pave.

paviator :—a paviour.

parilio :—a tent.

pavimentatio :—paving.

pavire :—to pave.

pax :—a small tablet presented by the priest at mass to be kissed by the people.

paxeria :—a pier ; a floodgate.

paxillum :—a staff ; a landmark ; a tent pole.

peccum :—a peck.

pecia :—a piece or small quantity.

peciatum :—a peck.

peconus :—a hook or clasp.

pectorale :—a breastplate ; an ornament worn by a bishop ; a horse's poitrel.

pectrix :—a woman comber.

pecuarius :—a grazier.

pedagium :—pedage ; toll paid by travellers, esp. through forests.

pedale :—a footcloth ; a duty exacted at Bordeaux ; a shoemaker's last.

pedalis pons :—a footbridge.

pedana :—gaiters or stockings.

pedaticum :—a toll on passengers ; any toll.

pedatus :—having a foot.

pedellum :—a pightell or picle (?). See *pictellum.*

pedica :—a fetter ; a trap for catching wolves ; a calthrop.

pedicator :—a trapper.

pedicru :—a pedigree.

pediles :—stockings.

pedilusor :—a football player.

pedinus :—a pawn at chess.

pedisgradum :—a pedigree.

pedis pulveris, or *pulverisati, curia* :—Piepowder Court.

pedo :—a foot soldier.

pedules :—stockings.

pego :—a candlestick.

peisa, peisea, peisia :—a wey. See *waga.*

pela :—a peel, a castle ; a baker's peel.

peletarius :—a pelterer.

peletria :—peltry, skins.

pelfare :—to pilfer.

pelfra :—booty ; pelf.

pella :—a booth ; a shop.

pellagium :—duty on hides.

pellefridus :—a palfrey.

pelletria :—fur ; the wardrobe of furs in the royal household ; the trade of peltry.

pellica :—a baker's peel.

pellicia, pellicies, pellicium :—a pilch ; a fur gown.

pelliparius :— a pelterer, a skinner.

pelliris :—a palet, a headpiece of *cuir bouilli.*

pellura :—fur.

pellus :—a shovel ; a peel.

pelota, pellota :—a ball ; the ball of the foot.

pelum. See *pela.*

penalitas :—penalty.

pendicia :—appurtenances.

pendicula :—a plumb-line.

pendiculum :—a timber arch over a doorway.

pendulus :—a pendant jewel.

penerarius :—an ensign-bearer.

penitenciaria :—penitentiaryship.

penitenciarius :—a penancer.

penitimus :—inmost.

penitior :—inner.

pennarium :—a penner.

pennula. See *penula.*

pennum :—a pennon.

pensa :—a wey. See *waga.*

pensionarius :—liable to payment.

pensum :—a weight.

pentecostalia : — Whitsuntide offerings, or a payment in lieu of them.

Pentecoste :—Whit Sunday.

penticium :—a pentice or penthouse.

penucella :—a pensell or penoncell, a small banner.

penula :—a hood.

penularius :—a maker of hoods ; a parmenter.

penulatus :—hooded ; furred.

pera :—a purse ; a bag ; a pier.

peracula :—a little bag or purse.

perambulata, perambulatio :—survey ; a walk in a forest (?).

perambulum :—a walk ; an alley.

perapsis :—a platter.

peraria. See *petraria.*

perca :—a perch of land. See *pertica.*

percaminarius : — a seller of parchment.

percaptura :—stakes set in a river for catching fish.

percata :—a perch. See *pertica.*

percella. See *parcella.*

perchia :—a perch (*perca fluviatilis*) ; a perch or pole. See *pertica.*

percursum :—pursuit ; the right of following game beyond one's own bounds.

perdica :—used for *pertica.*

perdona :—pardon ; discharge ; remission.

perdonare :—to pardon.

perdonatio :—pardon.

perdonista :—a pardoner, an official from whom pardons can be obtained.

perdricarius :—a man employed in taking partridges.

perecia :—a piece, a fragment.

peregrinatio :—a pilgrimage.

peregrinus :—a pilgrim.

perempnis :—used for *perennis.*

perendinare :—to delay ; to remain, to reside ; to redouble.

perequare :—to level.

performare :—to perform.

pergamena :—parchment.

pergamenarius : — a parchment maker.

pergulum :—a lodge ; a pound.

perhendinare. See *perendinare.*

peribolus :—a circuit ; a compass ; a gallery.

peridota : — a peridot, a gem, colour green.

periermeniæ : — interpretation (περὶ ἑρμηνείας.)

perillum :—part of the machinery of a mill.

perinus. See *perrinus.*

peritus : —tried ; sometimes used to mean " guilty."

perla :—a pearl.

permentarius. See *parmentarius.*

peronizare :—to purchase.

perpacare :—to pay in full.

perperus : — a Byzantine coin, worth half or a quarter of a mark.

perplacitare :—to decide.

perplicar :—a garter.

perpunctum :—a doublet.

perquirere :—to purchase, to acquire otherwise than by inheritance.

perquisitio :—purchase.

perquisitor :—a purchaser.

perquisitum :—purchase; perquisite ; profit.

perreator :—a lapidary.

perreia :—a precious stone.

perreria :—a stone quarry.

perrinus :—stony ; shining like a precious stone.

perseus, persicus : — peach - coloured.

persona :—a person ; a parson or rector.

persona impersonata :—a parson imparsonee, a lawful incumbent in actual possession.

personabilis :— able to maintain a plea.

personagium :—a parsonage ; a benefice.

personatus :—the office of a parson ; a benefice.

pertica : — a perch or pole of land, now 16½ feet, in the thirteenth century 24 or 25 feet ; a square perch, now 30¼ yards ; a crossbeam ; the beam of a buck's head or branch of a stag's.

perticalis :—a percher candle, placed on a crossbeam.

perticarius :—a beadle ; an apparitor.

perticata :—a square perch. See *pertica.*

perticia terre :—the same as *perticata.*

perticulus :—a staff ; a bat.

pertinentia :—appurtenance.

pertizona : — distribution of alms (?).

pertum :—a broom.

perula :—a pearl.

pervisum. See *parvisa.*

pesa. See *pensa.*

pesagium :—pesage, custom paid on weighing goods.

pesarius :—a weigher.

pesor :—a weigher, an Exchequer officer.

pessagium. See *pesagium.*

pessellum :—a bolt (*pessulum*).

pesso, pessona : — mast.

pessularia :—a stockade.

pestellus :—a leg of pork. O. E. pestle.

peta : — peat.

petagium. See *pedagium.*

petalum :—a paving stone.

petancia. See *pietancia.*

petilio, petilla :—a crossbow bolt ; a pestle.

petillarius :—a boltmaker.

petillium :—a crossbow bolt.

petitorium :—a claim ; a writ of right.

petra :—a stone weight.

petraria :—a stone quarry ; an engine to cast stones.

petrima :—a gun.

pettum :—a crack of a whip ; a report of a gun.

petulium :—a bolt.

petulus :—with white feet.

peytrellum :—a poitrel.

phalesia :—a cliff on the seashore.

phano : — a banner.

pheliparius :— a fripperer.

phila :—a file.

philaterium, philaternum : — a phylactery ; an amulet ; a reliquary, worn suspended from the neck.

philipparius :—a fripperer.

phoracra. See *foracra.*

pica :—an index, pyebook ; rules for saying divine service ; a peck.

picagium, piccagium :—payment to the owner of the soil for breaking ground to erect booths, &c.

picesium :—a pickaxe.

picheria :—a pitcher.

picherius :—a fish, perhaps pilchard (*clupea pilchardus*), but more probably the gilthead (*chrysophrys* or *sparus aurata*), called in old French *picarel*, O. E. cackerell.

pichoisium, picoisum :—a pickaxe.

pictaciare :—to mend, to patch.

pictaciarius :—a cobbler.

pictacio :—painting.

pictare :—to paint.

pictellum :—a pightell, or picle, a small piece of land, enclosed with a hedge.

picturare :—to paint.

picula :—pickle.

pietancia :—a pittance, an addition to the usual food in collegiate churches or convents ; the pittance for two was given in one plate.

pietanciaria :—the place where pittance is distributed ; the office of the pittancer.

pietantiarius :—a pittancer, an officer who distributes the pittance.

piga :—the forearm.

pightellum. See *pictellum.*

pikerellus :—a pickerel, a small pike.

pila :—a pile (heraldic) ; the reverse of a coin.

pilare :—to drive piles.

pilarius :—a pillar.

pilatus :—a blunt arrow, bolt, or quarel.

pileo :—a hatter, a capper (?).

pilettus :—an arrow with a knob at the head.

pillare :—to plunder.

pillaria :—plunder ; devastation.

pilleus :—for *pileus*, a hat.

pillorium, piloria, pilorium :—a pillory.

pilum :—cloth.

pilus :—a stake.

pinaculum :—a pinnacle.

pinca :—a jug ; a bodkin ; a granary.

pincella :—a pencil.

pincerna :—a butler ; a cup-bearer.

pincernaria :—a buttery ; the office of butler.

pincernarius :—an officer of the buttery.

pinnare :—to notch ; to cut niches.

pinsa :—a pestle.

pinsella :—a brake or braye, a kneading machine.

pinsis :—a grimace.

pipa :—the great or pipe roll of the Exchequer ; a pipe of wine, two hogsheads.

piperarius :—a pepperer.

pipum :—a pipe of wine.

pira :—an arch of a bridge.

piratum, piretum :—perry.

piritegium :—curfew.

pisa :—a wey. See *waga.*

pisaria :—a stock of peas.

piscaria :—a fishery.

piscaricea navis :—a fishing boat.

piscenarius :—a fishmonger.

pischaria :—a fishery.

piscina :—a small lavatory in a church near the altar.

pistare, pistrinare :—to bake.

pistrinum :—a bakehouse; part of a church, error for *piscina* (?).

pitacio :—a document; a letter.

pitancia, pitencia, &c. See *pietantia,* &c.

placea :— a place ; a plot of ground.

placeum. See *placius.*

placitabilis :—impleadable.

placitare :—to plead.

placitatio :—pleading.

placitator :—a pleader.

placitum :— a plea ; obligation to attend courts.

placium :—a piece of flat ground.

placius :—a plaice (*platessa vulgaris*).

plada :—a plaice.

plagiare :—to wound.

planare :—to plank.

planatorium :—a plane.

planca, plancha :— a plank ; a measure of land.

planchagium :—planking ; camp-sheathing.

planchera :—a plank.

planchia :—a plank.

planchiare :—to plank.

planchicium. See *planchagium.*

plancium. See *planchagium.*

planctura :—planking.

planeta :—a chasuble.

plangnum :—a plank.

planicies :—a field (heraldic).

planula : — staunchegreyne, a preparation like pounce, used by scriveners.

planus :—plain, in the sense of unornamented.

plastrare, plastriare :—to plaster.

plastrum :—plaster.

plata :—a flat piece of unwrought metal, ingot.

platellus :—a platter.

platera :—an open space (?).

platiper :—a game played with stones.

platoma :—a metal plate.

plaustrata :—a wagon-load.

plaustrum :— usually a wagon, but sometimes a two-wheeled cart.

plebania :—a church having subordinate chapels ; a parish.

plebanus :—(adj.) parish.

plebanus :—a rural dean; a parish priest.

plecta :—a plait.

plectrum :—pewter.

plegagium, plegiagium, plegiatio :—suretyship ; pledgery.

plegium, plegius : — a pledge ; surety.

plenarius miles :—fully armed.

plevina :—replevin ; bail ; surety.

plostrum. See *plaustrum.*

plumbarius :—a plumber.

plumbatio :—plumbing.

plumerus :—a plover (*charadrius pluvialis* or *vanellus cristatus*).

pluscula, plustula :—a buckle.

plutum :—rain.

pluviale :—a cope.

pluvina. See *plevina.*

pobles :—used for *poples.*

pochia :—a pouch ; a purse.

poderis :—an alb, a linen vestment worn under the chasuble ; a rochet.

podium :—anything to lean on ; a staff ; part of the seat in a choir stall.

podoris. See *poderis.*

pœnacius :—purple.

poketta, pokettum :—a pocket.

pola :—a perch or pole ; a bank ; a pool.

polana, polena :—the pointed toe of a shoe ; a pulley-piece, armour for the knee.

polentriticare :—to sift flour.

poletarius :—a poulterer.

poletria :—poultry.

poletta :—a pullet.

poliandrum :—a grave, a gravestone.

polimitarius :—a stainer.

politrudinare :—to boult flour.

pollardus :—a pollard, bad money, used in the 13th century.

pollex :—an inch.

poltarium :—poultry.

poltarius :—a poulterer or keeper of fowls.

polteria :—poultry.

polus :—an axle.

pomacium :—apple-moss, a dish made of stewed apples ; cider.

pomellatus :—dappled.

pomellum, pomelum :—a pommel ; a boss.

pompina :—a kitchen.

pondagium :—poundage.

ponderare :—to weigh.

ponderatio :—pesage.

ponderator :—a pesour, weigher, an officer in the Exchequer.

pondus :—a pound, a pinfold.

pontagium :—tax for repairs of a bridge ; toll taken on a bridge.

pontarius :—a bridgemaker or bridge keeper.

pontifex :—a bishop ; a pope.

pontificalia : — episcopal vestments.

pontificalibus, in :—under stole.

pontificatus :—bishopric ; popedom.

pontonagium :—bridge toll.

pontum :—used for *punctum.*

popinator : — a tippler, *i.e.*, an alehouse keeper or a drinker.

porca terræ :—a balk of land.

porcaria :—a pigsty.

porcarius, porcator : — a swineherd.

porcellatus :—born (of pigs).

porchettus :—a porker, a little pig.

porchia :—a porch.

porkaria :—a pigsty.

porpecia, porpesius :—a porpoise (*phocœna communis*).

porportum :—purport.

portabilis :—portable.

portagium :—toll taken at a gate ; porterage ; wear and tear.

portamentum :—behaviour.

portaria :—the office of porter.

portarius :—a porter.

portatio :—the entry of a bishop into his cathedral town ; bearing arms.

portator :—a porter.

portatus :—carriage.

portella :—a small gate; a basket; a reliquary.

portgrevius :—a portreeve.

porticulus :—a truncheon.

porticus :—an apse or porch, not a peristyle as in classical Latin.

portiforium :—a breviary.

portimotus. See *portmota.*

portionarius :—a joint holder of a benefice.

portmota :—a portmote, a court held in towns.

porus :—a pore.

positio :—an impost ; a tax.

posse (*subst.*) :—power.

possessionatus :—in possession of.

posta :—a station ; a post.

postarum, magister : —Master of the Post.

postdisseisina :—postdisseisin.

postela :—a crupper.

postergare :—to leave behind, to abandon.

posterna :—a postern gate.

posterula, posticum :—a postern gate.

postilla :—a homily.

postillare :— to interpret, to comment on.

postorellus :—a name given to robbers in Gascony, temp. Edw. II.

postsellium :—the hinder part of a saddle.

postulare :—to transfer a man in possession of or elect of an episcopal see, to another.

potagium :—pottage ; a tax on drink.

potata :—a pot or pottle.

potellum :—a pottle, two quarts.

poteria :—pottery ; a pottery.

potestas :—a king, chief ruler, or magistrate.

poticarius. For *apothecarius.*

potionare :—to poison.

potissare :—to sip.

pottarius :—a potter.

pottata :—a pot or pottle.

pottus :—a pot.

potura :— pasture ; drink.

poudratus :—powdered ; salted.

poutura. See *potura.*

powenatius :—a garment of cloth.

practisare, practizare :—to practise.

præbenda :—commons ; a prebend ; provender.

præbendarius :—a prebendary.

præceptor :—an officer of the knights of the Temple.

præcantare :—to sing beforehand.

præceptoria :—the benefice assigned to the office of præceptor.

præcessor :—vanguard.

præcipitaria :—a battering ram.

præconia :—superiority ; fame.

præconisare : —to foresee; to foretell ; to proclaim.

præconsa :—some vestment.

præcontestis :—a previous fellow-witness.

præfectus :—a mayor.

præferentia : —preference; the right of receiving firstfruits.

præferrementum : —a prerogative ; a privilege.

prælata :—an abbess.

prælatia :—ecclesiastical dignity.

prælatus : —a magistrate ; a bishop ; an abbot or abbess ; a prior or prioress.

prælibare :—to mention before.

præmasticare : —to discuss beforehand.

præmiabilis :—deserving of reward.

præmunire :—to cite (for *præmonere*).

præpositura :—a reeveship, constableship ; a district under the jurisdiction of such an officer.

præpositus :—a provost; a constable or reeve; a warden (of a church) ; a bailiff ; the prior of a Benedictine Abbey.

prærogativa :—prerogative.

præsellum :—a saddle bow.

præsentare :—to present.

præsentia :—a present, a gift.

præsentialiter :—immediately ; in presence of; as a gift.

præstare :—to let.

præstitum :—an advance of money.

præsul :—a chief ; a bishop ; an abbot ; a judge.

præsulatus :—a bishopric ; an abbacy.

prama :—a prame, *i.e.*, a barge or lighter.

pramo :—a bargee.

precaria, precarium :—a request by a lord to his tenant for aid or tax ; extra service performed by tenants in ploughing and harvest, boonday, benewerk. See *bedrepium.*

precentaria :—precentorship.

precentor :—a precentor, a chanter.

precipitaria :—a battering ram.

precis. See *precaria.*

preciunt :—they cost.

preco :—a crier.

precula :—a rosary.

premorium :—a primer.

prenticius : —an apprentice.

prenum :—a press for wine, &c.

prephatia :—used for *præfatio.*

presbyter :—a priest.

presbyteragium :—the income of a parish priest.

presbyteratus :—priesthood.

presbyterium :—priesthood ; a presbytery ; the choir of a church.

presentum :—a present, a gift.

primitiare :—to begin.

princeps :—a prince.

principalium :—an heirloom ; a mortuary.

principatus :—principality.

principissa :—a princess.

principium burgi :—a town hall.

prior :—a monastic officer, next to the abbot in an abbey, head of a priory.

prioratus :—a priory.

priorissa :—a prioress.

prisa :—a prize ; booty ; a fine ; prisage.

prisagium :—prisage, a share of prizes ; a right of taking prizes ; a duty on wine and provisions.

prisalia :—reprisals.

prisia :—prisage.

priso :—a prisoner of war ; a prison ; imprisonment.

prisona :—a prison.

prisonare :—to keep in prison.

prisonarius :—a prisoner.

privatus :—privy.

privicarnium :—fasting ; Lent.

privilegiare :—to grant a privilege to.

proaula :—a porch.

probare :—used for *propriare.*

probaticus : — connected with sheep.

probator :—an accuser ; an approver.

probatum :—a sheep.

probi homines :—good men, an elected body of citizens forming a common council.

proceres :—ornamental heads of beams on house fronts.

Processio :—Rogation week.

processionale :—a book containing directions for and music to be used in processions, the service for gangdays, litanies, or intercessions.

proclamator :—a crier ; in the Court of Common Pleas, proclamator.

proconsul :—a justice in eyre.

procuratio :—procuration, a payment, originally in victuals, by the inferior clergy to bishop or archdeacon at visitations ; a proxy ; necessaries, as food and clothing ; a meal.

procurator :—a proctor.

procuratorium :—procuratory ; a proxy.

proditio :—treason.

proditionaliter :—treasonably.

profectus : —profit.

profestum :—the eve of a feast.

proficuum :—profit.

profrum : — profer, time appointed for officers to make their accounts.

promarius :—a waiter.

promtorium, promptuarium :—a buttery ; a storehouse.

propalare :—to publish.

propars, propartia :—pourparty, purparty.

prophetare :—to prophecy.

propiare. See *propriare.*

propina :—salutation.

proportare :—to purport; to show.

proportatio :—a verdict; a declaration.

proportionabiliter : — proportionally.

proportionare :—to divide.

proportionatio :—proportion.

proportum :—purport.

proprestura :—the 12th century form of *purprestura.*

propriare :—to claim; to appropriate; to make fit for use; to grind (of tools).

propriatio :—appropriation.

propriator :—an impropriator.

proprietarius :—a proprietor.

propunctum :—a doublet.

proretha :—a master of a ship.

prosecutor :—a prosecutor; a pursuivant.

prostrare :—to throw down.

protocollum : — a preface; a charter.

protoforestarius : — a c h i e f forester.

protonotarius, protonotator :—a prothonotary.

protractura :—drawing a picture before colouring.

providentia :—provision.

provisio :—a grant by the Pope of the succession to a benefice.

provisor :—a purveyor.

psalterium :—a psalter.

puca :—a gown. O. E. pewke.

pucellagium :—maidenhood.

pucha :—a pouch.

puchea :—a pouch.

pucio :—a child.

puctura. See *putura.*

puellagium. See *pullagium.*

pugnalis :—the size of a fist.

pugnata :—a handful.

pulcinus :—a chicken.

puletarium :—a poultry yard.

puletarius :—a poulterer.

pullagium :—a tax or rent paid in fowls.

pullanus :—a foal.

pullarius :—an officer of the royal household in charge of the poultry.

pullenata :—a mare which has foaled.

pulletarius :—a poulterer.

pulletria :—poultry.

pulletrus :—a foal.

pulliolus, pullus : — a young horse.

pulo :—a foal.

pulsare :—to accuse; to ring a bell.

pulsatio :—bell ringing.

pultrella :—a filly.

pultura :—poultry.

pulveris, pulverisatipedis, curia :— Court of Piepowder.

pulvis tormentarius : — gunpowder.

pulverizare :—to powder.

pumata :—a handful.

punctum :—the fourth or fifth part of an hour.

pundfalda :—a pound, a pinfold.

pundo :—a pinder.

punfauda. See *pundfalda.*

puniata :—a handful.

punicare : —to paint red.

punio. See *punzunus.*

puntum :—a point ; the chape of a scabbard.

punzunus :—a punshion, stud or quarter, an upright timber used in building houses.

puralla :—purlieu.

purare :—to clear (ground).

purcachium, purchacia : — purchase, acquisition.

purcivandus :—a poursuivant.

purgacium :—purchase.

purila :—the tip of the nose.

purportare :—to extend.

purportum :—purport.

purprestura :—pourpresture, encroachment.

purprisa, purprisum :—an enclosure.

purpunctus :—a doublet. (Fr. *pourpoint.*)

putacius :—a polecat.

putagium : —fornication.

putura :—food for cattle, &c. ; food for men, horses, and hounds, exacted by officers of a forest from the inhabitants ; timber.

pyrgus : —a dice-box.

pyritegium :—curfew.

pyxis :—a pyx, a casket to contain the Host.

Q.

quaccum :—cream.

quachetus :—a sort of bread used in Scotland.

quactum : —cream.

quadra :—a square loaf ; a quarter of a loaf.

quadragena :—forty ; a period of forty days.

quadragesima :—Lent.

quadragesimalia :—Easter offerings ; or a rate paid in their stead.

quadrans :—a farthing.

quadrantata :—the quarter of an acre, a farthingdeal.

quadraria :—a quarel or quarry of glass ; a stone quarry.

quadrellus :—a quarel, a square-headed bolt ; a carrell, a small chamber for study in the cloister of a monastery.

quadrigarius :—wide enough for a waggon.

quadriporticus :—a peristyle.

quæsta :—an indulgence ; a tax.

quæstabilis :—taxable.

quæstionarius :—a collector of alms; a seller of indulgences.

quæstus : —acquired by purchase.

qualificare :—to entitle ; to describe.

qualus : —a thead, a strainer used in brewing.

quarellus. See *quadrellus.*

quarentena :—quarentine, a space of forty days ; Lent ; a shot or shute, *i.e.*, a square furlong, a space of 40 perches.

quarrera :—a stone quarry.

quarrerius :—a stonecutter.

quarruria :—a stone quarry.

quarta :—a quart.

quartale :—a quart.

quartarium :—a quarter of corn.

quartarius terræ :—eight acres.

quartenarius :—suffering from quartan ague.

quarteragium :—quarterage, quarterly payment.

quarteria :—a quarter of land.

quarterisare :—to cut into four quarters.

quarterium :—a quarter ; a soam of corn.

quarterizatio :—quartering, part of the punishment of treason.

quaternum :—a quire.

quarteronus :—a quarter ; a quarter of a hundredweight.

quartilatus :—divided into four parts.

quartus :—a quart.

quassare :—to annul, to quash.

quassillarius :—a pedlar.

quaternio, quaternum :—a folded sheet of paper (Fr. *cahier*) ; a quire.

quaternis, in :—in quarto.

quaterno, in :—in quarto.

quatriplicare :—to quadruple.

quaxillarius :—a pedlar.

quentesia :—a device.

querela :—a party ; a faction ; a fine.

querquera :—ague.

querraria :—a quarry.

querulare :—to complain.

questa :—an inquest or inquisition.

questionarius :—a palmer. O. E. " quistron."

quieta clamancia or *clamatio* :—a quitclaim.

quietantia : — an acquittance ; abandonment; immunity.

quietare :—to quit ; to acquit.

quietatio : — exemption, discharge, acquittance.

quiete, quietum clamare :—to quit claim, to renounce.

quietus :—freed, acquitted, quit.

quietus redditus :—quit rent.

quindecia. See *quindena*.

quindena :—a quinzaine, fifteen days.

quinio :—a bundle of five ; a sheet made of five leaves.

quintale, quintallus :—a weight used for metals, &c., varying from 96 lbs. to 120 lbs.

quintana :—Quintaine, the first Sunday in Lent.

quintena :—the game called quintain.

quinterna :—a cittern.

quirea :—the hounds' reward at the death of a stag (Fr. *curée*) ; a cuirass ; something connected with a cart.

quirinarium :—a quintain.

quisinum :—a cushion.

quitancia :—an acquittance ; a quittance ; a discharge.

quittacio. See *quitancia*.

quittare :—to acquit ; to remit.

quorespondens :—used for *correspondens*.

quota :—a share ; a tax to be levied equally.

quota litis :—a bribe received by a judge.

quotare :—to divide into chapters ; to repeat ; to mark.

quotator :—a chronicler.

quyschenus :—a cushion.

R.

racenius :—raisin.

racetus :—erased.

racha. See *ragana.*

rachaptare :—to ransom.

rachatum :—compensation ; ransom ; relief.

rachetare :—to ransom.

rachetum. See *rachatum.*

radiatus :—rayed, striped ; ray, a striped cloth.

ragana :—a ray (*raia clavata*) or a skate (*raia batis*).

raglorium :—the jurisdiction of a *raglotus.*

raglorius, raglotus :—a steward. (Welsh, *rhaglaw.*)

ralla :—a rail ; a thin tunic.

ramia, ramilla, ramilia :—twigs.

rangeator :—a ranger.

rapa :—a rape, a division of a county, especially Sussex.

rapagulum :—railing.

rappus. See *rapa.*

rapum :—rape (crime).

rapus. See *rapa.*

rasa :—a rase, a measure of corn ; land requiring a rase of seed.

rasare :—to scrape, to rase.

raseria. See *rasa.*

rasorium :—a razor.

rastillare :—to rake.

rastillum :—a rake.

rastrare :—to rake.

rastura :—shaving.

rasurus :—a razor.

rata :—an agreement ; a share ; a rate.

ratificare :—to ratify, to confirm.

ratificatio :—ratification.

ratihabere :—to confirm.

rationale :—a peculiar form of the pontifical pallium.

ratis :—error for *crates* (?).

rato :—a rat.

ratula :—a landrail (*crex pratensis*).

ratus :—a rat.

rauba :—a robe.

raubare :—to rob.

raubaria :—robbery.

raucisonare :—to speak hoarsely.

rayus :—a ray or skate (*raia clavata* or *batis*).

reafforestare :—to make land into a forest after it has been disafforested.

realis :—royal.

reattachiamentum :—a reattachment of one who has been dismissed the court.

rebroccator :—a cobbler.

recaptio :—taking a second distress.

M.

X

recatiare :—to restore.

recatum :—relief.

reccare :—to rack wine, to draw it off the lees.

reccus :—wine thus treated. (Fr. *vin raqué*.)

recepta :—receipt; receiving in the sense of harbouring.

receptamentum :—receiving; entertainment.

receptare, recettare :—to harbour; to entertain.

rechaciare :—to drive out; to separate gold or silver from the ore.

rechatum. See *rachatum.*

recidiva :—retribution.

recidivare :—to fall back.

recitare :—to revoke.

reckus. See *reccus.*

reclusa :—an inclosure; an anchoress.

reclusagium :—a cell.

reclusorium :—a cell; a pound or pinfold.

reclusus :—an anchorite.

reclutare :—to reglue (*reglutinare*).

recognitio : — acknowledgment; recognizance, recognition.

recognitor :—one who enters into a recognizance; a juror impanelled on an assize; a recognisor, recognitor.

recognoscere :—to acknowledge; to take cognizance of.

recokillatus :—curled. (Fr. *recoquillé*.)

recollecta :—gathering; harvest.

recommenda :—recommendation.

recompensare :—to repay, to recompense.

recordator :—a recorder.

recordum :—a record; a memorial.

recreantisa :—recreancy.

recredencia :—recreance, a provisional possession given to one of the parties till a suit be determined.

recta :—right; jurisdiction.

rectare :—to set straight; to cite, to accuse.

rectitudo :—right in the sense of compensation.

rector :—the rector of a parish, or college.

rectoria :—a rectory; a rector's house.

recuperamen :—a recovery.

recuperare :—(subst.) recovery.

recuperatio :—a recovery.

recussorium :—a hammer.

recusum :—rescue.

reddare :—to clean, to scour (a river).

redditarium :—a rental.

redditarius :—a renter.

redd{i}tualis :—rent (adj.).

redditus :—rent.

redditus assisæ or *assisus* :—rent of assise.

redemptio :—ransom.

redimere :—to ransom, to purchase the freedom of; sometimes, to set free for a ransom.

redisseisina :—redisseisin.

reditus, &c. See *redditus.*

refare :—to rob, to deprive.

refectorarius :—a caterer ; a refectorer, refectioner.

refectorium :—a refectory, fratry or frater ; a dining-hall.

refeoffare :—to enfeoff again.

referendarius :— an officer who exhibits petitions to the king, Master of the Requests.

refletum :—an osier bed.

refollum :—the outlet of a pond ; an overflow.

refortiuncula :—a fortress.

refullum. See *refollum.*

refutancia. See *refutatio.*

refutatio:—a quittance, a receipt.

rega terræ :—a measure of land in Guienne. (Fr. *rége.*)

regale, regalia :— royalty ; the temporal rights of a bishop ; some kingly ornament, that used by Henry III. was of white " diaspre " or silk.

regalitas :—royalty.

regardare :—to examine, to inspect ; to regard.

regardator :—the regarder of a forest.

regardere. See *regardare.*

regardor. See *regardator.*

regardum :—the regard, or inspection of a forest ; the extent of the regarder's charge ; the impost levied by him ; a reward.

regardus. See *regardator.*

rege et regina, ludus de —chess.

regestum :—a register ; a book-marker ; a safe for jewels, &c.

registrare :—to register.

registrarius :—a registrar.

registrum :—a register ; a book-marker.

regrataria :—sale by retail.

regratarius :—one who buys to resell in the same market, a regrator.

regratiare :—to give thanks.

regrator. See *regratarius.*

reguardum, &c. See *regardum.*

regula :—a reglet, a narrow flat moulding.

regulare :—to rule ; to rule lines.

regulare:—an instrument used in the mint.

regularis :—belonging to a monastic order.

regulus :—a prince ; an earl.

regwardum. See *regardum.*

rehabilitatio:—restoration to former ability.

reia :—a swathe, a row.

reintrare :—to re-enter.

reintratio :—re-entry.

reisa :—a journey ; a campaign.

rejunctio :—a rejoinder.

relaxare :— to release.

relaxatio:—a release ; relief.

relevamen, relevatio, relevium :— relief, a payment to the lord by a feudal tenant on entering his fief.

religio :—a religious order.

religiosus :—a member of such an order.

rella :—ray, striped cloth.

remanentia :—remainder.

remasilia vaccarum :—cowdung.

remedium :—recreation.

remembrancia :—remembrance.

rememoratio :—a remembrance.

rememorator :—a remembrancer.

remissus :—careless.

remocium :—rowing.

remuabilis :—removeable.

remulus :—a rudder, an implement used in mixing malt.

renga :—a belt; a baldric.

rengia, rengiata :—a strip of land.

rengum :—a rank; a row.

reno :—a short cloak, usually fur.

rentale :—a rental; a rent-roll.

rentarius :—a renter, a tenant paying rent.

reparium :—a fortified place; a harbour (for deer); repair, *i.e.* recourse, visit.

repassagium :—return.

repassare :—to return.

repastum :—a repast, a meal.

repatriare :—to return to one's country.

repausare :—to nourish; to be still, to repose; to make still.

repeciare :—to patch.

repellare :—to repeal.

repellum :—repeal.

reperium. See *reparium*.

replacitare :—to plead what was pleaded before.

replegiabilis :—replevisable, bailable.

replegiamentum :—replevin.

replegiare :—to redeem by giving surety; to replevy.

reportagium :—carrying back.

reportare :—to report.

reportus :—report.

reprisa :—deduction.

reprisale :—taking one thing in satisfaction for another, reprisal.

reprisare :—to remit; to deduct.

reragia. See *arreragium*.

resaisire. See *reseisire*.

rescuere :—to rescue.

rescussa, rescussio :—recovery; rescue; attack.

rescussor :—a rescuer.

rescussura :—rescue.

rescussus :—rescue.

rescutire :—to rescue.

reseantia :—residence.

reseisire :—to retake lands into the king's hand; to replace in seisin.

resiantia, resiantisa :—residence.

residensurus :—about to reside.

resolvere :—to pay.

resortire :—to be in the jurisdiction of; to revert; to resort to.

resortum :—the jurisdiction of a court; return.

respecta :—respite.

respectare, respectuare :—to respite.

respectus :—respite.

respiciatus : — considered; decreed.

respiciens :—reguardant (heraldic).

respicium :—respite.

responsalis :—one who answers for another in court.

restare :—to arrest. For *arestare.*

restauramentum :—restocking.

restaurare :—to repair ; to restore ; to restock.

restaurus :—reparation ; store.

resummonire:—to summon again.

resummonitio :—resummons.

retabulum. See *retrotabula.*

retallia, retallium :—retail.

retare. See *rectare.*

retenementum :—withholding.

retentio, retinentia :—retinue.

retiaculum :—a small net.

retinementum :—withholding.

retirare :—to retire.

retondarius :—a clipper of coin.

retonsura :—clipping.

retorna :—return of writs, &c.

retornare :—to return.

retornus :—profit ; return.

retracta :—withdrawal.

retrocomitatus : — rier-county, a place appointed by the sheriff for receipt of the king's money, after the close of the county court.

retrofeudum : — a mesne fee or mesne tenure.

retrogarda :—a rearguard.

retropannagium :—pannage from Martinmas to Candlemas.

retrotabula, retrotabulum : — a retable, a shelf above an altar or a frame on such a shelf.

retrovenda :—a sum paid on purchasing an estate in addition to the price.

retta. See *recta.*

rettum :—a charge, an accusation.

returna, &c. See *retorna, &c.*

reugia : — a measure of land (error for *rengia* (?)).

revella, revelles :—revels.

revelus :—a pedlar.

reventio :—revenue.

reversatus :—turned inside out.

reversio : — reversion, the right of succession.

revestiarium :—vestry ; sacristy.

revestire :—to reinfeoff.

revestitorium :—a vestry.

revestitura : — putting into possession again.

revolus :—a pedlar.

rewardum. See *regardum.*

rewennio :—rennet.

reysa :—a journey ; a campaign.

ribaldus:—a light-armed soldier; a rogue, a vagrant.

ribinare :—to bank up (?).

ridare :—to clean.

ridellus :—a curtain.

ridmicus (rhythmicus) : — in metre ; in rhyme.

rifflare :—to take away by force; to plunder.

riffletum :—an osier bed.

rifflura : — plunder See also *rufflura.*

riga : —a ridge.

rima : — rhyme.

rimagium : — error for *riviagium* (?).

ringa : — a soldier's belt.

ringeldus, ringildus : —a bailiff. (Welsh *rhingyll.*)

ringildria : —office of *ringildus.*

rinsura : —washing.

riota : —a riot.

riotosus : —riotous.

riottum : —a riot.

riparia : — water flowing between banks.

riparius : —one who conveys fish from the coast to inland towns.

ripator : —a reaper.

risa : —rice.

rismus : —rhyme.

ritare. See *rectare.*

rivagium : —toll taken on rivers for the passage of boats, or on the shore for landing goods.

rivaria : —a river bank.

riveare, riviare : — to fish and fowl on a river; to have the right of doing so.

riviagium : — the above-mentioned right. See also *rivagium.*

rivera : —a river.

rivola : —a stream, a rivulet.

rixa : —rice.

roba : — a robe.

robare : —to rob.

robaria : —robbery.

robator, roberator : —a robber.

roberia : —robbery.

robigalia : — Rogation week.

roborare : —to confirm.

robur : — often means a dead oak for firewood, while *quercus* is used for a live one, to be cut down for timber.

rocca : —a spinning rock, or distaff.

rochea : —a roach.

rochettum : —a rochet, a frock of white lawn without or with tight sleeves.

rochia, rochus : —a roach (*leuciscus rutilus*).

rocus : —a rook or castle at chess.

roda : —a perch, 16½ feet ; a rood, a quarter of an acre.

rodata : —a quarter of an acre.

rogationes : —public prayers or processions.

rogatorium : —an almonry.

rogatorius : — a beggar ; an almoner.

rogus : —a pile of wood ; a beacon ; a rogue.

rolla : —a roll.

rollagium : —rolling ; money paid therefor.

rollare : —to enrol ; to roll.

rolliare : —to roll.

romancium : —a French book ; a romance.

Romano, in : —in French.

romea : —a room.

romipeta : —one who has appealed unto Rome.

roncalis, roncaria. See *runcalis.*

rondella :—a roundel.

ropa :—a rape, a division of a county.

rosa, rosarius :—base money imported from abroad in the reign of Edw. I. A penny of base money in Q. Mary's reign bears a rose instead of the Queen's head ; a rosette.

rosatum vinum :—*vin rosetique* from Nerac in Gascony.

rosera auca :—a species of wild goose.

roserellum :— a rosary (?), a rosette (?).

rosetum :—a rushy place ; thatch.

rossinum :—rosin.

rossus :—red.

rotabulum :—a firefork.

rotagium :—wheelage, toll on wheeled vehicles.

rotarius :—a soldier ; a robber ; a wheelwright.

rotula :—a roll ; a rowel ; a mullet (heraldic) ; a candle.

rotulare :— to turn round ; to enrol.

rotularius :—a notary ; a secretary.

rotulus :—a roll.

routa, routum :—a rout ; an unlawful assembly.

rubbosa :—rubbish.

rubea, rubettus, rubetus :—a ruby.

rubiginator :—a furbisher.

rubius :—red.

rubrica :—a rubric.

rubricella :—a little rubric.

rucha. See *rutta.*

rucillaria :—a skep (?) ; same as *ruscatia* (?).

rudera :—rubbish.

ruelium :—a taper.

rufflura : —a scratch.

ruinus :—ruinous.

rumagium :— rummaging, unloading a ship.

rumigerulus : —bearer of tidings.

rumphea :—a dart.

runagium : — error for *riviagium* (?).

runcalis, runcaria :—land overgrown with brambles, &c.

runcilus, runcinus :—a draughthorse, or pack-horse.

runsus. See *runcilus.*

ruptarius :—a husbandman ; a mercenary soldier; a robber.

ruptura :—arable land.

rusca :—a skep ; a hive.

ruscatia :—a place where broom grows.

ruscubardum : — some kind of broom.

ruscum :—filth ; gorse.

russetus :—russet.

russus :—red.

rusticus :—used as the opposite to *liber* in the 12th century.

ruta. See *routa, rutta.*

rutta :—a troop of mercenary soldiers.

S.

sabaia :—small beer.

sabbatarius :—a Jew.

sabbatis dies :—Saturday.

sabbatum : — sometimes means peace.

sabelinus :—(adj.) of sable fur.

sabellum, sabelum : — a sable (*mustela zibellina*).

saber :—(adj.) rough ; (subst.) gravel.

sablinus. See *sabelinus.*

sablona :—sand.

sablonare :—to strew with sand.

sabracia :—sabras, a mixture used in dressing parchment.

sabulonarium :—a gravel pit ; liberty to dig gravel, and money paid for the same.

saca :—sac, a lord's right of holding a court for pleas of trespass among his tenants.

saccare :—to pack.

saccha. See *saca.*

saccinus :—wearing sackcloth ; a monk.

sacculus :—a satchel ; a hood.

saccus :—a sack ; a cloak.

sacellarius :—a keeper of a purse.

sacer :—a female saker falcon (*falco sacer*), the male being called a sakerett ; a cannon, of various sizes.

sacramentalis :—a compurgator.

sacrarium :—a small lavatory near the altar in a church.

sacrifugus :—some trade.

sacrista :—a sacristan ; a sexton.

sacristaria, sacristia :—a sacristy or sextry.

sæcularis :—not belonging to a monastic order.

saenna :—a seine net ; a fishery.

saga :—say, fine serge.

sagemannus. See *sagibaro.*

sagena. See *saenna.*

sagibaro :—an elder, a judge.

sagimen : —fat, lard.

saginarius. See *sagmarius.*

sagitta :—an arrow ; the shaft of a cart ; a small swift ship.

sagittamen :—a stock of arrows.

sagittaria :—a small swift ship.

sagittarius :—a bowman ; a fletcher ; a shafter, *i.e.*, the horse next the cart in a team.

sagma :—a soam. See *summa.*

sagmarius :—a packhorse.

sagmen :—fat, lard.

sagum :—say, fine serge.

saio :—a tipstaff.

saisio :—season.

saisire, &c. See *seisire.*

saisona :—season.

sala : —a hall.

salare :—to salt.

salaria. See *salarium.*

salariare :—to ebb.

salarium :—a saltcellar ; pay, salary.

salcia :—a sausage.

salina : —a salt pit ; a tax on salt.

salinare :—to salt.

salinarius :—a salter.

salire :—to salt.

salitus :—salted.

salix :—active.

salma :—a seam of corn, 8 bushels.

salsa :—a salt marsh ; seasalt ; sauce.

salsaria, salseria :—a salt pit ; the saucery, an office in the royal household.

salsarium :—a saltcellar ; a saucer ; a measure of dry goods.

salsarius :—the officer in charge of the saucery, " le sauser."

salsatio, salsatum :—salting.

salsea :—sauce.

salsinia, salsutia :—a sausage.

saltatorium :—a deer leap, a leapyeat ; a stirrup ; a saltire.

alteria :—a salt house ; a saltery.

salterium :—used for *psalterium*.

saltorium, salturum. See *saltatorium*.

salutia, salutium :—a salute, a French gold coin of the 15th century, with the Annunciation or Salutation on the obverse, weight 60 grains Troy, coined also by Henry V. and Henry VI.

salvagardia :—safeguard, safe keeping.

salvagina :—deer ; venison.

salvagium :—salvage.

salvagius :—wild, savage.

salvistrum :—saltpetre.

salvus conductus :—a safe conduct.

samba :—a cittern.

samictum, samitum : — samite, rich silk cloth, often woven with silver or gold.

samo :—a salmon (*salmo salar*).

sanctimonialis :—a nun.

sanctuarium : — a sanctuary ; consecrated ground.

sandax : —madder (*sandix*).

sandalium :—cendal or sendal.

sanguinarius : —a bloodhound.

sanna :—derision.

saponarius : — a soap maker.

sappus :—sap ; moisture.

sarabaitæ :—men calling themselves monks, who belong to no rule.

sarabarda :—a pilgrim's cloak, O.E., slaveyne ; coarse cloth.

sarclare :—to weed, to hoe.

sarclo :—a hoe.

sarculare. See *sarclare*.

sarculatura :—a day's work at weeding.

sargens. See *serviens*.

sargia :—serge ; a mat.

sargire :—to sift.

sarkellus :—an engine for catching fish.

sarpeleria :—packing wool.

sarpilarium :—coarse cloth ; a cloak of such material.

sarplare :—a sarpler of wool, half a sack ; in France, larger than a sack.

sarplerium. See *sarpilarium ; sarplare*.

sarracum :—a tumbrel, a dung cart.

sarrator :—a sawyer.

sartare :—to clear ground of wood, &c. See *assartare*.

sartatectum :—thatch.

sartor :—a tailor.

sartorium :—a tailor's shop ; a room in a monastery where the clothes were made.

sartrinum. See *sartorium.*

sartum :—woodland brought into cultivation. See *assartum.*

satiare :—to impound.

saticulum :—a seedlip.

satifiare :—to ratify.

satitolum :—a seedlip.

satorium :—a seedlip, or basket used in sowing.

satrinum :—a bakehouse.

saugma, sauma :—a soam. See *summa.*

saurus :—a hawk until her first moult.

sausaria :—a saucer.

savagina. See *salvagina.*

savina :—a measure. In some cases perhaps an error for *saugma.*

saxifragium :—a stone quarry.

saysire, &c. See *seisire, &c.*

sayum :—serge ; silk (?).

scabinus :—the wardens of the town of Lynne were so called. (Fr. *échevin.*)

scaccarium :—a chessboard ; the Exchequer.

scacci :—chessmen.

scaccificare :—to play chess.

scachia :—the body of a tally.

scafila :—a boat.

scala :—a goblet ; a scale for weighing.

scalarium :—a staircase.

scaldria :—a scalding house.

scalera, scaleria, scalerna :—a stile (?).

scalinga :—a slate quarry.

scambium, scambum. See *escambia.*

scamella :—a butcher's block or stall.

scamellum :—a bench or stool (*scabellum*).

scamnarium :—a banker, a carpet or cloth to cover a bench.

scandalum :—prejudicial report ; scandal.

scangium. See *escambia.*

scansile :—a stirrup.

scansillum :—a stile.

scantilio :—a piece ; a sample.

scapha :—a measure of corn.

scaphalda :—a scaffold.

scapilus :—a measure of corn.

scapulare :—a scapular, a garment worn by Benedictines when at work, instead of the cowl ; a vestment made of two woollen bands, one down the breast, the other down the back.

scapulare :—to beat.

scara :—underwood ; a troop.

scareta :—a vine prop.

scaria :—a troop of soldiers.

scarioballum :—the cog of a mill.

scarlateus, scarlatus, scarletus :—scarlet.

scarra :—a share.

scarta :—a measure of corn, in use in Bordeaux, equal to an English quarter.

scatarigo :—a spring of water.

scatera :—a creek.

scavagium :—scavage or schewage, toll exacted from merchants for goods exposed for sale, or paid when imported goods are shown at the Custom-house.

scavaldus :—a collector of scavage.

scawanga. See *scavagium.*

sceithmannus :—a pirate.

scelda. See *selda.*

scenerium :—a courtyard (?).

sceppa :—a skep. See *esceppa.*

sceurum :—a granary; a repository.

schaffa :—a sheaf.

schavaldus. See *scavaldus.*

schaveldarius :—a moss trooper.

schela :—a bell; a strap.

schilla :—a small bell; a dish.

schillingus :—a shilling.

schira :—a shire; a shire court; payment for exemption from attending thereat.

schirmannus :—the ruler of a shire; a sheriff.

schopa :—a shop.

scilicet :—to wit.

scindallum :—cendal.

scindifaber :—a bladesmith.

scinditorium :—trencher bread.

scindula :—shingle for roofing; lath; a blade.

scindularius :—a bladesmith.

sciper, sciprus :—a skipper, a captain of a ship.

scira. See *schira.*

scisellum :—a chisel.

scisimus :—a fur, gris.

scissor :—a tailor.

scissorium :—a trencher.

scitus :—site. For *situs.*

sclauma :—a cloak.

sclavus :—a slave.

sclopeta :—a gun.

sclopetarius :—a musketeer.

sclopetum :—a gun; an arquebus.

sclusa :—a dam; a sluice.

scochia :—a scutcheon.

scolastizare :—to study.

sconcha, sconsa :—a sconce.

scopellus :—a knife; a chisel; a lancet; used for *scapilus.*

scopeta :—a gun.

scoppa :—a shop.

scorcium :—bark.

scoria :—dross; a score.

scorium :—a mat.

scortum :—escort.

scota :—scot; tax.

scotagium. See *scutagium.*

scotalla, scotallum :—a contribution for liquor for forest officers; a feast provided by contribution.

scoticare :—to naturalise a man in Scotland.

scotta. See *scota.*

scottare :—to pay scot.

scottum. See *scota.*

scribania :—an office in Guienne, registry.

scrinea, scrineum :—a screen.

scrinialis, scriniarius :—a scrivener.

scrinium :—a shrine.

scriptorium :—a writing room.

scrivabile paperum :—writing paper.

scrobula :—a robe worn by female pilgrims.

scrofa :—a sow ; a machine for digging at the base of the walls of a fortress.

scrotula :—a scroll.

scrutator : — an examiner ; a watchman.

scrutinium :—search ; examination.

scrutlanda :—land assigned for providing clothes.

scucheo :—an escutcheon.

scultetus :—a governor, "schout."

scura :—a stable.

scurare :—to scour.

scurellus :—a squirrel.

scurgia :—a whip (?).

scuria :—a stable.

scurio :—a stableman.

scutagium :—a tax paid in lieu of military service by those who held lands by knight-service.

scutarius :—an esquire ; a shield maker.

scutella :—a dish ; a scuttle ; a basket ; a coin (?).

scutellarium :—a scullery.

scutellarius :—a scullion; a monk or other person in charge of crockery and other table things ; a dealer in such ware.

scutifer, scutiger :—an esquire.

scutillarius. See *scutellarius.*

scutra :—a metal chafing dish.

scutularius. See *scutellarius.*

scutulatus :—dapple grey.

scutum : — a shield ; the coin called a crown; a coat-of-arms.

scyra. See *schira.*

scyremotum : — a shiremote, a meeting of the qualified men of a shire.

scytheaticum molendinum : — "a blade mylle."

seasina :—seisin.

seca :—a saw ; perhaps also hair cut from the tails of oxen.

secerniculum :—a portcullis.

seckillo :—thorns, brambles (?).

secretarium :—a strong room in a convent for keeping relics, plate, &c. ; a sacristy.

secretarius :—a secretary ; a sacristan, a sexton.

secta :—suit, in all senses.

sectare :—to sue.

sectarius :—a suitor.

sectator : — an executioner ; a suitor.

secundarius : — a secondary, second clerk of the sheriff.

secuntur :—sometimes used for *sequuntur.*

securantia :—assurance.

securare :—to warrant ; to make secure.

securatio :—surety ; security.

securiare. See *securare.*

sedes :—used for *cædes.*

sedua :—used for *cædua.*

sedula :—a schedule.

seforniculum :—a portcullis.

segutius canis :—a sleuth hound.

seignior :—senior ; a lord.

seignoragium :—lordship.

seillo :—a strip of land ; a furrow. See *selio.*

seisiare. See *seisinare.*

seisina :—seisin, possession.

seisinare :— to put in possession.

seisire :— to take possession ; to put in possession.

seisona :—season.

selda :—a shop ; a stall ; a shed ; a willow wood ; a salt pit.

selio :—a butt of land, an uncertain quantity; a strip in the open field.

sellarius :—a saddler.

semella :—a shoesole.

semiquarta :—a pint.

semispata, semispathum :—a small sword.

semitorium : — often used for *cæmeterium.*

semitorius :—a seedlip (basket).

semotim :—separately.

sempectæ :—senior monks, of fifty years' standing, in the Benedictine order.

semus :—imperfect ; mutilated.

senagium :—money paid for synodals.

sendellium. See *cendalum.*

senescalcia, senescaldia :— stewardship.

senescaldus :—a steward.

senescallia :—stewardship.

senescallus :—a steward.

senescaria :—stewardship.

seneucia :—widowhood.

senevectorium :—a wheelbarrow, a mud cart (*cenivectorium*).

senglarius :—a wild boar.

sententiare :—to sentence, to condemn.

sentinarum domus :—" houses of office."

seolda :—a shop, a stall.

seosinabilis :—seasonable.

sepa. See *cepa.*

separalis, seperarius, separius :— several.

seperalitas :—severalty.

sephalanaxia :—chief requirements ; commands.

seplassarius :—a merchant ; a grocer.

septimana :—a week.

septimanarius :—taking weekly turns of duty (*hebdomadarius*).

septipliciter :—sevenfold.

septor :—a hedger.

sepultura :—burial fee.

sepum :—tallow.

sequela :—result ; suit ; retinue ; issue of a *nativus*, or bondman.

sequentia :—a sequence, a hymn sung after the gradual and before the gospel.

sequestrare :—to sequester ; to renounce.

sequestrum :—sequestration.

seratura :—a bolt or lock ; a locksmith's trade.

serchia :—search ; hue and cry.

sergancius :—a serjeant.

serganteria :—serjeanty ; tenure by honourable service.

serganterium :—" *unum sergante-rium, s. tres solidos per annum.*" (Fine, Suffolk, Ric. I., No. 11.)

sergenteria. See *serjanteria.*

seriere :—to settle.

serifaber :—a locksmith.

seriolius : —in order.

serjanteria :—the fee or benefice of a *serviens;* the office of apparitor.

serjantia, serjeantia :—serjeanty.

serjantius :—a serjeant.

sermonium :—an interlude or pageant.

serpigo :—crawling.

serplera :—a sarpler of wool, half a sack.

serrare :—to lock.

serrura :—a bolt, a lock.

serum : —evening.

servagium :—the obligation of providing workmen for the lord.

servatorium :—a stew; a chest.

servicia :—ale (*cervisia*).

serviens :—a servant; an infantry soldier; a sergeant.

serviens ad legem :—a serjeant at law.

servisia :—ale (*cervisia*).

servitium :—service, the duty owed by the tenant to his lord.

servorium. See *servatorium.*

servus :—a bondman; a servile tenant.

sesona, sesso :—season, esp. for sowing.

seuda. See *selda.*

seueare :—to drain.

seuera. See *sewera.*

severundæ :—eaves.

seweare :—to drain.

sewera :—a trench to preserve land from floods; a sewer.

sexhindeni :—men whose wergyld was 600*s.*

sexogonus :—with six corners or angles.

sextertium :—used for *sextarius.*

seylo. See *selio.*

seysire. See *seisire.*

shaffa :—a sheaf of arrows, fourteen or twenty-four.

shava alei :—a chive of garlic.

shelfa :—a bank where mussels are found.

shippare :—to ship.

shira :—a shire. See *schira.*

shopa :—a shop.

shotea :—a workman of some kind.

shouta :—a schuyt or scout, a Dutch fishing boat.

sibula :—an awl (*subula*).

sica :—a sike, a ditch, a furrow; a marsh.

sica :—a gisarme, according to Matthew Paris, I. 470.

sicera :—beer or cider.

sichetum : — a little stream of water; a piece of meadow.

siclus :—a coin worth a shilling; a shekel.

sigalis, sigalum :—rye.

sigillare :—to seal.

sigillarius : — the keeper of a seal; a chancellor.

sigillator pannarius :—an alnager of cloth.

sigillum :—a seal.

sigla :—a sail.

siglare :—to sail.

siglatura :—a day's sail.

signare :— often used for *significare;* to make the sign of the cross.

signetum :—a signet.

significare :—to signify.

signum :— the sign of the cross; a bell.

sika :—a sike (Yorks.).

sikettus. See *sichetum.*

sila :—a sill ; a ditch.

silarium :—the ceiler of a bed ; a canopy.

silentiarius :— a privy councillor; an usher ; a papal secretary.

silina :—a measure of corn.

silvicedium :—coppice wood, under 30 years' growth.

similari :—to assemble.

simina :—a chamber.

siminellus :—simnell bread, fine white bread ; a cake.

simonia : — simony, traffic in spiritual things.

sincatio :—digging (a well).

sincellus (σύγκελλος) : — sharing the same cell ; a coadjutor.

sincubare :—to cut short (*syncopare*).

sindicus :—an advocate.

sindula. See *scindula.*

singillatim :—one by one.

singnifacere. See *signifacere.*

singnificare : — used for *significare.*

singnum :—used for *signum.*

sinistrare :—to turn to the left; to walk on the left of.

sinimum :— cinnamon.

sinodogium :—an inn (*xenodochium*).

sira. See *schira.*

sirgia :—an instrument of torture.

sirographum. See *chirographum.*

sirotheca. See *chirotheca.*

sirurgicus :—a surgeon (*chirurgicus*).

sisara. See *sicera.*

sistarchia :—a bag or basket.

sitarius, sitator :—a summoner.

situare :—to be situate.

situs :—site.

skamberlengeria : — chamberlainship.

skarkalla :—an engine for catching fish.

skella, skelletta :—a small bell.

skerda :—a scar.

skermia :—swordplay, fencing.

skilla :—a small bell (*schilla*).

skippagium :—embarkation; passage money on board ship ; hire of a ship.

skirmia :—fencing.

skuvinagium, skyvinagium :—the revenue of a *scabinus;* some due at Calais harbour.

slippa :— a stirrup.

smakka : — a smack, a small ship.

smeltus, smyltus : — a smelt (*osmerus eperlanus*).

snacca, snecca :—a ship (*esnecca*).

soca :—the jurisdiction of a lord; the liberty of tenants excused from customary impositions.

socagium :—socage ; plough service, a tenure inferior to tenure by knight-service.

socca. See *soca.*

socenagium. See *socagium.*

socha. See *soca.*

sochemannus. See *socmannus.*

sochemanria :—tenure by socage.

socmannus :—a socman or socager, a tenant by socage, or tenant in ancient demesne ; a sokereve.

socnum. See *soca.*

soffrancia. See *sufferentia.*

soinus :—essoin.

soka. See *soca.*

sokerevus :—a sokereve, rent collector for the lord of a soke.

sokmannus. See *socmannus.*

sola :—a sole (*solea vulgaris*).

solagium :—a due paid for use of soil.

solanda :—a plough land. (A. S. *sulung.*)

solarium :—an upper story or room.

solda :—a piece of land. See also *selda.*

soldarius :—serving for pay ; a soldier.

soldata :—pay.

soldum :—pay.

soldus :—a shilling ; a sou.

solecizare : — to speak bad grammar.

solemne :—the mass.

solicitator :—a solicitor.

solidarius :—serving for pay ; a soldier.

solidata :—a shilling's worth ; pay.

solidatum :—property.

solidatus. See *solidata.*

solidus :—a shilling ; a sou.

solidos suos, ad :—at his expense ; in his pay.

solinum :—a meal for one person.

solinus :—a measure of land about 160 acres, a plough land (?).

solium :—an upper room ; a loft.

solinga. See *sullinga.*

solivagus girus :—the sun's orbit. In classical Latin, *solivagus* is derived from *solus,* and means wandering alone.

solta :—payment.

somarius :—a sumpter horse, a pack horse.

sometarius :—the officer in the king's household who attended to carriage.

sonare :—to snore.

sonium. See *essonium.*

sopa :—a shop (*shopa*).

sorceria :—sorcery, witchcraft.

sornecca :—some kind of ship.

sornus :—red.

sororius :—a brother-in-law ; a sister's son.

sors :—sort, kind ; principal.

sorus :—red. See *saurus, sourus.*

soscallus :—some kind of hound used for stag hunting.

sotillares, sotulares :—shoes.

sottus :—a fool, a sot.

sourellus :—a sorel, a buck of three years old.

sourus :—a sore, a four-year-old buck.

spada :—a sword.

spado :—a gelding.

sparro :—a spar, a stake.

sparrus :—a hobbyhawk (*falco subbuteo*).

spartha :—an axe.

sparverius :—a sparrow hawk (*accipiter fringillarius*).

spata :—a sword.

spatularia :—apparels round the neck and wrists of an alb.

specialitas :—a bond or deed.

speciarius :—a spicer; a druggist.

specieria :—spicery.

species :—spices.

specietarius. See *speciarius*.

spectacula :—spectacles.

speleum :—a cell.

spelta :—spelt (*triticum spelta*).

spengabulum :—a duty on mill wheels.

spera :—a sphere.

spervarius :—a sparrow-hawk.

spiciaria :—spicery.

spicurnancia :—the office of spigurnel.

spigurnellus :—the sealer of the king's writs.

spinacium :—a pinnace.

spindula, spinula :—a gold pin used with the archiepiscopal pall.

spira bissi :—a hatband.

spirasmus :—a tag.

spiritualia :—the profits which a bishop or other spiritual person receives as an ecclesiastic, not as a lord.

spiritualitas :—the clergy.

spirula :—a ferrule ; a chape ; a gimlet.

spolia :—a shuttle ; a spool.

sponda :—a bier ; a pier ; a partition.

springaldus :—a springald, a kind of cannon.

sprottus :—a sprat (*clupea sprattus*).

spurarium aureum :—a gold coin called a spur royal, or spurrial, value 15*s.* in the reign of James I.

spurgellum :—a box or trunk.

squarrare :—to square.

squelenarius :—a keeper of baskets.

squillaria :—a scullery.

squillarius :—a scullion.

squinancia :—quinsy.

squinatus :—a sequin or zechin, a Venetian gold coin.

squirellum :—a squirrel.

stabellum :—a stool.

stabilamentum, stabilia, stabilitio :—a buckstall, or deer-hay, a stand for shooting deer.

stablia :—a stall.

stabula :—a stable.

stabularius :—an ostler.

stabulatum. See *stabilamentum*.

stabulum :—a stable.

staca :—a stake ; a measure of corn.

stachia :—a stage for catching fish.

stacnaria. See *stannaria.*

stadium :—a furlong; a floor, a story.

stafa :—a stirrup.

staffeta. See *stoffeta.*

stagga :—a small quantity of hay or straw.

staggus :—a swan, half grown (?).

stagia :—a stage; a story of a house.

stagiarius :—a canon in residence.

stagium :—a story of a house.

stagmen :—tin.

stagnaria :—a tin mine.

stagnator :—a tin miner.

stagnum :—a pond; tin.

staka. See *staca.*

stalaria :—a fixed engine for catching fish.

stalinga :—same as *stalaria* (?).

stalla :—a stall.

stallagium :—stallage, the right of erecting a stall and payment for it.

stallangiarius, stallangiator :—a seller of goods at a stall.

stallare :—to put off; to give respite.

stallarius :—a groom; master of the horse; a stallkeeper in a market.

stallatio :—installation.

stallum :—a stall.

stalo :—a stallion.

stamen, stagmen :—tin.

stamen :—linsey woolsey cloth. O. E. *stamine.*

stamina, staminea, stamineum :— the same; a garment made of such cloth.

stancilla :—stirrups (?).

stancum :—a pond, a tank.

standardum :—a banner; legal weight and measure.

stangneus, stanneus :—of tin.

stannaria :—a tin mine.

stannarius :—a pewterer; a tin-man.

stannator :—a tin miner.

stannatus :—dyed.

stannum :—tin.

stanso :—a stanchion (?).

stantiva fenestra :—a window reaching to the floor (?).

stapellum :—a staple, a bolt.

stapha :—a stirrup.

stapula, stapulum :—a market or staple.

stara :—8 bushels, or 2 gallons.

starrum :—a Jew's deed or bond.

stationarius :—a canon in residence.

statutum :—a statute.

stauramentum :—the stock of a farm.

staurus :—stock; store.

stella :—a kiddle, a weir for fishing; a rowell, a trendle, a hoop with candles thereon.

stellata camera :—the Star Chamber.

sterilensium solidi :—shillings sterling.

sterlingus :—sterling; an English penny; money.

stermannus :—a steersman.

sternium :—a bedstead.

steynare :—to stain.

stibiare :—to starch.

stica :—a brass Saxon coin, worth half a farthing; a stick of eels, *i.e.*, 25.

stiga :—a pricket for a candle.

stika. See *stica.*

stillatorium :—a distillery.

stina :—the handle of a plough.

stinarius :—a ploughman.

stingus :—a shrimp.

stipa :—a metal bar, as on a belt.

stipes :—a tally.

stipula :—stubble.

stiremannus :—a steersman.

stivale, stivallum, stivella :—a boot.

stochia. See *stachia.*

stockarius :—a stockfishmonger.

stoffare :—to stuff.

stoffeta :—stubble.

stoffura :—equipment; provisions; material; stuff.

stola :—a stole.

stolium :—a fleet or army.

stonda :—staddles.

stophare :—to store; to stuff.

stoppa :—tow; a stoup.

storea :—straw.

storium. See *stolium.*

stotarius :—a keeper of horses or oxen.

stottus :—a horse or an ox.

stowagium :—stowage.

straciatus :—striped.

stracus :—a strake; a tire.

strada :—a stripe.

stragulare :—to strangle; to embroider of divers colours.

stragulati fratres :—Carmelite Friars, whose clothing was parti-coloured when in Palestine.

stragulator :—an embroiderer.

stragulus :—variegated.

straiatus :—strayed.

stramere :—to strew.

straminare :—to strew with straw.

stramura :—straw for the floor.

strandagium :—strandage, payment for leave to beach a boat.

stranglinum :—squirrel fur.

strangulum :—ray, a striped cloth.

stranlingum :—squirrel fur.

strata :—a street, a high road.

stratilectilia :—bedding.

strator :—a groom.

strenare :—to send a New Year's gift.

strepa :—a stirrup.

strepare :—to strip.

strepitus :—destruction; estrepement.

streppum. See *strepitus.*

striaballum :—a cog of a wheel.

striatus :—engrailed. See *engrallatus.*

stricatus :—striped.

stricum :—a strike, a stick used for levelling corn in the measure; the eighth of a quarter.

strigil :—a currycomb.

strikum. See *stricum.*

stroda :—sands.

strofa :—a stirrup.

strublus :—a staff ; a goad.

structus :—a suit (of clothes).

stuba :—a stove ; a stew.

stubula :—stubble.

studium :—a university ; a study (room).

studium generale :—a university.

stufa, stuffa ;—a stove ; a stew ; a hot bath.

stuffare :—to stuff; to give a hot bath to.

stuffura. See *stoffura.*

stupula :—stubble.

sturemanus. See *stiremannus.*

sturgio :—a sturgeon (*acipenser sturio*).

suanimotum : — a swainmote, a forest court.

suaria :—a horsecloth (*sudaria*).

suatim :—among themselves ; by himself. The word occurs in classical Latin, but derived from *sus* not *suus.*

subalternus :—subordinate.

subarrare :—to plough up ; to espouse ; to give a pledge, or earnest ; sometimes to take a pledge.

subboscus :—underwood.

subdiaconus :—a subdeacon.

subductura :—lining or trimming.

subescaetor :—an under-escheator.

subfalcum :—aftermath (?), or a field after mowing or reaping.

subharrare :—to plough up.

subjugalis :—a beast of burden.

sublarvare :—to act in a mask.

sublegerius :—guilty of incest. (A. S. *sibleger.*)

subligacula : — breeches, stockings.

subligar :—a garter, in classical Latin a waist band.

submonere :—to summon.

submonitio :—summons.

submonitor :—a summoner.

subnervare :—to hamstring ; to hough.

subpedium :—a treadle.

subplacitare :—to cite before a court of law.

subprior :—an officer of a convent next in authority to the prior.

subprisia :—surprise.

subregulus :—a baron, a lord.

subrubeus :—reddish.

subsannatio :—derision.

subsidium :—an aid, a subsidy.

subsisternium :—a litter.

subtiliare :—to diminish ; to act craftily.

subucula :—a bodkin. (In classical Latin *subucula* is a shirt, and *subula* an awl.)

suburbanus :—a countryman, a rustic.

subvassor :—an esquire, a tenant of a knight.

succellerarius:—an undercellarer.

succentor : — assistant to the *armarius* in a monastery.

succidia :—a flitch of bacon.

succidium :—sowse, pickle.

succurrum candidum : — sugar candy.

succursarius:—a courser (horse).

succursus :—help.

suchia :—a stump.

sucura :—sugar.

suera. See *sewera.*

suetta, suettum :—suit.

suffalum. See *subfalcum.*

sufferentia:—a grant; sufferance; a suspension of arms, armistice.

sufflum :—a whistle.

suffraganeus :—a suffragan or subsidiary bishop, who assists the bishop of a diocese.

suffrago :—a pastern.

suffurrare :—to trim with fur.

suissimus :—very own.

suitor :—a follower ; a suitor.

suliva. See *sulliva.*

sullinga, sullingata :— a ploughland (A. S. *sulung*), used as equivalent to hide or carucate.

sulliva :—a beam, a sill.

sullo :—a furrow.

suma. See *summa.*

sumelarius :—a butler ; a scullion.

sumeracius, sumericius equus :— a packhorse.

sumetarius. See *summetarius.*

summa :—a load ; a soam or seam, 6 or 8 bushels; an abstract.

summa mensa :—high table.

summagiare :—to carry loads.

summagiatio :—carrying loads.

summagium :—a horse-load, a soam ; obligation to supply pack-horses; toll for horses.

summarius :—a pack-horse, a sumpter horse.

summata :—a load.

summetarius :—a man in charge of pack-horses.

summista : — a compiler of a *summa* or abstract.

summitas :—the top of a hill.

summonere :—to summon.

summonitio :—summons.

summonitor :—a summoner.

summus :—a soam. See *summa.*

suparum :—a linen sleeve; a shirt.

superædificium:—an upper building.

superaltare :—a portable altar ; the shelf at the back of an altar.

superannatus:—more than a year old.

superaudire :—to overhear.

superculum :—a coverlet.

superdemanda :—excess of claim.

superdicere :—to accuse.

superexceptus :—despised.

superfactum:—profit.

superfidere :—to trust too much.

superfossorium :—a drawbridge.

superfrontale :—a superfrontal, a cloth hanging above a frontal.

supergabulum :—overgavel.

superhidagium : — superhidage, the extra rate per acre imposed upon a hide of small extent.

superlabium :—the upper lip.

superonerare :—to overload.

superpellicium :—a surplice.

superplus, superplusagium : — a surplus ; the amount which a sheriff or other officer has spent beyond his receipts.

superprisia :—seizure by surprise.

superseminatus : — measled (of pork).

supersisa :--sursise, penalty for neglect, esp. for not paying castle-ward at Dover.

supertenere :—to hold over ; to neglect.

supertunica :—a garment worn over a tunic.

supervidere ;—to survey, to examine.

supervincere :—to conquer.

supervisor :—a surveyor ; an overseer.

supervisus :—survey.

supparum. See *suparum.*

suppeditare :—to trample on.

suppositio :—a support ; a prop ; a hypothesis.

supprior. See *subprior.*

suppriserunt :—they surprised.

supprisia :—used for *superprisia.*

supra :—before, in a reference in a book. This meaning and the corresponding meaning of *infra* and *inferius* were originally used for a roll.

supravisor :—an overseer.

sura :—a coarse loaf.

surigicus :—a surgeon (*chirurgicus*).

surplusagium. See *superplus.*

surrejunctio :—a surrejoinder.

surrogatus :—a surrogate, one appointed in the room of another.

sursa :—a spring, a fountain.

sursumreddere :—to surrender.

sursumredditio :—a surrender.

susanus :—worn out.

susceptor :—an undertaker.

suspeditare :—to trample on.

suspendicula :—hangings.

suspendium :—hanging.

suua :—a soam. See *summa.*

swagium :—aid.

swainmotus, swanemotus : — a swainmote, a forest court.

swolinga, swulinga. See *sullinga.*

sya :—a load ; a seam. See *summa.*

synaxis :—an assembly, a congregation ; church service or office.

syndicus :—an advocate ; a burgess.

syngraphus :—a deed signed by all the parties.

synodale : — payment by the clergy to the bishop or archdeacon at a visitation.

synodus :—a meeting of ecclesiastical persons.

syra. See *schira.*

syrografum :—a chirograph.

syua. See *summa.*

T.

tabacum :—tobacco.

tabardarius : — a tabarder or tabiter, a scholar at Queen's College, Oxford.

tabardum :—a tabard, a short tunic worn by heralds, priests, and others.

tabellarium :— a board for the game of tables.

tabellatum :—a boarded partition.

tabellio :—a notary.

tabellionatus : — the office of notary.

taberna :—a tavern ; a brewery.

tabernaculum :—a tabernacle or pyx for reserving the sacrament.

tabernarius :—a tavernkeeper.

tabula :—a board ; the cover of a book.

tabulamentum :— a tablement, a projecting course of stone to hold a roof.

tabularium :—a chess-board, or board for the game of tables.

tabulatus :—boarded.

tabuletta :—a tablet.

taburcinum, taburcium :—a drum.

tacella :—a tassel.

tachiamentum :—attachment.

tactare :—to confirm.

tailla :—brushwood, a copse ; a tally.

taillagium. See *tallagium.*

taillia :—a tally.

tailliare. See *talliare.*

tainus. See *thainus.*

talare :—to cut ; to devastate.

talea :—a tally.

taleator :—a teller.

talentum :—sometimes a pound. See *marabotinus.*

tallagium :—tallage, tax.

tallator. See *talliator.*

tallea, tallia :—a tally ; a tallage ; a stated allowance of provisions, commons ; tail (legal).

talliare :—to cut ; to limit ; to tax.

talliator :—a teller ; a cutter of tallies ; a tailor.

talliatum feodum :—feetail.

talliatura :—talwood ; firewood.

talliatus :—in tail.

tallium :—entail ; retail.

talmus :— an eye (*ophthalmus*).

tamenetallum. See *tenemenetallum.*

tanaliter :—mortally.

tanator :—a tanner.

tancardus :— a tankard.

tannare :—to tan leather.

tannarius, tannator :—a tanner.

tanneria :—a tannery.

tannerius :—a tanner.

tannum, tanum :—oakbark for tanning.

tanquam :—in the Universities, "a person of worth and learning, fit company for the fellows of colleges."

tapatium :—tapestry work.

tapeta, tapetium :—a carpet, in the middle ages used for covering tables, benches, or beds, not the floor.

tapheta :—taffety, a thin silk.

tapiceria :—tapestry.

tapicerius :—a tapestry maker.

tapinagium :—concealment.

tapisterium : — the tester of a bedstead.

tappa :—a tap.

taragium :—the foot of or a stand for a piece of plate.

taratantarizare :—to boult flour.

tarcha :—a targe ; a target.

tarenus :—a Sicilian gold coin, 20 gr.

targa :—a small shield, a target.

targia :—a ship of burden ; a target.

targus. See *targa.*

tarida :—a ship of burden.

tarifa :—a list of prices; customs.

tarkosia :—a quiver.

tarta :—a tart, pastry.

tartenus pannus :—cloth of tars, perhaps China silk crape.

tasca, taschia :—a task ; a tax.

tassare :—to put hay into cocks.

tassellus :—a fringe ; a tassel ; a hood.

tassus, tassum :—a rick.

tastare :—to try ; to taste.

tastum :—taste ; choice.

taxa :—a tax ; a task.

taxare :—to name ; to describe ; to heap up ; to appraise ; to tax.

taxatio :—valuation, assessment.

taxator :—an assessor ; a tax collector.

taxus :—a badger.

techa :—a chest (*theca*).

techellatus :—pied ; spotted.

tector :—a thatcher, not as in classical Latin, a plaisterer.

tedinga :—a tithing.

tegnio :—a thane.

tegnum :—apparently used for τέχνη, art, fraud.

tegula :—a tile ; a slate ; a brick.

tegularius, tegulator :—a tiler, a bricklayer.

teignus :—a thane.

tela :—a tile.

telaria :—the tiller or stock of a *balista*, made of wood.

telarius :—a weaver.

teldum :—a tent.

telligraphia :—written evidence.

telonium :—toll.

telum :—a tile.

temantale :—a tax of 2*s.* on every plough-land. See *tenemenetallum.*

templarius :—a knight of the Temple.

temporalia :—temporalities, the revenues, &c., held by a bishop as a baron.

temptatio :—trial ; proof.

tena :—a coif; a cap ; the pendants of a mitre.

tenaculum :—a hook or clasp.

tenalia :—pincers.

tenandria :—a vill, a town.

tenatura :—a tenancy, a holding.

tencellare :—to cover with metal.

tenda :—a trace.

tendicula :—a long net or tunnel for catching birds, esp. partridges.

tenditor :—a man who attends to hawks.

tenella :—tongs ; pincers.

tenellus :—a banqueting-hall.

tenematallum. See *tenemenetallum.*

tenemenetallum :—tenmentale, a tithing; frithburgh, frankpledge.

tenementum :—a holding, a tenement.

tenenciarius :—a tenant.

tenendria :—a vill, a town.

tenens :—a tenant.

tenentia :—tenancy, tenure.

teniludus :—tennis.

tenisia :—tennis.

tennus :—a thane.

tenor :—purport ; a copy.

tenorcula :—the stock of a cross-bow.

tenorculus :—a notch, a nock.

tensabilis : — defended ; prohibited.

tensamentum :—a tax.

tensare :—to protect, to defend; to exact, to extort.

tensaria, tenseria :—tax ; tallage; exaction.

tensum :—toll.

tenta :—a tent for a wound.

tentum :—a tent.

tenuale :—a barbican.

tenura :—tenure ; a tenant's service.

teoloneum :—toll.

terbichetum :—a tumbrel, a cucking-stool. See *trebuchettum.*

tercelettum :—a young tiercel.

tercellus, tercillus :—a tiercel, a male hawk.

tercionarius :—a farmer with a third share (?).

tereus :—earthen.

terga :—a targe, a target.

tergotenus :—on the back, endorsed.

terminarius :—a termor, one who holds lands for a term.

terminatus :—a boundary.

terminus :—a term.

termisium. See *tremagium.*

terragium :—land tax; groundwork.

terrare :—to fortify with earth ; to block up ; to cover.

terrarium :—a terrier, a landroll.

terrarius :—a landholder ; a terrier dog.

terratus :—banked up.

terricidium :—fallen branches.

tersorium :—a duster, a towel ; a broom.

tesso :—a badger (*meles taxus*).

testa :—a head.

testamentalis :—devisable by will.

testamentum :—a will; testimony.

testator :— the maker of a will.

testerium :—a tester, a flat canopy over the end of a bed, a tomb, &c.

testicare :—to testify.

tethinga :—a tithing.

tetrizare :—to tether.

texera :—the sign of the Chequers.

textus :—a copy of the gospels ; a register ; type.

teysa, teysia :—a fathom.

thainus :—a thane.

thalamus :—a chamber, a room, as compared with *aula*.

thalassiarcha :—an admiral.

thanagium :—land belonging to the king of which the governor was a thane.

thaxa :—a tax ; a task.

thaynus :—a thane.

thedinga : —a tithing.

theloneum, thelonium :—toll.

thelonmannus :—a toll-collector.

themicium :—a hedgerow.

themmagium : —a duty paid by inferior tenants to be free from the lord's jurisdiction.

themum :—theam, the right of having and judging one's bondmen and their issue, or of following them to other lord's lands ; vouching to warranty, part of the legal process for recovering stolen property among the Anglo-Saxons.

thenecium :—a hedgerow.

theodum : —error for *feodum* (?).

theoloneum, theolonium :—toll.

Theophania : —the Epiphany.

thesare :—to worry.

thesauraria, thesaurarium : — a treasury.

thesaurarius :—a treasurer.

thesauria :—a treasury.

thesaurizarius :—a treasurer.

thesaurum :—a treasury.

thethinga :—a tithing.

thimagium. See *themmagium.*

thingus :—a thane.

thollia :—thowlpins.

tholneum, tholonium :—toll.

tholta :—extortion.

Thomipeta :—a Canterbury pilgrim.

thorale. See *torale.*

thorallia :—a mattress.

thorallum. See *torale.*

thrava, thravus. See *trava.*

threngus. See *drengus.*

thrimsa :—a drachm ; an Anglo-Saxon coin worth three pence.

thumelum :—a thumb.

thurem dexteram :—some part of the body (error for *sura*, shin (?)).

thuribulum :—a censer.

thymallus :—a smelt (*salmo eperlanus*) ; a grayling (*salmo thymallus*).

tia :—an aunt on the mother's side.

tibialia :—stockings.

tibisare :—to address in the singular.

ticendulum :—a wick of a lamp.

tilerium :—a trigger (?); a tiller (?).

tillagium :—tillage.

timbrellus :—a small assembly (Skene, *De verborum significatione*). See *tumbrellum*.

timbria : — a timber of fur, a bundle of 40.

timorare :—to frighten.

timoratus : —God-fearing.

tina :—a cask, a tun, a tub.

tinata :—a cask full.

tinctor :—an oxherd, perhaps an error for *tractor*.

tinellus :—a cowlstaff.

tinettum :—brushwood for repairing hedges.

tinneum :—tin.

tiparium. See *typarium.*

tipetum :—a tippet, a scarf, generally black, and furred.

tiplare :—to tipple.

tippulator :—a tippler.

tipularia domus :—an alehouse.

tipus (τῦφος) :—pride.

tira :—a tier, used of the lines of skins in a fur cloak.

tiriaca :—treacle (*theriaca*).

tiro :—a young man intending to become a knight; a young knight, a champion.

tirocinare :—to be a *tiro*; to serve in war.

tirocinium :—knighthood.

tissutum :—tissue.

tithinga :—a tithing.

titulare :—to make a heading or title.

titulus :—a title.

toacula, toale, toalle :—a towel.

todda :—a tod of wool, 28lbs.; a certain quantity of grass.

toftmannus : — the holder of a toft.

tofta, toftum :—a toft; a place where a house formerly stood.

togella :—a towel.

tolcestrum :—tolsester, payment to the lord of the manor for liberty to brew and sell ale.

tolia :—toll.

tollagium :—forcible exaction of illegal toll.

tolletum :—toll.

tollum :—toll.

tolnetum :—toll.

tolnetum de pixide :—toll pixy, a customary payment by artisans and dealers in Gower to the lord.

tolonarius :—a tollkeeper.

tolonium :—toll.

tolta :—wrong, extortion.

tolta placiti : — a writ removing a cause in a Court Baron into the County Court; the removal of a cause from temporal jurisdiction.

tolumen :—a tumbrel.

tonare :—to intone.

tonellarius :—a cooper.

tonellum, tonellus :—a tun, a vat; a prison on Cornhill.

tonna :—a tun of wine.

tonnagium :—tonnage.

tonsor :—a shearman.

topare :—to top trees.

topettum :—a knob ; a knop.

tophta. See *tofta.*

torale :—bedding ; a mound ; a kiln.

torallum :—a mound.

torcare :—to clean.

torcha : — cob, straw and mud used for roofing.

torchea, torchetus, torchia : — a torch.

torchiare :—to plaister.

torchiator : — a plasterer, a dauber.

torcia :—a torch.

tormentum :—a catapult; a cannon ; a fowling piece.

tormentura :—torture.

tornare :—to turn.

tornator :—a turner.

tornatilis pons :—a swingbridge.

torneamentum :—a tournament.

torneare :—to tilt at a tournament.

torneator :—a tilter or jouster; one who attends a tournament.

tornus. See *turnum.*

torta :—extortion ; a cake.

tortellæ :—tourteaux (heraldic).

tortica, torticia :—a torch ; a winch, a windlass.

tortua : — a turtle (*chelone mydas* or *imbricata*).

tortum :—wrong ; injustice.

totsectus. See *cotsethus.*

tottum :—rent ; toll ; a day's work for rent.

toualus :—a towel.

towagium :—toll paid for towing.

traba :—a thrave. See *trava.*

trabaria :—a small boat, a "dug-out."

trabeatio : — the Incarnation, from *trabea*, a robe, not *trabs*, a beam.

trabeatura :—beams.

trabes :—a thrave, 12 or 24 sheaves.

tracea :—search ; pursuit ; a trail.

traceare :—to track.

traco :—a cavern.

tracta :—a horse's trace.

tractagium :—towing, hauling.

tractilis pons :—a drawbridge.

tractula, tractulus :—a little tract or treatise.

tractum, tractus : — a horse's trace ; a haul ; a drag-net.

tractus :—struck out.

trada :—a haven.

traditio :—treason.

traga, traha :—a sledge ; a dray.

trahicium :—a trace.

trainellum :—a shoehorn.

trama :—a path (*trames*).

tramaricia :—a boundary ; a landmark.

tramellum :—a trammel, a net used for catching birds.

tramerium :—a travers, the shed in a smithy where horses are shod.

tramesio. See *tremesium.*

tranetarius :—a tranter, a carrier.

transeptum :—a transept.

transeuntes :—passant (heraldic).

transfretare :—to cross a strait.

transgressio :—trespass.

transitus : — noon ; death ; a judge's *iter.*

transnavare :—to cross the sea.

transvadare :—to wade across.

trappa :—a trap ; a trapdoor.

trassa :—a dungeon ; a fetter.

trassans canis :—a sleuth-hound.

trassare :—to follow.

trava :—a thrave of corn, 24 or 12 sheaves.

travatura :—beams.

traversia : —a traverse.

traversum :—a ferry.

traxus :—a trace.

treacha :—treacle.

trebuchettum :—a catapult ; a trebuchet, for casting stones ; a cucking stool.

trebuculus : — a catapult.

trefa :—meat refused by Jews.

trega :—a truce.

treingum :—a riding.

tremagium :—the season for sowing summer corn ; spring ; spring corn.

tremellum :—a granary.

tremesium :—corn cut after three months' growth.

tremiscum. See *tremagium.*

tremulum :—a granary.

trencatum :—a ditch ; a trench.

trenchea, trencheia :—the right of cutting wood ; a trench.

trencheator :—a carver.

trenchura :—a slice.

trenga :—a dray ; a sledge.

trentale :—an office of 30 masses said for the dead.

treparium :—a trivet.

trepha. See *trefa.*

tresancia :—a passage; a cloister; part of the cloister reserved for reading.

trescentia :—rent or tax from land.

tresentia. See *tresancia.*

tressorium :—a tress of hair ; also some article of dress.

trestella, trestellus :—a trestle.

trestornare :—to turn aside.

trethinga. See *tridingum.*

treuga, treuia : — a truce ; tribute.

trialitas :—a bull of "trialyte," allowing a clerk to hold three benefices.

triallum :—trial.

trialogus :—a conversation between three persons ; the title of a book by John Wycliffe.

triare :—to try ; to select.

triatio :—trial.

triator :—a trier ; a witness.

tribrica :—braces.

tribuculus :—a catapult ; a trebuchet.

tribulagium :—tribulage, a custom payable to the Crown
on tin in Cornwall.

tricare :—to hinder ; to complain.

tricatura :—twisted work (used
of chain armour).

tricennale, tricennare :—a trental.

tricesima :—a trental, "month's
mind."

triculator :—a treasurer.

tridens :—a harrow.

tridingum, tridlingum :—a tri-
thing, or riding, the third
part of a shire.

triforiatus :—having a *triforium.*

triforium :—a thoroughfare ; a
gallery or arcade over the
arches of the nave of a
church.

trigeldum :—a triple fine.

trigintale :—a trental, a month's
mind.

trillabus :—a birdbolt.

trimagium. See *tremagium.*

trimestrium :—a quarter of a
year, three months.

trinoda necessitas :—the threefold
tax, for repairing bridges,
maintaining castles, and re-
pelling invasion.

triparium :—a three-legged stool ;
a trivet.

triplarius :—triple.

tripodium :—a length of three
feet.

triroda :—three rods or perches.

trisancia. See *tresancia.*

trisilis :—a three-legged stool.

trista :—a place where hounds
are posted during a deer
drive ; the service of placing
or holding them there. See
Manwood, Part I., p. 86.

tristega, tristegum :—a house of
three stories ; an engine
used in sieges, consisting
of a tower in three stories.

tristellum :—a trestle.

tristra. See *trista.*

tritennale :—a trental.

trithinga :—a riding, a third of a
county.

triturare :—to thresh.

Trium Regum dies : — Twelfth
day.

triumvir :—a constable of three
hundreds.

trivium :—the study of grammar,
logic, and rhetoric.

trochus :—a cluster, a band, esp.
of precious stones.

trocus :—a top.

trogga :—a trough ; a measure
of corn (*Welsh*).

trogulus :—a cowl.

troillium :—an oil or wine press.

trona, tronum : — the Tron, a
beam for weighing.

tronagium : — toll for weighing
wool and other goods.

tronare :—to weigh at the Tron.

tronator :—the officer who weighs
wool.

troparium, troperium :—a book containing *tropi,* verses sung at certain festivals before the Introit.

trua :—a sow.

trubechettum. See *trebuchettum.*

trubla :—a sieve.

trublagium. See *tribulagium.*

trublechettum. See *trebuchettum.*

trubuculus :—a catapult.

trubula :—a sieve.

trufare :—to deceive.

trufatorius :—trifling.

truffa :—trifles.

truga :—a measure of corn.

truia :—a sow.

truncagium :—a payment to Bamborough Castle by the townships near.

trunculum :—a bench.

truncus :—a money-box ; the pillory ; a candle end.

trunso :—a truncheon.

trusellum :—a bale.

trussa :—a truss.

trussare :—to truss.

trussellum :—a bale.

trussula, trussum :—a truss.

trutannicus :—worthless, false.

trutannus, trutanus :—truant, vagrant.

trutta, trutus :—a trout (*salmo fario* and *salmo trutta*).

tryinkus :—a net used in the Thames.

tuallium, tuellium :—a towel.

tuare, tuisare :—to address in the singular. (Fr. *tutoyer.*)

tuitorius :—seeking protection.

tumberalis pena : — the punishment of the tumbrel.

tumberellus : — some military engine.

tumbrellum :—a tumbrel, a cucking stool.

tumpilloralis pena :—the pillory.

tunellum :—a tun or ton.

tunicella, tuniculus : — a short tunic.

tunnagium :—tonnage.

turba :—turf.

turbagium :—the right of digging turf.

turbare :—to turf.

turbaria :—the right of digging turf ; a place where turf is dug.

turbarius :—kerne.

turbido :—a tempest.

turbo : — a turbot (*Rhombus maximus*).

turcasia :—a quiver.

turcoplerius, turcopoliarius : — a Turcopolier, an officer in the Order of the Knights of St. John of Jerusalem, originally the commander of the *Turcopuli,* light cavalry.

turella, turellus :—a turret.

turetti :—tirrets.

turgiolum :—a boss.

turkesius :—Turkish ; a turquoise.

turnarius :—a turner.

turnatus pons :—a swingbridge.

turneamentum :—a tournament.

turneare :—to joust, to hold a tournament.

turneicius pons :—a swingbridge.

turniamentum :—a tournament.

turniare :—to joust.

turnum, turnus : — a turn; the king's leet through a county; a winch, as on a crossbow.

turqueizare :—to favour the Turk.

turratus :—having towers.

turrella. See *turrellus.*

turrellare :—to build turrets.

turrellus :—a turret, a tourel, a small tower.

turtarius :—a baker of tourte, *i.e.,* coarse brown bread.

turtra :—trout (*salmo fario*).

turtus :—tourte bread.

tussimulus :—a door knocker.

tutibarum :—a tumbrel.

twigeldum :—a double fine.

tymbrium. See *timbria.*

tyna :—a tub; part of Gloucester town.

typarium :—a seal bearing the image of its owner.

tyro. See *tiro.*

U.

ulcus :—a hull.

uliare :—to remedy a default.

uligo :—a marsh.

ulmetum :—an elm grove.

ulna :—an ell.

ulnagium : — alnage, duty on cloth.

ulnator, ulniger : — an alnager, examiner of cloth and collector of alnage.

ulnus :—for *ulmus.*

ulphus :—hassock, coarse grass.

ultragium :—outrage.

umbra :—an umbrer or umber, part of a bacinett, which protected the face ; a grayling (*salmo thymallus*); precincts, outskirts.

umbraculum. See *umbra.*

umbraria, umbreria : — some office in Bordeaux, perhaps prefect of the *umbra* or suburb.

umpirator :—an umpire.

unare :—to bring together, to collect.

uncia :—an ounce; an inch ; a measure of land, perhaps 12 *modii.*

uncialiter :—in capital letters.

unciata. See *uncia.*

uncina sagitta :—"a swalowe tayle or a brode arrowe," *i.e.,* barbed.

unire :—to unite.

unitio :—union.

uplanda :—upland.

ura :—ore.

urigenator :—a furbisher (*eruginator*).

urla :—a border ; an orle.

ursarius :—a bearward ; a beardog.

usagium :—usage.

usia :—being.

ustilamentum :—a loom.

usuagium :—usage.

utensilium :—a loom.

uterennium :—a space of two years.

uthesium :—hue and cry.

uthlega, &c. See *utlaga, &c.*

uthundredum :—the outlying parts of a hundred.

utinatio :—regret.

utlaga :—an outlaw.

utlagare :—to outlaw.

utlagaria, utlagatio : —outlawry.

utlagius :—an outlaw.

utterare:—to distribute, to utter.

uxorare :—to give in marriage.

uxoratus :—married.

uxorium :—a fine for not marrying.

V.

racanus :—vacant ; void.

vacare :—to be void.

vacaria :—waste ground.

vacatura :—a church benefice not yet vacant; provision thereto ; the next avoidance of a benefice.

vaccaria : — a cow-house or pasture.

vaccarius :—a cowherd.

vaccasterium :—a cowhouse ; a dairy farm.

vacuare :—to frustrate.

vadiare :—to pledge oneself ; to give security for ; to wage.

vadiare legem :—to wage his law.

vadimonizare :—to pawn.

vadium:—surety; wage; custom.

vafra :—a wafer.

vagium :—security.

valatorium, valatrum :—a churn.

valectus. See *valettus.*

valentia :—value.

valesium :—a travelling bag.

valettus :—a groom ; a yeoman ; a journeyman.

valibilis :—valuable.

valisona anguillarum : — eel-bucks (?).

valitor :—an assistant; an ally.

vallare :—to wall up.

valor : — strength ; courage ; value.

valvassor :—a vassal. See *vavassor.*

vana :—a weathercock.

vanga :—a shovel ; a spade.

vannatarius :—a winnower.

vannus :—a vane ; a winnowing-fan.

vantarius :—a footman who runs before his master.

vapulatio :—beating, cleaning ; perhaps also " whipping," binding with string.

varancia :—madder.

varectare. See *warectare.*

varium :—vair, an expensive fur, perhaps ermine.

varrare :—to value.

vasa :—a ship.

vasarius :—a keeper of crockery.

vascella : — some sort of ship, perhaps an error for *nascella.*

vaslettus. See *valettus.*

vassalagium :—the condition of a vassal.

M.

Z

vassallus:— a vassal, a feudal tenant.

vasseleria :—a vassal's tenure.

vassella :—plate.

vastare :—to waste.

vastellarium :—a b a k e h o u s e where wastel bread was baked.

vastellum :—a shade ; an arbour. See *wastellus*.

vastina :—waste land.

vastum :—waste.

vatila :—a scoop.

vavassaria. See *vavassoria*.

vavassor :—a vassal, next in dignity to a baron; a free tenant of a tenant in chief.

vavassoria : — land held by a *vavassor*.

vealtrarius, veautrarius. See *veltrarius*.

vehagium : — payment for carriage.

vehia :—a load.

vehitura :—carriage.

veicium :—a conduit or pipe (?).

veirium :—error for *veicium*.

velare :—to sail.

velle :—will (subst.).

veltraria :—the office of slipper when coursing.

veltrarius : — a lyme-hound ; a man who leads hounds, a slipper.

veltrea :—a leash.

veluellum, veluettum, velutum:— velvet.

venaria :—beasts and birds of chase.

venatio :—venison; the right of hunting.

venda : — payment to lord for licence to sell ; toll of goods for sale.

venea :—a vineyard.

venella :—a lane.

Veneris dies :—Friday.

venia curta :—a slight bow.

venia longa :—a low bow.

ventare, ventilare :—to winnow ; to air.

venticius :—wind (adj.).

ventilogium :—a vane.

ventosa :—a cupping glass.

ventosare : —to bleed by cupping.

ventriceum, ventriticum molendinum :—a windmill.

veragium :—verage, the right of the Marshal of England to all pied cattle taken in war.

verbale :—a dictionary.

vereda :—a carter.

veredarius :—a courier ; a thill horse.

veredictum :—a verdict.

veredis :—a ferret.

veredum :—a thill, the draught tree of a cart.

veredus :—a thill horse.

vergenta :—a measure used for spices.

verina :—a pane of glass.

vermiculus :—vermilion.

vermina :—vermin.

vernacio :—varnishing.

vernare :—to varnish.

vernellum :—varnish.

vero : — a minnow (*leuciscus phoxinus*).

veronica :—a vernacle.

verra :—war.

verrina :—a pane of glass.

versatilis pons :—a swingbridge.

versator :—a turnspit.

versor :—a turner.

versutius :—" fersouthe."

vertagus :—a tumbler dog.

vertebra :—a hinge.

vertebrum :—a reel.

vertevella, vertinella :—a hook ; a hinge ; shears.

vertitor :—a turner.

verugirus :—a turnspit.

veruversorium :—a roasting jack.

vervella :—vervels, gold or silver rings on a hawk's jesses.

vesca :—vetch.

vesperæ :—vespers, between the 9th hour of the day and night.

vesperus :—evensong.

vespilio :—a nocturnal robber.

vesselamenta :—plate.

vesta :—crop.

vestiarium : — a wardrobe ; a vestry.

vestibulum :—a vestry.

vestigabilis canis : — a sleuth hound.

vestiplicium :—a clothes press.

vestire :—to invest.

vestitura. See *vestura*.

vestitus :—a fee or benefice with which the holder is invested.

vestura :—crop ; possession.

vettrarius. See *veltrarius*.

vetuxuale :—toll (for *vectigal* ?).

veua, veuta :—a view.

veutrarius. See *veltrarius*.

vexillator :—a standardbearer.

vexillifer :—a standardbearer.

vexus : —a pack, a bundle.

viagium :—a voyage.

vians :—a traveller.

vibrella :—a cannon.

vibrellator :—a gunner.

vicaria :—a vicarage.

vicariatus :—the office of a vicar.

vicarius :—a vicar.

vicecancellarius : — a vice-chancellor.

vicecomes :—a viscount; a sheriff.

vicecomitilia :—vicontiels, rents farmed by a sheriff.

vicedominus : — a vidame, a bishop's deputy in temporal matters.

vicenarius. See *vintarius*.

viceplebanus : — a deputy to a parish priest.

vicinetum, vicinia :—neighbourhood ; venue.

victinella :—a bolt (from *vectis*).

victualarius :—a victualler.

vicus :—a street.

viduatus :—widowed.

vidula :—a fiddle.

vidulator :—a fiddler.

viella :—a viol.

viellator :—a player on the viol.

vigeria :—the jurisdiction of a vicar.

vigerius :—a vicar.

vigilarius :—a monk who woke the others.

vigilia :—the eve of or day before a feast.

vigiliæ :—matins or vigils.

villa :—a vill or village ; a town.

villanagium :—the tenure of a villein, villenage.

villanus :—a villein, a bondman.

villare :—a list of *villæ*.

villata :—a township, a village.

villaticus :—a peasant.

villatus pannus :—frieze.

villenagium :—the tenure of a villein.

villicanus, villicus :—a steward, a reeve.

villificare :—to build ; to wall in.

villosa :—velvet.

vilnetum. See *vicinetum.*

vina :—a fin.

vinagium :—rent paid in wine.

vinaria :—a vintry.

vinegrum :—vinegar.

vinetria :—a vintry.

vinitarius :—a vintner ; the custodian of the wine in a convent.

vinitor :—a vintner.

vinna :—a drag-net.

vintarius, vintenarius :—a vintner ; a commander of twenty soldiers.

virbius :—twice married.

virga :—a yard ; a wand ; the verge, the compass of the king's court.

virgarium :—an osier bed.

virgarius. See *virgatarius.*

virgastrum :—an osier bed.

virgata :—a yard-land, or verge, a quarter of a hide, varying from 12 to 40 acres ; the verge.

virgatarius :—originally a holder of a virgate or yard-land, but used for all small holders of land.

virgator :—a verger.

virgeus :—striped, brindled.

virgiferens :—a verger.

virgultarius :—an orcharder.

viridariæ dies :—days for surveying the *viridaria* in a forest.

viridarium :— a clearing in a forest ; a garden.

viridarius :—a verderer, a forest officer ; a hayward.

viride :—vert or greenhue, trees, &c. in a forest ; the right to cut green wood.

viridere :—to scour a river or ditch.

viridis :— sometimes used for *varium*, vair.

viridium, virificum :—varnish.

viro :—a boatman.

visitor :—a vejour.

visnetum. See *vicinetum.*

visor :—an inspector.

vispilio :—a nocturnal robber.

vista :—an interview.

visus :—a view.

vitellarius :—a victualler.

vitellium :—caudle.

vitillarius :—a victualler.

vitreare, vitriare :—to glaze.

vitriatio :—glazing.

vitriatus :—glazed.

vitulamen :—a graft.

vitulare :—to calve.

vitulinium :—vellum.

vivarium :—a park ; a fishpond. O. E. vever.

viverra :—a ferret.

vobisare :—to address in the plural.

vola :—the hollow of the hand ; a handful.

volatus :—falconry.

volsura :—vaulting.

volta :—a vault.

volticium :—an arch.

volupare :—to roll up (*volutare*).

volutus :—a vault.

vosare : — to address in the plural.

vota :—a drain ; a vault.

vouta :—a vault.

vulgariter :—in English.

vulpericia canis :—a foxhound.

W.

waccaria :—a cowhouse or cow-pasture.

waccarius :—a cowherd.

wacta :—watch.

wactare :—to watch.

wadda :—woad.

wadium. See *vadium.*

waerum :—a weir.

wafra :—wafer bread.

waftor :—a pilot.

waga :—a wey or weigh : of wool 256 lbs. or 2 sacks ; of cheese 168, 256, or 300 lbs. ; of barley or malt 6 qrs., temp. Edw. I. ; of salt 25 qrs. ; of tallow 168 lbs. ; a waif ; whey.

wagesium :—ooze, sea-ground.

wagha. See *waga.*

waia. See *waga.*

waida :—woad.

wainabilis :—passable by wag-gons ; tilled.

wainagium :—a stock of wagons, team, &c. ; wainage ; cart-age.

wainare :—to till ; to get a profit out of.

waineria :—farm implements (?).

waisda :—woad.

waivare :—to forsake ; to outlaw (a woman).

waiviamentum, waiviaria : — a waiver, waiviary ; refusal.

waiviare : — to waive, to aban-don.

waivium :—a waif.

waivius :—wandering.

walda, waldia :—a forest ; weald, wold.

walecheria :—Welshry.

waliscus :—a Welshman ; a ser-vant.

walla :—a wall.

wallare :—to wall ; to fortify.

wallia :—a wall.

wallum :—a wall.

wallura :—walling.

wambasarius :—a maker of gam-besons.

wambasium. See *gambeso.*

wannagium. See *wainagium.*

wannus. See *vannus.*

wantalius, wantarius :—a glover.

*wapentacium, wapentachium, wa-
pentacum, wapentagium* :—a
wapentake, a division of a
county similar to a hun-
dred, used in the north ;
suit of court and other
duties incumbent on the inhabitants.

wara :—a measure of land, a
gore (?) ; a weir.

warantia, &c. See *warrantia, &c.*

warda :—a ward of a city ; custody ; wardship ; ward-
penny.

warda castri :—castleguard.

wardagium :—contribution for
the custody of a castle,
wardpenny.

wardemotus :—a wardmote, a
court held in London.

warderoba :—a wardrobe.

warecta :—fallow land.

warectabilis :—fallow.

warectare :—to plough land intended for wheat in the
spring and let it lie fallow.

warectus :—fallow.

warengæ :—the ribs of a ship
(Fr. *varangue*).

warenna :—a warren.

warennarius :—a warrener.

warentiza :—warranty.

waretare. See *warectare.*

waretta, &c. See *warecta, &c.*

warfus :—a wharf.

wargus :—a banished rogue.

warnamentum :—a garment.

warnestura. See *warnistura.*

warnetum :—warnoth, a rent at
Dover doubled if not paid.

warniso, warnisona :—protection;
a garrison.

warnistura : — garrison ; provisions.

warpenna :—wardpenny.

warrantia :—warranty.

warrantisio :—warranty.

warrantizare :—to warrant.

warrantizatio :—warranty.

warrantum :—a warrant.

warrecta, &c. See *warecta.*

warrenna. See *warenna.*

warrentiza :—warranty.

wasshum :—a shallow arm of the
sea ; the Wash.

wastellus :—wastelbread, the second sort of white bread,
next in quality to simnel.

wastum :—waste.

watergagium :—a watergage, a
bank to keep off water ; a
watergauge, an instrument
to measure water ; a watercourse.

waterganga :—a watercourse; an
aqueduct.

watergangius :—a trench to carry
off water ; an aqueduct.

waterscopium. See *watergangius.*

watillum :—a wattle.

watlura :—wattling.

waulura :—fencing.

wavium, &c. See *waivium, &c.*

waynabilis. See *wainabilis.*

waynagium. See *wainagium.*

wayura :—a channel.

wayvium, wavium, &c. See
waivium, &c.

wdewardus :—a woodward.

wdiarius :—a woodman.

wegga. See *waga.*

weidia :—woad.

wela :—a bownet to take fish in ; a weir pool.

welcomare :—to welcome.

welkus :—a whelk.

welluetum :—velvet.

wendus :—a circuit of ground.

wera :—wergild, the fine paid for killing a man ; a weir.

werccum :—wreck.

werelada :—purgation of homicide by oath.

wergildus : — wergild, fine for homicide.

werra :—war.

wesda :—woad.

wesdarius :—a dealer in woad.

wexare :—to mend, to repair.

weyfa maris :—waif of the sea.

wharfa :—a wharf.

wharfagium :—wharfage.

wharva :—a wharf.

wharvagium :—wharfage.

whassum. See *wasshum.*

whitauwarius :—a white-tawer, a tanner of white leather ; a collar maker.

wica :— a country house, a farm.

wicarius, wikarius :—the keeper of a *wica.*

wikettum :—a wicket.

windare :—to hoist.

windarium :—hoisting.

winpla :—a wimple.

wiscare :—to mend, to repair.

wisda :—woad.

wista :—a measure of land, a quarter of a hide.

wita : — a fine ; an amerciament.

withernamium :—carrying off a distress, so that the sheriff cannot deliver it when replevied.

wittescalchus :—an officer who collects fines imposed by judges, a bailiff.

wixare :—to mend, to repair.

wodegeldum :—a tax paid on woods.

wodewardia :—the office of woodward.

wodewardus :—a woodward, a forest officer.

wodiarius :—a woodman.

wreccatum :—wrecked.

wreccum :—wreck.

wrectum :—wreck.

wrekum :—wreck.

wudewardus :—a woodward.

wullire :—to boil (*bullire*).

wulperettus, wulpericius canis :— a foxhound.

wyka. See *wica.*

wykettum :— a wicket.

wympla :—a wimple.

wyndare :—to hoist.

wyta. See *wita.*

X.

xenium : — a present. See *exennium.*

xenodochium:— an inn ; a hospital ; a convent.

xylopola :—a dealer in wood.

xysticus :—a champion ; a wrestler.

Y.

yarda :—a yard.

yconia :—an image.

yconomus :—a guardian.

yda. See *hida.*

ydolotrare :—to worship images.

ydor :—a water jar.

yems :—used for *hiems,* winter.

yepso :—" a little ipson," in Somerset, is a double handful, from A. S. *gespeon,* clasped.

ympnare :—a hymnal.

yvernagium. See *hibernagium.*

Z.

zabulum :—gravel, sand.

zabulus :—the devil (*diabolus*).

zeta :—a dining room; a chamber.

zibellus :—sable fur.

zigarus :—a gipsy.

zinziber, zinzuber :—ginger.

zourus :—a sore, a four-year old buck.

zucara :—sugar.

zucheus, zuschia : — the dead trunk of a tree ; a stub.

zygostata :—a clerk of a market.

zythum :—a drink made of corn.

A LIST OF THE LATIN NAMES OF PLACES IN GREAT BRITAIN AND IRELAND.*

A.

Aballaba, Aballiaba :—Appleby, Westmoreland; Watchcross, or Papcastle, Cumberland.

Abbandonia, Abbandunum :—Abingdon, Berks.

Abbas æstuarium :—River Humber, Yorks.

Abbendonia :—Abingdon.

Abbotesbiria :—Abbotsbury, Dorset.

Abbus :—Humber.

Abedesberia :—Abbotsbury, Dorset.

Abenduna :—Abingdon, Berks.

Aberconouium :—Aberconway; also the River Conway. See *Conouium.*

Aberdeia, Aberdona, Aberdonia : — Aberdeen, Scotland.

Aberdora, Aberdura:—Aberdore, and Aberdour, Scotland.

Abergennium :—Abergavenny, Monmouthshire.

Aberistyuium :—Aberystwith, Cardiganshire.

Abernæthum:—Abernethy, Scotland.

Aberuanus, Aberruanus. See *Abrauannus.*

Abindonia :—Abingdon.

Ablatum Bulgium : — Cardunnock, or Bowness, Cumberland; or Middleby, Dumfries.

Abomina : — Bodmin (?), Cornwall.

Abona Flu. : — River Avon, Hants.

Abone, Abonis :—Sea Mills, on the Avon ; Alvington-on-the-Severn, Abstone, or Aunsbury, Gloucestershire.

Aboya :—Athboy, Meath, Ireland.

Abrauannus, Abrauanus Flu. :—The estuary at Ravenglass, Cumberland ; or Glenluce Bay, Wigtownshire.

Abreconium : — Abercorn, Linlithgow.

Abredea :—River Dee, Aberdeen.

Abredesega Insula :—Bardesey Island, Carnarvonshire.

Abrenethæum :—Abernethy, Scotland.

---

* To the names of Roman Stations, upon the position of which there is a difference of opinion, several of the localities suggested have been appended, as their inclusion in this list is not for the purpose of giving information about Roman Britain, but to give the meaning of the names when used in later times. It has not been thought necessary always to insert Latin names where they are merely the common English names with a Latin termination. When no county is added to the English name, the reason usually is that there are more than one place of the same name.

Abretaum :—Swansea, Glamorganshire.

Abreuicum :—Berwick-upon-Tweed.

Abrinca :—Abernethy.

Abundena :—Abingdon.

Abus æstuarium :—Humber.

Acantium promontorium :—North Foreland.

Acastra :—Acaster, Yorks.

Accara :—Castle Acre, Norfolk.

Acemanni Civitas :—Bath.

Achada :—Achonry, Sligo.

Achadia : — Aghadoe, Kerry, Ireland.

Achathkonrensis, Achathronensis :—Of Achonry, Ireland.

Achelandia : — Bishop's Auckland, Durham.

Achilia :—Achill Isles, Connaught, Ireland.

Achinctona :—Ripe, Sussex.

Aclea : — Oakley, or Ocley, Surrey ; Aycliffe or Auckland, Durham.

Acmodæ Insulæ : — Seven Islands, mentioned by Pomponius Mela and Pliny. The name is used both for the Scilly and the Shetland Islands.

Acra :—Acre, Norfolk.

Ad Ansam : —Ithanceaster, Witham Barklow, Tolshunt Knights, or Halstead, Essex ; Wratting or Stratford St. Mary, Suffolk.

Ad Candidam Casam:—Catwade Bridge near Brantham, Suffolk.

Adcouecin. See *Comberetonium.*

Adelingia, Adelona :—Athelney, Somerset.

Ad-Lapidem : — Stoneham, Hampshire.

Ad-Latus Bouium :—Boverton, Glamorganshire. See *Bonium.*

Ad-Murum : — Walbottle, or Walton, Northumberland.

Ad-Pontem :—Paunton, Linc. ; Southwell or Farndon, Notts, or Zouch Bridge, over the Trent.

Ad-Portum Dubris : — Dover, Kent.

Ad-Portum Lemanis :—Lympne, Kent.

Ad-Portum Rutupas. See *Rutupæ.*

Adron Flu. :—River Adder, Berwickshire, or River Wear, Durham. See *Ouedra.*

Adros :—Bardsey Island, Caernarvonshire ; or Lambay, Dublin.

Adtanatos Insula : — Isle of Thanet.

Ad-Taum :—Tasburgh, Norfolk, or Norwich.

Ad-Tisam :—Piersbridge, Durham.

Adtropam :—Thrup, Abingdon.

Adurni Portus : — Porchester, Hants ; Aldrington, or Old Shoreham, Sussex.

Æbudæ :—Hebrides, West of Scotland.

Ædulfiberga : — Ellesborough, Bucks.

Ægelesbyri, Æglesburgus :—Aylesbury, Bucks.

Æiglea : — Iley Mead, near Melksham, Wilts.

Æilecuriana :—Vale of Aylesbury, Bucks.

Aelfete :—Adlingfleet, Yorks.

Aelfinensis :—Of Elphin, Ireland.

Aelfonensis :—Of Elphin, Ireland.

Ælia :—Ely. See *Elia*.

Ælia Castra :—Alcester, Warwickshire.

Æliani Porta :—A town near Hadrian's Wall.

Aemonia :—Inchcolme, in the River Forth.

Aera :—River Ayr, Scotland.

Æsycha, Æsica : — Netherby, Cumberland ; Great Chesters, Northumberland.

Ætona, Ætonia :—Eton, Bucks.

Afena :—Littleborough, Notts.

Afena Flu. :—River Avon.

Agamerium : — Aghamore, co. Mayo, Ireland.

Agelocum : — Littleborough, Notts.

Agmundishamum : — Agmundisham or Amersham, Bucks.

Agneda :—Edinburgh.

Ailenetona :—Aylton, Herefordshire.

Ailesberia :—Aylesbury, Bucks.

Ailesmera :—Ellesmere, Shropshire.

Aiscaranus : — Of Aysgarth, Yorks.

Aissoura :—Ashover (?).

Aiwella :—Ewell, Surrey.

Aka :—Rock, Worcestershire.

Akelea :—Ockley, Surrey.

Akemancester :—Bath.

Ala Campi :—Wingfield ; Winkfield.

Alachda :—Killalla, bishopric in Connaught.

Alaenus Flu. : — River Axe, Devon ; R. Stour, Dorset ; R. Alne, Warwickshire.

Alana :—Alloway, Ayrshire.

Alannius :—River Avon, Wilts.

Alata Castra, Alatum Castrum :— Tain, Ross ; Edinburgh ; or Burghead, Moray.

Alauna Civitas :—Alnwick, Northumberland ; A l c e s t e r, Warwickshire ; Allchester, Oxon ; Camelon, Stirling ; a place near Poole, Dorset.

Alauna Flu. :—River Stour, Dorset; Alne, Northumberland.

Alauna Silua : — Borders of Hampshire and Dorset, or perhaps Stourhead, Dorset.

Alauni fluuii ostia :—Alnmouth ; Tweedmouth.

Alaunicastrum :—Alcester, Warwickshire.

Alaunicus Pons :—Maidenhead, Berks.

Alaunicus Portus :—M i l f o r d Haven, Pembrokeshire.

Alauniuadum : — A y l e s f o r d, Kent.

Alaunodunum :—Maidenhead.

Alaunouicus :—Alnwick, Northumberland. See *Alauna*.

Alaunus :—Maidenhead.

Alaunus Flu. :—R. Alne or R. Tweed, Northumberland.

Alba Domus :—Whiteland, Caermarthenshire.

Albalanda :—Whiteland, or Ty Gwyn ar Taf, Caermarthenshire ; Blanchland, Northumberland.

Alba Lundy :—Blanchland, Northumberland.

Albana :—Scotland.

Albania : — Scotland, or Britain north of Humber.

Albi Equi Mons :—White Horse Hill, Berks.

Albinunno Civitas :—Caer Nonou or Whitewalls, Monmouthshire.

Albion :—Britain.

Album Castrum : —Whitchester, Northumberland; Oswestry, Shropshire.

Album Monasterium : — Whitchurch, the seat of the Stranges ; Oswestry, Shropshire, of the FitzAlans.

Alcheseia :—Alchester, Dorset.

Alcluith : — Dunbritton, on the Clyde.

Alcmundeberia :—Almondbury, Yorks.

Aldeburia :—Oldbury or Woldbury, Warwickshire.

Aldedelega : — Audley, Staffordshire.

Aldithelega :—Audley, Staffordshire.

Aldud :—Dumbarton.

Alecana :—Ilkley, Yorkshire.

Alectum :—Dundee.

Alencestria : — Alcester, Warwickshire.

Alenus Flu. See *Alaenus.*

Alexodunum. See *Axelodunum.*

Alincestria : — Alcester, Warwickshire.

Alicinca :—Ilkley (?). See *Olicana* and *Alecana.*

Aliennia :—Athelney, Somerset.

Alione, Alionis : — W h i t l e y Castle, Northumberland ; Ambleside, Westmoreland ; Kirkbride or Allonby, Cumberland.

Alitacenon Civitas :—Elgin, Scotland.

Alkesia :—Halsway, Somerset.

Allectum :—Dundee.

Alna : — Alne, Yorks ; River Alne, Northumberland.

Alnetum :—Llangerniw(?) on the Elwey, Denbighshire ; Dodnash Priory, Suffolk.

Alneuicum :—Alnwick, Northumberland.

Alone :—Bowness, Cumberland ; Whitley Castle, Northumberland ; Ambleside, Westmoreland.

Alone Flu. :—River Alne, Northumberland.

Alongium, Alouergium Civitas :— Carnbrea, Cornwall.

Alpes Peneni Montes :—Pendle Hill, Lancashire.

Alre :—Aller, near Bridgwater, Somerset.

Alrene : —Alderney.

Alta Clera :—Highclere, Hants.

Alta Prisa :—Haltemprice or Howdenprice, Yorks.

Altum Peccum :—The Peak, Derbyshire.

Aluerodunum Brigantum :— North Allerton, Yorks.

Aluertonia :—North Allerton, Yorks.

Aluestana :—Olveston, Gloucestershire.

Aluion. See *Albion.*

Alunna :—Castleshaw, Yorks.

Alunus :—River Alan, Wales.

Ambegianna. See *Amboglanna.*

Ambesbiria :—Amesbury, Wilts.

Amboglanna :—Ambleside, Westmoreland ; Burdoswald, Cumberland.

Ambresbiria:—Amesbury, Wilts.

Ambreslega :—Ombersley, Worcestershire.

Ambrosia, Ambrosii Burgus, Ambrosii Mons :—Amesbury, Wilts.

Ammera :—Anmere, Norfolk.

Anachoreticus Vicus :—Ankerwick, Bucks.

Anandia Vallis:—Annandale, Scotland.

Ancalites :—A tribe near Henley, Oxfordshire.

Anchoreticus Sinus :—Ankerwick, Bucks.

Anderelio. See *Anderida.*

Anderida:—Newenden, Kent ; Pevensey, Eastbourne, or Arundel, Sussex.

Andeuera, Andouera:—Andover, Hants.

Andium. See *Adros.*

Andreapolis :—St. Andrew's, Scotland. See *Fanum Reguli.*

Andreseya :—An old monastery on the site of Burton Abbey, Staffordshire.

Andrium, Andros :— Bardsey Island, Caernarvonshire. See *Adros.*

Anecastrum : — Ancaster, Lincolnshire.

Anegus :—Angus, Scotland.

Angelocum :—Ancaster, Lincolnshire.

Anglesega :—Anglesey.

Anglia :—England.

Angra, Angria :—Ongar, Essex.

Anguillaria Insula : — Isle of Ely.

Anguillarianus :—Of Ely.

Angulia :—Flintshire.

Angusia :—Angus, Scotland.

Anicetis Civitas :—In Dorset.

Ansoba :—River Galway, Ireland.

Antiuestæum promontorium :— Land's End, Cornwall.

Antona : —River Avon, Northants ; River Anton, Hants.

Antona Australis :—Southampton.

Antona Borealis :—Northampton.

Antrum Flu. : — The Erme, Devonshire.

Apaunaris Civitas :—In Devonshire.

Apelbia :—Appleby, Westmoreland.

Apiacum : — Hexham, Northumberland ; Papcastle, Cumberland.

Apletrea :—Appledore, Kent.

Applebeia, Applebera:—Appleby, Westmoreland.

Apultrea :—Appledore, Devon.

Aqua Rubra:—Redbourn, Herts; Redbourne, Lincolnshire.

Aquæ Calidæ :—Bath, Somerset.

Aquæ Solis, Sulis :—Bath.

Aquædonum : — Eton, Bucks ; Aikton, Cumberland.

Aquædunensis Saltus :—Waterden, Norfolk.

Aquædunum:—Waldron (?), Sussex ; Waterden, Norfolk.

Aquæuadensis Pons : — Eye Bridge, Dorset.

Aquapontanus : — Bridgwater, Somerset.

Aquelmum :—Ewelme, Oxfordshire.

Aquila :—Eagle, Lincolnshire.*

Aquilodunum :—Hoxne, Suffolk.

Aquis Civitas. See *Aquæ Calidæ.*

Aramis, Aranus Civitas :--In Dorset.

Arbeia : — Moresby or Ireby, Cumberland ; Armley or Castleford, Yorks.

Archfordensis :—Of Ardfert, Co. Kerry.

Archmachia :—Armagh.

Arclouium :—Arklow, co. Wicklow, Ireland.

Arcmacensis :—Of Armagh.

Arcmorensis : — Of Ardmore, Waterford.

Arcubus, Curia de :—Court of Arches.

Ardacha :—Ardagh, co. Longford.

Ardahachdensis : — Of Ardagh, Ireland.

Ardaoneon Civitas:—Old Sarum; Silchester, Hants.

Ardatum :—Ardat or Ardathen, co. Kerry.

Ardefertensis :—Of Ardfert, co. Kerry.

Ardgathelia : —Argyle, Scotland.

Ardmacha :—Armagh.

Ardmoria :—Ardmore, co. Waterford.

Ardræum :—Ardee, co. Louth ; Ardree, co. Kildare, Ireland.

Ardraicum: —Ardagh, co. Longford.

Ardua :—Lostwithiel, Cornwall.

Arewa :—River Orwell, Suffolk.

Argadia, Argathelia : — Argyle, Scotland.

Argistillum : — In Gloucestershire, or perhaps Arwystli, Powys.

Argita:—Lough Foil, Londonderry. Camden applies this name to Lough Swilley.

Ariconium :—Kenchester, Ross, or Penyard Castle, Herefordshire.

Armaca :—Armagh, Ireland.

Armanothia : — Ardmeanach, Scotland.

Armethua:—Armathwaite, Cumberland.

Armis :—Bath.

Armone :—Caernarvon.

Arnemega : — Willoughby - on - the-Wolds, Notts. See *Verometum.*

Arrania :—Isle of Arran, Scotland.

---

* The preceptory of the *Ballivus Aquilæ.* *Honor Aquilæ* is the honour of Laigle, in Normandy.

Arregaidela :—Argyle.

Arthferdensis, Arthfertensis :— Of Ardfert, co. Kerry.

Arthmorensis :—Of Ardmore, co. Waterford.

Arundelia, Arundellum :—Arundel, Sussex.

Arundinis Vadum :—Redbridge, Hants.

Aruntina Vallis :— Arundel, Sussex.

Arunus Flu. :—River Arun, Sussex.

Aruone :—Caernarvon.

Aruonia :—Caernarvonshire.

Arus :—River Aire, Yorks.

Asaphopolis :—St. Asaph, Flintshire.

Ascaranus. See *Aiscaranus.*

Ascdala :—Eskdale.

Athanaton, Athanatos :—Isle of Thanet. See *Tanathos.*

Athesis Flu. :—River Tees. See *Tesa.*

Atholia :—Athol, Scotland.

Athra :—Athenry, co. Galway.

Atina Insula : — Thanet. See *Adtanatos.*

Atrebati :—People of Berks.

Atrium Dei :—Hinton, Somerset.

Attacotti :—Conquered tribes N. of the Roman wall.

Aualana : — Watchcross. See *Aballaba.*

Aualonia :—Glastonbury, Somerset.

Auchelandia : — Bishops Auckland, Durham.

Aue : — River Avon, or Avin, Scotland.

Auena Flu. :—River Avon, Wilts.

Auenina, Auenna Flu. :—River Afan, or Avon, Glamorganshire.

Auenmorus :—Blackwater river, Cork.

Auennus :—River Avon, a tributary of the Clyde, Scotland.

Auentio Flu. :—River Aun, or Avon, Devon.

Aufona : — River Avon, Northants.

Augusta : — Aust, Gloucestershire.

Augusta Trinobantum, Augusta : —London.

Augustaldia :—Hexham, Northumberland.

Auinus :—River Avon, or Avin, Scotland.

Aula, vel Villa Antiqua :—Aldbury, Herts.

Aula Cervina :—Hart Hall, Oxford.

Aumodishamum : — Amersham, Bucks.

Auna :—Awn, bishopric in Ireland.

Aunest' :—Elstow, Beds.

Auona : — River Avon ; River Nen, Northants.

Auona :—Bungay, Suffolk.

Auona, Auondunum :—Hampton Court, according to Leland.

Auona Littoralis, sive Australis :—Southampton.

Auona Mediterranea, sive Borealis :—Northampton.

Auonæ Vallis :—Oundle, Northants.

Auondunum Limenorum : — Southampton.

Auonii palatium :—Winchester House, Southwark.

Aura :—Awre, Gloucestershire.

Aurauanus. See *Abrauannus.*

Aurea Vallis : — Golden Vale, Herts.

Aurenium :—Alderney, or Herm Island.

Aureum Vadum : — Guildford, Surrey.

Ausoba. See *Ansoba.*

Ausona : — R i v e r A v o n, Northants.

Auteri, Auterii :—People of Galway and Roscommon, Ireland.

Autona :—Avon, Northants.

Axelodunum :—Hexham, Northumberland ; B u r g h-b y-Sands, or Bowness, Cumberland.

Axeministra : — Axminster, Devon.

Axiholma :—Axholme, Lincolnshire.

Axium Flu. :—River Axe, Devon.

B.

Ba, Baa :—Bath.

Babaglanda :—Burdoswald. See *Amboglanna.*

Babbegraua :—Baggrave, Leicestershire.

Bachelagana, Bacheleia Sylva :— Bagley Wood, Berks.

Bada :—Bath, Somerset.

Baddanbyrig : — Badbury, Dorset.

Badecanwella : — Bakewell, Derbyshire.

Badiza : — Bath. See *Aquæ Calidæ.*

Badonicus Mons :—Badon Hill, or Bannesdown, a hill near Bath.

Badunum :—Bath.

Baenburgus : — Bamborough, Northumberland.

Bagilogana Sylva : — Bagley Wood, Berks.

Bainardi Castellum :—Baynard's Castle, London.

Bainus Pons :—Bainbridge, Yorks.

Bala :—Bala, Merionethshire.

Balingium : — Bowes-upon-Stanmore, Yorks.

Balmuræum : — Balmerinach, Fife.

Balnea, Balneodunum :—Bath.

Baltifordia : — Waterford, Ireland.

Bamfum :—Banff, Scotland.

Bana Insula :—An island opposite the mouth of the River Taff, Glamorganshire.

Banatia :—Bean Castle, Murray ; Comrie, Perthshire ; or near Inverness.

Bancornensis :—Of Bangor.

Banesinga Villa :—Bensington, Oxfordshire.

Banna :—River Ban, Ulster.

Banna :—Cambeck, or Castlesteeds, Cumberland.

Bannauenna, Bannauentum :— Borough Hill, near Daventry; or Weedon, Northants ; or Banbury, Oxfordshire.

Banneberia :—Banbury, Oxford-shire.

Bannio : — Abergavenny. See *Gobannium.*

Bannochorus, Bangorium :—Ban-gor, N. Wales.

Bannouallum. See *Bannauenna.*

Banua :—Bannow, Ireland.

Banus Flu. :—River Bain, Lin-colnshire.

Bara :—Dunbar, Scotland.

Barangæ. See *Brangonia.*

Barcsciria :—Berkshire.

Bardeneia :—Bardney. Lincoln-shire.

Bardunus :—River Bure, Nor-folk.

Barnastapula :—Barnstaple, Devon.

Baromaci. See *Cæsaromayus.*

Baruicus, Barwicus :—Berwick-upon-Tweed.

Basenga, Basingum : — Basing, Basingstoke, Hants.

Basselawa :—Baslow, Derby-shire.

Batalia :—Battle Abbey, Sussex.

Batersega :—Battersea, Surrey.

Batha, Bathonia :—Bath.

Batilfordia :—Waterford, Ire-land.

Batonicus :—Of Bath.

Bdora :—River Dore, Hereford-shire.

Beanflota :—Bamfleet, Essex.

Bearrocscira :—Berkshire.

Beatitudine, Abbatia de :—Bectiffe Abbey, co. Meath.

Bebba, Bebbanbyrig :—Bambo-rough, Northumberland.

Bechewrda : — B a d g w o r t h, Somerset.

Bechlanda :—Byland, Yorks.

Bedeforda :—Bedford.

Bedericia, Bedericum :—St. Ed-mundsbury, Suffolk.

Bedfordia :—Bedford.

Begesse :—A town on the Wall of Antonine.

Beggewurda :—Badgworth, Somerset.

Belaisena :—Ballinasloe, co. Galway.

Belerium promontorium : — The Land's End.

Belgæ :—Inhabitants of Somer-set, Wilts, and Hants, in Cæsar's time occupying the South Coast.

Belgæ :—Wells, Somerset.

Belinus Sinus :—Billingsgate.

Belisama : — River Ribble, or Mersey, Lancashire.

Bella Vallis :—Beauvale, in Gresley Park, Notts.

Bellalanda :—Byland, Yorks.

Bellesitum :—Oxford.

Bellisama. See *Belisama.*

Bellocliuum, Bellodesertum :— Beldesert, or Beaudesert, Warwickshire.

Bellomariscus :—Beaumaris, Isle of Anglesey.

Bellositum :—City of Oxford.

Bellum :—Battle, Sussex.

Bellum Beccum :—Beau Bec, co. Meath.

Bellum Caput :—Beauchief, Derbyshire.

Bellum Verum :—Belvoir, Leicestershire.

Bellus Campus :—Bulcamps, Suffolk.

Bellus Locus:—Beaulieu, Hants; Beaulieu, Moddry or Mylbrook, Beds.; Beauly, Inverness; Beaudesert, Warwickshire; Killagh, Kerry, Ireland.

Bellus Locus Regis :—Beaulieu Abbey, Hants.

Bellus Portus : — Kilclehin, co. Kilkenny.

Beluerum :—Belvoir, Leicestershire.

Benethleya :—Bentley, Middlesex.

Bennauenna. See *Bannauenna.*

Bennones. See *Venonæ.*

Bentensis :—For *Ventensis.* See *Venta.*

Beohrtforda :—Burford, Oxon.

Bera:—Bere Forest, Hants; Beer, Dorset.

Berca :—Barcombe, Sussex.

Berceia, Berceria :—Berkshire.

Bercheleia :—Berkeley, Gloucestershire.

Bercheria :—Berkshire.

Bercheya :—Barraway, Cambridgeshire.

Berclea :—Berkeley, Gloucestershire.

Berdeniya :—Bardney, Lincolnshire.

Berdeseia :—Bardsey Island, or Ynys Enlli, Caernarvonshire.

Berdestapla : — Barnstaple, Devon ; Barstable, Essex.

Berechingum :—Barking, Essex.

Bereda. See *Voreda.*

Berekingum :—Barking, Essex.

Berga :—Bridgnorth, Shropshire.

Bergefelda :—Burghfield, Berks.

Bergonium :—A vitrified fort, opposite Connell Ferry, at the mouth of Loch Etive, Lorne.

Berkeria :—Berkshire.

Berkleia:—Berkeley, Gloucestershire.

Bermundesaia, Bermundsheia, Bermundi Insula :—Bermondsey, Surrey.

Bernardi Castellum :—Barnard Castle, Durham.

Bernia. See *Hibernia.*

Bernicia : — Province reaching from the River Tees to the Frith of Forth.

Berogomum :—A castle in Lorn, Scotland.

Bersetelawawapentagium : —Bassetlaw Wapentake, Notts.

Berua :—River Barrow, Ireland.

Berubium promontorium :—Duncansby Head, or more probably Noss Head, Caithness, Scotland.

Beruchensis :—Of Berkshire.

Beruicium, Berwicus :—Berwick.

Betesdenna :—Bediston, Devon.

Beuerlacum, Beuerlea : — Beverley, Yorks.

Bibrocassi, Bibroci : — A tribe near Bray, Berks.

Bimonium : — Binchester, Durham. See *Vinnouium.*

Bindogladia. See *Vindocladia.*

Binonium, Binouia, Binouium :—
Binchester, Durham. See
Vinnouium.

Birgus :—River Barrow, Waterford.

Biria :—Berryn Arbor, Devon.

Birila Insula : — Burril Island,
co. Down, Ireland.

Birnwda :—Burnham Wood.

Bishamum : — Bustlesham, or
Bisham, Berks.

Bistaghnensis :—Of Glendalough,
co. Wicklow.

Blacamora :—Blackmore, North
Riding of Yorks.

Blacinctona : — Blatchington,
Sussex.

Blacna :—Blakeney.

Bladinæ Montes :—Sliabh Bladh-
ma, now called Slieve Bloom
Mountains, in the barony
of Ossory, Queen's County,
Ireland.

Bladunum :—Malmesbury. See
Maidulphi Curia.

Blakingraua : — A hundred of
Wilts, temp. H. II.

Blancaforda :—Blandford, Dorset.

Blancalanda : — Blanch Land,
Northumberland ; White-
land, Caermarthenshire.

Blancum Castrum :—White Castle, or Blane Castle, Monmouthshire.

Blanii :—A tribe about Dublin.

*Blatum Bulgium, Ablatum Bul-
gium* : — Middleby, Dum-
fries ; or Bowness, or Cardunnock, Cumberland.

Bledewurda :—Blidworth, Notts.

Blengata hundredum :—Black-
heath hundred, Kent.

Blestium : — Monmouth ; Old-
town, Herefordshire.

Blia, Blida :—Blythe, Notts.

Blidberia, Blieberia :—Blewbury,
Berks.

Blithodunum :—Blyton, Linc.

Blokelega : — Blockley, Worcestershire.

Blya :—Blythe, Notts.

Boanda, Boandus : — River
Boyne, Ireland.

Bobium. See *Bomium.*

Boccania, Boccinia, Boccinum :—
Buckingham ; Buckenham,
Norfolk.

Bodenna :—Bodmin, Cornwall.

Boderia. See *Bodotria.*

Bodianum :—Bodiam, Sussex.

Bodotria :—Frith of Forth.

Boduni. See *Dobuni.*

Boena :—A town in the west of
Scotland.

Boghania :—Buchan, Aberdeenshire, Scotland.

Boisgraua :—Boxgrove, Sussex.

Bolbenda :—R. Beaumont, Durham.

Bolerium :—The Land's End.

Boleshouera, Bolesoura : — Bol-
sover, Derbyshire.

Boluelaunio :—Poole, Dorset.

Bomina :—Bodmin, Cornwall.

Bomium : — Cowbridge, Boverton, or Bridgend, Glamor-
ganshire ; or Axbridge,
Somerset.

Bonium, Bonuium : — Stretton,
Bangor, or Queenhope,
Flintshire ; Bunbury,
Cheshire ; or Whitchurch,
Shropshire.

Bonno. See *Bomium.*

Boræum prom. :—Malin Head, Ireland.

Borcouicum, Borcouitium, Borcouium:—Housesteads, Northumberland ; Berwick.

Bosco, Domus S. Egidii in :— Flamsted, Herts.

Boscus Arsus : — Brentwood, Essex (Fr. *Boisars*).

Boselawa:—Baslow, Derbyshire.

Bosmanacha : — Bodmin, Cornwall.

Bosphorus Picticus :—Pentland Frith, Scotland.

Bosuenna :—Bodmin, Cornwall.

Botelega :—Botley, Hants ; Bolney, Oxfordshire.

Bothmenia.—Bodmin, Cornwall.

Botis:—Bute Island, West Coast of Scotland.

Bouenia :—Boveney, Berks.

Bouium. See *Bomium, Bonium.*

Boxelega, Boxeleia :—Boxley, Kent.

Boxora :—Boxford, Berks.

Braboniacum. See *Bremetonacum, Bremeturacum, Brouonacis.*

Bracchium :—Burgh, or Bainbridge, Yorks.

Brachilega :—Brackley, Northants.

Bradeweya :—Broadway, Worcestershire.

Brage. See *Brige.*

Braitha :—River Brathay, Lancashire.

Bramenium. See *Bremenium.*

Bramptonia :—Brampton, near Huntingdon.

Branconium. See *Branoricum.*

Brangonia, Brannogenium : — Bangor. See also *Branoricum.*

Brangoria :—Bangor.

Branodunum :—Brancaster, Norfolk.

Branoricum, Branouium, Brauinium, Brauonium:—Worcester ; Ludlow, Leintwardine, or Onibury, Shropshire.

Brechinia :—Brecknock.

Brechinium:—Brechin, Scotland.

Bredenestreta :—Broadways, Worcestershire.

Brehinium. See *Brechinium.*

Breinensis :—Of Brechin, Scotland.

Brembra :—Bramber, Sussex.

Bremenium : — Newcastle or High Rochester, Northumberland ; Brampton, Northants.

Bremesgraua : — Bromsgrove, Worcestershire.

Bremetonacum : — Overborough, Lancaster, or Clitheroe, Lancashire.

Bremeturacum : — Either the same as *Bremetonacum;* Old Penrith or Bromfield, Cumberland ; or Ribchester, Lancashire.

Brendanici Montes :—Knock Brandon, Kerry.

Brendanicum Mare :—The Atlantic.

Brenna :—Breubege or Brynabege, Glamorgan.

Brentœ Vadum : — Brentford, Middlesex.

Bresnetenati Veteranorum. See *Bremeturacum* and *Bremetonacum.*

Brexarum : — Burgh, Lincolnshire.

Bribra :—Perhaps the same as *Bremeturacum.*

Brigantes :—Inhabitants of Yorkshire, Lancashire, Durham, Westmoreland and Cumberland; also of Waterford and Kilkenny, Ireland, and Galloway, Scotland.

Brigantium :—York.

Brige:—Bridgnorth, Shropshire; Broughton, or Titchfield Bay, Hants ; Ryde.

Briges. See *Brigantes.*

Brigewatera : — Bridgwater, Somerset.

Brigomono : — Bargeny, Wigtown.

Brigus:—Barrow River, Ireland.

Brillendunum : — Bridlington, Yorks.

Brimesgraua : — Bromsgrove, Worcestershire.

Brincaburga :—Brinkburn, Northumberland.

Brinchelawa :—Brinklow, Warwickshire.

Briodunum :—Bredon, Worcestershire.

Bristelmestuna : — Brighton, Sussex.

Bristoldum :—Bristol.

Bristolia, Bristolium, Bristollum, Bristowa :—Bristol.

Britanni :—People of Britain.

Britannia Prima :—Britain south of the Thames.

Britannia Secunda :—Britain west of the Severn ; or from Bristol Channel to Mersey, and from Thames to Humber.

Britannicus Oceanus :—English Channel.

Britannodunum : — Dumbarton, Scotland.

Brithania. See *Britannia.*

Britones :—People of Britain.

Britonum Castrum : — Dunbritton, or Dumbarton, Scotland.

Brocara, Brocauo :—Brough or Brougham-on-the-Eamont, Westmoreland.

Broconiacum : — Brougham, Westmoreland.

Brodenestreta : — Broadways, Worcestershire.

Bromfelda : —Bromfeld, Denbighshire.

Brouonacis : — Aldstone Moor, Brough, Brougham, or Kirkbythure, Westmoreland.

Brueria:—Bruerne Abbey, Oxon.

Bruga :—Bridgnorth, Shropshire.

Bruga Walteri:— Bridgewater, Somerset.

Brugia :—Bridge, Devon.

Bruhella :—Brill, Bucks.

Brutannia. See *Britannia.*

Brycstowa :—Bristol.

Brygiona :—Boxgrove, Sussex.

Bubris. See *Dubris.*

Buccinghania :—Buckingham.

Buchania :—Buchan, Scotland.

Bucostenum : —Buxton, Derbyshire.

Budeforda :—Bedford.

Buellium :—Boyle, Ireland.

Buffestra : — Buckfastleigh, Devon.

Buksiria :—Buckinghamshire.

Bulgium : — Bowness, Cumberland.

Bullæum :—Builth, Brecknock ; or Usk, Monmouth.

Bumsteda :—Bumpstead, Essex.

Bungehia :—Bungay, Suffolk.

Burgamera :—Bolmer, Sussex.

Burgensis Pons : — Boroughbridge, Yorks.

Burgodunum : — Burton, Staffordshire.

Burgus :—Brough, Westmoreland ; Peterborough ; Burgh, Norfolk ; Bridgnorth, Shropshire.

Burgus Regine :—Queenborough, Kent.

Burgus super Zabulum :—Burgh-by-Sands, Cumberland.

Burhella. See *Bruhella.*

Buroauerus. See *Durouernum.*

Buroleuo. See *Durolenum.*

Burrio :—Usk, Monmouthshire ; Ledbury, Hereford.

Burwardescota :—Buscot, Berks.

Buseneia :—Binsey, Oxon.

Bustelli Domus : — Bustlesham or Bisham, Berks.

Buuenia :—Boveney, Berks.

Buuinda :—River Boyne, Ireland.

Byligesleaga :—Billingsley, Shropshire.

Byrdena :—Burdon, Durham.

C.

Cacaria:—Tadcaster or Aberford, Yorks.

Caerdiffa:—Cardiff, Glamorganshire.

Caerdigania :—Cardigan.

Caer-Lincoit : — Lincoln. See *Lincolinum.*

Caermardinia : — Caermarthen, Wales.

Caerperis :—Porchester, Hants.

Caerseuerus :—Salisbury, Wilts.

Cæsarea, Cæsaria :—Jersey.

Cæsaris Burgus :—Searbyrig, Old Sarum.

Cæsaromagus:—Chelmsford, Writtle, Widford, Burntwood, Canvey Island, or Billericay, Essex.

Calacum. See *Galacum.*

Calaterium :—R. Calder, Yorks.

Calaterium Nemus :—Forest of Galtress, Yorks.

Calatum. See *Galacum.*

Calcaria :—Tadcaster or Aberford, Yorks.

Calcetum :—A monastery near Lewes.

Calcoensis, Calchouensis : — Of Kelso, Scotland.

Calcua, Nalcua. See *Calleua* and *Galleua.*

Caldei Insula :—Ynys Pyr, or Caldey Island, Pembroke-shire.

Calderus Flu. :—River Calder, Yorks.

Caledonia :—Callander, Perth-shire. It is also used for the whole of Scotland.

Caledonia Sylva:—Argyle, Loch-aber and Moray.

Caledonii : — Inhabitants of north-west of Scotland.

Caledonium Castrum:—Dunkeld.

Calgachi Roboretum : — Doire Chalgaich, Derry, Ireland.

Calidoniæ Sylvæ:—Florus applies this name to the interior of England.

Calkoensis :—Of Kelso.

Calleua :—Basingstoke, Hants.

Calleua Attrebatum. See *Galleua Atrebatum*.

Calna :—Calne, Wiltshire.

Calonia:—Coldingham, Berwick.

Calunio :—Same as *Galacum;* or Wakefield, Yorks.

Camaldunum, Camalodunum :—Maldon, Colchester, or Lex-den, Essex.

Camaletum :—Camel, Somerset.

Cambium Regale :—Royal Ex-change, London.

Cambodunum : —- Almondbury, Greetland, or Elland, West Riding of Yorkshire.

Camboricum, Camborium :—Ick-lingham, Suffolk ; or Cam-bridge.

Cambretonium. See *Combere-tonium*.

Cambria :—Wales.

Cambula :—R. Camel, Cornwall.

Camelodunum :—Doncaster, Yorks.

Camerum :—Castell Cwm Aram, Denbighshire.

Camestrum :—Campsterne, Dorset.

Camolodunum. See *Camaldunum*.

Campodunum. See *Cambodunum*.

Campus Altus :—Hatfield, or Hautfield, Herts.

Campus Fabrum :—Smithfield, London.

Campus Nouo-Forensis :—New-market Heath, Cambridge-shire.

Camudolanum. See *Cambodu-num*.

Camulodunum. See *Camaldu-num* and *Cambodunum*.

Cana Insula : — Sheppy. See *Counos*.

Canachina Silva : — Cannock Chase, Staffordshire.

Canani Terra :—Merioneth.

Cancani :—People living in Car-narvonshire.

Cancanum. See *Canganorum*.

Cancia :—Kent.

Candalia:—Kendal, Westmore-land.

Candida Casa : — Whitehorn, Whithern, Wigton-shire.

Candida Ecclesia:—Whitchurch, Salop.

Canewella :—Canwell, Stafford-shire, a Benedictine Priory.

Canganorum promontorium : — Braichy Pwll Point, Car-narvonshire. The same as *Ganganum*.

Cangi :—A tribe in Somerset, or perhaps the same as *Cancani.*

Caninga : — Bishop's Canning, Wilts.

Canonium :—Canewdon, or Fambridge, or near Kelvedon, Essex.

Canouaci :—People in Argyle, Lorn, and Lennox.

Cantabrigia :—Cambridge.

Cantæ :—A tribe in Sutherlandshire.

Cantebrigia :—Cambridge.

Cantia, Cantium :—Kent.

Cantiuenti :—A tribe probably in Westmoreland.

Cantium promontorium : — The North Foreland, Kent.

Cantuaria :—Canterbury.

Cantuaritæ :—Kentish Saxons.

Canubio. See *Conouium.*

Capræ Caput, Caprocephalia :— Gateshead, Durham. See *Gabrocentum.*

Capreolum :—Cheverell, Wilts; some place in Brecon (?).

Carbantium : — Caerlaverock, Dumfriesshire.

Carbantorigum :—Drummore, Dumfries ; Caerlaverock.

Carbonarius Collis : — Coleshill, Flintshire.

Carcaria. See *Calcaria.*

Cardelum :—Carlisle.

Cardigania :—Cardigan, Wales.

Careni :—Inhabitants of Caithness.

Carleolium, Carleolum : — Carlisle.

Carmarthinia :—Caermarthen.

Carnaruonia :—Caernarvon.

Carnetum :—Carnedon Prior, Cornwall.

Carnonacæ : — People of Ross, Scotland.

Carphillis :—A castle, supposed to have been built by the Romans, Glamorganshire.

Carricta :—Carrick, Scotland.

Carrum :—Charmouth, Dorset ; Carham, Northumberland.

Carsuilla :—Kerswell, Devon.

Cartusia :—Witham Charterhouse, Somerset.

Carugia :—Kerry, Ireland.

Casa Candida. See *Candida Casa.*

Casella :—Cashel, Ireland.

Cassi, Cassii :—A tribe in Hertfordshire.

Cassilia :—Cashel, Ireland.

Cassiterides :—Scilly Islands.

Cassiuelauni oppidum :—St. Alban's. See *Verolamium.*

Casta Silua :—Kilcreunata, co. Galway.

Castellum Haroldi :—Haroldeston, in the deanery of Ross.

Castra :—Caistor, Lincolnshire.

Castra Alata. See *Alata Castra.*

Castra Exploratorum : — Burgh by Sands, Netherby, Old Castle, or Bowness, Cumberland.

Castrodunum : — Chesterton, Cambridgeshire.

Castrum Britonum : — Dunbritton, Scotland.

Castrum Caledonium :—Dunkeld.

Castrum Cubii:—Holyhead.

Castrum de Aruon:—Caernarvon Castle.

Castrum Dei:—Fermoy Abbey, Ireland.

Castrum de Vies:—Devizes, Wilts.

Castrum Episcopi: — Bishop's Castle, Shropshire.

Castrum Godrici:—Goodrich, Herefordshire.

Castrum Legionis, Leonis:— Holt Castle, Denbighshire.

Castrum Matildis:—Painscastle, Herefordshire.

Castrum Oscæ: — Usk, Monmouthshire.

Castrum Puellarum:—Edinburgh.

Cataracta, Cataractonium:— Thornbrough, near Thirsk, Allerton, or Catterick Bridge, Yorks.

Cataracta Flu.:—River Swale, Yorks.

Catenessa:—Caithness.

Cateracta:—Catterick, Yorks.

Cateuchlani. See *Catuellani*.

Catguilia:—Kidwelly, Carmarthenshire.

Cathania:—Caithness, Scotland.

Cathinensis:—Of Caithness.

Catini:—People of Caithness.

Catteleia:—Catley, Lincolnshire.

Catuellani, Catyeuchlani: — People of Buckingham, Bedford, and Hertfordshire.

Cauci:—Tribe living in Wicklow, Ireland.

Cauda:—R. Calder, Cumberland.

Cauda Alicii:—La Quealiz, a wood in Brill Forest, Bucks.

Cauna. See *Counos*.

Caunonio. See *Canonium*.

Causennæ, Causennis: — Boston, Ancaster, Brig Casterton, or Swineshead, Lincolnshire.

Caua:—Cave, Yorks.

Cauæ Diræ: — Holderness, Yorks.

Cauerna Viperina:—Aspeden, Herts.

Cauoda:—Cawood, Yorks.

Cawda. See *Cauoda*.

Cealchithe:—Chalk, Kent; Chelsea.

Cealtide:—Chelsea.

Ceangi. See *Cangi*.

Ceastra:—Chester; Chester-le-Street, Durham.

Celerion: — Callander Castle, Perthshire.

Cella Canici:—Kilkenny.

Cella Reguli:—Kilreule, St. Andrew's.

Cella S. Brigittæ:—Kilbride.

Celnius Flu.:—River Findhorn, or River Spey, Elgin.

Celouion. See *Celerion*.

Celunno. See *Cilurnum*.

Celurca:—Montrose, Forfar.

Cenenensis:—Of Kells, Ireland.

Cenimagni:—The same as the Iceni, a tribe in the east of Britain.

Cenion Flu. : — River Falle, Cornwall.

Centum fontes : — Hundreds-kelde, or Hinderwell, Yorks.

Ceolesega :—Selsey, Sussex.

Ceolesegia :—Cholsey, Berks.

Cerda :—Chard, Somerset.

Cerda Selyouarum :—Dumfries.

Cerdici Vadum :—Chardford, Hants.

Ceretica : — Ceredigion, a pro-vince of S. Wales; Car-diganshire.

Cerneia :—Charney, Berks.

Cernelium :—Cerne, Dorset.

Cernualia, Curnualia : — Corn-wall.

Cerones, Ceronii : — Inhabitants of Lochaber and Ross.

Cerota Insula : — Chertsey, Surrey.

Cerqueyum :—Sark.

Cerringa :—Charing, Kent.

Certesia :—Chertsey, Surrey.

Cerui Insula : — Chertsey; also Hartlepool, Durham.

Cesarea, Cesaria :—Jersey.

Cesaris Tumulus :—Carn Ceasra, Connaught.

Cestratona :—Chesterton.

Cestre :—Is used for York, Ches-ter, and Chester-le-Street.

Cestrescira :—Cheshire.

Cestria : — Chester; Cheshire ; Chester-le-Street, Durham ; Castle Knock, Dublin.

Cestrisiria :—Cheshire.

Chaluelea : — Cheveley, Cam-bridgeshire.

Chanani Terra :—Merioneth.

Chanrea, Chanoricum :—Chan-onry, Ross-shire.

Chardum :—Chard, Somerset.

Chathania. See *Cathania.*

Chauci. See *Cauci.*

Chauseya :—Cheausey, or Chol-sey, Berks.

Cheleswurda : — Chelworth, Wilts.

Chelmerium : — Chelmsford, Essex.

Chemesinga :—Kemsing, Kent.

Chentenses :—Kentish men.

Chepstouium :—Chepstow, Mon-mouthshire.

Chesterfelda : — Chesterfield, Derbyshire.

Chestria, Chestrum. See *Cestria.*

Cheua :—Kew, Surrey.

Chibii Castrum :—Holyhead, Anglesey.

Chicum :—St. Osith, Essex.

Chienfernensis : — Of Clonfert, Ireland.

Chimela :—Keymer, Sussex.

Chineglissi Castrum : — Kenil-worth Castle, Warwick-shire.

Chingesordia :—King's Worthy, Hants.

Chingestona :—Kingston.

Chingeswuda :—Kingswood.

Chingeswurtha : — King's Wor-thy, Hants.

Chirca :—Chirk, Denbighshire.

Chirchbeia :—Kirkby, Kirby.

Chiringecestra :—Cirencester, Gloucestershire.

Chonderensis :—Of Connor, co. Antrim.

Chorfa :—Corfe, Dorset.

Choro Benedicti, Abbatia de :— Chore or Middleton Abbey, Cork.

Chridiantune :—Crediton, Devon.

Cibra :—A town on or near the Antonine Wall.

Cica :—Chich St. Osyth, Essex.

Ciceastria, Cicestria (Cissaceastre) :—Chichester, Sussex.

Cilurnum, Cilurinum : — Walwick Chesters, or Collerton, Northumberland.

Cindocellum :—A town in Scotland, north of Antonine's Wall.

Cirecestria, Cirencestria, Cirinium :—Cirencester, Glouc.

Cirnea :—Charney, Gloucestershire.

Cissaceastre : — Chichester, Sussex.

Ciuella :—Cheveley.

Ciuitas Legionum :—Caerleon, Monmouthshire ; Chester.

Clandensis :—Glendalough, Wicklow.

Clanouenta :—Lanchester, Durham ; Cockermouth or Ellenborough, Cumberland.

Clara :—County of Clare, Ireland.

Clarentia :—Clare, Suffolk.

Claria :—Clare County, Ireland.

Clarofontanus, Clarus Fons :— Sherborne, Dorset ; Moycoscain, co. Derry.

Claudia Castra, Claudia :—Gloucester.

Claudiana provincia :—Gloucestershire.

Claudiocestria :—Gloucester.

Clausentum : — Bishop's Waltham ; Southampton ; Bittern, Hants ; Chichester, Sussex.

Clauinio :—A town probably in Dorset.

Clauwurda :—Clayworth, Notts.

Cledhea Flu. :—River Cleddy, Pembrokeshire.

Cleituna :—Clayton, Sussex.

Cleocestria :—Gloucester.

Clera Regis : — Kingsclere, Hants.

Cletlinga :—Cleatlam, Durham.

Cleuum : — Gloucester. See *Claudia.*

Clidum : — Ardoch, Perthshire. See *Lindum.*

Cliua :—King's Cliff, Northants.

Cliuelanda :—Cleveland.

Clocheria, Clocherium : — Clogher, Ireland.

Cloenensis : — Clonmacnois, King's County, Ireland.

Clokorna :—Clogher, Tyrone.

Clona :—Clone or Cloone, Ireland.

Clonfertum :—Clonfert, Cork.

Clota :—River Clyde.

Clouesho :—Cliffe at Hoo, Kent.

Cluainfertensis :—Clonfert, Cork.

Cluainvanea, Cluanania, Cluanum : — Cloyne, co. Cork, Ireland.

Cluanumensis :—Of Cloyne, co. Cork.

Cluda :—River Clyde.

Cluenerardensis : — Of Clonard, co. Meath.

Cluida, Cluta: —R. Clwyd, Denbighshire.

Clunererardensis :—Of Clonard, co. Meath.

Clutina Vallis :—Diffryncloyd, Wales.

Cnapa :—Knepp, Surrey.

Cnaresburgus:—Knaresborough, Yorks.

Cnobheriburgus :—Burgh Castle, Suffolk.

Coantia :—R. Kent, Westmoreland.

Cocarus : — R. Coke, Yorks.; Cocker, Lancashire.

Coccium -—Blackrode, or Ribchester, Lancashire.

Cocuneda Civitas:—On the River Coquet, Northumberland.

Cocwuda :—R. Coquet.

Cognacta :—Connaught, Ireland.

Coguuensuron Flu. :—R. Soar, Leicestershire.

Coila :—Kyle, W. of Scotland.

Cokarus. See *Cocarus.*

Colania :—Carstairs, or Crawford, Lanarkshire ; Coldingham, Berwickshire.

Colanica :—Coldingham, or Colchester.

Colcestria :—Colchester, Essex.

Coldania :—Coldingham.

Coleceastra, Colecestra : — Colchester, Essex.

Collis Magnus : — Crug Mawr, Pembrokeshire.

Collis Victoriæ :—Knockmoy, a Cistercian Abbey, co. Galway.

Colmonora. See *Cumanora.*

Colnia Flu. :—River Colne.

Colonia :—Colchester, Maldon, or Mersea Strood, Essex.

Colonia Victricensis :—Maldon, Essex.

Coludum :—Coldingham, Berwickshire.

Colunum :—Colnbrook, Bucks.

Comberetonium : — Brettenham ; Stratford St. Andrew ; or Hadleigh, Suffolk.

Combretouium. See *Comberetonium.*

Comparcus :—Combe Park, Surrey.

Conacta :—Province of Connaught, Ireland.

Conallea :—Tirconnell, Ireland.

Concangios :—Watercrook, near Kendal ; or Chester-le-Street, Durham ; or Burgh, near Woodbridge, Suffolk.

Concani :—People of Munster, Ireland.

Condate : — Congleton, Northwich, Kinderton, or Arley Hall, Great Budworth, Cheshire.

Condercum : —Chester-le-Street, Durham ; Benwell, Northumberland.

Congauata :—Stanwix, or Drumburgh, Cumberland.

Congericuria :—Congersbury, Somerset.

Connaccia, Connachtia : — Connaught, Ireland.

Connarta :—Connaught.

Connaria :—Connor, co. Antrim, Ireland.

Connatium :—Connaught.

Conneria, Connertum. See *Connaria.*

Cononium :—Chelmsford, Essex.

Conouium:—Caer Rhyn, or Caerhen, on the Conway, Caernarvonshire.

Conouium, Conouius : — River Conway, North Wales; also used for the Town of Conway.

Contaracta :—River Swale, Yorks.

Conuennon, Conuennos Insula. See *Counos.*

Conuentria : — Coventry, Warwickshire.

Conuetoni. See *Comberetonium.*

Coqueda, Coquedus : — Coquet River, in Northumberland.

Coqueda Insula :—The Isle of Coquet, on the coast of Northumberland.

Corcagia :—Cork, Ireland.

Corcensis :—Of Cork.

Corda : — Cumnock, Ayrshire ; Lynekirk, Peebles, or some town near Loughcure, Scotland.

Coria : — Corbridge, Northumberland.

Coria, Curia Ottadinorum :— Jedburgh, Roxburghshire ; or Currie, Edinburghshire.

Coria Damniorum : — Carstairs, Lanark ; or Kirkurd, Peebles.

Corie :—Patrington, Yorks.

Coriendi :—A tribe in Wexford, Ireland.

Corinea :—Cornwall.

Corinium, Corinium Dobunorum : —Cirencester, Gloucestershire.

Corinus Flu. : — The River Churne, Gloucestershire.

Coriondi :—Folk in South Ireland.

Coritani, Coritaui : — People of Northampton, Leicester, Rutland, Derby, and Nottingham shires.

Cornabii :—Tribe in Strathnavern, Scotland.

Cornauii, Cornabii : — Inhabitants of Warwick, Worcester, Stafford, Shropshire, and Cheshire.

Corneliensis :—Of Cerne, Dorset.

Cornualia, Cornuallia : — Cornwall.

Cornubia :—Cornwall.

Cornutum Monasterium:—Hornchurch, Essex.

Corragia :—Cork.

Corstopilum, Corstopitum :—Corbridge, Morpeth, Gorbet, or Corchester. Northumberland.

Corsula Insula :—Perhaps Holyhead.

Coruesgeata :—Corfe, Dorset.

Coterinus Mons :—Cotterdale, North Riding of Yorkshire.

Cotteswoldia :—Cotswold, Gloucestershire.

Cottona : —Cotham, near Yarm, Durham.

Coualia :—Kyle, Ayrshire.

Couentria:—Coventry, Warwickshire.

Couesgraua : —Cosgrove, Northants.

Couiburchelega:—Coverly, Gloucestershire.

Couintrea:—Coventry, Warwickshire.

Counos : — Isle of Sheppey, Kent; or Canvey Island, Essex.

Cranburna, Craneburgus :— Cranborne, Dorset.

Crativallis :—Cratundene, Cambridgeshire.

Craua, Crauena : — Craven, Yorks.

Creccanforda:—Cricklade, Wilts.

Crecolada :—Cricklade, Wilts.

Credigone :—Caerriden, on the Wall of Antonine.

Credio :—Crediton, Devon.

Crenodunum :—Crendon, Bucks.

Creones :—Tribe living in Ross. See *Cerones.*

Cricgealada :—Cricklade, Wilts.

Cridea, Cridia, Cridiatunum, Cridiodunum : — Crediton, or Kirton, Devonshire.

Crococalana, Crocolana :—Ancaster, Lincolnshire ; Brough, near Collingham ; or Car-Colston, Notts.

Croucingo :—Crosby.

Crowlandia, Croylandia, Cruilandia : — Crowland, Lincolnshire.

Croyreys :—Royston.

Crucelandia :—Crowland.

Crukeri Castrum :—Pen-y-Crug, Radnor.

Crulandia:—Crowland, Lincolnshire.

Crux Chariniana : — Charing Cross.

Crux Oswaldi : — Oswestry, Shropshire.

Crux Roesiæ :—Royston.

Cubii Castrum :—Holyhead, Anglesey.

Cucufelda :—Cuckfield, Sussex.

Culenum :—Cullen, Banff.

Culerna :—Colerne, Wilts.

Cumanora:—Cumnor, Berks.

Cumberlandia :—Cumberland.

Cumbremara :—Combermere, Cheshire.

Cumbri : — People of Cumberland.

Cumbria :—Cumberland.

Cunacia :—Connaught.

Cunctona :—Compton, Sussex.

Cunecacestre :—Chester-le-Street, Durham.

Cunetio :—Marlborough, Mildenhall, or Ramsbury, Wilts.

Cunetio Flu. :—River Kennet.

Cunga :—Cong, Ireland.

Cunia :—River Conway.

Cunio :—Mull of Cantire.

Cuprum :—Coupar in Angus.

Cuprum Fifæ :—Cupar Fife.

Curia. See *Coria.*

Curia Edmundi :—Bury St. Edmunds, Suffolk.

Curnualia :—Cornwall.

Cuuichelmeslawa : — Cuckhamsley, Berks.

Cyneta :—River Kennet.

D.

Dabrona : — River Avonmore, Cork, Ireland.

Dacorum hundredum :—Hundred of Upper and Lower Deans, Herts, de Aneis or de Daneis, 12th cent.

Dacorum clades : — Danes-end, Herts.

Dammucensis : — Of Dunwich, Suffolk.

Damnii :—People of Clydesdale and Stirling.

Damnium, Damnonium promontorium : — Lizard, or Dodman Point.

Damnonia, Domnania :—Devon.

Damnonii :—People of Devon and Cornwall.

Danacastra :—Doncaster, Yorks.

Danecastria :—Doncaster, Yorks.

Daneia :—Denny, Cambridgeshire.

Danica Sylva : — Andredswald Forest, Sussex ; also the Forest of Dean, Gloucestershire.

Danmonii. See *Damnonii.*

Danubiæ Sylva :—Forest of Dean.

Danum :—Doncaster, Yorks.

Danus Flu. :—The Dane. Lincolnshire ; Dan, or Daven, Cheshire ; Don, or Dun, Yorks.

Darbia :—Derby.

Darensis :—Of Kildare.

Darentiuadum:—Dartford, Kent.

Darentus Flu. :—Darenth, or Dart River, Kent.

Darinum :—Estanford, Strangford (?), Ulster.

Darnii :—A tribe in Ulster.

Darotenses :—People of Dorset.

Daruentia :—River Derwent, Derbyshire.

Daruenum :—Canterbury. See *Daruernum.*

Daruernum :—Canterbury ; Rochester.

Daumuicensis : — Of Dunwich, Suffolk.

Daurona. See *Dabrona.*

De Fontibus :—Wells, Somerset.

Dea :—River Dee, Cheshire.

Debba. See *Bebba.*

Decha :—A town in Scotland, North of the Forth.

Decuaria. See *Petuaria.*

Deia : — River Dee.

Deidonum :—Dundee.

Deilocum :—Godstow, Oxfordshire.

Deira :—Abbey of Deer, in Buchan.

Deira :—The part of the kingdom of the Northumbrians on the south side of the Tyne.

Deira Sylva :—Deerhurst, Gloucestershire.

Deirorum Sylva :—Derewald, or Beverley, Yorks.

Dela :—Deal, Kent.

Delgouitia :—G o o d m a n h a m, Fimber, Millington, or Market Weighton, East Riding of Yorks.

Deluinia :—Delvin, Westmeath, Ireland.

Demerosesa :—Dumfries.

Demetæ, Dimetæ : — People of South Wales.

Demetia, Demetica :—Dyved, a province in South Wales, Pembrokeshire, and a part of Caermarthenshire.

Dena, Foresta de :—Forest of Dean.

Dena Victrix :—Chester. See *Deua.*

Denæa Sylva :—Forest of Dean.

Denbighia :—Denbigh, Denbighshire.

Deomedum :—South Wales.

Deorbeia :—Derby.

Deræ :—Derry, Ulster.

Derbentione : — Little Chester, near Derby.

Derebisciria :—Derbyshire.

Derelega :—Darley, Derbyshire.

Derentiuadum :—Dartford, Kent.

Dereta :—River Dee (?) or Derwent (?).

Derewenta :—River Derwent.

Derstemuta : — Dartmouth, Devon.

Derte Ostium, Dertmuta : — Dartmouth, Devon.

Deruentione : — Holtby, Kexby, or Stamford Bridge, on the Derwent, Yorkshire ; Pap Castle, Cumberland.

Desmonia, Dessemonia : — Desmond, Ireland.

Dessia :—Decies, co. Waterford, Ireland.

Deua :—Dundee ; Chester.

Deua Flu. : — River Dee, Cheshire.

Deuana :—Aberdeen ; Chester ; Doncaster.

Deuania :—Cheshire.

Deucaledonii :—The Scots.

Deucaledonius oceanus :—The sea on the W. of Scotland.

Deuenescira :—Devonshire.

Deui Flu. :—River Dovey, Wales.

Deuionisso :—Devonport.

Deuna :—Chester. See *Deua.*

Deunana :—Doncaster.

Deuonia :—Devonshire.

Deuouicia. See *Delyouitia.*

Deuus Flu. :—River Dovey.

Dewi :—St. David's.

Dextralis Cambria : — Deheubarth, *i.e.* South Wales.

Deya :—River Dee.

Dicelinga :—Ditchling, Sussex.

Dicetum :—Diss, Norfolk.

Dicia :—Diss, Norfolk.

Dictis :—Ambleside, Westmoreland.

Dictum :—Diganwy, Caernarvonshire.

Dimetæ :—People of South Wales.

Dineuour :—South Wales.

Diona :—River Dee, Scotland.

Dirtouicum :—Droitwich, Worcestershire.

Diuana. See *Deuana.*

Diuilena, Diuilina :—Dubh-lein (the Black Pool), now called Dublin.

Diuisæ, Diuisio :—Devizes, Wiltshire. See *Castrum de Vies.*

Dixio. See *Dictis.*

Dobaria :—Dover.

Dobuni, Boduni : —People of Gloucestershire and Oxfordshire.

Docestria :—Dorset.

Doffra, Dofris :—Dover.

Dolocindo :—A town in Dorset.

Domnania. See *Damnonia.*

Domnia :—Dunwich, Suffolk.

Domus Sanctæ Crucis :—Holyrood House, Edinburgh.

Donalmum :—Durham.

Donewicum :—Dunwich, Suffolk.

Donus :—River Done, Durham.

Dorbeia :—Derby.

Dorcadæ :—The Orkneys.

Dorcestria :—Dorchester, Dorset.

Dorcinia :—Dorchester, Oxfordshire.

Dorcinni Civitas :—Dorchester, Oxfordshire.

Doresetesciria :—Dorset.

Dorfris :—Dover, Kent.

Doris Cantiorum :—Dover.

Dorkcestria, Dorkecestra :—Dorchester, Dorset.

Dornaceaster :—Dorchester.

Dornocum : — Dornock, Dumfriesshire, Scotland.

Dornsetta :—Dorchester, Dorset.

Dorobellum. See *Daruernum.*

Dorobernia : — Canterbury ; Dover.

Dorobreuum. See *Durobriuis.*

Dorobrina :—Dover.

Dorocina :—Dorchester.

Dorouentio. See *Deruentione.*

Dorouernum : — Canterbury ; Dover.

Dorpendunum :—Orpington, Kent.

Dorseta, Dorsetania, Dorsetia :—Dorset.

Doruantium, Doruatium : — River Dart, Darenth, or Derwent.

Dorubernia : — Canterbury ; Dover.

Doruenta :—River Derwent or Darenth.

Doruentani :—People of Derbyshire.

Doruernum. See *Daruernum.*

Dorus Flu. :—The Dor, Herts.

Doruuernia. See *Dorubernia.*

Douaria, Douera, Douerha, Doueria, Douoria :—Dover.

Doura :—Dover.

Dourus :—Dingle Bay.

Douus Flu. : — River Dove, Derbyshire.

Dromoria :—Dromore, co. Down, Ulster.

Duablisis, Duabsisis :—Dupplin, Perthshire.

M.   B B

Duacum :—Kilmacduagh, Galway, Ireland.

Dublicensis :—Of Dublin.

Dublinia, Dublinium, Dublinum :—Dublin. See *Diuilena.*

Dubris :—Dover, Kent.

Dufelda :—Duffield, Derbyshire.

Duflinum :—Dublin.

Duglassus Flu. :—River Douglas, Clydesdale.

Dulce Cor, Suauicordium :— Sweetheart, or New Abbey, Kirkcudbrightshire.

Dulma. See *Magiouinium.*

Dulmanum :—Durham.

Dumbarum : — Dunbar, Haddingtonshire.

Dumbinensis :—Of Dunblane.

Dumblanum : — Dunblane, Perthshire.

Dumbrosa :—Bundroose, or Bundoram, Leitrim.

Dumbum promontorium :—Bengore Head, or Fair Head, Antrim.

Dumera :—Dummer, Hants.

Dumna :—Fair Island, one of the Orkneys.

Dumnonia : — Devonshire. See *Damnonia.*

Dumnonii. See *Damnonii.*

Dumwicus :—Dunwich, Suffolk.

Duna :—Down, Downpatrick.

Dunamum :—Downham, Cambridgeshire.

Dunamutha : — Tynemouth, Northumberland.

Duncheldinum :—Dunkeld. See *Caledonium Castrum.*

Duncheranum : — Dunkerrin, King's County, Ireland.

Dundalcum :—Dundalk, Louth, Ireland.

Dunedinum :—Edinburgh.

Dunelmia, Dunelmum, Dunelmus :—Durham.

Dunestaplia :—Dunstable, Beds.

Dunestor :—Dunster, Somerset.

Duneuetum : — Launceston, Cornwall.

Dunfreia :—Dumfries, Scotland.

Dungallum :—Donegal, Ulster.

Dunholmum, Dunholmus :—Durham.

Dunistabulum : — Dunstable, Bedfordshire.

Dunium :—Dorchester, Dorset. See *Moridunum.*

Dunmonii. See *Damnonii.*

Dunolmum :—Durham.

Dunouicum : — Dunwich, Suffolk.

Dunrodunum : — Dornoch, Sutherland.

Dunuicus :—Dunwich, Suffolk.

Dunum :—Down, Downpatrick, Ulster ; Doncaster, Yorks ; Dundalk, co. Louth ; Salisbury ; Waterford, Ireland.

Dunum Sinus : — Scarborough Bay, Yorks, or Teesmouth.

Dunus Flu. :—River Doon, Ayrshire.

Dunus Sinus. See *Dunum Sinus.*

Dunwicus :—Dunwich, Suffolk.

Dura :—Derry, Ireland.

Duracastrum :—Dorchester, Oxfordshire.

Durbis :—River Dour, Kent.

Durcinate. See *Durolipons.*

Durelmum :—Durham.

Duri, Duris :—" That part of the Bay of Dingle where is the mouth of the River Maing," co. Kerry.

Duria :—Dorset.

Duris :—Dover.

Durius :—River Stour.

Durnium :—Dorchester.

Durnonouaria : — Dorchester, Dorset.

Duroauerni :—Canterbury.

Durobrabis, Durobreua. See *Durobriuis.*

Durobriuas :—Caistor, Lincolnshire; or West Lynne; or Wiggenhall St. Germain's, Norfolk.

Durobriuis :—Rochester, Strood, or Cuxton, Kent.

Durobrouæ. See *Durobriuis.*

Durobrus. See *Durobriuis.*

Durocastrum : — Dorchester, Oxon.

Durocobriuis : — Dunstable, Beds; Hertford, Great Berkhampstead, or Redbourn, Herts.

Durocornouium :—Cirencester.

Durolani Flu. : — River Len, Kent.

Durolenum, Duroleuum :—Newington, Lenham, or Westwell, Kent.

Durolipons :—Cambridge, Godmanchester, or Ramsey, Hunts.

Durolitum :—Old Ford, Leyton, Romsey, or Purfleet, Essex.

Duronouaria :—Dorchester, Dorset.

Duroprouis. See *Durobriuis.*

Durosipons. See *Durolipons.*

Durotriges : — Men of Dorsetshire.

Durouernum :—Canterbury.

Durus Flu. :—River Stour.

Dusceleberga, Dusteleberga :— Desborough hundred, Bucks.

Duthena :—River Duddon, Lancashire.

Duuelescense Castrum :—Duleek, Meath.

Duuelina :—Dublin.

Duuere :—Dover.

Dwthena. See *Duthena.*

Dyrwenta :—R. Derwent.

E.

Eadmodum :—Emmet, Yorks.

Earipolensis :—Jerpont, co. Kilkenny.

East-Sexena :—Essex.

Eathelingiana Via : — Watling St.

Eaxanceastra :—Exeter.

Ebbecastrum : — Bamborough Castle, Northumberland.

Eblana :—Dublin. See *Diuilena.*

Ebodia :—The Isle of Alderney.

Eboracum :—York.

Ebuda Insula :—Two islands are thus named by Ptolemy, of which one is Skye or Islay, the other Lewis or Jura.

Ebudæ :—Used for the Western Isles of Scotland generally.

Eburacum :—York.

Eburocastrum :—Near Rochester, Northumberland.

Edenburgus :—Edinburgh.

Ederosum Monasterium :—Ivychurch, Wilts.

Edmundi Burgus :—Bury St. Edmunds, Suffolk.

Edra :—River Whitadder.

Edros Insula :—Bardsey Island, Caernarvonshire, or Ireland's Eye.

Edulfesberga :—Ellesborough, Bucks.

Edwella :—Ewell, Surrey.

Edwiniburgus :—Edwinstow, Notts.

Efenewuda :—Evenwood, Durham.

Egelesforda :—Aylesford, Kent.

Eia :—Eye, Suffolk ; Eye, near Westminster.

Eidumania Flu. : — Blackwater River, or mouth of the Stour and Orwell, Essex.

Eilecuriana Vallis : — Vale of Aylesbury, Bucks.

Eilecurium :—Aylesbury.

Eiluius, Eluius :—St. Asaph's.

Eiudensca : — Jedburgh, Roxburghshire.

Eladunum :—Eildon, Roxburghshire.

Elauiana :—Islay.

Elconium :—A town in Cornwall.

Eldunum :—The Eildon Hills (?).

Eleueinia. See *Eluemia.*

Elginum, Elgis :—Elgin, Scotland.

Elgotii, Elgouæ :—Inhabitants of Liddisdale, Ensdale, Eskdale, Nidisdale, and Annandale, in Scotland.

Elia :—Ely, Cambridgeshire.

Eliensis Insula :—The Isle of Ely.

Ellandunum :—Allington, near Amesbury, or Wilton, in Wilts.

Ellebri :—People in Kerry, Ireland.

Ellesmara :—Ellesmere, Shropshire.

Elmelega :—Elmley, Worcestershire.

Elnicestria :—Alceter, Warwickshire.

Eltabo. See *Voluba.*

Elteshamum :—Eltham, Kent.

Eltherburna :—Halterburn, Roxburghshire.

Eluadunum :—Elphin, Roscommon.

Eluemia :—Elvael, a cantref in Powys, Radnorshire.

Eluium, Elwa :—St. Asaph's.

Elys :—Ely, Cambridgeshire.

Embesea :—Embsay or Emshaw, Yorks.

Emelia :—Emly, co. Tipperary.

Emonia :—May Isle, in the Firth of Forth.

Enachdunensis :—Annadown, co. Clare, Ireland.

Encheyallia :—Inisgall, *i.e.* Iona, Tiree, Coll, Canna, and Rum.

Engleschyria :—England.

Englewria :—England.

Ennabrensis :—Of Kilfenora, co. Clare.

Eouercon :—Abercorn, Scotland.

Eouerwicum :—York.

Eouesum :—Evesham, Worcestershire.

Eoyrus :—River Nore, Ireland.

Epeiacum, Epiacum :—Hexham, or Papcastle See *Apiacum*.

Epidii :—Tribe living in Cantire.

Epidium Insula :—Islay.

Epidium promontorium :—Mull of Cantire.

Epocessa :—Perhaps Upper Stanton, Herefordshire.

Erchenefelda :—Irchingfield, Herefordshire.

Erdingeleya :—Ardingley, Sussex.

Erdini :—People of Fermanagh. Ireland.

Ergadia :—Argyle.

Eripolensis :—Of Jerpont, Ossory.

Ermonia :—Ormond, Tipperary.

Ernulphi Curia :—Eynesbury, Hunts.

Erpeditani. See *Erdini*.

Esca :—River Esk, Dumfries.

Esica. See *Æsycha*.

Esse Insula :—Stourmouth (?), Kent.

Esselega :—Ashley.

Essendona :—Ashdon, Essex.

Essexa :—Essex.

Estantona :—Stanton.

Estlega :—Astley, Worcestershire.

Estratona :—Stratton, Bedfordshire.

Estreia :—Eastry, Kent.

Estrindia :—East Riding.

Estsexia :—Essex.

Esturministra :—Sturminster, Dorset.

Ethandunum :—Heddington, Wilts.

Ethelingia :—Athelney, Somerset.

Ethona :—Nuneaton, Warwickshire.

Etlingeleia :—Athelney, Somerset.

Etocetum :—Kingsbury, Warwickshire; or Wall, Staffordshire.

Etona :—Nuneaton, Warwickshire.

Euania. See *Meuania*.

Eubonia :—Isle of Man. See *Mania*.

Euenlodus Flu. :—River Evenlode, in Oxfordshire.

Euerwica, Euerwika :—York.

Eufania :—Isle of Man.

Euonium :—Dunstaffnage, Argyle.

Eura :—River Ure or Yore, Yorks.

Exa Flu. :—River Exe, Devonshire.

Exancestria :—Exeter.

Excambium Regium :—The Royal Exchange, London.

Excestra :—Exeter.

Exexa :—Essex.

Exoche :—Gunfleet, Essex ; or Wintertonness, Norfolk.

Exonia :—Exeter.

Exosades :—Islands off Norfolk or Essex.

Exploratorum Castra :—Burgh by Sands, Cumberland.

Extensio. See *Exoche.*

Eya :—Eye, Norfolk.

F.

Fayrovella :—Fairwell, Staffordshire.

Fala Flu. :—River Fal, Cornwall.

Falensis Portus :—Falmouth.

Fanocodi :—A town in Cumberland.

Fanum ad Taffum :—Llandaff, Glamorganshire.

Fanum Andreæ :—St. Andrew's, Scotland.

Fanum Canici :—Kilkenny.

Fanum Christi :—Christchurch, Hants.

Fanum Germani :—Llanarmon, Denbigh.

Fanum Iltuti :—Llantwit, Glamorganshire.

Fanum Iuonis Persiæ :—St. Ive's, Hunts.

Fanum Leonis : — Leominster, Herefordshire.

Fanum Neoti :— St.Neot's, Hunts.

Fanum Oswaldi :—Nostal, Yorks.

Fanum Reguli :—St. Andrew's, Scotland, also called Kirkrule and Kilrule.

Fanum S. Albani :—St. Alban's, Herts.

Fanum S. Asaphi :—St. Asaph's, Flintshire.

Fanum S. Botolphi :—Boston, Lincolnshire.

Fanum S. Edmundi :—Bury St. Edmund's, Suffolk.

Fanum S. Johannis :—St. John's, Roscommon, Ireland.

Fanum S. Mauditi :—St. Mawe's, Cornwall.

Fanum Stephani :—Kirkby-Stephen, Westmoreland.

Fanum Teclæ :—Llandegla, Denbigh ; S. Tecla's Chapel, an island at the mouth of the Wye.

Farina :—Fearn, Ross.

Farlega : — Farley or Farleigh Monkton, Wilts. A cell to Lewes Priory.

Fauoria :—Faure, Meath, Ireland.

Faustini Villa. See *Villa Faustini.*

Fawenses :—Inhabitants of Fowey, Cornwall.

Felicia :—Felixstow, Suffolk.

Felicis Oppidum :—Flixton, Suffolk.

Ferberga :—Farnborough.

Ferlega. See *Farlega.*

Ferleia. See *Farlega.*

Fermedona :—Farringdon, Hants.

Fernæ :—Ferns, Wexford, Ireland.

Fernlega. See *Farlega.*

Fernum. See *Fernæ.*

Ferulega :—Hereford.

Fibrilega, Fibrolega :—Beverley, Yorks.

Fifburgensis :—Of the Five Boroughs—Lincoln, Nottingham, Derby, Leicester, and Stamford.

Finnabrensis :—Of Kilfenora, *alias* Edumabrach, *alias* Fenabore, co. Clare, Ireland.

Fisela :—Fishlake, Yorks (?).

Flagaflora, Flauflor :—Sparsholt, Berks.

Flaua Cæsariensis :—Province of Roman Britain between the Thames, Humber, and Mersey; or between Humber, Mersey, and Great Wall.

Flexelega, Flexlega :—Flaxley, Gloucestershire.

Flintia :—Flint.

Fluentanus Carcer :—Fleet Prison, London.

Flumen Dei : — Kilbegain, co. Meath.

Fons Amnensis :—Amwell. Herts.

Fons Brigidæ :—Bridewell, London.

Fons Clarus :—Sherborne, Dorset.

Fons Clericorum :—Clerkenwell, London.

Fons Interfraxinus :—Ashwell, Herts.

Fons Limpidus :—Fairwell, Staffordshire.

Fons Sacer :—Holywell.

Fons S. Patricii :—Ballintobber, co. Mayo.

Fons Scotiæ : — Scotland-well, Kinross.

Fons Vivus :—Maur, co. Cork.

Fontanæ :—Fountains Abbey, Yorks.

Fontanetum, Fontanensis Ecclesia :—Wells, Somerset.

Fontes : — Wells ; Fountains Abbey, Yorks.

Fonticuli :—Wells.

Fontis, Villa :—Holywell, Flintshire.

Fordunum :—Fordoun, co. Kincardine, Scotland.

Forenna :—Part of the city of Wells.

Forgium :—Kilmoney Abbey, co. Clare.

Forneseta :—Forcett, Yorks.

*Fors** de Caritate*:—A Cistercian house in Wensleydale, Yorks.

Forthæ æstuarium, Fortheia :— Firth of Forth.

Forum :—Cheap, London.

Forum Jouis :—Marazion, Cornwall.

Fouera, Fouria :—Fore, Westmeath.

Fraxula Flu. :—In Derbyshire.

Freskewattera : — Freshwater, Isle of Wight.

Fretum Britannicum, Fretum Gallicum, Fretum Morinorum :—The Straits of Dover.

Frigidum Mantellum : — Freemantle, Hants.

Frigmareventus : — Winchelsea, Sussex.

Friscodunense cœnobium :—Freston Abbey, Lincolnshire.

Frodrenela : — Fotharta, Leinster, Ireland.

Fromus, Froma :—River Frome.

Frumentarius Mons :—Cornhill, London.

---

* Query, *Fons* ?

G.

Gabaglanda. See *Amboglanna.*

Gabrantonicorum, Gabrantouicorum Sinus :—Bridlington or Filey Bay, Yorkshire.

Gabrocentum, Gabrosentis :—Gateshead, Durham ; Black Dyke or Drumburgh, Cumberland.

Gadeni :—Inhabitants of Fife, Tweeddale, March, and Lothian, in Scotland.

Gadiua :—Aberffraw, in the Isle of Anglesey.

Gaelwallia : — Galloway, Scotland.

Gaidingtona :—Geddington, Northants.

Gaingtona—Geddington.

Gaini : — People of Lincolnshire.

Gainiburgus :—Gainsborough, Lincolnshire.

Galacum :—Appleby, Kendal, or Whallop Castle, Westmoreland.

Galaua :—Old Town, Keswick, or Wythburn, Cumberland; or Walwick, Northumberland.

Galensis :—A Welshman.

Galetum : — Langley Gale, Sussex.

Galewegia :—Galloway.

Galienses :—Men of Galloway.

Gallaua. See *Galaua.*

Galleua Atrebatum :—Guildford, Silchester, Henley, Reading, Wallingford, Calve Pit Farm, near Reading, or Haslemere, Surrey.

Galliua :—Galway, Ireland.

Gallouidia : — Galloway, Scotland.

Gallunio : — Aldborough. See *Isurium.*

Gallutum. See *Galacum.*

Galueia :—Galloway.

Galuia :—Galway.

Galwalenses :—People of Galloway.

Galwedia, Galwegia : — Galloway.

Galweia :—Galloway.

Gangani : — People of Connaught, Ireland.

Ganganum promontorium : — Braichy Pwll Point, Caernarvonshire.

Garbantorigum :—Caerlaverock, Scotland.

Gareotha :—Gaury or Gowrie (?), Scotland.

Gariannonum :—Yarmouth, or Burgh Castle, Norfolk.

Garmundi Via :—Garmondsway, Durham.

Garrienis, Garyenus, Flu. :—Yare River, Norfolk.

Garryeni Fluvii ostium :—Yarmouth.

Gauinga :—Wenge, Bucks.

Gaurouicum :—Warwick. See *Verouicum.*

Gausennæ, Gausennis. See *Causennæ.*

Gauelforda :—Camelford, Cornwall.

Gedewurda :—Jedburgh, Roxburghshire.

Gegenforda :—Gainford, Durham

Geldeforda :—Guildford, Surrey.

Genesborwia :—Gainsborough, Lincolnshire.

Genunii :—People living on the border of Scotland.

Gereseya :—Jersey.

Gerewedona :—Garendon, Leicestershire.

Gernemua, Gernemutha :—Yarmouth, Norfolk.

Gerneria :—Guernsey.

Geroldona :—Garendon, Leicestershire.

Gersuium :—Jersey.

Geuentonæ :—Chevington, Suffolk.

Geuini :—A river in Wales that runs into the River Usk.

Geuissi :—West Saxons.

Gipeswica, Gippeuicum :—Ipswich, Suffolk.

Girouicum :—Jarrow, Durham.

Giruii :—Inhabitants of the Fens.

Giruum, Girwa :—Jarrow, Durham.

Giuela :—Yeovil, Somerset.

Glamorgania, Glamorgantia :—Glamorganshire.

Glandelacum :—Glendalough, Wicklow, Ireland.

Glannibanta, Glanouenta. See *Clanouenta.*

Glasbiria :—Glasbury, Brecknock.

Glasconia :—Glastonbury, Somerset.

Glascouium :—Glasgow.

Glascua :—Glasgow.

Glascum :—Glascwm, Radnorshire.

Glasquum :—Glasgow.

Glastincbiria :—Glastonbury, Somerset.

Glastonia :—Glastonbury.

Glaudiocestra :—Gloucester.

Glauorna, Glaworna :—Gloucester.

Gleastonia :—Glastonbury.

Glenus :—River Glen, Northumberland.

Glessoburgus :—Glastonbury.

Glestingia, Glestonia :—Glastonbury.

Gleuum :—Gloucester.

Glocestria, Gloecestra :—Gloucester.

Glota :—Isle of Arran.

Glota, Glottiana :—River Clyde, Scotland.

Gloueceastria, Glouernia, Glowecestria :—Gloucester.

Gobannium : — Abergavenny, Monmouthshire.

Goccium. See *Coccium.*

Goderici Castrum : — Goodrich Castle, Herefordshire.

Godestoua :—Godstow, Oxfordshire.

Godritona :—Codrington, Gloucestershire.

Gouheria :—Gower, Glamorganshire.

Græcolada :—Cricklade, Wilts.

Grampius Mons :—The Grampians.

Grangia :—Gransha, Down, Ireland.

Granta : — River Cam, Cambridgeshire.

Granta, Grantanus Pons:—Cambridge.

Grantebreggia : — Cambridge, sometimes Cambridgeshire.

Graua :—Grovebury, Beds.

Grauesenda :—Gravesend, Kent.

Greglada :—Cricklade, Wilts.

Grenewicum : — Greenwich, Kent.

Grenouicus, Grenouicum :— Greenwich, Kent.

Grenteburga :—Cambridge.

Greua :—Gravesend.

Greuanus :—River Girvan, Ayrshire.

Grimboldesessa : — Grombold Ash, Gloucestershire.

Grinuicum :—Greenwich.

Grossus Mons : — Grosmont, Monmouthshire.

Grubba : — Gubeon, Northumberland (Gullane ?).

Guala, Guallia :—Wales.

Guaræ, Guarus :—Ware, Herts.

Guella : —Wells, Norfolk.

Guerfa Flu. : — The River Wharfe, Yorkshire.

Guidonicus Cliuus :—Guy's Cliff, Warwickshire.

Guildhalda Teutonicorum :—The Steel Yard, London.

Guilon Flu. :—River Will, or Wiley, Wiltshire.

Guincestria :—Winchester.

Guinethia : —Wales.

Guinta :—Gwent, a province in South Wales, between Usk and Wye.

Guinuga :—Wenge, Bucks.

Guiramutha :—Wearmouth, Durham.

Guiunga : —Wenge, Bucks.

Guldeforda :—Guildford, Surrey.

Gumicastrum :—Godmanchester, Hunts.

Gwallia :—Wales.

Gwirchia :—Chirk, Denbigh.

Gyruum :—Jarrow, Durham.

H.

Habenduna :—Abingdon, Berks.

Habitancum : — Risingham, Northumberland.

Habus :—The Humber.

Hadriani Murus :—Picts' Wall, or Wall of Hadrian.

Hæbuda. See *Ebuda.*

Hæmodæ. See *Acmodæ.*

Hafren Flu. :—The Severn.

Haga :—The Hay, or Hasely, in Brecknockshire.

Hagulstada :—Hexham, Northumberland ; Alston, Cumberland.

Hagustaldunum : — Hexham, Northumberland.

Haia : — Eye, Suffolk ; Hay, Brecknockshire.

Halænus :—River Avon, Hants.

Hamonis Portus :—Southampton.

Hamptonia, Hamtona : —Southampton ; Northampton ; Hampton.

Hancstesia :—Hinksey, Oxford-shire.

Hansus Flu. :—River Hans, Staffordshire.

Hantonia :—Hampshire.

Haraia :—Harris, one of the Hebrides.

Harefordia :—Hereford.

Harlecum :—Harlech, Merion-ethshire.

Harlepolis : — Hartlepool, Dur-ham.

Haroldi Crux :—Harold's Cross, near Dublin.

Haruicum :—Harwich, Essex.

Hastinga :—Hastings, Sussex.

Hauerberga :—Harborough, Warwickshire.

Hauerfordia : —Haverfordwest, Pembrokeshire.

Haugustaldium. See *Hagustal-dunum.*

Hauma :—Hamme, Berks.

Hauteuorta :—Highworth, Wilts.

Hauxoniensis :—Of Hawkshead, Lancashire.

Haya :—Hay, Brecknockshire.

Heastinga :—Hastings, Sussex.

Hebrides :—A cluster of Isles on the West side of Scotland.

Hebuda. See *Ebuda.*

Hederosum Monasterium :—Ivy-church, Wilts.

Hedros. See *Edros.*

Hedwa :—Hythe, Kent.

Hegdunensis :—Of Annaghdown, co. Clare, Ireland.

Heia :—Hythe, Kent.

Heisa :—Hayes, Kent.

Helaturnum : — Ellerton (?), Yorkshire.

Helenum promontorium :—Land's End.

Helia :—Ely, Cambridgeshire.

Helma :—Helmington, Durham.

Helmanensis : — Of Elmham, Suffolk.

Helmelum :—Elmley.

Hengestesdunum : — Hengston Hill, Cornwall.

Henlega : — Henley - upon - Thames, Oxfordshire.

Henoforthum :—Hereford.

Herboldona : — Harbledown, Kent.

Hernleia :—Hurley, Berks.

Heortforda :—Hertford.

Heoueshamnensis :—Of Evesham, Worcestershire.

Heppa :—Shap, Westmoreland.

Herculis promontorium :—Hart-land Point, Devonshire.

Herdingheleia : — Ardingly, Sussex.

Herefordia :—Hereford, formerly *Ariconium.*

Herkeloua:—Arklow, Connaught.

Herlaua :—Harlow, Essex.

Hertfordia :—Hertford.

Hesperides :—Scilly Isles.

Hestelega : — Astley, Warwick-shire.

Hestinga :—Hastings, Sussex.

Hestingi :—East Angles.

Hetha Pratorum :—Maidenhead, Berks.

Hetha Regine :—Queenhithe.

Heya :—Eye, Suffolk.

Hibernia :—Ireland.

Hichelendunum:—Ickleton,Cambridgeshire.

Hichena :—River Itchen, Hants.

Hichia cœnobium :—Newbiggin, or Hitchin, Herts.

Hicthteslapa :—Islip, Oxon.

Hichtredeberia : — Heytesbury, Wilts.

Hida :—Hyde, near Winchester.

Hieron Promontorium :—Greenore Point, or Carnsore Point, Wexford.

Hildesleia :—Ilsley, Berks.

Himba :—One of the Acmodæ Islands.

Hinchisega :—Hinksey, near Oxford.

Hirtha :—One of the Hebrides.

Histesleapa:—Islip, Oxfordshire.

Hitha Regine :—Queenhithe.

Hithinus portus :—Hythe, Kent.

Hlediæ :—Leeds, Kent.

Hludense Monasterium :—Lough Park Abbey, Lincolnshire.

Hodneius Flu. : — Honddhu River, Brecknockshire.

Hoilandia, Hollandia :—Holland, a part of Lincolnshire.

Holyoti, Castrum de : — Castle Holdgate, Herefordshire.

Holmus :—Hulme, or St. Bennet's-in-the-Holme,Norfolk.

Homdeleia :—Hundsley, Yorks.

Homelea Flu. :—River Hamble, opposite the Isle of Wight, Hants.

Horesti :—People living north of the Firth of Forth.

Horka :—Dunnet Head, Caithness.

Hornecastra :—Horncastle, Lincolnshire.

Horspada :—Horspath, Oxon.

Hospitium Leonis :—Lyon's Inn, London.

Hothenia : — Rivers Hodni or Honddu, in Brecknockshire and Monmouthshire.

Houendena :—Hoveden, Yorks.

Houlandia. See *Hoilandia*.

Hripum :—Ripon, Yorks.

Hrofi, Hrosi Civitas :—Rochester.

Hulla, Hullus:—Kingston-upon-Hull, Yorkshire.

Hultonia :—Ulster, Ireland.

Humbra Flu. :—River Humber.

Hundesdena :—Hunsdon, Herts.

Hundredeskelda : — Hunderthwaite, Yorks.

Hunegetona : — Honington or Hunnington, Staffordshire.

Hungreforda : — Hungerford, Berks.

Hunnum :—Sevenshale, or Halton Chesters, Northumberland.

Hunsdona :—Hunsdon, Herts.

Huntendonia, Huntundona :— Huntingdon.

Hurstanum Castellum : — Hurst Castle, Hants.

Hurstelega :—Hurley, Berks.

Husseburna :—Hurstbourne, Hants.

Huya :—Holy Island.

Hwerwella :—Wherwell, Hants.

Hwiccii :—People of Worcestershire, and about the Severn.

Hydropolis :—Dorchester, Oxon.

Hymalia : — Achad-Fobhair, co.
Mayo.

Hymbrionenses, Hymbronenses :—
People of Northumberland.

Hyrebothla :—Harbottle,
Northumberland.

Hyrtha :—One of the Hebrides.

Hyta :—Hythe, Kent.

I.

Iberni :—People of Desmond,
Ireland.

Ibernia :—Ireland.

Ibernio :—Bere Regis, or Iwerne,
Dorset.

Ibernium :—Iwerne, Dorset.

Ibernis :—Dunkerrin, King's Co.,
Ireland.

Iberran :—A town in Scotland,
north of the Forth.

Icannum : — Boston, Lincolnshire.

Iceni :—People of Suffolk, Norfolk, Cambridge, and Hun-
tingdon shires.

Iciani, Icinos :—Chesterford,
Essex ; Thetford or Ig-
borough, Norfolk ; or
Southwold, Suffolk.

Icini. See *Iceni.*

Ictis Insula : — St. Michael's
Mount, Cornwall ; or, per-
haps, the Isle of Wight
(*Vectis*).

Idumanus :—Blackwater River,
or the mouth of the Stour
and Orwell, Essex.

Iena æstuarium :—Wigton Bay,
Galloway.

Ierne, Iernis :—Ireland.

Iernus :—River Erne, or Ken-
mare Bay, Ireland.

Igenia : —Part of Flintshire.

Ihona. See *Iona.*

Ila Flu. :—River Wick, Scotland.

Ila Insula :—Isla, west of Scotland.

Illega Combusta :—Brent Eleigh
or Illegh, Suffolk.

Illega Monachorum : — Monk's
Eleigh, Suffolk.

Imelaca :—Emly, co. Tipperary.

Imelensis :—Of Emly.

Imensa æstuarium :— Mouth of
the Thames.

Imlaca :—Emly.

Immemera :—Mere, Wilts.

Incuneningum : — Cunning-
ham (?), Scotland.

Inderauuda :—Beverley, Yorks.

Ingetlingus :—Gilling, Yorks.

Ingiruum :—Jarrow, Durham.

Ingoluesmera : — Ingoldmells,
Lincolnshire.

Inmeleccensis :—Of Emly, Tipperary.

Innerlothea :—Inverlochy, Inverness.

Insula :—Eynesham, or Ensham,
Oxfordshire ; Axholm, Lincolnshire ; Isle, near Stock-
ton, Durham ; Little Island.
Waterford Harbour.

Insula Cervi :—Hartlepool, Durham.

Insula Sacra : — Ireland ; also Holy Island, Northumberland.

Insula Missarum :—Inchaffray, Perthshire.

Insula Sancti Columbæ : — Columbkill, Iona.

Insula Sanctorum :—Ynis Enlly, Bardsey, Caernarvon.

Insula Vectis :—Isle of Wight.

Insularis Villa :—Islington.

Interamna, Interamnium:—Christ Church, Hants.

Inuernessus : — Inverness, Scotland.

Iona :—Iona, or Icolmkill Isle, West Coast of Scotland.

Iphletha :—Evelith, Shropshire.

Ircenefelda : — Archenfield, or Irchingfield, Herefordshire.

Iris :—Ireland.

Isaca :—River Exe, Devonshire ; also River Esk, Scotland.

Isamnium : — St. John's Foreland, or Point, co. Down, Ireland.

Isannauantia, Isannauaria, Isannauatia :—Stony Stratford, Northants, or the same as *Bannauenna ;* Allchester, Oxon, between Wendlebury and Bicester.

Isannium. See *Isamnium.*

Isca :—River Exe ; River Usk.

Isca :—Liskeard, Cornwall.

Isca Dumnoniorum : — Chiselborough, Somerset ; or Exeter.

Isca Legio II. Augusta, Iscelegua Augusti, Isca Silurum, Iscamum : — Caerleon, Monmouthshire.

Iscalis :—Ivelchester, now Ilchester, Somerset.

Iscamum :—Caerleon.

Ischalis. See *Iscalis.*

Isiacum :—Oxford.

Isiburna : — Woburn, Bedfordshire.

Isidis Insula :—Ousney, or Oseney, near Oxford.

Isidis Vadum :—Oxford.

Isis Flu. :—River Isis, Oxford; the Ouse, Buckinghamshire; and the Ouse, Yorkshire.

Istelhorda :—Isleworth, Middlesex.

Isubrigantum. See *Isurium.*

Isuria :—Yorkshire.

Isurium :—Aldborough, or Boroughbridge, Yorkshire.

Isurouicum :—York.

Ittingaforda :—Hitchin, Herts.

Itucadon : — A town between Tyne and Forth.

Ituma, Ituna : — River Eden, Cumberland ; or Solway Firth.

Itys :—Loch Eu, Torridon, or Duich, Scotland.

Iuecestra : — Ilchester, Somerset.

Iuerianus Pons :—Iford Bridge, Hants.

Iuernia :—Ireland.

Iuernis : — Dunkerrin, King's Co., Ireland.

Iuorus :—Newry, co. Armagh.

J.

Jaciodulma. See *Magiouinium.*

Jamesa, Jamissa : — River Thames.

Jano :—A town in Caithness.

Jarum :—Yarm, Yorks.

Jernmuthia :—Yarmouth, Norfolk.

Jerouallæ :—Jervaulx, Yorks.

Joriuallis :—Jervaulx, Yorks.

Judaismus :— Old Jewry, London.

Jugantes. See *Brigantes.*

Jugo Dei, de :—Jude or Gray, a Cistercian Abbey, co. Meath, a cell of Holme Coltram.

Jugum Fraxinetum :—Ashridge, Bucks.

Julia Strata :—A Roman road in South Wales, from Newport to Caerleon, Caerwent, and the Wye.

Julianus Pons :—Julian Bridge, Wimborne Minster.

Juliocenon. See *Tunnocelum.*

Jumanius. See *Eidumania.*

Juuerna :—Ireland.

K.

Kaerperis :—Porchester, Hants.

Kanna :—Calne, Wilts.

Kanus Flu. : — River Ken, or Kent, Westmoreland.

Karintona :—Catherington, Hants.

Karlegion :—Chester.

Karlenefordia :—Carlingford, Louth, Ireland.

Katenessa, Kathenessia :—Caithness, Scotland.

Katinensis : — Of Caithness.

Kauna :—Calne, Wilts.

Kenceleia :—Hykinselagh, a district in Leinster.

Kenelcunillia : — Tirconnel, Ulster.

Keneleonia :—Cinel-Eoghain, Ulster.

Keneta Flu. : — River Kennet, Berkshire.

Kenintona : — Kennington, Kempton.

Keresburga : — Carisbrook, Isle of Wight.

Keretica : — Ceredigion, a province of South Wales ; Cardiganshire.

Kermelum : — Cartmel, Lancashire.

Kerriensis Comitatus :—County of Kerry, Ireland.

Kerrigia :—Kerry.

Kesteuena : — Kesteven, a division of Lincolnshire.

Kiemela :—Keymer, Sussex.

Kilchennia, Kilchennium :—Kilkenny, Leinster, Ireland.

Kildabewensis : — Of Killaloe, Ireland.

Kildareuensis :—Of Killaloe (?).

Kildaria :—Kildare, Ireland.

Killathensis :—Of Killalla, Ireland.

Kilmalochum :—Kilmallock, Limerick.

Kilmora : —Kilmore, co. Cavan, Ireland.

Kinardeferia :—Kinardferry, Axholm.

Kinebantum Castrum :—Kimbolton Castle, Hunts.

Kinetus fluvius :—R. Kennet.

Kirchuallum : — Kirkwall, Orkney Islands.

Kirketona : — Kirton, Lincolnshire.

Koila. See *Coualia.*

Korcensis :—Of Cork.

Kubii Castrum :—Holyhead.

Kyenfernensis :—Of Clonfert (?).

Kyma :—Kyme, Yorks.

Kynlathensis :—Of Killalla.

Kynemeresforda :—Kempsford, Wilts.

Kyrieleyson :—Odorney Abbey, Kerry.

Kyuela :—Keevil, Wilts.

L.

Laberus :—Killare Castle, Westmeath, Ireland.

Lacra :-- Castle Acre, Norfolk.

Lactodorum, Lactorodum :—Towcester, Northants; Stony Stratford, Bucks; Bicester, Oxfordshire; Bedford; or Loughborough or Lutterworth, Leicestershire.

Ladeni. See *Gadeni.*

Ladensis Episcopatus : — The bishopric of Killalla, co. Mayo, Ireland.

Laentonia :—Lanthony.

Lætus Locus :—Netley, Hants.

Lagecium : — Castleford, near Pontefract, Yorks.

Lagenia. See *Laginia.*

Lagentium. See *Lagecium.*

Laghlinum :—Leighlin, co. Carlow, Ireland.

Laginia :—Leinster, Ireland.

Lagubalium. See *Luguvallum.*

La Hyda :—Hyde, Hants.

Lamea, Lamheya, Lamitha, Lamithus, Lampheia : — Lambeth, Surrey.

Lamyrii Montes :—Lammermuir Hill, Scotland.

Lancastra, Lancastria : —Lancaster.

Landa :—Launde, Leicestershire.

Landava : — Llandaff, Glamorganshire.

Landinium :—London.

Lanelvensis :—Of Llanelwy, *i.e.* St. Asaph, Wales.

Langanum promontorium. See *Canganorum.*

Langeleia :—Langley.

Lanhondenum : — Lanthony, Monmouthshire.

Lanhondenum Claudianum : — Lanthony, Gloucestershire.

Lania :—Lancashire.

Lanicolæ :—Lancashire men.

Lannotaua :—Llandaff, Glamorganshire.

Lanstuphadonia, Lanstauentum : —Launceston, Cornwall.

Lantodhenia :—Llanthony, Monmouthshire.

Lantonia : — Llanthony, Monmouthshire.

Laodonia :—Lothian.

Laonia : — Killaloe, co. Tipperary.

Lapis Tituli :—Stonor, in the Isle of Thanet, Kent.

Lathelada :—Lechlade, Gloucestershire.

Latisaquensis :—Lewes, Sussex.

Latum Bulgium. See *Blatum Bulgium.*

Lauatres, Lauatris, Lauaris :— Bowes, North Riding of Yorkshire; or Barnard Castle, Durham.

Laudenia, Laudonia : —Lauden, or Lothian, Scotland.

Lawedra : — Lauder, Berwickshire.

Lccefelda :—Lichfield, Staffordshire.

Lechenlada, Lechelada :—Lechlade, Gloucestershire.

Lechlinia:—Leighlin, co. Carlow, Ireland.

Lectoceto. See *Etocetum.*

Ledanum Castrum :—Leeds Castle, Kent.

Ledesia :—Leeds, Yorkshire.

Ledone :—Dunbar.

Legacestra :—Chester.

Legacestria, Legecestria: —Leicester.

Lege Dei, B. V. M. de :—Leix Abbey, Queen's co.

Legeolium :—Pontefract, Castleford, Goole, or Ferrybridge, Yorks. See *Lagecium.*

Legercestria :—Leicester.

Leghelensis, Leghglensis :—Of Leighlin.

Legio VI. Victrix :—York.

Legio XX. Victrix :—Chester.

Legionum Urbs:—Chester; Caerleon.

Legoria :—Leicester.

Legra :—River Soar, Leicestershire.

Legrecastrum :—Leicester.

Legrecestria : —Leicester ; Chester.

Lehecestria :—Leicester.

Leicestria :—Leicester.

Leis : —Leix, Leixlip, co. Kildare, Ireland.

Lelannonius, Lelamnonius Sinus : —Loch Fyne.

Lelienus Flu. :—River Rother, Kent.

Lemana Flu. :—The Rother, Kent; the Loman, Devon.

Lemanis portus, Lemauio :— Lympne, Kent.

Lemaus:—Lympne, Kent; Lynn, Norfolk.

Lena :—Monkland, Hereford.

Lenes :—Lessness, Kent.

Leofense Cœnobium :—Leominster, Herefordshire.

Leofrici Villa :—Leverington, Cambridgeshire.

Leogereceastria :—Leicester.

Leogoria :—Leicester.

Leogus :—Lewis, one of the Hebrides.

Leonense Cœnobium :—Leominster.

Leonis :—Lothian.

Leonis Castrum :—Lyons, *alias* Holt Castle, Denbighshire.

Leonis Monasterium :—Leominster, Herefordshire.

Leouechenora : —Lewknor, Oxfordshire.

Leouense Cœnobium : —Leominster.

Lesinæ :—Lesnes or Lessness, Kent.

Lesmoria :—Lismore, co. Waterford.

Lestinga :—Lastingham, Yorks.

Lesua :—Lewes, Sussex.

Letha :—Leith, co. Edinburgh.

Lethglensis :—Of Leighlin, co. Carlow.

Leuarum. See *Leucarum.*

Leuca :—River Low.

Leucarum :—Glastonbury, Somerset ; Loughor, Glamorganshire ; or Llandybi, Caermarthenshire.

Leucobibia. See *Lucopibia.*

Leucomago. See *Verlucio.*

Leuena :—River Leven, Lancashire.

Leugosena : — River Loughor, South Wales.

Leuinia :—Lennox, Stirlingshire.

Leuinus :—River Leven, Scotland.

Leuiodanum :—Livingstone, Linlithgow.

Leuioxana :—Lennox.

Leuissa : — Lewis Island, Hebrides.

Leuisum :—Lewes, Sussex.

Lewæ :—Lewes.

Lewensis : —Of Lewes.

Leya : — Canon Leigh, Burlescombe, Devon.

Liar Flu. :—River Liver, Lancashire.

Libæus :—Sligo Bay.

Libnius :—River Liffey, Ireland.

Licestria :—Leicester.

Licetfelda, Lichfeldia : — Lichfield, Staffordshire.

Lichia :—Leach, Gloucestershire.

Lichinus Campus :—Lichfield.

Liddenus Flu. :—River Leadon, Herefordshire.

Lideforda :—Lydford, Devon.

Lidocollina :—Lincoln.

Ligea :—River Lea.

Ligeria :—Leicester.

Ligrecastrum :—Leicester.

Limenus :—R. Rother, Kent.

Limericum :—Limerick, Ireland.

Limes Prætorius : — Gravesend, Kent.

Limnos, Limnus :—Dalkey Isle, or Lambay Isle, Dublin.

Limodomus :—Limehouse, near London.

Limonius Mons : — Plinlimmon, Cardiganshire.

Limpida Sylva :—Sherwood Forest, Notts.

Lincolinum, Lincolnia, Lindecolina :—Lincoln.

Lindeseia : — Lindsey, Lincolnshire.

Lindicolinum :—Lincoln.

Lindis : — River Witham, Lincolnshire.

Lindisfari :—Lindsey.

Lindisfarnea, Lindisfarnum :—Holy Island, or Farn Isle, on the coast of Northumberland.

Lindisgia, Lindisi :—Lindsey, Lincolnshire.

Lindisseia :—Lindsey.

Lindocollinum :—Lincoln.

Lindonium :—Lincoln ; London.

Lindum, Lindum Colonia :—Lincoln. See *Lincolinum.*

Lindum Damniorum :—Linlithgow, or Ardoch, Perth.

Linia :—Bardsey Island, Caernarvonshire.

Liniennus :—River Rother, Kent.

Linum Regis :—King's Lynn, Norfolk.

Linus :—River Lin, Notts.

Liserpalus :—Liverpool, Lancashire.

Lisia :—See *Lissia.*

Lismora :—Lismore, co. Waterford.

Lismoria :—Lismore, Argyleshire ; Lismore, co. Waterford.

Lissia : — The Wolf Rock, or the Seven Stones, between the Scilly Islands and the Cornish coast.

Litana :—Linlithgow.

Litecota :—Littlecote, Wilts.

Litinomago :—Linlithgow.

Littus Altum :—Roxburgh.

Littus Saxonicum :—Eastern and southern coasts of Britain.

Llanlienis :—Leominster, Herefordshire.

Locherinum stagnum : —Lough Owel, Westmeath.

Locus Benedictus :—Stanlawe, Cheshire.

Locus Dei :—Hethorp, Gloucestershire ; Hinton Charterhouse, Somerset.

Lodanum Castrum : — Leeds Castle, Kent.

Lodeneium, Lodoneium, Lodonis (dat.) :—The Lothians, Scotland.

Loegria : — England between Humber and Severn.

Loennais :—Lothian.

Logi : —A tribe in Sutherland and Strathnairn.

Logia Flu. :—River Bann, which flows north from Lough Neagh. Camden applies the name to Lough Foyle.

Logus :—River Llugwy, Wales.

Loidis :—Lothian.

Lokerleia :—Lockerley, Hants.

Lomandus. See *Lomundus.*

Lombormora :—Lammermoor, Midlothian.

Lomea :—The Goodwin Sands.

Lomithis : —Lambeth.

Lomulla :—Lemallyon, Cornwall.

Lomundus :—Loch Lomond.

Lonais :—Lothian.

Loncastria :—Lancaster.

Londa :—Launde, Leicestershire.

Londinia, Londinium, Londinia Augusta :—London.

Londino-Deria :—Londonderry, Ireland.

Londinum, Londonia, Londoniæ : —London.

Longa Leta :—Longleat, Wilts.

Longouicariorum, Longouico :— Lanchester, or Chester-le-Street, Durham ; or Lancaster.

Longum Æstuarium :—Loch Linnhe, Argyleshire.

Longus Pons :—Longbridge, Gloucestershire.

Loonia :—Lothian.

Louentinum :—Powysland, in Wales. See also *Luentinum.*

Lounecastra :—Lancaster.

Loxa :—River Lossie, Elgin ; or the Loth, Sutherland.

Loxa Civitas :—Inverlochy, Scotland.

Luceni :—The people of West Munster.

Lucga :—River Lugg, Herefordshire.

Lucopibia :—Whitherne, Galloway. See *Candida Casa.*

Lucus Benedictus : — Stanlawe Abbey, Cheshire.

Luda :—Louth, Ireland ; Louth, Linc. ; Ludlow.

Luddolocus, Ludelawa :—Ludlow, Shropshire.

Luentinum :—Llanddewybrefy, Cardiganshire.

Lugas :—River Lug, Herefordshire.

Lugdunum :—Louth, Ireland.

Lugensis :—Of Louth, Ireland.

Lughbelunensis :—Of Louth, Ireland.

Lugi :—People in the north of Scotland.

Luguballia, Luguballium :—Carlisle, or Plumpton Wall, Cumberland.

Lugundinum :—Lanchester, Durham.

Luguuallum :—Carlisle, Cumberland. See *Luguballia.*

Luia :—Louth (?).

Luia :—River Lea, Herts.

Lumbricus :—Limerick.

Lummalea :—Lumley, Durham.

Lumniacum, Lumpniacum :— Limerick.

Luna :—Lynn, Norfolk.

Lunda :—Monk Bretton, Yorks.

Lundinium, Lundonia :—London.

Lunia :—Lancashire.

Lutudarum :—Tapton, near Chesterfield, Derbyshire.

Lutum :—Louth, Ireland.

Luua :—Louth County, Ireland.

Luueth :—Louth (?), Ireland.

Luuius :—River Lee, Cork.

Lychefeldia :—Lichfield, Staffordshire.

Lyssa :—Liss, Hants.

M.

Macatonion :—The same as *Ariconium.*

Machui :—Mayo, Ireland.

Macolicum :—Mallow, co. Cork, Ireland.

Madus :—Maidstone, Kent, or Strood. See *Vagniacæ.*

Mæata :—People living near the Wall of Antonine.

Mayesetæ :—The people of Radnorshire, or Herefordshire.

Magiouinium, Magiouintum :—Dunstable or Ashwell, Beds; or Fenny Stratford, or Aylesbury, Bucks.

Magis :—Pierce Bridge, Durham, or Lonsdale Hundred, Lanc.

Magium :—Nenay, co. Cork.

Maglonæ, Maglouæ :—Machynlleth, Montgomeryshire; Greta Bridge, Yorks; or Lancaster.

Magnis :—Bowness, Cumberland; Caervoran or Chester-in-the-Wall, near Haltwhistle, Northumberland; Kenchester, or Old Radnor, Herefordshire.

Magnitum. See *Magiouinium.*

Magnus Portus :—Portsmouth.

Maia :—May Island, in the Firth of Forth.

Maidulphi Curia, Maidulphi Urbs :—Malmesbury, Wilts.

Maigonensis :—Of Mayo, Ireland.

Mailenia :—Maelienydd, a province in Powys, North Wales.

Mailoria Wallica :—Maylor, Flintshire.

Maina Flu. : — The Mintern, Dorset.

Maionensis :—Of Mayo.

Malaca :—Isle of Mull.

Mala Platea :—Near Wenlock, Shropshire.

Malbanus Vicus, Vicus Malbus :—Wyz Mauban, Nautwich, Cheshire.

Malcolicum :—Mallow, co. Cork.

Maldunense Cœnobium :—Malmesbury Abbey, Wilts.

Malea Platea : — Ill Street, Cheshire.

Malesbergia : — Marlborough, Wilts.

Maleos :—Isle of Mull, west of Scotland.

Malmesbiria :—Malmesbury.

Malum Oppidum :—Yeovil, Somerset.

Malus Passus : — Malpas, Cheshire.

Maluerna, Maluernia, Maluernum:—Malvern, Worcestershire.

Mameceastra : — Manchester, Lancashire.

Mamucium :—Manchester.

Manapia :—Wicklow, or Wexford, Ireland.

Manaui. See *Meneuia.*

Mancunium :—Manchester.

Manduessedum :—Mancetter, or Kenilworth, Warwickshire.

Mania, Manna, Mannia :—The Isle of Man.

Mannechestria : — Mancetter, Warwickshire.

Mantauis :—St. David's, Pembrokeshire.

Mantio :—Manchester.

Manucium :—Manchester.

Mara, Foresta de : — Delamere Forest, Cheshire.

Marawuda:—Marwood, Durham.

Marchenium :—Roxburgh.

Marchia : — March, or Mers, Scotland.

Marchia Walliæ :—The Marches or Borders of Wales.

Marchidunum :—Roxburgh.

Marcotaxon :—A town north of the Wall of Antonine.

Mare Britannicum : — The English Channel.

Mare Caledonium :—The Scotch Sea.

Mare Hibernicum :—The Irish Channel.

Mare Sabrinianum :—The Severn Sea.

Mare Virginium, Verginium :— The sea on the south of Ireland.

Margaberya : — Marlborough, Wilts.

Margidunum, Margitudum : — East Bridgeford, Notts ; or Mount Sorrel, Leicestershire.

Maridunum :—Caermarthen.

Mariscallia :—The Marshalsea, London.

Marlebrigia :—Marlborough.

Marnia :—Mearns, Kincardine, Scotland.

Marria :—Marr, Aberdeen, Scotland.

Martona :—Merton, Surrey.

Masona :—A town probably in Devonshire.

Massamensis Pons : — Masham Bridge, Yorks.

Matillis Castellum :—Painscastle, Herefordshire.

Matouion :—A town north of the Wall of Antonine.

Mauditi Castrum :—St. Mawe's Castle, Cornwall.

Maulion : — A town north of the Wall of Antonine.

Mauordina :—Marden, Herefordshire.

Mauia :—River Maw, Merionethshire.

Mauritanea :—probably Llanbadarn Vaur, Cardiganshire.

Mauthia :—Meath, Ireland.

Maxima Cæsariensis :—Province of Britain, north of the Humber and Ribble, and south of Tyne ; or the Scotch Highlands, north of the Wall of Severus.

Mealdunum :—Maldon, Essex.

Mealmesbiria :—Malmesbury.

Mealtuna :—Malton, Yorks.

Meandari. See *Meanuari.*

Meanuari :—A tribe living in Hampshire, whose name remains in Estmeon and Westmeon Hundreds.

Mearlsberga :—Marlborough, Wilts.

Meatæ :—People of Lothian.

Meaudunum :—Maldon, Essex.

Medeguaia :—River Medway.

Medena : — Newport, Isle of Wight.

Medeshamstundensis :—Of Peterborough, Northants.

Media :—County of Meath, Ireland.

Mediamnis : — Medmenham, Bucks.

Medimna : — Christchurch, Hants.

Mediolanium : — Middleham, Yorks.

Mediolanum : —Llanvyllin or Meifod, Montgomery; or Nantwich, Cheshire; Drayton, Whitchurch, or Bearstone, Shropshire; or Chesterton, Warwickshire.

Mediomanum : — The same as *Mediolanum*, or Maentwrog, Merionethshire.

Medionemeton :—On the Wall of Antonine.

Mediterranei Angli :—People of the Midland Counties.

Medius Vicus : — Middlewich, Cheshire.

Meduaga, *Medweacus* : — River Medway.

Mela :—Isle of Mull.

Melamon :—In Devonshire.

Melanclani, *Melanchlani* : — People of the Scilly Islands.

Melduna :—Maldon, Essex.

Meldunum :—Malmesbury, Wiltshire.

Melesburia :—Melbury, Dorset.

Melezo :—In Dorset.

Mella monasterium : — Meaux Abbey, Yorks.

Mellifons :—Mellifont, Louth.

Melsa :—Meaux, Yorks.

Memanturum :—A town north of the Wall of Antonine.

Menan :—Meneg, Cornwall.

Menapii : — Tribe inhabiting Wexford.

Menauia :—Isle of Man.

Menes :—Meon, Hants.

Meneuia : — St. David's, Pembrokeshire.

Menna :—Meneg, Cornwall.

Menstra :—Minster, Kent.

Mentæ :—People on the Scotch Border. See *Meatæ*.

Meodewega : —River Medway.

Mercia :—Middle part of England.

Mercii :—Inhabitants of Mercia.

Merionithia :—Merionethshire.

Merleberga :—Marlborough, Wilts.

Merleberia, *Merlebrigia* :—Marlborough.

Merscum :—Marske, Yorks.

Mersia : —River Mersey, Cheshire.

Mertæ : — Tribe inhabiting Sutherland.

Meruinia :—Merionethshire.

Metaris Æstuarium :—The Wash, Norfolk.

Meuania :—Isle of Man ; Anglesey.

Miba :—Midhurst, Sussex.

Micelnia, *Michennia*, *Michlania* : —Muchelney, Somerset.

Mictis. See *Ictis*.

Mida :—Meath, Ireland.

Midcelania :—Muchelney, Somerset.

Middlesexia :—Middlesex.

Midia :—Meath.

Mildeshala :—Mildenhall, Suffolk.

Mildetunensis :—Of Middleton, Dorset.

Milidunum : —same as *Meldunum* (?).

Milfordiensis Portus :—Milford Haven.

Milidunum :—In Devonshire.

Milleferda :—Milford, Pembrokeshire.

Miluerdicus Portus : — Milford Haven.

Minarii Montes:—Mendip Hills, Somerset.

Mincheneleya : — Canonleigh, Burlescombe, Devon.

Mineruæ Insula :—Peninsula of Morvern, Argyleshire.

Mira Vallis : — Merevale, Warwickshire.

Mirmanton : —According to Nennius the same as *Cair Segeint,* which Henry of Huntingdon says is Silchester ; but one MS. of Nennius adds, " *Id est urbs Eboraca.*"

Mitfordia :—Mitford, Northumberland.

Mochinga :—Mucking, Essex.

Modanus :—River Liffey, Ireland.

Modarnus:—River Mourne; once applied to the Foyle.

Moina :—Man.

Molis Flu. :—The Mole, Surrey.

Momonia :—Province of Munster, Ireland.

Mona :—Anglesey.

Mona Ulterior :—Isle of Man.

Monachodunum :—Monkton, Yorks.

Monachopolis :—Newcastle - on - Tyne (Munekeceastre).

Monæda, Monapia :—The Isle of Man.

Monasterium Cornutum:—Hornchurch, Essex.

Monasterium Hederosum :—Ivychurch, Wilts.

Monega :—Anglesey.

Monemuta :—Monmouth.

Monia :—Anglesey ; Man.

Monmuthia :—Monmouth.

Monocotona :—Monkton, Kent.

Monomia. See *Momonia.*

Monouaga :—Monmouth.

Mons Acutus :—Montacute, Somerset.

Mons Altus :—Mold, Flintshire.

Mons Arenosus:—Sandon, Herts.

Mons Dives:—Richmond, Surrey.

Mons Dolorosus :—Stirling.

Mons Draconis :—Mount Drake, Devon.

Mons Gaudius :—see *Mons Jouis.*

Mons Gomericus:—Montgomery, Wales.

Mons Grampius :—Grampian Hills.

Mons Jouis :—Mountjoy, or Monge, Norfolk.

Mons Michaelis :—St. Michael's Mount, Cornwall.

Mons Rosarum:—Montrose, Forfarshire.

Mons S. Andreæ :—Sallay, or Sawley, Yorks.

Mons Solis :—Bath.

Mont Dolerus, Chastel de :—Montrose.

Montarcola :—Near Caermarthen.

Monte Gilberti, Foresta de :—The Wrekin, Shropshire.

Montgomeria :—Montgomery.

Monumethia :—Monmouth.

Mora :—More, Shropshire.

Moravia :—Moray or Murray, Scotland.

Morbium :—Moresby, Cumberland ; Hornsea, or Temple Brough, Yorkshire.

Morda : —River Meole (?), which joins the Severn near Shrewsbury.

Moricamba, Moricambe Æstuarium :— Morecambe Bay, Lancashire.

Moridunum :—Seaton, or Honiton, Devon ; Eggerton, Dorset.

Morpitium :—Morpeth, Northumberland.

Morsiburgus :—Bridgenorth, Shropshire.

Mortuus Lacus :—Mortlake, Surrey.

Mucletona :—Mickleton.

Mula :—Isle of Mull, west coast of Scotland.

Munekacastra : — Newcastle-on-Tyne, Northumberland.

Munemuta :—Monmouth.

Munus :—River Monnow, which divides Herefordshire from Monmouthshire.

Murevia :—Moray, Scotland.

Muridunum. See *Moridunum.*

Muridunum : —Caermarthen.

Murimintum, Muriuindum :—Silchester, Hants.

Murionio : In Dorset.

Murotriges. See *Durotriges.*

Murrevia :—Moray, Scotland.

Murthlacum :— Murtley, Aberdeen.

Murus :—River Vere, Herts.

Murus Picticus :—The Picts' Wall. See *Hadriani Murus.*

Muscomaria :—Mossdale Moor, Yorks.

Mussalburgum :—Musselburgh, co. Edinburgh.

Mutuantonis :—Lewes, Sussex ; Whitewalls, Wilts.

Mygensis :—Of Mayo, Ireland.

N.

Nabæus. See *Nauæus.*

Næomagus. See *Neomagus; Nouiomagus.*

Næsbeia :—Naseby, Northants.

Nagnata :—Sligo, or Limerick.

Nalcua :—The same as *Galleua.*

Nanæus. See *Nauæus.*

Nantouicum :—Nantwich, Cheshire.

Nasense Castrum :—Naas, Kildare.

Nasi Enei Colleyium :—Brasenose College, Oxford.

Nauæus :—River Naver, Sutherland.

Nauesbia :—Naseby, Northants.

Naurum : —The Nadder, Wilts ; the Naver, Sutherland.

Nautgallum :—Walbrook, London.

Nauticus Sinus :—Rotherhithe.

Neagora :—Newmarket.

Neddercota : —Nethercote, Oxfordshire.

Nemedus : — Barrymore, near Cork.

Nemetotacio :—A town in Cornwall.

Nemus Aquilinum : — Elstree, Herts.

Nemus Boreale :—North - hall, Herts.

Neomagus :—Buckingham, See also *Nouiomagus.*

Neoportus : — Newport, Isle of Wight ; Newport, Essex.

Neoportus Paganellicus :—Newport Pagnell, Bucks.

Ncorus :—Lagan Water, Ulster.

Nerigon Insula :—Isle of Lewes.

Neslandia :—West of Scotland.

Neuarca, Newerca : — Newark, Notts.

Nicholia, Nicole :—Lincoln.

Nicolesciria :—Lincolnshire.

Nidum : — Portbury, Somerset ; Neath, Glamorganshire.

Nidus :—River Nid, Yorks.

Nigera :—Blakeney, Norfolk.

Nincolia :—Lincoln.

Niomagus. See *Nouiomagus.*

Nithia :—Nidisdale, Scotland.

Niuburia :—Newbury, Berks.

Niuicollini : — Snowdon Mountain, Caernarvonshire.

Niwebota :—Newbottle, Durham.

Niweburia :—Newbury, Berks.

Nobius. See *Nouius.*

Nocteleia :—Nutley, Bucks.

Nordhumbra, Nordhumbria :— Northumberland.

Nordoricum : — Norton Hall, Yorks.

Nordouicum :—Norwich.

Nordouolca :—Norfolk.

Norflita :—Northfleet, Kent.

Norhamtuna :—Northampton.

Norhantescira : — Northamptonshire.

Norhumbria :—Northumberland.

Northaluertonia : — Northallerton, Yorks.

Northamptonia, Northamtuna :— Northampton. See *Bannavenna.*

Northanimbria :—Northumberland.

Northantonia :—Northampton.

Northimbria :—Northumberland.

Northumbria :—Northumberland.

Northwicum :—Norwich.

Northymbria :—Northumberland.

Nortmannabia : — Normanby, Yorks.

Nortobricum : — Norton Hall, Yorks.

Nortouicum : — Northwich, Cheshire.

Noruicum :—Norwich.

Norwallia :—North Wales.

Norwicia, Norwicus :—Norwich.

Notium Promontorium :—Mizen Head, Wicklow, Ireland.

Nottingamia :—Nottingham.

Noua Aula :—Newhall, Essex.

Noua Porta :—Newgate, London.

Noua Terra :—Newland, Gloucestershire.

Noua Villa : — Newtown, co. Down.

Nouantii, Nouantæ, Nouantes:—
The inhabitants of Gallo-
way, Carrick, and Arran.

*Nouantum Promontorium, No-
uantum Chersonesus* :—Mull
of Galloway ; Cockermouth.

Nouia :—River Rother, Sussex.

Nouiodunum :—Newenden, Kent.

Nouiomagus, Nouiomagnus :—
Woodcote, Surrey ; Chi-
chester ; Holwood Hill,
Keston, or near Plumstead,
Kent.

Nouius Flu. :—River Nid, Scotland. See also *Conouium.*

*Nouum Castellum, Nouum Cas-
trum* : — Newcastle - upon -
Tyne, Northumberland ;
Newcastle - under - Lyme,
Staffordshire.

*Nouum Forum, Nouum Merca-
tum* : — Newmarket, Cam-
bridgeshire.

Nouum Oppidum sub Lima :—
Newcastle-under-Lyme.

Nouum Oppidum super Tinam :—
Newcastle-on-Tyne.

Nouus Burgus :—Newport, Isle
of Wight ; Newport, Mon-
mouthshire ; Newhaven or
Rye, Sussex ; Newbury,
Berks ; Newburgh, Yorks ;
a Benedictine convent near
Llandaff.

Nouus Locus:—Newark, or New
Place, near Guildford ; New-
stead, Notts.

Nouus Portus:—Newport ; Newhaven, Kent ; Rye, Sussex.

Nuba :—Midhurst, Sussex. See
Mibu.

Nubiria, Nuburia : —Newbury,
Berks.

*Nulla Ejusmodi, Nulli Par, Nulli
Secunda*:—Nonsuch, Surrey.

O.

Oboca Flu. :—River Avoca, Ireland.

Occidua Wallia :—Cornwall.

Oceanus Verginius :—The Irish
Ocean.

Ocellum Promontorium:—Spurn-
head, Holderness, Yorks.

Ocetis : — Shetland, Pentland,
Skerries.

Ochthe Hupsele :—Ord of Caithness.

Ocite :—Baz Island on the West
of Ireland (Bear Isle, Ban-
try Bay ?).

Ockhamptonia : — Okehampton,
Devon.

Ockus :—River Okement, Devon.

Ocrinum, Ocrium Promontorium :
—Lizard Point, Cornwall.

Octapitarum Promontorium : —
St. David's Head, Pem-
brokeshire.

Odrona :—Idrone, co. Carlow.

Oestrymnicus Sinus : — Mount's
Bay, Cornwall.

Oestrymnides Insulæ : — Scilly
Islands.

Offalaia :—Offaly, co. Kildare.

Offedena :—Howden, Yorks.

Offelana :—Offaly.

Offelawa:—Offlow,Staffordshire.

Oissereia :—Ossory, Ireland.

Okesseta :—Oxshot, Surrey.

Olanega :—Olney, Bucks.

Oleiclauis :—Ogle Castle, Northumberland.

Olenacum : — Old Carlisle, or Ellenborough, Cumberland; Ilkley, Yorks.

Olerica :—Ilkirk, Cumberland.

Olfinum :—Elphin, co. Roscommon, Ireland.

Olicana : — Ilkley, or Halifax, Yorks.

Omire :—Southampton.

Omnium Sanctorum ad Fœnum Parochia :—Allhallows the Great, London.

Omnium Sanctorum de Barking : —Allhallows, Barking, London.

Omnium Sanctorum Garscherch : — Allhallows, Lombard Street.

Omnium Sanctorum in Mellis Viculo :—Allhallows, Honey Lane, London.

Omnium Sanctorum in Vico Longobardico :—Allhallows, Lombard Street, London.

Omnium Sanctorum in Vico Pistorum :—Allhallows, Bread Street, London.

Omnium Sanctorum Pictorum Delibuentium : — Allhallows Staining, London.

Omnium Sanctorum super (or *ad*) *Celarium* :— Allhallows the Less, London.

Omnium Sanctorum supra Murum :—Allhallows - The - Wall, London.

Onna : — Andover, or Alton, Hants.

Onno. See *Hunnum.*

Ophelania :—Offaly, Leinster.

Ora :—Ore, Sussex.

Orcades Insulæ :—The Orkney Islands.

Orcaneia :—Orkney.

Orcas Promontorium :—Dunnet Head, Caithness.

Orchadia. See *Orcades.*

Ordeuices, Ordolucæ :—People of North Wales.

Ordouicæ :—Tribe near Berwick.

Ordouicum :—Norwich. See *Nordouicum.*

Orkeneia :—Orkney Islands.

Ormondia :—Ormond, Ireland.

Orrhea :—Orrock, Fifeshire.

Orsteda : — Horsted Keynes, Sussex.

Orus Flu. :—River Ore, Suffolk.

Osca :—River Usk, Wales.

Oseneia :—Oseney, Oxfordshire.

Osseria, Ossoria :—Ossory, Ireland.

Ossonia :—Oxford.

Ostium Sturæ :—Stourmouth, Kent.

Ostuthus :—River Ystwith, South Wales.

Oswaldeslawa :—Osbaldstow, Worcestershire.

Oswaldi Arbor :—Oswestry, Shropshire.

Oswaldi Crux :—Oswestry.

Oteleia :—Otley, Yorks.

Othona :—Ithanchester, or Brad-well-juxta-Mare, Essex.

Otreuum :—Up Ottery, Devon.

Ottadeni, Ottadini, Ottalini :— People on the coast from Tyne to Forth.

Ottanforda :—Otford, Kent.

Otthea :—Otham, Kent.

Ottodani. See *Ottadeni.*

Ouedra : — River Adder, Ber-wickshire.

Ousa :—River Ouse, Yorks, and Bucks.

Outerini :—People of Desmond, Ireland.

Ouinia Insula:—Isle of Sheppey, Kent.

Oxebea :—Christchurch, Hants.

Oxefordia, Oxenforda :—Oxford.

Oxenhala:—Oxenhall, Durham.

Oxeneia :—Oxney, Lincolnshire.

Oxeria :—Ossory, Ireland.

Oxinega :—Oxney Isle, Kent.

Oronia, Oxonium :—Oxford.

Oza :—River Ouse.

P.

Pagula, Pagula Fleta :—Paules Flete, now Paghill or Paull, Yorks.

Palus Argita : — Lough Derg, Ireland.

Palus Salsa :—Pwllheli, Caer-narvonshire.

Palustris Vicus : — Fenchurch Street, London.

Pampocalia :—The same as *Calcaria.*

Pangorensis :—Of Bangor.

Panhovius :—Penhow (?), Monmouthshire.

Panteneia :—Pentney, Norfolk.

Parathalassia :—Walsingham, Norfolk.

Parcus Ludus :—Louth Park, Lincolnshire.

Parisi :—People of Holderness, Yorks.

Parva Cella :—A monastery in Ireland.

Parvus Burgus :—Littleborough, Notts, and Lancs.

Pascia :— Pacey, Leicestershire.

Pasletum, Passeletum :—Paisley, Renfrewshire.

Paterni Magni Ecclesia :—Llan-badarn Vawr, Cardigan-shire.

Patricii Purgatorium :—Ellanu Frugadory, on an island in Lough Derg, Donegal.

Pecchum:—The Peak, Derby-shire.

Pedicoria :—

Pedreda : — Penenden Heath, Kent.

Pedridon Flu. :—River Parret, Somerset.

Pegelandia : — Peakirk, Northants.

Pembrochia, Penbrochia :—Pem-broke, Wales.

Pencricum : — Penkridge, Staf-fordshire.

Pendinas : — Pendennis Castle, Cornwall.

Penguernum :—Shrewsbury.

Penlinnia :—A place in Merionethshire, the source of the River Dee.

Penmona :—Priestholme, Anglesey.

Penna :—Penselwood, Somerset; or Stourhead, Wilts.

Pennocrucium :—Penkridge, or Lichfield, Staffordshire.

Pennorinum :—Penrhyn, Merionethshire; Penryn, Cornwall.

Pente Flu. :—River Pant, Essex.

Peonnum :—Pen, Somerset. See *Penna.*

Perscora, Persora : — Pershore, Worcestershire.

Perthum : — St. Johnstone, or Perth, Scotland.

Peterillus, Peterus Flu. :—The Peterill, Cumberland.

Petra Duacensis :—Kilmacduagh, co. Clare.

Petra Fertilis : — Corcumroe, Clare.

Petriana:—Castle Steeds,Plumpton Wall, or Cambeck Fort, Cumberland; WaltonHouse; Lanercost.

Petriburgus, Petroburgum, Petropolis : — Peterborough, Northants.

Petuaria :—Beverley, or Brough Ferry on the Humber, Yorks.

Peuenesea :—Pevensey, Sussex.

Pexa :—A town near Dumbarton.

Picalia :—Pickhill, Yorks.

Pictauia, Pictandia :—The country of the Picts.

Picti :—The Picts, a people living north of the Antonine Wall.

Pilais :—A town in Cornwall or Devon.

Pilla : — Pille, a Benedictine Priory in Stainton, Pembrokeshire.

Pincanhale :—Finchale Priory, Durham.

Pinnatis Civitas. See *Alata Castra.*

Piona Canonicorum : — Canon Pyon, or Pewen, Herefordshire.

Piona Regis :—King's Pyon.

Pirri, Insula :—Ynys Pyr, or Caldey Island, Pembrokeshire.

Piscaria :—Fish Street, London.

Piscaria Vetus, Piscenaria :—Old Fish Street, London.

Placentia :—A palace at Greenwich, built by Humphrey, Duke of Gloucester.

Placeto, Castellum de :—Pleshy, Essex.

Plimmuta, Plymutha : — Plymouth, Devon.

Pohanlech :—Poughley, Berks.

Pohhela :—Poughley, Berks.

Pola. See *Strata Marcella.*

Poleslawa :—Polleshoe, Devon.

Poletria :—The Poultry, London.

Pomona :—Mainland, one of the Orkney Isles.

Pons Ælii :—Ponteland, or Newcastle, Northumberland.

Pons Belli :—Stamford Bridge, Yorks.

Pons Burgensis, Pons Burgi : —Boroughbridge, Yorks.

Pons de Burc :—Boroughbridge.

Pons Episcopi :—Bishopsbridge, Lincolnshire.

Pons Ferie : — Ferrybridge, Yorks.

Pons Fractus :—Pontefract, or Pomfret, Yorks.

Pons Fractus Super Tamisiam : — Pomfret, near Stepney Marsh.

Pons Stephani :—Lampeter, Cardiganshire.

Pons Vianus : — Cowbridge, Glamorgan.

Pontaquinum : — Bridgwater, Somerset.

Ponte, de :—A house of Dominican friars in Armagh dioc., perhaps at Drogheda.

Pontes :—Colnbrook, Old Windsor, Staines, Reading, or Byfleet.

Pontuobici : — Cowbridge, Glamorganshire.

Pontus Flu. : — The Point, Northumberland.

Populorum Lapis :—Folkestone, Kent.

Porcestra :—Porchester, Hants.

Poreoclassis : — Orrock, Fife ; Forfar ; or Barry.

Porteseia :—Portsea, Hants.

Portesmua, Portesmuda : —Portsmouth, Hants.

Portesmutha, Portesmuta : — Portsmouth.

Portesoka : — The Portsoken, London.

Portlandia :—Portland, Dorset.

Portlargium : — Waterford, Ireland.

Portlocon :—Porlock Bay, Somerset.

Portunia Insula :—Isle of Portland, Dorset.

Portuosus Sinus : — Sewerby, Yorks.

Portus Adurni : — Porchester, Hants ; Aldrington, or Old Shoreham, Sussex.

Portus Ammonis : — Sandwich, Kent.

Portus Britanniarum : — Portsmouth ; or Richborough, Kent.

Portus Ecgfridi :—Jarrow Slake, Durham.

Portus Lemanis : — Lympne, Kent.

Portus Magnus :—Portsmouth.

Portus Novus :—Rye, Sussex (in the Roman period) ; Newhaven, Sussex.

Portus Ostium :—Portsmouth.

Portus Patrum :—Abbey at Enachdune, co. Galway.

Portus Salutis :—Cromarty, Scotland.

Portus Sistuntiorum. See *Setantiorum Portus.*

Pouisia, Powisa, Powisia : — Powys, Wales.

Præsidium :—The same as *Prætorium.*

Præsidium Civitas : — Camelon, co. Stirling.

Prætorium : — P a t r i n g t o n, Broughton, Flamborough, or Hedon, Yorks.

Pratis, S. Maria de :—S. Mary de Pré or de la Pré, or S. Mary of Prees.*

Prata Domini Regis :—Kingsmead, Derbyshire.

Prestona, Prestonium :—Preston, Lancashire.

Pridania :—For *Britannia.*

Princiduela :—Prittlewell, Essex.

Pritannia :—For *Britannia.*

Priuotes Flu. : — River Privet, Hants.

Procolitia :—Prudhoe Castle, or Carrawburgh, Northumberland.

Profundum Vadum :—Deptford.

Pteroton Stratopedon : — Edinburgh. See *Alata Castra.*

Puellarum Castrum : — Edinburgh.

Pulchra Vallis : — Beauvale, Notts.

Pulchrum Vadum : — Fairford, Gloucestershire.

Pulchrum Visu : — B e l v o i r, Leicestershire.

Pulla. See *Pilla.*

Punctuobice : — Cowbridge, Glamorganshire.

Purocoronauis :—A town in Cornwall or Devon.

Putewurtha :—Petworth, Sussex.

Puttenega :—Putney, Surrey.

Pyonia. See *Piona.*

Q.

Quadraria, Quarrera, Quarera :— Quarre, Wight.

Quentona :—Quinton, Northants.

R.

Ractomessa :—River Racon.

Radecotanus Pons :—Radcot Bridge, Oxon.

Rademora :—Radmore, Staffordshire.

Radenawra, Radenoura :—Radnor.

Radinge :—Reading, Berks.

Radnoria :—Radnor.

Rædinga :—Reading.

Raga, Ragæ :—Leicester ; Retford.

Raganeia :—Rayleigh, Essex.

Ramense :—Of Ramsey.

Ramesburia :—Ramsbury, Wilts.

Ramesia, Rameseya :—Ramsey, Hunts.

Ranatonium. See *Rhetigonium.*

Randuaria :—Renfrew.

---

* There were two nunneries of this name, a Benedictine house near St. Albans, and a Cluniac house in Northants ; also an abbey of Austin Canons near Leicester.

Rapa, Rapotum :—Raphoe, Donegal, Ireland.

Ratæ :—Leicester ; Ratby, or Brinklow, Warwickshire.

Ratecorion. See *Ratæ.*

Rathpotensis, Rathpothensis:—Of Raphoe, Donegal, Ireland.

Ratostabius. See *Rhatostathybius.*

Ratupis. See *Rutupæ.*

Rauenatone :—A town in Cornwall or Devon.

Rauendala :—Ravensworth, Durham (?).

Rauimagum. See *Nouiomagus.*

Ranius :—River Erne, Connaught.

Rauonia :—A town probably in Cumberland.

Rebodunum :—Ribchester, Lancashire.

Reculsum :—Reculver, Kent.

Redingum :—Reading, Berks.

Redmella :—Rodmell, Sussex.

Regaina Insula :—Isle of Arran.

Regalis Locus:—Riallieu, Rewley, Oxon.

Regata :—Reigate, Surrey.

Regentium. See *Regnum.*

Reginæ Burgus :—Queenborough, Kent.

Regiodunum Hullinum :—Kingston-upon-Hull, Yorks.

Regiodunum Thamesinum :—Kingston-upon-Thames.

Regis Burgus :—Queenborough, Kent.

Regis Comitatus :—King's County, Ireland.

Regni :—People of Surrey, Sussex, and the sea coast of Hampshire.

Regni Sylva:—Ringwood, Hants.

Regnum :— Ringwood, Hants ; Chichester, or Steyning, Sussex.

Regulbium :—Reculver, Kent.

Reguli Fanum :—St. Andrews, also called Kirkrule and Kilrule.

Reodburna :—Rodburne, Wilts.

Reofhoppa :—Ryhope, Durham.

Reopadunum :—Repton, Derbyshire.

Repandunum :—Repton.

Retha :—Ryde, Isle of Wight.

Reuedala. See *Rauendala.*

Rhæba:—Rheban or Rheib, Queen's County, Ireland.

Rhage :—Leicester.

Rhatostathybius Flu. :—River Taff, Glamorganshire, Wye, or Ogmoor.

Rhauius. See *Rauius.*

Rhedus Flu. :—River Read, Northumberland.

Rhemnius :—River Remny, Glamorganshire.

Rherigonius Sinus :—Loch Ryan, or Luce Bay.

Rhesi Civitas:—Rochester, Kent.

Rhetigonium :—Barlan or Stranraer, Galloway.

Rhibellus Flu. :— The Ribble, Lancashire.

Rhicina :—Isle of Rum, or Rathlin. See *Richina.*

Rhigia : — Limerick, Ireland ; Railstown, Tipperary.

Rhigodunum :—Ribchester, Warrington, or Manchester.

Rhitubi Portus, Rhitupis Portus : —Richborough or Sandwich, Kent. See *Rutupæ.*

Rhius :—River Rye, Yorkshire.

Rhobodunum. See *Rhigodunum.*

Rhobogdii :—People of Donegal, Ireland.

Rhobogdium Promontorium : — Fair Foreland, now called Malin Head, co. Donegal.

Rhofi Civitas:—Rochester, Kent.

Rhutubi, Rhutupiæ. See *Rutupæ.*

Richala :—Riccal, Yorks.

Richemundia, Richmondia : — Richmond, Yorks ; also Richmond, Surrey.

Richina, Ricina, Ricinia, Ricnea : —Rathlin Isle, co. Antrim ; or Rum, one of the Hebrides.

Ridumo. See *Moridunum.*

Riduna. See *Richina.*

Rievallensis :—Of Rievaulx, Yorkshire.

Rigia. See *Rhigia.*

Rigmundia :—St. Andrews. See *Fanum Reguli.*

Rigodunum:—Richmond, Yorks ; Ripon, Yorks ; Ribchester, Lancashire.

Ripa :—River Ribble.

Ripa Alta :—Ordhill, near Findhorn.

Ripa Regine :—Queenhithe.

Ripadium, Ripandunum :—Repton, Derbyshire.

Riparia Regine :—Queenhithe.

Ripensis : —Of Ripon.

Ripodunum, Ripodum :—Ripon, Yorks.

Ritupis Portus. See *Rutupæ.*

Rium :—Rye, Sussex.

Roberti Pons, Robertinus Pons:— Robert's Bridge, Sussex.

Roboretum, Campus Roborum :— Derry, Ireland.

Rochesburga : —Roxburgh.

Rodecotanus Pons : — Radcot Bridge, Oxfordshire.

Rodolanum :—Rhuddlan, Flintshire.

Roesperra :—Rusper, Sussex.

Roffa :—Rochester, Kent.

Roibis. See *Roffa.*

Roisiæ Oppidum, Villa de Cruce Roesiæ : — Royston, Cambridgeshire.

Rokesburga :—Roxburgh.

Rosæ Castellum :—Rose Castle, Cumberland.

Roscomia :—Roscommon.

Rosea Vallis :—Monaster - evin, Ireland (Ware I. 455); Ross Glass, co. Kildare.

Rosenensis :—Of Ross, Scotland.

Rosensis :—Of Ross, Ireland ; of Rhos, Pembrokeshire.

Rossa, Roscrea :—Ross, Wexford County, Ireland.

Rossia : —Rosse Land, Cornwall ; Ross, Herefordshire; Ross, Scotland ; Rhos, Pembrokeshire.

Rotelandia :—Rutland.

Rothelanum :—Rhuddlan, Flintshire.

Rothesia : — Rothesay, Isle of Bute, west coast of Scotland.

Rotibis :—Rochester or Maidstone, Kent.

Rouecestria :—Rochester.

Rouensis :—Of Rochester.

Rouia :—River Rother, Sussex.

Rowleia :—Rothley Temple, Leicestershire.

Ruber Cliuus : — Redcliffe, or Ratcliffe, near London.

Ruda :—Routh, Yorks.

Ruelega :—Rowley Regis, Staffordshire.

Rugnitunia, Ruitonia :—Ryton-upon-Dunsmoor, Warwickshire.

Rumabo Civitas : — Drumburgh Castle, Cumberland.

Rumeseia :—Romsey, Hants.

Rupa :—Roch, Pembrokeshire.

Rupe, de :—Roche, an Abbey in Yorks.

Rupes Fergusii :—Carrickfergus, Ireland.

Rupis Aurea :—Goldcliffe, Monmouthshire.

Ruscomia : — Roscommon, Ireland.

Ruthunia :—Ruthin, Denbighshire.

Rutlandia :—Rutland.

Rutunia. See *Rugnitunia ; Rutunium.*

Rutunium :—Wem, Shropshire ; Chesterton, Staffordshire ; Rowton, Shropshire.

Rutupæ, Rutupi, Rutupiæ, Ritupis Portus :—Richborough, Kent ; or Sandwich.

Rutupinum littus :—The coast between the North and South Forelands, Kent.

Ruturugum Stagnum :—Bay of Dundrum, County Down.

S.

Sabaudia :—The Savoy, London.

Sabriana, Sabrina : — River Severn.

Sabulovicum :—Sandwich, Kent.

Sacana :—River Shannon, Ireland.

Sacra Capilla :—Halifax, Yorks.

Sacra Insula : — Holy Isle, Northumberland.

Sacra Sylva :—Halifax, Yorks.

Sacrum Nemus :—Halywood Monastery, Galloway.

Sacrum Promontorium :—Greenore Point, or Carnsore Point, Wexford.

Sadberga :—Sadberge, Durham.

Safteberia :—Shaftesbury, Dorset.

Salebeia :—Selby, Yorks.

Salenæ :—Chesterton, near Sandy, Beds.

Salesburia :—Salisbury, Wilts.

Salicetum, foresta de :—Salcey Forest, Northants.

Salimnos Insula :—Sulmey Isle, near Milford Haven.

Salinæ :—Droitwich, Worcester-
shire; Nantwich, Cheshire;
Slaughter, Gloucestershire.
See also *Salenæ*.

Salisbiria :—Salisbury; Shrewsbury.

Salopesburia :—Shrewsbury,
Shropshire.

Salopescira, Salopesiria :—
Shropshire.

Salopia :—Shrewsbury.

Saltria :—Sawtry, Hunts.

Saltus Andreda :—The Weald of
Sussex.

Saltus Salmonis :—Leixlip, co.
Dublin.

Salutaris Portus :—Sewerby,
Yorks.

Salwarpus :—Salwarpe River,
Worcestershire.

Samairus :—River Erne, Ireland.

Samothea :—Britain.

*Sancta Anna intra Portum
Alneani* : — St. Anne's,
Aldersgate, London.

*S. Anna Nigrorum Monacho-
rum* :—St. Anne's, Black-
friars, London.

S. Crux :—Holyrood, Edinburgh.

S. Genovefa : — Fornham St.
Genevieve, Suffolk.

S. Katarina de Colmancherche :
—St. Catharine Colman,
London.

S. Katarina Trinitatis : — St.
Catharine Cree Church.

*S. Margareta a Caligarum
Venditione* : —St. Margaret
Pattens, London.

S. Margareta extra Fossam :—St.
Margaret Outditch, Rochester.

Sancta Margareta juxta Pontem:—
St. Margaret, Bridge Street,
or St. Margaret, New Fish
Street, London.

S. Margareta Moysi :—St. Margaret Moses, London.

S. Maria a Lintris Statione :—St.
Mary Bothaw, London.

S. Maria Abbatis Ecclesiæ, or *de
Abbecherch* :—St. Mary Ab-
church, London.

S. Maria ad Collem :—St. Mary-
at-Hill, London.

S. Maria ad Lanæ Trutinam :—
St. Mary Woolchurch,
London.

S. Maria ad Villam Insularem:—
St. Mary, Islington.

S. Maria ad Villam Novam :—St.
Mary Newington, London.

S. Maria de Alba. Capella :—St.
Mary Whitechapel, London.

S. Maria de Arcubus:—St. Mary-
le-Bow, London.

S. Maria de Insula :—Alceter,
Warwickshire.

S. Maria de Monte Alto : —St.
Mary Mounthaw, London.

S. Maria de Newcherche :—St.
Mary Woolchurch, London.

S. Maria de Rupe : —Kirkheugh,
St. Andrews.

S. Maria de Sabaudia :—St. Mary
Savoy, London.

S. Maria de Wlchershawe :—St.
Mary Woolchurch, London.

*S. Maria in Aldermannorum
Burgoparochia* : —St. Mary's
Aldermanbury, London.

S. Maria in Campis :—St. Mary
in the Fields, Edinburgh.

Sancta Maria Salvatoris in Australi Opere :—St. Mary's Southwark.

S. Maria Senioris Mariæ :—St. Mary Aldermary, London.

S. Maria Wolnothi :—St. Mary Woolnoth, London.

S. Maria Maydalena de Bermendi Insula :—St. Mary Magdalen, Bermondsey, London.

S. Maria Magdalena in Veteri Piscario Foro : — St. Mary Magdalen, Old Fish Street, London.

S. Maria Magdalena in Vico Lacteo :—St Mary Magdalen, Milk Street, London.

S. Ositha :—St. Osyth's, Essex.

Sancti Botolphi Oppidum :—Boston, Lincolnshire.

S. Clari Castellum : —St. Clear's, Caermarthenshire.

S. Columbæ Insula :—Icolmkill, Iona.

S. Davidis Oppidum: —St. David's, Pembrokeshire.

S. Edwardi Abbatia :—Shaftesbury, Dorset.

S. Edwardi Villa:—Shaftesbury; Corfe Castle (?), Dorset.

S. Egidii in Bosco, domus :— Flamsted, Herts.

S. Vinini Ecclesia : — Kilwinning, Ayrshire.

Sancto Johanne, Villa de : — Perth, Scotland.

Sanctus Ægidius ad Portam Membris-captorum :—St. Giles Cripplegate, London.

S. Albanus :—St. Alban's, Herts.

Sanctus Albanus in Vico Ligneo : —St. Alban's Wood Street, London.

S. Andreas:—St. Andrew's, Scotland.

S. Andreas ad Vestiarium :—St. Andrew's by the Wardrobe, London.

S. Andreas sub Malo Cereali :— St. Andrew's Undershaft, London.

S. Asaf :—St. Asaph, Flintshire.

S. Bartholomæus pone Peristylium : — St. Bartholomew's near the Exchange, London.

S. Benedictus in Graminoso Vico : —St. Benet's Gracechurch Street, London.

S. Benedictus Shorhog : — St. Bennet's Sherehog, London.

S. Boscus :—Holywood, Belfast Bay.

S. Botolphus ad Episcopi Portam : —St. Botolph's Bishopsgate, London.

S. Botolphus ad Portam Bellini : —St. Botolph's Billingsgate, London.

S. Botolphus ad Veterem Portam: —St. Botolph's without Aldgate, London.

S. Botolphus Alneæ Portæ :—St. Botolph's without Aldersgate, London.

S. Clemens Dacorum :—St. Clement Danes, Strand.

S. Edmundus:—Bury St. Edmund's, Suffolk.

S. Edmundus in Vico Longobardico :—St. Edmund's, Lombard Street, London.

Sanctus Gabriel in Vico Palustri:
—St. Gabriel's Fenchurch
Street, London.

S. Jacobus ad Clericorum Fontem:—St. James' Clerkenwell, London.

S. Jacobus ad Ducis Hospitium:
—St. James', Duke Place,
London.

S. Jacobus ad Montem Allii:—
St. James' Garlickhithe, or
Hill, London.

S. Joannes Zakarie:—St. John
Zachary, in Aldersgate
Ward.

S. Johannes Baptista super Walbroc: — St. John Baptist's,
Walbrook, London.

S. Laurentius in Judaismo:—St.
Lawrence Jewry, London.

S. Laurentius Pountneus:—St.
Lawrence Pountney, London.

S. Martinus ad Luddi Portam:
—St. Martin's Ludgate,
London.

S. Martinus de Pomerio:—St.
Martin's Pomeroy, London.

*S. Martinus in Ferrariorum
Viculo*:—St. Martin's Ironmonger Lane, London.

S. Martinus in Vinariis, or *de
Vinetria*: — St. Martin's
Vintry, London.

S.Martinus juxta Charinge Crosse:
—St.Martin's-in-the-Fields,
London.

S. Martinus Ogari:—St. Martin's
Ogars, London.

S. Martinus Outwichi, or *Ottewish*:—St.Martin's Outwich,
London.

Sanctus Michael ad Blada :—St.
Michael's at the Quern,
London.

S. Michael ad Ripam Reginalem :
— St. Michael's, Queenhithe, London.

S. Michael de Woudestrete :—St.
Michael's, Wood Street.

S. Michael extra S. Trinitatis :—
St. Michael's without the
Holy Trinity.

S. Michael in Curuo Viculo :—
St. Michael's Crooked Lane,
London.

S. Michael in Foro ad Bladum :
—S. Michael's-atte-Corn, or
le Quern.

S. Michael in Hordeaceum Collem :—St. Michael's Cornhill, London.

*S. Michael Paternoster Cherch in
Riola*:—St.Michael's Royal.

S. Mundus :—Kilmund, Argyleshire.

S. Neothus:—St. Neot, Cornwall;
St. Neot's, Hunts.

S. Nicholaus ad Macella :—St.
Nicholas' Fleshambles, London.

*S. Nicholaus Aldrethegate ad
Macella* : — St. Nicholas'
Fleshambles, London.

S. Nicholaus Aureæ Abbatiæ :—
St. Nicholas' Cole Abbey,
London.

S. Nicholaus Hakun:—St.Nicholas Acon, London.

S. Nicholaus Olof:—St. Nicholas
Olave's, London.

S. Olauus in Argenteo Vico :—
St. Olave's, Silver Street,
London.

Sanctus Olauus in Australi Opere:
—St. Olave's, Southwark.

S. Olauus in Ceruina Platea :—
St. Olave's, Hart Street,
London.

S. Olauus juxta Turrim :—St.
Olave's, Hart Street.

S. Oswaldus de Nostellis :—Nostal, Yorkshire.

*S. Pancratius in Vico Smeg-
matico*:—St. Pancras
Soper's Lane, London.

S. Paternus :—Llanbadarn, Cardiganshire.

S. Paulus in Conuentuali Horto:—
St. Paul's Covent Garden,
London.

S. Petrocus :—Petrockstow,
Devon.

S. Petrus de Grano Piaco :—
St. Peter's Cornhill.

S. Petrus in Foro :—St. Peter's
Cheap, London.

S. Petrus super Tamisiam :—
St. Peter's Paul's Wharf,
London.

S. Stephanus in Vico Colmanni:—
St. Stephen's Coleman
Street, London.

Sandicum :—Sandwich, Kent.

Sandouicum, Sanwicius :—Sandwich.

Sarebria :—Salisbury, Wilts.

Saresburia, Sarisbiria :—Salisbury, Wilts.

Sarnia—Guernsey.

Sartis, de : — Wardon Abbey,
Beds.

Sarua :—River Severn.

Sauerennus :—River Bandon or
River Lee, Cork.

Sauerna :—River Severn.

Sauranus Flu. : —River Avonmore, Cork.

Saxonicum Littus :—The eastern
and southern coast of
Britain.

Scadum Namorum. See *Isca
Dumnoniorum.*

Scala Celi:—St. Wolstan's Abbey,
co. Kildare.

Scandia :—Sanday Island, one
of the Orkneys.

Scapeia :—Sheppey, Kent.

Scardeburgum, Scardus Burgus :
—Scarborough, Yorks.

Scartheburga :— Scarborough,
Yorks.

Sceaftesbiria :— Shaftesbury,
Dorset.

Sceargeta :— Sarratt, Herts ;
Shearsby, Leicestershire (?).

Sceftonia:—Shaftesbury, Dorset.

Scena :—River Shannon.

Sceptonia:—Shaftesbury,Dorset.

Scetis :—Isle of Skye.

Schafbera :—Shebbear, Devon.

Schaftesberia :— Shaftesbury,
Dorset.

Schellus Flu. :— River Skell,
Yorks.

Schelsega :—Chelsea, near London.

Schepeia :—Sheppey.

Scireburna :—Sherborne.

Scona :—Scone, Perthshire.

Scorberia, Scorbesberia :—
Shrewsbury.

Scornæ :—Shorne, Kent.

Scoti :—The Scots.

Scotia :—Ireland ; Scotland.

Scrobesberia, Scropesbyria :— Shrewsbury.

Searesbiria :—Salisbury.

Sebasta Altera Legio :—Liskeard, Cornwall.

Secandunum :—Seckington, Warwickshire.

Sedes Animarum :—Soulseat, Galloway.

Seftesberia, Seftonia :— Shaftesbury, Dorset.

Segedunum :—Sedghill; Cousinshouse, or Wallsend, Northumberland.

Segelocum :—Ollerton, or Littleborough, Notts.

Segeswalda :—Seckington, Warwickshire.

Seggesfelda :—Sedgefield, Durham.

Segontiaci :—A tribe living near Silchester.

Segontium, Seguntium :—Cairseint, Caernarvon ; Silchester.

Selburgi Tumulus :—Silbury Hill, Wilts.

Selebia :—Selby, Yorks.

Seletuna :—Monk Hesleton, Durham ; Silton, Yorks.

Selyouæ :—People of Nithsdale and Annandale.

Sellinæ Insulæ :—Scilly Islands.

Seluestuna :—Selston, Notts.

Sena :—River Shannon.

Senna :—River Senni, or River Usk, Brecknockshire.

Senus :—River Shannon.

Seolesia :—Selsea, Sussex.

Sepes Inscisa :—Hay Castle, Brecknock (?).

Serberia, Serbyria :—Salisbury.

Serduno. See *Segedunum.*

Seresberia :—Salisbury.

Setantiorum Portus :—Windermere, or the mouth of the Ribble, Lancashire.

Seteia Æstuarium :—The mouth of the Dee, Cheshire.

Seueria :—Salisbury.

Sewardeslega :—Sewesley near Towcester, Northants.

Shaftonia :—Shaftesbury, Dorset.

Shaga :—Shaw, Berks.

Sharpenora :—Sconce Point, Isle of Wight.

Shenum :—Shene, or Richmond, Surrey.

Siambis :—River Shannon.

Sibbetonum :—Sibton, Suffolk.

Sienus :—River Shannon.

Sigdeles :—The Scilly Isles.

Silamesteda :—Sulhamstead, Berks.

Silesia :—Selsea, Sussex.

Silionnus. See *Limnos.*

Sillinæ Insulæ :—Scilly Islands.

Silura Insula :—Scilly Islands.

Silures :—People of South Wales.

Simeni :—A tribe in Norfolk and Suffolk.

Sineius Flu. :—River Shannon, Ireland.

Sinnenus :—River Shannon.

Sinnodunum :—Sinodun Hill, near Wallingford, Berks.

Sinomagus. See *Sitomagus.*

Sinus Felix :—Bridlington or Filey Bay, Yorks.

Siresburna :—Sherborne, Dorset.

Siriolis :—St. Cyriol, Bangor.

Sirwuda :—Sherwood, Notts.

Sitomagus :—Thetford, Norfolk ; Woolpit, Stowmarket, Dunwich, or Eye, Suffolk.

Slana :—River Slaine, Wexford.

Slepa :—St. Ives, Hunts.

Slicheius :— River Gitley, *olim* Sligo.

Slopesberia :—Shrewsbury ; Shropshire.

Smedefelda :—Smithfield.

Snaudonia :—Snowdon Forest, Caernarvonshire.

Sobrica :—Ardnamurchan, Argyleshire.

Socinus :—River Shannon.

Sodera :—Sodor, islands on the west coast of Scotland.

Soltra, hospitale de :—Soutra, between Edinburgh and Kelso.

Soluathianum Æstuarium, Soluæum Flumen :—Solway Firth.

Somaridunum :—Somerton, Lincolnshire.

Somersata, Somerseta, Somersetania, Somersetensis, Somertunensis Comitatus : — Somerset.

Sorbiodunum, Soruiodunum : — Old Sarum ; Carisbrooke ; also Shrewsbury.

Southamptonia :—Southampton.

Southeria :—Surrey.

Southerlandia : — Sutherland, Scotland.

Southriana :—Surrey.

Southsexena, Southsexia : — Sussex.

Southwella :—Southwell, Notts.

Spea :—River Spey, Elgin, Scotland.

Spinæ :—Speen, near Newbury, Berks.

Spinarum Insula :—Thorney Isle, the site of Westminster Abbey.

Spinetum : — Spinney, Cambridgeshire.

Spinodunum : — Thornton, Lincolnshire.

Staffordia :—Stafford.

Stanfordia, Stanforda : — Stamford, Lincolnshire.

Starkelea :—Startley, Wilts.

Starus :—River Stour.

Statiarius Lapis :—Clough, co. Antrim.

Statio Deventia : — In Devonshire, Totness (?).

Steafordensis :—Of Stafford.

Stellata, Camera : — The Star Chamber.

Stenum :—Stean, Northants.

Steofordensis :—Of Stafford.

Stinsiarius : — River Stinchar, Ayrshire.

Stiuentona :—Staunton, Gloucestershire.

Stokeporta, Stokeportus :—Stockport, Cheshire.

Stourus :—River Stour.

Strata Florea, Strata Florida:— Ystrad Flûr, or Stratflower, now Mynachlogfur, or Caron-llwch-Clawdd, Cardiganshire.

Strata Marcella :—Strat Margel, or Ystrad Marchel, Montgomeryshire.

Stratcluttenses : — Britons of Strathclyde.

Streoneshalf :—Ancient name of Whitby Abbey.

Stretgledwali. See *Stratcluttenses.*

Stretlea :—Streatlam, Durham.

Strigulense Castrum :—Striguil Castle, Monmouthshire.

Strigulia, Stringulia : — Chepstow, Monmouthshire.

Striuellina, Striuilingum :—Stirling, Scotland.

Stroda :—Strood, Kent.

Stubeheda, Stubhutha :—Stepney.

Stuccia, Stucia Flu. : — River Ystwith, or Dovey, Cardiganshire.

Stura :—River Stour.

Sturodunum : — Stourton, and Stourminster, Dorset.

Sturus Flu. :—River Stour.

Sualua :—River Swale, Yorks.

Suauicordium, Dulce Cor : — Sweetheart, or New Abbey, Kirkcudbrightshire.

Subdobiadon :—A town on the Wall of Antonine.

Sudereia :—Surrey.

Sudesexia :—Sussex.

Sudhamtonia :—Hampshire.

Sudouerca :—Southwark.

Sudouolca, Sudouolgia :—Suffolk.

Sudria :—Surrey.

Sudsexa :—Sussex.

Sudwallia :—South Wales.

Sudwercha :—Southwark.

Suella :—Southwell, Notts.

Suelloniaca :—Brockley Hill, near Elstree, or Chipping Barnet, Herts.

Suffolicia :—Suffolk.

Suiftus :—River Swift, Leicestershire.

Suina :—Swinhey, Yorks.

Suirus :—Suir River, near Waterford, Ireland.

Sukius :—River Suck, Connaught.

Sulcalua Flu. : — River Swale, Yorks.

Sulloniaca, Sullonica. See *Suelloniaca.*

Sumersetanea, Sumertunensis, Summurtunensis Paga :— Somerset.

Sunningum :— Sonning, near Reading, Berks.

Surium :—Inislaunagh, co. Tipperary.

Surra, Surria, Surreia :—Surrey.

Sussexia :—Sussex.

Susura :—Isle of Jura (?).

Suthamtonia :—Southampton.

Suthamtunensis Provincia :— Hampshire.

Suthburia :—Sudbury, Suffolk.

Sutheria :—Surrey.

Suthesexia :—Sussex.

Suthimbria :—England south of the Humber.

Suthregia, Suthreia :—Surrey.

Suthriona :—Surrey.

Suthsaxonia :—Sussex.

Suthsexia :—Sussex.

Suthumbria. See *Suthimbria.*

Suthwalonia :—South Wales.

Suthwella :—Southwell, Notts.

Suthweorca :—Southwark.

Suwallia :—South Wales.

Suwella :—Southwell, Notts.

Sweynesia :—Swansea, Glamorganshire.

Swina :—Swinhey, Yorkshire.

Swthwella :—Southwell, Notts.

Syli :—People of S. Wales.

Syllina, Sylina :—Scilly Isles.

Syreburna :—Sherborne, Dorset.

T.

Tabu :—Teignmouth, Devon.

Tadecastrum :—Tadcaster. See *Calcaria.*

Tadoriton :—A town between the Walls of Hadrian and Antonine.

Taffus Flu. :—River Taff, Glamorganshire.

Tagea :—Monteith, Perthshire.

Taisa :—River Tees.

Taizali :—The people of Buchan, Scotland.

Taizalum Promontorium :— Buchanness, or Kinnaird Head, east coast of Scotland.

Tama :—Thame, Oxfordshire.

Tama Flu. :—River Tame, Oxfordshire; River Teme, Worcestershire.

Tamara :—Tamerton-Foliott, Devon; or Saltash, Cornwall.

Tamara Flu. :— River Tamar, Cornwall.

Tamare :—Tavistock, Devon.

Tamaris. See *Tamara.*

Tamaris Fluvii Ostia :— Plymouth.

Tamarus :—River Tamar.

Tamawordina :—Tamworth, Staffordshire.

Tambra :—River Tamar.

Tameia :—Dunkeld, Perthshire.

Tamensis :—River Thames.

Tamese :—Kingston, Surrey, or Streatley, Berks.

Tamesia, Tamesis :— Rivers Thames and Medway.

Tamewrda :— Tamworth, Staffordshire.

Tamion :—River Tavy (?).

Tamisa, Tamisis :— River Thames.

Tamworthia :—Tamworth, Staffordshire.

Tanarus :—River Tamar.

Tanathos Insula :— Isle of Thanet, Kent.

Tanaus :—The Firth of Forth.

Tanetos. See *Tanathos.*

Tanfelda :—Tanfield, Yorks.

Taniatidæ. See *Tanathos.*

Tanodunum :—Taunton, Somerset.

Taodunum :—Dundee.

Tarensis :—Of Derry, Ireland.

Tarenteforda :—Dartford, Kent.

Taruedum, Taruisium : — Duncansby Head, Caithness.

Tarxa :—Torksey, Lincolnshire.

Tatecastra :—Tadcaster, Yorks.

Taua :—Teignmouth, Devon.

Taua :—River Tay, Scotland.

Tauistokia : —Tavistock, Devon.

Taus :—River Tay.

Tawus :—River Taw, Devon.

Teauus :—River Tavy, Devon.

Tedfordia :—Thetford, Norfolk.

Techelesberia : — Tewkesbury, Gloucestershire.

Tegæus Lacus :—Lake Tegid, or Bala, Merionethshire, Wales.

Teisa, Teisis :—River Tees, Durham.

Temdus :—River Teme.

Temesforda :—Tempsford, Beds.

Templum Florum :—Kynloss, or Kilfloss, Moray.

Tenos :—Isle of Thanet.

Teodforda :—Thetford, Norfolk.

Terdebigga : —Tardebigg, Worcestershire.

Terentus Flu. :—River Trent.

Terna : — River Tern, Shropshire.

Tesa :—River Tees, Durham.

Tesedala :—Teesdale.

Tesobius :—River Conway.

Tethfordum : — Thetford, Norfolk.

Tetocuria : — Tetbury, Gloucestershire.

Teuidalia : — Teviotdale, Scotland.

Tewiensis fluvius :—River Tywi, Caermarthenshire.

Texali : — People of Buchan, Aberdeenshire. See *Taizali.*

Teysa :—River Tees.

Thamesis, Thamisia :—Thames.

Thanatos, Thanathos :—Thanet.

Theisa :—River Tees.

Themis :—River Teme, Worcestershire.

Thenodunum :—Taunton, Somerset.

Theobaldenses Ædes : — Theobalds, Herts.

Theoci Curia :—Tewkesbury, Gloucestershire.

Theodforda :—Thetford, Norfolk.

Theodorodunum :—Wells, Somerset.

Theokebiria, Theokesberia :—Tewkesbury.

Theorodunum. See *Theodorodunum.*

Theostrota :—Toccotes, Yorks.

Thermæ :—Bath.

Theta :—Little Ouse River, Norfolk.

Thetfordia :—Thetford, Norfolk.

Thewda :—River Tweed.

Thiletheya :—Tiltey, Essex.

Thinemutha :—Tynemouth, Northumberland.

Thinus Flu. : — River Tyne, Northumberland.

Thongum :—Thong, Yorkshire.

Thonodunum : — Taunton, Somerset.

Thonus :—River Tone, Somerset.

Thornega :—Thorney Isle, the site of Westminster Abbey.

Thorncia : — Thorney, Cambridgeshire.

Thorp Comitisse :—Countessthorpe, Leicestershire.

Thuemia :—Tuam, Galway.

Thuenensis :—Of Down, Ireland.

Thuetmonia : — Thomond, Ireland.

Thule :—Shetland Isles, or Iceland.

Thweda :—River Tweed.

Tibius, Tybius Flu. : — River Teify, Cardiganshire.

Tibraccia : — Tibraghny, Kilkenny; perhaps sometimes Tipperary.

Ticcelea :—Thickley, Durham.

Tichehella, Tichehulla : — Tickhill, Yorks.

Tichfelda :—Titchfield, Hants.

Tietforda :—Thetford, Norfolk.

Tignea : —Teign Canon, Devon.

Tikehilla :—Tickhill, Yorks.

Tilæ. See *Thule.*

Tileburgum :—Tilbury, Essex.

Tiliapis. See *Tolapia.*

Tina Flu. :—River Tyne, Northumberland ; or the Eden, Fifeshire.

Tindolana :—Winchester in the Wall, Northumberland.

Tinea Flu.:—River Teign, Devon.

Tinemutha:—Tynemouth, Northumberland.

Tinna. See *Tina.*

Tinomoutum :—Tynemouth.

Tintagium : — Tintagell, Cornwall.

Tinus. See *Tina.*

Tiretia :—Tiltey, Essex.

Tisa :—River Tees.

Tisis, Tisobis Flu. :—River Conway, N. Wales.

Tistonia :—Tisted, Hants.

Tiueteshala :—Titshall, Norfolk.

Tiwa Magna :—Great Tew, Oxfordshire.

Tobius Flu. :—River Towy, Caermarthenshire.

Tœsobis. See *Tisis.*

Tolapia, Toliapis, Toliatis : — Sheppey, or Thanet.

Toller Porcorum :—Swinetoller, Dorset.

Tomewordina:—Tamworth, Staffordshire.

Tomondia :—Thomond, Ireland.

Tonbrigium :—Tonbridge, Kent.

Tonellum:—The Tun, a prison in Cornhill.

Torcestria :—Towcester, Northamptonshire.

Torkesega :—Torksey or Torsey, Lincolnshire.

Tornai, Torneia:—Thorney, Cambridgeshire.

Tornetuna :—Thornton, Yorks.

Torteoda :—Tortworth, Gloucestershire.

Tortuna : —Thornton - le - Street, Yorks.

Totonesium Littus : —Coast of Hampshire, opposite to Totland's Bay (?) ; Totness.

Trajectus:—Henbury, Hanham, or Bitton, near Bristol.

Trajectus Augustæ :—Austcliff, or Henbury, Gloucestershire.

Treanta :—River Trent.

Trecastellum :—Beaumaris, Anglesey.

Trefontana :—Three Fountains, Lammermuir.

Trehenta :—River Trent.

Trellinum : —Welshpool, Montgomery.

Trenovantum :—London.

Trenta :—River Trent.

Trepelawa : — Triplow, Cambridgeshire.

Treska :—Thirsk, Yorks.

Triburna :—Kilmore.

Trimontium, Trimuntium :—Annand, Dumfriesshire, or Eildon.

Trinoantes, Trinobantes, Trinouantes:—The people of Middlesex and Essex.

Tripontium :—Towcester, or Lilbourne, Northants; Rugby, Cave's Inn, or Kineton, Warwickshire.

Trisanton :—River Test, Hants ; River Ouse, Sussex.

Trisanton, Trisantonis Portus : —Southampton. See *Clausentum*.

Triuerium :—Truro, Cornwall.

Trumense castrum : — Trim, Meath.

Trutulensis Portus : —Probably an error for *Rutupensis*, or the Humber.

Tuai Æstuarium:—Mouth of the Spey, Scotland.

Tuama, Tuaima :—Tuam, Galway, Ireland.

Tueda :—River Tweed.

Tuemia :—Tuam, Galway.

Tueoxbea, Tueoxnea : — Christchurch, Hants.

Tuerobis Flu. :—River Teify.

Tuesis:—River Tees, Berwick.

Tuesis:—Beancastle, near Nairn, or Bellie, cos. Elgin and Banff.

Tuessis :—Berwick-on-Tweed.

Tuggahala :—Tughall, Northumberland.

Tuhetmonia :—Thomond.

Tuida, Tuidus :—River Tweed.

Tulina :— Inchtuthill, on the River Tay, Scotland.

Tunnocelum :—Bowness, or Cardornock, Cumberland; Tynemouth, Northumberland.

Turfeia :—Turvey, Bedfordshire.

Turobius Flu. :— River Teify, Cardiganshire.

Tutesbiria, Tuttebiria:—Tutbury, Staffordshire.

Tweda, Tweodum :— River Tweed.

Twomondia :— Thomond, Ireland.

Tybius :—River Teify, Cardiganshire.

Tykeilla :—Tickhill, Yorks.

U.

Ubbanforda :—Norham, Northumberland.

Udiæ :—People about Cork.

Uffintona :—Ufton, Berks.

Ugrulentum :—A town north of the Wall of Antonine.

Ugueste :—A town north of the Wall of Antonine.

Ulidia :—The province of Ulster, Ireland.

Ullerwuda :— Ollerton, Cheshire (?).

Ulmetum :—Elmley, or Emley, Yorks ; North Elmham, Norfolk.

Ultonia, Uluestera :—Ulster, Ireland.

Umalia :—Achad Fobhair, co. Mayo, Ireland.

Umber :—River Humber.

Undalium, Undola :— Oundle, Northants.

Uniuallis. See *Ureuallis.*

Urbs Legionum :—Chester.

Ureuallis :—Jervaulx, Yorks.

Urgalia :—Louth, Ireland.

Uriconia :—Wrottesley, Staffordshire.

Uriconium. See *Virioconium.*

Uriponium :—Ripon, Yorks.

Urithlesia :—Wrexham, North Wales.

Uriuallis :—Jervaulx, Yorks.

Uroconium. See *Virioconium.*

Urolanium. See *Verolamium.*

Urosullum :—Wressell, Yorks.

Urouicum :—York.

Urus :—River Ure, or Yore, Yorks.

Usa :—River Ouse.

Usocona, Usoconna :—Sheriff Hales, Oaken Gates, Shropshire ; or Bednall, Staffordshire.

Uterni :—A tribe living in South Desmond.

Utriconion. See *Virioconium.*

Uxacona. See *Usocona.*

Uxela :— Exeter, Bridgewater, or Lostwithiel.

Uxelis :—Lostwithiel, or Launceston, Cornwall.

Uxelludamum:—Hexham, Northumberland.

Uxelum :— Caerlaverock, or Wardlaw, Dumfriesshire.

Uxena :— Crockherne Well, Devon.

Uxinus Pons :—Uxbridge, Middlesex.

Uzela Æstuarium. See *Vexala.*

Uzelium. See *Uxelum.*

Uzella. See *Uxela.*

V.

Vacomagi :—People of Murray and Athol, Scotland.

Vadum Boum : —Oxford.

Vadum Ceruinum :—Hertford.

Vadum Pulchrum :—Fairford, Gloucestershire.

Vadum Rubrum :—Hertford.

Vadum Salicis :—Wilford ; Walford, Herefordshire (?).

Vadum Saxi :—Stanford.

Vaga Flu. :—River Wye, Herefordshire.

Vagniacæ, Vagniacum :—Maidstone, Wrotham, Northfleet, or Strood, Kent.

Valeia :—Whalley, Lancashire.

Valentia :—Province of Britain between the Walls of Hadrian and Antonine, *i.e.*, the Forth and the Tyne ; or between the Walls of Hadrian and Severus.

Vallidena :—Saffron Walden, Essex ; Walden, Lincolnshire.

Vallis Anangia :—Annandale, Scotland.

Vallis Aurea :—Golden Vale, Herefordshire.

Vallis Crucis :—An abbey at Llan Egwestl or Egwast, Denbighshire.

Vallis Dei :—Vaudey, or Walden, Lincolnshire ; Killenny, co. Kilkenny.

Vallis Doloris :—Wedale, Scotland.

Vallis Longa :—Combehire, or Cumhil, Radnorshire.

Vallis Lucis :—Glenluce, Galloway, Scotland.

Vallis Regalis :—Vale Royal, Cheshire.

Vallis Salutis :—Baltinglass, co. Wicklow.

Vallis S. Andreæ :—Pluscardin, Moray.

Vallis S. Mariæ in Snaudonia :—Beddgelert, Caernarvonshire.

Vallis Virtutis :—Charterhouse at Perth.

Vallum :—The Picts' Wall. See *Hadriani Murus*.

Valteris. See *Verteræ*.

Vanatinga :—Wantage, Berks.

Vandalis Flu. :—River Wandle, Surrey.

Vandelbiria :—Vandlebury, or Wandlesborough, a hill near Cambridge.

Vanduaria :—Paisley.

Vara Flu. :—Murray Firth.

Varæ Castrum :—Dunbar.

Varia Flu. :—River Frome, Dorset.

Varingtonium :—Warrington, Lancashire.

Varis :—Bodvari, Flintshire ; Llanfair, Denbighshire.

Varuicum :—Warwick.

Vecta, Vectesis :—Isle of Wight.

Vectis Insula :—Whitehorn Island, Galloway ; Isle of Wight.

Vecturiones :—Picts.

Vedra, Vedrus :—River Wear, Durham, or the Tyne.

Velabri :—People of Munster.

Velox Flu. :—River Ivel, Somerset.

Velunia :—A town in Scotland.

Veluntium :—Arless, Queen's
Co., Ireland.

Venantodunia :—Huntingdon-
shire.

*Venantodunum, Venatorum
Mons* :—Huntingdon.

Venedotia :—Gwynedd, North
Wales.

Veneris. See *Verteræ.*

Venicnium, Vennicuium :—Ram's
Head, or Horn Head, Done-
gal.

Venicontes :—People in Fife.

Vennicnii :—People of Tyrcon-
nel, Ireland.

Venonæ, Vennones :—Claybrooke,
near Bensford Bridge,
Leicestershire; or Southam,
Warwickshire.

Venta Belgarum :—Winchester
or Havant, Hants.

*Venta Icenorum, Simenorum,
Cenomum* :—Caistor or Norwich, Norfolk.

Venta Silurum :—Caer-went,
Monmouthshire.

Ventanum :—Winchester.

Ventolacensis :—Of Wensleydale,
Yorks.

Ventusfrigetmare :—Winchelsea,
Sussex.

Ventus Morbidus :—Windsor,
Berks.

Venutio :—The same as *Banatia.*

Veratinum :—Cressage, Shropshire; Warrington; or the
same as *Verometum.*

M.

Verbeia :—River Wharfe, Yorks.

Vergiuius, Verginius Oceanus :—
The sea to the south of
Ireland.

Verlucio : — Warminster, Leck-
ham, Spy Park, or Sandy
Lane, Wilts.

Vernalis :—A town in Cornwall
or Devon.

Vernemetum. See *Verometum.*

Vernicones :—The Picts.

Verolamium :—Verulam, now St.
Albans, Herts.

Verometum :—Burrow Hill, or
Cosby, Leicestershire; or
Willoughby, Notts.

Veromum :—A town north of the
Forth.

Verouicum :—Warwick.

Verregraua :—Wargrave, Berks.

Verteræ, Verteris : — Brough-
upon - Stainmore, West-
moreland; Watgarth, Dur-
ham; or Bowes, Yorks.

Verteuia :—A town in Cornwall
or Devon.

Vertis :—Bourton-on-the-Water,
Gloucestershire (?).

Veruedrum Promontorium :—
Strathy, or Duncansby
Head, Scotland.

Veruicum :—Warwick.

Verulamium :—Verulam, or St.
Albans, Herts.

Verus :—River Wear, Durham.

Veruuium. See *Berubium.*

Vetadunum :—Watton, Yorks.

Veteleganus Pons :— Wheatley
Bridge, near Oxford.

Vetilingiana Via :—Watling St.

Vetta Insula :—Isle of Wight.

Vetus Burgus :—Elvet, Durham; Aldborough, Yorks.

Vetus Piscaria :—Old Fish St., London.

Vexala, Uzela Æstuarium :—The mouth of the Yeo or Ivel, or of the Brent, Somerset.

Vexfordia :—Wexford, Ireland.

Via Caua :—Holloway, Middlesex.

Via Noua :—Monaster o Gormogan, co. Clare.

Vicanum :—Etchingham, Sussex.

Viconia. See *Vinnouium.*

Victesis :—Isle of Wight.

Victoria :—Wigton ; Abernethy, Perthshire ; Inchkeith ; or Dealgin Ros, Strathern.

Victuarii, Vectuarii :—Men of the Isle of Wight.

Vicumba :—Wycombe, Bucks.

Vicus Albanus, Malbus, or *Malbanus* :— Nantwich, Cheshire.

Vicus Orientalis :— Eastwick, Herts.

Vicus Saxeus :— Staindrop, or Stainthorp, Durham.

Vidogara, Vidotara, Æstuarium : —Mouth of the River Ayr or River Irvine, Ayrshire.

Vidua :—River Crodagh, Donegal.

Vieruedrum :—See *Veruedrum.*

Vigornia :—Worcester.

Villa Albani :—St. Albans.

Villa de Cruce Roesiæ :—Royston, Herts.

Villa de S. Johanne :—Perth.

Villa Faustini : — Dunmow, Woolpit, Bury St. Edmunds, or Orford in Suffolk.

Villa Noua :—Newnham, Herts ; Newtownards, co. Down.

Villa Novi Castri super Tinam :— Newcastle-upon-Tyne.

Villa Regia :—Kingston-upon-Hull ; St. Edmundsbury, Suffolk.

Vilsedonum :—Willesden, where there was a celebrated image of the Virgin Mary.

Vilugiana Provincia :—Wiltshire.

Vimutium :—Weymouth, Dorset

Vinchelsega : —Winchelsea, Sussex.

Vindagora :—Windsor.

Vindediuii :—Drogheda, Ireland.

Vindelis :—Winchelsea.

Vindelisora :—Windsor, Berks.

Vindelocomum : — Winchcombe, Gloucestershire.

Vinderius :—Bay of Carrickfergus, or Loch Strangford.

Vindesorium :—Windsor.

Vindobala :—Rutchester, or Rouchester, Northumberland.

Vindocladia, Vindogladia : — Cranbourne, Wimborne, or Blandford, Dorset ; or Alum Bay, Isle of Wight.

Vindolana, Vindolanda :—Little Chesters, or Chesterholm, in Northumberland.

Vindomora :—Ebchester, Durham ; Dod's End, Northumberland ; or Killhope Cross, Durham.

Vindomus, Vindonum :—Silchester; Farnham; near Whitchurch; or Winchester.

Vindouala. See *Vindobala.*

Vindugladia. See *Vindocladia.*

Vinduglessus :—River Gaunless, Durham.

Vinetria :—The Vintry, London.

Vinnouium, Vinouia :—Binchester, or Egglestone, Durham.

Virdogladia. See *Vindocladia.*

Virecinum, Virecium. See *Virioconium.*

Viride Lignum :—Newry, Ireland.

Viridis Sinus :—Greenwich.

Viridis Stagni Monasterium :—Soulseat, Galloway.

Virioconium, Viroconium :—Wroxeter, Shropshire; or Stone, Staffordshire.

Virolamium. See *Verolamium.*

Virosidum :—Ellenborough, Old Carlisle, or Workington, Cumberland.

Viruedrum. See *Veruedrum.*

Visimonasterium :—Westminster.

Visi-Saxones :—West Saxons.

Vitrea Insula :—Glastonbury.

Vituli Insula :—Selsey, Sussex.

Viurus :—River Wear.

Viuidin :—River Fowey, Cornwall.

Vodiæ :—People about Cork.

Volantium. See *Olenacum.*

Voldia :—Cotswold, Gloucestershire.

Voliba. See *Voluba.*

Volitanium :—Probably on the Wall of Antonine.

Volsas Sinus : — Loch Broom, Ross-shire, or Loch Assynt.

Voluba :—Lostwithiel, Tregony, Falmouth, Bodmin, or Grampound, Cornwall.

Volucrum Domus : — Fulham, Middlesex.

Voluntii :—People of Ulster, Ireland.

Voluntium : — Ardglass, Down, Ireland.

Volurtion. See *Borcouicum.*

Voluicum :—Woolwich.

Voran : — Caervoran, Northumberland, or Warran, Forfar.

Voreda :—Old Penrith, Plumpton Wall, or Kirk Oswald, Cumberland; or Whelp Castle, Westmoreland.

Vosargia :—Herm Island in the Channel.

Vusa :—River Ouse.

W.

Wabruna :—Weybourne, Norfolk.

Wachefelda :—Wakefield, Yorks.

Waga, Waia :—River Wye; River Wey.

Wakefeldia :—Wakefield, Yorks.

Walalega : — Whalley, Lancashire.

Walani :—Welshmen.

Waldena : — Saffron Walden, Essex.

Waldintona : — Waldington, Yorks.

Walensis :—A Welshman.

Walia :—Wales.

Walingforda :—Wallingford, Berks.

Walkenesteda : — Godstone, Surrey.

Walla Londoniarum : — London Wall.

Waliscus, Wallanus :—A Welshman.

Wallia :—Wales.

Walonicus :—Welsh.

Waltifordia :—Waterford, Ireland.

Wanlokensis :—Of Wenlock, Shropshire.

Wanneforda :—Wangford, Suffolk.

Wara :—Ware, Herts.

Warengeforda :—Wallingford, Berks.

Warewella :—Wherwell, Hants.

Warle Septem Molarum :—Warley, Essex.

Warsopa :—Worksop, Notts.

Waruicus :—Warwick.

Wasfordia :—Wexford, Ireland.

Watafordia :—Waterford, Ireland.

Watelega :—Wheatley.

Waterfordia :—Waterford, Ireland.

Watria :—Wavertree, Lancashire.

Wauerlega :—Waverley, Hants.

Waya :—River Wye ; R. Wey.

Wdestochia, Wdestoka :—Woodstock, Oxfordshire.

Weableia :—Weobley, Herefordshire.

Weda :—River Tweed.

Welandus :—Welland River, Northants.

Welcomestowa : —Walthamstow, Essex.

Wella, Welliæ :—Wells, Somerset.

Wendoura :—Wendover, Bucks.

Wennescoita :—Coedowen, Brecon.

Wenta :—Winchester. See also *Winta.*

Wenti :—People of Monmouth.

Wera :—Weare, Somerset.

Werkewurda :—Warkworth, Northumberland.

Werregraua :—Wargrave, Berks.

Werreministra :—Warminster, Wilts.

Wertemora :—Stainmore, Westmoreland.

Werwella :—Wherwell, Hants.

Wesefordia :—Wexford.

Weskus :—Esk River, Yorks.

Wessefordia :—Wexford, Ireland.

Westberia :—Westbury.

Westmaria :—Westmoreland.

Westmonasterium :—Westminster.

Westmoria, Westmorlandia :— Westmoreland.

Westmulna :—Westmill, Herts.

West-Walani :—Cornish men.

Wetha :—Isle of Wight. See *Vecta.*

Weuerus :—River Wever, Cheshire.

Weum :—Wem, Shropshire.

Wherfus :—River Wharfe, Yorks.

Wheta :—Isle of Wight.

Wiableia :—Weobley, Hereford-shire.

Wibigginum :—Wigan, Lanca-shire.

Wiburti Villa :—Wiveton, Nor-folk.

Wiccia :—Worcestershire.

Wiccii :—People living in Wor-cestershire.

Wichcombia :—Wycombe, Bucks.

Wichia :—Droitwich.

Wichium :—Northwich, Cheshire.

Wichum :—Wick, Gloucester-shire.

Wictona :—Witton, Durham.

Wicumba :—Wycombe, Bucks.

Wicus. See *Vicus.*

Wienornis :—Wimborne, Dorset.

Wigornia :—Worcester.

Wika Hamonis :—Wyke Hamon, Northants.

Wilda Sussexiæ :—The Weald of Sussex.

Willensis :—Of Wells.

Wilsates :—Inhabitants of Wilts.

Wiltenses :—Inhabitants of Wilts.

Wiltesciria :—Wiltshire.

Wiltonia :—Wilton ; Wilts.

Wimundhamia :—Wymondham, Norfolk.

Winburna :—Wimborne, Dorset.

Wincelcumba :—Winchcombe, Gloucestershire.

Wincestria :—Winchester.

Winchelcumba :—Winchcombe.

Winchelseya :—Winchelsea.

Windesora, Windleshora, Wind-resora :—Windsor, Berks.

Winta :—Gwent, a province in S. Wales, between Usk and Wye.

Winternia :—Whithern, Wigton-shire, Scotland.

Wintonia :—Winchester.

Wira :—R. Wear, Durham.

Wiramutha : — Wearmouth, Durham.

Wirecestrescira : — Worcester-shire.

Wirecestria :—Worcester.

Wiremunda : — Wearmouth, Durham.

Wirus :—River Wear, Durham.

Wistendena :—Withdean, Sussex.

Witebia :—Whitby, Yorks.

Witerna, Witernia :—Whithern, Wigtonshire.

Witlesia : — Whittlesey, Cam-bridgeshire.

Witteneia :—Witney, Oxon.

Witternensis : — Of Whithern, Wigtonshire.

Wluestera :—Ulster.

Wodnesberia : — Wednesbury, Staffordshire.

Wodneslega : — Wendesley or Wensley, Derbyshire.

Wotha :—Isle of Wight.

Wrekus :—River Wreke, Leicestershire.

Wudestocha:—Woodstock,Oxon.

Wulfrunehantona : — Wolverhampton, Staffordshire.

Wychium : — Northwich, Cheshire.

Y.

Yarienis :—River Yare, Norfolk.

Yarmuthia : — Yarmouth, Norfolk.

Yarum :—Yarm, Yorkshire.

Yeogerieceastria :—Worcester.

Yetzhamsteda :—Easthampstead, Berks.

Ylvernis :—Inverness, Scotland.

Ymiliacum :—Emly, Tipperary.

Ypocessa :— Lower Stanton (?), Herefordshire.

Ysteleswurda :—Isleworth, Middlesex.

Yuelcestria :—Ilchester, Somerset.

Yxninga :—Exning, Suffolk.

Z.

Zeviota :—The Cheviots.

LATIN NAMES

OF THE

BISHOPRICS IN ENGLAND.

Asaphensis, Assauensis :—St. Asaph's.

Bagarensis, Bangorensis, Bannochorensis :—Bangor.

Bathoniensis, or *Bathoniensis et Wellensis* :—Bath and Wells.

Bristoliensis :—Bristol.

de Burgo Sancti Petri :—Peterborough.

Cantuariensis :—Canterbury (Archbishopric).

Carleolensis :—Carlisle.

Cestrensis :—Chester.

Cicestrensis :—Chichester.

Couentrensis :—Coventry and Lichfield.

Dunelmensis :—Durham.

Eboracensis, Eburacensis :—York (Archbishopric).

Eliensis :—Ely.

Exoniensis :—Exeter.

Glocestrensis :—Gloucester.

Heliensis :—Ely.

Herefordensis, Herfordiensis :—Hereford.

Landavensis :—Llandaff.

Lichfeldensis :—Coventry and Lichfield.

Lincolniensis :—Lincoln.

Londiniensis, Lundoniensis :—London.

Meneuensis :—St. David's.

Noruicensis, Norwicensis :—Norwich.

Oxoniensis :—Oxford.

Pangorensis :—Bangor.

Petriburgensis :—Peterborough.

Roffensis, Rouecestrensis :—Rochester.

Sarisburiensis, Saz :—Salisbury.

Sodorensis :—Sodor and Man.

Vigorniensis :—Worcester.

Westmonasteriensis :—Westminster.

Wigorniensis :—Worcester.

Wintoniensis :—Winchester.

BISHOPRICS IN SCOTLAND.

Aberdeiensis, Aberdonensis :— Aberdeen.

Archadiæ, Argadiæ :—Argyle.

Argatheliæ, Argeuelensis :— Argyle.

Berechinensis, Brechynensis, Brikanensis :—Brechin.

Caledoniensis :—Dunkeld.

Candidæ Casæ :—Whithern, Galloway.

Catenensis, Cathanensis :—Caithness.

Cella Reguli :—St. Andrew's.

Dubleinensis, Dumblanensis, Dunbliuensis :—Dunblane.

Dunkeldensis :—Dunkeld.

Æbudæ :—The Isles.

Edenburgensis :—Edinburgh.

Ergadiensis, Ergaliensis :— Argyle.

Galeweiensis, Gallouidiensis :— Galloway.

Galueia, Candida Casa de :— Galloway.

Glascuensis, Glasguensis :—Glasgow (Archbishopric).

Hebudensis :—The Isles, or Sodor.

Lismorensis :—Lismore.

Manniæ et Insularum :—The Isles.

Morafensis, Morauiensis, Mureuensis :—Moray.

Murthlaci :—Mortlach.

Orcadiensis, Orchadensis :— Orkney.

Rosmarkiensis :—Ross.

Rossensis :—Ross.

S. Andreæ, Sanctandreanus :—St. Andrews (Archbishopric).

Sodorensis :—The Isles, or Sodor.

Witternensis :—Whitherne, Whithorn.

BISHOPRICS IN IRELAND.*

Acadensis, Achadensis :—Achonry.

Achadiensis, Achatensis : — Aghadoe.

Achathkonrensis :—Achonry.

Ælfinensis :—Elphin.

Airthermuighensis :—Armoy.

Akadensis :—Achonry.

Alachdensis, Aladensis : — Killala.

Alfinensis :—Elphin.

Anachdunensis :—Annaghdown.

Aondruimensis :—Nendrum.

Aras-Celtair :—Down.

Archfordensis :—Ardfert.

Archmorensis :—Ardmore.

Arcmacensis :—Armagh (Archbishopric).

Arcmorensis :—Ardmore.

Ardacensis, Ardachadensis, Ardahachtensis :—Ardagh.

Ardartensis :—Ardfert.

Ardbrekensis : — Ardbracchan, Meath.

Ardcarnia :—Ardcarne,

Ardecadensis :—Ardagh.

Ardefertensis :—Ardfert.

Ardmacanus :—Armagh.

Ardmorensis :—Ardmore.

Ardsrathensis :—Ardstraw, Ardrath.

Armacanus, Armakensis :—Armagh (Archbishopric).

Arthferdensis, Artfertensis : — Ardfert.

Artmorensis :—Ardmore.

Athrumensis :—Trim.

Aunensis :—Awn.

Baltifordia, Batilfordia :—Waterford.

Bangorensis :—Bangor.

Bistayniensis :—Glendelough.

Brefiniensis : — Brefiny, or Kilmore.

Campulus Bovis :—Aghavoe, or Achadboe, in Ossory.

Canic :—Kilkenny.

Carkagensis :—Cork.

Cashelensis :—Cashel, Munster ; Cassiol Irra, Connaught.

Casselensis, Cassiliensis :— Cashel, Munster (Archbishopric).

* Many bishoprics in Ireland were consolidated with others, or became extinct, the cathedrals becoming mere parish churches, as early as the 12th and 13th centuries.

Cellaiaro :—Cellaiar, in the province of Tuam.

Cellumabrath :—Kilfenoragh.

Cenanus, Cenenensis :—Kells.

Charensis :—Derry.

Chienfernensis :—Clonfert (?).

Chonderensis :—Connor.

Cinana :—Error for *Cluana*. See *Cluainensis*.

Clochorensis, Clogharensis :— Clogher.

Clonardensis :—Clonard, Meath.

Clonensis :—Cloyne, co. Cork.

Clonfertensis :—Clonfert.

Cluainensis, Cluanensis :—Clonmacnois, or Seven Churches, King's County.

Cluanumensis :—Cloyne.

Cluanuama :—Cloyne.

Cluenerardensis :—Clonard.

Coigners :—Connor.

Conactensis :—Connaught.

Conamy :—Cinani, or Clonmacnois.

Conga :—Cong.

Connerensis, Conorensis :—Connor.

Corcagiensis, Corcensis :—Cork.

Corcumrothensis :—Corcumroe, afterwards at Kilfenora.

Cuilectrannensis .—Culfeightrin.

Cuilrathensis :—Coleraine.

Dalnliguirensis, Damhliagensis : —Duleek.

Darensis :—Kildare.

Dearrhiensis, Derensis :—Derry.

Diuilensis :—Dublin (Archbishopric).

Domnachmor :—Donoghmore.

Donnaclsacheling :—Dunshaughlin, Meath.

Doune :—Down, or Dundalethglas.

Droncliuensis :—Drumclive.

Drumorensis :—Dromore.

Drunimorensis :—Dromore.

Duacum, Duatum :—Kilmacduagh, Galway.

Dublinensis :—Dublin (Archbishopric).

Dulicensis :—Duleek, Meath.

Dundalcensis :—Dundalk.

Dundalethglas, Dunensis :— Down.

Dunkerrensis :—South Kerry, *i.e.*, Ardfert.

Edumabragh :—Kilfenoragh.

Elnamirand :—Error for *Cluanard*, or *Clonard*.

Elphinensis :—Elphin.

Emiliensis :—Emly.

Enachdunensis :—Annaghdown, or Enaghdune.

Ennabrensis :—Error for *Fennabrensis*, Kilfenoragh (?).

Ergallia :—Clogher.

Eripolensis :—Jerpont.

Favoria :—Fore, Meath.

Fernensis :—Ferns.

Finnabrensis :—Fenabore, or Kilfenoragh.

Furensis :—Fore, Foure.

Fynnaborensis :—Fenabore, or Kilfenoragh.

Gathay, Insula de :—Inniscathay, or Inniscattery.

Glandelacensis :—Glendelough, or Glendalach.

Hymlacensis :—Imelaco-Ibhair, or Emly.

Iarmuanensis :—Of West Munster.

Imelacensis :—Imelaca-Ibair, Emly.

Inmelettensis :—Emly.

Iniscathrensis :—Inis-scattery.

Kenanusensis, Kenlis : — Kells, Meath.

Kildabewensis :—Error for Killdalua (?).

Kendaluam :—Killaloe.

Kildarensis :—Kildare.

Kildareuensis :—Killaloe (?).

Kildelo :—Killaloe.

Kilfenorensis :—Kilfenoragh.

Kilkenensis :—Kilkenny.

Kill-Aladh, Killaleth :—Killala, co. Mayo.

Killdalua :—Killaloe.

Killmunduach : — Kilmacduagh, or Kilmacough.

Killruaidhensis :—Kilroot.

Kilmorensis :—Kilmore, Kilmore Moy.

Kyenfernensis :—Clonfert (?).

Kynlathensis :—Killala.

Kyry :—Kerry.

Ladensis : —Killala, co. **Mayo.**

Laginiensis :—Leinster.

Laonacensis :—Killaloe.

Laoniensis :—Killaloe.

Leclinensis, Leghelensis, Leghglensis :—Leighlin.

Lessemore :—Lismore.

Lethlegensis :—Leighlin.

Limricensis :—Limerick.

Lismorensis :—Lismore.

Lugdunensis :—Louth, united to Clogher.

Lugundunensis :—Louth.

Lumbricensis, Lumniacensis, Lumpniacensis :—Limerick.

de Mageo, Maigonensis :—Mayo.

Maghbilensis : — Moville, co. Down.

Medensis :—Meath.

Melicensis :—Emly.

Middensis, Midiensis :—Meath.

Ofiachramuy : — afterwards at Killala.

Omanensis :—Omaine, Clonfert.

Osseriensis :—Ossory.

Rapotensis, Rathbocensis, Rathbotensis :—Raphoe.

Rathasithensis :—Rashee.

Rathaspicensis : — Ratheaspuic-
    innic.

Rathbothensis :—Raphoe.

Rathlucensis, Rathlurensis :—
    Rathluraigh.

Rathmurbhulgensis : — Rathmur-
    bholg.

Rechrannensis :—Rathlin.

Rosalither :—Rosscarbery, united
    to Cork.

Roscomon :—Roscommon.

Roscreensis :—Roscrea.

Rosensis :—Ross.

Rossiensis :—Roscrea.

Ruscomia :—Roscommon.

Saigerensis :—Saiger, Seirkeran,
    translated to Aghavoe, in
    Ossory.

Skrynensis :—Skreene.

Slanensis :—Slane, Meath.

Tarensis, Tharensis :—Derry.

Thuenensis :—Down.

Tighbonensis :—Tighbohin.

Tiramalgaid :—Tirawley.

Triburnensis : — Another name
    for the See of Brefiny, or
    Kilmore.

Trimensis :—Trim, Meath.

Tuaimensis, Tuenensis :—Tuam
    (Archbishopric).

Tullagensis :—Tulach.

Tume :—Tuam.

Ulagensis :—Down.

Umalia :—Achadfobhair, Mayo.

Wasefordensis :—Wexford.

Waterfordensis :—Waterford.

Wexfordensis :—Wexford.

Ymlagh : —Emly.

LATIN FORMS OF ENGLISH SURNAMES.

A.

Aba :—Abbott.

de Abbacia :—Abbess, Dabbs.

de Abbaneio :—Abney.

Abbas :—Abbott.

de Abrincis :—D'Avranches.

Acutus :—Hawkwood.

de Adurni Portu :—Etherington.

de Agnellis :—Agnew, Dagnall.

de Agnis :—Aignes, Ains.

de Aillio :—D'Aile, Alley.

Ala Campi :—Wingfield.

de Alba Mara, de Alba Marla :—
Albemarle, Aumarle.

de Albeneio :—D'Aubeney, Albiney, Albeney.

Albericus, Albrea, Albræus :—
Awbrey.

de Albineio, Albiniaco :—D'Aubeney, Albiney, Dolben.

de Albo Monasterio : — Blanc-
muster, Whitchurch.

Albus :—White.

de Aldedelega :—Audley.

de Aldithelega, Alditheleia : —
Audley.

Alec :—Herring.

de Alemania :—Dalmaine.

Alemannicus :—Allman.

Alesius :—Alane.

de Alneto :—Dawnay, Dannay,
Dennett.

de Alno :—Daunay.

Alselinus :—Ansell, Ancell.

de Alta Ripa :—de Hauterive,
Dawtrey, Daltry, Hawtrey.

de Alta Riva. See *de Alta Ripa.*

de Alta Villa : —De Hauteville.

de Alto Menillo :—de Haut-
mesnil.

de Amblia : — De Amblie,
Hamley.

Anastasius :—Anstis.

de Ancariis :—Dancer.

de Andeuilla :—Hanwell.

Anglicus :—Inglis, England.

de Angulis :—Angell.

de Angulo :—del Angle, atte
Cornere.

in Angulo :—atte Noke.

de Ansa :—Daunce.

de Apibus :—Bee, Bye (?).

Apotecarius :—Lespicer, Spicer.

Apparitor :—Sumner.

de Aqua Blanca :—Egeblaunch,
Aygueblanche.

de Aqua Frisca :—Freshwater.

Aquapontanus :—Bridgwater

de Aquila :—Eagle, D'Eagles, Diggles.

Arbalistarius :—Arblaster, Alabaster.

Archidiaconus :—Archdeacon, Arcedeckne.

de Archis, Arcis :—D'Arques, Arch, Dark.

de Arcla :—Harcla, Argles.

Arcuarius :—Archer, Larcher.

de Arcubus :—de Arches, Bowes.

de Arenis :—Darens, Darayns, Sandes.

de Argentomo :—Argentoune.

de Arida Villa : — Dryton, Dryden.

de Ariete :—Herriott.

Armiger :—Arminger.

de Armis :—Harms, Armes.

Arundelius :—Arundel.

Ascelinus :—Ansell, Ancell.

Asculphus :—Ayscough, Askew.

de Asneriis :—Daniers, Denyer.

de Atrio :—Hall.

de Aubemara :—Albemarle.

Aubericus :—Awbrey.

de Auca, de Auco :—Owe.

de Augo :—D'Eu, Auge, Agg, Dagg.

Augustinus :—Austin, Hotine.

de Aula :—Hall. See *de Haula.*

ad Aulam :—atte Halle, Hall.

Auonius :—Of Northampton.

de Aurea Valle : — Dorival, Dorvell, Darvall.

de Aureis Testiculis :—Orescuilz.

de Aureo Vado :—Goldford or Guldeford.

Aurifaber :—Orfeur, an ancient name in Cumberland.

de Aurilla :—Overall.

de Autrico :—d'Auxerre, Oxier.

de Aynecuria : — Daincourt, Deyncourt.

B.

de Ba, Baa :—Baugh.

Bacchus :—Backhouse.

de Bada :—Bath.

de Baha. See *de Ba.*

de Bailolio :—Baliol.

de Bajocis :—de Bayeux, Bews, Baines.

de Ballio :—Bailey.

cum Barba :—Witheberd, Beard.

Barbatus :—Barbet, Barbey.

Bardulfus :—Bardolph.

de Barra :—de la Barre, de Barre.

Barrarius : — Le Barrer, Le Barrier.

de Batonia :—Bath.

de Baudribosco :—Boldrewood.

de Beeuilla :—Beville, Beavill.

de Belesmo :—de Belesme.

de Bella Aqua :—de Bealeawe, Bellew.

de Bella Camera :—Belchambers.

de Bella Fago :—de Bealfo, Beaufoe, Belfou.

de Bella Fide :—Beaufoy.

de Bella Villa :—Belville.

de Bello Alneto :—Bellany.

de Bello Campo :—de Belcamp, Beauchamp.

de Bello Capite :—Beauchief.

de Bello Foco :—Beaufeu.

de Bello Loco :—Beaulieu, Bewley, Bowley.

de Bello Manso :—Beaumains, Beaumeis.

de Bello Marisco :—Beaumarsh.

de Bello Monte :—Beaumont.

de Bello Portu :—de Baupere.

de Bello Praio :—de Beaupre.

de Bello Situ :—Bellasis.

de Bello Vero :—de Beuvar, Beauver.

de Bello Visto :—Belvoir.

de Bello Visu :—de Beauvise, Bevers.

Benedictus :—Bennett.

de Benefactis :—Benfield.

de Beneuolis :—Benlows.

Bercarius :—Le Bercher, Barker.

Bercator :—Barker.

Berengarius :—Barringer.

de Bereuilla :—de Berville, Burfield, Berewell.

de Berneriis :—Berners.

de Beuerlaco :—Beverley.

Bituricensis :—de Bourges.

de Blanco Pane :—Whitbread.

de Blauia :—de Blaye.

de Blithoduno :—Blyton.

de Blosseuilla, Blosteuilla :—Blovile, Blofield.

de Bloys :—Blew, Bligh.

de Blundeuilla :—Blundeville, Blomfield.

Blundus :—Le Blond, Blundel, Blount. In the case of a lady, the feminine *Blunda* is used.

de Boceo :—de Bocy.

de Boeuilla :—Bovill.

de Bologna :—Bullen.

de Bona Villa :—Bonville.

de Bono Fassato :—Goodrick.

Bononius :—Boleyn.

de Boonia :—de Bohun.

de Borgeis :—Burges.

Borlasius :—Borlace.

de Bortano :—Burton.

de Bosco :—Boys, Boyce, Busk, Wood.

de Bosco Arso :—Brentwood.

de Bosco Roardi :—Borhard.

de Boseuilla :—Boswell.

de Botellis :—Butler.

de Boterellis :—Botreaux, Bottrel.

de Boularia :—de Bollers, Buller.

de Bouis Villa :—Bovill.

de Braiosa :—de Braose, Brewis, Brewhouse.

Brito :—Le Bretun.

de Broilleio :—de Bruilly, Briley.

de Brueria :—Bryer, Briewer, Brewer.

Brunelli :—Burnell.

Brunus :—Le Brun, Brown.

de Bucca :—Buck.

de Bucca Uncta :—de Bouchaine, Buccointe, Budgen.

de Bucis :—de Buces, Bouche, Bush.

Budellus :—de Buelles, Boyle.

de Buesuilla :—Bouville, Bousville, Boseville, Bousfield.

de Bulemara :—Bulmer.

de Buliaco :—Buisly, Builly.

de Burco :—de Burgh.

Burgensis :—Burges.

de Burgo :—de Burgh, Burke, Bourke.

de Burgo Charo :—Bourchier.

Burgundiensis :—de Bourgogne, Bourgoyne, Burgon.

de Burnauilla :—Bernwell, Barnwell.

de Burtana :—Burton.

de Bussa Villa :—de Boseville, Beuzeville, Boscherville.

C.

de Cabanisio :—de Chalbeneys.

de Cadomo :—de Caen, Caine.

de Cadurcis : — de Chaorces, Chaworth.

Cæcilius :—Cecil.

de Cahagnis, Cahannis :—Keynes, Keine, Cain.

de Caineto, Cainneto :—de Quesnay, Chainei, Keynes (?), Cheyne.

de Caisneto. See *de Caineto.*

Calcearius : — Le Chaucier, Chaucer.

Calixtus :—Killick.

de Calleio :—de Cailly, Cayley.

Caluinus :—Caffyn, Chaffyn.

de Caluo Monte :—Chaumond.

Caluus : — Baud, Bald, Cafe, Calf, Calver, Callow.

de Camera :—Chambers.

de Cameraco :—Gomery.

Camerarius :—Chamberlayne.

de Campania :—de Champaigne, Champneys.

Camparnulphus, de Campo Arnulphi :—Champernoun.

de Campis :—Descamps, Kemp.

de Campo Auene : — Campdaveine, Otfield.

de Campo Bello :—Campbell.

de Campo Florido, Florum :—Champfleur.

de Camuilla :—Camvil.

de Canceio :—Chauncey.

de Cancellis :—Chaunceus.

de Caneto :—Cheney.

de Caniueto :—Knevitt, Knyvett.

Canonicus :—Le Chanoin, Cannon.

de Cantilupo : — de Cantelou, Cauntelow, Cantlow, or Cantello.

Cantor :—Le Chaunter, Singer.

de Canuilla :—Camville.

de Capella :—Capel.

Capellanus :—Caplin, Chaplin.

de Capis :—de Chappes, Cope, Capes.

Capito :—Grostete, Grosse Teste, Grosthead, Grouthead.

Capra :—Chevre.

de Capra : — de la Chievre, Cheevers, Chivers.

de Capreolo :—Roebuck.

de Capreolocuria, de Capricuria :—Chevercourt.

Caractacus :—Craddock.

Caradocus : — Caradock, Cradock.

Carbonarius :—Carbonel.

Caretarius :—Carter.

de Cariloco :—Cherlewe.

de Carisio :—de Cerisy.

Carnotensis :—de Chartres.

de Carnotto : — de Carnoth or Crennach.

de Caro Loco :—Carelieu.

de Casa Dei :—Godshall.

de Casineto, Casneto. See *de Caineto.*

Castellanus :—Catlin.

de Castellis :—de Chasteus.

de Castello :—de Chastell, Castle, Castell, Chatto.

de Castello Magno :—Castlemain.

Castor :—Bever.

de Castro :—Castell.

de Castro Nouo :—de Castelnau.

de Catherege :—Catherick, Cartwright.

de Cauo Monte :—de Caumont, de Chaumont.

Cecus :—Cheke.

Cenomannicus :—Maine.

de Ceraso, de Cericio :—de Cerisy, Cherry.

de Cestria :—Chester.

de Chahaignis. See *de Cahagnis.*

de Chaisneto. See *de Caineto.*

de Chaluennio : — de Clavigny, Clabone.

de Chaorcis, Chaurcis : — Chaworth.

de Chauwurcis :—Chaworth.

Cheligreuus :—Killigrew.

Chenesis :—Chaigne, Le Chesne, Cheyny.

Chentiscus :—Kentish.

de Chesneto. See *de Caineto.*

de Cheueriis :—de Chevrieres, Chaffers.

Chirchebeius :—Kirkby, Kirby.

de Christi Ecclesia :—de Crissechirche, de Cristecherche.

Cinomannicus :—Maine.

de Clara Villa :—Clareville.

Claranus :—Clare.

de Clarifago :—Clerfay.

de Claris Vallibus :—Clerevaux, Clarival.

de Claro Fayeto :—Clerfay.

de Claro Monte : — Clermont, Clermund.

Clauiger :—Clavinger.

de Clauilla :—de Clavile, Cleville.

de Clauso :—Close, Class.

Clericus :—Clarke, Cleary.

de Clintona :—Clinton.

de Cliuo Forti :—Clifford.

de Coarda :—de Cowert, Coward.

Cocus :-- Cook, Coke, Cocks.

de Codria :—Cowdry.

de Coisneriis :—de Coiners

de Colauilla :—Colville.

de Coldreto :—de Coudray.

Collinus :—Knollys.

de Collo Medio :—de Colmieu.

de Columbariis :—Columbers.

de Conchis :—Shelley.

de Conductu :—Chenduit.

de Conigeriis, Conneriis : — de Coignieres, Conyers.

Constabularius :—le Cunestable, Constable.

Corbaldus :—Corbould.

de Corcella :—Churchill.

de Cormeliis :—de Cormayles, Cormie.

de Corniola :—Cornell.

de Cornubia :—Cornwayle.

Cornutus :—Horn.

Coruesarius :—Corveser, Corsar.

de Coruo Spinæ :—Crowthorn.

de Cramauilla :—Cranwell.

Crassus :—Le Gros. See *Grassus.*

de Craucumba :—Crowcombe.

de Creauso : — de Granson, Grandison.

de Crepito Corde :—Crevecœur, Crowcour.

de Criwa :—Crewe.

Crocus :—Croke.

de Crotis :—Croot, Grote.

de Cruce :—Cross.

Cruciarius :—Crocker.

de Cuillio :—Colley.

Cullus de Boue :—Oxenstern.

de Cuminis :—Comyn.

Cunetius :—Kennett.

de Curceo, Curci :—de Courcy.

de Curia :—Delacour, Cure.

de Curleio :—Curley.

de Curua Spina :—Crowthorn.

de Cusancia :—Cussans.

D.

Dacus :—Le Daneis, Dennis.

Daincuriensis, de Aynecuria :— Daincourt, Deyncourt.

Dalenrigius :—Dalegrig.

Daniscus :—Dennis.

de Daviduilla :—D'Aville, D'Eyville.

Decanus :—Dean.

Deuon' : — Le Deveneis, Devenish.

Diabolus :—Dayville, De Eyville, Deeble, Dibble.

de Diceto :—de Disci, Diss.

Dispensarius, Dispensator, Dispenserius :—Le Despenser, Spencer.

de Diua :—Dive, Dives, Deaves.

Diuitius :—Riche.

Doderigus :—Doddridge.

de Doito :—Dwight, Brook.

de Douera :—de Douvres, Dover.

Draco :—Drake, Drage.

de Drocis :—de Dreux, Drew.

Drogo :—Drew.

Duchtius :—Doughty.

de Dumouilla :—Domville, Dunville.

de Duna :—Don, Down.

de Dunestanuilla :—Dunstanvill.

Durandus :—Durrant, Durand.

Duridentis : — Duredens, Durdans.

Dutentius :—Doughty.

Dux :—Ducy, Duck, Duke.

E.

Easterlingus :—Stradling.

de Ebroicis, de Ebrois :—D'Evreux.

Ecclesiensis :—Churche.

Eliseus :—Ellis.

Elyota :—Elliott.

de Ericeto :—Briewer.

de Ermenolda Villa :—d'Ermenonville.

de Ermenteriis :—Darmenters.

Ernaldus :—Ernaut, Arnold.

de Erolicto :—Erliche.

de Escaleriis : — de Escales, Scalers, Scales.

de Escardeuilla :—Scarvell.

de Eschouilla :—Escoville, Schofield, Scovell.

de Escrupa :—Le Scrope, Scrope.

Esperuerius :—Le Sperver, Sparver.

de Essartis :—Essart, Sart.

de Esseleia :—Ashley.

de Estlega, Estleia :—Astley, or Estley.

Eudo :—Eade, Eades.

Extraneus, de Extraneo : — L'Estrange, Strange.

F.

Faber :—Lefevre.

Facetus :—Le Facet.

de Fago : — Beech, Beecher, Fagge.

de Faia :—de Fai, Fay.

Falconarius :—Falkner, Fachney.

Falkasius :—Fawkes.

Falterellus :—Futerel, Fewtrell.

Fantasma :—Fantosme.

Faucus :—Folkes, Vaux.

Faukesius :—Fawkes.

Ferchardus :—Farquhar, Forker.

Ferdinandus :—Farrant.

Ferrarii :—Ferre.

de Ferrariis :—Ferrars, Ferrier.

Ferratus :—Fairy, Ferrie.

Fiber :—Bever.

Fierebrachius :—Ferbras.

de Fieruilla : — Fierville, Fairfield.

de Filiceto :—Fernham.

Filius Adelini : — Fitz-Adelin, Edlin.

Filius Alani :—Fitz-Alan.

Filius Aluredi :—Fitz-Alard, or Fitz-Alfred.

Filius Amandi :—Fitz-Amand.

Filius Andreæ :—Fitz-Andrew.

Filius Baldewini : — Baldwin, Bolderson, Bowdon.

Filius Baldrici :—Baldry.

Filius Bernardi :—Fitz-Barnard.

Filius Bricii :—Bryson.

Filius Bogonis :—Bewes.

Filius Briani :—Fitz-Brian.

Filius Coci :—Cookson.

Filius Comitis :—Fitz-Count.

Filius Dauidis :—Dawson.

Filius Draconis :—Drake.

Filius Drogonis :—Drewes, Drew.

Filius Edmundi :—Edmunds.

Filius Eustachii :—Fitz-Eustace.

Filius Fulconis : — Fitz-Fulk, Faulke.

Filius Galfridi :—Fitz-Geoffry.

Filius Gerardi :—Fitz-Gerrard.

Filius Gilleberti :—Fitz-Gilbert.

Filius Godescalli :—Godshall.

Filius Gualteri :—Fitzwalter, Walters.

Filius Guarini :—Fitz-Warren.

Filius Guidonis : — Fitz-Guy, Fitzwith.

Filius Gulielmi :—Fitz-William, Williamson, Williams.

Filius Hamonis :—Fitz-Hamon, Hammond, Hampson.

Filius Hardingi : — Fitz-Hardinge.

Filius Henrici : — Fitz-Henry, Harrison, Harris.

Filius Herberti :—Fitz-Herbert.

Filius Hugonis : — Fitz-Hugh, Hughes, Hewes, Hewish, Hewson.

Filius Humfredi : — Fitz-Humphrey, Humphreys.

Filius Ibotæ : — Ibbotson, Ebison.

Filius Isaac :—Isaacs, Higgins, Higginson, Hickson.

Filius Jacobi : — Fitz-James, Jameson.

Filius Johannis : — Fitz-John, Johnson, Jones.

Filius Katerinæ :—Katlynson, Cattlin.

Filius Laurentii :—Lawson.

Filius Letitiæ :—Lettson.

Filius Lucæ :—Fitz-Lucas.

Filius Luciæ :—Lucy.

Filius Mauricii :—Fitz-Maurice, Morison.

Filius Michaelis :—Fitz-Michael.

Filius Nicolai : — Fitz-Nichol, Nicholson. Nichols.

Filius Odonis : —Fitz-Otes.

Filius Oliueri :—Fitz-Oliver.

Filius Osburni :—Fitz-Osburn.

Filius Osmondi :—Fitz-Osmond.

Filius Othonis or *Ottonis* :— Fitz-Otes.

Filius Pagani :—Fitz-Pain.

Filius Patricii :—Fitz-Patrick.

Filius Petri :—Fitz Peter, Peterson, Peters.

Filius Philippi : — Phillips, Phipps, Phipson.

Filius Radulfi :—Fitz-Ralph, Raphson.

Filius Reginaldi : — Fitz-Raynold, Reynolds.

Filius Ricardi :—Fitz-Richard, Richardson, Richards.

Filius Roberti : — Fitz-Robert, Robertson, Roberts, Robinson.

Filius Rogeri : — Fitz-Roger, Rogerson, Rogers.

Filius Saheri :—Searson.

Filius Simonis :—Fitz-Simon, Simonds.

Filius Stephani :—Fitz-Stephen, Stephenson, Stephens, Stiffin.

Filius Suani :—Swainson.

Filius Thomæ : — Fitz-Thomas, Thomson.

Filius Viduæ :—Widdowson.

Filius Walteri : — Fitz-Walter, Walters, Waters, Watson, Watts.

Filius Warini : — Fitz-Warin, Warison.

de Firmitate :—de la Ferté.

de Flammauilla :—de Flamville.

Flandrensis :—Flemyng.

Flauillus :—Flavell.

Flauus : — Blund, Blount; Fleuez.

Flecharius :—Le Flechier, Fletcher.

Florus : —Flowers.

de Fluctibus :—Flood.

de Folia :—Foley.

de Foliis :—Foulis.

de Fonte :—Font, Faunt.

de Fonte Australi :—Southwell.

de Fonte Ebraldi :—Fontevraud.

de Fonte Limpido :—Sherburn.

de Fontibus :—Wells.

de Forda :—Ford.

Forestarius : - Forester, Foster.

de Forgia :—de la Forge.

Formannus :—Formes.

de Fornellis :—de Furnel.

de Forti Scuto :—Fortescue.

de Fortibus :—de Fort, de Forz, Force.

de Fossa Noua :—Newdike.

de Fraisneto, Fraxineto : — de Fraine, du Fresne.

de Francheuilla :—de Freville

Francus :—Franks.

de Fraxino :—del Freine, Frean, Ashe.

Frescoburnus :—Freshburne.

de Freuilla :—Fretchvile, Frevile.

de Frigido Mantello : — Freemantle.

de Frigido Monte :—de Fremond, Fremont.

de Frisca Villa :—Fretchville, Frevile, Freshfield.

de Frisco Marisco :—Freshmarsh.

Fulcherii :—Fulcher.

de Fulgeriis :—de Fougeres, de Filgeres, Fudger, Fulcher.

de Furnellis :—Furneaux, Furness.

G.

de Gaio :—Gai, Gay, Jay.

de Gandauo, Gandauensis :— Gaunt.

Ganterius :—Glover.

de Gardaroba :—Wardroper.

de Gardinis :—Garden.

Garnerus :—Guarnier, Warner.

de Gasconia :—Gascoyne.

de Guweia :—Gower.

de Geinuila :—de Geynville.

de Geneua :—de Genevile.

de Genisteto :—Bromfield.

de Gerardi Villa : — Greville, Graville.

Geruasius :—Gerveis, Jarvis, Jervis.

Giouanus :—Young.

de Girbirti Villa :—de Gerberville.

de Gisneto :—de Gisney, Gynney.

de Gisortio :—de Gisors.

de Glanuilla :—Glanvil.

Gobio :—Gudgeon.

de Gorniaco :—Gorney, Gurney.

Gosselinus :—Gosling.

de Gouheria : —Gower.

Grammaticus :—Grammer.

de Grana :—Graine, Grain.

de Granauilla, Greenuilla :— Greenvil, or Grenvile.

de Grandauilla :—Granvile.

de Grandisono :—de Graunson, Grandison.

Grandis, or *Magnus Venator* :— Grosvenor.

Grandus :—Le Grand, Graunt, Grant.

Granetarius :—Grenet.

de Grangia :—Grainge.

Grangiarius :—Grainger.

de Grano Ordei, Granum Ordei : —Greindorge.

Grassus :—Le Gras, Grace, Le Gros.

de Graua :—de la Grave, Graves.

de Grendona :—Greendon.

de Grento :—Grente, Grinde.

de Greylliaco : —de Greilly, Grelley.

Grimbaldi :—Grimbaud.

de Grinnosa Villa :—de Grinville.

de Griperia :—Gripper.

Grisius :—Le Grice.

de Grosso :—de Gruce, Gross.

de Grosso Monte :—Grosmond, Grismond.

de Grosso Venatore :—Grosvenor.

Grossus :—Le Gros.

Grotius :—Grose.

de Grue :—Crane.

Guarini :—Guerin.

Guido :—Guy, Gee.

de Guidouilla :—Wydville, Wyville.

Gulaffra : — Golofre, Golfer, Gulfer.

de Gundeuilla :—Gonville.

de Guntheri Sylua : —Gunter.

de Guti :—del Got.

H.

de Haia :—de la Haye, Hay.

de Hambeia :—Hamby, Hanby.

de Hanoia :—de Henau, Hanway.

de Hantona :—Hanton, Hampton.

de Harcla :—Harkley.

de Haricuria :—Harcourt, Harecourt.

Hastifragus :—Brakespere.

Hauardus :—Howard.

de Haula :—de la Hale, Hall, Hawley.

de Haya :—de la Haye, Hay.

Heremita :—Armit.

Heres :—Le Hare, Eyre.

Herueus :—Harvey.

Hieronymus :—Jerome, Jerram.

de Hirundine :—Arundel.

Hispaniolus :—Aspinall.

de Hoga :—de la Hoge, Hogg.

de Holmo :—Holmes.

de Hosata, de Hosa :—de la Hose, de la Huse.

Hosatus :—Hose, Huese, Hussey.

Howardus :—Howard.

Hugo :—Hook.

Husatus, Hussatus : — Hoese, Huese, Hussey.

I.

de Illeriis :—de St. Hellier, Hillier.

Infans :—L'Enfant, Child.

de Ingania :—Engaine.

de Insula :—Lisle.

de Insula Bona :—Lislebone.

de Insula Fontis :—Lilburne.

de Ipra :—de Ipres.

de Ispania :—Spain.

J.

de Janua :—Janeway.

Joannis :—Johnson.

de Joannis Villa :—de Jehanville, Geneville, Ganville.

Joannus :—Jones.

Jodocus :—Joice.

Juuenis :—Lejeune, Young.

K.

de Kahagnis :—Keynes.

de Kaineto, de Kaisneto :—Chesney, Cheney, Keynes.

Kentesius : — Le Kenteis, Kentish.

de Keyneto. See *de Kaineto.*

de Kima, Kyma :—de Kyme, Keymer.

L.

de Lacella :—Lascales, Lacelles.

de Lacu :—de Lake, Lake.

de Lada :—de la Lade.

de Læto Loco :—Lettley.

de La Mara :—Delamare.

de Laga :—Lee, Lea, Leigh.

Lambardus :—Lambard, or Lambert.

de Landa :—de la Lande, Land.

de Landalis :—Landal, Landels.

de Langdona, Landona :—Langdon.

Larderarius :—Lardenier, Lardner.

de Largo :—Large.

Latimarius, Latinarius : — Latimer, Latomer.

de Lato Campo :—Bradfield.

de Lato Vado :—Bradford.

de Lato Pede :—Braidfoot.

Lauremarius :—Lorimer.

de Lecha :—Leke.

de Lega :—Leigh, Lee.

Legatus :—Leggatt.

de Leica :—Leke.

de Leicestria :—Lester.

Leslæus :—Leslie.

Leuchenorius :—Lewkin, Lewknor.

de Lexintuna :—Lexington.

de Leziniaco :—de Lezinan.

de Liberatione :—Liverance.

de Lienticuria :—de Liancourt.

de Limesia :—Limsie.

de Linna :—Linne.

de Lisoriis, Lisoris :—Lizurs, Lisors.

de Loco Frumenti :—Whethamstede.

de Logiis :—Lodge.

de Longa Spatha :—Longespee.

de Longa Villa :—Longueville, Longville, Longfellow.

de Longo Campo :—Longchamp, Longshanks.

de Longo Prato :—Longmede.

Lotharingius : — Le Loreyne, Lorraine, Lorriner.

Lotharius :—Lowther.

de Luceio :—Lucy, Lewsey.

Ludouicus :—De Lues, Lewis.

de Luera :—Lower.

de Lunda :—Lund.

de Lupellis :—Lovel.

Lupellus :—Lovel.

Lupus :—Le Loup, Love, Loo, Woolf.

de Lusoriis :—Lusher.

de Luxa :—De Los.

M.

Macer :—Le Meyre.

Macnisius :—Mackness.

de Maderiaco :—de Mezieres, Measures.

de Magna Pena : — de Magne Peine, Moneypenny, Mappin.

de Magna Villa :—Mandeville, Mannwille.

de Magno Monte :—Grosmount, or Groumount.

Magnus Venator :—Grosvenor.

Mainfelinus :—Meinfeuin.

de Maino :—Maine, Maoun.

de Mala Bissa :—de Malebisse, de Malebiche.

de Mala Fide :—Maufé.

de Mala Herba :—Malherbe.

de Mala Opera :—Mallop.

de Mala Platea :—Malpas.

de Mala Terra :—Mauland, Eveland.

de Mala Villa :—Melville.

de Malchenceio :—Munchensy.

Malconductus :—Malduit, Mauduit.

Maledoctus :—Maudoit.

Maleductus :— Malduit, Mauduit.

Malisius :—Malis.

de Malis Manibus :—Malmains.

de Malis Operibus :—Maloor.

de Malo Leone :—Mauleon.

de Malo Conductu :—Malduit.

de Malo Dumo :— de Maubusson.

de Malo Lacu:—Mauley.

de Malo Vicino.   See *Malus Vicinus.*

de Malo Visu :—Malveys.

de Malpassu :—Malpas.

Malus Catulus :—Malcael, Malchael, Malchein, Machel.

Malus Leporarius :—Maleverer, Mallieure, Mallyvery.

Malus Lupellus : — Maulovel, Mallovel.

Malus Vicinus:—Malveisin, Malvoisin, Mavesyn, Mason.

de Mandauilla : — Mandeville, Manneville.

de Maneriis : — de Mengues, Menzies, Manners.

de Manibus :—de Mans.

de Mannauilla : — Mandeville, Manhill, Manwell.

de Mara :—Mare, Marre.

de Marchia :— de La Marche, March.

de Marci Vallibus :—Martival.

de Marco :—Mark.

Marescallus :—Marshal, or Le Marshal, Merrishaw.

de Marinis :—Maryon, Marwin.

de Marisco :—del Mareis, Marsh.

Marruglarius :—Le Marler.

de Martiuallis : — Martivaux, Martival, Martivast, Martwas.

de Masura :—Le Massor, Measor.

Mauclerus :—Lacklatin.

Maurenciacus : — de Montmorency.

de Mauritania :—de Morteine.

de Media Villa :—Middleton.

Medicus :—Leech.

de Meduana :—Maine, Mayenne.

de Melsa :—de Meaulx, Meux, Mews.

Mentulamanus : — "Toulmaine *alias* Hancocke."

de Mercato :—de Marche, March.

Mercator :—Mercer.

de Mesleriis, de Meuleriis :—Mellers.

de Micenis :—Meschines.

Milesius, Miletus :—Miles.

de Mineriis :—Miners.

de Minoriis :—Minours.

de Moelis : — de Moelles, or Moels, Mills.

Molendinarius :—Miller, Milner.

de Molendinis :—Molines.

de Molis :—de Moelles, or Moels, Mills.

Monachus :—Le Moigne, Monk.

de Monasteriis : — Musters, Masters.

de Moncellis : — Monceaux, Monson, Monser.

de Monemutha :—Monmouth.

de Montana :—de Montaignes, de Montaigne, Mountain.

de Monte :—Mount, Mont.

de Monte Acuto :—Montacute, Montague.

de Monte Alto :—Montalt, Muhaut, Moald, Maude.

de Monte Aquilæ :—Mounteagle.

de Monte Begonis :—Montbegon.

de Monte Britonum :—de Monbreton.

de Monte Canasio, Canesio, Canisio : — Montchesney, Munchensi.

de Monte Dei :—Mundy.

de Monte Dublelli :—de Mont Dubleaux.

de Monte Fixo :—Montfitchet, Munfitchet.

de Monte Florum :—de Monteflour.

de Monte Forti :—Montfort.

de Monte Gaii, de Monte Gaudii :—Montjoy, Mungy.

de Monte Gomerico :—Montgomery.

de Monte Hermerii :—Monthermer.

de Monte Jouis :—Montjoy,

de Monte Kanesio : — Montchensey, Munchensi.

de Monte Marisco :—Montmorency.

de Monte Martini :—de Montmartre.

de Monte Moraci, Morentio :—Montmorency.

de Monte Pessono, de Monte Pessulano, de Monte Pissonis, de Monte Pissoris :—Montpinzon, Mompesson.

de Monte Reuelli :—Monterville.

de Montibus :—Mount, Mont.

de Morauia :—Moray, Murray.

de Morisco :—Moore.

de Mortiuallis :—de Martivaux.

de Mortuo Mari :—Mortimer.

de Mota :—de La Motte.

de Moubraia :—Mowbray.

de Muchelegata :—Micklegate.

de Mumbraio :—Mowbray.

Murdacus :—Murdoch.

ad Murum :—Walton.

de Musca :—Mus, Mosse.

de Musco Campo :—Muschamp.

Mustela :—Musteile.

N.

Nappator :—Le Naper, Napier.

de Naso :—de Nes, Ness.

Nepos :—Le Neve.

Nequam :—Neckham.

de Neuilla :—Nevil.

Nigellus :—Niele, Neal.

Nigeroculus :—Blackey.

de Nodariis, Nodoriis :—Nowres.

Norensis :—Noreis, Nordman, Norman.

Normandus :—Norman.

Norriscus :—Norris, Nurse.

de Noruico :—Norwich.

de Noua Terra :—Newland.

de Noua Uilla : — Neufville, Neville, Newell.

de Nouiomo :—Noon.

de Nouo Burgo : — Newburgh, Newborough.

de Nouo Castello :—Newcastle.

de Nouo Foro :—de Neumarche, Newmarch.

de Nouo Loco :—Newark.

de Nouo Mercato : —de Neumarche, Newmarch.

de Nouo Oppido :—Newton.

Nouus :—Newman.

Nouus Homo :—Newman.

Nutricius :—Nurse.

O.

de Oburuilla :—de Abbeville, Appeville.

de Oileio, Oili, Oilius :—D'Oyly, Olley.

de Omnibus Sanctis :—Toussaint.

de Ortiaco :—del Ortyay, Lorty.

Ostiarius : —Le Huissier, Usher ; Durward (Scotch).

de Oughtia :—Doughty.

P.

de Paceio :—de Pasci, Pacy.

Paceus :—Pace.

Paganellus : -- Pagnell, Painel, Paynell.

Paganus :—Payne.

Palmarius :—Le Paumier, Palmer.

Palmiger :—Palmer.

de Palo :—del Pau.

de Palude :—Puddle, Marsh.

de Parco :—Park, Perck.

Parmentarius : — Parmenter, Taylor.

de Parua Turri :—Torel, Tyrrel.

de Parua Villa :—Littleton.

Paruus :—Le Petit, Petty.

de Pascuo Lapidoso :—Stanley.

de Pauilliaco :—Paveley.

de Pauliaco :—Paveley.

Peccatum, de Peccato, Peccatus :— Peche, Pecche, Pecke.

de Pede Planco :—Pauncefoot.

Peitonus :—Peyton.

Pelliparius :—Skinner.

Pentecostes :—Wytesoneday.

Perfectus :—Parfey, Parfitt.

de Periis :—Piers.

de Perona :—Perowne.

de Perrariis :—Perrers.

de Petra :—Petre.

de Petraponte, Petroponto : — Pierrepont, Perpoint.

Peuerellus :—Peverell.

Phiscerus :—Fisher.

de Pictauia, Pictauiensis :—Peytevin, Peyto, Peto.

Pincerna :—Butler.

de Pinibus :—Dupin.

de Pinu :—Pine, Pyne.

Piperellus :—Pepperell, Peverell.

Piscator :—Fisher.

de Pisce, de Piscibus :—Fish.

de Pissiaco :—Poysey.

Placidus :—Placett.

de Planca :—De la Planche.

de Plantagenista :—Plantagenet.

de Plessetis, Plesseto :—de Ple-
seys, Plesseiz, Plessez,
Plaiz, Place.

de Podio :—des Pus.

Poherius. See *Puherius.*

de Pola :—de la Pole.

de Poleio : —Poley.

Polus :—Pole, Poole.

de Pomario :—Appleyard.

Ponderator :—Le Balauncer.

de Ponte :—Bridge.

de Ponte Fracto :—Pomfrey.

ad Pontem : — Atte Brigge,
Brigge, Paunton.

de Pontibus :—Bridgeman,
Bridges.

de Pontissara, Pontissera :—
Sawbridge ; Pontoise,
Pontys.

Pontius :—Pons, Pounce.

Porcarius :—Le Porcher.

de Porcellis :—Purcell.

ad Portam :—Porter.

Pottarius :—Potter.

le Poure :—Power.

Pouteneius :—Poultney.

de Praellis. See *de Praeriis.*

Præpositus :—Prevot.

de Praeriis :—Praeres, Prahors.

de Pratellis : — des Pres, Des-
preaux, Diprose, Meadows.

de Pratis :—Praty, Prettie.

de Prato :—Dupre, Mead, Pratt.

de Precariis. See *de Praeriis.*

Preco :—Price.

Puherius, Puherus :—Le Poher,
Poer.

de Puilleta :—Paulet.

de Pulchro Capellitio :—Fairfax.

Puletarius : — Le Poleter,
Poulter.

Puntius :—Pons, Pounce.

de Purcellis :—Purcell.

de Puteaco :—de Pusat, Pudsey,
Pusey.

de Puteis :—Pittes.

de Puteo :—Pitt.

de Pysanis :- -de Pessaigne.

Q.

de Quatuor Maris :—de Quatre-
mer.

de Querceto :—Cheney.

de Quercu :—Quirk, Kirk, Oake.

de Quinciaco :—Quincey.

R.

de Raalega :—Ralegh.

de Radeneio :—de Reyney, Rodney.

de Radeona :—Rodney.

de Radio :—Raye.

Ragotus :—Le Raggide, Raggett.

de Raimis :—de Reimes.

de Ralega :—Ralegh.

de Rea :—de Ree, Ray.

de Redueriis :—Rivers.

Reginaldi :—Renaud, Reynolds.

Reginaldus :—Reynold.

Regiosyluanus :—Kingswood.

Reinardus :—Rayner, Reyner.

Renoldus :—Reynold.

Rex :—King, Reeks.

Rheseus :—Ap Rhys, Ap Rice, Price.

de Ria :—de Rie, Rye.

de Rico Monte :—Richmond.

Rigidius :—Rivers.

de Riperia, Ripariis, Riueria, Ri-ueriis :—de Ripers, Rivers, Driver.

Robertiades :—Roberts.

de Roca :—Rock.

de Rodeneia :—Rodney.

Rodericus :—Rothery.

de Rodolio :—de Roel, Rolle.

de Roillio:—de Roilli or Reuilly, Rowley.

de Roka :—Rock.

de Rokela :—Rockley.

de Romeliolo : — de Romilli, Romilly, Rumley.

Rotarius :—Wheeler, Rutter.

de Rotis :—Rote, Roots.

de Rotundo, Rotundus :—Ronde, Round, Rounce.

de Rua :—Rue.

de Rubeo Monte :—Rougemont.

de Rubra Manu :—Redmayne.

de Rubra Spatha : — Rospear, Rooper, Roper.*

de Rubro Cliuo :—Radcliffe.

de Ruda :—Routh.

de Ruella :—Ruel, Rule.

Ruffus, Rufus :—Le Roux, Le Rus, Rous, Ruff.

de Rugehala : — Rugeley, Ruggles.

de Rupe :—de la Roche, Roche, Droope, Drope, Rock.

de Rupe Cauardi :—de Roche-chouard.

de Rupe Forti :—Rochfort.

de Rupe Scissa :—Cutcliffe.

de Rupella :—de la Rochelle, Rokell, Roupell.

de Ruperia. See *Rupetra.*

de Rupetra : — de Rupierre. Rooper, Roper.

de Rupibus, Rupinus :—Roche, Rock.

---

* "There is a very ancient family of the Ropers in Cumberland, who have lived immemorially near to a quarry of red spate there, from whence they first took their surname of *Rubra spatha.*" This is the explanation of the name given in the 8th ed. of "Wright's Court Hand Restored"; but "Cowell's Interpreter" translates *de Rubra Spatha*, Rouspee, Rospear, Rooper, Roper. The present editor has been unable to find any confirmation of the story about the quarry of red spate; but in the parish of Castle Sowerby, Cumberland, there are certain estates called Redspears, the owners of which were called by the same name, and did service by riding through Penrith on Whit-Tuesday, brandishing their spears (Jefferson, Hist. of Cumberland, i. 139). Though *spatha* properly means a sword, *de Rubra Spatha* is doubtless the Latin equivalent for Redspear, just as the Norman name *Sake Espee* appears in England as Shakespeare.

S.

de Sabaudia :—Savoy.

de Sacca Villa :—Sackville.

de Saceio :—de Sace, de Sauce.

de Sacheuilla :—de Sacquenville, Soucheville, Sackville.

de Sacra Fago : — Hollebech, Holbeach.

de Sacra Quercu :—Holyoak.

de Sacro Bosco :—Holywood.

de Sacro Fonte :—Holybrook, Holbrook.

Sagittarius :—-Archer.

de Saio :—Say.

de Sakenuilla :—Sackville.

de Salceto :—Saucey.

de Salchauilla :—Salkeld.

de Salicosa Mara :—Wilmore.

de Salicosa Vena :—Salvein.

de Salso Marisco :—Saumarez, Saltmarsh.

de Saltu Capellæ :—Sacheverel.

de Saltu Lacteo :—Melkeley.

Saluagius :—Savage.

Sancho :—Sankey.

de Sancta Barba or *Barbara* :— Senbarb, Simberb.

de Sancta Clara :—St. Clare, Sinclair.

de Sancta Cruce :—St. Croix, Cross.

de Sancta Ermina :—Armine.

de Sancta Fide : — St. Faith, Faith, Fiddes.

de Sancta Geneuefa :—Jeneway.

de Sancta Terra :—Holyland.

de Sancta Villa :—Sent Vile, Sainneville.

de Sancto Albano :—St. Alban.

de Sancto Albino :—Seyntabyn, St. Aubyn.

de Sancto Alemondo :—Salmon.

de Sancto Amando :—St. Amand, Samand.

de Sancto Audemaro :—St. Omer.

de Sancto Audoeno :—St. Owen.

de Sancto Bricio :—Brice.

de Sancto Cinerino :—Chinnery.

de Sancto Claro :—Senclere, Sinclair.

de Sancto Claudo : — Clodd, Clode.

de Sancto Crispino :—Crispin, Crisp.

de Sancto Dionysio :—Dennis.

de Sancto Edmundo :—Edmunds.

de Sancto Edolpho :—Stydolph.

de Sancto Edwardo :—Edwards.

de Sancto Eustacio :—Stacey.

de Sancto Gelasio :—Singlis.

de Sancto Germano :—Germain.

de Sancto Hilario :—Hillary.

de Sancto Johanne :—St. John, Singen.

de Sancto Judoco :—de Joyeuse, Jorz, Joyce.

de Sancto Laudo :—St. Laud, Sentlo, Senlo.

de Sancto Leodeyario :—St. Leger, Sallenger, Ledger.

de Sancto Leonardo :—Lennard.

de Sancto Lizio :—St. Lys, Senliz.

de Sancto Lodo. See *Sancto Laudo.*

de Sancto Lupo :—Sentlow.

de Sancto Luzo :—Sentluke.

de Sancto Martino :—de Danmartin, Semarton, Martin.

de Sancto Mauricio :—St. Morris.

de Sancto Mauro :—St. Maur, Seymour.

de Sancto Medardo :—Semark.

de Sancto Neoto :—Sennett.

de Sancto Olauo :—Toly.

de Sancto Paulo :—Sampol, Semple.

de Sancto Petro :—Sampier, Semper, Symper.

de Sancto Phileberto :—Filbert.

de Sancto Quintino :—St. Quintin.

de Sancto Remigio :—de St. Remy, Remy.

de Sancto Serennio :—Chinnery.

de Sancto Vedasto :—Foster.

de Sancto Vigore :—Vygour.

de Sancto Wallerico :—St. Wallere, Waller.

de Sanduico :—Sandwich.

Sapiens :—Le Sage.

Saracenus :—Sarazin, Sarson.

Sartorius :—Sartoris, Sartres.

Sauagius :—Savage.

Sauaricus :—Savory.

de Sauiniaco :—de Savigny, Saveney.

de Saxo Ferrato :—Ironston, Ironzon.

de Scalariis :—de Scaliers, Scales.

de Scoleio :—Scully.

de Scuris :—Lescures.

de Seinlicio, Senlycio :—de Seinliz.

de Sella :—de Salle, Sale.

Senescallus :—Stewart, Stuart.

de Septem Hidis :—de Sethides.

de Septem Vallibus :—de Setvaux.

de Septem Vannis :—Setvans.

Serlo :—Searle.

de Seuecurda :—Seacourt.

Sewallus :—Sewell.

de Sicca Villa :—de Sechevile, de Sacheville, Satchwell, Sackville.

ae Sideuilla :—Sidwell.

Siluanus :—Silvain, Salvin.

Sine Auerio :—Sanzaver.

Siwardus :—Seward.

de Smalauilla. See *Malauilla.*

de Sola :—Sole.

de Solariis :—Solers.

Sophocardius :—Wischeart.

de Spada :—Speed, Speedy.

de Spineto :—Spine, Spinney.

de Stagno : — Stanhow, Poole, Pond.

de Stampis :—d'Estampes, Stamp.

de Stella :—Stel, Steele.

Stephanides :—Fitz Stephen.

Stiganaus :— Stiggins.

de Stipite Sicco :—de la Zouche.

de Stoteuilla : — d'Estoteville, Stutfield.

Strabo :—Louch.

de Stratauilla : — d'Estréeville, Streatfeild.

de Stratona :—Stretton.

Sub Nemore :—Underwood.

de Sudburia :—Sudbury.

de Suilleio :—de Suilli, Sully.

Super Tysam : — Surteys, Surtees.

de Sureuilla : — Surville, Sherville.

de Suthleia, Sutleia :—Suthley, Sudley.

de Sylua :—Weld.

Syluanectensis :—Seyton.

T.

de Taberna :—Taverner.

Talliator :—Taylor.

de Tanaia :—Taney.

de Taneo :—de Tani, Tawney.

de Tankardi Villa : — Tankerville.

Tannator :—Le Tanur, Tanner.

Taxo :—Tesson, Tyson.

Telarius :—Taylor, Tylor.

de Tertia Manu :—Tremayne.

Teutonicus :—Tyes, Teys.

Thamarius :—Thame, Tame.

de Thaneto :—Thanet, Tanet, Tent.

Theobaldus :—Tipple.

Theodoricus :—Terry, Derrick.

de Thornamusa :—Tornemue.

de Tirnisco :—de Terouisch.

de Toleta :—Tollitt, Tullet.

de Tona :—Touny, Tony.

de Torto :—Turt.

de Tosca :—Tosh.

de Tribus Minetis :—Treminet.

de Trubleuilla : — Troubleville, Turberville.

de Tulka :—Tuke, Toke.

de Turbida Villa :—Turberville.

Turchetillus :—Turchill.

de Turpi Vado :—Fulford.

de Turri :—Towers, Torry.

de Turribus :—de Turs, de Tours.

de Tylia :—Tille, Tyley.

U.

de Uffintona :—Ufton.

de Umbrosa Quercu :—Dimoak, Dimock.

de Urtiaco :—de Lorty, Lort, Hort.

de Usseio :—Ducie.

Ususmare :—Hussey.

V.

de Vaaceio :—de Vaacey, Vaizey.

Vaca :—de la Wac, Wake.

Vacarius : — Vacher, Levaque, Livock.

de Vaccaria :—Vicary, Vickery.

de Vado :—Wade.

de Vado Boum :—Oxford.

de Vado Saxi :—Stanford.

Valchelinus :—Wakelin.

de Valeia :—de Valle, Wall.

de Valencia :—Valence.

Valesius :—Walsh.

de Valle :—Wale, Wall.

de Valle Torta : —Valetor, Vautort.

de Vallibus :—de Vals, Vaux.

de Vallo :—Wall.

de Valoniis :—de Valognes, Valoines.

de Valuinis :—Wauwain, Walwyn.

de Vannario :—Le Vanner.

de Varauilla :—Varvill, Warwell.

Vardæus :—Ward.

Velox :—Swift ; Fogarty.

Venator :—Vendore, Venour.

de Venetia :—Venesse.

de Verineio :—de Verigny, Verney.

de Vernaco :— de Vernai, Ferney.

de Vesci :—Vesey.

de Vetere Aula :—Oldhall, Oldham.

de Vetere Ponte :—Vieuxpont, Vipont, Veepount.

de Vetula :—Vale, Viel, Vyel.

de Vetulis :—de Vielles.

Vetulus :—Viel.

de Vicariis :—Viccars.

Vicinus :—Le Veysin.

de Vico :—de Vicques, Vick.

Vidulator :—Le Vielur.

de Vigneio :—de Vigny, de Wignai.

de Villa :—Veal.

de Villa Magna :—Mandeville.

de Villa Mota, Mouta :—Wilmot.

de Villa Torta :—Croketon.

de Villariis :—Villiers.

de Vindino :—de Vendome, Phantam.

de Vino Saluo :—Vinsauf.

de Viridi Campo :—Greenfield.

de Viridi Villa :—Grenville.

Vitulus. See *Vetulus.*

Vulpis :—Renard, Rainer.

Vulsæus :—Wolsey.

W.

de Wacellis :—Wasel, Vassall.

Walchelinus :—Wakelin.

Wallensis :—Le Walleis, Wallace.

de Wanceio :—Wansey.

de Warenna :—Warren.

Warennarius :—Warrender.

de Warneuilla :—Warneville.

de Warteuilla. See *de Wateuilla.*

M

de Wasa :—Wace.

de Waspria :—de Guaspre, de Waspre, Vosper.

de Watelega :—Wateley, Wheatley.

de Wateuilla : — Wateville, Waterfield.

de Wellebo :—de Wellebof, Welbore.

Wiscardus :—Wishart.

Wollæus :—Wolley.

Wolsæus :—Wolsey.

Woluesæus :—Wolsey.

de Wyuilla :—Wyville, Weevil, Whewell.

A FEW LATIN CHRISTIAN NAMES WITH THEIR ENGLISH EQUIVALENTS.*

A.

Abbalota :—Abelote.

Acceptus :—Accepted.

Aceslina :—

Acharius :—

Acheolus :—Acheul.

Acilia :—

Acius :—Ace, Ach.

Adam (gen. *Adæ*) :—Adam.

Adelardus : —Alard.

Adelheidis :—Adelaide.

Adelicia :—Same as *Aelizia*.

Adelmus :—Aleaume, Elesme.

Ademarus :—Aymer.

Adenettus :—Edneved (?).

Adhelina :—Adeline.

Adomarus :—Aymer.

Ægidia :—Giles.

Ægidius :—Giles.

Aelipdis :—Alice (?).

Aeliuedha :—Aled, Elined.

Aelizia :—Alice.

Affabellus, Affabilis :—Affabell.

Agatha :—Agace, Agas.

Agelwinus :—Aylwin.

Agilbertus :—Ailbert.

Agilda :—

Agiricus :—Agri.

Agna :—Agnes.

Agnes (gen. *Agnetis*) :—Agnés, Annyce, Anneys, Annes.

Agneta :—Agnes.

Ailbertus :—Ethelbert, Albert.

Ailmaricus :—Emery.

Ailmerus :—Aylmer.

Ailwinus :—Ethelwin.

Aitropus :—

Aiulfus :—

Akina :—

Alanus :—Aleyn, Alan.

Albaria :—Aubrey.

Alberedus :—Alfred.

Alberia :—Aubrey.

Albericus, Albricus, Albrius :— Albri, Aubrey.

Albinus :—Aubyn.

---

* The compiler of this list has inserted some Latin names occurring in English documents of which he has found no English equivalent, in the hope that some one who uses the book may be more fortunate than he has been. There are some Irish and Welsh names, as well as English.

Albrea :—Aubrey.

Albreda :—Aubrey.

Albredus :—Aubrey.

Albricus :—Aubri.

Alburga :—Aubrey (?).

Alda :—

Aldezina :—

Aldricus :—Audri.

Aldrida :—Etheldreda, Audrey.

Alecia :—Alice.

Alesia :—Alice.

Alexander :—Saunder (Irish).

Alexandra :—Alisandre.

Aleysia :—Alice.

Alheydis :—Adelaide.

Alic' (masc.) :—

Alicia :—Alice.

Alienora :—Eleanor.

Alina :—Aline.

Alionora :—Eleanor.

Almaria :—

Almaricus : — Amalri, Amauri, Aumary, Emery.

Alnoua :—

Aloysius :—Lewis.

Alphesia :—

Alricus :—Elfric.

Aluinus :—Aylwin.

Aluredus :—Alfred.

Aluricus :—Elfric.

Alyna :—Aline.

Amabilia, *Amabilla* :—Mabel.

Amarius, *Amauricus*. See *Almaricus*.

Ambrosius :—Ambrose.

Amerigus :—Emery.

Amfelisa :—Amphyllis.

Amfridus :—Amphrey.

Amia :—Amy.

Amica :—Amy.

Amicia :—Amice.

Amicius :—Amyas.

Amiotus :—Amyot.

Amiria :—

Amisius :—Amyas.

Ampholisa :—Amphyllis.

Amyas :—Amie.

Amyota :—Amy.

Anabilia :—Anable, Annabell.

Anania :—a feminine name.

Anastasia :—Anastese, Anastasse.

Andreas :—Andrew.

Andrina :—

Anelauus :—Anlaf.

Anfredus :—Amphrey.

Angilbertus :—Engelbert.

Angnes :—Agnes, Annes.

Aniana :—

Anianus :—Agnan.

Anicia :—Annis.

Ankareta :—

Anna :—Anne.

Annora :—

Aphabelus :—Affabell.

Apre :—Evre.

Apsolo :—Absalom.

Araldus :—Harold.

Arcturus :—Arthur.

Aredius :—Yrier.

Arigius :—Areg.

Armetrua :—Ermentrude.

Artorius :—Arthur.

Ascelina :—

Ascelota :—

Athelina :—

Auanus :—Afan, Avan.

Aubereya, Aubraya :—Aubrey.

Aubreia :—Aubrey.

Auda :—

Audebertus :—Aubert.

Audoenus, Audoinus :—Owen.

Audomarus :—Omer.

Auelina :—Aveline.

Auericus :—Avery.

Aufrica :—Ælfrith.

Augerus :—Ogier (?).

Augulus :—Aule.

Augustinus :—Austin.

Auicia :—Avis, Avice.

Aumaricus. See *Almaricus.*

Aumflesia, Aunfelisa : — Amphyllis.

Auntelina :—

Austregisilius :—Outrille.

Aymericus :—Aymer.

B.

Baclerus :—

Banabulus :—

Barbeta, Barbota :—

Bartholomæus :—Bartholomew.

Basilia :—Basile.

Basilius :—Basil.

Basolus :—Basle.

Batillda :—Bautour, Bate.

Bauclerus :—

Baudwinus :—Baldwin.

Beanus :—Beyn.

Beatricia, Beatrix :—Beatrice, Betune, Bete.

Bega :—Bees.

Belebora :—

Benedictus :—Bennet; Berachyah (a Jewish name).

Benigna :—

Bercarius :—Bercaire.

Bernacus :—Brynach.

Bernardus :—Bernard, Brian (Irish).

Beuicius :—Bevis.

Blaceus, Blasius :—Blaise.

Bledhericus :—Bledri.

Bojo :—Boeges, Beges, Bevis, Bew.

Boidinus :—

Bonabulus :—

Bonus Amicus :—Bonamy (Jewish).

Botild' :—Same as Batillda (?).

Brechanus :—Brychan.

Bricius :—Brice.

Brictina :—

Brigida, Brigitta :—Bridget, Bride.

Briocus :—Brieu.

Brithena :—

Brito :—

Brunellus :—Burnell.

Burga :—
Burna :—Bruna (?).
Buticia :—
Bya :—

C.

Cæcilia :—Cecily, Cecil.
Cæcilius :—Cecil.
Caius :—Kay.
Caluarius :—Baldy (Irish).
Cana :—
Cananus :—Kynan.
Canutus :—Cnut.
Caraunus :—Cerau.
Carilefus :—Calais.
Carolus :—Charles.
Castanea :—Castan, Castane.
Cedde :—Chad.
Celestria :—(feminine).
Celia :—Syly (Irish).
Chagnoaldus, Chanulfus :—
Cagnou.
Chalactericus :—Caltry.
Chera :—(Jewish).
Chetellus :—Ketel.
Childeloua :—
Chlodesindis :—Glossinde.
Chlodualdus :—Cloust, Cloud.
Christiana :—Christian.
Christina :—Christine.
Christophorus :—Christopher.
Cissota :—Syssot.
Claremunda :—
Claricia :—Clarice.

Claudius :—Clud, Clut.
Clementia :—Clemence.
Clodulfus :—Clou.
Colandus :—Colin.
Colecta, Coleta :—Colette.
Columbanus :—
Columbina :—
Columbus :—Columb, Colyn.
Comitissa :—Ha-Nasiah (a
Jewish name).
Constantia :—Constance.
Cosmas :—Come.
Cresus :—Cresse (Jewish).
Cuenburga :—Cwenburg.
Cunanus :—Cynan.

D.

Dametta, Damietta :—Damiot.
Datius :—Dace.
Denisia :—Deonise, Denyse,
Dyot.
Dermicius :—Dermot.
Desiderata :—Desirée.
Desiderius :—Didier, Dresery.
Desil' :—
Dionisia. See *Denisia.*
Dionysius :—Denis.
Diota :—Dyot.
Direta :—
Dominicus :—Dominick, Sunday.
Domuelus :—Dogmael.
Donatus :—Donagh, Donell.
Dorothea :—Dorothy, Dolly.

Dorotheus :—Dorothe.

Dousa :—Douce.

Drago :—Drieu, Drue, Drew.

Droco, Drogo :—Drieu, Drue, Drew.

Druco :—Drue.

Druetta :—

Drugan :—Drue.

Dubricius :—Dyfrig, Devereux.

Dulcia, Dulicia :—Douce.

Dulcibella :—Dowsabell.

Dunechanus :—Duncan.

Duuenaldus :—Donnell, Donald.

Duuianus :—Dyfan.

E.

Eadburga :—Edborrow.

Eadgitha :—Edith.

Eadmundus :—Edmund.

Eadwardus :—Edward.

Ebba, Sancta :—St. Tabb.

Eberhardus :—Erhard.

Ebrulfus :—Evroul.

Ebulo :—Eble, Eubold, Euball.

Eda :—

Edania :—Edene.

Edekina :—

Edelota :—Ydelot.

Edeneuettus :—Edneved.

Ederodus :—

Edina :—

Editha :—Edith, Edy.

Edonia :—Edoyne.

Edusa, Edussa :—

Egelwinus :—Ailwin.

Egidia :—Giles, Gille.

Egidius :—Giles.

Elena :—Ellen.

Elfleda :—Efflet.

Elfredus :—Alfred.

Elianora :—Eleanor.

Elias :—Ellis.

Eliphius :—Elof.

Elisabetha : —Elizabeth, Isabella.

Elisanta :—

Elizeus, Ellicius :—Elys, Ellis.

Elmua :—

Eltutus :—Illtyd.

Elyas :—Ellis.

Emelina :—Emily.

Emericus :—Aymer, Emery.

Emeterius :—Madir.

Emicia :—Amice.

Emicina :—

Emmenia :—

Emmota :—Emmotte.

Eneas :—Einon.

Engelerus :—

Engelramus, Engelrannus, Engeramus : — Engelram, Ingram.

Eniandus :—Enian.

Ennes :—Agnes.

Erminus :—Armin, Erme.

Ernisius, Ernisus :—Ernest (?).

Estrangia :—

Estrilda, Estrulda :—

Etha, Sancta :—St. Teath.

Ethelburga :—Aubrey.

Etheldreda, Etheldritha : — Audrey. Audrey is also used as a masculine name.

Eua :—Eva, Eve.

Eubulo. See *Ebulo.*

Eudo :—Eudes, Hudde.

Eudoardus :—Edward.

Eulalia :—Olaille.

Eularia :—

Euodius :—Yved.

Euota :—Evette.

Euphemia :—Effame.

Euphronius :—Eufroy.

Euphrosyne :—Euphroyne.

Eusebia :—Ysoye.

Eustachius :—Eustace.

Eustathia :—

Eustrichea :—

Exclamodia :—

Eymerus :—Imary.

Ezota :—Isotte.

F.

Falcho :—Falk.

Falkasius :—Fawke.

Fanchea :—Fane.

Fanus :—Fane.

Felicia :—Felise, Phelyse.

Felmeus :—Phelim.

Femisia :—

Ferchardus :—Farquhar.

Ferminus :—(Jewish).

Fiacrius :—Fiacre.

Fides (gen. *Fidis*):—Faith.

Fidolus :—Fale.

Filamyna :—

Filletta :—

Fina :—

Fingola :—

Fitzeus :—

Flandrina :—

Flodobertus :—Frobert.

Florianora :—

Florina :—

Fluria :—

Folcho :—Fulk.

Foulconus :—Fulk.

Frambaldus :—Frambourd.

Francisca :—Frances.

Franciscus :—Francis.

Francus :—Frank.

Frarius :—(Jewish).

Frethesauta :—Frideswide (?).

Fridericus :—Frederick.

Fulco :—Fulk.

Fullanus :—Foignan.

Fulqueyus :—Fulk, Fulcui.

Furseus :—Fursey, Furce.

G.

Galfridus :—Geoffrey.

Galia :—

Galiena :—

Galterus :—Walter.

Galwanus :—Gawain.

Garinus :—Warin.

Garsiana :—

Gartenetus:—Gratnach, Gratney.

Gaufridus :—Geoffrey.

Gaugericus:—Geri, Gerz.

Gena :—

Genesicus :—Genes.

Genofeua:—Genevieve, Jenofeffe, Jenefefe.

Genulfus :—Genou.

Gerardus :—Gerard.

Gerinus :—

Germanus :—Germain, Garmon.

Geroldus :—Gerald.

Geruasius :—Gervase.

Geua :—Eve.

Gilebertus :—Gilbert.

Gilemota :—Wilmot.

Giliana :—

Gilo :—Gilly.

Gineura:—Guenever, Wenhover.

Gislebertus :—Gilbert.

Gislenus :—Guislain.

Gladusa :—Gladys.

Glicerius :—Lizier.

Goda :—

Godefridus :—Godfrey.

Godeheuta :—

Godelacius :—Guthlac.

Godeleua :—

Godescallus :—Godescalde.

Godreda :—

Godusa :—

Goisfridus :—Geoffrey.

Gondulfus :—Goudon.

Gonnilda :—Gunhild.

Gorreia :—Another form of *Godreda.*

Goscelina :—Joscelyne.

Goscelinus :—Jocelin.

Gosfridus :—Geoffrey.

Gouda :—

Grahamus :—Graham.

Gralandus :—

Granta :—(Irish).

Gratia :—Grace.

Griffinus :—Griffin, Griffith.

Grimolfus :—Grimulf.

Gualaricus :—Velery.

Gualterus :—Walter.

Guarinus:—Warin.

Gudila :—Goule.

Guendoloena, Guenliana :— Gwenllian.

Guichardus :—Wicher.

Guido :—Guy.

Guillelmus, Gulielmus :— William.

Guinailus :—Guenau.

Gunnilda :—Gunhild.

Gwendoloena :—Gwenllian.

H.

Habet :—

Hadewisa :—

Haluatheus :—

Hamo :—Hamon, Ham.

Haraldus :—Harold.

Hasculfus :—Hascoil, Hasculf.

Hawisia :—Hawis, Hays, Hawes.

Heilewisa :—Helewis.

Heleca :—

Helena :—Helen.

Helewisa :—Helewis, Helwis.

Helewisus :—

Helisanta :—

Heltus :—Helt.

Helyas :—Ellis.

Hendricus, Henricus :—Henry.

Hereweccus :—Hervey.

Hermelandus :—Erbland.

Hersius :—

Herueius, Heruicius, Heruicus :—
Hervey.

Hieremias :—Jeremiah.

Hieronymus :—Jerome.

Hilaria :—Hillary.

Hilarius :—Hillary.

Hodierna :—

Hoelus :—Howell.

Honesta :—Honesty.

Honoria :—Honour.

Hosto :—

Huelina :—

Huga :—

Hugo :—Hugh.

Humelina :—

Humetta :—

Humfredus :—Humfrey.

Hunniua :—Hunneve.

Hychecosus :—

I.

Ibbota :—Ebote.

Ibria :—

Idaburga :—Edburge.

Idonia :—Edene, Idoigne, Ideyn,
Iden.

Ignauus :—Ednevet.

Ilaria. See *Hilaria.*

Iltutus :—Illtyd.

Imania :—Emma.

Ingelata :—

*Ingeleramus, Ingelramus, Ingera-
mus, Ingerramus* :—Ingram.

Ingelesia :—

Ingoldus :—

Ingulfus :—Ingolf.

Ingusia :—

Ionius :—Yon.

Irilda :—

Isabella :—Isabel, Elizabeth.

Isamaya :—Ismay.

Isilia :—

Ismania :—Emma.

Isolda, Isota :—Iseult, Isoude,
Isote.

Iterius :—

Iuo :—Ives.

J.

Jacobus :—Jacob, James.

Jacomyna :—Jacquemine.

Jacquetta :—Jackett.

Janbertus : —Janbryht.

Janeta :—Janet, Janekin.

Jerberga :—

Jereuerdus, Jeruerdus :—Jor-
werth.

Jestinus :—Jestin.

Joceus :—Joice.

Jocosa :—Joice.

Jodoca :—Joice.

Jodocus :—Joice.

Johanna :—Joan, Jane.

Johannes :—John.

Joldanus :—

Jordana :—

Joscelinus :—Gezelin.

Josias :—Josiah.

Jouetta. See *Juetta*.

Joylanus :—

Judas :—Jude.

Judocus :—Josse.

Juetta :—Jowet, Ivote.

Juetus :—Jowett.

Juguetha :—Jowett.

Juisa :—

Julia :—Syly (Irish).

Juliana :—Juliane, Gillian.

Julita :—Juliet.

Junana :—Jane.

Jursella, Jursola :—

Justina :—Justine.

K.

Kananus :—Kynan.

Kanaucus :—Cynog.

Karadocus :—Caradog.

Kenanus :—Cianan.

Kenewricus :—Cynvrig, Kenric.

Kenoldus :—

Kenulmus :—Kenelm.

Killanus :—Killeen, Kylian.

L.

Laderena :—

Lætitia :—Lettice.

Lancilottus :—Lancelot.

Landebertus :—Lambert.

Laua :—

Laudus :—Lo.

Laurentius :—Lawrence.

Laureta :—

Lecia :—Lettice (?).

Leffeda :—

Legardis :—

Lena : — Short for *Alina* or
Euelina.

Leobinus :—Lubin.

Leodgardus, Leodegarius :—Ledger, Leger.

Leonellus :—Lionel.

Leouegarus :—Leofgar.

Leouenothus :—Leofnoth.

Lesquena :—

Lessa :—

Letia :—Lettice (?).

Letitia :—Lettice.

Letuaria :—

Leubatius :—Leubasse.

Leuca :—

Leudocus : — Llawddog, Lleud-
dad.

Leuelinus :—Llywelyn.

Leuericus :—Leofric.

Leygarda :—

Licinius : —Lezin.

Licoricia. See *Lyquiricia.*

Lieba : —

Lietphardus : —Lifard.

Ligerius : —Leger.

Liniota : —

Lionhardus : —Leonard.

Lipwinus :—Lebwin.

Lorencia :—

Loreta :—

Loueda :—Loveday, Lowday (f.).

Luanus : —Lugid.

Lucas :—Luke.

Lucasius : —Luke, Lucas.

Lucia : —Lucy.

Ludouicus :—Ludwyke, Lewis.

Luelinus :—Llywelyn.

Lupentius : —Louvent.

Lupillo : —

Lupus :—Leu.

Lyquiricia :—(Jewish).

M.

Mabilia, Mabilla :—Mabel.

Macarius :—Macary.

Machutus :—Mawe.

Macia :—Same as *Mascia.*

Madelgarius :—Mauger.

Madelgisilus :—Maguil.

Madocus :—Madog.

Maggota :—Magote.

Magnobodus : —Mainbeu.

Magonius :—Mahon.

Maidocus :—Madog.

Mailgo :—Maelgwm.

Makinus, Makina :—

Malachias :—Malachy.

Malculinus :—Malcolm.

Malla :—

Manautus : —Menauld.

Mannicus : —Mannig.

Manserus, Manserius :—
Manasser.

Marculfus :—Marculf, Marcoul.

Marcus : —Mark.

Margareta :—Margaret.

Margeria :—Margery.

Maryota : —Margot.

Maria :—Mary.

Mariana :—Marion.

Mariota :—Mariot.

Marta : —Martha.

Martia :—

Martius : —Mars.

Mascia : —

Mascilia :—

Mascria :—

Mathias : —Macy, Mazy.

Mathila :—

Matilda, Matildis, Matillis :—
Matilda, Maud, Malkin.

Matthæus :—Matthew, Mawe in Yorkshire.*

Matthias :—Matthias.

Mauditus :—Mawe.

Mauricius :—Maurice, Morris, Merrick.

Maurilius :—Maurille.

Maya :—May.

Mazelina :—

Meilerius :—Meilyr.

Meliora :—

Memmius :—Menge.

Menautus :—Menauld.

Mercia :—Mercy.

Merdericus :—Merri.

Mereducius :—Maredudd, Meredith.

Mericia :—Mercy.

Meruinus :—Mervyn.

Meuricius :—Meurug, Maurice, Morris.

Meus :—(Jewish).

Michaela :—

Michaelis :—Michael.

Mildonia :—

Milesanta, Milesenta, Milicenta :—Midelsent, Millicent.

Milo :—Miles.

Mirabilla :—Mirabel.

Miracula :—

Misericordia :—Mercy.

Mitricus :—Mitry, Merre.

Modeua :—

Mondena :—

Mordacus :—Mordac.

Moreducus :—Maredudd, Meredith.

Morganus :—Morgan.

Morphita, last Abbess of Wherwell :—Morvethe.

Motto (gen. *Mottonis*) :—

Moyses :—Moses.

Murdacus :—Murdoch.

Muriella :—Muriel.

N.

Nalla :—

Natalicia :—

Natalis :—Noel.

Nauerina :—

Nesta :—Nest, Anneis.

Nicasius :—Nicaise.

Nicholaa :—Nichola, Nichole.

Nicholaus :—Nicholas.

Nicia :—

Nicolaa :—Nicola, Nicole.

Nicolaus :—Nicolas.

Nigasia :—

Nigellus :—Nigel, Niel.

Normannus :—Norman.

---

* There is also a feminine name, Mathue, which I have not found in Latin.

O.

Odo :—Eudes.
Odomarus :—Otmar.
Odonus :—Ede.
Oeneus, Oenus :—Owen.
Ogendus :—Oyant.
Olaus :—Olaf, Olave.
Olimpias (fem.) :—
Oliua :—Olive.
Orengia :—
Orframina :—
Oriolda :—
Osillis (fem.) :—
Otheus :—Otes.
Otho :—Otes.
Otto :—Otes.
Owinus :—Owen.

P.

Paganus :—Pain, Payne.
Palladius :—Palais, Padie.
Pancratius :—Pancras.
Pardulfus :—Pardou.
Pascha, Paschasia : — Easter (fem.).
Paternus : —Padarn.
Patricius :—Patrick.
Pauoltus :—
Pelerina :—
Pericia :—
Pero :—Piers.
Petronilla :—Parnel, Pernell.

Petrus :—Peter, Piers.
Pheliona :—
Pietancia :—
Pigotus :—Pigot.
Pipelota :—
Plesancia :—
Pontius :—Pounce.
Preciosa :—
Prejectus :—Prix, Prey.
Protensia :—
Prudentia :—Prudence.

Q.

Quaspatricius : —Gospatric.

R.

Rabotus :—Radbod.
Radulfus :—Randulf, Ralph, Rawlyn, Rades.
Ragnobertus :—Renobert.
Raineta :—Renee.
Randolphus :—Randolf, Randal.
Ranulfus :—Ranulf, Randolf, Randal.
Reginaldus : — Reginald, Reynold.
Regulus :—Rule.
Reinerus :—Rayner.
Remigius :—Remygie.
Remunda : — Used for *Claremunda*.
Renula :—Renell.

Resus :—Rhys, Rice, Reece.
Ricarda :—Ricarde.
Ricardus :—Richard.
Riceus :—Rhys, Rice, Rees.
Richarda :—Richarde.
Richerius :—Riquier.
Richolda :—
Risandina :—
Roberga :—
Roela :—
Roesia :—Rose.
Rogerus :—Roger, Roderick, Rory.
Rogo :—Roges.
Rohelendus :—Roland.
Rosa :—Rose.
Rosia :—Rose.
Rothericus :—Roderick.

S.

Saddocus :—Sadoth.
Saherus :—Saer, Saher.
Saluius :—Sauge.
Sapientia :—Wisdom.
Sarina :—
Sarra :—Sarah.
Saswallo :—Sewell.
Satiuola :—Sidwell, a saint to whom a church at Exeter is dedicated.
Sauaricus :—Savary.
Sauarus :—Saier.
Scientia :—
Scissibota :—
Scolastica :—Escholace, Scolas.
Secundinus :—Seachnal (Irish).
Sedulius :—Siedhuil (Irish).
Seisillus :—Seisyll, Cecil.

Selota :—
Semanus, Semannus :—Semeine.
Sequanus :—Seine.
Serlo :—Serle.
Sescilia :—Cecily.
Sewacus :—
Sewallus :—Sewall, Sewell.
Sexburga :—Sixburgh.
Sibella :—Sybil.
Sidneus :—Sidney.
Sigga :—
Sigo :—Seine.
Siliadicua :—
Siluanus :—Silas.
Siluester (fem.) :—
Similinus :—Semblin.
Simonettus :—Simonett.
Sindulfus :—Sendou.
Slana :—(Irish).
Solacia :—
Sperabilis :—
Stephanus :—Stephen.
Sticlea :—
Suanus, Swanus :—Swein.
Suspirus :—
Symon :—Simon.

T.

Teca, Tecia :—
Tecla :—
Tedbaldus :—Theobald.
Tedricus. See *Teodoricus.*
Tela :—
Teleaucus :—Teilo.
Teodoricus : — Thierri, Terence, Terry.
Terricus. See *Teodoricus.*
Tetildis :—

Teuredaucus :—Tyfrydog.
Thadeus :—Thady.
Thedridus :—
Theida :—
Theobaldus :—Theobald, Tybalt.
Theodoricus : — Theodore, Terence, Terry.
Theodorus :—Theodore, Tudor.
Theodulfus :—Thiou.
Theophania :—Tiffany.
Theophilus :—Teofle.
Therricus. See *Theodoricus.*
Thomasina :—Thomasine, Tamsin.
Thurketillus :—Thurkell.
Timotheus :—Timothy.
Tobias :—Toby.
Tudeleius :—
Tunnota :—
Turgiua :—
Turstanus :—Thurstan.

U.

Udalricus :—Ulric.
Ulitius :—Ulick, Willuk.
Umfridus, Unfridus :—Humfrey.
Ursella :—

V.

Vadinus :—Valentine.
Vedastus :—Fauster, Foster.
Villefredus :—Wilfrid.
Vincentius :—Vincent.
Vitalis :—Viel ; Hagin (a Jewish name).
Vodoalus :—Voel.
Vulstanus :—Wulfstan.

W.

Waco :—Wake.
Wadinus :—Valentine.
Walaricus :—Veleri.
Waldebertus :—Gaubert, Valbert.
Waldeuius :—Waldef, Wadef.
Waltheuus :—Waltheof.
Wandregisilus :—Wandril.
Wanthana :—
Warbora :—
Warnerus :—Warner.
Wenialus :—Guenau.
Wenliana :—Gwenllian.
Weruilla :—
Wido :—Guy.
Wilhelmus :—William.
Willelma :—Wilmyne, Wilmot.
Willelmus :—William.
Williametta :—Wilmot.
Winandus :—Wynkyn.
Wyllymota :—Welmet.
Wymerca :—Wymark.

Y.

Ylaria :—Hillary.
Ytho :—Ives.
Yuo :—Ives, Yvon.
Yuonus :—Ives.

Explicit, Expliciat,
Ludere Scriptor eat.